T0380595

Mainstream of America Series ★

EDITED BY LEWIS GANNETT

The Men Who Made The Nation

The Men Who Made
The Nation

John Dos Passos

PUBLISHED BY DOUBLEDAY
a division of Random House, Inc.

All characters in this book are fictitious,
and any resemblance to actual persons,
living or dead, is purely coincidental.

Copyright © 1957 by John R. Dos Passos

All rights reserved. No part of this book may be reproduced or transmitted
in any form or by any means, electronic or mechanical, including
photocopying, recording, or by any information storage and retrieval system,
without written permission from the publisher.
For information, address Doubleday, a division of Random House, Inc.

The lines from "St.George Tucker, Citizen of No Mean City" by Mary Haldene
Coleman are reprinted by permission of the author and The Dietz Press, Inc.

The lines from " A Diary of the French Revolution" by Gouverneur Morris,
edited by Beatrix Davenport are reprinted by permission of Houghton Mifflin Company.

The lines from "The Papers of Thomas Jefferson" are reprinted by permission
of Princeton University Press.

The lines from "Letters of Benjamin Rush" are reprinted by permission
of Princeton University Press.

DOUBLEDAY and the portrayal of an anchor with a dolphin are registered
trademarks of Doubleday, a division of Random House, Inc.

Original Jacket Design by Sydney Butchkes

The Library of Congress has cataloged the hardcover edition as:
LIbrary of Congress Catalog Card Number 57-5532

A hardcover edition of this book was published in 1957 by Doubleday
First shortrun edition published 2004
Shortrun Edition: 978-0-385-51362-3

146484122

For
E. H. D. P.
who typed and typed
with love

Contents

The Men Who Made
The Nation

" . . . I mean Politics in the great Sense, or that sublime Science which embraces for its Object the Happiness of Mankind . . . "
Gouverneur Morris to George Washington; Paris, January 24, 1790

I The Most Delightful Music

A little after nine o'clock in the morning of October 17, 1781, in the midst of the smoke and roar of the bombardment a drummer was seen beating a parley on the parapet of the hornwork that defended the most southerly corner of the British fortifications at Yorktown. "Had we not seen the drummer in his red coat," young Ebenezer Denny, who had been in the trenches all night with the Pennsylvania line, wrote in his diary, "he might have beat away till domesday. The constant firing was too much for the sound of a single drum."

Immediately an officer holding up a white handkerchief appeared outside the works. The drummer joined him, beating his drum. The French and American batteries ceased fire. An officer ran out from the American lines to meet the British officer and tied the handkerchief over his eyes. In the blessed silence all eyes watched the drummer boy sent back and the British officer led blindfolded through the lines to a farmhouse in the rear.

"When the firing ceased . . ." noted Ensign Denny, a sharpfaced Pennsylvanian with blue eyes and rusty hair, who, although he had barely turned twenty, had already seen service for the patriot cause smuggling dispatches across the Blue Mountains; and cruised on a privateer; and stood next to Anthony Wayne when a ball took the plume off that impetuous general's hat during his rash engagement with Cornwallis's troops at Green Spring. "When the firing ceased," noted Ensign Denny in his little diary, "I thought I never heard a drum equal to it, the most delightful music to us all."

In the trenches the Americans were reminding each other that the seventeenth was the anniversary of Burgoyne's capitulation at Saratoga.

THE MEN WHO MADE THE NATION

Next day Jefferson's genial Bermuda friend St. George Tucker, who had settled in Williamsburg to study law under George Wythe and had become a Virginian and was now serving as a lieutenant colonel in Governor Nelson's militia, took up the story in his journal: "At dawn of day the British gave us a serenade, with Bag-pipes I believe, and were answered by the French with the Band of the Regiment of deux ponts. As soon as the sun rose one of the most striking pictures of War was displayed which the Imagination can paint. From the point of Rock Battery on one side, our lines completely manned and our works crowded with soldiers were exhibited to view. Opposite them at a Distance of two hundred yards you were presented with a sight of the British works; their parapets crowded with officers looking at those which were at the top of our works. The Secretary's house with one of the corners broke off & many large holes through the Roof and Walls, part of which seems tottering from their weight, afforded a striking Instance of the Destruction occasioned by War."

Washington and Rochambeau had appointed Lafayette's brother-in-law, the fashionable Viscount de Noailles, and John Laurens as commissioners to treat with the pair of Scots Cornwallis chose to represent him in the negotiations in the cozy parlor at Moore's farm.

Young Laurens was the logical choice to represent the Americans. He was about the most popular officer in the army. Impulsive, full of generous sensibility, rashly courageous, he had defended his commander in chief against insult in a famous duel. He had brains too, as well as a good sword arm. He had just returned from a lightning mission to the French court to secure an immediate grant of money and munitions. He made the crossing in the company of Tom Paine on Captain Barry's swift frigate the *Alliance*, a crossing punctuated by a mutiny, a bolt of lightning that shivered the main topmast in a storm, the capture of numerous prizes and a desperate engagement in a dead calm with a British sloop of war and a well armed brig which ended with Barry wounded in the shoulder and both Britishers striking their colors to the Stars and Stripes.

John Laurens' father, Henry Laurens, recently President of Congress, had been captured while sailing on a mission to the Dutch and was at that moment held close prisoner in the Tower of London under accusation of high treason. Everybody who read the gazettes knew that the post of Constable of the Tower was one of the plums King George awarded Lord Cornwallis when he so far forwent his original whig principles as to consent to serve against the American rebels, so that his lordship's fortune was profiting at that very moment from the exorbitant charges the keepers of that most expensive of jails were levying on the wealthy Charleston merchant.

Young Laurens, too, had served in the unfortunate South Carolina campaign and capitulated with the rest when lumbering old Massachusetts Ben Lincoln surrendered Charleston. The officers and men of the forces in the Southern Department took particular satisfaction in being represented by a Charleston prisoner. When Cornwallis was forced to accept the same terms which the British had imposed on General Lincoln it was a blot wiped off their record. At Charleston the British, in a fit of whimsy, had insisted that the troops march out of town playing an American march. Smiles widened to broad grins of satisfaction among the besiegers when it was discovered that the capitulation arranged at Moore's farm specified that "The Garrison of York will march out to a Place to be appointed in front of the Posts at two o'Clock precisely with Shouldered Arms, Colors cased, and drums beating a British or German March."

Cornwallis, who was a belted earl and a member of one of the great whig families which had ruled England for nearly a century, evidently felt that he was too great a swell to appear in such an embarrassing situation. He announced himself indisposed, and when the British forces marched out of town on the afternoon of the nineteenth he was represented by a handsome Irish career officer named O'Hara.

The diarists among the Americans had their pens ready: "The British army parade and march out with their colors furled," wrote young Denny; "drums beat as if they did not care how." He added that there were riot and confusion among them. Lieutenant Feltman, also of the Pennsylvania line, noticed that the British prisoners appeared much in liquor. "The British officers," wrote a correspondent of *The New Jersey Gazette*, "in general behaved like boys who had been whipped at school; some bit their lips; some pouted; others cried, hiding their faces they were ashamed to show."

The doughty Cape Cod surgeon, Dr. Thacher, whom the truce relieved from the grim business of sawing off the arms and legs of the wounded, found that "some of the platoon officers appeared to be exceedingly chagrined when giving the word 'ground arms' and I am a witness," he wrote, "that they performed their duty in a very unofficerlike manner: and that many of the soldiers manifested a sullen temper, throwing their arms on the pile with violence as if determined to render them useless."

A sergeant from Anspach who marched out with the German mercenaries sketched a picture of the victorious allies in his notes: "On the right wing of each French regiment was gorgeously paraded a rich standard of white silk with three golden fleurs de lys embroidered on it. Beyond these standards stood the drummers and fifers, and in front of them, the band, which played delightfully. It must be confessed that the French troops altogether looked very well; they were all tall handsome men. They all wore white gaiters; a part of them were clad

in red; some also in green; most of them however wore white regimentals. The German or Alsacian regiments had blue regimentals . . .
The left wing of the line through which we had to march was formed
of Americans; in front of them their generals, Washington, Gates" —
the German sergeant must have mistaken Ben Lincoln for Gates: poor
Gates was home at Berkeley Springs skulking out his disgrace at
Camden — "Steuben and Wayne. They were paraded in three lines,
the first composed of the regulars who also had a band playing
moderately well. They looked passable, but the militia from Virginia
and Maryland, forming the second and third lines, were but a ragged
set of fellows, very ill looking."

Aedanus Burke, the crusty Irish democrat in the field with the South
Carolina militia, wrote in a more philosophic vein to his friend Arthur
Middleton, who was representing his state and the Middleton family's
vast plantations along the Ashley River in Congress at Philadelphia:
"To see these very men who had once reduced us to their power, and
treated us with cruelty and insult, I was prompted by a love of Revenge
natural to the mind of Man and in my opinion a very justifiable and
useful sentiment in a public War. But when I saw them reduced from
their former power and Consequence to their present miserable
melancholy plight, I for a moment forgot their insolence, their deprada-
tions and cruelty . . . They marched through both armies in a slow
pace and to the Sound of Music, not Military Marches, but certain
Airs w'ch had in them so peculiar a strain of melancholy, and w'ch
together w'th the appearance before me excited sentiments far different
from those I expected to enjoy. One must be something more or less
than a man not to be Serious on this occasion."

Most of the listeners agreed that the tune the redcoats most frequently played was an old English air known under the title of "The
World Turned Upside Down."

II   Washington's Combined
Operation

1. *The Dreary Station on the Hudson*

The appearance of that British drummer beating a parley on the hornwork at Yorktown was the result of a series of interlocking events that covered half the globe.

The farflung naval war between Britain and France had developed two main theaters, the Indian Ocean and the Caribbean. In each case the action of the armies on land depended on the fluctuating fortunes of the unwieldy squarerigged fleets that struggled for control of the sea lanes. It was not known whether Hyder Ali, who with French help was fighting the British in India, toasted George Washington; but it was public news that American patriots, like Dr. Rush, the humanitarian Philadelphia physician, were toasting Hyder Ali. In fact they named a privateer after him.

By the spring of 1781 it had become apparent to observers in America that King George's ministers in their struggle with France had taken on more enemies than they could cope with. After their declaration of war against the Dutch Republic early in the winter, His Majesty's navy found itself fighting all the maritime powers of Europe singlehanded. The shipyards of France were busy at work refitting the fleets that Chatham's masterly strategy had driven into drydock in the Seven Years' War twenty years before. Behind them lay the passive wealth of the Spanish dominions and their considerable though obsolete navy. Now the French were to be reinforced by the mercantile enterprise of the Hollanders and the armed neutrality of the nations round the Baltic.

In spite of the daily frustrations and disappointments he suffered trying to keep an army together for one more winter without money and without supplies, George Washington, reading his dispatches in what he referred to in those days as his "dreary station" at New Windsor, was beginning to feel that at last the American cause stood more than an even chance. He had chosen the bleak hamlet set in a fold of the hills south of Newburgh because it was near West Point, which he was building up as a fortress to deny the navigation of the Hudson to the British. Besides, it was far enough back from the river to be safe from surprise. As the feeling grew on him that great things were impending he picked himself out a fresh notebook with a pretty purple cover embellished with wavy lines, and, in his firm round hand, started a new diary. It was the first day of May 1781.

George Washington enjoyed keeping records just as much as Thomas Jefferson did. All his life he cultivated the habit of making notes on the weather and on the plowing and planting of his farms and the production of his mill, and on his travels as a surveyor and speculator in land. He put down how many drinks he drank in various taverns and how many grains of wheat he found in a bushel. It was usually his custom to keep a personal diary noting "how and where my time is spent"; but from the moment he took over command of the Continental Army at Wadsworth House in the Harvard Yard that showery Sunday in the summer of 1775, the press of military affairs had not left him a moment for private jottings.

"I lament not having attempted it from the commencement of the war," he wrote in his new notebook, looking as usual on the darker side, "and wish the multiplicity of matter which continually surrounds me, and the embarrassed state of our affairs which is momently calling the attention to perplexities of one kind or another, may not defeat altogether, or so interrupt my present intention and plan, as to render it of little avail."

When he sat writing these words on that May Day, George Washington was forty nine years old. He was at the peak of his powers. Except for his teeth he was in excellent health. Through all the years of the war he had hardly suffered a day's illness. The Cape Cod surgeon, Dr. Thacher, noted down a careful description of him in his journal: "Remarkably tall, a full six feet," he wrote. "The strength and proportion of his joints and muscles appear to be commensurate with the preeminent powers of his mind." Dr. Thacher was awed, as most men were, by the impression of dignity and grandeur the general gave him. "There is a fine symmetry in the features of his face, indicative of a benign and dignified spirit . . . His nose is straight and his eyes inclined to blue and he wears his hair in a becoming cue, and from his forehead it is turned back and powdered in a manner which adds to the military air of his appearance . . . His uniform dress is a blue coat with two brilliant epaulettes, buffcolored underclothes and a three-cornered hat with a black cockade. He is constantly equipped with an elegant smallsword, boots and spurs, in readiness to mount his noble charger."

Friends attributed the general's physical endurance to his continual exercise on horseback. Jefferson, who was no mean horseman himself, wrote unequivocally that Washington was the best horseman of the age. His fifteen-mile canters across the countryside before breakfast continued to be the despair of his younger aides.

A good horseman is at every instant in control of his horse. During these long years of the war's frustrations and defeats, Washington's physical stamina, this horseman's alert control had become the core of his mind's working.

The day of his appointment he told Congress that he did not think himself equal to the command they were honoring him with, but that he would exert every power he possessed in their service "for the support of the glorious Cause." For six heavyladen years he had done just that; he had exerted every power he possessed.

Under the provincial formality of the Virginia squire Washington was a plain country kind of man. There was nothing complicated about his motives. He had given his word. He stuck to it through summers and winters of stalling and defeat and the long agony of hope deferred. Now at last, amid the fresh leaves and the birds singing in the resurgence of spring along the Hudson, amid the bustle of the army shaking itself loose from the lethargy of winter quarters, he was daring to plot out on the chessboard of strategy he kept in the back of his head moves which might bring, not a fresh stalemate, but victory.

It was characteristic of the cast of his mind that when he started in his first entry in his new diary to list "our wants and our prospects," he took so long describing his lack "of magazines filled with provisions," of "arsenals well supplied with military stores," of "a regular system of transportation established upon credit" that he quite forgot to put down any prospects. As he often said: "I am not one of the sanguine ones." When he did have hopes he believed in keeping quiet about them. A couple of unfortunate events in the past winter had increased the clamlike reticence that grew on him with the years.

The British were getting much too clever at intercepting his mail. They had just printed in their *New York Gazette* a private letter to his cousin Lund Washington, the farm manager and confidential factotum at Mount Vernon, in which the general let himself go a little about how slow the French were in getting their fleet into effective action on the American coast. An admiral's feelings had been hurt, and it had taken all the virtuosity with English prose his secretary, young Alexander Hamilton, could muster, and all Rochambeau's candid good sense, to keep the matter from being blown up into an incident. Washington could bear with equanimity the damage the forged letters the British kept circulating did his reputation, because he knew they were forgeries, but when they got hold of something indiscreet he had actually written he could not help wincing.

Part of Washington's erect horseman's seat in the world was a fervid desire to be seen in a good light by his fellow citizens. He winced indeed, when a couple of months before he sat in these same headquarters reading a letter from his friend Benjamin Harrison from Richmond relating how that thorny old lady, Mary Ball Washington, the general's mother, had applied for relief to the Assembly, claiming she was in great want owing to the heavy taxes she had to pay. Washington answered immediately, requesting that any such proceedings be dropped and explaining that the family had done everything necessary to make the old lady comfortable.

About all he had in common with his mother was the love of horseflesh they both shared, and perhaps a certain graspingness in money matters which had been a cause of dissension between them ever since he was a boy. Though avid for money the old lady was a poor manager. There was no arguing with her. She never would keep her fences in repair. She let her farm run down but complained continually of her hard times. To have her make a public show of herself by appealing to the Virginia Assembly was a cross that must be borne with what patience he could summon.

Now fresh news from Virginia caused him even more painful humiliation. Cornwallis, ever since the start of his southern campaign, had been trying to bring the southern planters to their knees by a series of raids on their property. When a British armed sloop dropped anchor in front of Mount Vernon and carried off a bunch of slaves, Lund Washington, in a well meant effort to serve his cousin's interest, went out to the ship with supplies and begged to have the slaves returned to him.

"It would have been a less painful circumstance to me," the general wrote back huffily on the last day of April, "to have heard, that in consequence of non-compliance with their request, they had burned my House and laid the Plantation in ruins . . . To go on board their vessels; carry them refreshments; commune with a parcel of plundering scoundrels, and request a favor by asking the surrender of my Negroes, was exceedingly ill-judged and 'tis to be feared, will be unhappy in its consequences, as it will be a precedent for others, and may become a subject of animadversion."

These perplexities of course were nothing compared to great disasters like Arnold's treason, Cornwallis's victories in the Southern Department, Rodney's successes in the West Indies and the mutinies of the Pennsylvania and the New Jersey Line. Still the incident at Mount Vernon served to remind Washington that he could achieve no victory on land until he could get the help of a naval force superior to the British at some point along the coast.

The winter at New Windsor which had just come to an end, like every other winter since the general had taken up his command, was a period of frustration and strain. Tempers were ragged. On one of the dark days of February there occurred a painful incident with young Hamilton, the most valuable of his secretaries, that caused Washington more grief than he ever admitted.

Although happily married to his rich wife and devoted to his Custis stepchild's family, George Washington had no children of his own. He was a man who craved and needed children. One of the secrets of his effective command of his troops was the restrained though ardent affection he felt for the brilliant young officers he liked to gather round him in what he called his "military family."

Visitors to headquarters remarked on the convivial atmosphere of the meals. The commander in chief, never a talkative man himself, liked to forget his troubles listening to the prattle of the younger officers over the nuts and the wine after dinner. Chastellux, the most sophisticated of the French generals, a philosopher and encyclopedist in his own right, and a man with a taste for good conversation, in his account of his American travels left a pleasant description of a meal at the American G.H.Q. The general would sit back cracking nuts (sometimes he showed off the strength of his great hands by cracking them with his fingers) while the aide who had done the carving at the head of the table called out the toasts as the general suggested them.

The general's "family" usually sat a couple of hours after dinner, cracking nuts and munching apples and drinking madeira wine. A frugal Frenchman, Chastellux was a little shocked at the amount of time spent at the table. The day he was there, he complained that he had hardly escaped from the dinner table when he was called to supper. To his relief he found that the dishes were light and the toasts less solemn than at dinner when guests and strangers were present.

Chastellux was amazed by the number of nuts the general ate. The moment the cloth was taken off after supper Washington was at his nuts again as fresh bottles of claret and madeira started to move round the table. Chastellux wrote with evident relief that fortunately the glasses were small and that they didn't try to make him drink more

than he wanted to; his admiration for the republican commander was
so great that he was in a mood to be delighted with everything; even
the formal toasts, which most of the French found boring, seemed to
him to add, like the refrain to a song, a certain charm to the conversation. When the party broke up round eleven the last little formality
was what they called a sentiment. Each man drank to the lady of
his choice.

The general took great pleasure in this "father of a family" relationship to his officers. His immediate aides particularly returned his
affection with something like adoration. Like any good commander,
Washington knew how to pick his subordinates. His immediate aides
were young men with brains and dash. John Laurens, who served as
aide for a while, was the most promising young officer in the army.
Several of them had literary tastes. There was pompous and poetical
Humphreys, McHenry the cheerful physician, pious young Trumbull
from Connecticut, selfeffacing Tench Tilghman from the Eastern Shore
of Maryland, rich and romantic William Stephens Smith of New York,
and the bright hardworking rosyfaced amusing young man from the
islands who was the general's favorite.

Alexander Hamilton had come a long way since he turned up in the
mainland colonies at the age of seventeen to finish his schooling. He
thoroughly justified the reputation he brought with him from St. Croix
of being the island prodigy by the energy with which he followed the
courses at King's College, and the vigor with which he had sought
public notice in the press. As a very young man he became friendly
with Elias Boudinot's family and with witty Governor Livingston of
the great Livingston connection. When hostilities with what people
still liked to call "the ministerial troops" commenced, admiring friends
got him appointed captain of an artillery regiment in the New York
State militia. He was indefatigable, courageous; he had a good head
for tactics. He showed his mettle in the miserable winter campaign of
1776-77 in the Jerseys, and when his skill with his pen came to Washington's attention he found himself aide de camp and chief secretary
to the commander in chief.

Though he enjoyed a little literary conversation after dinner, Washington was no intellectual. His mind was essentially that of a practical
administrator. Abstract notions came to him slowly and painfully. As
the years went on he came to depend more and more on the speculative
brilliance of Hamilton's intelligence and on his cheerful appetite for
hard work.

One of Hamilton's charms for his friends was the candor with which
he admitted to overweening ambition. "Ned, my ambition is prevalent,"
he wrote his boyhood chum Edward Stevens, while he was still a lad

yearning among flour barrels and demijohns at Cruger's trading establishment on Danish St. Croix, "so that I contemn the grovelling
condition of a clerk or the like to which my fortune &c. condemns me,
and would willingly risk my life, though not my character, to exalt
my station . . . I wish there was a war."

Hamilton had found his war. Now his heart was set on greater
glories than could be reaped as mere amanuensis to the commander in
chief. He had made a brilliant marriage. In the course of a delicate
mission to Gates up above Albany in the year of Saratoga he became
an intimate of the family of the great upstate magnate Philip Schuyler.
It is hard to tell whether General Schuyler or his pretty daughters
were most impressed by the energetic young officer; when Hamilton
asked Elizabeth Schuyler to marry him, General Schuyler accepted him
as a soninlaw with almost boyish enthusiasm. Hamilton's marriage to
one of the lovely Schuyler girls immediately established him as a
character of importance on the New York scene, socially and politically.
His charm carried everybody away. The almost universal courtship
and admiration of so young a man by leaders of the revolutionary
cause could not have failed to turn his head.

The general could be trying. On the occasions when he lost his
temper he said things he afterwards regretted. This time Hamilton
refused to stand meekly silent while the general raged. He spoke up
and resigned.

Hamilton betrayed an agitated state of mind in the letter he wrote
his sympathetic fatherinlaw right after his run in with the commander
in chief. "I am no longer a member of the General's family," he wrote
from New Windsor. "This information will surprise you and the manner of the chance will surprise you more. Two days ago the General
and I passed each other on the stairs. He told me he wanted to speak
to me. I answered that I would wait upon him immediately. I went
below and delivered Mr. Tilghman a letter to be sent to the
commissary . . .

"Returning to the General, I was stopped on the way by the Marquis
de La Fayette, and we conversed together for about a minute on a
matter of Business . . ."

The lanternjawed marquis, whom Washington loved best of all the
Frenchmen about him, had his own command; but when not in the
field he was in the habit of rejoining the general's "family" at headquarters.

". . . He can testify how impatient I was to get back, and that I left
him in a manner which, but for our intimacy, would have been more
than abrupt. Instead of finding the General, as is usual, in his room,
I met him at the head of the stairs, where, accosting me in an angry
tone, 'Colonel Hamilton,' said he, 'you have kept me waiting at the

head of the stairs these ten minutes. I must tell you, sir, you treat me with disrespect.' I replied, without petulency but with decision: 'I am not conscious of it, sir; but since you have thought it necessary to tell me so, we part.' 'Very well sir,' said he, 'if it be your choice,' or something to this effect, and we separated. I sincerely believe that my absence, which gave so much umbrage, did not last two minutes."

The general may have allowed himself a few of the round oaths he was capable of. When Washington, like many another man of rigid selfcontrol, did fly off the handle, his rages were described as monumental. He was twice Hamilton's age; and under the strain of a thousand nagging responsibilities he probably felt the world owed him the luxury or a fit of temper now and then. He seems to have immediately repented and sent levelheaded Tench Tilghman to tell his injured young secretary that he had spoken in a moment of passion and would like to explain himself. To his surprise and mortification Hamilton refused to be conciliated.

Hamilton explained his bitterness to his fatherinlaw: "I always disliked the office of aid-de-camp as having in it a kind of personal dependence. I refused to serve in this capacity with two majorgenerals at an early period of the war. Infected however with the enthusiasm of the times, an idea of the General's character which experience taught me to be unfounded overcame my scruples and induced me to accept his invitation to enter into his family. It was not long before I discovered that he was not remarkable for delicacy nor good temper, which revived my former aversion to the station in which I had been acting, and it has been increasing since . . ."

This was not the first time the commander in chief lost his temper. Hamilton went on to explain that he had long since made up his mind to seize on the first opportunity for resigning from the general's staff.

". . . I resolved, whenever it should happen, not to be in the wrong. I was convinced the concessions the General might make would be dictated by his interest and that his selflove would never forgive me for what it would regard as a humiliation.

"I believe you know the place I had in the General's confidence and counsels, which will make it the more extraordinary to you to learn that for three years past I have felt no friendship for him and have professed none. The truth is, our dispositions are the opposites of each other, and the pride of my temper would not suffer me to profess what I did not feel. Indeed when advances of this kind have been made to me on his part, they were received in a manner that showed at least that I had no desire to court them, and that I desired to stand rather upon a footing of military confidence than of private attachment.

"You are too good a judge of human nature not to be sensible how this conduct in me must have operated on a man to whom all the world is offering incense . . . The General," he continued in a condescending tone, "is a very honest man. His competitors have slender abilities, and less integrity. His popularity has often been essential to the safety of America, and is still of great importance to it . . . I think it is necessary he should be supported."

For reasons of state, he explained, he intended to make no public mention of his break with the commander in chief, but he had told his friends that his resolution to refuse a reconciliation was inalterable. He did not want to quit the army while the war was on, and was thinking of reentering the artillery, even though he had lost his seniority there, as that might give him time "to resume studies relative to the profession" — of the law — "which, to avoid inferiority, must be laborious." He ended the letter by throwing out the suggestion, as if he hoped General Schuyler would take it up, that he might prefer "a handsome command in the light infantry."

Perplexities indeed. Any broken friendship is a painful business, but it was particularly painful to Washington's feelings to have his gruff fatherly affection spurned by the most brilliant member of his military family just at the moment when he needed every help he could muster for the great final effort of the campaign he was planning for that summer. And Lund's crawling before the enemy, and his mother's importunities. Subject enough for the sort of public "animadversion" he dreaded and hated. With a sigh he compressed his thin lips over the rotting teeth set painfully in his great square jaw and turned to the work in hand.

2. Rendezvous at Yorktown

As he looked over his maps and pondered the broad strategy of the war it looked as if, for once in George Washington's military career, luck might be with him.

On March 22 the Count de Grasse had sailed from Brest, in command of the major part of that great French fleet Vergennes had outfitted in a final effort to dispute Britain's mastery of the seas. His ships lumbered before a favorable wind across the Atlantic. De Grasse had high hopes of undoing the damage the gouty old British sea dog, Admiral Rodney, was doing the French cause in the West Indies. At the same time, a smaller detachment under de Suffren, another Provençal sailor in His Most Christian Majesty's service, sailed southward to reinforce the Dutch, hard pressed on the Cape of Good Hope, and to challenge the British squadrons off India and Ceylon.

It was high time the French bestirred themselves in the Caribbean. Rodney had taken advantage of the British declaration of war on the Dutch to pounce on St. Eustatius. His fleet had the place blockaded before the Dutch governor even knew hostilities had commenced. St. Eustatius, a rocky islet a little to the north of British St. Kitts, had become the center of a rich neutral trade — which Rodney claimed was all contraband — in munitions and supplies of all sorts between the Dutch and the French and the Spaniards and the revolting colonies on the North American coast. Not a few British merchants were doing a profitable business there too.

Rodney described his coup enthusiastically to his wife as "the greatest blow . . . that Holland and America ever received, we having taken the Dutch Islands of St. Eustatius, Saba, and St. Martin's. The riches of St. Eustatius are beyond all comprehension; one hundred and thirty sail of ships in the road, with one Dutch man-of-war of thirtyeight guns, and five other ships of war, from fourteen to twentysix guns, belonging to the Americans, and more than one thousand American prisoners."

The loss of St. Eustatius was a greater setback to the American cause than even the surrender of Charleston. It made Washington's army dependent on the French for munitions, and at the same time it broke up the profitable West India trade of the American privateers who by smart sailing had been managing to run the British blockade almost at will. As it turned out, the immensity of the booty captured on St. Eustatius became one of the links in the chain of events which led inexorably to Cornwallis's surrender.

As spring expanded into summer of that turning point year of 1781, Washington's orotund pen traced out further hopeful entries in his diary. The British fleet had become so absorbed in the pleasant work of shipping home prizes laden with sugar and tobacco that they let de Grasse slip past them, after a running fight in the channels between the islands, into Martinique. The lanky Provençal got his enormous convoy, loaded to the gunwales with troops and munitions, safe into port. As a result the British forces found themselves outnumbered in the Caribbean.

Meanwhile the British merchants whose vessels and cargoes Rodney had seized with the rest of the contraband in St. Eustatius Roads were filling the lobbies of Parliament with their clamors. They brought such a flock of suits against him in the courts of law that the admiral had to take advantage of an unusually bad fit of the gout — the convenient political distemper of that century — to cruise home to mend his political fences.

So it came about that de Grasse was able to reinforce the French garrisons in the islands during June and July and, when the time came to avoid the hurricane season, to sail unhindered through the Bahama Channel with the current of the Gulf Stream pushing his great wooden tubs northward at a decent clip, and to make a landfall on the American coast.

Guarding that station instead of stout old Rodney was only the sluggish Graves, who outranked Rodney's able lieutenant, Rear Admiral Hood, whom Rodney had ordered to spend the hurricane season cruising between New York and the Virginia Capes. At that Hood almost intercepted de Grasse. The British with their copper bottoms being smarter sailors reached the Chesapeake five days ahead of de Grasse's weedy battlewagons. Finding the coast clear, Hood sailed on to the northeast to forestall an attack on New York and to place himself, with proper naval decorum, under Admiral Graves' command. Without firing a shot, to the immense joy of the Virginians, not even hindered by one of the collisions between vessels that were so common in his fleet, de Grasse dropped anchor in Lynnhaven Bay.

Washington understood all along that the naval commanders, both French and British, considered their maneuverings off the American coast as sideshow; in their minds the important theater was the West Indies, where the prize money was, and where in the huge returns from the sugar crop the hard cash could be found that both governments needed to carry on the worldwide war. To relieve the suspense during July, Washington exercised his army and Rochambeau's in a reconnaissance in force of the defenses of New York. By mid August he had reconciled himself to the disappointing news that de Grasse had no intention of attempting anything so difficult as an attack on New York. The French admiral promised to spend a month in the Chesapeake and that was all.

"Matters having now come to a crisis and a decisive plan to be determined on," Washington noted in his diary August 14, he was obliged, "from the shortness of the Count de Grasse's promised stay on this coast, the apparant disinclination of his naval officers to force the harbour of New York and the feeble compliance of the States to my requisitions for Men," to turn his efforts towards Virginia.

It was now or never. Unless he defeated Cornwallis by the end of October, another unique opportunity would be frittered away.

For months Washington's mail had been full of letters begging him to come in person to help his home state in this hour of greatest need. The Virginia militia could not stand up against the well trained redcoats. Tidewater planters had to hide helpless in the woods while British raiders and loyalist privateers plundered their shorefront mansions and burned their tobacco barns. Cornwallis, whom the Virginians were beginning to call the American Hannibal, and his cavalry under

Banastre Tarleton were waging ruthless war against the plantations, burning crops, cutting the throats of horses and cattle they could not drive off, encouraging the slaves to revolt. Virginia's only protection lay in the great extent of her territory, in her decentralized economy, and in the unhealthy climate of the tidewater region. Chills and fevers struck down more Britishers than the Virginia sharpshooters. Smallpox and typhus dogged Cornwallis's steps like a curse. But organized resistance was at an end. Even earnest republicans like Richard Henry Lee were asking that Washington be invested with dictatorial powers.

Through all these importunities of old friends Washington, as was his custom, resolutely kept his mind on the broad strategy of the war. In this attitude, far from popular among the hard pressed Virginians, he was manfully supported by Thomas Jefferson, who was unhappily serving his second term as governor.

Jefferson at that time was a slender longlegged man of thirtyeight with blue gray eyes under a broad forehead. He had a long freckled face and red hair, which he wore powdered and combed plainly back and tied in a cue behind his long narrow head. He had the elastic stride of a man accustomed to long walks; he was an excellent horseman; though no speaker he had a great knack for committee work.

He was going through the most harrowing years of his life as wartime governor. Up to that moment, though his efforts to infect his fellow citizens with his libertarian creed had again and again met frustration, his career had been smoothly prosperous.

Through his mother he was kin to the great Randolph connection. From his father, a plain-minded man of great energy who had put together large landholdings as a pioneer surveyor in Albemarle County and in the Valley, he had inherited some wealth, vigorous health and a capacity for hard diligent application to business.

As a boy his ears had sung with the bloodheating talk of his father's associates in the Loyal Land Company, of the Indians and of expeditions along the warrior trails across the mountains to the Western Waters; and of their audacious project to explore the great rivers beyond and the dimly imagined mountains that barred the way to the Western Ocean. He was brought up on his father's new lands at Shadwell in Albermarle, with the prospect always before him of unlimited adventure in the great empty continent beyond the Blue Ridge. At the same time his eager reading of the classics and of the whig literature of eighteenth century England stirred in him an ardent belief in man's perfectability and in the imminent triumph of selfgoverning institutions.

His father's early death forced him to take over the management of his plantations while he was still a schoolboy. At fourteen he shouldered the responsibilities of the head of a family.

He had the good luck to find a couple of first rate teachers even in the ramshackle college at Williamsburg. William Small, an Aberdeen man who taught natural philosophy there for a few years, introduced him to the Scottish enlightenment at its moment of greatest vigor, with its passion for free inquiry, and the ramifications of its thought into free trade economics and scientific invention and discovery. The sturdy provincial classicist, George Wythe, taught him a scholar's approach to the study of law. Through Wythe's and Small's table companion, the deputy governor, Francis Fauquier, he heard echoes of Georgian music, and vicariously experienced some of the worldly and humane and scintillating conversation of the sect of philosophers who moved in the circle of the Royal Society in London.

His absorbent and curious mind did the rest. The Revolution found him a rising lawyer in his early thirties with the best cultivated, the most inquisitive, the most audacious set of brains in Virginia.

He had the further good luck to marry a woman of great charm who shared his taste for music and literature, and who brought him a personal fortune, in mortgaged lands to be sure, equal to his own. As an expression of happy selfconfidence he started building for himself and his family the hilltop mansion where he planned to adapt everything he found rational and elegant in Palladio's teaching of the antique styles to the needs of an American landowner.

As independence from Great Britain became instead of a possibility a certainty, he threw himself, with complete disregard of his own private interests, into the public service. The Virginia Whigs shared the cult of noblesse oblige with their cousins of the British gentry. With John Adams he had drafted the Declaration of Independence and, coming home to Virginia in the fall of the wonderful year of 1776, had initiated his great measures in the Assembly; to disestablish the Church and secure freedom of religious belief; to break up the great estates by repealing the law of entail; to abolish slavery; to codify and rationalize the body of law inherited from the colonial courts; and to secure universal free education for every citizen of Virginia.

Some of his measures succeeded and some failed, but as yet his fellow citizens, while they shied off from such of his radical measures as they feared would disturb their ease or cripple their incomes, regarded him with a sort of wondering admiration. The governor of Virginia, according to the constitution of 1776, was merely chairman of an executive council. Jefferson was elected to replace Patrick Henry, who had exhibited, along with his sweeping red Glasgow cloak and his gift for oratory, an appalling egotism in that office, and a lack of system and consistency very damaging to efficient administration.

As governor, with Virginia invaded first by Arnold and then by Cornwallis, Jefferson found himself frustrated by the exigencies of warfare, for which he had little aptitude, in the sort of statebuilding work he was thoroughly fitted for. He found himself a mere quartermaster for the militia and the Continental troops. He put all the patient attention to detail he was capable of into the task of outfitting the Continental Army, and managed to lay the foundation of a system of military supply which was to prove its effectiveness in the coming summer, but he was nothing of a soldier.

His natural distrust for the military way of doing things was intensified by his experience with the Baron von Steuben. That polished military adventurer, who fascinated the officers of the Continental Army with his tales of the martial elegances of the great Frederick's staff, was sent down to drill the Virginia levies being readied to reinforce Greene in the Carolinas. His Prussian methods and his peevishness and lack of tact when things did not go his way were producing more opposition in Virginia than they did discipline. When in June the baron and some of his recruits made a poor showing of themselves by losing to the British the stores they were supposed to be guarding at Point of Fork on the upper James, the ruffled feelings of the Virginians became vocal indeed.

Through the last miserable months of his second term as governor Jefferson made no secret of his intention to resign at the first opportunity. In this emergency, he wrote, the state needed a man who combined whig principles with military aptitude. In June, scampering out of Charlottesville into the hills with Cornwallis's raiders at their heels, the Virginia legislators managed to find just such a man in fleshy but energetic Thomas Nelson Jr., one of the welltodo Nelsons from Yorktown on the York River, who was already in command of the militia.

When they first reined their horses at Staunton in the Valley after their hurried flight across the mountains the delegates were in a mood to pin the blame for their humiliation on the first scapegoat they could find. Steuben, they shouted, ought to be hanged. Fat George Nicholas, the son of a family with which Jefferson always had most friendly relations, jumped up to move that a dictator be appointed. The motion was seconded by Patrick Henry in his red cloak. The motion failed. Then Nicholas, backed by approving glances from the gentleman in the red cloak, made a further motion that an inquiry be made into the recent conduct of the executive. The motion passed. Jefferson, who had to take to the hills himself to avoid being captured at Monticello, never got over the smart of that wound.

It was only the presence of Washington's favorite Frenchman that kept the Virginians from complete despair. Lafayette was twenty three. He was gay. He was wild with enthusiasm for the American cause. His manners were cordial. With the easy selfconfidence that came from his noble upbringing he allowed himself to treat men of all ranks with equal affability. Wherever he appeared men and women fell in love with him. Where Steuben was middleaged and quarrelsome in emergencies, Lafayette bubbled over with candor and high spirits. The campaign was the lark of his life. At his age to be commanding troops against the great Cornwallis was a continual marvel to him. To top it all, he was handling his small force with the shrewd economy of an old campaigner. It was not long before the Virginia planters, who had been resisting the demands of Steuben and Greene, were not only furnishing the marquis with their sons as volunteers, but with the use of their precious horses.

As summer advanced, by cleverly hanging on Cornwallis's flank without risking a general engagement, by playing hide and seek across the broad creeks and estuaries and through the winding forest paths, the marquis managed to turn Cornwallis's triumphal march through ruined tidewater farmlands into something that looked very much like a retreat. Washington kept writing his young friend encouraging letters. Already he had sent the redoubtable Anthony Wayne and his Pennsylvanians down to reinforce him.

Once Washington's mind was made up to seek a decision in Virginia, something almost lighthearted came into his correspondence. A certain gaiety even seeped into the general orders. The time had come to move, to move fast, "on the wings of speed," he wrote. He was staking everything on a single throw.

August 16, still on the Hudson, he was able to note in a fresh volume of his diary that he had received the encouraging news from Lafayette that Cornwallis was headed for Governor Nelson's tiny town of York on the York River. The earl, against his better judgment, was grudgingly carrying out Sir Henry Clinton's orders to seize and fortify a naval base with a deep water anchorage. With command of the sea the York River was perfect for that purpose, but it was obvious to every observer that, if the British lost the sea lanes even for a short time, the place would become, as Dr. Rush enthusiastically described it in a letter to Horatio Gates, "a mousetrap."

Three days later Washington had his army and Rochambeau's

assembled west of the Hudson. To keep Clinton guessing he had the French building bake ovens and setting up huts as if for an encampment on the Jersey shore opposite Staten Island. The British skill at intercepting dispatches proved their undoing. All the general's letters talked of an attack on New York.

August 30 Washington wrote in his diary, "as our intentions could be concealed one March more (under the idea of Marching to Sandy Hook to facilitate the entrance of the French fleet within the Bay) the whole army was put in motion" — in three columns, one of which, he explained, was detached to make a feint towards Staten Island.

Rochambeau was an able commander. He lacked the personal vanity that was the besetting sin of the French nobility. He accepted Washington's leadership with tact and good judgment. For once allied armies managed to cooperate without a single hitch. With their artillery and their baggage and their flatboats mounted on wheels Rochambeau's single column and Washington's two converged unbelievably fast on Trenton. There they crossed the Delaware. Washington ordered the cattle and horses swum across the river to save time. By September 5 he was able to note breathlessly that the rear of the French had reached Philadelphia and that the entire American army was already clear of the city.

"I left this city for the Head of Elk to hasten the Embarkation at that place and on my way received the agreeable news of the safe arrival of the Count de Grasse in the Bay of Chesapeake with 28 Sail of the line and four frigates with 3000 land troops which were to be immediately debarked at Jamestown and form a junction with the American army under the command of the Marquis de la Fayette."

Every man who was present on that day remembered the look of joy that came over the general's face when the dispatch rider caught up with him on the road out of Chester with the good news. Some claimed that when Washington hailed Rochambeau to let him know de Grasse was safe in harbor he shouted and waved his three-cornered hat like a boy.

The representatives of the states in Congress assembled, as usual at their wit's end for funds, had recently appointed Washington's close friend, the great Philadelphia merchant Robert Morris, Superintendent of Finance. It was felt that this son of an obscure Liverpool tobacco factor, who had arrived penniless from England and worked his way up by his miraculous skill in pyramiding one speculative venture on top of another, to a partnership in the powerful Willing firm of bankers and merchants, and thence to a position of wealth and influence in Pennsylvania, might perform some similar miracle for the public cause.

When he reached Head of Elk at the top of Chesapeake Bay, Washington put the prevalent high spirits of his troops on a firm foundation of hard cash. He had managed to chivvy the Financier, as they called him, into scraping them up a month's pay of silver, though the only way even that financial magician could find to lay his hands on any specie was to borrow it from Rochambeau's war chest. The stimulus to martial ardor was immense. Many of the Continental soldiers had not seen a coin in years. Paper money had become a bad joke. Men jingled the silver incredulously in their palms as they filed away from the paymaster's table.

September 6 the general allowed his optimism to overflow into the general orders:

"It is with the highest pleasure and satisfaction the Commander in Chief announces to the army the arrivals of the Count de Grasse in the Chesapeake with a very formidable naval and land force; at the same time he felicitates them on this auspicious occasion he anticipates the glorious Events which may be expected from the Combined Operation now in Contemplation."

Young Jonathan Trumbull, the pious son of Connecticut's pious governor, who was then serving as Washington's secretary, might well have added another flourish to his penmanship had he known that the day before de Grasse's fleet had worsted Admiral Graves in an engagement off the Virginia Capes, in which the Provençal had successfully employed the rigid line maneuver for which he was famous; and that while Graves was limping back to Sandy Hook for repairs, de Barras's squadron with Rochambeau's train of heavy siege artillery on board had slipped in through the Virginia Capes and joined the French fleet at anchor in the bay.

While General Lincoln's paymasters were counting out clinking French silver into the unaccustomed palms of the Continentals, and smacks and oysterboats and coasting vessels of all sizes and shapes were loading the troops aboard and sailing down the bay safe at last for American transports, Washington, followed at a slower pace by Rochambeau and Chastellux and the French staff, rode off at breakneck speed to Mount Vernon. He reached home after having ridden, with time out for business and public addresses in Baltimore, a hundred and twenty miles in three days.

"A numerous family now present," wrote young Trumbull in his minutes. "All accommodated. An elegant seat and situation, great appearance of opulence and real exhibitions of hospitality and princely entertainment."

It was six years and four months since Washington had seen his home plantation.

No time to visit his mill, to ride around the farms for a look at the crops, to check on the thousand dilapidations that must have happened during all these years of absence.

Next day, while his wife Martha and Lund Washington were busy marshaling the bountiful victuals the plantation, even in wartime, afforded for the entertainment of their highborn military guests, the general was back at his desk. He wrote the county lieutenants to put their militia to work to fill the mudholes on the Virginia roads so that the wagon trains could get through, and to improve the landings of the Georgetown ferry across the Potomac, and to remove obstructions from the ford on Occoquan Creek. He wrote to beg the governor of Maryland to expedite supplies. He sent off a reminder to slow Lincoln back at Head of Elk to hurry the embarkation of his troops. He found time to dictate to Humphreys a cheerful note for Lafayette: "I hope you will keep Lord Cornwallis safe, without provisions or forage until we arrive."

He gave the French officers a day for rest and high feeding in the comfort of Mount Vernon and then he was in the saddle again bright and early, riding off ahead of them to arrange for their accommodations at Fredericksburg.

A few days later Jack Custis, who since his sister's death before the war began was Martha Washington's only surviving child, followed the general down into the York Peninsula. The boy whose education he had watched over with tender care had turned out a disappointment. Years ago Washington had described his stepson hopefully to the schoolmaster Jonathan Boucher as "a promising boy, the last of his family, who would possess a very large fortune," and added that he was anxious to make him "fit for more useful purposes than horse races."

Jack Custis grew up without application, a flighty, headstrong, and rather sickly young man. He had raised a family of his own at Mount Vernon, but Washington still wrote of him affectionately as "an amiable youth." In the most crowded hours of his campaigns the general took time to write him long expostulatory letters, patiently trying to dissuade him from rash sales of his lands and from entering into the various risky deals he was inclined to. He never gave up the hope of at least teaching him how a plantation owner ought to conduct his business.

Martha Washington was an apprehensive and indulgent mother. Trying to cope gently with her son's vagaries was part of the tender consideration with which Washington treated his wife. Though the boy was no soldier, in fact he had turned out good for little except for fox hunting and dancing parties, the general invited him to come along as a volunteer aide to his headquarters. He probably felt that to take part even as a spectator in the "glorious Events" he anticipated might help make a man of him.

In spite of the uncertainty over the outcome of the naval battle off the Capes, the march on Yorktown was assuming a triumphal air. From every battlefront eager young officers were hurrying into tidewater Virginia to be in at the kill. Light Horse Harry Lee managed to get himself detached from the Carolina front for service with the commander in chief. Governor Nelson of Virginia notified the members of the executive council in Richmond that he would have to be absent from their sessions until this important business was settled. Handsome Arthur St. Clair was there with a huge cockade in his hat. Young Laurens led a regiment. Hamilton, who had sent in his commission in a pet earlier in the summer and had it politely returned to him by the commander in chief, had finally attained the "handsome command" in the light infantry he wrote his fatherinlaw about. Henry Knox, the stout Boston bookseller who had managed by sheer application to make himself an expert on ordnance, was in command of the artillery.

Surrounded by the camps of the allied armies, deserted Williamsburg came back to life. Officers were quartered in the college. Uniformed throngs packed the inns. Anthony Wayne, wounded in the leg by a triggerhappy sentry, was hobbling about the outskirts on a cane with a fresh plume on his threecornered hat. Steuben, laid low by gout and mortification, dragged himself out of bed to be present. Volunteers were trooping into the ranks of the Virginia militia. The French with their bent for the pomp and drama of war were beginning to endow the coming siege with the fashionable air of the great military events of the Grand Siècle in Europe.

A few weeks earlier St. George Tucker wrote his wife that at a party tendered the Virginians by their beloved marquis he had been amused by a certain Colonel Steward, "The same pretty fellow that he ever was and wears a plume almost as large as General Wayne's himself. I wrote you before that the Pennsylvania line abounded in these decorations. I will venture to affirm that all the ostriches that ever appeared on the table of Heliogabalus would be insufficient to furnish the whole army in the same profuse style. They put me in mind of the army marching on Dunsinane, when mistaken by Macbeth for Birnam's Wood; for the feathers appear before you can well discover the shoulders to which the head that bears them is annexed."

This same St. George Tucker was in the throng of officers who saw

the meeting between the commander in chief and his young protégé
at the French camp and saw the marquis, still pale and shaky from a
bout of malaria, throw himself from his horse and embrace the
general, kissing him from ear to ear, in a manner which the general
seemed to feel a little too demonstrative. This was the sort of moment
for which the French nobles, who saw their lives in terms of the great
battlepieces on the walls of Versailles, had been trained from their
cradles.

For the French nobility the prospect of victory at Yorktown meant
as much as it did for the Americans. A new generation was wiping
out the defeats their elders had suffered in Germany, at Louisburg,
on the heights at Quebec. Lafayette never forgot that his father was
killed by a British musketball at Minden.

For this new generation, too, there was more excitement in Yorktown than the mere pleasure of revenge against perfidious Albion.
From the rural gravity of Washington's behavior, from the talk of
men's rights and duties and of individual freedom which was commonplace with their American allies, they had been taking on a whole
new set of hopes and aspirations for themselves and for mankind.
Lafayette himself, de Lauzun who had unhorsed Tarleton in the woods
back of Gloucester Point, de Noailles, the Lameth brothers and a
dozen others were all to go back to France breathing out the spirit
of American liberty. In the political struggles to come, when the old
regime of Versailles started crumbling about their ears, they were to
take the side of freedom.

Among the French troops landed on the York Peninsula, serving as
an officer in the 7th Touraine Regiment, which his cousin, the head of
the great house of Saint Simon, commanded, there was an erratic
young aristocrat who was to become, in the course of a strange career,
not only the first instigator of European socialism, but of that nineteenth century religion of science which would be stamped with the
name of his pupil, Auguste Compte. From Rochambeau's winter quarters after Cornwallis surrendered, Claude Henri de Saint Simon wrote
his father: "I surmised that the American Revolution marked the beginning of a new political era and that this revolution would necessarily
entail an important progress in general civilization and that soon it
would bring about great changes in the social order in Europe."

It was one of those moments in history when young men wake in
their beds sniffing a fresh ozone in the morning air. It was a new sun
that broke through the clouds each dawn. They could feel the old
feudal world of privilege and pageantry being turned upside down
over their heads.

No wonder that, as the siege went on according to the careful prescriptions of the martial science of the period, people crowded in from far and near to see the show. The press of visitors became so great that Washington was forced to bar them by a general order: "The Commander in Chief having observed that the Trenches are constantly crowded by Spectators, who by passing and repassing, prevent the men from working and thereby greatly impede the operations of the Seige; He therefore orders that no officer not on duty shall enter the trenches except General Officers and their Aids. And that no inhabitant or person not belonging to the Army be suffered to enter the Trenches at any time without permission from the Major General of the Trenches."

As the fate of the British became certain, Washington was perplexed with the importunities of young men anxious to shine in these "great Events."

Lafayette had done his level best to induce him to shunt Benjamin Lincoln over to the Gloucester side of the river, so that, he volubly explained, he might add to his own military reputation by commanding the whole right wing. Goodnatured as ever, he acquiesced in the general's refusal with a smile and a shrug.

Hamilton, carried away by the drama of the moment, managed to push another colonel into the background and to assume command of the American forces attacking a British redoubt. The attack was a success and Hamilton exercised his literary skill in reporting it to Congress. John Laurens, needless to say, distinguished himself in the same operation without stepping into any man's light.

Even after the surrender the professionals of military glory kept elbowing themselves into the center of the stage. When, under the orders of his colonel, young Ensign Denny, who was keeping such a useful diary, was about to plant the regimental standard of the Pennsylvanians on the British fortifications, the Baron von Steuben came bustling up and snatched it out of his hand and planted it himself. A duel with Denny's testy commander, Colonel Butler of Carlisle, was barely averted.

3. Sentiments Far Different from Those I Expected

Before the wining and dining of the defeated British generals and of the exultant French allies that followed the surrender was over, before the bloated carcasses of the horses the British had killed and thrown into the river had been washed away by the tide, or the bodies of Negroes dead of smallpox or camp fever in the ruins of the little settlement had been properly buried, Washington was back at his desk writing gloomy letters again:

"My only apprehension, (which I hope may be groundless) is," he wrote Governor Nelson of Virginia, "lest the late important success, instead of exciting our exertions as it ought to, should produce such a relaxation in the prosecution of the war, as will prolong the calamities of it."

His apprehension was to a certain extent justified.

In spite of all Lafayette's persuasive charm de Grasse refused to let himself be convinced that he ought to linger long enough on the American coast to help in the operations against Wilmington or Charleston which Washington had set his heart on. In fact the Provençal showed so little interest in the American campaign that he stayed cooped up in his admiral's quarters on his magnificent flagship, the *Ville de Paris,* all through the siege. He did not even let himself be tempted by the great show of the surrender but, pleading some mysterious malady, had himself represented by the Count de Barras. Now his only interest seemed to be to get his table furnished with a few fresh vegetables and to sail south to the more congenial and lucrative encounters of the Caribbean. Even after having scored half a victory over Graves, he was none too anxious to risk a fresh encounter with the British fleet.

Washington had won a campaign but he knew the war still hung in the balance. A fresh British naval victory might tip the scales again. As if to confirm his worst apprehensions, Graves' fleet appeared off the Virginia Capes. This time neither admiral seems to have had stomach for a fight. De Grasse clung to his anchor lines and, in spite of a favoring wind, Graves made no effort to force an entrance into the bay. The moment the British sails went out of sight under the horizon, de Grasse hurried his troops aboard his ships and, without sending any further word to the American commander, took French leave to the southward.

With the Chesapeake open to the enemy again, Washington lost no time in starting his prisoners off on their march inland. His own troops were to return to their "dreary station" keeping watch on Clinton from West Point. Rochambeau was to spend the winter in the York Peninsula to guard Virginia. Cornwallis and his staff meanwhile were sent off under parole in a frigate, flying a flag of truce, to New York. Washington finished up the dreary business of reviewing the courtsmartial of deserters captured with the British, confirmed one death sentence, commuted the rest, and early in November got ready to ride home to Mount Vernon for a few days' repose before waiting on Congress in Philadelphia. At this stage of the war he deemed it more important to watch Congress than to watch the enemy.

He had hardly started on the road home when the joys of victory were all at once turned for him into bitterness and grief. The last entry for November 5, in the second little purplebound volume of the diary Washington started that spring to record "the happy Events" he hoped for in the Virginia campaign, broke off suddenly at the end of a page as if interrupted by some distracting message. The news that came must have been that Jack Custis was sick of camp fever at Colonel Bassett's house near Ruffin's Ferry. By the time Washington reached him he was dying. Martha and Jack's wife Nancy and his little girl Eliza and a couple of helpless physicians were at his bedside. Next day he died. He was a worthless young fellow, but he was the nearest thing to a son George Washington ever had.

Washington treated the deaths of those dear to him with stubborn silence. He kept close rein on his feelings as he did on the fine stallions he liked to ride. He abhorred any unmanly indulgence in grief.

The day after Jack's death he wrote the new President of Congress, John Hanson of Maryland, from Bassett's:

"Sir, After getting the detachment for the Southward on its March (which has been delayed longer than I expected on account of a want of Waggons, and other impediments) and having embarked the greatest part of the Eastern Troops for the head of Elk, getting the whole in readiness for it and making a distribution of the Ordnance and Stores; I set out yesterday on my return to the Northern Army; but an event which I met with at this place (very distressing to Mrs. Washington) will retard my arrival at Philadelphia a few days longer than I expected, which I hope Congress will have the goodness to excuse as I am not conscious that any important public duty will be neglected by it."

The detachment to the southward he referred tó was the body of Continental troops being sent down under Arthur St. Clair to reinforce General Greene in the Carolinas. In those last days at Yorktown the commander in chief had trouble keeping his more ambitious officers in harness. Hamilton immediately dashed home to his wife and to his new career in the law under the tender wing of the Schuyler family in Albany. Election to the Maryland Senate would soon furnish McHenry with an excuse to resign. Lafayette was getting ready to take off overseas to preen his victorious feathers at the court of Versailles. Anthony Wayne had requested leave to attend to his private affairs but had been induced to stay with his troops at least until they had joined Greene before Wilmington in North Carolina.

Now Washington set to work in his usual businesslike manner to attend to Jack Custis's funeral, to set plans in motion to get the estate settled, and to escort the bereaved ladies to Mount Vernon. There he allowed Martha a week of seclusion and mourning before he packed her into her carriage on the road to Philadelphia. By November twentyfirst they were in Annapolis, where the general was kept busy dictating to his secretaries answers to flamboyant addresses of welcome by the mayor and the two houses of the legislature.

III   The Careful Physician

1. Pater Patriae

The dinners and the toasts and the adulation of the ladies and the poetic recitations by little girls in white and the laurel wreaths let down on the general's head from triumphal arches that greeted their party at every turn of the road were having an appreciable effect on Mrs. Washington's spirits. She seems to have been a plump gentle person, indulgent of herself and her family, not too strong in the head, perhaps with a little more than her share of vanity. By Christmas the general was writing his old friend, the bibulous and scholarly New Yorker who had taken to himself the title of Lord Stirling, that Mrs. Washington was better than he could have expected after the heavy loss she had met with.

The day after New Year's the general and his lady were treated in Philadelphia to a grand theatrical evening which included a comedy by Beaumarchais, a ballet, and a transparency and tableau symbolizing the rise of a new nation in the West. This performance gave considerable scandal to the godly among the Quakers and some of the stricter sects. In fact it was pointed out in the press that the Assembly had passed a law against just such devilish temptations as this stage show.

The general, as was his custom, blandly ignored the criticism of the clerics. He had gone to some trouble to have Addison's *Cato* performed to cheer the troops at Valley Forge. All his life he took an almost childlike pleasure in the theater; it never occurred to him to miss a stage play when he could take one in, and it never occurred to him to pay attention to the opinions of a clergyman.

As it turned out, the Washingtons spent the entire winter in Philadelphia. There, while the general coped gravely with the protocol of congressional audiences and with his work with the committee that was reorganizing the army, Mrs. Washington was able to keep her spirits up in the company of the wealthy hostesses of the town, Mrs. Robert Morris, attractive Mrs. Bingham, and the ladies of the Willing family.

Philadelphia was full of gleaming harness and fashionable toilettes and formal entertainments. The local magnates, grouped round Robert Morris, who as Financier was building up his own fortune at the same time as he tried to stabilize the fiscal affairs of the confederation through the Bank of North America, came out of the war very wealthy indeed. Their wives were beginning to feel far too rich and wellborn to associate themselves with the aspirations of the lowly herd which found their expression in the Declaration of Independence and in the Pennsylvania constitution of 1776. Once the pressure from the enemy was relieved, class lines began to stiffen. The Revolution had left a lot of room at the top of the social heap. The merchants and the war speculators were crowding exultantly into the seats of power left vacant by the flight of the Tories and of the royal officials.

Though Washington was never "one of the sanguine ones," as he put it, he allowed himself a little more flattering unction than usual amid the comforts and the entertainments and the stately dinners of that Philadelphia winter. His dear friend Robert Morris seemed to have the finances in hand and was glibly claiming to have settled the problem of victualing the troops once and for all by farming procurement out to a number of individual contractors. Washington found the members of Congress agreeing with him perfectly on the need for a more efficient organization of the army. They appointed stolid General Lincoln, in whom he had every confidence, Secretary at War.

In January Washington wrote Lafayette to congratulate him, and through him the French minister, the great Vergennes, on the Marquis de Bouillé's brilliant coup in recapturing St. Eustatius, and to remind him that with a little more money from France to pay the Continental troops and a fresh naval force on the American coast during the coming summer they could complete the ruin of Great Britain in a single campaign. At the end of the letter he was able to add that he had just heard that the British had pulled out of Wilmington and were concentrating what was left of their southern force on the Charleston peninsula. Just the place, he did not need to add, where a French fleet could bottle them up again.

The third George, in his speech at the opening of Parliament in November, which was just being reported in the gazettes, had breathed defiance of the rebels and of the growing opposition in England but had given little indication of any plan for prosecuting the war.

When at the end of March the commander in chief arrived with Mrs. Washington to resume direct command of the army on the Hudson at his new headquarters in a pleasant stone house in the town of Newburgh, he found his staff seething with contention.

Winter quarters was always a time of quarrels and cabals. With Sir Henry Clinton's forces sunk in apathy in New York, the troops had only an occasional loyalist raid to keep them busy. As enemy pressure subsided, all the smoldering rancor and bitterness came to the surface. For years officers and men had been serving without proper clothing or equipment. Their pay, when they got it, was in paper money or in various kinds of certificates with a merely nominal value which soon sank to zero in the all-encompassing advance of inflation. Their appetite was whetted by a taste of specie at Head of Elk. Now that the war was nearly won they felt the time had come for Congress to consider their claim for compensation in some medium they could use for money.

Washington found the universal disgruntlement expressing itself in a row among his general officers. The row stemmed from the usual problem of who should take orders from whom. Major General Heath, the heavyhanded farmer from Roxbury, Massachusetts, who was Washington's second in command, had placed Major General McDougall under arrest.

McDougall — Sawney McDougall the milkmon's son, as he was known to his supporters — was a vehement Scot from New York who had been saluted in his youth as the American Wilkes. He had made his own way in the world. As a soldier he was an old campaigner in whom Washington had so much confidence that he put him in charge of West Point when Arnold's treason was discovered. Furthermore he had represented his state in the Continental Congress and had a large popular following.

In some postmortem argument over who was responsible for the loss of Manhattan early in the war, he intimated that Heath was "a knave." Heath promptly confined him to quarters. When General Stirling was appointed to preside over his courtmartial, McDougall threatened to call his selfstyled lordship out for a duel. Each man had a faction among officers and men. Barracks and billets echoed with disputing voices.

The one topic on which the commander in chief found his officers in agreement was that Comfort Sands, Robert Morris's contractor for the feeding of the forces along the Hudson, was a scoundrel.

While Washington with his usual paternal diplomacy was trying to quiet the contentious passions of his generals, news came from the

commissioners who were treating for an exchange of prisoners with
Sir Henry Clinton in New York that caused all patriots to close ranks.
A group of refugees, as the loyalist partisans who fought with the
British were called, had seized a Captain Huddy of the New Jersey
militia who was confined as a prisoner on a British prison ship in the
harbor and had taken him over to Middletown and hanged him with
a placard on his breast as a reprisal for the shooting of a loyalist.

Washington immediately demanded of Sir Henry Clinton that the
officer guilty of this outrage be punished. Meanwhile the Americans
drew a British officer by lot from among their prisoners to be executed
as a counter reprisal in case no action was taken against the murderer
of Captain Huddy.

It turned out that the man chosen, a comely youth of good family
named Asgill, was protected by the terms of the Yorktown capitulation. Washington stayed his execution.

This was a perplexity indeed. The last thing the general wanted
was to make another martyr like André. At the same time the loyalists
had to be taught a lesson.

In the midst of recriminations and counter recriminations Sir Henry
Clinton instituted a prosecution of Huddy's executioners which was
something less than halfhearted. It was obvious that the British commander had lost control of the loyalist partisans who, maddened by
the defeat of their cause, were carrying out ever more spiteful raids
against patriot communities. Clinton seems to have been glad enough
to escape this miserable tangle of hatreds and resentments by relinquishing his command in New York. A far abler man took charge.

The arrival of Sir Guy Carleton in early May to command the
British forces in America, with the express purpose of reaching a settlement, was the first visible result to the Americans of the upset that
had occurred in the administration at Westminster six weeks before.
Stubborn George had finally bowed to the inevitable and consented
to Lord North's resignation.

No government could have stood up under the series of defeats
that accompanied the surrender of Yorktown. Minorca, the great
British naval base in the Mediterranean, had fallen; Gibraltar was
besieged. In the West Indies de Grasse was carrying everything before him.

Grudgingly the King invited the Marquis of Rockingham to form a
ministry of Whigs. Lord North, one of the wittiest politicians ever to
bring this country to the edge of disaster, stepped out of office with
a jest. He was quoted as saying that, false as much of the information
was which he had published in the official gazette, he'd never told

such a lie as his successor, who prefaced the notice of his accession with the usual words: *His Majesty is pleased to appoint.*

Indeed for the popeyed flaxen-haired intriguer in St. James's Palace it was the bitterest moment of his life. In accepting North's resignation he was admitting defeat in his twenty years' struggle to reestablish royal rule in Great Britain. It was whispered round London that the royal yacht was being outfitted for a sea voyage, that George was going to retire to Hanover in a sulk. Instead he went on riding to his hounds at Windsor; but the strings of patronage that had animated the royal government had slipped from his hands forever and he knew it.

2. *Britannia Rules the Waves*

Had he been able to forecast the events of the next few weeks in the West Indies the third George might have tried to hold his crumbling tory administration together for a while longer.

Tortured with gout, stung by the invective of the whig politicians, and embarrassed financially by attachments at the hands of the St. Eustatius merchants, which made him all too conscious of the fact that only a great victory could save him from the prospect of a debtor's prison when he got home, Rodney on his flagship the *Formidable* led a freshly equipped fleet westward across seething Atlantic seas.

"Through storms and tempests and contrary winds," he wrote his wife from St. Lucia early in March, "we forced our way in five weeks to Barbadoes where my stay was only a few hours, till the breeze allowed us to sail."

His pen scratched with indignation when he described the ignominious surrender of St. Kitts. The West Indians were traitorous scoundrels; and he was crippled with gout. The press of duties left him no time to be ill. He was hoping, he told Lady Rodney, that the very violence of the present attack would insure him a few weeks of freedom from the disease. His hands and feet were swollen. It was agony to move. Even writing made him tired. His only pleasure was in the portraits of his daughters he had hung on his cabin walls. "I would not, for the world, have left the portraits of my dear girls behind me. They are the joy of my life and converse with me daily. By looking at them, they calm my mind, and even ease the torment of the gout, when it is upon me . . .

"The fleet," he went on, "I found here in want of everything; there is no villainy some of the merchants of these islands are not guilty

of, and they take every opportunity of carrying on a traitorous correspondence with the enemy, supplying them with provisions etc."

The gout, the lawsuits, the political attacks on his reputation in
England, the treachery of the West India planters, whose only idea
was to sell sugar and get rich, were lashing Rodney into a frenzy of
activity. Jamaica and Antigua and Barbados were the only important
islands the British had left. To save Jamaica he had to whip de Grasse.
The French and Spaniards were so confident that they could take that
richest of the sugar islands that a Spanish governor had already been
appointed.

The British admiral's first care was to establish a chain of fast sailing frigates to keep watch on the French, who as usual were hugging
their anchorage under the protection of the forts on the Martinique
shore. Meanwhile he cruised between the islands, waiting to pounce.

At last, in the second week in April, de Grasse's great expedition
against Jamaica ventured to put to sea. Rodney immediately made all
sail to intercept it. He caught up with the French fleet in the Saints'
Passage between Guadeloupe and Dominica.

"In the course of the two next days," wrote Rodney's personal
physician, Sir Gilbert Blane, who was on board the *Formidable* to
watch over the admiral's health, "the enemy, by dint of great efforts,
kept far to windward, and would probably have made their escape
had they not been brought down on the 11th to save one of their
ships which had dropped to leeward in consequence of being crippled
by running afoul of another ship in the night." — Another of the collisions for which de Grasse's fleet was notorious. — "By this casualty we
had the inexpressible pleasure at day-break on the 12th, to discover
that we were in a position to weather a large part of the enemy's
fleet . . . About half an hour before the engagement commenced, at
breakfast aboard the *Formidable,* the conversation naturally turned
on the glorious prospects of the day; and Lord Cranstoun remarked,
that if our fleet maintained its present relative position steering the
same course closehauled on the opposite tack to the enemy, we must
necessarily pass through their line in running along, and closing with
it in action."

Whether it was his own idea or that of one of his staff, Rodney,
seated in a chair on his quarterdeck to take the weight off his gouty
legs, decided to steer straight through the enemy's line of battle. "In
the act of doing so," continued Sir Gilbert, "we passed within pistol-
shot of the *Glorieux* of seventyfour guns which was so roughly handled that being shorn of all her masts, bowsprit and ensign staff but
with the white flag" — the French fleur de lis — "nailed to the stump
of one of her masts, breathing defiance as it were, in her last moments
become a motionless hulk, presenting a spectacle which struck our

Admiral's fancy as not unlike the remains of a fallen hero, for being an indefatigable reader of Homer he exclaimed that now was to be the contest for the body of Patroclus; but the contest was already at an end, for the enemy's fleet being separated fell into confusion, a total rout ensued and victory was no longer doubtful."

In the confusion of the encounter the *Ville de Paris* found herself surrounded by British ships. "De Grasse had lost his wits, made no more signals, sought every post of danger," wrote an embittered observer on one of the French ships that got away. Many of them had not waited for the admiral's "sauve qui peut" to take advantage of the last of the trade wind to crowd on all sail out of cannon shot to leeward. As the breeze died out in the fading glow of the short tropic twilight the lookouts on the *Formidable* saw that the French admiral had struck his flag.

"The Comte de Grasse," Rodney wrote to his wife a few days later, "who is at this moment sitting in my stern gallery, tells me that he thought his fleet superior to mine and does so still, though I had two more in number; and I am of his opinion, as his was composed all of large ships, and ten of mine only sixty fours . . . I am of the opinion," he went on, "that the French will not face us again in this war."

De Grasse had won the hearts of his British captors by his personal courage against overwhelming odds and by the nonchalance with which he took his defeat. They were surprised, when he was brought aboard the *Formidable*, by the lively interest he took in the antics of the sailors who were fishing for sharks that had been attracted in shoals by the dead bodies thrown overboard during the engagement. He delighted them by his disarming frankness when he talked on naval matters. "The Comte de Grasse said they were a hundred years behind us," wrote Sir Gilbert, "and added that were we not enemies he should have been charmed with the superior discipline, neatness and order that prevailed in our ships of war."

"You may believe," Rodney wrote Lady Rodney a couple of weeks after the battle, "my fatigues and anxieties have not been trifling. I begin now to feel the effects, but I hope a few days quiet at Grenada will restore me to perfect health. Tell my dearest girls they are never out of my mind; I see and converse with them hourly and such was my attention and my care of them, that I would not suffer them to be in danger in the battle. They took care of my wine in the store-room and seemed quite refreshed after their fatiguing duty. All the French officers were in love with them, particularly Count de Grasse."

The magnificent *Ville de Paris* was so badly damaged that she sank with her prize crew on the Atlantic crossing. De Grasse made his way to England, where he was presented at court and was the toast of the town during the London season. King George paid his hotel bills.

When he returned to France after the peace the nonchalant Provençal seems to have been surprised to find himself far from popular. At Versailles there was less talk of his courage than of the monumental blunders that had brought about his defeat. All the thanks Rodney got from the new administration at Westminster was a peremptory order to give up his command and come home.

3. The Title of King

The arrival of Sir Guy Carleton and the rumors of this great British victory in the Caribbean, to which that old America hand was giving full play in the New York gazettes, confirmed Washington's worst forebodings. The British were not beaten yet. He knew it had been Carleton's courage and skill and his astute handling of the Canadians that had defeated Arnold's and Montgomery's expedition against Quebec in the first year of the war. It was Carleton's peace propaganda he was thinking of when he wrote Robert R. Livingston, the enterprising head of the great Hudson River family of Livingstons whom Congress had appointed their first Secretary for Foreign Affairs: "We wanted no fresh opiate to increase that stupor into which we had fallen, but I much fear that the idle, and delusive offers of Peace with which the Country resounds, will, if it is not powerfully counteracted, be exceedingly injurious to us; not (I apprehend) from any disposition of the people to listen to improper terms, but from a misconception of what is really meant, and the arts which are used to make them believe that Independence, and what not, are preferred to them."

He was remembering Carleton's astute measures conciliating the Catholic Church and giving both the French and Englishspeaking settlers a measure of autonomy in their own affairs which had saved Canada for the Crown. The presence of Carleton in New York, backed up by Rodney's victory in the West Indies, was not a matter to take lightly. Washington knew that the settlers in the Green Mountain region, willing to take any means to free themselves from the conflicting jurisdictions of New York and New Hampshire, were already negotiating with the British on their own.

The commander in chief was taking advantage of the time it took his quartermaster to hunt through the army's stables for a fresh horse for the postrider who was carrying dispatches to Congress to unburden himself to Livingston. No delay could be brooked because these were dispatches from France that might disclose Vergennes' plans for next summer's campaign. While his pen scratched fast he was all too conscious of the fact that there lay on his desk a sheaf of papers that would cause him even more perplexity than Rodney's victory or the subtle machinations of the new British commander in New York.

These papers consisted of a carefully written memorial that summed up the army's discontents and grievances: "The injuries the troops have received in their pecuniary rights," the general read, "have been and will continue to be too obvious to require a particular detail, or to have escaped your Excellencies notice, tho' your exalted station must have deprived you of opportunity of information relative to the severe distress occasioned thereby."

After this well directed shaft at the eternal ignorance of the top command of the problems that beset the lower ranks, the general's correspondent pointed out that Congress had taken no effective action to find money for the arrears owed the army.

"This gives us a dismal prospect for the time to come," he read on, "& much reason to fear the future provision promised to officers, and the settling & satisfying their and their men's just demands will be little attended to, when our services are no longer wanted, and that the recompense of all our toils, hardships, expense of private fortune will be, to those who cannot earn a livelihood by manual labor, beggary; & that we who have borne the heat & labor of the day will be forgotten by such as reap the benefits without suffering any of the hardships."

His correspondent explained that officers and men, to eke out a living, had been forced to sell their pay certificates and their paper money to speculators for a small part of their value, "never more than one tenth, but often less." The correspondent went on to intimate in no uncertain terms that the patience of the army was exhausted. "I believe it is generally intended not to separate after the peace until all grievances are redressed, engagments and promises fulfilled . . . God forbid that we should ever think of involving that country which we have, under your conduct and auspices, rescued from oppression, into a new scene of blood & confusion, but it cannot be expected we should forego claims on which our future subsistence and that of our families depend."

This was threatening talk. The alarming thing about this memorial he had under his eyes was that it was not the work of some young hothead. It was in the handwriting of Colonel Lewis Nicola, whose covering letter was enclosed with it. This Colonel Nicola was a highly respected officer. He was an elderly Philadelphian of Huguenot extraction who had risen to the rank of major in the British army before emigrating to America. Before the war Nicola had edited the first magazine regularly published in Philadelphia. He was one of the

founders of the American Philosophical Society. He had written a
manual for the use of the troops. He had been well known to the
troops and to Congress as town major of Philadelphia during most of
the war and was at present in command of the Invalid Regiment — a
regiment made up of maimed and wounded veterans — which was on
garrison duty at West Point. Esteemed for his knowledge of military
affairs, he was often called upon to serve on courtsmartial.

Colonel Nicola's declaration made painful reading. "I own," he
wrote, "I am not that violent admirer of a republican form of government that numbers in this country are." He developed a carefully
reasoned argument, citing the decay of the aristocratic commonwealths
of Venice and Genoa and the weakness and disunion that were proving fatal to the Dutch Republic in the present war — "does not the
great similarity there is between her form of government and ours
give us room to fear our fate will be like hers?" he asked. He concluded that he considered a limited monarchy in the English style the
best model of government but suggested the improvement that all taxpayers should vote for annual parliaments. He expressed surprise that
none of the states had adopted it. "This war," he added, "must have
shown to all, but to military men in particular, the weakness of re-
publicks."

The plan he suggested to solve the army's troubles and to give
monarchical government a trial in America was that Congress should
pay the arrears owed to the officers and men, one third in cash and
the rest in public lands to the westward where the army should set up
a new state as a buffer against the British. His final suggestion made
a cold chill go down Washington's spine: "The same abilities which
have led us, through difficulties apparently insurmountable by human
power, to victory & glory, these qualities that have merited & obtained
the universal esteem & veneration of an army would be most likely
to conduct & direct us in the smoother paths of peace. Some people
have so connected the ideas of tyranny and monarchy as to find it very
difficult to separate them," he argued; "it may therefore be requisite
to give the head of such a constitution as I propose some title appar-
antly more moderate, but if all things are once adjusted I believe
strong arguments might be produced for admitting the title of king."

Washington was brought up as a Whig. His principles stemmed
from the Glorious Revolution. As much as any English country gentleman he believed that the military should be subordinate to the civil
power. During most of his early career as an officer of the Virginia
militia he saw the interests of the colonials sacrificed to the tory doctrines which the third George's manipulation of Parliament caused to
triumph at Westminster. If he ever felt much allegiance to the House
of Hanover, and he may have as a young man, that allegiance was

superseded, the day he took over command of the Continental Army, by his allegiance to the Continental Congress. He was no theorist about schemes of government but he had given his word to exercise every power he possessed "for the support of the glorious Cause." As the years wore on, the cause of independence became indissolubly associated in his mind with the cause of representative government in general and of Congress in particular. His heart was set on ending the war and going home to attend to his private business at Mount Vernon. He had already envisioned the final gesture of laying down his command without payment or reward. Reading Nicola's memorial shocked him to the marrow.

Immediately he wrote out a reply in his own hand: ". . . I am much at a loss to conceive what part of my conduct would have given encouragement to an address which to me seems big with the greatest mischiefs that can befall my Country. If I am not deceived in the knowledge of myself, you could not have found a person to whom your schemes are more disagreeable; at the same time in justice to my own feelings I must add, that no Man possesses a more sincere wish to see ample justice done to the army than I do, and as far as my powers and influence, in a constitutional way extend, they shall be employed to the utmost of my abilities to affect it, should there be any occasion. Let me conjure you then, if you have any regard for your Country, concern for yourself or posterity, or respect for me to banish these thoughts from your Mind, and never communicate, as from yourself, or any one else, a sentiment of the like Nature."

Washington found Nicola's proposals so alarming that for purposes of record he asked both Humphreys and young Trumbull to sign an attestation that the copy of his letter they sent off in reply was a true one. If this matter ever came out in the open he wanted to be in a position to counter the "animadversions" he dreaded.

It was proof of the sway Washington held over the minds of his officers that Colonel Nicola was so aghast at the tone of the commander in chief's reply that he wrote back three separate letters of apology during the next few days. They were forthright and manly communications; without exactly retracting his own opinions he bowed to Washington's superior judgment: "Since I find your sentiments so different from mine I shall consider myself as having been under a strong delusion & beg leave to assure you it shall be my future study to combat, as far as my abilities reach, every gleam of discontent."

From that day on, Washington knew that, as he had spent the last seven years raising an army and keeping it together, his preoccupation now would be to get the troops home again without an explosion. But the war was not over. Suppose the British launched a new attack. Perplexities indeed.

Meanwhile he went to work to try to remedy the supply situation. The contractor was not furnishing the troops at West Point with proper rations. "Why Sir," he wrote Comfort Sands in a rage, "are the Troops without provisions? . . . Why do you so pertinaciously adhere to all those parts of the Contracts as are promotive of your own Interest and convenience . . . and at the same time disregard the most essential claims of the public; thereby hazarding the dissolution of the Army, and risking the loss of the most important Post in America?"

At the same time he put the matter up to Robert Morris in friendly expostulation. It would be dangerous to drive the troops to despair. "Minds soured by distresses are easily rankled," he told him, taking the precaution to get his secretaries to put this part of the message into cipher, "as a specimen of it, the privates of the Connecticut line were the other day upon the eve of a general Mutiny; the vigilance of the Officers discovered it a few hours before they were to parade, and the ringleaders have been tried and executed; besides this desertions are more prevalent than ever." And this in spite of the savage military code of the time: deserters punished with a hundred lashes on the bare back; the courtsmartial almost continuously in session; the death sentence for repeated desertions which he approved as commander in chief again and again in his general orders.

Washington accepted the lash and the firing squad as part of the business of soldiering. He worked hard to see that punishment was applied justly but he suffered no humanitarian qualms at the sight of a flogged man's bloody back or of the weeping comrades of a mutineer cocking their muskets to shoot him. Yet as the year dragged on even he began to doubt the efficacy of too many floggings or too many executions.

Keeping the hungry army in a military posture when everyone knew that peace negotiations were beginning in Paris was a brutal business.

4.   An Assembly Truly Republican

Washington seized on the birth of a dauphin to the French King as an opportunity to cheer up the troops weary of close order drill and poverty and short rations, and at the same time to flatter the ally whose help was so crucial at Yorktown. He set the soldiers to work building an enormous bower of evergreens in which the commander in chief would entertain five hundred guests for dinner. The troops were paraded. Feux de joie were shot off and an extra gill of rum was served out all around. "A new edge to our swords, until they shall have opened the way to independence, freedom and glory; and then may be converted to the instruments of peace" was the favorite toast of the evening.

The Chevalier de la Luzerne returned the compliment in Philadelphia later in the summer by staging the most giant entertainment that had ever been seen on American shores. The ingenious Captain L'Enfant designed the decorations. Dr. Rush was present and described the party expansively to a lady of his acquaintance in a letter that was widely quoted in the newspapers:

"For ten days before the entertainment nothing else was talked of in our city. The shops were crowded with customers. Hairdressers were retained; tailors, milliners, and mantua-makers were to be seen covered with sweat and out of breath in every street.

"Monday, July 15, was the long expected evening. The morning of this day was ushered in by a corps of hairdressers occupying the place of the city watchmen. Many ladies were obliged to have their heads dressed between four and six o'clock in the morning, so great was the demand and so numerous were the engagements this day of the gentlemen of the comb. At half-past seven o'clock was the time fixed in the tickets for the meeting of the company. The approach of the hour was proclaimed by the rattling of all the carriages in the city . . . We were received through a wide gate by the Minister and conducted by one of his family forward to the dancing room . . . The numerous lights distributed through the garden, the splendor of the room we were approaching, the size of the company which was now collected and which amounted to about 700 persons, the brilliancy and variety of their dresses, and the band of music which had just began to play, formed a scene that resembled enchantment. Sukey Stockton said her mind was carried beyond and out of itself. We entered the room together, and here we saw the world in miniature. All the ranks and parties and professions in the city and all the officers of government were fully represented in this assembly. Here were ladies and gentlemen of the most ancient as well as modern families. Here were lawyers, doctors, and ministers of the gospel. Here were the learned faculty of the College, and with them many who knew not whether Cicero plead in Latin or in Greek, or whether Horace was a Roman or a Scotchman. Here were painters and musicians, poets and philosophers, and men who were never moved by beauty or harmony or rhyme or reason. Here were merchants and gentlemen of independent fortunes, as well as many respectable and opulent tradesmen. Here were whigs and men who formerly bore the character of tories. Here were the president and members of Congress, governors of states and generals of armies, ministers of finance and war and foreign affairs, judges of superior and inferior courts, with all their respective suits of assistants, secretaries, and clerks. In a word, the assembly was truly republican."

5. Ben Franklin's Gambit

Putting in an appearance at the French minister's party was far from being the first object of Washington's journey down to Philadelphia. The general was there for a much delayed conference with Rochambeau on plans for another campaign. Very little came of that conference. A French squadron, it turned out, was on its way to the American coast, but not a powerful enough fleet to risk an engagement with the British, who had been showing the confidence they had gained from Rodney's great victory by making a clean sweep of American shipping on the high seas. Washington was still urging that, if Versailles would furnish the money, the allied armies should try a sudden expedition to take Quebec, or if the French could marshal the naval force the allied armies could repeat the Yorktown operation against Charleston or New York.

With the best will in the world all that Rochambeau could do was to bow and smile. To avoid complete inactivity it was agreed that he would move his troops by slow and comfortable stages back to the Hudson.

In the worldwide war the prospects had changed since the great day at Yorktown. Vergennes at Versailles was beginning to have as many misgivings as the new government at Westminster about the wisdom of risking anything more on the American continent. Vergennes, a careful routinarian statesman of the old regime, saw himself essentially as a servant of the Bourbon monarchy. He had gone as far as he felt safe to help the revolting British colonies. The allied Bourbons of Spain were becoming uneasy about the potential threat of a new and aggressive Protestant nation to their holdings in the two Americas. With the dream of the conquest of the sugar islands gone by the board Vergennes was worrying about where the money would come from to prosecute the war. As he listened to young Lafayette, back from America full of idealistic talk about the revolution that would remake mankind, his misgivings undoubtedly increased. His life was dedicated to the strengthening of the bureaucratic despotism he had been brought up in, not to encouraging forces that might endanger its very existence. He had gone as far as he dared to encourage the philosophers' dream.

Franklin understood these things if Lafayette did not. The two old men understood and esteemed each other. Ever since Franklin had arrived in France, after slipping across the Atlantic with his two grandsons on an armed sloop, and landed unannounced in a small fishing port on the Breton coast in the fall of the year of many happenings, 1776, the American philosopher and the courtly bureaucrat had been matching wits in a friendly game of diplomatic chess. Now that they both felt the time had come to make peace each of them became very careful of his moves. Wartime mistakes could be remedied, but the peace was for keeps.

Franklin in his seventies had already lived enough lives for four men. Starting as a migrant printer, wandering from Boston to Philadelphia, from Philadelphia to London, and from London back to Philadelphia again, he took root in Philadelphia and into his forties lived the career of a successful storekeeper, of a publisher of newspapers, and a man of business. In the course of it he developed one of the sweetest styles of familiar writing ever attained in English.

As a philosophical hobby he led the way in experiments with electricity.

He had lived another life as colonial postmaster and public official. Again as agent for the Pennsylvanians in London he became one of the animators of the inventive and inquiring spirit that moved the discussions of the Royal Society and Lord Kames' breakfast table conversations outside Edinburgh and Matthew Boulton's experiments with manufacturing in Birmingham. He lived the high tide of the enlightenment in England.

Again, when the difficulties between the Crown and the colonies reached a breaking point, he made himself a full career as a revolutionary leader and as the protagonist of a radical plan for popular government. On his ocean crossings he initiated the study of the Gulf Stream.

Since arriving in France he had held in his knotted old hands the threads of all the intrigue through which the Americans acquired a fleet and munitions of war and funds and troops and an alliance with the court of Versailles. When rumor that North's ministry was tottering came hard on the heels of the news of Yorktown, he knew that the war was won. The peace which would establish the first independent European nation on the new continent overseas would be the crowning of his work.

Crippled by gout and by intermittent agonies from the stone in his bladder that was to cause him so much suffering for the rest of his days, he lurked in his hôtel de Valentinois in the quiet leafy suburb of Passy which his fame had made, for the philosophers of Europe at least, as much a hub of French life as Versailles itself; and waited, like the busy crafty old spider that he was, for overtures from England.

Naturally enough the first intimations came through a lady friend. A certain Lord Cholmondeley made the acquaintance in Nice of Franklin's dear Madame de Brillon, who was privileged to call him Papa and to sit on the aged philosopher's lap. It took more than worldwide war to keep the English milords from getting their glimpse of the sun on the Riviera. This gentleman appeared at Passy on his way home with a safe conduct from Versailles and assured Franklin of the high regard in which he was held by the liberal and devious Lord Shelburne.

Franklin already had letters from the Continental Congress appointing him, along with John Jay, who was in Madrid; with John Adams, who was negotiating a loan in Amsterdam; with Henry Laurens, who was shut up in the Tower of London; and with Thomas Jefferson, who was still refusing public office in Virginia, as plenipotentiaries to cooperate with the Bourbon foreign office in drafting peace terms with England.

A few days after the visit news came that North had resigned and that Lord Shelburne was Foreign Minister in Rockingham's whig government. Edmund Burke's contingent of pro-American Whigs was flocking into the administration. The turgid star of Charles James Fox was rising at Westminster. It looked as if Fox, who by his debater's skill in the Commons had kept radical whig doctrines alive through the years of King George's ascendancy, was at last just one step from becoming Prime Minister. Almost immediately Franklin received a call from Richard Oswald.

Oswald was a man of Franklin's own age, a Glasgow merchant with plantations in Jamaica and in the states, and a lifelong friend of Henry Laurens. He was no stranger to Franklin. Years before he had been introduced to him by Adam Smith. He had just proved the sincerity of his sympathy with the Americans by going Laurens' bail for fifty thousand pounds. He arrived fresh from escorting the ailing Charleston merchant across the Channel to Ostend after digging him out of his stony lodging. Laurens had found traveling too hard. His eighteen months' emprisonment had told on his health. He was waiting with John Adams at Haarlem to recover enough strength to risk the journey to Paris.

The two old men climbed into Franklin's carriage and went to call on old Vergennes at Versailles. There Oswald admitted that he had no formal powers to treat. Franklin announced that he did have formal powers and Oswald was sent off to London to report to Lord Shelburne. Before he left Franklin filled Oswald's ears with atrocity stories about the scalping and burning parties of Indians the British had let loose on the American settlers. Since reparations were in order Franklin suggested the cession of Canada to the United States.

Just to jog Lord Shelburne's memory, Franklin perpetrated one of the practical jokes he so much enjoyed. He had his own printing shop at Passy and his slender young grandson Ben Bache to operate it. They printed a spurious supplement to a facsimile of a number of *The Independent Chronicle* of Boston with a bloody tale of bags of scalps captured on their way from the Indians to British headquarters in Canada: 43 soldiers' scalps, 102 of farmers, 67 from very gray heads, 88 of women, 193 of boys, 211 of girls big and little, 29 of infants "ripped out of their mothers' bellies." Copies of the supplement were circulated throughout Europe wherever they would do the most good.

Meanwhile Fox, in an effort to get peace negotiations into his own hands, sent a younger son of the Grenville family over to Paris as his personal representative. When Oswald reappeared Franklin invited both envoys to breakfast, and made it quite clear that independence was already attained: "We do not consider ourselves as under any necessity of bargaining for a thing which is our own."

When news arrived of Rodney's victory over de Grasse, the Britishers began to hem and haw. Vergennes intimated to Franklin that he might as well go on negotiating a separate treaty. If all the treaties — that is, the treaties between Spain and England, between France and England, and between the United States and England — were signed on the same day Vergennes would be satisfied.

They had reached the point of drafting specific proposals when Lord Rockingham suddenly died and the government at Westminster was thrown into confusion until Lord Shelburne reappeared as Prime Minister. Fox had been forced out of the cabinet, so young Grenville's place in Paris was taken by Alleyne Fitzherbert to represent his lordship. Meanwhile, on account of his influence at Versailles and the affection Vergennes had for him, Lafayette was let in on the negotiations. John Jay arrived from Spain. Immediately he put his lawyer's mind to work on the wording of the clauses. He had come from Spain dead sure that favorable boundaries for the United States were the last thing either of the Bourbon courts was willing to grant. He suspected a plot was hatching to restrict the new nation to the territory between the Appalachians and the sea.

It was late October before John Adams drove into Paris. He arrived all puffed up from the success of his negotiations with the Dutch bankers. Adams was a stubby rotund New Englander, blue eyed, redfaced and shortnecked. He could have sat any day for a portrait of John Bull. He was a man of disinterested intelligence. The first public act of his career as a young lawyer was to undertake the defense of a British officer he felt was unjustly accused of being responsible for the deaths in the Boston Massacre. Right was right and wrong was wrong. He was vain. He was suspicious of foreigners. He was learned in the history of statebuilding. His brilliant unorthodox reasoning had happily matched Jefferson's when they worked together on the great state papers of the early Continental Congress. Before leaving on his mission to Europe he wrote, almost unaided, a constitution for his home state of Massachusetts. A pat phrase describing him, ascribed, as all such phrases tended to be, to shrewd old Franklin, was going the rounds: "always an honest man, often a wise one, but sometimes, in some things, absolutely out of his senses."

John Adams and his beloved sharptongued Abigail were New Englanders of the purest stripe. Wherever they went they carried Braintree along with them. They found Franklin's household at Passy repugnant to their notions of proper behavior. They deplored the levity, the risqué jokes, the lax behavior of the noble bluestockings who were forever cuddling the aged philosopher, the illegitimate children so frankly recognized, the looselaced tolerance of human frailties. Franklin was much too cozy with the French.

John Adams and John Jay, another puritan who had been brought up in the rigid ethics of the New York Huguenots, immediately put their heads together to keep old Franklin from being influenced by the rustle of petticoats into giving in too much to the French. Franklin intended nothing of the sort, but Adams' and Jay's suspicions stiffened the negotiations. The terms, so far as the United States were concerned, proved better than anyone dared hope for. No cession of Canada, but indefinite frontiers to the westward. Henry Laurens, still an ill man, dragged himself out to Passy on the last day just in time to affix his signature to the preliminary agreement.

6. Minds Soured by Distresses

Entirely ignorant of the details of the negotiations at Passy, Washington was continuing his vigil on the Hudson. When a French fleet finally did appear off Nantucket, it proved to be made up of only thirteen ships. Their commander wrote from his anchorage in Boston Harbor to suggest that to be doing something he might try a descent on the English posts on the coast of Maine. Washington immediately pointed out that so small an objective was not worth the risk of having the fleet bottled up by the British in Penobscot Bay.

The commander in chief was reconciling himself to the fact that the war was over so far as military movements went. As early as the middle of August of 1782 he wrote his retired aide de camp, Dr. McHenry, now Senator McHenry of Maryland, in the sarcastic and affectionate tone he used when he unbosomed himself to members of the inner circle of his military family: "If the Commanders of the Fleets and Armies of our late *most gracious* Soverign, in America are not guilty of more duplicity than comports with candid minds, we are now advanced to that critical and awful period when our hands are to be tried at the Arts of Negociation."

His role during "that critical and awful period" would be to use all the arts of leadership of which he was a master to hold the army in leash so long as it might be needed to hold up the hands of the American negotiators in Paris. He was getting no help from Congress or from the states; once the peace talks began, they seemed to expect the army to live on air. "The impolicy therefore of suffering ourselves to be lulled by expectations of peace," Washington wrote McHenry again, "because we wish it, and because it is the Interest of Great Britain to hold up the idea of it, will more than probably prove the ruin of our cause; and the disbanding of the Army; for it really appears, from the conduct of the States, that they do not conceive it necessary for the army to receive anything but hard Knocks; to give them Pay has been a matter which has long been out of the Question."

Comfort Sands had thrown up the famous contract in which Robert Morris had such confidence, and the army, so Washington put it, "had been at the very point of trying our hand at how we could live without Subsistence." Their horses, he added, had "long been without anything their own Thriftiness could not supply."

The general wrote in the same vein to his old subordinate, Secretary at War Lincoln, trying to appeal to his fellow feelings as a veteran campaigner: "Only conceive the mortification (even the general officers) must suffer when they cannot invite a French officer, a visiting friend or a travelling acquaintance to a better repast than stinking whiskey (and not always that) and a bit of beef without vegetables will afford them . . . Have not Military Men," he asked indignantly, "the same feelings of those in Civil line? Why then shd. one set receive the constant wages of Service, and the other be continually without them? do the former deserve less for their watchings and toils, for enduring heat and cold, for standing in Sunshine and in Rain and for the dangers they are continually exposed to for the sake of their Country, and by which means the Man in civil life sits quiet under his own vine and his figtree solacing himself in all the comforts, pleasures and enjoyments of life, free

and unrestrained? . . . The patience, the fortitude, the long and
great sufferings of this Army is unexampled in History: but there is
an end to all things, and I fear we are very near one to this."

He was looking forward with dread to the coming of the quarrelsome period of winter quarters. He feared movements of protest
would arise which he could not stifle as promptly as he had old
Nicola's. The army's discontents, he told McHenry, would oblige him
to stick very close to the troops that winter, "and try like a careful
physician to prevent if possible the disorders getting to an incurable
height."

His gloomy mood was heightened by a sad piece of news. Gay
young John Laurens was dead, killed in a trifling skirmish with a
group of plundering loyalists in South Carolina. As the news spread
Laurens' friends filled the mails with their lamentations. Hamilton and
Lafayette wrote pathetic letters. Everybody loved John Laurens. It
was characteristic of Washington that all he said when he wrote
Nathanael Greene, Laurens' commander, was that he considered his
death "a very heavy misfortune" to the public at large, to his family
and to his private friends and connections "to whom his amiable and
useful Character had rendered him particularly dear." Later he wrote
of him: "No man possessed more of the *amor patriae,* in a word he
had not a fault I could ever discover, unless Intrepidity bordering on
Rashness could come under that Denomination, and to this he was
excited by the purest Motives."

Washington was not given to expressing his religious feelings in
public. Although as a country squire he served as vestryman at
Alexandria and Pohick and took part as a matter of course in the
services of the Episcopal Church, he shared the low esteem in which
the deists held the clergy. Most of the stately references to a Divine
Providence that came to his lips during the latter part of the war
were in speeches or state papers composed for him either by young
Jonathan Trumbull, whose father intoned from the governor's chair
in Hartford like a preacher from the pulpit, or by David Humphreys.
Both of these secretaries had been raised in theocratic Connecticut,
where it was considered unseemly to make a public address without
invoking the Almighty.

When Washington spoke of Divine Providence in his letters it
was usually in connection with divine interposition on behalf of the
United States of America. Love of country, not only of his own
Virginia but of this American republic of the thirteen provinces he
was wearing out his years to serve, was his creed's first imperative.
When he spoke of young Laurens as the great exemplar of love of
country, it was the profoundest praise of which his mind was capable.

It was Washington's passionate faith in the "glorious Cause" he had

sworn to uphold the day he assumed command in Cambridge so
many weary years before, that enabled him by precept and example
to hold the army together through that long last winter while Jay
and Adams and Franklin and old Laurens in Paris labored to consoli-
date the preliminary articles into a permanent treaty. The army was
every day more restless and discontented. A committee of officers
under General McDougall sent to wait on Congress in Philadelphia
was eliciting only fair words and promises.

"The predicament in which I stand as Citizen and Soldier, is as
critical and delicate as can well be conceived," the general wrote in
early March of 1783; "the sufferings of a complaining Army on the
one hand, the tardiness of the States on the other, are forebodings
of evil."

Alexander Hamilton wrote him from Congress in Philadelphia to
warn him of strange plans afoot which might make the signing of a
peace treaty, now daily expected, a greater threat to the safety of the
United States than the war had been. Hamilton with his usual self-
assurance was trying to manipulate the great man to get him to fall in
with his own plans for using the discontents of civilian and military
creditors to force a more active executive on Congress. Washington
answered that he had confidence in the good sense of the troops, but
characteristically never neglecting the darker view, he added that
Hamilton's fears might be justified and hinted that "the old leaven"
was working again.

By the old leaven he meant that Horatio Gates, still smarting from
his disgrace after Camden, was back in service and might well, "under
a mask of the most perfect dissimulation and apparent cordiality," be
drawing all the discontented spirits into his orbit. From the old days
of "the Conway cabal" Washington had suspected that vain old Gates
wanted to supplant him.

Before he closed the long letter he explained to Hamilton that
though as a soldier he had no say, as a citizen he was for a strong
central government. "It is clearly my opinion, unless Congress have
powers competent to all *general* purposes, that the distresses we
have encountered, the expense we have incurred, the blood we have
spilt in the course of an Eight years war, will avail us nothing."

His letter to Hamilton was hardly in the pouch of the dispatch
rider when the discontents of the army boiled up with a vengeance.
In spite of the improved feeding and the fine new barracks Washington
kept the troops busy building all winter, schemes for desperate
measures smoldered in the officers' messes. They came to the surface
in an anonymous appeal for a mass meeting. An inflammatory address
appeared all at once in many copies passed from hand to hand. It
was Nicola's old scheme but couched in more violent language.

Washington denounced the anonymous document in his general orders and appointed the following Saturday afternoon as the time for a meeting of officers in the new building, familiarly known as the Temple, which the troops had just completed to use as a church and dancing academy. "After mature deliberation they will devise what further measures ought to be adopted as most rational and best calculated to attain the just and important object in view."

As if to challenge Washington's leadership, a fresh appeal was circulated. Washington wrote his friends in Congress in great perturbation of mind. In this extremity any coolness between him and Hamilton was forgotten. He wrote with his old confidence in the younger man's intelligence and good intentions that in his opinion these mysterious addresses that were stirring up the army were the work of "certain gentlemen from Philadelphia" who were trying to use the army's grievances for a political purpose.

He was soon to learn that the anonymous addresses were the work of General Armstrong's son, an impulsive young Pennsylvanian in his early twenties who was aide to General Gates. He had been right about "the old leaven." The impression was that young Armstrong was really trying to bring about a coup d'état, but that Hamilton and the Financier were merely trying to use this threat of a military uprising to impress Congress with the need for a properly funded debt and a strong central government. The congressional leaders, except the most extreme advocates of the supremacy of the states, were in agreement on that point. Washington went to work, as promptly as he had when he received Nicola's memorial, to draft a speech that would bring home to his officers the folly of these anonymous proposals.

At the same time he wrote a fresh batch of vehement letters to his friends in Congress telling them that something had to be done, and quickly, to relieve the necessities of the army. Could Congress not at least issue certificates of indebtedness to square the officers' accounts?

Their situation, he wrote, was "distressing beyond description. It is affirmed to me, that a large part of them have no other prospect before them than a Gaol, if they are turned loose without liquidation of accounts." Most of them had been forced to borrow money to support themselves and their families during the war, and according to the crude legal code of the day, the moment they stepped out of uniform they would be in danger of being clapped into jail as defaulting debtors. The only comfort he could offer them was a set of soothing resolutions which the friends of the McDougall committee had managed to put through Congress some weeks before, promising public creditors payment in the future. These the general had posted up in his general orders.

At the hour set for the meeting the commander in chief was seen striding in his buff and blue through the hall of the new building that still smelt of shavings and raw lumber. He was seen to be visibly agitated when he stepped up to the lectern.

He began his speech with an apology. He had not intended to take any part in the meeting. He had meant to let some other officer preside. It was the repetition of the addresses that turned them into a personal challenge. He felt they demanded a personal reply.

"Gentlemen," he said, "by an anonymous summons an attempt has been made to convene you together; how inconsistent with the rules of propriety! How unmilitary and how subversive of all order and discipline let the good sense of the Army decide." He admitted the sinister skill with which the addresses had been penned, but he pointed out that they were calculated "to impress the mind with an idea of premeditated injustice in the sovreign power of the United States," which was unthinkable. No man would do that without the blackest designs.

He tore the scheme to pieces: "The way is plain, says the anonymous Addresser. If War continues, remove into the unsettled Country; there establish yourselves and leave an ungrateful Country to defend itself. But who are they to defend? Our wives, our Children, our Farms, and other property which we leave behind us. Or in this state of hostile separation are we to take the two first (the latter cannot be removed) to perish in a Wilderness, with cold, hunger and nakedness? If Peace takes place, never sheath your Swords, Says he untill you have obtained full and ample justice . . . My God! what can this writer have in view, by recommending such Measures? Can he be a friend to the Army? Can he be a friend to this Country! Rather is he not an insidious Foe?"

He suggested that the addresses might well be the work of some emissary sent out by Carleton from New York to drive a wedge between the civilian government and the army.

"With respect to the advice given them by the Author, to suspect the Man, who shall recommend moderate measures and longer forbearance, I spurn it as every Man, who regards that Liberty and reveres that Justice for which we contend, undoubtedly must; for if men are to be precluded from offering their Sentiments on a matter, which may involve the most serious and allarming circumstances that can invite the consideration of Mankind, reason is of no use to us; the freedom of Speech may be taken away, and, dumb and silent we may be led, like sheep to the Slaughter."

In his opinion Congress had been doing all it could in view of the dreadful financial condition of the government and was preparing to do a great deal more to find funds to pay the army.

He pledged himself to exert whatever ability he possessed in the officers' cause.

Meanwhile he begged them to be patient and not to sully the reputation they had made themselves in the world: "And you will, by the dignity of your Conduct, afford occasion for Posterity to say, when speaking of the glorious example you have exhibited to Mankind, 'had this day been wanting the World had never seen the last stage of perfection to which human nature is capable of attaining.'"

It was the most moving speech of Washington's career. Men who were present told the story that after having finished his address he pulled out of his pocket a letter from a friend in Congress, which he intended to read to prove his statement that Congress was sincerely at work on the problem of army pay. He read a few words haltingly and then fumbled in his pocket for the reading glasses Rittenhouse had recently ground for him. He apologized for the pause while he fitted the glasses on his nose. "Gentlemen," he said, "I have grown gray in your service and now I find myself growing blind."

Many a man had tears in his eyes. In a magnificent gesture of self-confidence Washington, when he finished reading the congressman's letter, turned the meeting over to Horatio Gates, who was the senior officer present, and walked out of the hall. Enthusiasm for the anonymous addresses was dead. The general's faithful followers had the meeting in hand. They put forward a plan to work with McDougall's committee. It was unanimously accepted. A few days later Washington was able to forward a series of resolutions to the President of Congress and to report that the proceedings on the part of the army had terminated "with perfect unanimity and in a manner entirely consonant with my Wishes."

The spring of 1783 ripened into summer. Good news came in by every courier. The British had evacuated Charleston. A preliminary pact, provisional on the signing of a general peace, had been signed between Great Britain and the United States. As the reports of the terms trickled in it became evident that the American commissioners, who had been criticized as an ill assorted crew, had done their work well. They had worsted the professionals of British and French diplomacy. Independence recognized, a better frontier with Canada than anybody could have hoped for, the Newfoundland fisheries assured, the prospect of open navigation of the Mississippi. The patriot press exulted in the terms.

On March 29 Washington wrote gracefully to the Chevalier de la Luzerne, complimenting him on the part he had played and expressing regret that France had not come out better in a territorial way. "The news," he wrote, "has filled my mind with inexpressible satisfaction." The same day he informed his men through the general orders that the paymaster general was opening an office in Newburgh for settling the accounts of the army. The password he chose for that day was America, the countersigns Triumphant, Happy.

The summer days dragged by. All Robert Morris could do once the certification of the army's accounts was completed was to print a new batch of promissory notes in the hope that the states would honor them. Enthusiasm for peace was dampened in the minds of officers and men by the prospect of more worthless paper piled on the worthless paper they already had in their rucksacks.

In Philadelphia in June a minor riot occurred which took on great importance in the telling and retelling. Led by a couple of young featherbrains, about eighty men of the Pennsylvania Line marched in from Lancaster and laid siege to Congress, which was sitting as usual in the State House. After a lot of loud talk the mutineers were argued into submission. Once they submitted, arrests were made. Two of the ringleaders were condemned to death, though they were never executed. Congress meanwhile retired in a huff to the college buildings at Princeton.

To the troops on the Hudson, under the eye of that "careful Physician," the news of the Philadelphia riot brought fresh bitterness but no violence. Discharges were being issued. Furloughs had been liberally granted. Little by little the Continental Army melted away. Old comrades in arms said goodbye to each other and went home to face civilian life with empty pockets. In his letters to Congress, Washington cajoled, argued, stormed, but no money was forthcoming.

At last when Carleton announced he would evacuate New York in November, Washington felt the time to retire had come. Leaving Horatio Gates, whose ambition to become commander in chief was fulfilled at last, in charge of the dwindling army, Washington joined his old fat friend Knox from the artillery, who was waiting for him with a small force in Harlem. The general made it clear that he would be present only as a guest on Governor Clinton's staff. It was not the Continental Army but the State of New York that would take over the city.

When news arrived that the British barges had pushed off from the foot of the Bowery, Washington rode down the fire scarred and war dingy Manhattan streets with Governor Clinton and the New York state officials. They rode in procession, four abreast. They were followed by General Knox and the officers of the army, eight abreast, then by citizens on horseback, eight abreast. The Speaker of the Assembly and citizens on foot, also walking eight abreast, brought up the rear. So it was described by the Reverend William Gordon, first historian of the Revolution, who most likely walked among the citizens.

Governor Clinton entertained the commander in chief and the general officers at Fraunces'. Entertainments followed on succeeding days. There was a reception for the French Ambassador with fireworks "at the Bowling green on the Broad way, exceeding anything of the kind ever seen in the United States."

A few days later, again at Fraunces' Tavern, the general met his officers for the tearful scene of a last goodbye.

"General Washington came in," wrote Gordon, "and calling for a glass of wine thus addressed them — 'With a heart full of love and gratitude, I now take leave of you. I most devoutly wish, that your latter days may be as prosperous and happy, as your former days have been glorious and honorable.' Having drunk with moist eyes to the toast he suggested that the officers come up one by one to shake his hand. General Knox being nearest turned to him, Washington with tears rolling down his cheeks, grasped Knox's hand, and then kissed him; he did the same by every succeeding officer and by some other gentlemen who were present . . . The whole company was in tears."

In silence, "walking in solemn mute and mournful procession, with heads hanging down and dejected countenances," so the Reverend Gordon described them, "they followed the General past a corps of light infantry drawn up at attention down to the landing at White-hall." As the oarsmen rowed him across the bay past the British ships preparing to make sail he stood in the stern of the barge waving his hat to his friends on the shore.

Farewells, addresses of adulation, touching celebrations of esteem succeeded at every stage of his southward journey until at last the day so long waited for came when he could resign his commission to Congress.

Congress had kept away from Philadelphia since they had been thrown into such a humiliating fluster by the rioting soldiery. Washington found them in session in the gay little statehouse in Annapolis with his old opponent, the fastidiously dressed and hard drinking Pennsylvanian Thomas Mifflin, in the chair. There was the usual protocol. Jefferson and McHenry and Elbridge Gerry had sat in committee and decided that "when the General rises to make his address and also when he retires he is to bow to Congress which they are to return by uncovering without bowing."

The president remained seated with his hat on.

The general stood bareheaded, fumbling with his notes.

Only nineteen or twenty members were present. Not too many familiar faces under the threecornered hats; waspish Arthur Lee's thin buttoned mouth, rusty haired Jefferson's long face, solemn young Monroe's high cheekbones, dapper Gerry's long nose and furrowed brow, Virginian Sam Hardy's goodnatured countenance, ruddy as an apple. There was Dr. Tilton who had run the hospital in the old palace at Williamsburg during the siege of Yorktown and Dr. Hugh Williamson of North Carolina, and Samuel Osgood, the Massachusetts banker who had often visited the army on congressional committees, and dear McHenry's smiling phiz. In the gallery sat every Marylander and his lady who could be packed in.

McHenry described the scene in emotional terms when he wrote his fiancée Miss Caldwell of Baltimore that night: "It was a solemn and affecting spectacle and such an one as history does not present. The spectators all wept and there was hardly a member of Congress that did not drop tears. The general's hand which held the address shook as he read it . . . After a pause which was necessary for him to recover himself he proceeded to say in the most penetrating manner: 'Having now finished the work assigned me, I retire from the great theatre of action; and bidding an Affectionate farewell to this August body under whose orders I have so long acted, I here offer my commission, and take my leave of all the employments of public life.'

"This is only a sketch of the scene," McHenry went on to his intended bride, "but were I to write you a long letter I could not convey to you the whole. So many circumstances crowded into view and gave rise to so many affecting emotions. The events of the revolution just accomplished — the new situation into which it had thrown the affairs of the world — the great man who had played so conspicuous a figure in it, in the act of relinquishing all public employments to return to private life — the past — the present — the future — the manner — the occasion — all conspired to render it a spectacle inexpressibly solemn and affecting. But I have written enough. Good night my love. My amiable friend goodnight."

Washington resigned his commission at noon on December 23, 1783. Always a hard rider, in spite of a blustery crossing on the Potomac ferry he was in Mount Vernon Christmas Eve and next day ate Christmas dinner in front of his own fire with his wife Martha and her grandchildren.

IV   The Finance Office

1. *Good Executive Men*

When George Washington resigned his commission at the end of 1783 he left Robert Morris the most influential man in the congressional government.

Robert Morris was a sanguine hearty thicknecked man. He was openhanded, approachable, a bold trader who exuded that prime commercial quality described as confidence. He was married to a lady from a sound Maryland family. He had two town houses and a country house above the Schuylkill. The Hills was known for its fruit and for the products of the vegetable garden and greenhouse. His table was famous for good food and good drink and cheerful entertaining.

"You see I continue my old practice of mixing business and pleasure," he wrote one of his friends, "and ever found them useful to each other." His house was the social center of Philadelphia. From his office there radiated a web of commercial enterprises that included most of the banking and land speculation and shipping of the middle states. He was thought to be the richest man in America.

Very much the cheerful trencherman, he was always ready to crack a pot with a public man. He was obliging, particularly to people of influence. He made an opening for one of Washington's nephews in his countinghouse. He was helpful to the general and to many a member of Congress about discounting notes and cashing bills of exchange. When after his wife's death Jefferson left his eleven year old daughter in Philadelphia for her schooling Mr. and Mrs. Morris could not have been more considerate. The great magnate arranged loans for congressmen; he gave advice about investments; he was everybody's banker.

For Robert Morris the Finance Office came as the climax of a dashing career in business and politics.

With his practical knowledge of shipping and his flair for risks he had become the most active member of Congress's Secret Committee on Commerce and of the Marine Committee which improvised a continental navy. He saw to it that his firm's network of correspondents in the West Indies and in European ports should become indispensable in the procurement of war materials. He treated the Continental Congress and the State of Pennsylvania very much as he would commercial partners. While he procured the munitions they needed he indulged in profitable speculations on his own. In the network of secret wartime enterprises, in the intricacies of Beaumarchais's web of intrigue in the French ports, and in his operations with Silas Deane in Europe and with Holker, the French agent, in Philadelphia, it would have been a wise economist who could discover where the public business ended and where Robert Morris's private business began. At times he hardly knew himself.

Robert Morris's appointment was not without its critics. Joseph Reed had been Washington's aide in the days of the investment of Boston. He had studied law at the Middle Temple and had become a political power on the popular side in Pennsylvania. As a politician he was vain and thinskinned but he was a welleducated man and a shrewd observer. He described Morris to the Rhode Island general, Nathanael Greene, as a "pecuniary dictator . . . It would not be doing justice not to acknowledge that humiliating as this power is," he added, "it has been exercised with some advantage for the immediate relief of our distresses, and that the public have received a real benefit from Mr. Morris's exertions. At the same time those who know him will also acknowledge that he is too much a man of the world to overlook certain private interests which his command of the paper, and occasional speculations in that currency, will enable him to promote. It seems to have ever been a ruling principle with him to connect the public service with private interest and certainly he has not departed from it at this time of day."

Part of the confusion arose from the complexity of the commercial dealings of the time. Bookkeeping was rudimentary. Since merchants had to deal with the fluctuating paper currencies of thirteen separate states, transactions were basically by barter. A man would trade so many hogsheads of tobacco estimated in Maryland paper currency, say, for a shipload of molasses in St. Kitts estimated in pounds sterling. In default of other currency, bills of lading would have to pass as a medium of exchange, so that half the time the bill of lading for the shipload of molasses would be used to meet an obligation held by a broker in Leghorn. Bills of exchange circulated that could be met part in cash, part in commodities, part in credit. Due to the slowness in communications years might go by before any particular transaction was completed and liquidated. The hazards of wartime captures and confiscations and the sudden profits of privateering added an element of delirium.

Everything depended on the individual merchant's personal standing in the worldwide commercial community, what Robert Morris used to speak of as his "integrity." It was considered ethical for a merchant who had in his hands a shipload of lumber consigned to him, say, in Boston to exchange it, if he saw the chance for a good deal, with the bill of lading for a shipload of hides in Cádiz, without consulting the original owners, who might be merchants in St. Eustatius or in Baltimore or in Savannah. "The commonest things," wrote Morris, "become intricate where money has anything to do with them."

In dealing with public funds the Financier was never too curious to find out whether he was using the negotiable paper of the United States for a speculation to his own advantage or whether he was using his own funds for the benefit of the United States. He encouraged the legend to grow that he risked his private fortune to finance the Revolution.

2. Pennsylvania Politics

At the same time Morris was a vigorous partisan in local Pennsylvania politics. In the enthusiasm of 1776 the Pennsylvanians abandoned their old charter and, with the smiling approval of Benjamin Franklin, installed a constitution which merged most of the powers of government in a single chamber elected by popular vote. Their Assembly passed a test act practically disfranchising the Quakers and much of the property owning class. Immediately two parties sprang up: a party of western settlers and of the mechanics and artisans in the towns, mostly recent immigrants of Scotch-Irish origin and Presbyterians in religion, who called themselves Constitutionalists; and a party of merchants, Quakers, and Church of England people who wanted a revised constitution with a stronger executive and an independent judiciary. These called themselves Republicans. The Constitutionalists were for printing press money, price fixing, legal tender acts, and radical measures against suspected Tories; the Republicans were for the protection of property, freedom of opinion, and hard money.

The Constitutionalists had on their side the glamor of the distant

Franklin's name; David Rittenhouse, the mathematical instrument maker; the idealistic Dr. Hutchinson, later Dr. Rush's rival in the teaching of chemistry at the Philadelphia College; Tom Paine, who was serving as clerk of the Assembly; and Charles Willson Peale, the Maryland painter who had commemorated the Battle of Trenton by painting George Washington leaning on a cannon beside captured battleflags with Nassau Hall in the background. Peale was pushed into the forefront of the fray as a "furious Whig."

Morris, along with the scholarly Scottish lawyer, James Wilson, whose close arguments had done as much to give legal respectability to colonial resistance to Parliament in the early days, became a leader of the hard money Republicans in the state Assembly. Dr. Rush was one of their most voluble supporters.

Especially after the British occupation of Philadelphia, the party battle grew bitter. When Morris was elected to the Assembly he refused to take the oath to support the state constitution. His opponents accused him of war profiteering and particularly of cornering flour in defiance of the laws fixing prices. In Congress meanwhile his name was becoming anathema to the group of men who dreaded centralized government.

All through the war, since the state government and the continental government were seated in the same Philadelphia State House, Pennsylvania politics had a disproportionate influence on national affairs. Congress was the forum for a continuing debate between centralizers and decentralizers which sounded a sort of counterpoint to the discussions between the political parties in Pennsylvania. Usually on the decentralizing side in Congress were to be found the Stratford Hall Lees, Richard Henry and his brother Dr. Arthur Lee, and Samuel Adams of Massachusetts and his friends. One of the ablest advocates of the nationalist theory in Congress was the same James Wilson who was the theorist of the hard money Republican party in state politics and Morris's friend and legal counsel.

The acts of the Continental Congress could often be accounted for by the temporary dominance of one or the other of these factions. When John Laurens' father, Henry Laurens of South Carolina, a great merchant himself, was first elected President of Congress, the Lees convinced him that Morris was profiteering in the procurement of war supplies.

Arthur Lee hated Morris personally as much as he hated Benjamin Franklin. He was the eternal attorney for the prosecution. He began his political career in England as the American Junius and through his years in Congress had continued accusing all and sundry in the language of Cicero against Catiline. Though most of his accusations were

based on the profound conviction that nobody could be trusted with
the public funds but himself, he had sometimes been proved right;
he seems to have been the only public man to suspect that Franklin's
friend and emissary, Dr. Bancroft, was a double agent.

In this case an investigation was voted. Morris maintained the
attitude of the bluff goodnatured merchant unjustly accused by ill-
informed men incapable of understanding the intricacies of commerce.
To the disgust of the two Lees the committee reported back that
Morris had "clearly and fully vindicated himself."

The bitterness meanwhile between the two factions in Pennsylvania
reached the point of open violence. A crowd of Constitutionalists
attacked the house of a hard money man who had written an article
opposing them in *The Pennsylvania Packet*. Rival town meetings
shouted defiance at each other, with the Constitutionalists occupying
the State House yard and the hard money Republicans delivering
their speeches on the premises of the College of Philadelphia. There
were highhanded seizures of the homes of suspected Tories. A meeting
of the local militia was held on the commons, where a resolution was
passed to drive out the wives and children of all those who had
evacuated the city with the British.

By this time moderate men like the painter Peale and Rittenhouse
and Dr. Hutchinson on the Constitutionalist side were arguing to the
best of their ability against rash and brutal measures. Feeling ran so
high that leaders of both factions were waylaid on the streets. Even
peaceable Charles Willson Peale started carrying an ash club which
he named Hercules. He had to use it, too, when set upon one night by
some strongarm men of the opposing faction. The city was plastered
with Constitutionalist placards attacking businessmen as profiteers.
The most furious of the furious Whigs proposed that the hard money
men should be run out of town with the Tories.

The Republican leaders loaded their pistols. Threatened by a particularly vigorous burst of oratory from a Constitutionalist meeting,
Thomas Mifflin and Robert Morris and a group of twenty or thirty
retreated into James Wilson's house. The Philadelphia troop of light
horse, manned mostly by substantial citizens, rode out to protect them.
At dinnertime the light horsemen got hungry and scattered to their
homes. Their absence gave the Constitutionalists, who had been building up their courage in the surrounding taverns, a chance to rush the
house.

The place was known as Fort Wilson from then on. When the Constitutionalists tried to batter down the door they were shot at from
the windows. In the fusillade which followed, a man on each side was
killed and several wounded. At that point Joseph Reed, who was

President of the Supreme Executive Council and who had been roused from a sickbed, rode down the street astride a galloping horse, with his clothes all askew and waving a pistol above his head. He was followed by members of the light cavalry torn away from their dinner tables. At his direction they made arrests indiscriminately among defenders and attackers. Aghast at the bloodshed, the Philadelphians of both parties seem to have been glad enough to yield to higher authority.

"Poor Pennsylvania has become the most miserable spot upon the surface of the globe," wrote Dr. Rush a few days later. "Our streets have been stained already with fraternal blood — a sad prelude we fear of the mischiefs our Constitution will bring upon us. They call it a democracy — a mobocracy in my opinion would be more proper. All our laws breathe the spirit of town meetings and porter shops."

The Fort Wilson riot proved the beginning of the decline of the "furious Whigs." Moderate men of both parties began putting their heads together. The Assembly cut off prosecutions by an act of oblivion.

As the long war neared its end Pennsylvania politics became a seesaw. The hard money men carried the Supreme Executive Council. The Constitutionalists lashed back by repealing the charters of the College of Philadelphia, which they considered a Republican stronghold, and of Morris and Willing's Pennsylvania Bank. For the college they substituted an endowment out of confiscated Tory estates for the University of Pennsylvania. For the bank they substituted a state loan office which should lend money to farmers on better terms than penny-pinching Willing would allow. Even so the hard money Republicans were strong enough to reelect Robert Morris to the Assembly.

When Congress appointed him Superintendent of Finance, Morris gave notice that, since he could not hold both offices simultaneously, he would resign his seat in the Assembly only after voting there against a particularly obnoxious measure for a new issue of paper money. His further conditions were that he must be allowed to continue his private business and must be free to choose his subordinates. "If Congress means to succeed in this business," he wrote, "they must pay good executive men to do their business as it ought to be done."

High finance was regarded with awe and astonishment all over the world, almost as a form of sorcery. It was not only in America that a financial genius was supposed to be able to coax rabbits out of a hat. The court of Versailles, facing bankruptcy from the expenditures of the war — a considerable part of them in support of the American cause — had called in a famous Swiss banker named Necker to per-

form a miracle for the Bourbons. Washington went to the heart of the
matter when he wrote a friend: "I have great expectations of the
appointment of Mr. Morris, but they are not unreasonable ones; for
I do not suppose that by art magick, he can do more than recover us,
by degrees, from the labyrinth in which our finance is plunged."

Robert Morris set up his office in a building on Front Street next
to the large brick mansion where he lived. Immediately he became
known as the Financier. He was going to conduct the affairs of the
United States as he would his own business. The first thing he did
was to initiate a daybook or diary in a great ledger. He dictated an
opening statement to his Scottish clerk, who traced it out in a flowing
commercial hand:

"The Appointment was unsought and unsolicited, and dangerous
to accept as it was evidently contrary to my private Interest and if
accepted must deprive me of those enjoyments Social and Domestic
which my time of Life required and which my Circumstances entitled
me to, and as a vigorous execution of the Duties must inevitably expose me to the resentment of disappointed and designing Men and to
the Calumny and Detraction of the Envious and Malicious. I was
therefore absolutely determined not to engage in so Arduous an Undertaking. But the Solicitations of my Friends, Acquaintances and
Fellow Citizens and a full Conviction of the Necessity there was that
some person should Commence the Work of reformation of our Public
Affairs by an Attempt to introduce System & Economy and the per-
suation that refusal on my part would probably deter others from
Attempting this work so absolutely necessary to the safety of our
Country . . ."

He never managed to finish the sentence. Even before his appointment was confirmed his office filled up with contractors with long
bills demanding to be paid. Morris was beset by Continental officers
with pathetic stories of want asking for advances. Sea captains poured
out tales of capture and pillage on the high seas. Butchers, bakers,
clothiers, drovers crowded round his desk trying to turn their dog-
eared promissory notes into cash.

In September 1781, at the height of the march on Yorktown, Morris
had his secretary note in the daybook: "In the hurry of constant applications & interruptions I find it impossible to keep . . . minutes of
occurences as they happen and they are too numerous for Memory
to retain even for a short time because fresh Matter comes forward
every Moment . . . It seems as if every Person connected in the Public
Service," he added wryly, "entertains an Opinion that I am full of
Money for they are constantly applying even down to the common
express Riders and give me infinite interruption so that it is hardly

possible to attend to Business of more consequence . . ." They gave him no time to plan for the future. "The variety of business I am obliged to do in detail so engrosses my time," he wrote the President of Congress, "that I cannot pay attention to those general arrangements which are the proper subjects of my appointment."

3. *The Tall Boy*

To help him plan out these "general arrangements" Robert Morris called in a young New York lawyer who bore the same name as he did but who came from a very different family background. Gouverneur Morris was the son of the Second Lord of the Manor at Morrisania. These Morrises were one of the great patroon families. Gouverneur's mother was of Huguenot extraction and sent him to the famous Huguenot school in New Rochelle where he was steeped in French language and literature.

His father died an embittered eccentric while Gouverneur was still a small boy. "My Actions have been so inconsiderable in the World," the elder Morris wrote in his will, "that the most durable Monument will but perpetuate my Folly while it lasts. My Desire is that nothing be mentioned about me, not so much as a Line in a Newspaper to tell the World I am dead. That I have lived to very little Purpose my Children will remember with Concern when they see the small Pittance I have left them."

Gouverneur Morris grew up an eccentric but not an embittered one. "I have naturally a taste for pleasure," he wrote with the frankness that endeared him to his friends and was considered impious cynicism by his enemies. At the same time he was a hard student of the law and statesmanship. From early in life he had to contend with pain. An accidental scalding as a child left him with a crippled arm. Possibly it was this disability that kept him out of the army during the Revolutionary War, though the lawyers and the men trained in letters of the period felt no compulsion to serve as soldiers, no matter how intense their patriotic feelings.

He took his bachelor's degree at King's College and read law in the office of William Smith, a notable attorney of his day whose practice was linked with the affairs of the Livingstons. The boon companions of his youth were John Jay, the Westchester Aristides, and Robert R. Livingston, who was to head the great Livingston clan. With them, even though he already feared the excesses of the mob, he took the revolutionary side in 1775. He helped draft the New York State constitution and led the fight for religious toleration. He worked hard to get through measures abolishing slavery. All his life he was an abolitionist.

Well read, highspirited, witty, sarcastic, not a man to suffer fools gladly, he aroused considerable hostility when he appeared in Congress to represent New York. In spite of his disability he had a commanding presence. Years later in Paris he was to pose for George Washington when Houdon was working on the statue Congress had ordered. His gaiety was irrepressible. Too whimsical, men said. There was a self assurance about his language in debate that threw older men off. The delegates called him "the tall boy."

The ladies doted on him. Scandal hung round his name. He had the reputation of a headlong lover pushing himself into bedrooms where others feared to tread. He was a free spender, fond of the best in food and drink. Since what little revenue he had in his own right was cut off by the war, he had to do some speculating on the side to keep himself in cash. It was Gouverneur Morris's keen nose for moneymaking, combined with a congenial taste for women and wine and sprightly conversation after dinner, that first endeared him to the Financier. Perhaps the self made man took some pleasure in associating with someone of his own name who belonged so unequivocally to the rich and well born.

Gouverneur served two years in Congress. Appointed to the liaison committee that visited the army during the winter of Valley Forge, he formed there a warm unshakable affection for George Washington. Their friendship was mutual. The commander in chief had a ready appreciation of young men with brains. He enjoyed youthful high spirits.

Washington and Gouverneur agreed in putting the nation before anything. Possibly because Gouverneur refused to follow Governor Clinton of New York in his stubborn insistence on New York's claims to the region east of Lake Champlain where the Green Mountain settlers had already formed themselves into the independent state of Vermont, the New York Assembly failed to reelect him. The Clinton faction felt that he was too much interested in national affairs and too little in those of his home state. The tall boy's speeches punctured too many complacencies.

He returned to Philadelphia without holding any office and there was admitted to the Pennsylvania bar. There was not much for him in New York at that point in his career. He would have been handicapped in state politics even if local affairs had interested him. The New York Assembly under George Clinton was fanatically partisan. Gouverneur's mother was known to be at least a passive Tory. One of his half brothers was a major general in the British army. His home was occupied by the British. He was a man of metropolitan tastes.

Philadelphia at that point in the war was definitely the American metropolis.

It is not at all impossible, besides, that the attractions of a certain Mrs. Plater had a good deal to do with his settling in that city. Gossips linked that lady's name with an accident Gouverneur suffered the winter before he took up his duties at the Finance Office. In a hurry to be gone before the unexpected arrival of the injured husband, so the story went round Philadelphia, he let a pair of wild horses he was driving get out of hand. His phaeton turned over and his leg, caught in a wheel, was so badly shattered that the doctors insisted on an amputation below the knee. His friends were filled with admiration at his "becoming fortitude" during the agony of the operation but they could not help teasing him about the tender cause. Even the sober John Jay wrote, "I have heard that a certain married woman after much use of your legs was the occasion of your losing one."

Of one fact there was no doubt. It was into the Platers' house that he was carried after the accident. For the rest of his life Gouverneur Morris stumped about on a wooden peg.

Statebuilding remained his favorite hobby. The minds of the young men he had grown up with in New York were saturated with political speculation. He and Jay as college students were very much under the influence of the Livingstons. It was a family given to radical and explosive ideas. William Livingston, Robert R.'s cousin, who became the first governor of New Jersey after independence, was a sort of provincial Voltaire who for years in various private publications amused himself by jeering at the pretensions of royal officials and of Church of England divines. Secure in their great landholdings, the thoughtful and sharpwitted leaders of the Livingston connection cultivated the English country gentleman's conviction that political discussion was the noblest sport after foxhunting. With airy self confidence born of the independence of their lives they focused the extreme whig doctrines of the Wilkes and Fox factions in England on the new society which was developing under their eyes in America.

Eating and drinking, sleeping and waking, the young men of their circle, like the rising lawyers who frequented townmeeting in Massachusetts, and the Virginians arguing in the ordinaries round the backwoods courthouses of the Old Dominion, were entranced with the problem of how man should govern himself. Politics in the broad sense of the word was their hobby and their vocation. They read all the books ancient and modern; they sat up nights discussing them. They needed to convince others of the truth of their deductions. Appointed to Congress, they found themselves talking to likeminded men from each of the thirteen states.

Once settled in the Finance Office, the doubly crippled tall boy set to work with a will. Robert Morris was accustomed to partnerships. He exploited initiative in his subordinates. His younger namesake supplied the booklearning and the fertile mind forever bubbling over with impertinent notions. The Financier furnished the practical knowledge of trade and the sanguine front of the merchant prince, with assets in every part of the world at his beck and call, to whom nothing was impossible.

Part of Robert Morris's outgoing nature was a capacity for friendship. A bond of affection grew up between the two men of the same name that immensely stimulated their collaboration. "I do not know whether Gouverneur Morris writes to you by this opportunity," Robert Morris wrote at the end of an official communication to John Jay, who was spending a bleak Castilian winter as minister to the court of Spain. "You must cherish his friendship. It is worth possessing. He has more virtue than he shows and more consistency than anybody believes." The successful careerist came to the surface when he added, "He values you exceedingly, and hereafter you will be very useful to each other."

Between them the two Morrises projected a network of reforms calculated to introduce some semblance of a national administration.

The continental paper had reached the point in inflation where it cost more to print a bill than it was worth in the marketplace. Continental money had ceased to circulate as cash. The loan office certificates, which were the government bonds of the period, were on their way to the same fate; and foreign loans, which had been the mainstay of continental finances ever since the victory at Saratoga and the French alliance had established a certain credit for the new nation in the European money markets, were every day harder to come by. As the war emergency became less acute after Yorktown, it became more difficult for Congress to raise money from the states.

Paradoxically enough, at a time when Congress and most of the state governments were just about bankrupt, the country as a whole was prosperous. Privateering and wartime procurement had brought new wealth into the seaport towns. The rural districts, except where they had actually been laid waste by ravaging armies, were harvesting fine crops. Farmers were getting a good price for their wheat.

Cash had always been scarce in the American economy and the farmers and planters who could swap their grain and beef directly for durable goods through bills of exchange managed to do without it. Paper money they saved for taxes and for buying public lands. The war had brought more prosperity than ruin to the thirteen states. The problem that faced the Morrises was to turn the fundamental financial health of the new nation to account.

Their first measure was to establish a national bank. Alexander Hamilton had been agitating for a bank for some time. In a letter to James Duane, the staid New York lawyer who had been a public official under the Crown and who throughout his many terms in Congress consistently took his stand for a strong central government, Hamilton suggested that the bank be modeled on the Bank of Amsterdam. He had the Bank of England, that foundation stone of the whig oligarchy in Britain, in mind no doubt, but he was unwilling to outrage partisan feelings by bringing up an institution so characteristically British.

For a century the American colonists and been discussing banking. Their commerce had been plagued by fluctuating currencies. Paper money was the popular remedy for the lack of a circulating medium. Hard money had become associated in the minds of the farmers, and farmers were the majority of the population, with the cramping oppressions of the Board of Trade in London and of the tory magnates of the seaboard towns.

When Hamilton suggested a bank, the average farmer immediately asked the question: Whose bank? Would it be run for the benefit of the moneylenders or for the benefit of the creditors? So it came about, though most men agreed that its purpose was good, that the part of Robert Morris's fiscal operation which his opponents in Pennsylvania viewed with the most profound suspicion was the state bank he and Willing had set up to finance supply for the Pennsylvania troops.

Robert Morris went to work to push a charter for his new bank through Congress. "I mean to render this a principal pillar of American credit," he wrote Franklin, who was busy in Passy trying by his usual methods of wily indirection to coax a fresh loan out of the foreign office at Versailles, "so as to obtain the money of individuals for the benefit of the Union and thereby bind these individuals more strongly to the general cause by ties of private interest."

There was little opposition in Congress to the Bank of North America. The members were worn out with struggling with fiscal problems. They were willing to try anything. Even James Madison, Jefferson's scholarly little disciple from Orange County who was later to become such a suspicious watchdog of usurpation of power by the general government, was willing to have his constitutional doubts of Congress's right to charter such a bank quieted by a quibble.

"It's principal founder is R. M.," he wrote his and Jefferson's mutual friend, the acute Virginia lawyer Edmund Pendleton, "who has certain prerogatives with respect to it in his quality of Superintendent of

Finance. It is pretty analogous in its principles to the Bank of England. The stock supplied is $400,000 dollars."

Half of that sum was part of the French silver wheedled out of the French court for the Yorktown campaign by John Laurens and Tom Paine, the long awaited silver that Robert Morris had transferred with such tender care by oxtrain from Boston.

The Financier dominated the bank's operations from behind the scenes. Five of his close associates served as directors, with his old partner Thomas Willing in the chair; but he saw to it that several of his political opponents, such as Timothy Matlack, a convinced Constitutionalist, and the highly critical Samuel Osgood, who belonged to Sam Adams' anti-continentalist faction in Massachusetts, should sit on the board.

Robert Morris had the supreme effrontery to print notes of his own, backed only by the glamor of his name, to back up Congress's credit. The Robert Morris notes were generally accepted at a premium over the continental paper. Never since the days of the Mississippi Bubble had a financier trodden such dangerous heights. To build the edifice of credit he needed on such a small foundation in actual specie, he had to have recourse more and more to what Washington called "the art magick."

Year after year the two Morrisses kept having to postpone their "general arrangements." They did manage to reduce expenses and to put order into the paperwork of their department and to list and certify the heterogeneous congressional debt. They appointed continental collectors of taxes for the various states, thereby laying the foundation for an internal revenue system.

Invariably their plans for general arrangements were tabled when Congress forwarded them to the states. The state governments clung tightly to their prerogatives. The essential continental impost on imports was never ratified. Their proposals for the funding of the continental debt came to nothing. About all the Finance Office was able to accomplish was to set up the rudiments of the administrative machinery which was to be carried over into the federal government.

Robert Morris's hospitable table and the office where Gouverneur held forth sometimes after hours, fascinating sympathetic listeners by his hard commonsensical wit, became centers where members of Congress and army officers and public officials could gather to discuss ways and means of galvanizing the sluggish movements of the confederacy. The men who feared centralization well knew that the Finance Office was the source of the conviction, which was to become the main thread of Alexander Hamilton's political thinking, that government to be effective must be attractive and profitable to the rich.

4. *The Long Argument*

When Gouverneur Morris failed of reelection to Congress and before he joined his namesake in the Finance Office, he turned to the press as a pulpit from which to continue his argument for a strong continental government. He based his plea on economic grounds. The existence of thirteen disparate governments, all regulating trade, was a ruinous business. His articles signed "An American" came out in *The Pennsylvania Packet* and were reprinted up and down the coast.

The discussion was already under way when he entered it. His ideas had been stimulated by an essay that a certain Pelatiah Webster, whom Madison, alert as Morris to every fresh formulation of the relationship between finance and government, immediately described as "an obscure but able citizen," had published in the same paper during the preceding year.

Pelatiah Webster was a Connecticut man who, after studying for the ministry at Yale and preaching for a year at Greenwich in Massachusetts, moved to Philadelphia to go into the mercantile business. He was not too successful as a merchant. Lack of business gave him time for meditation on the problems of government.

Pelatiah Webster wrote a clear and homely style. He repeated the arguments of plain wayfaring men around the deep tavern fireplaces. He had suffered in his own hide the tribulations of wartime. He had felt the tyranny of what Dr. Rush called "the Spirit of town meetings and porter shops." As a small trader he had suffered from the stream of legislation regulating prices, making the use of paper money mandatory as legal tender, controlling imports and exports. He had suffered in his pocketbook from the impediments that stood in the way of trade between the states.

"Let trade be free as air," he wrote in 1779. "Let every man make the most of his goods and in his own way and then he will be satisfied. Let every man taste and enjoy the fruits of that liberty of person and property which was highly expected under an independent government. 'Tis a sad omen to find among the first efforts of independence, greater restraints and abridgements of natural liberty than ever we felt under the government we have lately renounced and shaken off."

He pointed out that freedom of trade could be attained only under a strong general government. His articles elicited praise and abuse.

This *Pennsylvania Packet* in which Gouverneur Morris's and Webster's articles appeared, edited by John Dunlap under an attractive masthead of a ship in full sail, was the center of the argument for a while. Letters to the editor echoed the unreported debates in Congress. Classical pseudonyms masked the identity of citizens who were carrying on the discussion in markets and in hairdressers' shops, on wharves and waiting for ferries or for the blacksmith to shoe the horses, or at mealtime in ordinaries and taverns.

The argument continued from day to day in communications and essays by men who were lending their best brains to the question of the relationship between government and the economy. Adam Smith's *Wealth of Nations* was stirring fresh ideas; free trade was still an untried and radical doctrine. From the Philadelphia newspapers the discussion spread as fast as the postriders could carry it into the rapidly proliferating press of the thirteen states.

Pelatiah Webster launched a theory of credit. Gouverneur Morris riposted with a disquisition on the nature of money. He explained how inflation produced a scarcity of goods. He demolished the theory that depreciation served a purpose by acting as a tax or capital levy. Throughout the "An American" series he developed the notion, which was to run like a thread through the long debate which would culminate ten years later in Hamilton's funding and assumption acts, that public finance could be the cement which would bind the thirteen states together as a nation.

Hamilton himself was already taking part in the argument. The moment he freed himself from the routine of headquarters paperwork his thoughts turned to the problems which had delighted him ever since his college days in New York. The summer after his tiff with the commander in chief, during the first transports of his marriage with his doting darkeyed Elizabeth, for the first time enjoying family life with the congenial Schuylers in their great square yellow brick mansion in Albany where he was the family pet; while wires were being pulled to procure for him that "handsome command in the light infantry" which would enable him to cut such a dashing figure at the siege of Yorktown, he found time to write a series of articles of his own.

They came out in the patriot edition of *The New York Packet*, printed in those days at Fishkill on the Hudson. He took up the argument where Gouverneur Morris left it in his "An American" series. Hamilton signed himself "The Continentalist."

Writing some of the best and plainest prose of his career, he put his great gift of clarifying issues to work to discuss the establishment of a federated government. He pointed out that the blunders and failures in the conduct of the war had resulted not from the disaffection of the people, who were ready to do everything for the "glorious Cause," but from the mismanagement of their government. When the members of a federation were more powerful than the head, a stable and unified command was impossible. The cure was to enlarge the powers of Congress.

Hamilton's contentions jibed completely with Robert Morris's profound convictions. "The inhabitants of a little hamlet," the Financier explained, "may feel pride in the sense of separate independence. But if there be not one government which can draw forth and direct the combined effort of United America, our independence is but a name, our freedom a shadow, and our dignity a dream."

Already Morris had noted down Washington's retired secretary as a young man who would fit into his plans. By inducing him to serve as collector of taxes for New York, he gave Hamilton a scrap of personal experience in fiscal administration which he was to make good use of later on.

Reading law in Albany the year Elizabeth's first baby was born, a boy they named Philip after her father, Hamilton continued his essays. At the same time he served in the Assembly. A seat in the Assembly was a prerogative of the great New York families. In spite of the fact that his time was taken up, so he wrote Lafayette, "rocking the cradle and studying the art of fleecing my neighbors" — that is, reading law; and that he was preoccupied with the uphill work of trying to induce the New Yorkers to pay their assessment to Congress, he found time to sketch out a plan for a rational system of continental taxation. Congress had to have the power to tax directly.

These arguments of Hamilton's were grist to the Financier's mill. Robert Morris had been telling everybody who would listen that paying just debts was the basis of that firm public credit which could become the source of fresh money. A proper funding of the debt would turn it into an asset instead of a liability. The war had cost more than it needed to, he tried to hammer his thesis into the head of any congressman he could buttonhole, because "the needy can never economize."

Before adjourning, the New York legislature elected young Hamilton one of its delegates to Congress. "I am now a grave counsellor at law, and shall soon be a grave member of Congress," he boasted lightheartedly in a letter to Lafayette in France. "The Legislature, at their last session, took it into their heads to name me, pretty unanimously, as one of their delegates." Philip Schuyler was responsible for his election; he stepped aside to allow the nomination of his favorite soninlaw. "I am going to throw away a few months more in public life," Hamilton went on in toplofty vein; — he was twentyseven, though he only confessed to twentyfive; who could blame him for being a little giddy with all these honors? — "and then retire a simple citizen and good paterfamilias." Then he added, referring, enviously perhaps, to Lafayette's dazzling position at the French court, "You are condemned to run the race of ambition all your life. I am already tired of the career and dare leave it."

One of his many occupations during that summer's session of the legislature was putting through a resolution calling for a convention to frame a new constitution for the general government of the confederation. In Philadelphia he set to work to steer a similar resolution through Congress. In this he was complying with the dearest wishes of his old commander in chief.

Washington, during all his years of struggle as a practical administrator with the inadequacies of the confederacy, threw his influence behind every movement for strengthening the central government by constitutional means. From the moment he took command of the Continental Army he thought of himself as an American first and a Virginian second. His letters were full of the subject.

In the carefully thought out last circular to the states which he dictated during his last summer at Newburgh, he said, "According to the system of Policy the States shall adopt at this moment, they will stand or fall, and by their conservation or lapse, it is yet to be decided whether the Revolution must ultimately be considered as a blessing or as a curse, not to the present Age alone, for with our Fate will be the Destiny of unborn Millions be involved."

Then he laid down the principles he felt essential for a successful government:

> . . . 1st An indissoluble Union of the States under one Federal Head,
> 2ndly A Sacred regard to Public Justice,
> 3dly The Adoption of a Proper Peace Establishment [for the Continental Army] and
> 4thly The prevalence of that pacific and friendly Disposition among the People of the United States, which will induce them to forget their local prejudices and policies, to make these mutual concessions which are requisite to the general prosperity, and in some instances, to sacrifice their individual advantages to the interest of the Community . . .

This was the central theme of the discussion of the seventeen eighties in Congress and out. At Washington's suggestion — the general had for years been trying to get some recognition for the inspired staymaker's great services during the war — Robert Morris hired Tom Paine at eight hundred dollars a year to promote the cause of a continental tax on imports. Even the greatest pamphleteer of the age failed to make much immediate impression on the public mind. Only gradually did the obscure citizens whom Pelatiah Webster spoke for, who had felt under popular rule in Pennsylvania "greater restraints and abridgements of natural liberty than we ever felt under the government we have lately renounced," begin to look to a general government to protect the liberties they had fought the war to attain.

Pelatiah Webster himself expressed some of the ideas which were eventually to prevail in a lucid little essay on "The Political Union and Constitution of the Thirteen United States of North-America" he published in *The Pennsylvania Packet* in February of 1783. There he laid down three basic propositions: "The supreme power must have power enough to effect the ends of its appointment . . . The supreme authority ought to be so limited and checked, if possible, as to prevent the abuse of power, or the exercise of powers that are not necessary to the ends of its appointment . . . A number of sovereign states uniting into one commonwealth . . . do necessarily and unavoidably part with and transfer over to such supreme power so much of their own sovereignty as is necessary to render the ends of the union effectual, otherwise their confederation will be a union without bands of union, like a cask without hoops."

The phrase "a hoop to the union" was suddenly in every man's mouth. It appeared in the army's addresses to Congress. It was a favorite toast at public dinners. Writers for the newspapers reported it lovingly. The conviction grew that a merely advisory Congress would not work as a national scheme of government.

V   The Decline of the Old Congress

1. *The Pride of Independence*

The day before Webster's timely article appeared in Philadelphia, Thomas Jefferson was writing unhappily from Baltimore to his old friend and colleague Edmund Randolph, who had been the first attorney general of independent Virginia: "I find also the pride of independence taking deep and dangerous hold on the hearts of individual states. I know no danger so dreadful and so probable as that of internal contests. and I know no remedy so likely to prevent it as the strengthening the band which connects us. we have substituted a Congress of deputies from every state to perform this task: but we have done nothing which would enable them to enforce their decisions. what will be the case? they will not be enforced. the states will go to war with each other in defiance of Congress; one will call in France to her assistance, another Gt Britain so we shall have all the wars of Europe brought to our own doors . . ."

Jefferson, like Washington when he spoke of "political probation" in his last circular, had the decline of the Dutch Republic in the back of his mind.

The political weakness the United Provinces had shown in the war now coming to an end filled every American who read the foreign news with apprehension and dread. The United Provinces had developed a system of government most like their own, and they saw the Dutch letting their land become a playground for all the power politics of Europe.

Jefferson was hoping that Randolph, who was about to be elected to the House of Delegates in Virginia, would influence his colleagues to forget the mood of resistance to authority which had been essential to the struggle with the King and Parliament at Westminster; now the need was to build up a new authority: "It is very important to unlearn the lessons we have learnt under our former government, to discard the maxims which were the bulwark of that, but would be the ruin of the one we have erected . . . my humble and earnest prayer to Almighty god will be that you may bring into fashion principles suited to the form of government we have adopted, not of that we have rejected, that you will first lay your shoulders to the strengthening the band of our confederacy."

2. *The Confederacy from a High Ground*

Though the Continental Congress was proving daily less capable of attaining any immediate practical ends, it continued to serve as a forum for the discussion of political theory. At one time or another every publicminded man in America sat among its members. There they joined in debate with the freshest minds from the other states. Amid all the detailed discussion from day to day through which the war's conduct was hammered out, there ran a thread of argument on basic political theory. Like Parliament in the great days of the whig gentry, Congress as well as being a legislative and administrative assembly was an academy of statesmanship. During stormy sessions, in leisurely conversations over the wine after dinner, in chance encounters in liverystable yards, men's thoughts were stimulated by friction with other men's minds. Even the continual turnover of membership, the coming and going which played hob with efficiency, enhanced Congress's position as a mart for the clash and exchange of ideas.

As plans for a federated republic matured in Congress, men could match their theories of what ideal government ought to be against the daily shortcomings of the confederacy. Necessarily the delegates came away with some of their sectional prejudices rubbed off. As Jefferson wrote Madison: "I see the best effects produced by sending our young statesmen here. they see the affairs of the Confederacy from a high ground; they learn the importance of the Union and befriend Federal measures when they return."

Though Hamilton served only eight months in Congress it was enough, to a man of his rapidly absorbent mind, to learn a great deal about the workings of that versatile assembly. When he arrived in Philadelphia in the fall of 1782 he found the sessions heavily weighted with men who took for granted the superiority of a government by the rich and wellborn over what they scornfully pointed out as the vagaries of the "mobocracy" they could observe daily in action at the other end of the Pennsylvania State House.

Elias Boudinot of New Jersey, a tall deferential lawyer with a deeply religious bent who came from one of the oldest and wealthiest Huguenot families in America, had just been elected president. He represented the scattering of landed men who controlled the heterogeneous Jerseys. In a state which at its eastern end fell under the influence of the great Hudson River families like the Livingstons, and at its western end was part of the Quaker community which centered in Philadelphia, public opinion had little chance to coagulate. The fact that most of the leadership had been educated in the Presbyterian republicanism of Princeton College was almost the only unifying factor. To President Boudinot's mind the divine government of the universe had ordained the government of the affairs of this world by the chosen few.

Representing Connecticut Hamilton found two middleaged men from the same neat white clapboard town of Windsor. Oliver Ellsworth, known for his excessive use of his snuffbox, was a downright countryman who had chopped wood and ploughed his own land in his youth and risen to prominence as a trader and businessman and of course as a lawyer. Physical labor was not considered degrading in the trim and prosperous little communities that clustered round the white churches in that green and rolling state; but nowhere was the distinction more rigidly drawn between the first families, who kept the public offices in their hands, and the low groveling herd. Ellsworth's colleague was to be one of Connecticut's perennial governors: the elder Oliver Wolcott, a darkcomplexioned puritan, who spoke of himself as a republican of the old school, meaning the school of Oliver Cromwell. Both men abhorred popular government. Land in Connecticut was held in small parcels, but the chosen few made up for their lack of great holdings by their skill in amassing hard cash.

Massachusetts had sent cautious Samuel Osgood. Osgood's sympathy with the state sovereignty faction of Sam Adams was tempered by his personal friendship with the continentalist John Adams, whose carefully balanced new constitution he had helped put through the state constitutional convention in Boston; and Nathaniel Gorham, the selfmade Charlestown merchant; and Elbridge Gerry from Marblehead.

Gerry had inherited a flourishing business in dried fish and marine supplies. In spite of his wealth he remained the mouthpiece of the fishermen and ship carpenters of his tight little port. Though somewhat erratic, he generally moved in the politics of his home state with the Sam Adams faction which dominated Boston townmeeting.

The booming shipping interests were on the scene in the shape of canny Stephen Higginson. Higginson had sailed out of his home port of Salem as supercargo and navigator and part owner on a number of successful cruises. He had retired from privateering with seventy thousand dollars, which he had invested in a mercantile business in Boston. His election to Congress was a recognition by his brother merchants that he was a rising man in the business community.

The fact that the small farmers and homesteaders of the western end of the state were insufficiently represented either in the state government or in Congress was soon to have unhappy results. Their discontent was on the edge of breaking out in rioting and insurrection.

New Hampshire was represented by a thorough moneyman in the shape of John Taylor Gilman, of a family long dominant in the politics of that state, which was divided much as Massachusetts was by a conflict of interest between the moneylending businessmen of the towns, the shipping interests of the seaports, and the money-borrowing farmers and settlers in the back country.

North Carolina, too, showed the same cleavage between the seacoast and the interior; in this case intensified by the fact that the coastal landowners were slaveowners and the upland farmers were not. State government there was rendered more than usually unstable by the continual movement of lumbermen and settlers across the mountains into the valleys of the Western Waters. In this present session of Congress, William Blount, a plainspoken backwoods character, represented the scattered frontiersmen who still burned with the selfgoverning spirit of 1776. At the moment Hamilton arrived in Philadelphia Blount's influence in Congress was offset by Benjamin Hawkins, who had been Washington's French interpreter, a lawyer in his late twenties who at that time found most of his clients among the coastal slaveholders. Though Hawkins was described as being "aristocratic, conservative, proud and wealthy," there was more to him than that. He became in due time, as Indian agent, the apostle of civilization to the Creeks.

The grandees of the great South Carolina rice plantations had a brilliant delegation; there was gouty, irritable and opinionated Ralph Izard, back from frustrating experiences as an American envoy in Europe; there was David Ramsay, the Charleston physician and historian; and John Rutledge, an Inns of Court lawyer profoundly versed in English constitutional law. Rutledge had carried on the government of his state singlehanded during the British invasion and had contributed mightily to the British defeat.

Pennsylvania's appointees were George Clymer and Thomas Fitzsimons, for whom business interests were uppermost; witty and self-deprecating Richard Peters, who as secretary had carried on the daily drudgery of the Board of War as long as the fighting lasted; and the mercurial Thomas Mifflin, whose keen mind his best friends admitted to be all too often clouded with wine. Though Mifflin was a leader of the hard money Republicans, his knack of personal popularity earned him support among the artisans and mechanics of the towns and in those western settlements beyond the mountains which were no better represented in Pennsylvania than they were in Massachusetts. When occasion demanded he could always evoke the spirit of 1776.

Rhode Island was the paper money state. The decentralizing point of view of its small farmers and seafarers was defended, and ably, by David Howell, a New Jersey man who had gone from the college at Princeton to teach at the Baptist school in Providence. A born pedagogue, he was developing a flimsy theological school into a real university. Howell was a man of wide learning, a witty speaker with a delivery so scorching that he twice irritated opponents in congressional debate to the point where they challenged him to duels. In Rhode Island the debtor interest tended to carry every election. Howell remained the most ardent spokesman for his state's debtor mentality as long as the old Congress lasted: the Rhode Islanders were addicted to cheap currency, low taxes, and the popular vote.

The Virginia delegation at that point combined enthusiasm for a stronger central government fomented by the influence of Washington and Jefferson with an understanding of the need to protect the settlers of the western lands against the speculators from the seaport towns. Joseph Jones of King George County, Jefferson's friend and Monroe's uncle, was a levelheaded country lawyer steeped in the interests of the planters of the Northern Neck. James Madison of Montpellier in Orange County, still mostly known as Jefferson's disciple, was an ardent continentalist.

Though he took no part in the debates, Charles Thomson, by his quiet industry as secretary, helped hold the rambling and migratory assembly together during the relaxed years after the war as he had helped give it vigor and energy during the times that tried men's souls. Described as a man of meager figure, with a furrowed countenance and hollow sparkling eyes, Thomson's scholarship, his fair-mindedness and his dedication to his task made him an important silent influence in everything that went on.

He was the son of an immigrant from County Derry who died on the ship that brought the family to America. When he was only ten years old he found himself put ashore at New Castle, Delaware, a penniless orphan. He worked for a blacksmith there at first; then he was befriended by another North of Ireland man, a Presbyterian minister named Alison who had made a name as a schoolmaster in Chester County, Pennsylvania. Young Thomson earned his keep as a tutor there as he went through the school himself. From a studious boy he grew up into a learned man and conducted a Latin school of his own in Philadelphia. Benjamin Franklin helped him along. He was elected to local offices. The fame of his plainminded honesty spread through the province. "It is true as if Charles Thomson's name were to it" became a popular saying.

His reputation caused the Indians of the Delaware tribe to ask him to report their case in the course of a dispute over lands with the proprietary government. He did so well by them that they adopted him into their tribe under the name of The-Man-Who-Tells-The-Truth.

In the struggle for independence his great influence with the common people made him known as the Sam Adams of Philadelphia. A man who combined great classical learning with an inquisitive mind, it was natural that he should be an early member of the American Philosophical Society. It was Charles Thomson who read the Declaration of Independence from the State House steps. Ever since that day he had buried his great abilities in the voluminous paperwork of the Continental Congress. His influence was quietly on the continentalist side.

On the whole the lines were drawn between men who represented tight political machines at home, who dreaded continentalism as a challenge to their authority, and the men who for a variety of different reasons held broader views.

In this body of men of considerable learning and of very various experience, Hamilton's ability was immediately recognized. Conversation and argument developed his knowledge of constitutional law and increased his confidence in the statebuilding ability of the rich and wellborn.

He immediately exhibited his facility for compelling phrases. His mind moved like lightning. Though he read a good deal, his thinking had none of the academic cast that Madison's had. His pleasure was to make complicated problems seem clear. In fact, he often made them seem clearer than they actually were. His critics claimed that in the heat of argument he sometimes forgot that the aim was to convince rather than to dazzle his opponent.

Hamilton found studious James Madison the most congenial man in the Congress. Matching his daily experience with the failures and successes of the confederacy with his study of the history of republican institutions of the past, the diffident young Virginian was reaching by a rigorous process of reasoning many of the conclusions Hamilton guessed at intuitively.

Although Madison was older than Hamilton, he looked at that time of his life so much younger than his age that a New England delegate meeting him for the first time wrote of him as a boy just out of college. Madison at Princeton in the company of such unruly companions as Philip Freneau and Hugh Henry Brackenridge had been very much the sort of "furious Whig" of Presbyterian cast as now dominated the Pennsylvania Assembly. During the period of his initiation into political life in Virginia he had fallen under the sway of Jefferson's broader theories of selfgovernment. In the course of his reading in the history of republican and particularly of federative institutions — as profound as that of any man in America except possibly John Adams — he had developed a close reasoning very much his own. Now gradually, without too much personal attraction to ease their association, Madison and Hamilton, working in committee and on specific problems, with the same general objects in view, fell into the intimate collaboration which was to reach its climax in *The Federalist*.

They agreed at this point that the first essential towards founding a stable government was that the states must live up to their obligations to their creditors, both military and civilian. As Madison put it in the address he drafted as a sort of valedictory before retiring when his three-year term in Congress expired in the winter of 1783: "The citizens of the United States are responsible for the greatest trust ever confided to a political society. If justice, good faith, honor, gratitude, and all other qualities which ennoble the character of a nation & fulfill the ends of government, be the fruits of our establishment, the cause of liberty will acquire a dignity and lustre which it has never yet enjoyed, and an example will be set which cannot but have the most favorable influence on the rights of mankind."

At this period in their lives, Hamilton and Madison and Jefferson all agreed on the need for a strong continental government. To that end Jefferson worked hard to induce the Virginians to cede their vast western lands to Congress. He lobbied in the Virginia legislature for Morris's impost. He so far approved of Morris's plan for the assumption and funding of the state and continental debts that he wrote Madison he hoped that measure would "sugar the pill" for the Virginians he was trying to induce to give up their claims to the westward. As in the argument over a national bank, it was the question of in whose interest funding and assumption should be carried out and in whose interest the continental government should be administered that brought a clash of opinion.

3. Concerned only with Affairs of Public Interest

Jefferson himself was appointed to Congress by the Virginia legislature in the spring of 1783.

He had been pulling himself up gradually, hand over hand, from the deepest pit of depression. He had given up his public life for good, so he believed, at the end of his second term as governor of Virginia. Smarting from the criticism of Patrick Henry's faction in the legislature, he had retired to Monticello, to his natural philosophy and his books and his music and his architecture and his farming and to the society of the frail vivacious wife in whose love his whole soul was engaged. When she died his private happiness was ruined forever. She left him three small daughters to tug at his heartstrings. For a while he tried to bury himself in his farming and the girls' education; but Monticello, his hilltop temple dedicated to the affection of a man and a woman divinely suited to each other, had no meaning without Patty. In the hope that fresh scenes in that Europe he had so often dreamed of seeing would bring back his taste for living he accepted the diplomatic post he had refused before. He clutched eagerly at an appointment, which his friends in Congress put through without a dissenting vote, to the commission which was negotiating peace in Paris.

Instead of an exciting excursion this first mission brought him only frustration. Leaving the two youngest girls with his wife's sister, Mrs. Eppes, he hurried to Philadelphia. He took Patsy, the oldest girl, along with him in his chaise. He was planning to leave her in school there under the care of his good friend Mrs. Trist, the daughter of the old lady who kept the boardinghouse where the Virginia delegates were in the habit of staying during their terms at the seat of government.

Although he was packed and ready, the congressional secretaries were not able to draft his instructions in time for him to sail with the French squadron that ran the British blockade to take home Rochambeau and his staff. As soon as his credentials were in order Jefferson posted to the booming new Maryland seaport of Baltimore to get aboard the Romulus, a French ship of the line, which was supposed to be sailing any day. It was an unusually cold winter. By the time he arrived the Romulus had dropped down the bay to avoid being frozen in. After some difficult communication by sloop and skiff through sheets of drifting ice, it came out that it was not the severe weather that was keeping the French captain from putting out to sea, but the British blockaders. Eighteen frigates and seven ships of the line of over fifty guns had been counted either at anchor in de Grasse's old anchorage in Lynnhaven Bay or cruising off the Virginia Capes. Too much for one poor Frenchman.

Weeks dragged by. There was talk of running the American envoy out of the Chesapeake by night in a swift frigate, but the frigate turned out to be waterlogged. Jefferson was exploring the idea of chartering a merchant ship under a flag of truce when word came from Congress that the preliminaries of peace had already been signed and that there was no need for him to make the trip.

Back in Virginia he tried to forget himself in an intense spate of work on a new constitution for the state. It was his old plan of 1776 refurbished. He wanted both houses of the legislature to be elected by free manhood suffrage. These were to choose a governor to serve for five years without reelection and a council of state to serve for seven years on the same terms. Civil rights were to be rigidly protected. Habeas corpus and freedom of the press were to be assured. The importation of slaves was to be forbidden. After December 31, 1800, all children born of slaves were to be free.

When Jefferson produced his new constitution in Richmond it evoked some praise from his friends, but the bill to call a convention to vote on it was quietly tabled in the legislature. Patrick Henry, furthermore, had set himself against Morris's impost and his funding and assumption scheme. When these measures failed too the delegates, who admired Jefferson as an ornament to their state but who felt his political notions were hopelessly ahead of his time, elected him to Congress as a sort of consolation prize.

Again he set out with Patsy in his chaise. The Continental Congress was no longer in Philadelphia. That assembly had moved to Princeton in a huff because of the slackness the Pennsylvania authorities had shown in protecting its dignity from the insults of the Lancaster mutineers. Unable to reach a decision in the sectional pulling and hauling over the location of an eventual national capital, the Continental Congress began to oscillate, like a pendulum, someone said, between Trenton and Annapolis.

Again leaving Patsy in Philadelphia, this time with the mother of the amiable musician, Francis Hopkinson, Jefferson drove off to Princeton and arrived there just in time to find the longsuffering Charles Thomson packing up his records to move to Annapolis. Madison had been writing Jefferson humorously about the close quarters "not ten feet square" members had to make shift in at Princeton, so great was the congestion there when Congress and the college were both in residence. Madison's term was over; he was starting home to Montpellier.

Jefferson settled down in Annapolis for a winter of hard work and ill health; he suffered from a succession of the migraine headaches that plagued him particularly in stressful times throughout his life. When friendly and admiring young Monroe arrived to join the Virginia delegation, Jefferson's solitude was relieved a little.

James Monroe was one of Jefferson's young men. He had appeared in Richmond as a bashful and unassigned officer during Jefferson's harried service as governor. Jefferson had put him to work to organize a dispatch service between the Virginia council and Greene's army in the Carolinas. He started him reading law and took over his general education with the enthusiasm he showed whenever he struck a responsive chord in a younger man. Monroe responded with all the singlehearted gratitude he was capable of. In Annapolis, Jefferson had discovered a firstrate French restaurateur; they messed together in style.

Congress was hampered as usual by lack of money that winter but particularly by lack of members to form a quorum. When General Washington arrived to resign his commission there was some question as to whether sufficient states were present to receive it. The delegates were thrown into a worse quandary when the very favorable treaty with England their commissioners in Paris had gone to such pains to negotiate was laid before them. For months they could not drum up enough members to ratify it.

Jefferson kept close to his quarters. As painful as his headaches, as the dreadful vacancy his wife's death had left in his life, was the frustration of presenting measures to an assembly that had no way of enforcing its decisions.

A young Hollander who visited him in the spring, one of the first of the endless train of European travelers visiting America to see with their own eyes this liberty men talked so much about, described him: "Mr. Jefferson during my attendance at the session of Congress was more busily engaged than anyone. Retired from fashionable society, he concerned himself only with affairs of public interest, his sole diversion being that offered by belles lettres. The poor state of his health, he told me occasionally, was the cause of his retirement: but it seemed rather that his mind, accustomed to the unalloyed pleasure of the society of a lovable wife, was impervious since her loss to the feeble attractions of common society, and that his soul, fed on noble thoughts, was revolted by idle chatter . . . He has the shyness that accompanies true worth, which is at first disturbing and which puts off those who seek to know him. Those who persist" — and evidently the young Hollander did — "in knowing him soon discern the man of letters, the lover of natural history, law, statecraft, philosophy and the friend of mankind."

The friend of mankind was an unhappy man during that session of Congress. He was only fortyone, but he felt old before his time;

it cost him a mighty effort to interest himself in the life he was living from day to day. Though he hardly knew it himself he was gradually putting his grief aside in his absorption in multifarious interests. He had a taste for close detail; before long he found himself loaded with all the complicated paperwork the other members avoided. Even in the frustration of congressional impotence there were moments when he could feel he was helping shape the nation that was coming into being.

One of Congress's lasting achievements was the settlement, by a series of complicated arbitrations during the years of the war, of territorial disputes between the states. The dispute between New York and New Hampshire over the Green Mountain territory had been settled in fact by the congressional benediction of the independent state government constituted in 1777 by the declaration of independence of the "New Hampshire Grants." The status of Vermont was to continue somewhat amorphous until the region was admitted to the Union as a state in 1791, but the danger of warfare between New York and New Hampshire was averted.

The other grave conflict that arose was between Connecticut and Pennsylvania. That too was in course of arbitration. Now Jefferson found himself joining in committee on the subject with a pair of highly talented physicians, the acidulous Dr. Lee, and Dr. Hugh Williamson of North Carolina who, besides being a friend of Franklin's and a collaborator in his electrical work, was an astronomer and one of the first Americans to put his mind to the study of public health. This new committee was appointed to deal with a fresh protest from Connecticut on the adjudication to Pennsylvania of the rich Wyoming Valley lands by the commissioners Congress had appointed to arbitrate the dispute.

The conflict of sovereignty in northern Pennsylvania, like most of such conflicts between the colonies, resulted from the overlapping boundaries of the early royal grants which had been drawn up with an enthusiastic disregard for geography. Land speculators had arrived early on the scene. In Connecticut they formed a Susquehanna Company which included a number of powerful figures round the Hartford statehouse. In Philadelphia the speculators worked through the Illinois-Wabash Company, in which Robert Morris and his friends were involved, represented by the great constitutional lawyer, who was a fanatical speculator himself, James Wilson.

The Connecticut people had brought in settlers. The Pennsylvanians had tried to enforce their claims with the militia. Two small border wars had followed in which settlers were driven from their farms by one party or the other, barns and houses were burned, with the resulting murders and shootings and feuding in the hills.

Congress scored an original success by inducing all parties concerned to submit their claims to the commissioners appointed at Trenton. Now all that was needed was to reaffirm the original decision against new legal moves originating at Hartford. When the negotiation showed signs of peaceful progress, Jefferson wrote down for his own satisfaction an exuberant note, "Perhaps history cannot produce such another proof of the empire of reason of right in any part of the world as these new states now exhibit. other nations have only been able to submit private contests to judiciary termination; but these new states have gone further. they have set the example of binding a court for the trial of nations."

4. *The Government of the Western Lands*

Next to the establishment of the habit of submitting disputes between the states to arbitration for judicial decision, which was later formalized by the Constitution in the shape of the Supreme Court, Congress's most enduring work during that winter, in which Jefferson also played a leading part, was the drafting of a plan of government for the western lands. This was the Ordinance of 1784.

Before this work could be undertaken Congress had to be induced, against the wishes of the land speculators who were well represented among its members, to accept the final deed of cession of Virginia's claims to lands northwest of the Ohio in the form in which it had been drawn up by Jefferson, Dr. Lee, Samuel Hardy and Monroe.

During the period of Jefferson's governorship of Virginia, in direct opposition to the short term interests of her own speculators, the Virginia continentalists had managed to shepherd the act of cession through the Assembly. Though Madison and Jefferson were not businessmen and had no great interests involved, Washington and George Mason and Benjamin Harrison and Monroe's uncle and guardian, Joseph Jones, were. In spite of their investments with various land companies they had all cooperated loyally. The willingness of these men to forget their private interest for the benefit of the nation was an immense step forward towards the establishment of a continental government.

Jefferson, who had had the frontier in his bones since his boyhood, was determined to protect the interests of the individual settlers who were risking their own scalps and their families' lives and everything they had to make the lands of the Western Waters part of the American nation.

Writing his old friend Governor Benjamin Harrison, he described with some humor the process by which they induced Congress to accept the Virginia terms. "We" — the Virginia delegation — "determined on consultation that our proper duty was to be still, having declared we were ready to execute, we would leave it to them to come forward and tell us they were ready to accept. we medled not at all therefore, and shewed a perfect indifference. N. Hampshire came to town which made us 9. states" — nine states were necessary for a quorum to do business — "a member proposed that we should execute the deed and lay it on the table . . . urging the example of N. York which had executed their deed, laid it on the table, where it remained 18. months before Congress accepted it. we replied, no, if these lands are not offered for sale the ensuing spring, they will be taken from us all by adventurers" — he meant speculators — "we will not therefore put it out of our power to sell them ourselves if Congress will not. a member from Rhode Island" — David Howell, always ready to rise up against speculators and the creditor interest generally — "then moved that Congress should accept. another from New Jersey proposed as an amendment a proviso that it should not amount to an acknowledgement of our right" — the land companies were putting forth a fanciful contention that New Jersey had a claim to part of the Virginia tract — "we told them we were not authorized to admit any conditions or provisos, that their acceptance must be simple, absolute and unqualified or we could not execute. on the question there were 6. ayes — the voting was by states, — Jersey no, S. Carolina and Pennsylvania divided. the matter dropped and the house proceeded to other business. about an hour after, the dissenting Pennsylvanian" — probably Thomas Mifflin, the somewhat unpredictible president — "asked and obtained leave to change his no into aye. the vote was then passed and we executed the deed."

So by a hair's breadth Congress accepted the Virginia conditions, which were that the territory should be laid out into states which should be eventually admitted into the Union under a republican form of government with the same rights of "Sovereignty, Freedom and Independence as the other States," that Virginia should be reimbursed for the expense of George Rogers Clark's expeditions which had driven the British out of Vincennes, that the French and Canadian inhabitants who had professed themselves Virginia citizens should enjoy their rights and liberties, and that George Rogers Clark and his men and the Virginia veterans of the Continental Army who had been granted lands there should retain them unmolested.

David Howell had been stimulated a few days before by Jefferson's

partisanship of the settlers on the western lands to write home an
enthusiastic description of him to Providence. After describing the
Virginian as "one of the best members I have ever seen in Congress,
has a good Library of French books, and had been so good to lend me
one," he exulted over the work of Jefferson's committees: "The western
world opens an amazing prospect as a national fund, in my opinion; it
is equal to our debt. As a source of future population and strength,
it is a guaranty to our independence. As its inhabitants will be mostly
cultivators of the soil, republicanism looks to them as its guardians."
Jefferson had loaned the Rhode Island schoolteacher more than his
French books; the letter read as if he had supplied him with a strong
dose of his private faith in small farmer democracy. "When the states
on the eastern shores, or Atlantic, shall have become populous, rich
and luxurious, and ready to yield their liberties into the hands of a
tyrant" — Howell rose to a burst of eloquence — "the gods of the
mountains will save us, for they will be stronger than the gods of the
valleys."

The territory in question included unfortunately no mountains. It
comprised the vast triangular plain, bounded on the east by the Ohio,
on the west by the Mississippi, and on the north by the Great Lakes,
where the British had not yet consented to relinquish their string of
posts that ran from Oswego and Erie to Detroit and Mackinac. This
was the region where old Lewis Nicola had dreamed for a mad
moment of setting up his monarchy with Washington as king, the
region that filled the heads of speculators with nightly visions of
uncountable profits from the sale of their acreage.

Already on foot and horseback, by wagon train and flatboat, the
movement west had begun. All through the war, pioneers had been
crossing into Kentucky from the settled lands of Virginia by Daniel
Boone's wilderness road that followed the warrior paths traced out
during Jefferson's boyhood in Albemarle by his father's friends in
the forgotten days of the Loyal Land Company. At the battle of
Kings Mountain a band of buckskin-clad men with long rifles led by
John Sevier had turned Cornwallis's flank by their fierce charge. They
had come across the hills to fight the redcoats from the clearings
along the Tennessee River. When they went home they organized
there the rebellious and shortlived State of Franklin. During the past
October the officer in command at Pittsburgh had reported that a
band of four hundred men had already crossed the Ohio to settle
on the Muskingum.

While Congress debated, men who had picked up stakes and moved
west to escape taxes and every other problem of government were
banding trees, burning off forest, shooting Indians, and planting crops

in the heart of the continent. With settlement some sort of organization of society would become inevitable. How would these people
govern themselves when they had driven off the savages and hewed
out their farms in the wilderness?

Even before the deed of cession was accepted Jefferson sketched a
plan of government for the newly settled lands. The matter had been
working in his mind ever since he had encorporated a scheme for
settling new states into the Virginia constitution of 1776. But his was
not the only scheme on the table.

The autumn before, George Washington, at the request of James
Duane, then chairman of the committee on Indian affairs, had sent
Congress a set of suggestions.

To avoid an Indian War, Washington's plan was for orderly settlement under military protection. "To suffer a wide extended country
to be over run with Land Jobbers, Speculators, and Monopolizers or
even with scatter'd settlers," he wrote, "is pregnant of disputes both
with the savages, and among ourselves, the evils of which are easier
conceived than described; and for what? but to aggrandize a few
avaricious men to the prejudice of many, and the embarrassment of
Government."

He proposed that the land should be settled in strips acquired by
negotiation with the Indians as they were needed, under the supervision of frontier garrisons, and that nobody should be allowed to
penetrate beyond the strip nearest the settled country until that section
was entirely occupied. He dreaded the pouring of uncontrolled immigrants into the western lands, "the overspreading of the western
country . . . by a parcel of banditti who will bid defiance to all
authority while they are skimming and disposing of the cream of the
country at the expense of many suffering Officers and Soldiers who
have fought and bled to obtain it."

These settlers whom Washington spoke of as "a parcel of banditti"
Jefferson thought of, much as Howell described them in his letter
home to Rhode Island, as the guardians of republicanism. In that
difference of opinion lurked the beginnings of a breach in the thinking
of patriotic men which was to loom ever larger in the years to come.

From the beginning Jefferson had hankered for title by occupancy,
or squatters' rights as they were derisively called by his opponents.
With his customary distrust of the military, he felt that every effort to
police that enormous frontier would fail. "They will settle the lands
in spite of everybody," he had written Edmund Pendleton years
before. He had faith in the settlers' ability to police themselves.

In his original draft of a constitution for his home state he had
wanted every nativeborn citizen and every immigrant to have a right

to enough acreage of the public land to qualify him as a voter. Another try for complete manhood suffrage in Virginia had failed with his second draft constitution the spring before. Now he saw the chance of making sure that when the settlers of the northwest territories reached the point of setting up their own governments it should be according to the principles of 1776.

Washington wanted primarily to avoid bloodshed and strife and to protect the grants which Congress and the states had made to veterans of his armies. On one point Jefferson's committee, poring over the not too accurate maps they had in hand, did follow Washington's suggestions. The states were laid out in tiers.

They were to be selfgoverning from the start. "Their free males of full age" were to meet together immediately to set up a temporary government at a time and place either directed by Congress or suggested by them in a petition to Congress. As each state reached a population of twenty thousand it should be admitted into the Union. The union would be irrevocable. The settlers should be subject to the United States in Congress assembled and to the Articles of Confederacy. They should pay their share of the federal debts. They could admit to citizenship no person who held a hereditary title. After 1800 slavery should be abolished in the new states.

By the time the report went through the congressional mill and appeared as an ordinance the sections on slavery and forbidding hereditary titles had disappeared and in their place had appeared provisions protecting the absentee holders of grants of land from interference or from discriminatory taxation by the new states.

Since the writing of the Declaration of Independence, Jefferson had never taken part in the drafting of a fundamental document without trying to slip in a provision for the eventual abolition of slavery. He was accustomed to having his proposals quietly discarded by the legislative majority, but he had never quite accustomed himself to the sting of these failures. He was convinced his cause was just; there were roundabout ways of having the last word.

A few days after Congress promulgated the ordinance, the readers of *The Pennsylvania Packet* found printed there, instead of the final approved text, the original resolution as reported by Jefferson's committee. Jefferson would seem to have had a hand in the leak, because in his next letter to congenial Francis Hopkinson he spoke ironically of an imaginary prosecution of the publisher for "scandalum magnatum" for printing as an act of Congress a paper "which certainly was no act of theirs, and which contained a principle or two not quite within the level of their politics . . . two of which as this forgery pretends were an exclusion of hereditary honors, and an abolition of slavery. when the true act shall be published you will find no such pettifogging ideas in it."

5. *The Society of the Cincinnati*

The restriction on "hereditary honors" in Jefferson's plan for the northwest territories was intended as a blow to the budding Cincinnati, a military order which Steuben was promoting among the veterans who had served as officers in the Continental Army during the Revolution. Perhaps the good baron, whose title was somewhat doubtful in Europe, hoped to make an aristocrat of himself in the New World. The institution of the Cincinnati raised a storm among republicans, radical and conservative alike.

The prototype was thought to be a hereditary association modeled on the old knightly orders formed in the more "enlightened" of the European courts among the young nobles who had fought for Polish liberty at the time of the first partition of that illfated country. A number of American officers, in the first flush of European enthusiasm for the American cause, were offered honorary membership, but Congress did not allow them to accept.

Henry Knox sketched out the first scheme of organization for the Cincinnati a few weeks after Washington quelled the uproar raised by the Newburgh addresses. It is possible that Washington encouraged the formation of the society as a way of finding an outlet for the energies of his officers still smarting from their shabby treatment by Congress.

Knox's plan was read to an enthusiastic meeting in the same "Temple" where the commander in chief had made his great speech. The society was officially constituted at Steuben's headquarters three days later. Among the charter members were Benjamin Lincoln and Nathanael Greene and Rufus Putnam and Steuben and Heath, and among field officers old Lewis Nicola, who had wanted a monarchy, and Knox's enterprising aide, Samuel Shaw, who was later to shine in the China trade. Washington of course was proposed as president, Knox as secretary, and Alexander McDougall as treasurer.

At first the society seems to have appealed mostly to the New Englanders, with their very special sense of social stratification, as something which would distinguish them from the rabble of farmers' and mechanics' sons they had had such difficulty in whipping into the shape of a disciplined army during the war.

Washington accepted his nomination as president general in much the same spirit of benevolent patience with which he accepted the flower petals strewn at his feet by little girls in white dresses, the odes of welcome spouted at him by deputations of townspeople, and the uncomfortable wreaths people placed on his head at public functions. He was full of affection for his staff and his officers. This harmless distinction would make them happy.

In France the institution was received with great enthusiasm. Rochambeau and Lafayette were overwhelmed with applications for membership. His Most Christian Majesty was induced to allow its badge to be worn by the French military. Up to that time the only foreign decoration so honored was the Order of the Golden Fleece. Everything American was in style at Versailles. Memories of the humiliation of the British milords at Yorktown were a balm to national prĩde wounded by the recent failure of the expedition against Gibraltar and by de Grasse's shameful defeat in the Saints' Passage. Every Frenchman who had drawn his sword on American soil, and a good many who had not, burned to appear at the court of Versailles wearing the handsome spread eagle badge which Major l'Enfant designed and which he was sent home to Paris to have executed. In the salons of Paris, on the promenades of the Palais Royale and at Marie Antoinette's private festivities at the Trianon, the Society of the Cincinnati was the last word.

American civilians of varied political complexions took it ill from the beginning. John Adams wrote home a horrified letter from Holland. John Jay agreed with him. Benjamin Franklin tried to laugh the idea out of court in a letter to his daughter. He complained that the bald eagle "was a bird of bad character" who spent his time perching on some dead tree waiting for a chance to snatch a fish out of the claws of hardworking fishhawks. He offered himself the mock consolation of suggesting that l'Enfant's eagle looked more like a turkey, "a much more respectable bird . . . a little vain and silly it is true . . . but a bird of courage who would not hesitate to attack a grenadier of the British Guard if he should presume to invade the farm yard with a red coat on."

There were still plenty of New Englanders ready to bristle at the word aristocracy. In Boston Sam Adams let it be known that it was not to start a hereditary nobility that he had instigated the committees of correspondence. The General Court appointed a committee to investigate the Cincinnati.

The nationwide opposition found voice in a pamphlet brought out in Philadelphia by the same Aedanus Burke, the vehement Irishman from County Galway, now a South Carolina judge, who had been moved to such mixed feelings by the sight of the beaten enemy at the surrender at Yorktown. Under the motto of "Blow ye the trumpet

in Zion" he dusted the jacket of aristocracies ancient and modern.
Grimly he signed himself "Cassius."

Aedanus Burke's pamphlet was widely read. Its influence was more
far reaching in Europe than in America. In London it was picked up
by a swarthy little Provençal count temporarily in exile from his
ungrateful country. In Mirabeau's free translation into French, along
with a letter of Dr. Price's praising American republicanism and
democracy, Aedanus Burke's argument went into edition after edition
and became, during the coming revolution in France, one of Mirabeau's chief engines for the destruction of the nobility.

Washington read Burke's argument with puckered brows. Animadversions again. Genuinely disturbed, he wrote a number of old
friends and comrades in arms, asking their opinions. "People are
alarmed, especially in the Eastern states," he told Jefferson, for whose
intellectual preeminence he felt real deference in those days, "how
justly, or how contrary to the avowed principles of the Society or the
purity of their Motives, I shall not declare, least it should appear I
wanted to biass your judgment, rather than to obtain an opinion."

Jefferson answered that he quite understood how men "who had
accompanied each other through so many scenes of hardship, difficulty and danger" would "seize with fondness any propositions which
promised to bring them together again at certain and regular periods
. . . I have no suspicion that they foresaw, much less intended those
mischiefs which exist perhaps in the forebodings of politicians only."

Then he went on to explain, a little condescendingly perhaps, that
such an institution was against the letter of most American constitutions and against the spirit of all of them, since they were founded on
"the natural equality of man, the denial of every preeminence but
that annexed to legal office, and particularly the denial of a preeminence
by birth." Opinion in Congress was unanimously against it. He advised
that the society be completely dismantled.

Washington was so much impressed by Jefferson's letter, and possibly
by what his fellow Virginian had to say privately in conversation
when Washington went through Annapolis on his way to the organization meeting of the society in Philadelphia, that he quoted Jefferson's
arguments in his speech to the officers assembled at the City Tavern.
He insisted that they strike out from their constitution "every word,
sentence and clause which has a political tendency." He urged them
to drop the provision that made membership hereditary. The constitution of the national organization was so amended. It was a measure
of the growth of class spirit among the "rich and wellborn" in the
thirteen original states that most of the local societies refused to
ratify Washington's revised constitution and stuck to the hereditary
principle.

6. *Hot Air Balloons*

Washington rode into Philadelphia for the first meeting of the Cincinnati on the first of May, 1784, a day already dedicated to celebration by the mechanics and artisans of the town who were banqueting in a grove on the banks of the Schuylkill. He was greeted by salutes of thirteen cannons and by shouts of "General Washington is arrived Huzza." After dinner at Robert Morris's comfortable abode, where he was dined and wined with all the abundance Mrs. Morris's kitchen and Robert Morris's cellar were capable of, a parade of the Sons of St. Tammany, an organization very much of the people, serenaded him with fife and drum.

Dreading "animadversions" as he did, the general was undoubtedly relieved to find that the peril of a military aristocracy was not the only topic of conversation in Philadelphia. What everybody was talking about was balloons. News of the successful ascents of Montgolfier's balloons from the gardens of the Château de la Muette in Paris echoed through every afterdinner conversation.

Jefferson's jocose correspondence with Francis Hopkinson, who had just been helping Robert Morris import a new harpsichord from Europe for the use of his daughters, was full of balloons that spring. Jefferson had laid hold of one of the first books on the subject that arrived on American shores. He was sending sketches and detailed accounts of the construction of hot air balloons to his relatives in Virginia. In Williamsburg his old schoolfellow, Madison of Montpellier's cousin, the Reverend James Madison from up in the Valley, was planning to build a balloon for the edification of his students at William and Mary.

In Philadelphia the general himself, a great lover of shows and curiosities of every kind, had the pleasure one morning of seeing a small fire balloon constructed by a certain Dr. Foulk rise successfully from Robert Morris's garden. It is likely that it was the ubiquitous Robert Morris that Hopkinson had in mind when he wrote Jefferson at the end of an aeronautical letter: "A highflying politician I think not unlike a Balloon — he is full of inflammibility, he is driven along by every current of Wind, and those who will suffer themselves to be carried up by them run a great risk that the Bubble will burst."

7. *Decimal Arithmetic*

Men of the most varied political opinions had become suspicious of the Financier's operations. One of the reasons why many

members were loath to have Congress return to Philadelphia was that
they felt it would be harder to shake loose there from Robert Morris's
all pervading influence. Governor Benjamin Harrison of Virginia wrote
Jefferson in confidence: "Philadelphia has been a continual drain to
us and will continue to be so if Congress is either in it or its
neighborhood. It is a vortex that swallows up our wealth and leaves
us no prospect of recovering a single shilling."

James Warren of Massachusetts wrote of the Financier bitterly as
"that sink of corrupt influence."

Marbois at the French embassy, whose business of the moment was
to try to induce the Americans to continue paying their interest on
the French debt, wrote home that Morris expected His Most Christian
Majesty to pay "all the illegitimate profits that he had taken to himself
and of which he is unhappily in possession."

During all that Annapolis spring when Jefferson, among other
duties, acted as chairman of Congress's Grand Committee on Finances,
he was in the middle of the controversy. Congress was as usual
wrestling with the problem of debts. The two Morrises had been using
their authority over the handling of funds and the payment of claims
to channel all public business through the Finance Office. Everyone
understood that where the current of financial power ran strongest
there too the political power would flow.

As the problems of peace began to displace the wartime emergency
in men's minds the pendulum of opinion which had swung towards
centralizing and continentalist policies in the year of Yorktown began
to swing back towards the protection of the sovereignty of the states.

The report of Jefferson's Grand Committee in the spring of 1784
advised the assumption by the states of the continental debt, rather
than the assumption of state debts by a central government which
the Finance Office was working for. The forces pulling towards
centralization were strong enough to check this trend. The parties at
either end of the tug of war were so evenly matched that congressional
action was paralyzed in every field. The states were neglecting to
supply Congress with funds.

According to the report of the Grand Committee in March of 1784,
South Carolina was the only state not in arrears in payment of the
latest financial requisitions agreed on. Delaware, North Carolina and
Georgia had not paid a cent. New Hampshire owed approximately
$277,000, Massachusetts $733,000, Rhode Island $94,000, Connecticut
nearly $429,000, New York $241,000, New Jersey $262,000, Pennsyl-
vania almost $500,000, Maryland $600,000, Virginia $865,000, North
Carolina $467,000.

It was this intentional starving out of Congress by the state legislatures that in the end made the great majority of Americans willing

to go along with the establishment of a strong general government.

By this time Jefferson had joined those opposed to Robert Morris's schemes; but he hardly went so far as David Howell who like Benjamin Harrison, wrote of the Finance Office as "a sinister vortex swallowing the wealth of the states." There remained areas of practical operation where Jefferson could cordially cooperate with Morris and his assistant. One of these was the problem of the currency.

During all the years of the Revolutionary War plans were discussed for currency reform but nothing was accomplished. Merchants continued to rack their brains with the staggering problems in arithmetic offered by the simplest interstate transaction. The Spanish dollar had even before the war been on the way to supplant the English pound as a unit of measurement, though both were still in use. The dollar was worth 8 shillings in New York and North Carolina, 6 shillings in New England and Virginia, 7/6 in the Middle Atlantic states, 5 shillings in Georgia, and 32/6 in South Carolina. Besides Spanish dollars, most of them originating in the Mexican mint at Guanajuato, there were current English guineas and exotic gold coins known as doubloons, joes, moidores, carolins, ducats, chequins: silver pieces of eight, pistareens and half pistareens; in copper there were the pence and ha'pence of old England, sous and picayunes, to say nothing of the various copper pennies stamped out in Vermont, Massachusetts, New Jersey, Connecticut and Pennsylvania. When a man traveled up and down the coast his wallet became a numismatic museum.

Ever since his first term in Congress Jefferson had been explaining to anyone who would listen that the thing to do was to scrap the whole business and adopt a decimal system. He referred to the arguments he had to contend with in a letter to Francis Hopkinson.

After suggesting that the date of the opening up of federal lands for sale, through the Land Office his committee had established immediately after Congress accepted the Virginia cession, would be a good time to introduce a geometric mile of ten furlongs divided into decimal subdivisions of chains and paces, he continued sarcastically, "but I hope it will be foreseen that should we introduce so heteradox a facility as the decimal arithmetic, we should all of us forget how to cypher. I have hopes that the same care to preserve an athletic strength of calculation, will not permit us to lose the pound as a money unit and its subdivisions into 20ths, 240ths, and 960ths . . . Certain innovaters" — he was referring of course to himself — "have been wishing to banish all this cunning learning, to adopt the dollar for our Unit, to divide that into 10ths. 100ths. &c . . . this is surely the age of innovation, and America the focus of it."

A report on the currency was one of the first jobs that Robert

Morris turned over to his assistant. Gouverneur made a painstaking study of the value of the various coins reckoned in pure silver. He suggested that the American currency should be based on a unit which would be the lowest common denominator of all the various currencies of the states. Immediately he ran into complications. If he included the undervalued pennies of South Carolina his unit would have to be $\frac{1}{18720}$ of a dollar, which was an arithmetical monstrosity. Even leaving the South Carolina pennies to shift for themselves, the lowest unit would be $\frac{1}{1440}$ of a dollar.

This report came under the scrutiny of Jefferson's committee. To head off its complications without heading off the whole project Jefferson drew up one of his most disarming state papers. He laid out the problems of setting up a currency in simple winning language. "The plan reported by the Financier is worthy of his sound judgment," he wrote — he was already in training for diplomacy — "it admits however of objection in the size of the Unit."

He suggested that the only real choice lay between the pound and the dollar, which were the two units people were accustomed to. He reminded his readers of their schoolboy headaches in trying to figure with pounds, shillings and pence. "Everybody knows the facility of decimal arithmetic." He seized on the fact that Gouverneur Morris had agreed with him on this point. "Certainly in all cases where we are free to chuse between easy and difficult modes of operation, it is most rational to chuse the easy." The dollar should be the unit and it should be divided into a hundred cents.

Congress adopted the dollar and the cent the following summer when Jefferson was in France, four thousand stormy Atlantic miles away, thereby setting up the first decimal currency in history. Washington had expressed his approval of Jefferson's plan and David Howell, who had published part of Jefferson's report in *The Rhode Island Gazette*, pushed it on the floor and managed to overcome the misgivings of the more timid members. Congress, even in the days of its doldrums, was capable of innovation.

When it came to establishing a mint under Robert Morris's supervision Congress balked. Morris, practical businessman that he was, had gone ahead and set up a trial plant. He had found an Englishman named Dudley who built stamping machinery and designed a set of coins embellished with a Masonic eye and thirteen stars and surrounded by the words *nova constellatio*. The members of Congress examined the sample coins and hastened to forget the whole matter.

Francis Hopkinson was so impressed by the imminence of a national coinage that, dreaming of Isaac Newton, he wrote Jefferson in Annapolis asking him to try to get him the job of superintendent of the new mint. "You are the only person to whom I have ever mentioned this

Business, except Mr. Morris, who in Truth first brought the object into my View."

Jefferson was not able to do anything for his friend because he had already been appointed a commissioner on a new diplomatic mission to France and was resigning from Congress. Robert Morris was unable to set up his mint because Congress was already up in arms against him. Congress itself continued to drift locked in a parallelogram of forces that could never be resolved. While Jefferson was packing a second time for the European journey, Congress was deciding to evade its problems by adjourning.

The congressional paralysis was brought home to the members most painfully through their pocketbooks. They found it almost impossible to get their pay and living expenses out of the state legislatures. Madison, like many another congressman, had time and again to borrow from a little Jewish broker named Haym Salomon in Philadelphia. Salomon refused to accept any interest on his money, saying that the members who borrowed from him were spending it in the public service.

Their eternal lack of cash to pay their board bills led some members to fall prey to the blandishments of the ever openhanded French ambassador, the Chevalier de la Luzerne; and, so men suspected, to the temptations of Robert Morris, who was always ready to let a penniless congressman in on some deal or other. Jefferson explained the difficulty of obtaining a quorum in one of his reports to Edmund Pendleton: "The true reason the delegates do not attend is that their states do not furnish them with money, and if they advance them some to get there they are then left in the lurch and obliged either to make mean shifts or to go home. spirited members prefer the latter and thus we are kept with a house incompetent to business . . . A committee of the states must be left to transact ordinary business."

In order to keep some central authority during the adjournment of Congress the plan was to leave an executive committee. For a while Jefferson had great hopes for this Committee of the States. He saw in it the beginnings of a truly federal administration.

Congress had come into being as an emergency body. It had been virtually in permanent session for nine years. It was a legislative, advisory and executive assembly.

The continentalists had all along been advocating the creation of some kind of executive organ. As far back as the Articles of Confederation which Benjamin Franklin had proposed in 1775 provision had been made for an executive council. Jefferson had embodied this plan in a fresh report to Congress early in the war and John Dickinson, when his turn came to make a proposal, had incorporated

Jefferson's wording in his own plan. He called the committee a Council of State but weakened its executive powers.

Jefferson, during this past session of Congress, had been struck by the all too obvious fact that in the five weeks that went by between the day he reported for duty at Princeton and the day sessions resumed in the Maryland statehouse, the United States had no general government at all. So he instigated a new committee to devise a central governing body when Congress, penniless and disheartened, should adjourn.

The committee to set up a Committee of the States resulted from a motion of Jefferson's, but to keep his continentalist ideas from running away with it, Congress chose two other members of a different cast of mind. One was Roger Sherman, the knotty old Connecticut storekeeper whom Pierce, the diarist of the Constitutional Convention, described a few years later as exhibiting "the oddest shaped character I ever remember to have met with." Sherman was a countryman who had risen from the shoemaker's bench to the judge's bench, a selfmade man with an enormous respect for his own opinions. He was dead set against any centralizing notions whatsoever. The other was the same Samuel Osgood of Massachusetts who had been such a bitter critic of Robert Morris's efforts to create a general government through the Finance Office. The result was that when Jefferson's committee reported back Jefferson's recommendations were stood on their heads. The act as passed used more words in ruling out the things the Committee of the States should not do than in stating what it should do.

Jefferson, before he left Annapolis, tried by amendment to give the committee a chance to perform at least one useful act: that of establishing a uniform currency. He failed.

The Committee of the States, though it did meet after Congress adjourned, turned out a complete fiasco. The members quarreled among themselves. Just at the moment in the middle of summer when the committee was about to attain a quorum the Connecticut and New Hampshire members walked out in a huff. Rufus King of Massachusetts amused himself by advertising for their recapture in the newspapers in the form of an advertisement for fugitive bond servants.

The members who did report for duty fumed out the summer in inactivity and frustration. John Francis Mercer, a selfseeking young Virginian who had ridden eagerly north through the heat and the dust with the idea of shining in the public service, summed up the general feeling in a letter home: "If I do not find the ensuing Congress of a very different complexion from the last, and disposed to be very decisive — I will no longer myself degrade the character of a human being by continuing a useless cypher among others who have become as contemptible to the world as they have long been to themselves."

From the time of the fizzle of the Committee of the States, Congress dragged out the existence of "a useless cypher." Men who wanted a nation instead of a squabbling congress of states turned their energies more and more towards the establishment of a new and separate government.

8. The Art Magick

For two years Robert Morris had been trying to force Congress to act on his proposals by threatening to resign. By the fall of 1784 it was obvious that not only were the states unwilling to levy Morris's impost on imports but that the new members they were sending to Congress were in a frame of mind not only to accept but to demand the Financier's resignation. He resigned November 1.

To add to Morris's troubles, his own enormous investments were endangered by the severe depression that the end of hostilities had brought to the seaport towns. Merchants found themselves overstocked with goods bought in Europe at inflated wartime prices. The carrying trade to the West Indies, which before the war had been the lifeblood of colonial shipping, was being choked off by the British through new interpretations of the Navigation Acts in reprisal for American independence. Shipbuilding was at a standstill. American merchants and shipowners had suffered staggering losses during the period of the British blockade from Rodney's defeat of the French to the signing of the peace. Morris's investments, which he was trying to protect by borrowing from Peter to pay Paul, had expanded to the danger point.

He held onto his office in the hope of at least balancing his books before resigning. With income insufficient to pay even the interest on Congress's multifarious indebtedness, and with Franklin writing from Passy that he had to have cash to keep up interest payments on the foreign loans, Morris was forced more and more to apply the "art magick" to meet current expenditures. His days were spent dreaming up recourses to bolster the value of the continental paper, and of his own Robert Morris notes. When credit faltered, men his illwishers claimed were his own agents were seen ostentatiously being paid in clinking silver at the Bank of North America.

He carried the art of kiting checks and bills of exchange to a high degree of perfection. The fact that sailing ships took so long to cross the Atlantic made it possible to meet an obligation in Philadelphia with a note drawn on some Dutch banker in Amsterdam. That would give Morris three months to find negotiable paper with which to appease the Dutchman should he threaten to protest the note.

In the end it was the loan John Adams raised in the Netherlands that extinguished the threat of a protest which would have ruined Congress's credit abroad and which enabled Robert Morris to resign with the books of the Finance Office tolerably balanced. He was not so happy in some of his other accounts. In the final statement of the affairs of the old Congressional Committee of Commerce it was found that Robert Morris still owed the United States $93,312.63.

Gouverneur had resigned as Assistant Superintendent of Finance sometime before. He turned his financial experience to good account in making money for himself. He continued as Robert Morris's agent and lawyer and worked hard to keep the topheavy structure of his patron's investments on an even keel.

With the return of the two Morrises to the pursuit of their own business congressional government fell back into the hands of men who feared and hated the continentalist view. The attempt by "good executive men" to put Congress's house in order had failed.

Richard Henry Lee was elected president that fall. Men were in the ascendant who saw in Morris's system a danger to liberty. They voted to put the Treasury back into commission. For some months they had trouble finding men rash enough to accept these unrewarding jobs.

Of the three commissioners who finally consented to serve, only one, Walter Livingston, one of the Hudson River Livingstons and an army contractor, could have had much sympathy with Robert Morris's operations. Arthur Lee had been devoting his life in and out of Congress to oppose him. The third commissioner, Samuel Osgood, enjoyed an insider's view as a director of the Bank of North America. He agreed with Lee. He wrote of Robert Morris in his roundabout way to his friend, the Boston shipowner, Stephen Higginson: "If you suppose that person had rendered to the public no valuable services, I acknowledge there is a very considerable difference in our sentiments. If you suppose that he may have rendered valuable services, but that his notions of government of finance and of commerce are incompatible with liberty we shall not differ. I think therefore the fort to be raised against him ought to stand on this ground."

Morris resigned before "the fort" was raised against him. Even Hamilton, the most ardent of continentalists, wrote Washington, whom he knew was a warm friend of Morris's, that he had not liked the way Morris had tried to bludgeon the members of Congress by holding the threat of his resignation over their heads. Still he had to admit that "no man in this country but himself could have kept the money machine a-going during the period he has been in office."

It was high time the Financier turned to his own affairs. Only he knew how desperately his own investments needed shoring up. He kept up the confident front. Men who had dealings with him came away awed and excited by the bustle of vast speculations that filled his life. In New York he was loading a vessel with ginseng, that mysterious root, cheap to gather in America, for which the Chinese mandarins were willing to pay enormous prices. Rumors trickled out of his scheme to corner the entire American tobacco market in a deal with the French farmers-general. He was putting out great sums to keep a controlling interest in several western land companies that were buying up hundreds of thousands of acres of land to be sold to the settlers who were imagined to be crowding in from all the world with cash in their hands to buy farms. Over the madeira after dinner his table hummed with talk of vast profits to come.

There were profits all right. The *Empress of China* sailed safely back into New York in 1785 after inaugurating the China trade. The grand old *Alliance*, taken over by private interests, among them Morris's, was off on another far eastern voyage.

Settlers were pouring into the western country. Dutch financiers were eager to buy land. Morris's corner in tobacco lowered the price disastrously for the planters in Maryland and Virginia, but the farmers-general made their advance payments on schedule in His Christian Majesty's good silver coin. The payments were never enough to keep up with the vast inflation of Morris's credit. The rest of his life was a race with the sheriff. He managed indeed to stave off his bankruptcy for a decade, but only by use of the "art magick" unexampled in financial history.

VI   Missionary of Liberty

1. *Mesmer's Chief Apothecary*

The appearance of the United States as a sovereign nation across the Atlantic did more than ruin King George's plans in England. It had profound repercussions in France. France, for all the shortcomings and corruptions of the court at Versailles, was still by far the most powerful the most populous and the richest country in Europe. Paris was the intellectual capital of the world. Both in Paris and at Versailles the signing of the American treaty set events in motion which would bring about the "great changes in the social order in Europe" that Saint Simon foresaw at Yorktown. For a while it seemed as if the "new political era" which was beginning had found embodiment in the engaging person of the young Marquis de La Fayette.

Arriving breathless from Cornwallis's surrender, Lafayette brought a breeze of victory into the stale antechambers of the Bourbon regime. The King stayed away from his hunting long enough to drape the ribbon of the Order of St. Louis round his neck. The marshals of France celebrated his homecoming with a dinner. He found himself upgraded in the army, over the heads of many older men, who took it far from kindly, to Chastellux's rank of maréchal de camp.

Already a major general in the American army, this fresh promotion made him a general officer in the army of His Most Christian Majesty before he had reached the age of majority for a French nobleman. The envious began to dub him scornfully le Vassington français.

As soon as he was twentyfive he celebrated his freedom from the dictates of the family council by buying himself a great town house in Paris in the rue de Bourbon, in the fashionable upper end of the faubourg St. Germain. There he took up family life à l'américaine.

Like so many other French officers, he was deeply impressed by the tenderness and confidence between husband and wife he had seen in the families of men like Washington and Henry Knox. Before his bolt for freedom to America he had played with the idea of setting up one of Marie Antoinette's ladies in waiting, a young woman of certain intellectual pretensions named Aglaé de Hunolstein, as his mistress. After a good deal of heartburning and declamation he broke off this somewhat desultory affair and settled down to being the affectionate husband of his sweet homekeeping Adrienne de Noailles and the father of his children. There was a girl named Anastasie and a boy whom Lafayette named for the American commander in chief he liked to think of as his own adopted father. Another child was soon on the way whom he named Virginie after the theater of his military exploits. He felt himself on the threshold of a great career and wanted to conduct it in a way he felt his American friends would approve.

The success of the American cause made him the leader of a new generation growing up in France impatient of the stagnation and corruption of the Bourbon regime. No man in Europe had greater prospects. He had a gift for impressing other men with the brilliance of his coming destiny. He was enormously rich. The income that poured in from the diligence of intendants and hommes d'affaires, without his lifting a finger, amounted to considerably more than the equivalent of a hundred thousand dollars a year. Through his wife's people he was allied to the de Noailles, one of the most powerful families in France.

The Minister for Foreign Affairs was his special protector. It was the great Vergennes who had privately encouraged the boyish rashness of Lafayette's first independent act, now so heroic in retrospect: the buying of a ship and setting sail with a lettre de cachet at his heels, so the story went, to join the American rebels. When he first reached home Vergennes encouraged him to hope he might lead a fresh expedition to conquer the West Indies and to help the American allies wrest Canada from the British. Rodney's victory put an end to that project. Vergennes was now more interested in patching up a peace than in outfitting new and costly armies.

Immediately Lafayette, never one to let himself be left out of a dramatic event, began to load the mails with letters to Washington and to his American friends begging them to send him as American commissioner for the ceremony of the signing of the peace in London. American patriotism did not take kindly to the notion of being represented by a foreigner in the mother country, so Lafayette had to keep himself busy organizing the French branch of the Society of the Cincinnati.

The marquis was incapable of idleness. He never wasted his time with the hectic gambling and the interminable love affairs which frittered away the nights of his contemporaries in the court circle. He had learned from Washington to be an early riser. He was always ready to leap on a horse or throw himself into his carriage to be off at a gallop on some noble enterprise.

Nothing was too much trouble where an American was involved. He wore out the road to Versailles to run errands for American merchants in Paris trying to clear shipments of champagne or Lyons silk through the interminable complications of the French customs. He even sat down at his desk to write a brochure on freedom for American trade with the French Antilles.

Socially he was the lion of the hour. The belles in powdered coiffures who crowded around him were all un peu philosophes. Diderot, Rousseau, Voltaire had made science as fashionable as they had good works. The Lafayettes' Monday dinners, where they affectionately entertained American diplomats and their wives and American merchants seeking concessions from the ministries at Versailles, became fashionable with the philosophic set. Dr. Franklin, the philosophe par excellence, could occasionally be induced to appear there.

The moment peace was signed the English gentry started to hurry across the Channel to Paris, which more than ever, as the decline of old sovereignties broke down class and feudal barriers, became the capital of the effervescence of Europe. Liberty was fashionable in England too. English milords, always greedy for European novelties after being pent up for a season in their tight green island, highly appreciated an invitation to the Lafayettes', especially if the Doctor were included in the party.

Their long table was even graced one day by the great Chatham's son, William Pitt, who though two years younger than the marquis had already climbed higher in Parliament than Lafayette had at Versailles; by Pitt's bosom friend Wilberforce, who was to devote his great talents to abolishing the British slave trade; and by Edward Eliot, Pitt's great friend. Lafayette wrote Washington in his baroque English, modestly for once, that Franklin "was the center upon which moved the whole party"; but he could not help feeling that it was on his own shoulders that the mantle of the liberator had fallen.

Deprived of a chance of military glory by the peace, he set out to emulate the great doctor's philosophy. When a Dr. Charles made a record flight of twentyseven miles out of the Tuileries Gardens in an improved version of Montgolfier's balloon, inflated with hydrogen instead of hot air, it was in Lafayette's carriage that the aeronaut drove up to the Palais Royale to compliment his patron, the sinister and illfated Duc de Chartres, who was to end his days on the guillotine as Philippe-Égalité. Lafayette promptly wrote up an account of the flight for the American Philosophical Society. Unluckily Dr. Franklin's own account had reached there before his.

When mesmerism swept the Paris drawing rooms, Lafayette, at the cost of a hundred gold louis, enrolled himself as one of the Viennese doctor's pupils. With Chastellux, the old dilettante of science, he joined an association of Mesmer's disciples known as the Order of Harmony. It was Franklin himself who pricked that balloon. When he was asked by the court at Versailles to head a commission to consider Mesmer's claims of miraculous cures through animal magnetism, although Lafayette tried to tell him that Mesmer's vital fluid was just another form of his own electricity, he brought in a skeptical report.

In spite of doubting Thomases the young marquis remained one of the most enthusiastic of Mesmer's instructed scholars. He wanted to initiate General Washington into the cult. He induced Dr. Mesmer to write his adopted father. "It seems to us," Mesmer pleaded "that the man who has deserved the most of his fellow men must be interested in the outcome of any revolution that has the welfare of humanity as its object." Washington was noncommittal. Lafayette may have suspected that his old commander in chief would be hard to convince because when he wrote, himself, he touched somewhat lightly on the *magnetism animal* as he called it. "I know as much as any conjuror ever did, which reminds me of our old friend's at Fishkills interview with the devil that made us laugh so much at his house . . ." He was already planning a triumphant return to America. "Before I go I will get leave to let you into the secret."

A story was circulating in the antechambers at Versailles that the King, who for all his sluggish behavior showed occasional flashes of humor, had cornered the marquis and asked him teasingly: "What will Washington think when he hears you have become Mesmer's chief apothecary?"

2.   A Canine Appetite for Popularity

After the excitement and the free and easy life of the American countryside Lafayette found he had lost his taste for Paris drawing rooms and the mummery and frustration of a courtier's life.

His heart was set on revisiting the land of his great achievements. He was delayed by fruitless efforts to get some official glamor thrown about his journey, but at last in the spring of 1784 he was able to announce: "Yes my dear General before the month of June is over you will see a vessel coming up the Pottomack, and out of the vessel will your friend jump with a panting heart and all the feelings of perfect happiness."

He relieved the boredom and seasickness of the voyage by putting Dr. Mesmer's secret instruction to good use. When one of the ship's boys fell from the rigging and lay stunned on the deck the marquis, according to his own account, brought him back from the dead by the use of animal magnetism. He hurried through a dinner of a hundred covers attended by all the Cincinnati in New York while the Stars and Stripes waved in the breeze overhead, and was off posthaste to Philadelphia to describe his miraculous cure to a hastily assembled meeting of the American Philosophical Society. The learned Philadelphians were already familiar with Franklin's report. They were cordial but unimpressed. Charles Thomson, detained in New York, wrote Jefferson in Paris that the marquis was "quite an enthusiast." He added dryly that mesmerism had brought to light one important discovery, "namely to what degree imagination could operate on the human frame."

Eagerly the marquis set out for Virginia. Wherever he stopped to rest his horses he was greeted by the hugs and handclasps of old comrades in arms, by salutes from the militia and the ringing of church bells and candles in the windows at night and toasts at public dinners in the taverns. The words liberty, republicanism, independence and glory rang in his ears from every welcoming address. In Baltimore a society of Irish exiles celebrated his services to the cause of oppressed humanity. At Mount Vernon he threw himself into the arms of his adopted father. When the two generals showed themselves to an indulgent public at a welcoming dinner in an Alexandria hostelry, Lafayette confided to a friend that some of the company claimed that both he and Washington had gotten a little tipsy together.

He had wanted his old commander in chief to accompany him on his triumphant tour, but Washington instead invited him to come along on a hard crosscountry ride he was planning over the mountains and out to the Ohio to visit his western lands. The marquis, who was familiar enough with American geography to know that there would be no public demonstrations along those shaggy and sparsely settled trails, pleaded other engagements.

Back in Philadelphia he fell in with James Madison, who invited him on a trip which was more to his taste. Madison had been stimulated by Jefferson to interest himself in Indian languages. He was on his way to a great Indian powwow convoked at Fort Schuyler. The little Virginian immediately saw that Lafayette would be a trump in the hands of the American commissioners. Many of the Indians still missed the fatherly French rule. Lafayette's name had spread to their tepees, where he was known as Kayewlaah.

The trip appealed to all the marquis's romantic aspirations. The long ride up the Mohawk Valley into upper New York State gave Madison an opportunity to talk the marquis into offering to use his good offices with the Bourbons of Spain to convince them that they should open the navigation of the Mississippi to the American settlers. This was the matter which Madison wrote Jefferson was uppermost in his own thoughts at the time. The sly Madison noted with some amusement that the newfangled cloak of gummed taffeta Lafayette wore to protect him from the rain had been wrapped, when his baggage was packed, in newspapers that still stuck to it, so that his companions could read snatches of Parisian news off his back as they rode. It was a dismal ride through the rainsoaked forest. Lafayette delighted everybody by his carelessness of civilized comforts and by his ingratiating manner with the savages.

Lafayette immediately, to the dismay of Guy Carleton's agents on the scene, became the leading figure in the complicated negotiations for a peaceful withdrawal by the Indians from frontier lands inside the state boundaries. Beside a crackling campfire in the cold October night, in declamatory French worthy of Chateaubriand he addressed a group of chiefs of the Six Nations while the tobacco smoldered in the peace pipes. Trust the Americans, he told them, and the great King Onontio — that was the Indian name for Louis XVI — who, shining like the sun across the water, had cleared away the clouds of war. As long as he stayed the young marquis quite eclipsed the actual commissioners. Dr. Arthur Lee, who was one of them, was particularly exasperated. It was a great moment in Lafayette's life.

Madison wrote Jefferson, who was just settling into his diplomatic post in Paris, that part of the marquis's pleasure in the dramatic scene was the thought that it "would form a bright column in the gazettes of Europe. The time I have lately passed with the M. has given me a pretty thorough insight into his character," he added. "With great natural frankness of temper, he unites much address; with very considerable talents a strong thirst of praise and popularity. In his politics he says his three hobbyhorses are the alliance between France and the United States, the union of the latter and the manumission of the slaves. The two former are the dearer to him as they are connected with his personal glory. The last does him real honor as it is the proof of his humanity. In a word I take him to be as amiable a man as his vanity will admit." Both Madison and Jefferson agreed that no other man was as well situated as the marquis to further American interests in the chancelleries of Europe.

Lafayette's American tour revived the celebrations of the peace. In

Hartford the whole town turned out to do him honor at Bull's Tavern. As far out as Watertown he was greeted by a delegation of Continental officers to escort him into Boston. Amid cannonading from the forts and from French warships in the harbor he was regaled with a banquet at Faneuil Hall on the Yorktown anniversary. He was made a citizen of three states and freeman of a number of cities. Even his best friends pointed out that some of the compliments he received did not come unasked. When the enthusiasm of welcome seemed to slacken he made no bones about suggesting fresh celebrations. For the crowds of Americans who cheered him on his prancing stallion he was the living symbol of the French assistance that had won the war for independence.

The French frigate *Nymphe* carried him back to Virginia to take formal farewell of George Washington. He made the sentimental journey to Yorktown with rotund Thomas Nelson, whose fortunes had never recovered from the losses his family's warehouses had suffered during the siege. General Washington met him in Richmond. For a whole week the raw little city was in an uproar with parties and balls and illuminations and the firing of cannon. Together they rode to Mount Vernon, where the marquis once more saluted his adopted American family. Dumpy Martha Washington, her daughter and her four grandchildren and her daughterinlaw's new husband Dr. Stuart, he declared, were his dearest kin. After a week, amid tears and kisses, he tore himself away to rejoin His Most Christian King's frigate, which was waiting for him in New York.

Washington was so moved that he rode with him all the way to Annapolis when he left. Back at Mount Vernon he wrote the marquis a letter which for him was highly emotional: thinking of the love and affection he felt for Lafayette, he said he had asked himself, as their carriages drove out of town on different roads, whether that was the last sight he would ever have of him. "And though I wished to say no my fears answered yes. I called to mind the days of my Youth, and found they had long since fled to return no more; that I was now descending the hill I had been 52 Years climbing, and that though I was blessed with a good Constitution, I was of a shortlived Family and might soon expect to be entombed in the Dreary Mansions of my Fathers. These things darkened the Shades and gave a Gloom to the picture, consequently to my prospect of seeing you again; but I will not repine, I have had my Day."

The fast traveling marquis bade his official farewell to America at a session of Congress held especially for him in the long room of the French Arms at Trenton. A committee made up of one member from each state presented him with a laudatory address and with one of the British standards captured at Yorktown. When he sailed from New

York amid a hail of plaudits he carried in his suite two Indian boys to serve as pages.

Back in France the marquis found that these fresh American triumphs had indeed formed "a bright column in the gazettes of Europe." Jefferson, who was beginning to learn the byways of diplomacy, saw to it that the fulsome accounts in the American gazettes (which Madison regularly forwarded him) of the marquis's triumphant progress should come to the attention of European editors. As Lafayette settled back into life on the rue de Bourbon with Adrienne and his children he somewhat ostentatiously loved, he set to weaving about himself the legend of the American Cincinnatus. He was the adopted son and disciple of the great liberator. "In everything I do," he wrote back to Washington at Mount Vernon, "I first consider what your opinion would be had I an opportunity to consult it."

To add a touch of authentic American color to the domestic scene, the Oneida halfbreed he met at Fort Schuyler and the Onondaga Indian boy he induced to follow him to Europe attended him in costume. In full Iroquois regalia they ran errands for him. At the evening parties of the philosophic set they demonstrated the war dances of the noble savages.

For a while it looked as if the Dutch might offer him a theater for the display of his talents as the Washington of France. The party of the republicans and the party of the royalists who backed the hereditary Stadholder of the ancient House of Orange were at each other's throats. Every ambitious court in Europe was sizing up the chance of getting some advantage out of the dissensions of the wealthy Netherlanders. Versailles was split between the Austrian faction round Marie Antoinette, which was for the royalists, and the adherents of Vergennes, who wanted to put France into the posture of a liberal monarchy ever ready to spring to the defense of European freedom. If the Austrians should back the Stadholder there was talk in the lobbies of the Ministry of Foreign Affairs of giving Lafayette command of a French army to establish the republican liberties of the Dutch. Rumors circulated that he would soon be called to lead a rebellion in Ireland.

3. The Grand Maneuvers

While war scares sizzled and spluttered in the European chancelleries, Lafayette tore himself away from his family long enough to show himself on a summer tour of the grand maneuvers in Germany. Washington's fame had stirred the curiosity of the enlightened despots. The marquis appeared at their courts with the glamor of Yorktown about him. He met old friends and old foes from the American war. Everywhere he talked up the advantages of the American trade and the greatness of General Washington.

It was the last year of the great Frederick's life. The Prussian army still offered the most brilliant military show in Europe. At Potsdam the aging Prussian King received the marquis as an equal. He dined at the royal table in a brilliant assembly gathered from all over Europe for the war games. Malicious Old Fritz had seated him between Lord Cornwallis and the English Duke of York. Lafayette described the great drillmaster to Washington as "an old broken dirty corporal, covered all over with Spanish snuff, with his head almost leaning on one shoulder and his fingers quite distorted with the gout . . . But what surprised me much more," he added after he had seen him ride at the head of his troops, "is the fire and sometimes the softness of the most beautiful eyes I ever saw."

He went on at length about the "good reception and flattering testimonies" he had met from "those crowns, staffs and other great personages." Every conversation on American affairs had started with an eulogium of General Washington. "Had we been unfortunate in the contest," he added with some humor, "we would have cut there a poor figure." To Henry Knox he summed up his feelings as an honorary American. "I had rather be the last farmer in America than the first General in Berlin."

At Old Fritz's martial court he met another self-appointed liberator. Francisco Miranda, a talkative Venezuelan exile, had been beating his way from country to country in search of support for his scheme to foment a revolution in South America. He had already visited Philadelphia and New York where his eloquence had elicited enthusiasm, and some handouts of cash to help him on his way, from Henry Knox and Hamilton and from Washington's old aide, William Stephens Smith. In London, Pitt had listened to his plans and advanced him a small subsidy. Miranda was making a tour of the German maneuvers in the company with this same Colonel Smith, now stationed in London as secretary of the American legation and soon to be John Adams' soninlaw.

Even at Potsdam liberty was à la mode.

4. American Principles Transplanted into Europe

Back in Paris, since the wars and rebellions he was interested in persistently hung fire, the marquis temporarily shelved his ambition to be the first general in Europe. Instead he went to work diligently to provoke reforms at home. For some time he had been involved with a number of court officials of a philosophic turn of mind in a quiet effort to put through some measure of religious toleration. The old liberal functionary Malesherbes for years had been trying to have Louis XVI reenact the Edict of Nantes so that the ban of outlawry might be lifted off the necks of the scattered groups of Huguenots that persisted in France. In the factious atmosphere of the Versailles bureaucracy any effort for reform had to be carried on through backstairs negotiations. Lafayette threw his energy and his taste for ciphers and conspiracies into the intrigue to such a degree that Washington, whom he kept posted on every detail, wrote him a guarded warning, "it is part of the military art to reconnoitre and feel your way before you engage too deeply."

Much as his American friends wanted to further the cause of toleration, they knew that stirring up the enmity of the vast vested interests that opposed it in France was a dangerous business. Jefferson went so far as to write Madison that it might be wise to induce the Virginia Assembly to make the marquis a gift of lands, not only as a gesture of gratitude for his services, but because he might shortly need an American estate as an asylum. "The time of life at which he visited America was too well adapted to receive good and lasting impressions to permit him ever to accommodate himself to the principals of monarchical government, and it will need all his own prudence and that of his friends to make this country a safe residence for him."

Lafayette and Jefferson became fast friends. They had first met somewhere near Richmond when Jefferson was a governor without a government during the scurry and confusion of the British raids along James River. On his return from his American triumph it was Lafayette's heavy duty to bring Jefferson the news of the death of his baby girl, Lucy Elizabeth. Immediately Lafayette, with the openhanded candor that was so engaging, put himself at the service of the American minister. Jefferson's prime business in that capacity was to induce Versailles to relax the complicated restrictions on American trade and shipping which were part of the general inhibition of commerce brought about by the mercantilist practices of the French officials. Lafayette knew every back door to every office; he knew where liberal policies could find a hearing and he knew where they could not. He became indispensable to the reticent redhaired Virginian.

Lafayette was twentyeight. Jefferson was fortytwo. Perpetually in search of a father, Lafayette missed Washington's paternal advice. Jefferson liked nothing better than to tutor young men in the arts of politics and statebuilding. What started as a hospitable gesture on Lafayette's part became a firm collaboration. From trying to pry loose the trammels the bureaucracy had fastened about the American trade, the two men found themselves plotting to free the French from the whole complex of the vested interests of the old regime.

In spite of his delight in the courtesy of the Parisians and in the concerts, the architecture, the painting and the sculpture, Jefferson led a dreary existence that winter in his first cramped lodgings in the cul-de-sac Têtebout. It was hard for him to get used to the lack of sunlight. His fresh bereavement threw him back into the mood of solitary misery of the year after his wife's death. The departure of his fellow commissioners, of Franklin for America and his dear friend John Adams for London, left him in Paris in lonely state as sole American minister. Though he read French fluently he was finding it hard to understand and to make himself understood in the spoken language. He saw more misery than splendor in the clattering streets of the great capital. His health was bad. With all his enthusiasm for science and literature and the arts, Jefferson was, like Washington, a countryman at heart. He was never easy in a city. His seasoning, he came to call his first years in France.

Jefferson's unconquerable curiosity never deserted him. Lafayette found the American minister in a mood to discover everything that could be discovered about the people of France. He had moved the legation to an airy and beautiful mansion out at the end of the Champs Elysées where he could enjoy the freshness of trees and the smell of country gardens. At the same time from the windows of the hôtel de Langeac he could see with his own eyes at the nearby barrier the oppression of the farmers-general whose agents took toll of every poor countrywoman who carried a basket of eggs into the city for sale.

Agreeable young Short, whom he had coached in the law after Short had graduated from William and Mary and for whom he intended a great career, had arrived to serve as his secretary. He had begun to form friendships with men and women whose conversation he enjoyed. He was viewing the life about him with increasingly friendly curiosity. Now Lafayette was able to open many a door for him which he had found closed before.

The marquis was happy to do everything in his power to make Jefferson's life pleasant in Paris. Furthermore he felt he was winning the esteem of the author of the Declaration of Independence by the sacrifices he was making for its principles.

The abolition of slavery was one of the great causes that stirred Jefferson throughout the early part of his life. Lafayette was spending a hundred and twentyfive thousand livres to buy a plantation in the remote French colony of Cayenne which he intended to settle with emancipated slaves. It was not for mere show that he kept a framed copy of the Declaration of Independence on the wall of his study.

He viewed this gesture as a mere beginning. When people asked him why the empty frame beside the American declaration he would answer that it was waiting for a charter of liberties for the people of France.

Jefferson gradually replaced Washington as Lafayette's guiding star. Jefferson believed that American principles could be made, with some adjustments, to apply universally to all mankind. He tried to show the marquis how to make practical application of all these great ideas for human betterment. It was easy for Lafayette to fall into the position of eager pupil. The passion of Jefferson's life was molding the minds of younger men. As they worked together trying to make headway against the tobacco monopoly and the whale-oil interests to open a French market for American products, Lafayette found himself happily falling into the same sort of filial relationship he had enjoyed so much when he was Washington's lieutenant.

Lafayette particularly needed Jefferson's advice since he had been appointed, through the tender care of Vergennes, to an important committee to report ways and means to increase French trade with America. Immediately this became known as the American Committee.

Lafayette's education, outside of a fair grounding in Latin, was purely military. His upbringing as a wealthy noble gave him no practical experience of life. Now Jefferson saw building a good society as a practical business, like building a house. Plans must be adapted to the limitations of the materials. Through Jefferson's critical eye and through the day to day work with him in trying to blast a passage through the privileges and monopolies of the farmers-general, Lafayette began to understand how the dead hand of the past throttled every effort to adjust the creaking machine of the absolute monarchy to the needs of the French people. Jefferson wrote Madison enthusiastically of Lafayette's quick understanding of every problem that was explained to him.

Though they managed between them to undermine Robert Morris's scheme for cornering the American tobacco market, they could only reach a stalemate with the tobacco monopoly in France. In the case of whale oil and spermaceti candles the interests involved were less powerful. Lafayette managed to obtain concessions for the American minister that earned the marquis the present of a five hundred pound cheese made up specially for him by the grateful whalers of Nantucket out of the milk of their own cows.

Lafayette's friendship introduced Jefferson into all the salons of the French enlightenmant. With the tireless consideration of the perfect aristocrat the marquis saw to it that his friend met the people he wanted to meet. Lafayette knew everybody; through Adrienne he was related to everybody. His wife's aunt, the Comtesse de Tessé, the friend of Voltaire, in her great drawing room and in her rose gardens at Chaville near Versailles, formed the hub of all the most sparkling society of the day. The mode was intelligence, information and personal charm. Jefferson, who loved good conversation, was delighted by the intellectual effervescence of that world, by the unstudied good manners of a regime that had ceased to take itself too seriously, where personality counted for more than protocol.

Madame de Tessé was a witty, possessive, highly understanding woman. In spite of a complexion marred by smallpox and a slight tick in the corner of her mouth that gave a strangeness to her smile she had immense social attractiveness. She dearly loved her nephew; she saw in him the saviour of France. She sympathized with his Americanism. She could not do too much for his preceptor, the tall reticent American minister who turned out to be so unexpectedly learned, so filled with boyish enthusiasm for Greco-Roman architecture and natural philosophy.

Jefferson was at his best in sprightly unengaging relationships with charming women of whatever age. Madame de Tessé immediately understood that the friendship of the American philosopher diplomat, who so ably carried on in his own way the tradition established by the adorable Franklin, would add new luster to her nephew's career. In the end she came to love Jefferson for himself; they remained friends as long as she lived.

In France as in America 1787 proved to be a landmark year. A few months before some forty Americans met in the Philadelphia state House to debate the theory and practice of the politics of freedom, Lafayette found himself engaging in the ceremony of the opening of an Assembly of Notables in the Hall of Fugitive Pleasures at Versailles under the presidency of the Bourbon princes. He was determined to take his part in the debates in a way that Jefferson and Washington would approve. Although the fluid society of the American frontier had little in common with the stratified society of France the immediate causes that brought the two assemblies together were the same: ruined finances and restraint of trade.

No more than Robert Morris of Philadelphia, had the Swiss banker Necker been able to make government expenditures match government revenues by the use of the "art magick." Versailles was bankrupt. The Notables were called together to find fresh ways of raising money. Jefferson, who was present at the opening sessions, saw in the Assembly of Notables an opportunity for a gradual reform of Bourbon autocracy into something like the constitutional monarchy of England.

He was seizing on the opportunity afforded him by the success of his negotiations, in which Lafayette had been so helpful, to take a vacation. After three years under the leaden Parisian sky he felt starved for sunlight.

He set off alone in late February in a hired chaise for the South of France, determined for once to escape the diplomatic protocol that cut him off from the people wherever he went. Before he left he hurriedly scribbled a note to Lafayette, outlining a plan of reform for the Notables.

From Nîmes, where he spent hour after hour sitting in the sun among the silkspinners and stockingweavers of the marketplace looking up — "like a lover at his mistress" — at the goldfluted columns crowned with the acanthus of the Augustan temple he considered the most beautiful building in the world, he wrote more at length to Madame de Tessé.

He knew that her salon at Chaville would be the headquarters of the reforming element among the Notables and that her nephew and his friends would be influenced by her opinion. After some rhapsodic sentences on the passion they had in common for the beauties of classical architecture he returned to the plan for reform he had sent Lafayette: "My journey has given me leisure to reflect on this Assembly of Notables. under a good and a young King, as at present, I think good may be made of it. I would have the deputies then, by all means, so conduct themselves as to encourage him to repeat the call of this assembly. their first step should be to get themselves divided into two chambers instead of seven; the noblesse and the commons separately." The chambers should be elected instead of appointed. "Two houses so elected would contain a mass of wisdom which would make the people happy and the king great . . . they would thus put themselves in the track of the best guide they can follow" — he meant the English constitution — "they would soon overtake it, become its guide in turn, lead to the wholesome modifications wanting in that model."

He advised against moving too fast. "Should they attempt more than the established habits of the people are ripe for, they may lose all, & retard indefinitely the ultimate object of their aim."

He saw in the regime's fiscal crisis an opportunity for the Notables to seize hold of the power of the purse which had been the foundation of the British Parliament. Knowing how volatile the charming marquis was, Jefferson was already puzzling over how to keep him on the track of moderate and reasonable reform. Driving along the dry flowering hillsides, looking out over the azure Mediterranean that had been the highway and the battleground of the antique republics whose virtues he wanted to see restored to mankind, his mind kept dwelling on the political possibilities of the moment. Much as he loved

Lafayette, Jefferson continually dreaded the result, when Lafayette should be called to take a hand in the rebuilding of France, of his ignorance of the lives and motives of the ordinary run of unprivileged men. How could a man govern a nation when all he knew of the people whose affairs he would be trying to manage was the deputations that met him with band music and drums and pretty speeches round the decorated tables of a "vin d'honneur" wherever he moved in princely state through his feudal domains in Auvergne or Brittany.

"Your head my dear friend," he wrote him from Nice, "is full of Notable things . . . I am constantly roving about, to see what I have never seen before & shall never see again . . . From the first olive fields of Pierrelatte to the orangeries of Hières, has been a continual rapture to me. I have often wished for you. I think you have not made this journey. it is a pleasure you have to come & an improvement to be added to the many you have already made. it will be a great comfort to you to know from your own inspection, the condition of all the provinces of your own country, & it will be interesting to them at some future day to be known to you. this is perhaps the only moment in your life in which you can acquire that knoledge & to do it most effectively you must be absolutely incognito. you must ferret the people out of their hovels as I have done, look into their kettles, eat their bread, loll on their beds in the pretense of resting yourself, but in fact to find if they are soft. you will feel a sublime pleasure in the course of this investigation & a sublimer one hereafter, when you shall be able to apply your knoledge to the softening of their beds, or the throwing a morsel of meat into their kettle of vegetables."

5. Les Américains

The Assembly of the Notables furnished more comedy than it did "wholesome modifications." When Jefferson returned to Paris he found all the salons poking fun at it. A pun was being circulated that gave the French liberals a chance to show off their knowledge of English. The Notables were not able.

Though some useful recommendations were made these worthies scattered to their chateaux and to their hunting lodges without having accomplished anything definite. The government did promise to revive the provincial assemblies, which with the States-General of the realm had been the nearest the French had come to parliamentary institutions in the days before the absolute bureaucracy of the Bourbons ate up every other organ of government.

Lafayette distinguished himself with a courageous speech exposing graft in the management of the royal estates. His speech caused the downfall and the flight to England of the finance minister, Calonne. It caused the marquis to be marked down as a dangerous man among the conservatives at court. It earned him the eternal hatred of Marie Antoinette, who was fond of Calonne. From then on a courtier's career, promotion in the army, service in the ministry were closed to him. His protector Vergennes had died that same spring. Lafayette had come into the open as a dedicated reformer, one of the men who more and more, from their enthusiasm for American institutions and from the fact that many of them were young nobles who had served in the American war, were becoming known as les américains.

"I had the misfortune to displease their Majesties, the royal family, and a set of powerful men and courtiers," the marquis wrote Washington, "while that conduct of mine, much criticized there, made me very popular among the Nation at large."

From that day on Lafayette looked to the nation, that novel entity in a French noble's thoughts, for promotion rather than to the court. He looked forward with immense optimism to the growing wave of reform. "Liberal ideas are cantering about from one end of the kingdom to the other," he scribbled lightheartedly to Washington. "The ideas of liberty have been since the American revolution spreading very fast. The combustible materials have been kindled by the Assembly of Notables."

Combustible materials indeed. The nation was taking an interest in its destiny with a vengeance. "All tongues in Paris have been let loose," Jefferson wrote John Adams in London, "& never was a license in speaking against the government exercised in London more freely or more universally. caricatures, placards, bon-mots have been indulged in by all ranks of people & I know of no well-attested instance of a single punishment. for some time mobs of ten, twenty & thirty thousand people collected daily, surrounded the parliament house, huzzaed the members, even entered the doors & examined their conduct, took the horses out of the carriages of those who did well & drew them home . . . The queen, going to the theatre at Versailles with Mme. de Polignac, was received with a general hiss. the king, long in the habit of drowning his cares in wine, plunges deeper & deeper. the queen cries but sins on."

A new scandal, following the famous affair of the diamond necklace, which had first besmirched the character of Marie Antoinette with the French people, was again showing up the venality and incompetence of the Austrian party at court.

6. The Fall of a Republic

The proud Dutch Republic, whose institutions Jefferson and Adams and Madison had studied with such care, had reached a crisis. A few years before, the Francophile liberals there, in a last flareup of republican energy, had ousted their hereditary Stadholder. Their party became known as the Patriots. Even a degenerate William of Orange found sympathy among the English Whigs, whose whole tradition dated from the "Glorious Revolution" of 1688. Furthermore this particular William was married to the sister of the Frederick William of Prussia who had inherited Old Fritz's magnificently drilled army. With some slight backing from William Pitt, who as he grew into the office of Prime Minister had outgrown his early penchant for parliamentary reform and was more interested in curbing the power of the French than in the liberties of the Dutch; and with the enthusiastic backing of King George, who hated the word patriot as much as Dr. Johnson did, the Prussian army was marching to reinstate the Stadholder. Versailles had promised to back the Patriots. Vergennes was said to have been planning to put his young American paladin Lafayette in command of the Dutch army which France was subsidizing, but Vergennes was dead.

One of the most stupid of Calonne's stupid moves before he bolted for a Channel port was to get a Parisian rounder of Marie Antoinette's inner circle appointed to command the Patriots instead of Lafayette. This was the Rhinegrave of Salm-Kribourg, a gentleman of some taste in the arts but of absolutely no morals. It was the Rhinegrave's reconstruction of his dainty domed hotel on the left bank of the Seine that so delighted Jefferson that he went, so he wrote his friends, every day to sit on the parapet of the Tuileries gardens and gaze across the river at it. Though of ancient Rhenish lineage, Salm-Kribourg had already made himself a laughingstock for brazen poltroonry by appearing to fight a duel encased in a complete suit of mail. Before he left Paris he extorted from Calonne an enormous sum in advance of pay, which he claimed he needed to satisfy his creditors before they would allow him to leave the city. He no sooner took command at Utrecht than the rumor began to spread that he was selling out that vital fortress for cash to the Stadholder's party. The Rhinegrave took his bribe with the quip that much as he enjoyed the lemon color of the lilies of France he liked oranges too.

Lafayette had been fuming in his feudal halls in Auvergne. At the last moment, determined to do or die in spite of everything at the head of the Patriot troops, he threw himself into his carriage and, urging on the postilions to crack their whips on the sweating backs of the posthorses, drove all night and part of a day towards the Dutch border. At Varennes he learned that he was too late. Fait accompli. The Prussians were in Utrecht. The Hague and Amsterdam had capitulated. The great Dutch Republic, the pride of every liberal in Europe, had come to an end with hardly a whimper.

While the crestfallen liberator jogged slowly home to Paris, a constitutional monarchy modeled on England's took over at the Hague. The Stadholder became a puppet of Pitt's. Vergennes's successor, the Comte de Montmorin, with tears streaming down his face, assured the British ambassador that the French would not resort to arms to help their allies. The Patriot leaders poured out of their tulip gardens to take refuge in Brussels and Paris. Jefferson heard their sad tales. So much for monarchy as a defender of popular liberties. For John Jay, Congress's Secretary for Foreign Affairs, he drew a moral in his next dispatch: "It conveys to us the important lesson that no circumstances of morality, honor, interest or engagement are sufficient to authorize a secure alliance on any nation."

VII   A Hoop for the Barrel

1.   "...the inconveniences of the present government"

On Wednesday, May 9, 1787, George Washington set out reluctantly in his carriage to drive to Philadelphia. He had intended to leave the day before, but he let the bad weather detain him.

One source of his reluctance was that he was not a man who liked to change his mind. He had been determined not to let himself be coaxed out of Mount Vernon that spring. For four years he had been settling down to the slow rhythms of plantation life, enlivened, at a cost in money and produce even he could hardly afford, by the constant flow of the visitors he entertained so lavishly at his table. He was trying to find ways of keeping up the failing fertility of his land. He had experiments with crop rotation under way. He had just learned a new trick about sprouting Irish potatoes.

Planting was early that season; he was about through planting corn, but in some fields the birds were eating his corn as fast as it came up. Times were bad for the farmer. The peace had brought a depression in prices. Money was tight. Large sums were owed him that he was unable to collect. Obligations were coming due. He had been trying to sell land to raise cash, had advertised lots but found no takers. His Potomac fishery was doing well, but since nobody came to buy the fish he had to salt it away in barrels.

It had been an unhappy winter. He had suffered from rheumatism. As late as May 1 he had made a most uncharacteristic entry in his diary: "Notwithstanding my fatigue I rid to all the plantations today." Fatigue, at fiftyfive, was a new word in his vocabulary. There had been deaths in the family. His favorite brother Jack was gone; his nephew had lost a baby. His mother was dying and his sister was desperately ill in Fredericksburg.

Every mail brought him new perplexities about the coming convention. As he often did when he had to make a decision he wrote in all directions to his friends asking their advice. Some were for his going to Philadelphia, some against. Prominent Virginians were set against the convention. Patrick Henry refused to go. Richard Harry Lee found the convenient excuse that, since as a member of Congress he would have to pass on the product of its deliberations, it would not be fitting for him to attend. George Mason was proving hard to detach from Gunston Hall. The Virginia continentalists urged that these abstentions, added to the fact that Jefferson and John Adams were in Europe, made the general's presence even more essential.

He held off all winter. His final plea was that since he had refused an invitation to preside over the Philadelphia meeting of the Cincinnati that spring, on account of the "animadversions" of so many patriots against the aristocratic trend of that organization, if he consented to preside over the convention he feared his old officers would be offended. In spite of all that, in the end he had let himself be argued into going.

The summer before he had been full of hope that the meeting at Annapolis, so sedulously promoted by James Madison and Edmund Randolph to concert common measures for trade and commerce, might begin to remedy the paralysis into which the congressional government had fallen. His hopes were disappointed. Only five states showed up.

He was not "one of the sanguine ones"; always he would rather envisage disaster than run the risk of hope deferred. Leaving Martha at Mount Vernon, he was starting his journey full of misgivings about this fresh convention.

"I very much fear," he wrote Edmund Randolph, newly elected governor of Virginia, "that all the states will not appear in convention, and that some of them will come fettered so as to impede rather than accelerate the great object of their convening which, under the peculiar circumstances of my case, would place me in a more disagreeable situation than any other member would stand in." The father of his country did not want to risk seeing his laurels wilted. "As I have yielded however to what appeared to be the earnest wishes of my friends, I will hope for the best," he added a little ungraciously.

Behind most of the letters he received from Virginia was the busy little figure of James Madison, now serving in the House of Delegates. Madison had worked hard to produce results at Annapolis, but all he was able to bring about was a call, which Hamilton drafted and which Madison induced the irresolute Randolph to approve, for a new convention in Philadelphia. Madison in Virginia and Hamilton in New York worked tirelessly as beavers this time to ensure attendance. They felt Philadelphia was the last chance for the Union.

Far more than Madison's and Randolph's theoretical arguments, it was news from Massachusetts that convinced the general he had to go. The government of that state was taking the opposite course from the governments of Pennsylvania and Rhode Island, where the debtor interest predominated in the legislatures. The hard money party of the merchants and magnates of the towns ran roughshod over the small farmers. In the depressed state of business the farmers found no way of getting their hands on any cash. If great landowners like Washington were hard pressed for money, what must the situation be of a man trying to make a living off a few mortgaged acres?

The courts had been enforcing decisions against debtors. Farms were being sold for taxes, hardworking men were being imprisoned for debt. The farmers and settlers of the western part of Massachusetts began to take the law into their own hands. Armed men with evergreen twigs in their hats prevented the circuit court from sitting at Northampton. An insurrection under the leadership of a scattering of retired Continental officers threatened to seize the muskets stored in the Continental arsenal at Springfield. Washington's old associate, General Benjamin Lincoln, marched to the arsenal's relief at the head of some regiments of militia. At Exeter in adjoining New Hampshire a crowd of angry farmers held the legislature under siege.

Even after Lincoln scattered the main body of the insurgents under Daniel Shays into the snowy night at Petersham, Washington's correspondents feared that the Massachusetts rebellion might be merely a prelude to "some awful crisis" in which the advocates of paper money and of the distribution of lands and of leveling generally would seize the state governments. The debtors could still outvote their creditors if they had a mind to.

A letter from his old artillery general, ponderous Henry Knox, clinched the matter for Washington. The poetical David Humphreys, who had been his aide and confidential secretary, had been reminding him that the meeting was sanctioned by a resolution of Congress. He assured the general that no "personal ill consequences" were to be feared from his attendance. Now Knox wrote in most alarming terms: "It is the general wish that you should attend . . . The mass of the people feel the inconveniences of the present government and ardently wish for such alterations as would remedy them. The alterations must be effected by wisdom and agreement, or by Force . . . Were you not then to attend the convention, slander and malice might suggest that force would be the most agreeable mode of reform to you."

Knox knew his man. What the general most dreaded for his country was the sort of Cromwellian coup d'état he had nipped in the bud at Newburgh during his last year as commander in chief. What he most dreaded for himself were the animadversions of slander and malice. A month to a day after Knox sent off his letter the general was ferrying his carriage and horses across the Potomac "a little after Sun rise."

He pursued his way to Baltimore next morning in spite of a violent headache and sick stomach. In Baltimore he lodged with his old friend and aide, Dr. McHenry, now set up with a wife and growing family, who was himself a delegate from Maryland. The weather proved bad on the whole trip; the general was delayed half a day at Havre de Grace by squalls on the Susquehanna. He was traveling slowly; it was not one of the dashing rides that were his wont. Not till the sixth day did he reach the graveled road that led from Chester into the metropolis.

2.   ". . . the great business now before us"

At Chester, while the general was eating a good dinner at Mrs. Whitney's renowned Columbia Hotel a welcoming group of old wartime associates joined him. There was frothy General Mifflin, now Speaker of the Pennsylvania Assembly, with whom his differences were gradually being forgotten — Washington was not a man to hold grudges — and Henry Knox, stouter than ever, and General Varnum, the Rhode Islander, apologizing for his state's refusal to attend, and the Major Jackson who was to be secretary of the convention. At Gray's Ferry the cavalcade was greeted by the Philadelphia Light Horse. By the time the general reached the entrance to the city there was no more doubt of the popular approval of his decision. A large concourse on foot and on horseback escorted his carriage. The artillery gave him a thirteen-gun salute. As he rode through the streets he noticed that church bells were chiming.

He alighted from his carriage into a cheering crowd in front of Mrs. House's boardinghouse, Madison's and Jefferson's favorite lodging, where Virginians on public business in Philadelphia usually put up. There Robert Morris and his wife were waiting for him. They would not hear of the general's staying anywhere except among the polished brasses and the rubbed mahogany of their hospitable house.

The general's first call was on the president of the Supreme Executive Council of Pennsylvania, the venerable Dr. Franklin.

Franklin had been home more than a year. Among his grandchildren and greatgrandchildren and the affectionate crowd of his sisters' families, he had hardly had a chance to rest up, in his house that had been so long abuilding, from the long sea journey when Constitutionalists and Republicans had joined with the Mechanics Society to elect him president. John Dickinson, the serene old Quaker, had already in his several terms done a great deal to quiet the factional strife among the Pennsylvania parties. Now Franklin, full of years and experience of men and cities; of the London of the Royal Society; of the Paris of the philosophers and of the Bourbon court of Versailles; and of Passy where he had held sway over a special philosophical court of his own, was joking the Philadelphia politicians into harmony by his shrewd stories and his quiet smiling ways. He was eightyone. Colonel Pierce of Georgia, who saw him in the convention, said he had the activity of mind of a youth of twentyfive. The stone in his bladder made it painful for him to ride in a carriage so he walked to the council meetings at the State House.

May 14 was the day set for the convention's opening. Always punctual, Washington presented himself early at the State House only to discover that no one was on hand except the impatient Madison, a couple of other Virginians and a few Pennsylvania delegates. They blamed the bad weather and adjourned. So it went on day after day. "These delays," Washington wrote Arthur Lee, "greatly impede public measures, and serve to sour the temper of the punctual members, who do not like to idle away their time."

Philadelphia was full of animation that month of May. Washington found old friends at every corner. Besides the Constitutional Convention and the general meeting of the Cincinnati, there were gathering at the same time the Pennsylvania Society for the Abolition of Slavery, the Presbyterian synod and a convention of Baptists. In spite of the commercial depression brought about by the collapse of the high prices of wartime and by the measures the government at Westminster was taking to choke off the competition of American shipping, the city resounded with hammering and sawing. New houses were going up in all directions.

The general was somewhat at loose ends. He missed his wife and the family life at Mount Vernon and the daily ride round his farms; still he managed to idle away his time fairly pleasantly during the two weeks that went by before the convention collected sufficient members to get down to business. The Morrises' table was always lively and often crowded with guests for dinner. The madeira was of the best. The ladies of the town were agog to have the general drink tea with them.

The third afternoon after he arrived he dined with his old comrades in arms of the Cincinnati. Undoubtedly he explained the importance of the business that kept him from their meetings. As the toasts came fast and the bottles sped round after the table had been cleared he may have heard some of the rough talk Otto, the French chargé d'affaires, reported to his government: if the convention failed the military would take arms in their hands and establish a central government, a monarchy maybe, as Knox had written Washington, by force.

Another day Benjamin Franklin dined all the delegates so far arrived in town in his new dining room and set them up to a particularly fine cask of porter a friend had sent him from England. Mrs. Morris, who was full of good works, dragged the general off to hear an Irish lady "in reduced circumstances" give a reading at the college hall, and again to a benefit concert at the City Tavern.

His first Sunday he rode out with the Morrises to their country place across the Schuylkill. He was always happy looking at orchards and garden crops.

Monday he "dined and drank Tea at Mr. Bingham's in great splendor." William Bingham had served as Robert Morris's agent in Martinique. He came back well heeled and married Thomas Willing's charming and domineering daughter and bought bank stock and became one of the financial nabobs of Philadelphia. It was giddy Mrs. Bingham whom Otto, the eyes and ears of the French legation, saw some years before ride off from her home in a one-seated sulky, sitting in the lap of the irrepressible Gouverneur Morris; Otto retailed the scandal with some satisfaction in his next report to Versailles. The Binghams already were leaders in the growing cult of the rich and wellborn and in "the etiquette and nonsense so fashionable in this city" that George Mason complained of in his letters home. The Sunday that followed, always eager for shows, the general attended high mass at the Romish church.

By the end of the first week all the Virginia delegates had reported and George Mason was writing his son George Jr. from the old Indian Queen, where in spite of the crowding of the city he said he found good accommodation at a reasonable price: "The Virginia deputies (who are all here) meet and confer together two or three hours every day to grow into some acquaintance with each other."

At these meetings they molded the Virginia proposals that were to present the convention with a basis of discussion from the first. "The most prevalent idea in the principle States," George Mason explained, "seems to be the total alteration of the present federal system, and substituting a great national council or parliament, consisting of two branches of the legislature founded upon the principles of equal proportionate representation, with full legislative powers upon all the subjects of the Union and to make the several state legislatures subordinate to the national . . . and an executive. It is easy to foresee that there will be much difficulty in organizing a government on this grand

scale, and at the same time reserving to the state legislatures a sufficient portion of power for promoting and securing the prosperity and
happiness of their respective citizens; yet with a proper degree of
coolness, liberality and candor (very rare commodities by the bye) I
doubt not but it may be effected."

George Mason went on in his aloof amused way to point out what
he described as a very extraordinary phenomenon. "We are likely to
find the republicans on this occasion issue from the Southern and
Middle States and the anti-republicans from the Eastern." He accounted for this eccentricity of opinion by the fact that "the people
in the eastern states starting out with more republican principles, have
consequently been more disappointed than we have been," and as a
result had run into the opposite extreme. So the great dilettante of
freedom, with a palate fine as a winetaster's for political shades,
assessed the state of mind of the gathering convention.

From the table talk at the Indian Queen he gathered that men of
business, merchants, bankers and creditors generally sought from the
new government protection from a flood of paper money and from the
riots and tumults of the debtor element that went with it. The people
who thought of themselves as the rich and wellborn were sated with
townmeetings and direct democracy. As a newspaper writer put it: in
1776 the times had demanded liberty, now they demanded government.

For George Mason liberty was an intellectual passion. Already he
feared the reaction against selfgovernment would get out of hand.
Though he admitted in his next letter, "I have the pleasure to find in
the convention, many men of fine republican principles," he was looking forward apprehensively to the part he would have to play. "I
declare I would not, upon pecuniary motives, serve in this convention
for a thousand pounds per day. The revolt from Great Britain and the
formations of our new governments at that time, were nothing compared to the great business now before us; there was then a certain
degree of enthusiasm, which inspired and supported the mind; but to
view through the calm sedate medium of reason the influence which
the establishment now proposed may have upon the happiness or
misery of millions yet unborn . . . in a manner suspends the operations
of the human understanding."

3.   ". . . a strong consolidated union"

At last on a rainy Friday it was found that enough delegates
had assembled to pronounce themselves a quorum. The convention was

called to order in the large hall in the east end of the State House. The Pennsylvania authorities had considerately spread earth over the cobbles of the adjoining streets so that the speakers should not be disturbed by the rumble of market carts or the clatter of hoofs. Sentries were posted on the vestibule to keep the curious out of the hall. The windows were kept tightly closed. As soon as silence fell on the twentyseven men in the highceilinged room with its tall arched windows, Washington's host, Robert Morris, rose and nominated him for the presidency. John Rutledge seconded the motion. The members wrote out their ballots and it was found that George Washington had been unanimously elected.

This nomination was a special tribute from the Pennsylvania delegation; Franklin would have been their logical candidate. The doctor stayed home that day, he claimed on account of the rain, but possibly because he wanted to be sure that the honor would fall to Washington.

Promptly the general was conducted to the chair by his two old friends. Much moved, he explained in a few disjointed words that it embarrassed him to be so lacking in the qualifications needed to preside over such a gathering and asked their indulgence of any involuntary errors he might fall into. As it turned out, most of the work of the convention was done in committee of the whole, where Nathaniel Gorham, who had had parliamentary experience as Speaker of the Massachusetts legislature, presided. All the general had to do during the first half of the convention was sit and listen.

Next Alexander Hamilton, who had arrived in town considerably put out by the fact that his election as delegate through the efforts of the Schuyler faction in the New York Assembly had been counterbalanced by the election of two anticontinentalists by the Clinton faction, nominated his old associate on Washington's staff, Major Jackson, for secretary. Then a committee was appointed to prepare a set of rules for the convention consisting of Hamilton, George Wythe, the classical teacher of law to the youth of Williamsburg, and Charles Pinckney of the South Carolina Pinckneys, who, though younger even than the prodigious Hamilton, was already renowned for his legal scholarship. They chose a doorkeeper and a messenger and adjourned till the next day. George Washington went off to dinner at Thomas Willing the banker's house.

On that auspicious Monday the delegates went to work with such a will that by the end of the second session they had passed the rules which, succinct and practical, have constituted a model for future assemblies. No member could read papers or whisper comments while another member had the floor. No man could speak more than twice on the same subject. All proceedings should be secret.

And secret they were. It was regarded one of history's miracles that the forty-odd men who eventually assembled were able to keep their counsel so religiously during the four months the convention continued. A colonel in the Continental Army who was now a merchant in Savannah, William Pierce, who enlivened the notes he kept on the debates with little sketches of personalities he found striking, told a story about George Washington in the chair that went far to explain the scrupulous silence of the delegates. The general was not a man to be trifled with. One day after adjournment, while the delegates were following their rules by remaining in their seats until their president had left the hall, Washington announced that a copy of one of the sets of resolutions had been picked up from the floor.

"I must intreat gentlemen to be more careful," he said in the voice that had terrified officers and men in chancy moments in the field, "lest our transactions get into the NewsPapers . . . I know not whose paper it is but there it is" — throwing it down on the table — "let him who owns it take it." Nobody stirred. "At the same time he bowed, picked up his Hat and quitted the room with a dignity so severe that every person seemed alarmed."

Pierce added that he himself reached guiltily for the copy on his desk and was horrified to find that it was in somebody else's handwriting. He was not easy in his mind until he found his own copy in the pocket of the coat he had pulled off that morning at his lodgings at the Indian Queen.

The next day Governor Randolph of Virginia took the floor and presented the fifteen Virginia propositions which were to be accepted as the frame round which the debates of the coming weeks were to revolve. Edmund Randolph had a handsome presence and an agreeable voice. He had the breeding and assurance of a man brought up to the public service in a family that had been for several generations part of the very structure of the colonial government. He had a first rate education. He had studied law under George Wythe. When his father, the tory King's attorney of Virginia, sailed for England his son elected to throw in his lot with the rebels and was chosen to hold his father's office under the new government. He was one of Washington's first aides. He had held public office ever since in Congress and in Virginia. Perhaps as a result of the strenuous coaching of Madison and Hamilton at Annapolis the year before, he had done more than any man to bring the Constitutional Convention about. He was one of those men who make a magnificent first impression; it was only when people got to know him that they discovered a certain weakness and lack of decision in his character. A chameleon, Jefferson called him. Governor of the most populous state, a lawyer of renown and a speaker of great polish, he was just the man to open the proceedings.

The scheme of government he proposed was somewhat more "high-toned," as Hamilton put it, than most of the delegates expected. The national legislature was to take the form sketched by George Mason in his letter to his son; but in his speech Randolph emphasized his opinion that the aim should be for a national instead of a federated government. Judge Yates, who had been sent to Philadelphia by George Clinton of New York particularly to oppose this kind of national government, wrote apprehensively in his notes: "He candidly confessed . . . that he meant a strong consolidated union in which the idea of states should be nearly annihilated."

Charles Pinckney followed Randolph and read his draft of proposals, which agreed with Randolph's as to the need for centralization, but went into greater detail as to the powers of the executive. Both propositions called for a highly authoritarian government with a veto over legislation in state assemblies, and demanded high property qualifications for holding office. Pinckney, with the South Carolina landowner's confidence in the virtue of the rich and wellborn, suggested an estate worth a hundred thousand dollars as the minimum for a candidate for the presidency.

The delegates referred both sets of proposals to their committee of the whole and adjourned. The project so long debated in Congress and in the press was on the floor. Now it was the job of the "men of fine republican principles" to whittle it down to size.

4.   "... the danger of the levelling Spirit"

As the argument continued from day to day, Washington heard, probably with some approval, delegate after delegate denounce the turbulent democracies that had been unleashed by the Declaration of Independence. His friend McHenry pointed out how the powers of government exercised by the people were tending to swallow up the other branches. Elbridge Gerry, the dapper Marblehead fish merchant, agreed: "The people do not want" — that is, lack — "virtue but are the dupes of pretended patriots. In Massachusetts it has been fully confirmed by experience that they are daily misled into the most baneful measures by false reports circulated by designing men, and which no one on the spot can refute."

Small shy James Madison, who in a fantastic burst of intellectual energy was not only conducting a large part of the debate but keeping

careful stenographic notes of what was said, added that "Gerry
confessed that he had been too republican before. He was still however
republican, but had been taught by experience the danger of the
levelling spirit."

George Mason, the tall squire of Gunston Hall, with his snapping
black eyes under a mop of white hair; Madison himself; James Wilson,
with his spectacles askew on his nose, whom they had nicknamed
"the Caledonian" in Philadelphia on account of his stiff Scottish
reasoning so deeply rooted in the old Scots kirk; and, to the surprise
of many of his friends who thought him a hopeless monarchist,
Gouverneur Morris, in attendance as a delegate from Pennsylvania,
came out in favor of direct election, by the people, of at least the
lower house.

"Mr. Mason," wrote Madison, "argued strongly for an election of
the larger branch by the people. It was to be the grand depository of
the democratic principle of the Govt . . . our House of Commons . . .
It ought to know and sympathize with every part of the community
. . . We ought to attend to the rights of every class of the people. He
had often wondered at the indifference of the superior classes of society
to this dictate of humanity & policy, considering that however affluent
their circumstances, or elevated their situations might be, the course
of a few years . . . certainly would distribute their posterity throughout
the lowest classes of Society. Every selfish motive therefore, every
family attachment, ought to recommend such a system of policy as
would provide no less carefully for the rights of the lowest than of the
highest orders of Citizens."

James Wilson backed him up and shrewdly pointed out that the
opposition of the states to federal measures proceeded much more
from the officers of the states than from the people at large.

The believers in selfgovernment carried the day. Already by the end
of May the plan had crystallized that one branch of the national
legislature should be elected by the people and the other by the state
legislatures. Even Hamilton, whose heart was set on a British-type
constitution, and who made no secret of his distrust of democracy,
went along with the principle of direct popular election of the lower
house.

This convention was an assembly in which it was hard for one man
to hold the center of the stage. Hamilton seems to have sat there
fuming. Before adjournment one day, in a fit of pique perhaps, he let
drop an observation which rang oddly in the mouth of a convinced
continentalist. He suggested scornfully that before the convention took
up the Virginia propositions there should be some inquiry as to
"whether the United States were susceptible of one government, or

required a separate existence connected only by leagues offensive and defensive and treaties of commerce." William Paterson, the attorney general of New Jersey, one of those state officers whom James Wilson had spoken of as opposed to federal measures, quoted him approvingly in the notes he was taking on the discussion. The last thing the Virginians who were working for a national union wanted was to bring this conflict out on the floor.

As the delegates worked over the Virginia plan section by section, it was becoming obvious that the dangerous split in the convention was not between the advocates of more or less selfgovernment for the new nation but between the men who were willing to make almost any concessions of individual preferences to attain a central government and the men who wanted no part in any kind of consolidation.

Day after day Randolph and Madison, often abetted by Gouverneur Morris's lighthearted cynicisms, managed to steer the argument past a direct collision on this basic issue. It was understood that when they came to the end of the Virginia propositions the opposition was to have the floor. In spite of every effort at diplomatic management the debates were becoming more and more heated. Personalities had begun to bristle.

No report came down of the conversation the afternoon of June 7 when George Washington dined privately with some convention members at the Indian Queen, which Manasseh Cutler, that irrepressible lobbyist for the land companies, who was in Philadelphia to try to find out how the proceedings of the convention would affect his business, was describing as being kept in elegant style and as spreading a sumptuous table, "the attendance in the style of noblemen." As that spacious old tavern had become the campaign headquarters for the Virginia delegation the talk over the wine that evening could hardly have avoided ways and means of meeting the contest to come. Washington, to whom secrecy was second nature, did not even confide his forebodings to his diary.

He felt the growing tension as the opposing bands maneuvered for position. His entries for the following Sunday expressed his relief at escaping into the country after the confinement of sitting ramrod stiff in his chair for seven hours a day, listening to arguments often abstruse and longwinded. He breakfasted with his good friend Samuel Powel, who was soon to be mayor of Philadelphia, and rode out with him afterwards to see the Bartrams' famous botanical garden, which he found small and badly laid out. With real relish he noted that afterwards "we rid to the farm of one Jones to see the effect of the plaister of Paris, which appeared obviously great." Liming land to improve the crop was just coming into use among progressive experimental farmers in England. The general observed with pleasure the thick growth of clover on the land that had been limed in contrast to the naked stubble and skimpy weeds where it had not. Nothing pleased him like good crops. Increasing fertility was the great problem of his management of Mount Vernon. Jones told him with a straight face that the lime must be spread when the moon was on its increase. "But this must be whimsical," Washington noted. From Jones' farm they rode to Powel's own place and ended a fine day with an ample dinner with the Morrises at The Hills. "Returned to the City abt. dark."

5.   *"Positiveness and warmth . . ."*

Next morning when the convention was called to order Benjamin Franklin asked James Wilson to read a statement for him. He was too feeble, he said, to make his voice heard in the large hall. He had observed with great pleasure that until the question of representation came up the debates had been carried on with great coolness. The question now was whether the states should be represented according to their wealth or according to their population. Behind that argument lurked slavery, an issue on which no man could control his passionate feelings. "Positiveness and warmth on one side naturally beget their like on the other," said Franklin, pleading for reasonableness. He asked the delegates to remember that they had been sent to Philadelphia "to consult not to contend with each other."

In spite of the old doctor's cozening words, the debate grew hotter with the weather during the last weeks of June. The representatives of the small northern states put up a stubborn battle against representation according to population. They found eager allies from South Carolina and Georgia. The question of whether to treat Negro slaves as property or as population had hopelessly embittered the discussion.

Luther Martin of Maryland, whom Colonel Pierce described as being extremely prolix "and tiring the patience of all who hear him," and Roger Sherman of Connecticut, with his sly Yankee twang, had become the big guns of the anticontinentalist party.

June 15 William Paterson read his proposals, which had been concocted in their chambers by a group of delegates from the Jerseys and from Connecticut, New York and Delaware, with the assistance of the vehement and longwinded Luther Martin. William Paterson was a sawedoff little North of Ireland man from County Antrim. His father was supposed to have been a tinker. Graduated from the college at Princeton, he had made a name for himself as a lawyer. Colonel

Pierce described him as a man of great modesty "whose powers break in upon you and create wonder and astonishment." The Paterson plan was "to review, correct and enlarge" the Articles of Confederation.

In the debate which followed, the opponents of a strong continental government joined ranks behind the Paterson proposals. The convention set to work to compare the two sets of propositions clause by clause. Again differences of opinion appeared which seemed hardly reconcilable. Alexander Hamilton declared in a petulant tone that neither Paterson's nor Randolph's proposals were continental enough for his taste.

6. ". . . an elective monarchy . . ."

The following Monday Hamilton made his only important speech. He explained that he had kept silent heretofore on account of his delicate situation with the other two delegates from his home state, whom he knew disagreed with him. He agreed with Mr. Necker, the great financier of France, that the British constitution was the only one in the world "which unites public strength with individual security." He had observed that even the members most tenacious of republicanism were loud in declaiming against the vices of democracy. "Give all power to the many, they will oppress the few. Give all power to the few, they will oppress the many." The problem was to set up a republic which would check both types of oppression.

He found no resolution of that problem in any of the proposals at present before the house. The New Jersey plan offered no advantage over the present confederacy, which everybody agreed to be ineffective.

According to Judge Yates' notes, which of course reflected the partisan attitudes of the Clinton faction, Hamilton admitted that the New Jersey plan was nearest to what the people had been led to expect. The Virginia plan Hamilton described as nothing but democracy, checked by democracy, or "pork still, with a little change of sauce."

Hamilton then read his own sketch for a national government. He wanted a lower house elected by the people for three years, to be checked by an upper house appointed for life. "Let one executive be appointed" — also for life — "who dares execute his powers . . . It may be said this constitutes an elective monarchy . . . But by making the executive subject to impeachment, the term monarchy cannot apply. This," he explained, "would be going the full length of republican principles."

Hamilton's propositions were not too well received by his colleagues. In spite of his quiet voice, something about his delivery

offended them. The young man was too cocksure. Colonel Pierce
described him as "of small stature . . . and lean." He found him "rather
a convincing Speaker, than a blazing Orator . . . there is no skimming
over the surface of a subject with him, he must sink to the bottom to
see what foundation it rests on. — His language is not always equal,
sometimes didactic like Bolingbroke's at others light and tripping like
Stern's." He complained of Hamilton's manners as "tinctured with
stiffness, and sometimes with a degree of vanity that is highly disagreeable." Since his two colleagues could outvote him on any proposition, Hamilton's unhappiness in the legislative strait jacket he found
himself in caused him to show himself in a poor light.

When Hamilton finished speaking the convention adjourned. Washington went on to dinner with the Sons of St. Patrick and drank tea
at Dr. Shippen's afterwards.

Next day and for the following week the debate was mired again in
the problem of whether the convention had a right to report a national
government. The continentalists kept brushing the question off and
trying to keep the discussion on the virtues and shortcomings of the
various proposals for such a government. Madison and Charles Pinckney in a pair of brilliant speeches reviewed the history of federative
and republican forms of government. George Mason and James Wilson replied by a firm reiteration of the fundamental principles of their
republicanism, which was that sovereignty must stem from the mass
of the people. The balloting was inconclusive. The deadlock reached
such a point that Benjamin Franklin rose to make the motion that they
had better have recourse to prayer.

"The small progress we have made after 4 or five weeks close
attention," he read in his quavering old voice, ". . . is methinks a
melancholy proof of the imperfection of the Human Understanding.
We indeed seem to feel our want of political wisdom, since we have
been running about in search of it. We have gone back to ancient
history for models of Government, and examined the different forms
of those republics which, having been formed with the seeds of their
own dissolution," he pointed out dryly, "now no longer exist. And we
have viewed Modern States all round Europe, but find none of their
Constitutions suitable to our circumstances . . . how has it happened,
sir that we have not hitherto once thought of applying to the Father
of Lights to illuminate our understandings?"

Dr. Hugh Williamson, who represented North Carolina in the convention as he had in Congress, answered tersely that the reason for
the lack of prayers was that the convention had no funds to hire a
minister. Edmund Randolph suggested, in his rounded tones, that they
should all listen to a sermon on the Fourth of July. "After several

unsuccessful attempts for silently postponing the matter by adjourning," noted Madison, "the adjournment was at length carried without any vote on the motion." The same treatment had been applied to Hamilton's proposals.

At this point in the proceedings that busy young man picked up and went home to New York. He was nettled because the delegates would not debate his scheme of government. He was short of cash, he had important cases pending in his law office. He had a family to support. Why waste his time in an assembly where his advice was not taken and where his talents were not appreciated? As Dr. Johnson, the Connecticut college professor, put it, "although he has been praised by everybody he has been supported by none."

7. *". . . an astonishing revolution for the better"*

After adjournment the afternoon that Hamilton went off in a huff, Washington dined with the Morrises, as usual, "in a large company." Robert Morris had sat in convention day after day without taking part in the proceedings. Perhaps he felt he had shot his bolt during his tenure in the Finance Office when all of his long term projects had failed of acceptance, or perhaps his mind was too taken up with financial worries and difficulties. His contract to furnish tobacco to the French farmers-general was meeting opposition in France. He had been in a continual dither these last few years to raise money to protect his investments in western lands. Dinner that day at Robert Morris's house was a Nebuchadnezzar's feast. "The news of his bills being protested," noted Washington in his diary, with maybe a trace of malice, "arriving last night a little mal-apropos."

During the week that followed Gouverneur Morris, back on the floor after a short absence, took up the argument for a "hightoned" government where Hamilton had dropped it in disgust. To balance a popular lower house, he was for an aristocratic senate frankly representing wealth. "History proves, I admit, that the men of large property will uniformly endeavor to establish a tyranny. How then shall we ward off this evil? Give them the second branch and you will secure their weight for the public good."

Everything by that time was bogged down on the problem of representation. In the matter of the choice of an executive the members were so far from agreement that they tried the expedient of turning all the questions on which they failed to agree over to a "Grand Committee" for solution.

The Fourth of July they trooped in a body to the Calvinist Church to hear an oration delivered by a Mr. Mitchell, a student of law. Washington, the same day, took advantage of his leisure to visit the anatomical figures exhibited by a certain Dr. Chovet.

In his spare time he had been sitting for his portrait, first to the Englishman, Robert Edge Pine, who had aroused sympathy on a portrait-painting tour of Virginia by giving out that he had lost a lucrative clientele at home through his espousal of the American cause, and then to Charles Willson Peale. Washington had become reconciled to having his picture painted, as he had to the declamatory verses and the singing school children and the laurel wreaths, as part of his position as Father of his Country. Writing earlier from Mount Vernon to Francis Hopkinson, who was one of those people to whom everybody wrote amusingly, he said: "In for a penny, in for a pound is an old adage. I am so hackneyed to the touches of the painter's pencil that I am now altogether at their beck, and sit like patience on a monument while they are delineating the lines of my face . . . At first I was impatient at the request, and as restive of the operation as a colt is of the saddle. The next time I submitted very reluctantly, but with less flouncing. Now, no dray moves more readily to the thill" — thill was an eighteenth century word for the shaft of a wagon — "than I to the painter's chair."

As he sat there under the north light, in the smell of linseed oil and pigments, while Charles Peale sat at his easel and the young Peales crowded around with their sketch pads, the General had time for anxious musings, behind his impenetrable countenance, on the contentions of the states in convention.

Hamilton had written him as soon as he reached New York that talking to chance acquaintances on his ride home through the Jerseys had brought him to the conclusion "that there has been an astonishing revolution for the better in the minds of the people. The prevailing apprehension among thinking men is, that the Convention from a fear of shocking the popular opinion, will not go far enough . . . Men in office are indeed taking all possible pains to give an unfavorable impression of the Convention, but the current is running strongly the other way."

This was encouraging news. Popular opinion, nourished by a decade of discussion in the press, was running ahead of the professionals in politics.

In spite of the favorable turn of opinion, Hamilton expressed little hope that any good would come of the convention he had abandoned. "I am seriously and deeply distressed at the aspect of the councils which prevailed when I left Philadelphia," he wrote the general. "I fear we shall let slip the golden opportunity."

Washington was forced to agree with him. He answered Hamilton's letter in a pessimistic mood: "they are now, if possible in worse train than ever . . . I *almost* despair of seeing a favorable issue . . . and do therefore repent having had any agency in the business . . . I am sorry you went away. I wish you were back" — the general had always been tolerant of the egotisms and vagaries of younger men, and particularly those of Hamilton, whom he loved and esteemed; still he added sternly: "No opposition under such circumstances should discourage exertions till the signature is fixed." What he meant was: "Young man come back and put your shoulder to the wheel."

The report of the Grand Committee merely gave rise to further arguments and to more tie votes. Fresh committees were chosen to mull over disputed clauses. Representation was the stumbling block. As they felt the tide turning against them, the men who made their stronghold in the state governments began to drag their feet. Some went so far as to try to obstruct the proceedings. July 10 Hamilton's two colleagues, Judge Yates and John Lansing, walked out of the convention and went home. One less vote against the new government.

Through the hot summer days the work dragged on while the bluebottle flies buzzed in the tall windows. The afternoon sun broiled the delegates stooping over their desks. Madison's informed and logical mind hummed steady as a dynamo under the babel of contention. Persistent George Mason kept patiently reminding the delegates that their business was to establish a government, not for the benefit of officeholders or of this or that special interest, but for the people at large. James Wilson backed him up by weaving his steely web of Scottish logic round the central proposition that sovereignty stemmed from the people.

The argument covered the entire field of social and political life. Economic interest was topmost in every man's mind. Adam Smith's *Wealth of Nations* was being very much read. Four years before the first extracts had appeared in the *New Haven Gazette* and had been copied up and down the coast. Perhaps the preoccupation these men had most in common was how to use conflicting economic interests to further their plans for a good society.

In the long tussling discussions it happened sometimes that the contestants spun clean around until they were taking positions oppocite from those they had started from. Though a fervent continentalist, Gouverneur Morris, in the course of his argument that representation should be based upon wealth instead of on population counted by the head, found himself giving aid and comfort to the opposition.

The "tall boy's" thinking hinged on the dominance of the economic motive. Wealth must be the political basis. His oratory was so fluent he was apt to go off on a tangent. Colonel Pierce wrote of him with amazement: "He winds through all the mazes of rhetoric, and throws around him such a glare that he charms, captivates, and leads away the senses of all who hear him . . . But with all these powers he is fickle and inconstant."

In the crisis of the debate on whether representation should be by population or wealth Gouverneur's friends were appalled to find him giving encouragement to the conservatives, who were in a panic for fear the new states sure to be formed to the westward would outvote them in a continental government. Already the turbulent pioneers were fomenting trouble with Spain over the navigation of the Mississippi. They were denouncing Gouverneur's friend John Jay, who as congressional Secretary for Foreign Affairs had agreed with a Spanish representative to let the American claims drop for twentyfive years. Morris admitted that he too dreaded the ascendancy of the teeming backwoodsmen. "A parcel of banditti," Washington had called them; now his urban young friend declared that "the Western States will not be able to furnish men equally enlightened to share in the administration of our common interests. The busy haunts of men not the remote wilderness are the proper school of political talents."

James Wilson answered promptly that all men wherever placed had equal rights. All men were equally entitled to confidence: "the majority of people wherever found ought in all questions to govern the minority."

He explained that it was the shortsighted thinking which Gouverneur Morris was displaying that had caused England to lose her American colonies. America must avoid that error. The West must be treated equally with the East. He concluded with a statement that went to the root of selfgoverning institutions. "He couldn't agree that property was the sole or the primary object of Governt. & Society. The cultivation & improvement of the human mind was the most noble object."

James Madison broke off his notetaking to skewer Morris's argument with a rejoinder: "Apparently the gentleman determines the human character according to the points of the compass."

One aspect of Gouverneur's inconsistency was a refreshing willingness to admit he was wrong if someone proved a point against him; slaves were wealth too. That stopped him. One of his most consistent convictions was a hatred of slavery. Much as he wanted to curb the slave trade and abolish the institution, he knew, as every man who

agreed with him in that hall knew — and altogether they constituted a
majority — that if they tried to force through measures abolishing
slavery Georgia and South Carolina would join the small northern
states in opposition to any constitution whatsoever.

In the course of the debate as to whether slaves should be treated
as population or as wealth Pierce Butler of South Carolina, alarmed
by the abolitionist atmosphere of Philadelphia, came out with the flat
statement: "The security the southern states want is that their negroes
may not be taken from them which some gentlemen within and without doors, have a very good mind to do."

Gouverneur went along with the compromise by which representation for the lower house at least should be on the number of free
persons and three fifths of "all other persons." The dread fact of
slavery was masked under the euphemistic phrase "other persons." On
July 12 all states present voted for representation by population,
except Delaware, which was divided.

8. *Unanimity Hall*

The deadlock continued for the rest of the week, but the
basic compromise had begun to take shape. The states should each
have two votes in the Senate. Senators should be elected by the state
legislature. The people should be represented in the House propor-
tionately to their numbers. From then on both sides began to yield.
Candor there had always been; now the "coolness and liberality"
George Mason had called for became the order of the day. Give and
take. The legislative arm was to be balanced by a strong executive,
by an independent judiciary. The authoritarians and the republicans
could each feel satisfied.

In spite of the curtain of secrecy so rigidly adhered to, by July 21
the fresh turn of events in convention found an echo in the press. A
writer in *The Pennsylvania Journal* pointedly dubbed that tortured
unventilated chamber in the State House "Unanimity Hall."

The next day, a Sunday, as if to conform to the sweet breeze of
concord that was renewing the muggy Philadelphia air, Washington
got up at five in the morning to ride out to Thomas Mifflin's
place in the country for breakfast. Together they spent the day riding
to Spring Mill to visit Peter Legaux's vineyard and his beehives, and
back to the Mifflins' for dinner. So were buried the last rancors of
the Conway cabal.

Monday, July 23, when the general called the convention to order
at the usual hour he found that the delegates were already taking a

constitution for granted. The discussion now was: how should it be ratified?

During these same middle weeks in July, as if galvanized by the sudden spurt of achievement in the Philadelphia convention, the rachitic old Continental Congress, sitting in New York, was finding strength to pass the last great act of its career. This was the Ordinance of 1787 for the government of the Northwest Territory.

Jefferson's original proposals of 1784 were worked over during the winter and spring to give a little more satisfaction to the land companies, but his favorite measure was at last enacted into law. His provision prohibiting slavery in the states north of the Ohio had been dropped out by the Congress sitting in Annapolis. It was restored by the Congress in New York owing largely to the persuasive tongue of a spirited young Harvard man named Rufus King, the son of a sea captain and lumberman from Scarboro, Maine, who astounded his colleagues by the polish and learning of his addresses. This was the Rufus King who had taken some of the gloom out of the debacle of the Committee of the States by his comic advertisements for the missing members.

Fresh from his work at the Congress in New York, and fresh too from long conversations with Alexander Hamilton, who had filled him with his own enthusiasm for building a nation out of the ruins of the confederacy, Rufus King and appeared in Philadelphia to represent his home state. He kept notes. He entered energetically into the debates. In contrast to Elbridge Gerry's procrastinations and picayune faultfinding, he was the member of the Massachusetts delegation whose criticisms tended to make the work roll faster instead of slower. Colonel Pierce described his "strong expressive Eye, and a sweet high toned voice." He spoke with admiration "of something strong and rich in his expression"; in public speaking, "his action is natural, swimming, and graceful."

King joined what was fast becoming a nationalist majority to set up a Committee of Detail whose business it would be to organize in logical sequence the confused mass of enactments already completed. The idea was to take advantage of the new spirit of accommodation to set down in plain simple English what had already been agreed on. The tactic of the fait acompli. The nationalists were taking advantage of the fact that the delegates were worn out by the scope and complication of their discussions. Everybody needed a breath of fresh air. Without too much debate a committee was chosen with the widest possible geographical distribution. It was made up of John Rutledge of South Carolina, Edmund Randolph of Virginia, Nathaniel Gorham of Massachusetts, James Wilson of Pennsylvania, and Oliver Ellsworth of Connecticut. The entire record was put in their hands for digestion. Dazed by the struggle and contention of the past weeks, the rest of the delegates voted themselves a ten-day vacation.

George Washington went fishing. First he had to spend a couple of days in his lodgings at the Morrises' catching up on his correspondence, but on Monday, July 30, instead of repairing to his hard seat in the convention hall, the general rode happily out of town in Gouverneur Morris's phaeton, driving his own horses, he notes in his diary, to Jane Moore's farm near Valley Forge. Gouverneur, lighthearted, salty of speech, in spite of his learning given more to pithy paradoxes than to the sort of prolonged ideological discussions the general's mind recoiled from, was the best company in the world. All his life he had been an enthusiastic angler.

Next day, while Gouverneur teased the trout in the adjoining brooks, the general in reminiscent mood "rid over the whole Cantonment of the American Army of the Winter 1777 and 8, visited all the Works wch. were in ruins; and the Incampments in woods where the grounds had not been cultivated."

The diary says not a word of the brooding recollections that must have come to his mind, the memories of cold and hunger and courts-martial and floggings, humiliation and discord, of the clash of personalities among loved friends and subordinates now long dead and buried; if the American cause had triumphed over all that, it could well triumph over the disagreements of these voluble and learned men in convention assembled. No hint in his diary of such profound meditations; but a sprightly account of a talk he had with some farmers he found at work at Mrs. Moore's about the cultivation of buckwheat and the use of that grain mixed with potatoes to fatten beeves and hogs. It was like being home again.

At Mrs. Moore's he found the Robert Morrises, who had driven out to dine and spend the night. After dinner Gouverneur set the general to fishing one of the trout streams. Next day rain set in, so the whole party left for the city and arrived in time for dinner at the Morrises'. This fishing party with Gouverneur was such a success that a couple of days later the general and all the Morrises were at it again up at Trenton, lodging at the ironworks and fishing for perch in the Delaware.

9.   "... a rising and not a setting sun"

Monday, August 6, the general called the convention to order to hear from John Rutledge, whom a French embassy report called "the most eloquent, the proudest, the most imperious man in the U.S.," what was actually a rough first draft of the Constitution. The result of the committee's work was placed in the members' hands in a printed broadside. The continentalists had control of the parliamentary machinery. Instead of contention, a spirit of bargaining, "the calm sedate medium of reason" George Mason had hoped for, continued to prevail.

A rational regulation of commerce was one of the prime motives for the organization of a general government. As the convention debated the report of its Committee of Detail on the new Congress's power to pass navigation acts and to tax imports and exports a fresh conflict of interest flared in the hall.

The southern states were exporters of raw materials, tobacco, rice and indigo. Shipbuilding and the carrying trade were the chief businesses of the eastern states. From Virginia to New York interests were more mixed. The delegates from South Carolina and Georgia again took fright at the notion that Congress might tax their exports.

Luther Martin frightened them worse by suggesting a tax on the importation of slaves. If their importation of slaves remained unrestricted the southern states could swell their population until they outvoted the rest by importing more slaves, he stormed. Slavery was "inconsistent with the principles of the revolution and dishonorable to the American character."

John Rutledge of South Carolina replied that "religion and humanity had nothing to do with this question — Interest alone is the governing principle with Nations. The true question at present is whether the Southern States shall or shall not be parties to the Union."

Ellsworth of Connecticut, whose home state had already prohibited the importation of slaves, backed up Rutledge. "Let every state import what it pleases. The morality and wisdom of slavery are considerations belonging to the States themselves."

George Mason cried out that slavery was "an infernal traffic." He denied that slavery was in anyone's interest. His mind was on far reaching questions of morality and wisdom. "The present question concerns not the importing states alone, but the whole Union," he declared. "Slavery discourages arts and manufactures. The poor despise labor when performed by slaves. They prevent the immigration of Whites, who really enrich and strengthen a Country. They produce the most pernicious effect on manners. Every master of slaves is born a petty tyrant. They bring the judgement of heaven on a Country. As nations can not be rewarded or punished in the next world they must in this. By an inevitable chain of causes & effects providence punishes national sins, by national calamities."

Edmund Randolph declared he would rather risk the Constitution than consent to an unrestricted slave trade. Rufus King brought the argument down to the bargaining level again by pointing out that the northern states would object to paying taxes on their imports if the Southerners paid none on the slaves they brought in. Gouverneur, again the smooth cosmopolite, suggested reference to a committee. "These things," he insinuated, "may form a bargain among the Northern & Southern States."

That bargain was to form the basis of a long entente between the New England merchants and the slaveowners of the deep South. The immediate result of the committee's deliberation was a fresh compromise by which Congress should be denied the authority to prohibit the slave trade for twenty years.

As one successful compromise followed another the hopes of the delegates rose. They were tired of the heat and contention. They wanted to finish their work and go home.

Since a motion to refer the proposals of the detail committee to a committee of the whole failed, the hard work of presiding over the decisive terminal debates fell to Washington. To speed the final stages the delegates passed a resolution fixing the daily sessions at from ten in the morning to four in the afternoon: no motions to adjourn to be made before that hour, no matter how hungry the delegates were for their dinners.

Another month went by before the convention was ready to turn the completed document over to a Committee of Style and Arrangement. William Samuel Johnson, the learned college teacher from Connecticut, who was the son of the first president of King's College and was himself to be the first president of Columbia, was chairman. Alexander Hamilton, back again once the sessions of the circuit court of New York had come to an end; Gouverneur Morris, James Madison, and Rufus King made up the remaining four members. Colonel Pierce, who was much taken with King, noted that "tout en semble he should be ranked among the Luminaries of the Present Age." From among these "luminaries" the convention could hardly have chosen five men more apt to the work in hand.

Gouverneur was the chief draftsman. Years later he wrote Timothy Pickering: "That Instrument was written by the Fingers which wrote this Letter. Having rejected redundant and equivocal Terms, I believed it to be as clear as our Language would permit. He added that he was unhappy about the section that dealt with the judiciary. "Conflicting Opinions had been maintained with so much professional astuteness" — was he thinking of James Wilson or Dr. Johnson? — "that it became necessary to select Phrases, which expressing my own Notions would not alarm others, nor shock their selflove."

That letter gave only an inkling of the final compounding of diverse opinions that went into the drafting of the document. The five men worked incredibly fast. A loose mass of notes was referred to the committee when the convention adjourned Monday afternoon, September 10. By Wednesday morning they not only had copies of the Constitution all set up and printed for the perusal of the delegates, but they had a letter ready to accompany the finished document when it should be signed, sealed and delivered to Congress:

"We have now the honor to submit to the consideration of the United States in Congress assembled that Constitution which has appeared to us the most advisable.

". . . Individuals entering into Society must give up a share of Liberty to preserve the rest. The Magnitude of the Sacrifice must depend as well on Situation and Circumstances as on the object to be obtained. It is at all times difficult to draw with Precision the Line between those Rights which must be surrendered and those which may be preserved. And on the present Occasion this Difficulty was increased by a Difference among the several States as to their Situation Extent Habits and particular Interests.

"In all our deliberations on this subject we kept steadily in our View that which appears to us the greatest Interest of every true American — namely, the creation of a nation."

The rest was all detail. The delegates gnawed at the printed document for five more days. They went over it paragraph by paragraph. Dissenters spoke up. Elbridge Gerry objected to certain details. Edmund Randolph and George Mason announced that neither of them could conscientiously sign the document unless it should be amended by state conventions and finally passed on by another convention, a proposition so impractical as to give the nationalists cold chills.

George Mason noted down his objections on the blank pages of his printed copy of Gouverneur Morris's draft:

"There is no Declaration of rights . . . nor are the people secured even in the enjoyment of the benefit of the common law . . . In the House of Representatives there is not the substance but the shadow only of representation . . . The Judiciary . . . is so constructed and extended as to absorb and destroy the judiciaries of the several States; thereby rendering law as tedious, intricate and expensive, and justice as unattainable, by a great part of the community, as in England, and enabling the rich to oppress and ruin the poor . . . The President of the United States has no Constitutional Council . . . He will therefore be unsupported by proper information and advice, and will generally be directed by minions and favorites . . . or a Council of State will grow out of the principal officers of the great departments; the worst and most dangerous of all ingredients for such a council in a free country; for they may be induced to join in any dangerous or oppressive measures, to shelter themselves, and prevent enquiry into their own misconduct in office . . . By declaring all treaties supreme laws of the land, the Executive and Senate have, in many cases, an exclusive power of legislation; which might be avoided by proper distinctions with regard to treaties, and requiring the assent of the House of Representatives . . . There is no declaration of any kind for preserving the liberty of the press, or the trial by jury in civil causes; nor against the danger of standing armies in time of peace . . . The general legislature is restrained from prohibiting the further importation of slaves for twenty odd years, though such importations render the United States weaker, more vulnerable, and less capable of defence."

George Mason's mighty dissent was to provide the basis for the first ten amendments and for many a political contest in the years to come.

With the exception of these three men, the Constitution was unanimously agreed to. On Monday, September 17, the final engrossed copy was read to the convention. Benjamin Franklin rose with a paper held in his withered hands and asked James Wilson to read it for him. No words could have better summed up the hopes and misgivings of the assembly:

"Mr. President:

"I confess there are several parts of this constitution which I do not at present approve, but I am not sure I shall never approve them: For having lived long I have experienced many instances of being obliged by better information or fuller consideration, to change opinions even on important subjects, which I once thought right but found to be otherwise . . . In these sentiments Sir I agree to this Constitution with all its faults, if they are such; because I think a general Government necessary for us, and there is no form of Government but what may be a blessing to the people if well administered; and believe further that this is likely to be well administered for a course of years, and can only end in Despotism, as other forms have done before it, when the people shall become so corrupted as to need despotic Government, as being incapable of any other. I doubt too whether any other Convention we can obtain will be able to make a better Constitution. For when you assemble a number of men to have the advantages of their joint wisdom, you inevitably assemble with those men, all their prejudices, their passions, their errors in opinion, their local interests, and their selfish views . . . I hope therefore that for our own sakes as a part of the people, and for the sake of posterity, we shall act heartily and unanimously in recommending this Constitution."

A ripple of contention crossed the hall after Franklin's speech. What number of inhabitants should elect a representative? Nathaniel Gorham moved thirty instead of forty thousand.

George Washington from the chair spoke up for the first time in those long summer months. He apologized for giving his opinion but said he hoped the alteration would carry.

It was agreed to unanimously. After some discussion of the scruples of the dissidents, and a nightmarish speech by Elbridge Gerry, who claimed to foresee that the document they were about to sign would bring about civil war in Massachusetts, the members filed up to the table to put their signatures to the engrossed copy.

"Whilst the last members were signing," wrote Madison in his notes, "Doctr. Franklin looking towards the Presidents Chair, at the back of which a rising sun happened to be painted, observed to a few members near him, that Painters had found it difficult to distinguish in their art a rising from a setting sun. I have, said he, often and often in the course of the Session, and the vicissitudes of my hopes and fears as to its issue, looked at that behind the President without being able to tell whether it was rising or setting: But now at length I have the happiness to know it is a rising and not a setting sun."

"The business being thus closed," wrote Washington lightheartedly in his diary, "the Members adjourned to the City Tavern, dined together and took a cordial leave of each other." After dinner he walked back to his lodgings at the Morrisses' and, he added, "retired to meditate on the momentous work."

VIII   Of the Making of Constitutions

1.   *The Nine States Needed*

As soon as the copies of the new Constitution which Franklin and Washington and Madison had each hurried on board ship for him reached Jefferson at the American legation on the Champs Elysées in Paris, he began to correspond with Lafayette on the subject. The mercurial marquis was down in his native Auvergne getting himself elected to the assembly of the provincial noblesse. When Lafayette wrote Washington his impressions, he found himself voicing Jefferson's two principal objections: "I read the new proposed constitution with an unspeakable eagerness and attention . . . I have admired it and find it is a bold, large and solid frame . . . I am afraid of only two things — 1st the want of a Declaration of Rights 2ndly the great powers and possible continuance of the President, who may some day become a State Holder."

The collapse of the Dutch Republic had left a tender spot in the mind of every liberal in Europe.

Lafayette went on to exclaim that Washington was the one man who could set these errors right: "In the name of America, of mankind at large, and of your own fame, I beseach you, my dear General, not to deny your acceptance of the office of President for the first years. You only can settle the political machine, and I forsee it will furnish an admirable chapter in your history."

He could not finish his letter without telling his adopted father how happy he was in his collaboration with Jefferson. "I am more and more pleased with Mr. Jefferson. His abilities, his virtues, his temper, everything of him commands respect and attracts affection. He enjoys universal regard and does the affairs of America to perfection. It is the happiest choice that could be made."

Jefferson had been prepared to be discouraged. Madison had written him ominously in a gloomy moment while the convention was still in session that the plan would "neither effectively answer its national object nor prevent the local mischiefs which everywhere excited disgusts against the state governments." As soon as the convention rose he would be no longer bound to secrecy and could explain to Jefferson what he meant.

"There are things in it which stagger all my dispositions to subscribe," Jefferson wrote John Adams in London after his first perusal. "The house of federal representatives will not be adequate . . . Their President seems a bad edition of a Polish king . . . I wish that at the end of 4. years they had made him forever ineligible for a second term."

John Adams had been poring over his own copy and had misgivings on a very different score: "You are afraid of the one; I of the few," he replied. He was afraid the Senate would turn into an aristocracy like that of Venice. "You are apprehensive that the President when once chosen, will be chosen again and again so long as he lives. So much the better as it appears to me . . . Elections, my dear Sir, Elections to offices which are great objects of Ambition, I look at with terror."

Working the document over paragraph by paragraph, Jefferson gradually became reconciled to its terms. Madison's explanatory letters profoundly colored his opinion.

Immediately after the engrossed copy was handed to the postboy to deliver to Secretary Thomson of the Continental Congress in New York, Madison hurried across the Jerseys to take his seat in that body. It was natural that he should turn for advice to Hamilton, with whose thinking he had been so much in sympathy when their terms in Congress overlapped. Between them they came to the conclusion that Franklin was right in his final summary; the Constitution was not perfect, but there was no reason to believe any other convention could produce a better one. Every man who wanted a general government must throw everything he had into getting this Constitution ratified as it stood. Amendments could come later.

Hardly pausing for breath, Madison and Hamilton went to work, with some assistance from John Jay, to draft the series of articles they brought out in *The Independent Journal* in New York under the signature of "Publius." The following year they published them in book form as *The Federalist*. As soon as he was free from the nagging detail of debating and notetaking in the stifling end room of the Philadelphia State House, Madison began to see that he and his fellow delegates had built better than they could possibly have hoped.

Hamilton was a natural advocate. The moment he started to plead a cause every doubt vanished. His enthusiasm was catching. At the end of a month's careful cogitation under the stimulus of Hamilton's lively mind Madison had his arguments in favor of the form of government the Philadelphia convention had invented sufficiently clear to send Jefferson an abstract of them. He dated his letter October 24, 1787, a couple of days before Hamilton's first Publius piece appeared in the newspaper.

"The great objects," Madison wrote, were energy in the executive and stability in the legislative departments. They had tried to draw a line of demarkation between them that would "give the General Government every power requisite for general purposes and leave to the States every power which might be beneficially administered by them." They had tried "to provide for the different interests of different parts of the Union" and "to adjust the clashing pretensions of the large and small States." He described the scheme as "a feudal system of republics . . . the Senate will represent the States in their political capacity, the other House will represent the people of the States in their individual capacity."

He launched into his theory of the economic nature of political interests which he was to round out in the tenth number of *The Federalist*:

"It may be asked how private rights will be more secure under the Guardianship of the General Government than under the State Governments, since both are founded on the republican principle which refers the ultimate decision to the will of the majority . . . Those who contend for a simple Democracy, or a pure republic . . . suppose a case which is altogether fictitious. They found their reasoning on the idea that the people composing the Society enjoy not only an equality of political rights; but they have all precisely the same feelings in every respect . . . We know however that no Society ever did or can consist of so homogenious a mass of Citizens . . . There will be rich and poor; creditors and debtors; a landed interest, a monied interest, a mercantile interest, a manufacturing interest. These classes may again be subdivided according to the different productions of different situations and soils, and according to different branches of commerce and of manufactures. In addition to these natural distinctions, artificial ones will be founded on accidental differences in political, religious and other opinions, or an attachment to the persons of leading individuals . . . It remains then to be enquired whether a majority having any common interest, or feeling any common passion, will find sufficient motives to restrain them from oppressing a minority."

He explained that the motives for restraint were: first, the fact that each man's personal fortunes were tied up in the "permanent good of the whole"; "experience however shows that this motive has little effect on individuals and still less on a collection of individuals, and least of all on a majority with public authority in their hands."

The second motive he called "respect for character." He found it as insufficient as the first to restrain individuals from injustice: "Besides as it has reference to public opinion, which is that of the majority, the standard is fixed by those whose conduct is to be measured by it."

The third motive was religion. "The conduct of every popular assembly, acting on oath, the strongest of religious ties, shews that individuals join without remorse in acts against which their consciences would revolt, if proposed to them in their closets . . . If then there must be different interests and parties in Society; and a majority . . . cannot be restrained from oppressing the minority, what remedy can be found in a republican Government, where the majority must ultimately decide, but that of giving such an extent to its sphere, that no common interest or passion will be able to unite a majority of the whole number in an unjust pursuit? . . . The same security seems requisite for the civil as for the religious rights of individuals."

This reasoning led Madison to that final compact formulation of his theory of government, as compelling in its field as Newton's law of gravitation in the field of physics: "The great desideratum in Government is, so to modify the sovereignty as that it may be sufficiently neutral between different parts of the Society to controul one part from invading the rights of another, and at the same time sufficiently controuled itself, from setting up an interest adverse to that of the entire Society."

He added hopefully: "In the extended Republic of the United States the General Government would hold a pretty even balance between the parties of particular States, and be at the same time sufficiently restrained by its dependence on the community, from betraying its general interests."

Madison wound up his long letter with a summary of the prospects for ratification. New Hampshire was favorable. "Boston is warm and almost unanimous in embracing it . . . The paper money faction in Rh. Island is hostile . . . Its passage through Connecticut is likely to be very smooth and easy . . . N. Jersey takes the affirmative side . . . Penna. will be divided . . . Maryland . . . strongly in favor." Virginia was doubtful. A great deal depended there on Patrick Henry's attitude. There was no news from the states to the southward.

As it turned out, little Delaware on December 7, 1787, was the first state to ratify. The debate in Pennsylvania was opened by James Wilson, who addressed a massmeeting in the State House yard to answer George Mason's objections which had been printed in *The Pennsylvania Packet*. Their convention was dominated by continentalists from the first. The opposition filled the newspapers with denunciations of the document as "a scheme of the wealthy and ambitious, who in every community think they have the right to lord it over their fellow creatures."

Good Dr. Rush, as usual seeing everything as all white or all black, came out dogmatically in favor of a general government. "Plurality in politics," he declaimed, "is what plurality of gods is in religion, it is the idolatry, the heathenism of government."

The moneymen were for it for commercial reasons, but so were the artisans and mechanics of the towns. Both in the convention and in the general popular debate it was the close Scots reasoning of James Wilson that carried the day. "My position is, that the sovereignty resides in the people . . . This constitution rests upon this broad principle . . . the people have hitherto been shut out of the federal government" — he was referring to the Continental Congress, which represented only the state legislatures — "but it is not meant that they should be any longer dispossessed of their rights . . . the proposed system sets out with a declaration that its existence depends on the supreme authority of the people alone." Rush echoed him: "I have now a vote for Members of Congress. I am a Citizen of every State." The ayes had it on December 12.

New Jersey followed hard on the heels of Pennsylvania, and with the new year Georgia and Connecticut; and Massachusetts in February 1788.

Unlike Pennsylvania, where ratification was hurried through by a group of men trained in the partisan disputes which had kept the chandeliers of the State House shaking all through the war, the Massachusetts debates, in a Boston church that had a large gallery for the public, were leisurely and extensive. The speakers represented every segment of the community. Farmers from down east and from the western hills made themselves heard as much as Boston lawyers and Essex County magnates.

"Shall we swallow a large bone for the sake of a little meat?" asked a Maine settler. "These lawyers, and men of learning, and monied men," shouted another, "that talk so finely and gloss over matters so smoothly to make us poor illiterate people swallow down the pill, expect to get into Congress themselves; they expect to be managers of their constitution, and get all the power and all the money into their own hands, and then they will swallow up all us little folks, like the great *Leviathan*, Mr. President: yes, just as the whale swallowed up *Jonah*."

These men were answered in their own terms by one Jonathan Smith of Berkshire County who announced himself as a plain man who got his living by the plow: "I beg your leave to say a few words to my brother ploughjoggers . . . I am going, Mr. President, to show you my brother farmers," he cried out in recollection of the scenes he had lived through during Shays' rebellion: "People, I say, took up arms, and then, if you went to speak to them, you had the musket of death presented to your breast . . . Our distress was so great we should have been glad to snatch at anything that looked like a government . . . When I saw this constitution, I found that it was a cure for these disorders . . . I got a copy of it and read it over and over . . . Suppose two or three of you had been at the pains to break up a piece of rough land, and sow it with wheat — would you let it lay waste because you could not agree on what sort of a fence to make? Would it not be better to put up a fence that did not please every one's fancy, rather than not to fence it at all, or keep disputing about it, until the wild beasts came and devoured it? . . . Gather fruit when it is ripe. There is a time to sow and a time to reap: we sowed our seed when we sent men to the federal convention . . . now is the time to reap the fruit of our labor."

This was the sort of support at the roots that won over the old revolutionary leaders. John Hancock was elected to preside but took to his bed with a fit of the diplomatic gout until he could feel how the public wind was blowing. Rufus King slyly convinced him that if Massachusetts ratified and Virginia did not, he would be the logical candidate for the first President. Samuel Adams had always thrown his great influence in the Continental Congress, along with the Virginia Lees, in favor of state sovereignty. It was only when Paul Revere marshaled the mechanics and artisans and small manufacturers who were the heart of Boston townmeeting in its favor that he gave the Constitution his grudging support.

Meanwhile in Maryland, with intemperate Luther Martin and Judge Chase and John Francis Mercer opposed and Washington's friend McHenry and the whole booming port of Baltimore in favor, every crossroads tavern rang with the argument and vituperation of the campaign to elect delegates to a convention. In spite of an effort to tack on a series of amendments in the form of a bill of rights, the convention in Annapolis ratified unconditionally after six days of debate.

A couple of weeks later news sped up the coast by sloop and postrider that South Carolina had ratified.

On June 22 Washington's secretary, Tobias Lear, the son of a Portsmouth sea captain, who was on a visit to his home state of New Hampshire, wrote the general: "The Constitution was ratified on Saturday at one o'clock P.M. I am thus particular, as Virginia might have adopted it the same day, and, in that case, the hour must be known to determine which was the ninth State." Lear was anxious that his own New Hampshire should have the honor of putting the Constitution into effect. And so it turned out.

Jefferson in Paris, suffering as he so often did from lack of spending money that winter on account of the great expense which he had been put to in setting up the legation, for which Congress had not yet seen fit to reimburse him, was writing Madison asking him to jog John Jay's memory on that score and begging for news of the progress of ratification. He was now seeing more to like than to dislike in the scheme: "I like the power given the Legislature to levy taxes . . . preserving inviolate the fundamental principle that the people are not to be taxed but by representatives chosen immediately by themselves. I am captivated by the compromise of the opposite claims of the great and little states." What he did not like was the lack of a bill of rights.

As news of the ratification by successive states reached him he became more sanguine. "I sincerely wish that the 9 first conventions may receive, and the 4. last reject, the former will secure it finally, while the later will oblige them to offer a declaration of rights in order to complete the union."

At the same time as they exchanged ideas on the problems of government Madison and Jefferson were shipping each other all sorts of things back and forth across the Atlantic. Jefferson bought Madison a watch which he sent him through the kind offices of the new French minister, the Marquis de Moustier. He was shipping him boxes of books, a pedometer to measure his walks with, some acorns of the cork oak, and a bag of peas for his garden. In return he was asking for the antlers and skin of a moose to prove to Monsieur Buffon how wrong his theory was on the puny size of American animals, for a barrel of cranberries and one of Newtown pippins to prove to the Parisians the excellence of American fruits, and for a long list of American trees and plants to distribute among the philosophical French friends he was making through Lafayette's assiduous attentions. They had turned out, many of them, to be as enthusiastic botanists and gardeners as Jefferson himself. "Red birds for the ladies," he added in one letter, "and Opossums for the naturalists would be great presents, if any passenger would take charge of them."

2.　The Key to the Bastille

While Americans on both sides of the Atlantic avidly followed the debates on the ratification of their new Constitution in the state assemblies, in France the gilded coach of the Bourbon regime rumbled on towards disaster.

Ministries rose and fell.

Necker, who in spite of his ill success with the finances of Versailles was still the richest man in Europe, and whose virtues as a financier were loudly publicized through his wife's salon and through the trumpetings of his intellectual daughter, famous among the drawing rooms of Europe as Madame de Staël, was called back from the quiet shores of the Lake of Geneva to make one more try with his "art magick." He alighted from his traveling carriage shaking his head. "I see a great wave advancing," he was reported as saying. "Will it swallow me up?"

The Notables were summoned back to the Hall of Fugitive Pleasures. The provincial assemblies were already clamoring for a meeting of the States-General. The press and the pamphleteers, who in the general relaxation of government had lost any fear of the police, echoed their cry.

The States-General had not met since 1614, when they had put in a final feeble appearance during the tumultuous years while Richelieu was consolidating the monarchy into a great bureaucratic machine centered at Versailles. Suddenly the name became magic. Lafayette from among the Notables signed a demand for the States-General. Necker could think of nothing better than to back him up. His Most Christian Majesty liked the idea. It appealed to the antiquarian tastes of some of his enlightened courtiers. It was like the revival of a very old play. A great deal of archaeological research went into reconstituting the costumes and finding the old prompt books.

While all France waited for the opening performance bitter debate raged over the methods of voting. In the old days nobles, clergy and commons had voted as corporate bodies. Now individualism was the mode. Each vote must be counted individually. Already the prospective members of the commons, the Third Estate, were demanding that, as they furnished most of the taxes, their votes should be counted twice. His Most Christian Majesty, who trusted in the Third Estate to squeeze funds out of the church and the nobility, was not averse to this arrangement. Thereby King Louis became a great liberal.

"The representation of the people will be perfect but they will be alloyed by an equal number of nobility and clergy," Jefferson wrote, full of optimism, to David Humphreys, who had served as secretary of the legation during his early days in Paris. "The first great question they will have to decide is whether they will vote by orders or persons, & I have hopes that the majority of the nobles are already disposed to join the tiers état in deciding that the vote shall be by persons. this is the opinion à la mode . . . all the handsome young women for example are for the tiers état, & this is an army at present more powerful in France than all the 200,000. men of the king . . ."

The French people were taking part in the constitutional argument as eagerly as the public in Philadelphia or New York. Jefferson greedily read the publications that poured from the presses. "The writings published on this occasion are some of them very valuable because unfettered by the prejudices under which the English labor, they give full scope to reason, and strike out truths as yet unperceived & unacknoledged on the other side of the channel. the Englishman dosing under a kind of half reformation, is not excited to think by such gross absurdities as stare a Frenchman in the face wherever he looks, whether it be towards the throne or the altar. in fine I believe this nation will in the course of the present year have as full a portion of liberty dealt out to them as the nation can bear."

The American faction was determined to use the States-General to produce a constitution that would deal out a generous portion of liberty to the nation. A constitution was their cure for all evils. When the entrenched interests blocked the work of the American committee, Lafayette and his brotherinlaw de Noailles formed a club known as the Club of the Thirty to debate on constitutional topics. De la Rochefoucauld was a member; and Condorcet, the Master of the Mint whose abstract mind was already at work on a study of American parliamentary institutions; and Mirabeau the stormy Provençal aristocrat, whose private war with his father was turning into a public war against aristocracy as an institution. A group of lawyers from the Parlement de Paris joined them and a couple of old members of the Order of Harmony. It was in the Club of the Thirty that Talleyrand, the clubfooted babyfaced Bishop of Autun, made his first appearance as a reformer on the public stage. In the salons they became known as the conspiracy of well intentioned men.

Lafayette and his friends were continually applying to Jefferson for news of the progress of statebuilding in America. America was supplying them with the models they needed. By mid July in 1788 Jefferson was able to assure them that the new government was complete. He could not quite breathe easy yet: until he had news of ratification by the great states of Virginia and New York there was still a chance that the Constitution would bring a schism instead of union.

"The Plot thickens fast," Washington wrote Lafayette from Mount Vernon in May. "A few short weeks will determine the political Fate

of America for the present Generation and probably produce no small
Influence on the happiness of Society through a long succession of
Ages to come . . . Should everything proceed with Harmony and Consent I will confess to you sincerely, my dear Marquis; it will be so
much beyond anything we had a Right to imagine or expect eighteen
months ago, that it will demonstrate as visibly the Finger of Providence, as any possible Event in the course of human Affairs."

The Virginia convention sat in the hall recently erected on Shockoe's
Hill in Richmond for a French academy projected by a grandson of
Quesnay the physiocrat. Lame old Edmund Pendleton presided.
George Wythe, whose fingers were already crippled with gout, was in
the chair during the long periods when the meeting sat as a committee of the whole. In spite of Patrick Henry's tempestuous oratory and
George Mason's libertarian fire, diffident little Madison, reading his
notes out of the bottom of his cocked hat, and Light Horse Harry Lee
with the glamor of his wartime exploits still about him, and a tall
shambling young backwoods lawyer named John Marshall carried the
day for the Constitution.

Changeable Edmund Randolph, still state governor, whose scruples
had kept him from signing in Philadelphia, tipped the scales by coming over, to everybody's amazement, to the continentalist side. To
their ratification the Virginians tacked on a demand for a national bill
of rights modeled on George Mason's preamble to their own constitution of 1776.

In New York, Hamilton managed the campaign for ratification.
Against him he had Governor Clinton's upstate machine and most of
the lords of the manor of the Hudson River estates who were accus-
tomed to voting their tenantry like the pocket boroughs of England.
Behind Hamilton were John Jay and Robert R. Livingston, who
brought along the power and influence of his family's farflung lands.
Almost from the first the debate settled down into a dialogue between
Hamilton and a selftaught merchant with a candid mind named
Melancton Smith. Smith represented Dutchess County, though his
business was in the city.

While the delegates debated in Poughkeepsie, in New York City
Hamilton's supporters were marching. L'Enfant designed the floats for
a vast parade on July 23 which was to demonstrate public support for
a close federal union. Merchants gave money, artisans donated their
time. The shipbuilders of the port constructed a model frigate, forty-
six feet long, mounting thirtytwo guns, named the *Alexander Hamilton*, which was drawn in full sail through the streets by ten horses.
Old Commodore Nicholson of Revolutionary War fame stood at the

helm. All the trades and occupations of the city followed in the order of march. The tailors marched under a representation of Adam and Eve, sewing fig leaves on a huge flag. The brewers drew a dray loaded with casks of ale surmounted by a curlyhaired boy dressed as Bacchus in vine leaves over flesh colored tights. The upholsterers exhibited a chair of state seven feet tall festooned with light blue satin.

To Poughkeepsie, along with accounts of the great parade, came news of Virginia's accession. Melancton Smith declared himself convinced by Hamilton's arguments and himself put the motion to ratify.

By early September, Jefferson in Paris learned that elections for President and Vice President and for the House and Senate were proceeding in an orderly way. By November he had read *The Federalist*, which he declared to Madison was "the best commentary on the principles of government ever written. Here," he added, "things are going on well . . . the misfortune is that they are not yet ripe for receiving the blessings to which they are entitled. I doubt, for instance whether the body of the nation, if they could be consulted would accept of a Habeas corpus law."

He added that he was applying for leave of absence to attend to his affairs in Virginia, explaining for Madison's private ear that his daughters were reaching an age where he wanted them home among their own people. He had left home planning a five months' trip and had been abroad four years. He asked Madison to use his influence with Congress in that direction. His plan was to settle his daughters with their relatives in Virginia and then to go back to Paris to watch the process of reform.

Like Washington, he felt that Lafayette was the man to lead the way. Late in the year he wrote to Mount Vernon: "The Marquis de La Fayette is out of favor with the court but high in favor with the nation. I once feared for his personal safety but I hope he is on safe ground at present."

As events in France speeded their pace Lafayette's American friends loaded him with advice. Washington's letters were full of guarded warnings. *Festina lente* had been George Mason's motto for the Philadelphia convention. Jefferson had right along been urging on the marquis some sort of adaptation of the British limited monarchy. Despotism was bankrupt. Parliament's control over taxation was the foundation of individual liberty under the British constitution. If the French people could get hold of the purse strings they could buy from Versailles whatever dose of liberty they felt the country could absorb.

Gouverneur Morris had lately arrived in Europe on a complication of missions. Washington made him his informal representative to the

Court of St. James to see what could be done to induce the British to evacuate the line of forts along the Great Lakes which they should already have given up according to the terms of the peace treaty. He was representing Robert Morris in an effort to rebuild his monopoly of the sale of American tobacco to the farmers-general which Jefferson and Lafayette had been busy undermining. He was trying to organize a consortorium of European bankers to trade in securities. He had lands to sell and speculations of his own to promote.

Gouverneur was in Europe for the first time. He was plunging with eager curiosity into the swirling life of the disintegrating regime. With his inborn taste for cosmopolitan existence, his knowledge of the language, his flair for raffish adventure he was boring into the heart of this effervescent Parisian society so full of promise and so full of danger. He was enjoying himself. At last he was in a world where he could live as he pleased.

He was already deep in a love affair with the bright passionate browneyed Adele de Flahaut. Madame de Flahaut, a young woman of literary gifts who was to develop into a novelist of some talent, lived in the Louvre with an elderly and complacent husband. Her formal lover and the father of her son was Talleyrand, the subtle scornful Bishop of Autun. She was a much courted lady. Vigée-Lebrun, the portrait painter, said she had "the wittiest eyes in the world." The day he met his Adele, Gouverneur wrote in his diary: She speaks English and is a pleasing Woman. If I might judge by Appearances, not a sworn enemy to Intrigue."

She still, it turned out, had room for another lame man in her heart. They talked and walked together in the pleached avenues of the royal gardens. She took him to see the paintings. They admired the statuary. It was the beginning of a long relationship that filled Gouverneur's life with a great deal of pleasure and a great deal of pain.

While he was writing tender verses for the velvet eyes of the lovely Adele, Gouverneur was also casting appraising glances on the charms of the Duchess of Orleans. This was the wife of the libertine royal duke — erstwhile de Chartres, now d'Orléans — who had thrown himself into the camp of the fashionable reformers and was lavishing funds on enterprises of a frankly revolutionary cast, out of idealism, out of pique against the powers that were at Versailles, out of sheer wickedness: nobody knew just why. "She has something or other which weighs very heavy at her Heart." Gouverneur wrote of the duchess, "Perhaps the besoin d'être aimée." The tall boy was ready to love them all.

At the same time he was keeping Washington informed of every turn of affairs. Late in April of 1789 he wrote the general that their friend Lafayette was "returned from his political campaign in Auvergne crowned with Success. He had to contend with the Prejudices and the interests of his order and with the Influence of the Queen and Princes (except the Duke of Orleans) but he was too able for his Opponents. He played the Orator with as much Éclat as he ever acted the Soldier and is at this Moment as much envied and hated as his Heart could wish." Gouverneur was not yet a cynic about the French Revolution: "I say that we have an Interest in the Liberty of France. The Leaders here are our Friends. Many of them have imbibed their Principles in America and all have been fired by our Example."

Even as he wrote, the second thoughts crowded upon him: "The Materials for a Revolution in this Country are very indifferent. Every Body agrees that there is an utter Prostration of Morals but this general Position can never convey to an American mind the Degree of Depravity." Even the squire of Morrisania was shocked by the society he was plunging into so recklessly. High or low, he found no man whose word he could trust. "The great Mass of the common people have no Religion but their Priests, no law but their Superiors, no Moral but their Interest. These are the Creatures who led by drunken Curates, are now on the high road a 'la Liberté' and the first Use they make of it is to form Insurrections everywhere for want of Bread."

The dinner table of the Lafayettes on the rue de Bourbon was the center of reform. While the well intentioned conspirators debated their high hopes men not so well intentioned were airing their woes at street corners and in the taverns of the workingclass districts. They too had heard about the rights of man. Man's first right was the right to eat. While the salons of the enlightenment argued fine points of procedure the working people starved. The winter of 1788-89 turned out unusually cold. Laborers were laid off. There was nothing new about starvation in France, but this winter the French were no longer willing to starve quietly. There were riots in the provinces.

In Paris, while the carpenters and the upholsterers were at work preparing the Hall of Fugitive Pleasures for the coming meeting of the estates a riot was touched off by the rumor of a wage cut by a paper manufacturer. The press and the paper business were booming as the flood of publications on political subjects swelled to a Niagara. The working people were beginning to ask why their wages should not be enough to keep their children from hunger. They had not been educated in the methods of selfgovernment. The only way they knew to express their feelings was to sack the manufacturer's house and to burn his factory. Troops were called in. In the course of the scrimmage the unruly learned that the square pavingstones of Paris could be put to good use: barricades.

These riots shocked Jefferson as much as they did Gouverneur Mor-

ris. Jefferson wrote Carmichael, the American chargé d'affaires at the
Spanish court, that probably a hundred people had been killed. "It
was the most unprovoked & is therefore justly the most unpitied
catastrophe of the kind I ever knew. nor did the wretches know what
they wanted except to do mischief." As a practical American he was
horrified by wanton destruction, particularly of a commodity he
valued as much as paper. "It seems to have had no particular connection with the great national question now in agitation," he added; "the
want of bread is most seriously dreaded throughout the whole kingdom."

The convocation of the States-General on a fine May day in 1789
at Versailles turned out to be a brilliant affair. Jefferson wrote it
lacked only lamps and chandeliers to be an opera. Gouverneur wrote
Mrs. Robert Morris in Philadelphia a detailed account of what he
called the "dress and hattery" of the occasion. "A great Number of
fine Women and a very great Number of fine Dresses ranged round
the Hall. On a kind of Stage the Throne . . . Behind the Throne a
Cluster of Guards of the largest Size dressed in antient Costume taken
from the Times of Chivalry . . . In front of the Ministers on Benches
facing to the opposite Side of the Hall sat the representatives of the
Clergy, being Priests of all Colors, Scarlet, crimson, black, white and
grey to the Number of three hundred. In front of the Maréchals of
France on Benches facing the Clergy sat an equal number of representatives of the Nobility dressed in a Robe of Black, Waistcoats of
Cloth of Gold, and over their Shoulders so as to hang forward to their
Waist, a kind of Lappet about a quarter of a Yard wide at Top and
wider at Bottom, made of Cloth of Gold. On benches which reached
quite across the Hall and facing the Stage sat the Representatives of
the People, clothed in black . . . When the King . . . had taken his
Seat he put on his Hat, a round Beaver ornamented with white
Plumes, the Part in front turned up with a large Diamond Button in
the Center."

The King read a short speech and was cheered. Mr. Necker made
a very long speech and was cheered. Nobody cheered the Queen. Had
he been a Frenchman he would have cheered her, wrote Gouverneur.
"The King rises to depart. The Hall resounds with a long loud Vive le
Roi! He passes the Queen who rises to follow him. At this Moment
someone imbued with the Milk of human Kindness originates a faint
Vive la Reine. She makes a humble Curtsey and presents the Sinking
of the high Austrian Spirit . . . Here drops the Curtain on the first
great Act of this Drama in which Bourbon gives Freedom. His Courtiers seem to feel what he seems to be insensible of, the Pang of Greatness going off."

Lafayette, with his tall sloping forehead and his horsetoothed smile, made a fine figure all draped in cloth of gold over the sable robes of the nobility. In spite of his fine vestments the day of the great show was for him a day of torment and indecision. He had explained his predicament to his friends. "His principles," Jefferson wrote Washington, "you know are clearly with the people, but having been elected for the Noblesse of Auvergne they have laid him under express instructions to vote for the decision by orders & not persons. this would ruin him with the tiers état."

There was no equivocation about Jefferson's advice to his young friend. He wrote the marquis the next morning: "You will in the end go over wholly to the tiers état because it will be impossible for you to live in a constant sacrifice of your sentiments to the prejudices of the noblesse. but you would be received by the tiers état at any future day coldly & without confidence. this appears to me the moment to take at once that honest & manly stand with them which your own principles dictate."

Lafayette still hesitated. Everybody gave him advice. Gouverneur, who had known him since Valley Forge, told him bluntly to resign and be done with it. As the days slipped by and as the temper of the factions rose, some of his friends of the club des Trente felt he had gone over to the enemy. "If you go to Lafayette's house," Condorcet wrote the Italian liberal Mazzei, who had set himself up as an expert on American affairs because he had been a neighbor of Jefferson's in Albemarle County, "try to exorcize the devil of aristocracy that will be there to try to tempt him in the guise of a councillor of parlement or a Breton noble. For that purpose take along in your pocket a vial of Potomac water and a sprinkler made from the wood of a Continental Army rifle and make your prayers in the name of Liberty, Equality, Reason, which are but a single divinity in three persons."

Lafayette's head swam with conflicting advice. In America, Washington had always been there to make his decisions for him. Still full of doubts as to whether or not he ought to resign his seat, he went to work to put the committee to phrase a declaration of rights for the French people in touch with the American minister. No better adviser than Jefferson. Lafayette fell eagerly into the happy posture of errand boy between his committee and the author of the great Declaration of Independence.

Jefferson promptly sat down at his desk to draw up a suggested charter; annual assemblies; the States-General alone to levy taxes, to make laws with the royal consent; no arrests without legal warrant; subordination of the military to the civil authority; abolition of all special privileges.

The King must offer this charter in person to the estates and to the nation; the States-General must grant him funds for the year in return, and then promptly dissolve and go home. "You will carry back to your constituents more good than was ever effected before without violence," he wrote Lafayette's friend and fellow committee member, the Protestant Rabaut de St. Etienne, whose position in a responsible post was a sign of how far the revolution had already gone, "and you will stop exactly at the point where violence would otherwise begin. time will be gained, the public mind will continue to ripen & to be informed. a basis of support may be prepared with the people themselves, and expedients occur for gaining still more at your next meeting, & for stopping again at the point of force."

The last thought in the minds of the impatient men gathered at Versailles was to go home. Lafayette had hardly time to ride clattering out over the cobbles from Paris with Jefferson's charter in his pocket when events took the very turn towards violence Jefferson dreaded. Already, while Jefferson sat at his desk drafting his minimum charter for them in his clear nervous handwriting, the Third Estate had constituted themselves a National Assembly. Let the nobles and the clergy join them if they would.

One morning in June they found the doors barred to them when they arrived at the Hall of Fugitive Pleasures. From within came the sound of hammering as the carpenters and upholsterers prepared a new décor for a royal session.

Overnight the liberal King had listened to the advice of the faction grouped around Marie Antoinette and the Bourbon princes. Poor Louis had no head for politics. He liked hunting and eating and tinkering with clocks. He would have made a good mechanic, but he could not remember his political decisions from one day to the next. When he had to make a decision he drank.

Necker was rumored to be packing his trunks. The Bourbon was to qualify the freedom he gave. From that moment on there was no more question of gaining time or ripening the public mind. The Americans overseas had written themselves a constitution. Now the deputies of the National Assembly stormed into the covered tennis court at Versailles and swore never to go home until they had drafted a constitution for the French.

In the months to come, while occasional summer sunlight brightened the gray streets of Paris and the broad avenues of Versailles, drama reigned among the surging crowds. In the frightening acceleration of events it became, for the men who had sworn the oath of the tennis court, less a question of who should direct the revolution than who should ride the avalanche.

That Fourth of July, Jefferson entertained the American colony at the legation. As he was daily awaiting his leave of absence it was thought of as his farewell dinner. It was an enthusiastic gathering. The Lafayettes were the guests of honor. There was Joel Barlow, who had recently risen to fame as the first American poet with his *Vision of Columbus*. Like every other American, he had western lands to sell. He brought with him a letter from George Washington introducing him to Lafayette as "one of those Bards who hold the keys of the gate by which Patriots, Sages and Heroes are admitted to immortality." He was traveling around Europe as an agent for William Duer's illfated Scioto settlement scheme. John Paradise was there, a charming and winesoaked member of the Royal Society. Jefferson esteemed him as a classical scholar; and because he was of part Greek origin, and had married a Ludwell of Virginia, treated him as an honorary American citizen. There were merchants and shipowners. Except for John Paradise, who was borrowing money, they all had land or securities or American products to sell. They were ready to speculate in anything.

The ratification of the Constitution and Washington's inauguration as the first President filled the heads of every American businessman with dreams of El Dorado. The credit of the new nation was rising daily with the bankers of Europe. As Americans they were pleased with themselves and their country. They felt they were experts in the practice of liberty. Liberty paid. Every American dreamed of making himself a fortune. Every American wanted to see liberty spread over the world. Every American felt he could advise the French about how to conduct their revolution.

Gouverneur took the marquis aside after dinner: "I urge him to preserve if possible some constitutional Authority to the Body of Nobles as the only means of preserving any Liberty for the People." An aristocratic and money interest like the British gentry, to counterbalance demagoguery from below and despotism from the executive, had been Morris's political hobby all through the long debates in Philadelphia.

A few days before Gouverneur had refused to sign an elaborate testimonial which John Paradise had drawn up to present to Jefferson at that very dinner. As a representative of Robert Morris's business interests Gouverneur was disgusted with Jefferson's and Lafayette's campaign against the tobacco monopoly. He was there to sustain Robert Morris's end of the business. He claimed that Robert Morris, by breaking the hold of the Glasgow merchants in the market, was really benefiting the tobacco growers. He was becoming daily more alarmed by the course of events at Versailles; he was in no mood for the phrasemaking of idealists.

While Gouverneur stumped on his pegleg from banker's office to banker's office, in pursuit of his own speculations and of financial combinations to bolster his friend and namesake's declining credit, what he saw of men and events was convincing him that the constitution-making at Versailles was about to end in bloody disaster.

"I have steadily combated the Violence and Excess of those Persons who, either inspired by an enthusiastic Love of Freedom or prompted by sinister Designs, are disposed to drive everything to extremity," he wrote Carmichael in Madrid on that same Fourth of July that he dined with Jefferson. "Our American Example has done them good; but like all Novelties Liberty runs away with their Discretion if they have any. They want an American Constitution with the Exception of a King instead of a President, without reflecting that they have not American citizens to support that Constitution."

In his enthusiasm for a declaration of rights Lafayette forgot the technicalities of his position as an Auvergnat noble so far as to take a leading part of the work of the National Assembly. The evening of that same July 4 he scribbled a hurried note from Versailles asking Jefferson for another copy of his proposed charter. Things were happening fast, he explained. "It is very hard to navigate on such a whirling." On July 11 he moved the adoption of the completed text of the Declaration of the Rights of Man in the National Assembly.

That same night the Bourbon princes met in the Queen's boudoir to plan a counterrevolution.

From two deputies of the noblesse whom he met at his club Gouverneur heard the story: "The Queen, Count d'Artois and Dutchess de Polignac had been all Day tampering with two Regiments who were made almost drunk and every Officer was presented to the King, who was induced to give Promises, Money & c.a. & c.a. . . . Their Music came and played under her Majesty's Window. In the mean time the Marechal de Broglio was tampering in Person with the Artillery. The Plan was to reduce Paris by Famine and to take two hundred Members of the National Assembly Prisoners."

The King forgot his liberalism. The Declaration of Rights gave him a fright. He was always ready to listen to advice. This time it was the advice of his brothers. Necker was dismissed. Troops were marched into Paris.

Morris and Jefferson, drawn together as reasonable Americans in this time of crazy passions out of control, compared notes. They each saw the Swiss guard deploying their cannon on the Champs Elysees. A cavalry charge. Pavingstones were thrown. The troops joined the people.

At Versailles, Lafayette was president of the Assembly, but the Assembly had no control of the streets. Armorers' shops were pillaged. The attack on the prisons began. July 13 Morris stumped about like one of Daniel Shays' mutineers with a twig of green leaves in his hat in honor of the Third Estate. "It is somewhat whimsical," he wrote in his diary, "that this Day of Violence and Tumult is the only one in which I have dared to walk the Streets but as no carriages are abroad but the fiacres I do not hazard being crushed and I apprehend nothing from the Populace."

The next day the populace stormed the Bastille.

A liberal duke forced his way into the King's bedchamber in the middle of the night and convinced him that his only safety lay with the National Assembly. Louis turned reformer again.

The Bourbon princes fled.

Messengers were sent off to recall Necker already prudently posting towards the Swiss border. The Bishop of Autun was requested to prepare a speech for the King. Lafayette was appointed to command the National Guard.

Not even Gouverneur could restrain his enthusiasm. When Americans met on the street they congratulated each other on the great blow struck for freedom. A retired Continental colonel called to say how happy he was to be in Paris at this great moment. "So am I," Gouverneur noted in his diary, "considers as I do the Capture of the Bastille to be an instance of great intrepidity."

A couple of days later he dined with Madame de Flahaut, with her husband and the Bishop of Autun at the Louvre. "A very Agreeable Party." After dinner she took Gouverneur and Talleyrand and the rest of her guests to visit David's studio. After admiring that revolutionary painter's perspective Gouverneur with his usual brashness suggested that instead of painting Helen among the vestal virgins for the King he should paint the great event: "I tell him he had better paint the Storm of the Bastile, it will be a more fashionable Picture, & that one Trait will admit of a fine Effect. It is one of the Gardes Françaises who, having got hold of the Gate and unable to bring it down, cries to his Comrades of the Populace to pull by his Legs, and the Man has the Force and Courage to hold while a dozen of them pull him like a Rope, and bring down the Gate, so that he actually sustains the Rack. To represent him drawn out of Joint with his Head turned round, encouraging them to draw still harder, must I think have been a fine Effect. L'Evêque d'Autun agrees with me entirely in this Sentiment."

The night after the fall of the Bastille, Gouverneur ate supper at his club in the Palais Royale with his friends the deputies. He told them the Count d'Artois should be sent out of the country. They agreed.

"The Claret being better than I have tasted in France I gave them as a Toast the Liberty of the French Nation and then the City of Paris . . . This has been a Fine Day."

Lafayette's first official act was to order the Bastille's demolition. They were installing a revolutionary municipality at the hôtel de Ville. Necker was on his way back to resume the practice of his "art magick" at Versailles.

It was announced that the liberal King would show himself to his faithful subjects.

While Gouverneur was allaying Madame de Flahaut's fears as he escorted her through the press to a house where she had reserved a window on the rue St. Honoré to see the royal procession, he had his pocket picked of a handkerchief he valued as a keepsake from another lady friend. They waited in their window from eleven in the morning until four in the afternoon to see the procession in which Louis XVI entered Paris to congratulate his loyal subjects on the failure of the reactionary plot. Lafayette led the way on a white horse. He had acquired his adopted father's taste for white horses. Cockades in the city's red and blue colors were on every hat.

Lafayette had attained the dearest wish of his heart. He was the most popular man in France.

He spent the summer hurrying between his headquarters in the hôtel de Ville and the court and Assembly at Versailles. The deputies were working hard to keep ahead of events. Everyone was in a hurry. He would have to do without Jefferson's advice; the American minister was returning home. While his daughters packed their trunks Jefferson prepared careful notes on the American jury system for the committee which was writing the French constitution. The jury system, he explained, was the cornerstone of selfgovernment.

Gouverneur meanwhile drafted his own set of suggestions for a constitution. His conviction of the usefulness of an aristocracy was putting him in the bad books of the liberals, but the ferocity of the Paris mob was giving them pause. After a visit to Lafayette's aunt and Jefferson's dear friend Madame de Tessé he noted, "I find that the high Democrats begin to cool a little and I think that by degrees they will feel, tho they would not understand, Reason."

For all his aristocratic theories, Gouverneur was essentially a tenderhearted man. Stumping in and out of his carriage on sordid errands of business and pleasure that took him to all parts of the city, he saw things his revolutionary friends did not see.

"After Dinner walk a little under the Arcade of the Palais Royal waiting for my Carriage." The arcade of the Palais Royale was the paradeground for the filles de joie of those days. Undoubtedly he was casting a probing eye about him. What he saw made him forget the bulbs and curves of the little ladies of Paris.

"In this Period the Head and Body of Mr. de Foulon are introduced in Triumph. The Head on a Pike, the Body dragged naked on the Earth. Afterwards this horrible Exhibition is carried thro the different Streets. His Crime to have accepted a Place in the Ministry. This mutilated Form of an old Man of seventy five is shewn to Bertier, his Son in Law, the Intend't. of Paris, and afterwards he also is put to Death and cut to Pieces, the Populace carrying about the mangled Fragments with a Savage Joy. Gracious God what a people!"

While Lafayette at Versailles was trying to behave as Washington would have behaved in "the whirling" of the National Assembly, throughout France the country people were taking the law in their own hands, dividing up feudal lands, burning manors and châteaux and taking particular care that the title deeds should not escape the flames. In the Assembly the night of August 4 Adrienne's brother, the Vicomte de Noailles, and Lafayette's bosom friend de Lameth moved the abolition of titles and feudal privileges. The young nobles who had fought in America rose to back them up.

The old regime was tumbling. In heady phrases the Assembly put the seal of its approval on each separate act of demolition. France was without a government.

The first result of the crash of the Versailles bureaucracy was the stalling of the economic machinery of the whole of France. Nobody got paid. The cost of living soared. In Paris there was no bread. "For some days since," Jefferson wrote Jay at the end of August, "the people have besieged the doors of the bakers, scrambled with one another for bread, collected in squads all over the city & need only some slight incident to lead them to excesses which may end in nobody can tell what."

Early in September, Lafayette scribbled a hasty note to Jefferson begging him "for liberty's sake" to arrange a dinner for himself and a group of deputies at the American legation. They wanted his advice. They wanted a neutral spot where they could quietly talk over plans for a coalition with common aims tightly enough linked to drive a workable constitution through the Assembly. There was no time to be lost. Lafayette and his friends must furnish France with constitutional government before the fabric of society broke down entirely.

Thirty years later when he was writing his autobiography Jefferson still remembered vividly "the coolness and candour" of these men's arguments, their "logical reasoning and chaste eloquence." They decided for a limited monarchy with a single legislative chamber, for a "suspensive" veto by the King on all laws passed. Lafayette proudly declared that as head of the National Guard he would see to it that whatever constitution they established would have the force of law. His adopted country had written a constitution; he would see to it that his native land had one too.

A few days later, after Jefferson and his daughters had already left for Havre in the phaeton, while Petit his French steward and the colored servants followed in the chariot, Gouverneur dined at the Lafayettes'. He took the ci-devant marquis aside after they arose from the table to urge "that he must immediately discipline the Troops and make himself obeyed, that this Nation is used to be governed . . . On the subject of Discipline," he noted in his diary, "his Countenance shews the Self Accuser for he has given the Command to Officers who know nothing of their Business." He went on to talk about the great pressing need of the moment: "I mention to him the Subject of Subsistance."

Instead of immediate practical plans for feeding the city all Gouverneur could get out of Lafayette was an invitation to meet with a new committee that would be sitting on the subject during the next week.

Before next week came the people of Paris had taken the question of subsistence into their own hands. While Jefferson was at Havre waiting for a storm to subside so that he could sail to England on the packet, he received an excited letter from young Short, whom he had left in charge of the legation: "the scarcity of bread continuing on sunday evening the 4th inst. crowds assembled as on former occasions in the Palais Royale . . . on monday morning a number of women assembled at the place de Grève and took possession of the hôtel de ville — there they found some old arms &c — the Marquis de la fayette, informed of this circumstance, went to the hôtel de ville, recovered possession of it & endeavored though in vain, to recover also the place de Grève — the women to the number of 5 or 6 thousand marched off to Versailles . . . the people & soldiers joined in insisting that the Mrqs. de la fayette should march with them to Versailles — he . . . was forced to yield & about half after five set off at the head of his troops — the women had arrived at Versailles crying du pain du pain."

The crowd broke into the palace. Gentlemen of the King's bodyguard were chased through the corridors and shot down. The Queen had to run in her nightgown to take refuge in the King's chamber. The cry was that the King must come to Paris. Next day Louis agreed and Lafayette, somewhat shamefaced perhaps, led a second parade into the city. They brought the Queen and the royal children along. "We have the baker and the baker's wife and the little baker," was the chant of the crowds returning in triumph. The royal family remained under arrest in the Tuileries. The pang of greatness passing off.

Versailles overnight became a museum. The Assembly followed the King to Paris and set to work in the riding school of the Tuileries to elaborate a constitution according to the sketch Lafayette and his friends had drawn up at Jefferson's dinner table, which they hoped would combine the best features of European monarchy with the best features of American republicanism.

When the huge walls of the Bastille were torn down stone by stone Lafayette saved the great key of the main gate to send to his adopted father in America.

"How often, my beloved General," he found time to write to Mount Vernon from the midst of the debates on royal veto, "have I wanted your wise advices and friendly support . . . Now that everything that was is no more, a new building is erecting, not perfect by far but sufficient to ensure freedom." "As everything has been destroied, and not much new building is yet above ground, there is much room for critics and calumnies," he admitted in the letter he entrusted to Tom Paine to forward to Washington from England along with the key. "Give me leave, my dear General," he added with a flourish, "to present you with a picture of the Bastille just as it looked a few days after I ordered its demolition, with a main kea of that fortress of despotism — it is a tribute which I owe as a son to my adoptive father, as an aide de camp to my General, as a Missionary of Liberty to its Patriarch."

3.   " . . . the Systems taken out of Books . . ."

"This Country is as near to Anarchy" Gouverneur wrote Washington, "as Society can approach without Dissolution. There are some able Men in the national Assembly, yet the best Heads among them would not be injured by Experience . . . They have all that romantic Spirit and all those romantic ideas of Government, which happily for America, we were cured of before it was too late." The Assembly, which was now affectionately known as la constituante, was hard at work in the old Tuileries riding academy: "with much Imagination," so he put it, but "little Knowledge, Judgement or Reflection," on the constitution of a limited monarchy supposed to combine the best features of the unwritten code that ruled Great Britain, which Montesquieu had taught the French to admire, with some of the new republican institutions inaugurated in America.

Administration stagnated as the constitution advanced clause by
clause. The King was still a prisoner. Gouverneur described him
scornfully to Washington: "If this reigning prince were not the small
beer character that he is, there can be but little Doubt that watching
Events and making a tolerable Use of them he would regain his Authority, but what will you have from a Creature who situated as he is eats,
drinks and sleeps well, and laughs and is as merry a Grig as Lives?"

The King was governed in everything by the Assembly. The Assembly was made up of disgruntled aristocrats, of middleclass people
who were "really friends of good government, and of what are called
here the Enragés, that is the Madmen . . . of that Class which in
America is known as pettifogging Lawyers, together with a Host of
Curates . . . This 1st Party is in close Alliance with the Populace
here . . . They have already unhinged every Thing . . . The middle
Party who mean well, have unfortunately acquired their Ideas of Government from Books and are admirable Fellows upon Paper; but as
it happens somewhat unfortunately that the Men who live in the
World are very different from those who dwell in the Heads of Phi-
losophers, it is not to be wondered at if the Systems taken out of
Books are fit for Nothing but to be put into Books again."

Gouverneur had spent hour after hour listening to their debates:
"They discuss Nothing in their Assembly. One large half of the Time
is spent Hallowing and bawling . . . Such as intend to hold forth write
their Names on a Tablet . . . and are heard in the Order that their
Names are written down, if the others will hear them, which very
often they refuse to do but keep up a continual Uproar till the Orator
leaves the Pulpit."

The speeches were written more with an eye to publication than
for practical legislative purposes: "There is another Ceremony which
the Arguments go through and which does not fail to affect the Form
at least, and perhaps the Substance. They are read before Hand in a
small Society of young Men and Women, and generally the fair Friend
of the Speaker is one, or else the fair whom he means to make his
friend, and the Society very politely give their Approbation, unless
the Lady who gives the Tone to that Circle chances to reprehend
Something, which is of course altered, if not amended. Do not suppose I am playing the Traveller. I have assisted at some of these
Readings . . ."

Gouverneur and his Adele of the brown velvet eyes moved in the
circle of the constitution makers. At one point he noted in his diary
that Adele had proposed to him, half jokingly, that the two of them
should rule France by manipulating the Queen through the Queen's
physician, who was a devotee of Adele's. The regime Adele was going

to prescribe for Marie Antoinette was a man every night and a mass every morning. *"Enfin,"* she told Gouverneur, *"mon Ami, vous et moi nous gouvernerons la France."* "It is an odd combination," wrote Gouverneur in his diary, "but the Kingdom is actually in much worse Hands."

"At present the People are fully determined to support the Assembly," Gouverneur explained to Washington, "an Extension of Priviledges and a Remission of Taxes to the lower Class has marked every Stage of their Progress . . . In Lieu of Taxes remitted other Taxes must be paid . . . Hence must arise Bickerings and Heartburnings among the different Districts . . . Hence will result a Loss of public Credit . . . As to Mr Necker he is one of those People who has obtained a much greater Reputation than he has any Right to . . . his writings on Finance teem with that Sort of Sensibility which makes the Fortune of modern Romances, and which is entirely suited to this lively Nation, who love to read but hate to think. Hence his Reputation . . . He is utterly ignorant also of Politics, by which I mean Politics in the great Sense, or that sublime Science which embraces for its Object the Happiness of Mankind. Consequently he knows not what constitution to form nor how to obtain the Consent of others to such as he wishes. From the Moment of convening the States General he has been afloat upon the wide Ocean of Incidents. But what is most extraordinary is that Mr Necker is a very poor financier . . ."

Ever since the convening of the States-General, Necker had been dodging the problems of national bankruptcy (in the Assembly it was only Mirabeau who had the courage to pronounce the dreadful word: banqueroute) and inflation. When he could borrow no more he had proposed a patriotic capital levy which, being voluntary, had been unproductive, to say the least. Now he was attempting to raise a fund from the sale of lands confiscated from the Church and the Crown. Since there was no way of immediately realizing the ten or twelve millions of pounds they were supposed to be worth, Necker was selling anticipations of this hoped for revenue which he called *assignats*. Gouverneur Morris hardly needed to point out to George Washington that this maneuver would reduce the value of the lands, if it did not make them altogether unsalable. Consequently the value of the *assignats* must go tumbling too.

If Necker resigned the prospects were even worse: "I sincerely wish I could say there were able Men at Hand to take the Helm, should the present Pilot abandon the Ship . . . The new Order of Things cannot endure." He had no good news to tell: "All Europe just now is like a Mine ready to explode"; so he ended his letter.

Necker, as Gouverneur put it, was "ineptious." The King was impotent; the ministers were donothings. It was the gaudy Mirabeau's oratory that ruled the Assembly; any decision that was reached resulted from Mirabeau's connivings. Gouverneur despised him. Mirabeau was a venal scoundrel: "His understanding is I believe impaired by the Perversion of his Heart." One of Mirabeau's compelling motives was jealousy of Lafayette.

"Our friend Lafayette . . . acts now a splendid but dangerous Part," Gouverneur told Washington in another letter. "Unluckily he has given in to Measures as to the Constitution which he does not heartily approve, and he heartily approves many Things which Experience will demonstrate to be injurious. He left America, you know, when his Education was but half finished . . . he did not learn to be a Government Maker."

4. *The Festival of the Federations*

Lafayette's popularity reached its climax in the great Festival of the Federations held on the Champs de Mars on the first anniversary of the taking of the Bastille. The Constituent Assembly had completed its work. Lafayette had contrived a confederation of the men of the National Guard from all over France. It was the guardsmen who were to assure the stability of the new regime. Every unit sent its representatives to Paris to swear allegiance to the constitution. The Channel packets were crowded with English radicals and reforming Whigs hastening to take part in the triumph of enlightened liberty. Revolutionists from every European nation pressed into Paris. Tom Paine arrived in time to carry an American flag in the parade.

The constitution was read to an enormous concourse of guardsmen from all the departments of France and from all the sections of Paris, drawn up in a hollow square on the immense parade ground. The French constituted themselves a federated nation with a constitutional king at their head. The King swore to support this constitution. Assisted by four hundred priests with red white and blue sashes thrown over their white vestments, the Biship of Autun performed High Mass on the towering altar of the fatherland. He blessed the banners of the eightythree departments.

Lafayette read out the oath: "We swear to be forever faithful to the Nation, to the Law and to the King, to protect persons and property, and the circulation of grain within the kingdom; the collecting of public contributions under any form; to remain united to all Frenchmen by the indissoluble bonds of Fraternity."

To Liberty and Equality, Fraternity was added.

With tears streaming down their faces the guardsmen shouted: "Je le jure." Cannon roared. There were discharges of musketry. At dusk fireworks filled the sky.

Some of the English complained about the poor marching order of the troops, but stocky bushyhaired young William Short who had been mingling with the crowds all night wrote Gouverneur Morris: "the spectacle of that day was really sublime & magnificent — the most perfect order and harmony reigned as well then, as at the illuminations & bals of the Sunday following — but the streets & Palais Royale presented every evening during the course of the week such collections of people in uniform, returning after numerous dinners and parading with the women they had picked up in their way, as excited reflections of a disagreeable nature to those who wished to see a patriot & sober legislator in every *fédéré* . . . Instead of this the Palais Royale had the air of the general rendezvous for the votaries of Mars, Bacchus & Venus."

"The People will never continue attached to any Man who will sacrifice his Duty to their Caprice," Gouverneur had written Short from London. In a rapid exchange of letters they had been deploring the rift that was appearing between Lafayette and his old friends Lameth and Barnave, who were becoming leaders of the new political club which had taken to meeting in the abandoned convent of the Jacobins. "I remember in one of the early Addresses of Congress something was said about the Luxury of being free. Now the french Genius may perhaps refine as much upon this Luxury as they used to upon the other . . ." He was beginning to wonder where this refinement of the idea of liberty would lead them.

Short was writing from the château of the enlightened duc de la Rochefoucauld where he had been adopted into the family to the point of falling desperately in love with the duke's lovely young wife, Rosalie. In the country quiet he was thinking over his conversations with the National Guardsmen "in the hurry bustle & confusion of those orgies." "One thing which was very observable however among these *fédérés*," he told Gouverneur, "was their principles of Royalism . . . they were far from shewing these democratic principles which prevail in a part of the national Assembly . . . The marquis de la fayette seemed to have taken full possession of the *fédérés* — his popular manners pleased them beyond measure & of course they approved his principles — When I left Paris he was adored by them — that moment may be regarded as the zenith of his influence — he made no use of it . . . the time will come perhaps when he will repent having not seized that opportunity of giving such a complexion to the revolution as every good citizen ought to desire.

"I saw your friends at the P. Royal the day before I left Paris," he added, "you are their Magnus Apollo in whatever relates to Politics & Government & Revolutions — they quote you frequently to prove that the constitution can never march, notwithstanding the new song of *ça ira, ça ira.*"

"It will work, it will work," sung to an old tune that Marie Antoinette had made popular at her fêtes at the Petit Trianon, turned out to be the popular refrain of the whole festival.

> "Ça ira, ça ira, les aristocrates à la lanterne,
> Ça ira, ça ira, les aristocrates on les pendra,"

the guardsmen and their girlfriends sang as they marched with torches over the cobbles of the deep stone streets.

It worked so badly that before three months were out Monsieur Necker was once more, and for the last time, packing his bags to seek the seclusion of his Swiss lake. The wave that engulfed him was a wave of *assignats*.

IX The President's Court

1. Homecoming

Thomas Jefferson landed from Europe at Norfolk, Virginia, about noon on November 23, 1789. He came ashore with his daughters and his servants and his forty odd cases of furniture and books and diplomatic records, and the crates of plants for Monticello and the Normandy sheepdog he bought while waiting for the packet at Havre and the pups she produced during the crossing.

The tobacco port was full of ships. Wharves and warehouses burned during the war were in the midst of rebuilding. The town was so crowded that some gentlemen had to vacate their rooms at Lindsay's hotel to give the returning envoy and his family a place to lay their heads. Jefferson had hardly time to get the smell of pitch and bilge out of his nostrils, or the lurching and creaking of the ship during the twentysix day crossing out of his head, when the news reached him that President George Washington had chosen him for Secretary of State in the new general government and that the Senate had confirmed his appointment.

The news came as a shock to him. His plan had been to settle his daughters at home, to take six months off to straighten out his plantation affairs, and then to go back to Paris to finish out his tour of duty as minister. He had learned to enjoy Paris; the cookery, the concerts, the architecture, the conversations with men of learning and wit, the excursions with charming women in which the pleasures of sightseeing and landscape were spiced with just the right spice of flirtation; and the sensation that Europe's misty capital gave every foreigner, of being at the great world's hub.

By his enthusiasm for learning and the grace of his conversation and his passionate libertarian convictions he had won himself a role in the events being enacted there, a role that suited him, the role of mentor and counselor to the principal actors from behind the scenes. He had undergone the excitements and the hopes and fears of the opening of the great drama. It was his dearest wish to watch the unfolding of the remaining acts and to applaud the happy conclusion he expected.

His friends and the local committees gave him little time to think out his plans for the future. At every stage he was met by addresses of welcome. There were moisteyed reunions with old associates; at Williamsburg with George Wythe and with the Reverend James Madison, the astronomer and surveyor and Episcopal minister who was now president of William and Mary; with the dear Eppes family linked to his by such tender ties; with the Tuckahoe Randolphs, Thomas Mann and his sallow gangling son of the same name.

Everywhere he went he found Virginia full of stir, new houses building, canals under construction. As communications improved, young men were packing up their families and moving west in search of fresh land. From the Eppes place he wrote young Short that Short's brother Peyton had married and was moving to Kentucky. The new locks in the James River canal were complete. A pontoon bridge twentytwo hundred feet long had been built at Richmond.

"There is one street in Richmond," he proudly added, ". . . which would be considered as handsomely built in any city in Europe . . . Our new capitol" — the building he drew the plans for with the help of Clérisseau, the French antiquarian and architect in whose studio he had steeped himself in the study of the Hellenic revival — "when the corrections are made, of which it is susceptible, will be an edifice of first rate dignity, whenever it shall be finished with the proper ornaments belonging to it (which will not be in this age) will be worthy of being exhibited alongside the most celebrated remains of antiquity . . . it's extreme convenience," he added with understandable satisfaction, "has acquired it universal approbation."

The Jeffersons found so many friends to entertain them on the way that they barely reached Monticello by Christmas. Martha Jefferson, in an account she wrote years later of the trip home, told how a crowd of Negroes from all the Jefferson plantations met their carriage and four at the foot of the mountain. "When the door of the carriage was opened, they received him in their arms and bore him to the house, crowding around and kissing his hands and feet — some blubbering and crying — others laughing. It seemed impossible to satisfy their anxiety to touch and kiss the very earth that bore him . . . They believed him to be one of the greatest, and they knew him to be one of the best of men and kindest of masters."

2. *". . . the greatest man in the world"*

After Christmas James Madison rode over from Montpeleier. Although the two friends had corresponded continually Jefferson must have been struck by how the diffident young bookworm he had known in Congress and in the Virginia legislature had matured in the five years since he had seen him. Madison's face had rounded out and his small figure had become stocky and well set. His complexion had become ruddy. He walked with a peculiar bouncing stride that made him look taller than he was. In his struggle to put Jefferson's legislative program through the recalcitrant Assembly in their home state he had become a master of parliamentary infighting. He was now serving in the House of Representatives in the first session of the new Congress. He had become Washington's closest adviser on legislative matters and as majority leader was showing the skill and assurance of a prime parliamentarian. He played a large part in the squelching of the effort by John Adams and some of his "hightoned" New England friends to puff up the dignity of federal officials by titles borrowed from the ceremonious Dutch.

It was Madison who had put the first ten amendments to the Constitution through the first session of the First Congress. In New York during the spring of 1788 he spent laborious weeks weeding the clauses he considered most essential out of the welter of suggestions which the states had tacked onto their ratifications.

Massachusetts and New York insisted on the need for setting forth in unmistakable terms the limits to the power of the general government. In Pennsylvania a dissident convention had gathered at Harrisburg for that particular purpose. South Carolina and North Carolina demanded that the rights of the states and of the citizens be itemized. Maryland and Virginia virtually made their ratifications contingent on the passage of a bill of rights.

The ten clauses, protecting freedom of religion, speech, press and assembly; asserting the citizens' right to bear arms; prohibiting unreasonable searches and seizures, excessive bail, cruel and unusual punishments, and imprisonment without due process of law; and reserving to the states or to the people all rights not explicitly vested in the general government, had passed the Senate and were now speeding through the various state legislatures.

American Whigs told each other that there was something particularly auspicious politically about the year '88. 1688 was the date of the Glorious Revolution in England. Now in 1788 that revolution was in the course of being completed in America by the addition of a bill of rights to the new Constitution. To Jefferson, who considered a bill of rights necessary indeed, all this was gratifying news.

Madison was becoming known for a humorous streak, for sly digs at personalities and saucy stories over the wine after dinner. Although his visit to Monticello was primarily a visit of friendship, he had been charged by the President to do his best to induce Jefferson to accept the office of Secretary of State. Jefferson admitted that he could handle the foreign affairs part of it but he claimed to be doubtful of his ability in domestic administration. He had not forgotten the miseries and frustrations of his second term as governor of Virginia. He dreaded exposing himself again to the criticism and backbiting inseparable from politics at home.

Madison laughed off the domestic part of the work. Jefferson's influence was needed. Every act of the new administration would mold the habits of the government for all time. New York was a nest of Tories. The monarchical faction there, which had launched three years before the ridiculous project of putting the Bishop of Osnaburg, the third George's son, on an American throne, was still active. Jefferson was needed to give the example of republican simplicity.

Madison can hardly have kept it to himself that Jefferson's old friend John Adams was considered a leader in these monarchical vagaries. He was making himself a laughingstock by the airs he was putting on as Vice President. The senators called him His Rotundity. If anybody could ease him out of this strange mood Jefferson could. By the time Madison rode home to start north for the winter session of Congress he had just about convinced Jefferson that, however much he would like to go on observing the experiments of the reformers of France, his duty lay at the seat of government.

"After three months of parleying," so Jefferson put it, he accepted the office. Washington begged him to lose no time in reporting for duty. "Your desire that I should come as quickly as possible is a sufficient reason for me to postpone every matter of business that admits postponement," Jefferson answered.

He readily postponed the unpalatable business of settling his own financial affairs, buying time by a not too advantageous agreement with his English creditors for interest payments on the debt which he had inherited along with his dead wife's plantations from her father John Wayles. To raise cash he wrote a Dutch banker to ask for a two thousand dollar loan. The one matter of business that did not admit postponement was an arrangement with Thomas Mann Randolph as to what settlements they should make on their respective children. Young Thomas Mann Randolph and Martha Jefferson had announced that they wanted to get married.

The match was the most Virginian conceivable. The young people were cousins. They had known each other all their lives. Young

Thomas Mann was a highstrung young fellow of some capacity and not too much application who had recently returned home from somewhat desultory political studies at the University of Edinburgh. Jefferson had been writing him letters of advice about a consistent plan of study for the law. Thomas Mann Randolph Sr., had been Jefferson's father's ward. He and Jefferson were raised together and had their first schooling side by side in the little plastered schoolhouse at Tuckahoe. Instead of losing a daughter by the marriage Jefferson was gaining a son.

He was more careful of his daughter's financial affairs than of his own. Perhaps already recognizing a certain lack of judgment about these matters in his soninlaw, he settled the thousand acres in Bedford County that was his part of the agreement directly on his daughter and her children. Martha was then a tall redheaded girl of seventeen. Some people called her homely. She had inherited Jefferson's looks along with a share of his brains. Since her mother's death she had been closer to her father than to anyone on earth. The marriage hardly affected their relationship. Thomas Mann Jr., for all his moods, proved an affectionate and appreciative soninlaw. Martha grew up everything a man could hope for in a wife and mother. The Randolphs eventually settled at Monticello and furnished Jefferson with a mob of grandchildren and with the closeknit family group he so craved and made his home a nest of refuge for him from the stings and galls of political conflict.

The young people were married February 23. A few days later, leaving them in charge of Monticello and of his younger daughter Polly, Jefferson started on the long wintry drive to New York. It was a snowy season. He found the roads so bad that he shipped his phaeton north by sea from Alexandria and continued his journey by the public stages. The jouncing and the coldfooted discomfort of the trip were made up to him by the interest he felt in mixing, free from the formalities of office, with the general run of his fellow citizens. He never missed such an opportunity when public life gave him a chance.

To break the journey he stopped off a couple of days in Philadelphia to call on old friends. He paid his respects to David Rittenhouse, the philosophical clock and instrument maker whom he esteemed so extravagantly for his model of the solar system and whom he was consulting about his plans for a thoroughgoing decimal system for coinage and for weights and measures. The congenial ladies at Mrs. House's boardinghouse, where he and Madison had been the star boarders in the days of the old Congress, undoubtedly inquired anxiously if Mr. Madison showed any signs of getting married. It worried the little man's friends that he stayed so long single. They had all played the frenzied matchmakers eight years before when young Madison was courting pretty Kitty Floyd, only to see him turned down, to Jefferson's especial chagrin.

Jefferson could hardly go through Philadelphia without visiting Benjamin Franklin. "I called on the venerable and beloved Franklin," Jefferson remembered when years later he was writing his autobiography. "He was then on the bed of sickness from which he never rose. my recent return from a country where he had left so many friends, and the perilous convulsions to which they had been exposed, revived all his anxieties to know what part they had taken, what had been their course, and what their fate. he went over all in succession with a rapidity and animation almost too much for his strength."

Since he had concluded his last public duties as a member of the Constitutional Convention and as president of Pennsylvania's Executive Council, Benjamin Franklin at eightyfour knew very well that the stone that had tortured him for years would soon be the end of him. He had been preparing himself for death by getting his papers in order. On fine days when he was well enough, he would still sit awhile under the great mulberry tree in his yard, chatting in his old joking commonsensical way with the endless procession of people who came to see him and to marvel at him as they would at Niagara Falls.

Washington, when he wrote him six months before, had expressed the feelings of every American: "Would to God, my dear Sir, that I could congratulate you upon the removal of that excruciating pain under which you labor and that your existence might close with as much ease to yourself, as its continuance has been beneficial to our Country and useful to mankind! Or if the united wishes of a free people, joined with the earnest prayers of every friend to Science and humanity, could relieve the body from pains or infirmities, you could claim an exemption on this score. But this cannot be, and you have within yourself the only resource to which we can confidently apply for relief: *a philosophic mind.*"

This from Washington was the extremest compliment. Franklin had been amusing himself writing his will. Maybe some hint of the monarchical rumors was in his mind when he wrote, matching compliments with the President: "My fine Crabtree walking stick with a gold head curiously wrought in the form of a cap of Liberty I give to the friend of Mankind, General Washington. If it were a sceptre, he had merited it, and would become it."

Jefferson found him bedridden and very weak, but with his mind untarnished. It was the last month of his life.

At his inn Jefferson received a visit from his old acquaintance of the early days of Congress, Benjamin Rush. Dr. Rush had been a great friend of John Adams. He was a man of many stubborn dogmas: republicanism was one. He had evidently been hearing tales of how

Adams had come home from the courts of Europe full of monarchical obsessions and had been making a holy show of himself by the splendor of his dress and by driving six horses to his coach and by the selfsatisfied simper he wore on his face as he sat under the crimson canopy to preside over the Senate.

Rush evidently feared some such aristocratic change might have come over Jefferson. "It was the first time I saw him since his return from France. He was plain in his dress and unchanged in his manners," the doctor noted with evident relief in his commonplace book. "He still professed himself attached to the republican form of government, and deplored the change of opinion on this subject of John Adams, of whom he spoke with respect and affection as a great and upright man. He said Mr. Madison was the greatest man in the world."

3.   The Seat of Government

The trip from Albemarle County to New York was turning out a long grueling journey through the worst of the winter weather. The stages, big springless wagons with benches across them and leather curtains to keep out the sleet, dragged and jounced through the mud and snow at two or three miles an hour by day and at half that speed by night. Jefferson had a couple of saddle horses along in charge of his personal servants so that he could relieve the tedium of the stage by occasionally riding. It was March 21 before he reached the ferry that carried him across from Paulus Hook to the huddle of tall brick houses, half hidden by the crowded masts and rigging of the shipping tied up in the slips at the tip of the beautiful rocky island that was the town of New York.

Although the day was Sunday, as soon as he left his baggage in the rambling frame buildings of the City Tavern, he walked up the Broad Way to the fine new mansion with balconies overlooking the North River which the erratic Count de Moustier had recently been filling with the scandal and splendor of the French legation. It stood a block below Trinity Church. It was considered the finest residence in the city. The President and Mrs. Washington and her grandchildren and the family secretaries and aides who made up the President's official family had recently moved there from Samuel Osgood's smaller house on Cherry Street which had been considered quite fine enough to be the official home of the president of the old Continental Congress.

The President himself attended to every detail of the placing of the great mirrors in the public rooms and the tinting of the new landscape wallpaper that was coming into fashion. The upholsterer for the

French legation furnished hangings in the latest Parisian style. "Which way soever I turn my eyes," Thomas Lee Shippen wrote his father after having been put up for the night in one of the bedrooms, "I find a triumphal Car, a Liberty Cap, a Temple of Fame, or the Hero of Heroes . . . on the hangings."

Jefferson found George Washington just home from morning services at St. Paul's. Jefferson had not seen him since their conference in Annapolis seven years before, when Jefferson explained to him his objection to the hereditary principle in the Society of the Cincinnati. Most likely the President was wearing a suit of the gray broadcloth he had bought from the Hartford mills as half mourning after his mother's death. He always wore American made goods when he could. Though his bearing was still erect and stately the man had aged.

Washington was only fiftyeight, but it was as if his life of ease since his retirement from command of the army had shaken the iron constitution that had stood up against all the fatigues and exertions of the war. His face showed traces of the illnesses of the last few years, the anthrax that had almost killed him during the past summer, the ague and rheumatism that had plagued him at Mount Vernon. The recent loss of a number of teeth gave a caved look to his cheeks. He was feeling the effects of lack of exercise and confinement as well as to the worries and perplexities that went along with his official duties.

The day he left home to take the oath of office Washington wrote in his diary, "I bade adieu to Mt. Vernon, to private life, and to domestic felicity and with a mind oppressed with more anxious and painful sensations than I have words to express, set out for New York." His year in office had not been all anxious and painful sensations: no man alive could fail to be affected by the love and adulation that surrounded him; but, with all his gift for administration, the task of inventing the daily routine of the new government was immensely wearing.

No one had ever been President of the United States before. He was thoroughly conscious that every move he made would set a precedent for the future. "I walk on untrodden ground. There is scarcely any part of my conduct which may not hereafter be drawn into precedent," he wrote in answer to a congratulatory letter from Mrs. Macaulay, the English bluestocking writer of popular histories who had visited him a few years before at Mount Vernon. He was tortured, as so often before in crucial moments of his career, by a feeling of inadequacy.

He was leaning heavily on his cabinet for advice. With the plausible and tireless Hamilton who held the prime post of Secretary of the Treasury, he had slipped back into the old confidential relationship. He had absolute trust in stout solid Henry Knox who was another holdover from his military staff. With John Adams his Vice President he was hardly congenial. Though he respected Adams' speculative mind and his learning he found in him a lack of the ordinary day to day common sense he prized so much. In his choice of Edmund Randolph for Attorney General he had deferred to a great Virginia name and to Randolph's reputation as a statesmanlike lawyer which had someway survived his backing and filling on the subject of the Constitution.

Washington's conception of the presidency was at that time that of a chairman of the board. He wanted the makeup of his cabinet to reflect the national consensus. After a good deal of consultation with Madison he had chosen Jefferson as a counterweight against the possibly too "hightoned" tendencies of Hamilton and Adams and Knox. It was with real relief that he saw the tall rawboned plainly dressed Virginian advancing to meet him across the fine new green carpet of his public room. He needed his help. Within a few months he was signing a note to his minister of state "affectionately yours." "I feel myself supported by able co-adjutors who harmonize extremely well together," he wrote Lafayette.

Jefferson met Washington again on the two following days to talk over the duties of his office. Immediately he plunged into the paperwork. "Much business," he wrote his soninlaw, "had been put by for my arrival, so that I found myself all at once involved under an accumulation of it."

His function as he saw it at that time was simply that of a secretary carrying out the President's policies. He felt that Washington's prestige was all important to the establishment of a national government. "If the President can be preserved a few years till habits of authority and obedience can be established generally, we have nothing to fear," he wrote when he in turn reported hopefully on the prospects of the new government to Lafayette. He consulted Washington on every detail.

To help him with these details in the two rooms of John Jay's old Department of Foreign Affairs, Jefferson found a chief clerk, a couple of underclerks and a messenger boy. In addition to foreign affairs he was charged with the custody of the great seal, with the publication and distribution of the acts of Congress, and with the correspondence with federal law officers, to which later were added the management of the Mint and the taking of the census. A few days after he arrived Congress charged him with the granting of patents and copyrights and asked him to prepare a report on coinage and on weights and measures. He wrote home that he feared the office would leave him little leisure.

New York was fast catching up with Philadelphia. With some difficulty, since the rebuilding had not kept up with the growth of population, Jefferson found himself a cramped little house on Maiden Lane where, as was his habit wherever he moved, he went right to work to give his architectural hobby free reign in redesigning the rooms. His location turned out to have one pleasant feature. He was living across from Mrs. Elsworth's where Madison boarded and the congenial Virginia Englishman John Beckley, who had been clerk of the House of Delegates and whom Madison had managed to get appointed clerk to the new House of Representatives, and where congressmen sympathetic to Jefferson's and Madison's notions tended to forgather.

In the quarter of a century since Jefferson, a law student on vacation, had first seen New York, the city had lost its quaint Dutch look. L'Enfant's Federal Hall, in the talented Frenchman's adaptation to the American scene of the styles recently fashionable at Versailles, dominated Wall Street with the great gold eagle of the Cincinnati ensconced in its pediment. There were new wharves and warehouses along the waterfront and great ships in the slips. Fortunes were being made in imports and exports.

That same spring Washington described the general prosperity enthusiastically to Lafayette. He told of the excellent prices farmers were getting for their last year's grain crop and the profits New York merchants were making on the triangular run the illfated John Ledyard had suggested to Robert Morris some years before: round the Horn to the northwest coast for sea otters; then to Canton with the pelts and back to New York with spices and tea. The skippers of two vessels had deposited a hundred thousand dollars in duty at the customhouse without too much cutting the owners' profits. "I mention this," he added apologetically, not wanting to seem too mercenary, "to shew the spirit of enterprize that prevails."

Jefferson himself must have been pleased to know that the whalers he saw anchored in the harbor owed some of the success of their ventures to the arrangements he and Lafayette had made with the court of Versailles to cut the import duty on their products.

The spirit of enterprise was everywhere. The merchants' countinghouses in the narrow streets below Wall were roaring with boom spirit. Even more than in the China trade, or in the western lands that were the perpetual objects of blue sky trading, the moneymen who crowded the Coffee House near Hanover Square were interested in what measures Congress would take to fund the new nation's war debts. The state debts and the continental debt were the prime speculation.

The city was full of men who had come out of the war more pros-

perous than their fellow citizens. Many of them were piling up speculative schemes which would, if they succeeded, bring them wealth no
American had ever yet dreamed of. They, and especially their wives,
yearned to set themselves up permanently above the common herd.
The old country offered a model. There the constitutional king sat at
the top of the social pyramid and aristocracy was considered part of
a divine order and tradesmen and commoners knew their place. While
Jefferson was in Europe the merchants and bankers of the seaport
towns had begun to think of themselves as the rich and wellborn,
ordained by God to top the social pyramid.

"We were educated in royalism," Jefferson had admitted in a tolerant mood, writing Madison from Paris, "no wonder if some of us retain that idolatry still." Hopefully he added, "Our young people are
educated in republicanism."

4. "... Splendour and Majesty ..."

His first months in New York made Jefferson doubt the truth
of those last words. "The President received me cordially and my Colleagues & the circle of principal citizens, apparently with welcome,"
he wrote years later in his preface to the Anas, "the courtesy of dinner parties given me as a stranger newly arrived among them, placed
me at once in their familiar society. but I cannot describe the wonder
and mortification with which the table conversations filled me. politics were the chief topic, and a preference of kingly, over republican,
government was evidently the favorite sentiment. an apostate I could
not be; nor yet a hypocrite; and I found myself, for the most part,
the only advocate on the republican side of the question, unless
among the guests, there chanced to be some member of that party
from the legislative houses."

The President's court was imbued with protocol. When George
Washington asked John Adams how he should conduct the social life
of the presidency, the Braintree lawyer answered in a written opinion, "Neither Dignity nor Authority can be supported by human
Minds, collected into Nations of any great Numbers, without a Splendour and Majesty in some Degree proportioned to them."

John Adams, whom with pert Abigail, his wife, Jefferson had come
to love dearly when he had so depended on their company during his
first year abroad, by the publication of his ponderous commentary on
Davila's French Civil Wars, had become the philosopher of the authoritarian party. What he had been trying to prove, he explained
years later, was not so much that monarchy was a desirable institu-

tion as that the people were not necessarily the best keepers of their own liberties. Liberty and order were his aims. He wanted America to imitate the balance of powers between various elements of the community that had somehow preserved civil liberty in England through all the ups and downs of her constitutional history. He had a genius for overstatement. Now he was announcing to all and sundry who came to visit him under the forest trees of the charming country house the Adamses occupied at Richmond Hill that he was "hostis republicani generis," an enemy of the republican breed.

Jefferson knew how much sound stuff there was under the froth and nonsense of his old friend's bombast. "During his mission to England," he tried to explain charitably, "the glare of royalty and nobility had made him believe their fascination a necessary ingredient of government." Other observers were not so charitable. "Is it not strange," Senator Grayson of Virginia had written home to Patrick Henry, who was still the fountainhead of southern suspicion of the general government, "that monarchy should issue from the East? Is it not still stranger, that John Adams, the son of a tinker, and the creature of the people, should be for titles and dignities and pre-eminencies, and should despise the Herd and the illborn?"

In one respect Washington had been happy to follow his Vice President's recommendation for "Splendour and Majesty." As a Virginian he had a congenital fondness for fine horseflesh. He never spared expense when it came to horses. When he drove to Federal Hall to deliver his opening message to Congress in January of 1790 it was in a canary yellow coach drawn by four creamcolored horses. Colonel Humphreys and Major Jackson, his military aides, decked out in their most resplendent uniforms, rode ahead on the two best white chargers in his stable. A chariot followed carrying two more secretaries driving a magnificent pair of matched bays. A third secretary rode behind them. There followed the Chief Justice, the Secretary of the Treasury, and the Secretary of War, each driven in the most brilliant equipage he could muster. A fine show for the citizenry backed up against the buildings along the narrow sidewalks.

Washington was much disturbed by the mounting criticism of his Vice President. From Virginia there had even been reported "animadversions" about the toploftiness of his own behavior. As he wrote in his revealing letter to Mrs. Macaulay, his aim was, through a mixture of prudence, conciliation and firmness, to establish the central authority the Constitution demanded "by accommodations as well as . . . Laws." Animadversions must at all cost be avoided.

He went to considerable trouble to explain the social behavior of his administration to David Stuart of Ossian Hall, who, since he married Jack Custis's widow, had become a member of the family circle at Mount Vernon. John Adams, he assured him, "though hightoned has never appeared with more than *two* horses to his carriage." Later he explained the alleged stiffness of his receptions, which were known as levees. Before he instituted them "gentlemen consulting their own convenience rather than mine, were calling from the time I rose from breakfast, often before, until I sat down to dinner." They left him no time to read his dispatches. An hour every Tuesday afternoon was all the time he could spare for casual callers. A congressman had railed at the stiffness of his bows. "Would it not have been better to throw the veil of charity over them, ascribing their stiffness to the effects of age or to the unskillfulness of my teacher, than to the pride and dignity of office, which God knows has no charms for me."

He described what went on at the levees: "Between the hours of three and four every Tuesday I am prepared to receive them." From all accounts he stood stiff as a ramrod before the fireplace in his black velvet suit with its silver buckles, his dress sword in its silver scabbard at his side, his cocked hat under his arm, his hair powdered and carefully tied into a black silk bag behind, with tight yellow gloves on his huge hands. Often the callers were introduced by the ceremonious Humphreys who, since the President was getting a little deaf, intoned their names in a sonorous voice. The President shook no man's hand. "Gentlemen often in great numbers come and go," he wrote Stuart, "chat with each other and act as they please . . . As many as I can talk to I do." Never in his life had George Washington been able to muster any small talk. "What pomp there is in all this I am unable to discover. Perhaps it consists in not sitting." The reason he could not ask his visitors to sit down was that there were not enough chairs.

The President's levees were stiff. His dinners, though the food his steward, the same Black Sam who had been host of Fraunces' Tavern, piled on the table was lavish to a degree, were dismal. According to a saying of Madison's that Jefferson often quoted, they were "wound up to a pitch of stateliness which nothing but his personal character could have supported."

Martha Washington's Fridays were more relaxed. She was becoming affectionately known as Lady Washington. With the help of Robert Morris and his wife, who had the knack of putting guests at their ease, she gave her receptions a little of the feeling of cozy hospitality of her own home at Mount Vernon. The President explained to his critics that he was invariably present on these occasions.

Washington faced the social obligations of his office as unflinchingly as he would have faced a charge of dragoons: it was too much for people to expect him to pretend to enjoy it. In criticism of his behavior he could see only one aim. "Enemies of the government," he complained bitterly to Stuart, "always more active than its friends, and always on the watch to give it a stroke, neglect no opportunity to aim one."

Jefferson at this period felt the most profound admiration for Washington one man could feel for another. "His was the singular destiny and merit," he wrote later, "of leading the armies of his country successfully through an arduous war, for the establishment of it's independence; of conducting it's councils through the birth of a government, new in it's forms and principles, until it had settled down into a quiet and orderly train." He was determined to give no aid and comfort to the enemies of the general government. He wrote Lafayette that he felt its stability depended on Washington's being spared a few years more until the habit of obedience was established throughout the states.

Taken up as Jefferson was with the pressing and immediate problems of foreign affairs — how to rescue the American seamen held captive by the Barbary pirates, how to straighten out the State of Georgia's land deals with the Creek Indians, how to induce the Spaniards to reopen the free navigation of the Mississippi after John Jay's unfortunate acquiescence in its closing — he had no time for matters of protocol or even to worry about the financial lobby round Federal Hall that so preoccupied his friend Madison. He tended to defer to others in matters of finance.

5. Funding and Assumption

Madison was coming to think that his close associate Hamilton's connection with the merchants and speculators of New York offered a far more urgent threat to the new government than John Adams' paradoxical dissertations on the need of authority to preserve liberty. On January 14 Hamilton had delivered the text of his Report on the Public Credit to Congress. It was due to Madison's vigilance that the Secretary of the Treasury did not read it in person; Madison knew Hamilton's plausible tongue and preferred to have the House mull the document over paragraph by paragraph.

Hamilton's recommendation was that the foreign debt of eleven million dollars and the domestic debt of a little more than forty million dollars inherited from the Continental Congress should be redeemed by new securities and that the war debts of the states, which he estimated at twentyfive million, should be assumed at par by the Treasury.

Funding was the rock on which Robert Morris had foundered in the Finance Office; it was up to Hamilton to make the prospect alluring. He suggested a variety of schemes for paying off the interest and principal. The interest payments could be met by an impost on luxuries; coffee and tea and imported wines and spirits; and by an excise tax on all spirits distilled within the United States. The report was written in Hamilton's usual limpid style. There was general agreement on the need for funding the debt and on the methods proposed for revenue, though many members felt that Hamilton's suggested methods were far too expensive.

The cleavage between Hamilton and Madison came on how the debt should be redeemed. Madison was in favor of discriminating in favor of the soldiers and farmers and producers who had risked their lives and fortunes in "the glorious Cause" and had been paid in then worthless paper for their pains. The original creditors had been forced to sell their debentures to dealers at two shillings to the pound. It was only right that they should be paid in full. At the same time, to ignore the claims of the present holders of the paper would destroy the public credit. "A composition then is the only expedient that remains," Madison wrote; "let it be a liberal one in favor of the present holders, let them have the highest price that has prevailed in the market; and let the residue belong to the original sufferers."

Madison argued his motion with all the dialectic skill at his command. The businessminded members were against him. Young Fisher Ames of Massachusetts particularly distinguished himself. He claimed discrimination would produce confusion, corruption and expense. "I think so highly of his probity and patriotism," he said of Madison, "that if he can be made to see that these consequences will follow, or only be apprehended, he will give up his scheme. But if government has this right what right of private property is safe?"

Livermore of New Hampshire appealed to scripture: Had not Esau bartered his birthright for a mess of pottage? The Almighty Himself had stood behind Jacob's contract. The inference was plain.

It was the beginning in the federal Congress of the unending argument between human rights and property rights. The debate became so intriguing that the members of the Senate trooped over from their chamber to listen. In the end Madison was defeated, and thereby lost his leadership of the administration forces in the House.

Hamilton, who never could understand how any man in his right mind could disagree with him, was disappointed and hurt. Since Madison had always been for funding and assumption he had expected him to be one of the strongest supporters of his report. As he wrote Jefferson's friend Edward Carrington sometime later, he attributed what he considered Madison's change to Jefferson's influence.

Throughout the thirteen states funding, assumption, and discrimination became clubs men beat each other over the head with. Farmers and veterans and the debtor classes generally sided with Madison. An anonymous rhymster in *The Columbian Sentinel* neatly expressed their feelings:

> In war to heroes let's be just,
> In peace we'll write their toils in dust;
> A soldier's pay are rags and fame,
> A wooden leg — a deathless name.
> To Specs both in and out of Cong
> The four and six percents belong.

6. "... Specs both in and out of Cong ..."

For the speculators in continental paper the stakes were immense. While the veterans and the farmers who had been the original holders of the various I owe yous of the armies and the procurement services were scattered all over the country, the speculators and their agents were right there in New York. Intermarried as many of them were with the great families of the state and of Boston and Philadelphia, they had behind them all the power of social prestige.

Robert Morris had been elected senator from Pennsylvania as a matter of course. In spite of the known shakiness of many of his ventures he still carried with him the glamor of vast wealth and of his financial dictatorship under the old Congress. Neither did he let anyone forget that he was one of the President's most intimate friends. At the social functions of the republican court he and his lively Maryland wife ranked immediately after the President and Lady Washington.

In matters of taste and etiquette, Washington, who with that odd diffidence that was so much part of his character sometimes feared that his own notions might be considered too rustic, tended to defer to the fashionable Morrises. When he wrote Gouverneur Morris in Europe to ask him to find a set of mirrors and figurines to ornament the center of his dining table for state dinners he told him, not feeling himself quite competent to describe what he wanted, "Recur to what you have seen on Mr. Robert Morris's table generally."

Gouverneur may not have felt that his good friend Bob Morris was quite so much the arbiter elegantiarum as the President thought him. When he attended to the commission in Paris, shipping three cases "containing a Surtout of seven Plateaux and the Ornaments in Biscuit" with careful instructions on how to clean them with warm water and a fine brush and explaining the order in which they should be set out on the dining table, he added a few hints of his own on the general question of taste:

"I could have sent you a Number of pretty Trifles for very little prime Cost . . . and your table would have been in the Style of a petite Maîtresse of this City, which most assuredly is not the style you wish." He was sending figurines in white bisque in a severely classical style. "Those now sent are of a noble Simplicity, and as they have been fashionable above two thousand Years, they stand a fair Chance to continue so during our Time . . . I think it of very great importance to fix the Taste of our Country properly, and I think your Example will go very far in that Respect," he explained to the President. "It is therefore my Wish that every Thing about you should be substantially good and majestically plain; made to endure."

Rivaling Robert Morris in ostentatious living and in influence in the countinghouses was William Duer. Having married the daughter of that remarkable Scottish New Yorker who in spite of the College of Heralds insisted all his life on calling himself Lord Stirling, he was a connection of the Schuylers'. Mrs. Duer, known everywhere as Lady Kitty, was much beloved in the circle of Livingstons and Jays. She was a cousin of Hamilton's darkeyed Elizabeth.

Though Duer himself was born in Devonshire and educated at Eton his family estate was in Dominica. After some experience as a young man with Clive in India, he turned up in New York to buy spars for the Royal Navy and went into the lumber business at Fort Miller above Saratoga with Lord Stirling and Philip Schuyler. Brought up an extreme Whig, when war came he harmonized his political convictions with his business interests by becoming a contractor for the Continental Army. His fortunes prospered as Robert Morris's did with the fortunes of the United States and he came out of the war holding vast amounts of continental paper and options on hundreds of square miles of public lands.

He served as secretary to the Board of the Treasury after Morris's resignation and was instrumental, when the ordinance for the settling of the Northwest Territory was passed in the last sessions of the old Congress, in obtaining a charter for Manasseh Cutler's Ohio Company. At the same time, on the foundation of this open and aboveboard Ohio Company which was successfully settling New England war veterans on the Muskingum, he erected in private a vast and shadowy edifice of speculative deals known as the Scioto Company.

At that moment Joel Barlow, with more good will than discretion, was selling to Frenchmen anxious to escape the political turmoil at home lands on the Ohio that Duer's company had not yet acquired title to. Unknown to any but their direct business associates, Duer and Robert Morris, working through Robert Morris's partner Constable, were combining with a consortium of European bankers to buy up American debentures abroad at a low figure. It was to this end that Gouverneur was acting at Robert Morris's agent at the same time as he sounded out Westminster for Washington on the touchy subject of the renewal of normal diplomatic relations. The moneymen were staking their shirts on the rise in the market that would surely come when Congress put Alexander Hamilton's recommendations into law.

In spite of the fact that Duer's traffic in government securities made it illegal, neither the President nor anyone else seems to have objected to his appointment as Assistant Secretary of the Treasury. He was thought of as a holdover from the old board who would instruct the new secretary in the details of the "art magick" of government finance.

Duer and Morris were merely the most conspicuous of the businessmen, in Congress and out, who combined their civic enthusiasm for the general government with a determination to get rich by it. Robert Morris, who liked to expatiate in the Senate lobbies on his own disregard of money when the public interest was at stake, was proclaiming it as his opinion that the speculators in state and continental paper should be congratulated for their demonstration of confidence.

7. The President's Prime Minister

Brilliant and plausible Alexander Hamilton was the darling of this hectic business community. As Philip Schuyler's soninlaw he was very much part of it. In the seven years since he had tacked up his shingle at 58 Wall Street he had made himself a name as one of the rising lawyers of New York. He had shown courage in espousing unpopular causes. He had stood up for the Tories against the lynching spirit of the popular party at the close of the war. He had gained in reputation by his able management of the campaign for ratification in his home state and had managed to take most of the credit for the articles signed "Publius" which were reprinted as The Federalist.

Now as Secretary of the Treasury Hamilton was entering on the brightest phase of his career. Even at thirtyfive, with his trim short figure and his fresh complexion, he found it hard to give up thinking of himself as the precocious boy. His boyishness, too, pleased the ladies, of whose attentions he was somewhat overfond.

From the moment the terms of his Report on Public Credit became known, the Secretary of the Treasury was the toast of the moneymen.

Unlike his supporters, he had no personal stake in funding or assumption. Although he liked to live well and brought in a good income from his legal work he had no taste for moneymaking. He neglected opportunities for profit his friends threw his way. His fees were moderate. For himself he was ambitious, as Plutarch's heroes, whose names he loved to use for pseudonyms when he wrote for the papers, and the great English Whigs like Robert Walpole and Chatham had been ambitious. Always a little under the surface of his other ambitions was a romantic craving for military glory. Often he must have reflected in private on the fact that his name was Alexander.

The establishing of the credit of the United States, which his measures were so successfully accomplishing, took second place in his mind to the use of a national debt as the core round which to build a ruling class for the nation.

Though his inner romantic reveries stemmed from Plutarch, in practical matters he kept the English model before him. The Bank of England, one of the first fruits of the Glorious Revolution, had been the heart of the moneyed interest that had formed the stable support of the long whig administrations. Now that the third George's reactionary efforts to rule as King in fact instead of in name had come to grief in the loss of the American colonies and of that unfortunate gentleman's wits, Chatham's precocious son (who, Hamilton must often have reflected, became Prime Minister at twentyfour) was setting the kingdom to rights again with the help of what could already be described as the capitalist class. A good many details of Hamilton's schemes for funding were taken from the Sinking Fund Act young William Pitt had put through Parliament four years before. Hamilton's theories on buying the support of moneyed men, through corruption if necessary, had been Robert Walpole's practice. Now as he threw the influence of the Treasury behind the speculators' lobby working on the members of Congress in Federal Hall to enact the measures recommended in his report, he was seeing himself more and more clearly as Washington's Prime Minister.

It was from the Treasury bench in the House of Commons that the great whig statesmen of England developed the office of Prime Minister. The Treasury was Hamilton's machine for power.

8.   The Landed Interest

The first obstacle Hamilton found in his way was the opposition of his friend James Madison. It was not that Madison disagreed with him about the importance of economic interests. It was Madison who in the tenth number of *The Federalist* had formulated the theory which he had first sketched out in his long letter to Jefferson while he and Hamilton were planning the work: "Those who hold and those who are without property have ever formed distinct interests in society . . . The regulation of these various and interfering interests forms the principle task of modern legislation, and involves the spirit of party and faction in the necessary and ordinary operations of government."

Madison's differences with Hamilton hinged on the question: whose economic interests shall profit from the operations of government?

As a Virginia landowner Madison was suspicious of bankers, speculators, moneylenders and of this whole new class of people who lived by manipulating currency instead of from production from the soil. His long association with Jefferson had given him respect for the needs of small farmers and western settlers. Hamilton was the only member of Washington's first administration who was not someway or other rooted in the land. Though he had married into the upstate clan of the Schuylers, Hamilton was a New Yorker of New York City. It was inevitable that the landed Virginian would sooner or later come into conflict with the businessman. Although they had only an inkling of the full amount of speculation that lay behind the fervor of the lobby for Hamilton's fiscal program the Southerners and the western-minded men in Congress already knew enough to make them suspicious.

After the defeat of Madison's motion for discrimination the debates in Congress hinged on the question of assumption. There was strong opposition from the states that had already paid off the major part of their indebtedness. A series of contradictory votes resulted in stalemate. "So high were the feuds excited by this subject," wrote Jefferson, "that on it's rejection business was suspended. Congress met from day to day without doing anything, the parties being too much out of temper to do business together."

Meanwhile an even more inflammatory issue was intruded into the business of an already irritated group of men. To Washington's great disgust and to the dismay even of men like Jefferson and Madison who, working as they were for a gradual abolition of slavery, dreaded the results of a frontal attack on the slaveholding interests, delegates from the New York and Philadelphia Quakers waited on Congress and on the President with a petition for the immediate end of the slave trade. At the same time the Pennsylvania Abolition Society presented to Congress an eloquent memorial signed by its president Benjamin Franklin demanding the abolition of slavery itself.

A new cleavage in Congress was immediately produced. The South

Carolina and Georgia delegations, already irritated by the operations of what they considered primarily an eastern lobby in favor of funding and assumption, lost their tempers completely. In a bitter debate which one member described as shamefully indecent, the slaveowners sprang to the defense of their peculiar institution. The eastern members retorted with heat. With great difficulty Madison, who wanted funding and assumption to take priority over any other business, managed to get the memorial, and the reports and counterreports it had occasioned, entombed in the journal.

Signing this petition to abolish slavery was Franklin's last public act. He died two months later. Madison steered a resolution through the House that the members should wear mourning for a month, but in the Senate the feeling among slaveowners against the old philosopher was so bitter that a similar resolution failed to pass.

9. Jefferson's Bargain

While Congress was caught in the toils of the great issues which were to keep Americans embroiled for the next hundred years, news came that gave every man pause. President Washington was at the point of death. An epidemic of influenza had been going through the city. On Sunday, May 9, the President stayed home from church. He made an entry in his diary: "Indisposed with a bad cold and at home all day writing letters on private business." The next day he took to his bed. On the fifteenth the doctors announced that pneumonia had set in and that he was dying. There was still enough iron left in his great frame to prove them liars. Around four the same afternoon he broke into a copious sweat. His pulse improved. His fever abated. Five days later he was pronounced out of danger.

"Within the last twelve months," he wrote Stuart, "I have undergone more and severer sickness than thirty preceding years afflicted me with." A third attack, more than probably, he declared, would put him to sleep with his fathers.

The thought that George Washington might have died before the law passed firmly establishing the credit of the United States gave the supporters of the Constitution cold chills. Jefferson as much as Hamilton felt that its passage in some form was essential. Without it the Union would fall to pieces.

A bill establishing the permanent residence of the general government had been kicked around between factions in the tugging and hauling over funding and assumption. The New Englanders were willing to have the capital remain in New York. Robert Morris, who owned an iron foundry and a large tract of land across from Trenton, wanted it on the Delaware. The western Pennsylvanians were suggesting a location on the Susquehanna. For years it had been one of Jefferson's darling projects, in which he had Washington's full approval, to establish the federal city at the head of navigation of the Potomac. From the vicinity of Georgetown easy communication could be opened through the projected canal to the Western Waters.

None of these sites had yet mustered enough votes. The congressmen influenced by the speculators' lobby had laid down the law that there should be no vote for funding unless assumption went along with it. At the last roll call assumption had lacked only three votes. Madison still held out against it. Jefferson felt the time had come to make his influence felt. He had been successful with legislative compromises before. Why not arrange a bargain by which Maryland and Virginia should trade their votes for assumption for the removal of the capital to the Potomac?

Hamilton had previously suggested a similar trade to Robert Morris, offering to establish the capital at Germantown or at Trenton on the Delaware, but Robert Morris had not been able to marshal the necessary votes.

"Going to the President's house one day I met Hamilton as I approached the door," Jefferson wrote in a memorandum found among his papers, "his look was sombre, haggard and dejected beyond description, even his dress uncouth & neglected, he asked to speak to me, we stood in the street near the door, he opened the subject of the assumption of the State debts, the necessity of it in the general fiscal arrangement & it's indispensible necessity towards a preservation of the union . . . if he had not credit enough to carry such a measure as that he could be of no use & was determined to resign, he observed at the same time, that altho' our particular business laid in separate departments, yet the Administration & it's success was a common concern, and that we should make common cause in supporting one another . . . I thought the first step towards some conciliation of views would be to bring Mr. Madison and Colo. Hamilton to a friendly discussion of the subject. I immediately wrote to each to come and dine with me next day . . . I opened the subject to them, acknoledged that my situation had not permitted me to understand it sufficiently but encouraged them to consider the thing together, they did so, it ended with Mr Madison's acquiescence in a proposition that the question should again be brought before the House by way of amendmt. from the Senate, that tho' he would not vote for it . . . yet he should not be strenuous but leave it to it's fate. it was observed, I forget by which of them, that as the pill would be a bitter one to the Southern States, something should be done to soothe them, that the removal of the seat of Government to the Potowmac was a just measure." To mollify the Pennsylvania members whose votes for it were needed and to give time for the construction of a new city the capital would first be moved to Philadelphia for ten years.

As soon as the bargain was made Jefferson put his powers of persuasion to work. Daniel Carroll of Maryland, who owned land on the projected site, was not too hard to convince. Two of the Potomac members from the Virginia side, Alexander White and Richard Bland Lee, agreed to change their votes, but White, so Jefferson put it with characteristic vehemence, "with a revulsion of stomach almost convulsive." Hamilton had agreed to carry the other point.

"In doing this, the influence he had established over the eastern members, with the agency of Robert Morris with those of the middle states, effected his side of the engagement; and so the Assumption was passed" — Jefferson noted years later in his preface to the *Anas*; forgetting, perhaps, that at that time he was still ignorant of the nature of the lobby behind Hamilton — "and twenty millions of stock divided among favored States, and thrown in as a pabulum to the stockjobbing herd."

Jefferson might have added that Robert Morris promptly sent off couriers to buy up land options for him below Georgetown on the Potomac.

The ultimate result of Jefferson's and Hamilton's bargain was that the funding bill passed.

10. *The Permanent Residence*

The doctors attributed Washington's illness to lack of outdoor exercise. He was hardly out of his bed when he took up his old habit of riding before breakfast. By early June he was feeling well enough to entertain the notion that some fresh sea air would do him good. He enjoyed catching fish and eating fish. He invited Jefferson and Hamilton to go deep sea fishing with him off Sandy Hook, possibly in Hamilton's own private sloop. He wanted to encourage the budding sympathy between his two secretaries. Jefferson had been suffering for the past month from one of the migraine headaches that were the curse of his life. He was often seasick at sea. Though no fisherman he went along explaining that he thought a good bout of seasickness would help him throw off his headache. They were out three days and came back with a good catch of sea bass and blackfish. Jefferson reported that the President was looking much better than he had before his illness.

There followed a short summer of good feeling in Washington's administration. Hamilton had been alarmed by the public outcry against his fiscal plans and against the speculators' lobby. When William Duer suggested it might be wise for him to give up his post of Assistant Secretary of the Treasury, possibly because he could no longer spare the time from the dizzy complication of his own affairs, Hamilton eagerly accepted his resignation and appointed Tench Coxe in his place.

Tench Coxe was a member of Benjamin Franklin's circle, a Philadelphian of some means who had devoted his life to encouraging American manufactures. He was a friend of Madison's. Although he had been suspected of Toryism during the war, he had redeemed himself, to Jefferson's and Madison's way of thinking, by his thoughtful writing on economic subjects. He served in Franklin's antislavery society, in the society for improving the jails, and in many other humanitarian causes. Though he had inherited his father's mercantile business he was thought of as an economist rather than a businessman. Choosing him for the post was a gesture of conciliation towards the Virginians.

The residence bill passed promptly. The funding bill was in the works.

Early in July the informal negotiations with the British government, which had been depressingly inconclusive, took an encouraging turn with the appearance in New York of a Major Beckwith who was an aide to the astute Guy Carleton, now ruling British Canada from Quebec under the title of Lord Dorchester.

Rumors had been coming in of difficulties between the Spanish and the British in the Northwest. The Spaniards, who laid claim to the entire northwest coast of America, had arrested some British fur traders who were buying sea otters from the Indians in Nootka Sound for the China trade. Through Hamilton, who was already considered the member of the cabinet most congenial to British ideas, Major Beckwith was cautiously sounding out the state of mind of the administration on the possibility of an alliance, and dropping hints about allowing the passage of British troops through United States territory in case of war with Spain. Jefferson immediately saw a bargaining point to be used in negotiations over the frontier posts with the British, and over the navigation of the Mississippi with the Spaniards.

Neither the President nor the Secretary of State was willing to talk to Beckwith officially because he was not an accredited representative. The conversations fell to Hamilton and were the beginning of the Secretary of the Treasury's encroachment on the State Department's domain.

At the moment both Jefferson and Hamilton agreed that a war between England and Spain would be in the best interests of the United States. Jefferson's glee over the prospect made him forget every other consideration. "Our object is to feed & theirs to fight," he wrote Monroe; "if we are not forced by England we shall have a gainful time of it."

One Saturday in July when Congress was not in session, the President, still working to promote the sort of cordial relations among the members of his cabinet he had enjoyed among his staff officers when he was commander in chief of the Continental Army, arranged an excursion. Washington and Hamilton and Adams and Knox and their families drove out through the farmlands of Manhattan Island to Fort Washington, which held such poignant memories for the President of the dark days of the war. The President's secretaries and all the children went along. Jefferson was a member of the party. After visiting the ruins of the fort they all dined in high good humor at a fine country mansion on a hill that had been confiscated from one of the tory Morrises and was now "in the occupation of a common Farmer."

A few days later John Rutledge's young son of the same name disembarked from Europe where he had been spending his father's money on the grand tour. He brought in his baggage the painting of the Bastille Lafayette was sending his adopted father and the famous dungeon's great key, letters from many of Washington's French friends and a note from Tom Paine in London regretting he had not been able to present the key in person. "That the principles of America opened the Bastille is not to be doubted," wrote Paine, "and therefore the key comes to the right place."

The French news on the whole was encouraging. Washington wrote back to Lafayette congratulating him that he had "address and fortitude enough to steer . . . safely through all the quicksands and rocks which threatened instant destruction on every side." He was relieved that the news brought by American travelers contradicted the bloody tales that filled the English gazettes. He sent him, not for their intrinsic value, but because they were of American manufacture, a pair of shoebuckles from New York. The President had the key hung on the wall in the state apartment where he held his solemn levees.

Undoubtedly it was exhibited with the other wonders of the President's house to a delegation of Creek Indians who appeared in the city led by their halfbreed chief McGillivray. Washington set great store by a settlement with this master of border intrigue who was very successfully playing off the conflicting interests of the British in the region of the Great Lakes, the Spaniards along the Mississippi, and the conflicting groups of landhungry Americans. The Creeks, in war paint and feathers, were entertained by the Society of St. Tammany and, under Henry Knox's careful and sympathetic management, signed a treaty relinquishing some of their lands to the United States.

August 4 the funding bill was ready for the President's signature. A few days later Secretary Knox presided over the ceremonies of the signing of the treaty with the Creeks in the parlor of his fine house on the Broad Way. August 12 Congress adjourned to meet again in Philadelphia in the fall. There were fireworks on the Common.

Two days later the President, taking Jefferson and George Clinton along with him, set sail on the packet for Newport. In the last days of May "the little vautrien," as Jefferson had described the stubborn little state in one of his confidential letters to Lafayette, had finally ratified the Constitution, thereby rounding out the original thirteen. Taking Jefferson, who had been intimate with such Rhode Islanders as Howell in the old Congress, and George Clinton, who had been one of the Constitution's bitterest opponents, was evidence of how carefully Washington was following his program of proceeding "by accommodation." By his informal behavior among the Rhode Islanders he gave the lie to rumors of stiffness and haughtiness in office.

"It is now no more that toleration is spoken of" he told the leaders of the Jewish community at Newport, "as if it was by the indulgence of one class of people that another enjoyed the exercise of their inherent national rights. For happily the government of the United States which gives to bigotry no sanction, to persecution no assistance, requires only that they who live under its protection should demean themselves as good citizens."

With Jefferson and Clinton he strolled through the towns, admired the public buildings and points of interest. Several times when invited into private homes he graciously drank a glass of wine or punch with the company. In Providence he walked around the streets and lanes for four hours until he had completely worn out his escort. He ventured out into the rain and the drizzle, although it was his habit now to keep indoors at night, to admire the illumination of the college. He reviewed the state militia standing in the doorway of a tavern. He left the equality-minded Rhode Islanders enchanted with his visit.

Ten days after the return of the presidential party to New York, days which Jefferson spent in arranging with his chief clerk for the transfer of the Department of State to Philadelphia, Jefferson and Madison set out together for home. They traveled in Jefferson's phaeton. They must have carried with them a bundle of the New York newspapers in which they found expressed in no uncertain terms the bitterness of the "Yorkers" at losing the national capital after all the expense they had been put to to prepare a home for it.

Tom Shippen, who had described the presidental draperies in such glowing terms, now on a jaunt south to visit his Lee cousins along the Potomac, described the trip in his letters home. He was one of a host of young men for whom Jefferson drafted educational travel guides for the European tour. He joined the two Virginians at Chestertown. They made a gay party. Jefferson and Madison always enjoyed each other's company, but this time they were in unusually high spirits.

"My journey was a delightful one," young Shippen wrote his father, "whether spoken of for the excellence of the society, my fare, the weather or the roads . . . At Rock Hall . . . we waited all day for want of a vessel to take us over" (to Annapolis from the Eastern Shore) "and I never knew two men more agreeable than they were. We talked and dined and strolled and rowed ourselves in boats and feasted on delicious crabs."

In Annapolis they found an inn which Shippen, though he was fresh from the grand tour of Europe, rated "among the most excellent in the world . . . I never saw so fine a turtle or so welldressed a dish as he gave us the second day for dinner . . . Old Madeira at £80 a pipe to season it."

On the road through southern Maryland they encountered bedbugs and wretched victuals, but at Bladensburg they ate a fine breakfast "with an old black woman who keeps the best house in town and calls herself Mrs. Margaret Adams. She diverted us with an account of the resentment which discovered itself towards her because the President and his family had preferred her house to lodge at as he passed through."

Washington and his suite had put up for the night there a few days before. After the President left, an angry crowd of whites led by some rival innkeeper had stormed about the black woman's inn and finally vented their rage by pulling down her "temple of Cloacina, and there was the demolished building when we arrived, a monument at the same time of the envy of her fellow citizens and her own triumph."

In Georgetown they were entertained by Congressman Carroll. In his company and followed by a cavalcade of local landowners already dizzy with the dream of rising real estate values, they rode over the tract of farmland and meadow between Rock Creek and muddy little Goose Creek, which Jefferson already was glorifying by the name of Tiber. After dinner they rowed in a boat up the Potomac. They admired the romantic reaches of the river up to the Little Falls. Jefferson, looking back from the water at the richly wooded slopes round the saucershaped depression which his imagination was filling with the

domes and the columns and the white porches of the federal city to
be, may well have been able, against the blue highlands that hemmed
it about, to count off seven hills.

The Virginians left their young Philadelphia friend at the ferry.
While they drove down to Mount Vernon he visited his Lee cousins.
"My having joined these two charming men," he wrote his father with
a request for an extra draft, "though it gave me infinite pleasure, cost
me money." Jefferson and Madison traveled in style.

At Mount Vernon when the cloth was removed and the toasts
disposed of, projects for the federal city must have been uppermost in
the conversation. It is likely that Jefferson's first little plat, showing
a gridiron of streets fronting on the creek, was sketched out in
connection with this conversation. All the time he was in Europe
he had been searching for a type of architecture that would express the dignity and simplicity of the republican scheme. It had to be
founded on the antique. He considered the temple at Nîmes, built in
that period of the early empire when the Roman architects themselves
were harking back to the elegance and simplicity of the Hellenic style,
the most beautiful building in the world. The statehouse he had
designed according to that same inspiration was already standing on
Shockoe's Hill in Richmond. Among the crates and crates of his
European acquisitions that were even then headed for Philadelphia
there was a collection he had made in Paris of engravings of what he
considered the best modern dwellings he saw in his travels where he
felt architects could find hints for the style of the private houses of the
federal city. He wanted a certain uniformity. The public buildings
should be modeled either on what he called the spherical style of the
Pantheon or the cubical style which stemmed from the Greek temples,
or a combination of both. He had a model all ready for adaptation in
the designs he had worked out for the Virginia capitol. He would
have the drawings shipped up from Richmond.

Washington had a taste for architecture himself. He gloried in the
spacious laying out of grounds. Both men agreed there was no time to
lose. Streets must be laid out and foundations laid right away. Congress
must be faced with an accomplished fact. Here was a project on which
they could work together wholeheartedly. From Washington's and
Jefferson's collaboration with L'Enfant, who based his city plan on
Versailles where he had grown up, and with Thornton and Hoban,
who won the competitions they instituted for the President's house and
for the building which was to accommodate the two houses of Congress,
grew not only the city as it was finally established on the muddy flats of
the Potomac, but a whole new style that younger men developed from
Jefferson's beginnings, the classical revival of the early republic.

X The Rights of Man

1. The Inspired Staymaker

During the first formative years of the general government, which his writings had done a great deal to promote, Tom Paine was back in the old England he sailed away from a ruined man on a fever-ridden emigrant ship the year before the Revolutionary War began. Landing sick and penniless in Philadelphia, with only a bundle of essays in his wallet and one of those letters of introduction from Benjamin Franklin which proved passports to fortune for so many young men of parts, he immediately made a name for himself as editor of *The Pennsylvania Magazine*. He found tutoring the sons of well-todo merchants quite profitable. He had prospects of opening a school. He always claimed that the Revolutionary War interrupted a promising literary career.

"Scarcely had I set foot into the Country but it was set on fire about my ears," he wrote in his memorial to Congress asking for financial assistance when he began to plan a trip back to England to see his old father before he died. "All the plans and prospects for a private life . . . were immediately disconcerted . . . From a principle devoted to the love of liberty, and a disposition to assist injured and suffering people, I felt a pleasure in sharing their fate without even troubling myself about consequences."

During the war years he proved himself the greatest journalist of his age. *Common Sense*, which Washington, who was no friend to journalists, described with unwonted enthusiasm as "a flaming argument," had put the case of the American provincials against the British Crown into terms every man could understand. The *Crisis* papers raised the spirit of the Continental Army in the winter of discouragement and despair. Paine's clear exuberant preachments over the signature "Common Sense," became one of the strongest threads in the web of American political thinking. With the peace Paine found himself accepted as one of the great men of the successful revolution. "Though my situation is in no ways advantageous," he wrote old Franklin, whom he knew enjoyed the success of his protégés, "it is nevertheless agreeable. I have the pleasure of being respected and feel a little of that satisfactory kind of pride which tells me I have some right to it."

The end of the war found him as penniless as the day he arrived in Philadelphia. "Trade I do not understand. Land I have none, or what is equal to none," he wrote Congress. "I have exiled myself from one country without making a home in another and I cannot help sometimes asking myself what am I better off than a refugee . . . from the country I have obliged and served to that which can owe me no good will."

Though he failed to get himself subsidized as "historiographer to the continent" to write a history of the war, the Commonwealth of Pennsylvania presented him with five hundred pounds in cash and New York deeded him a confiscated farm in New Rochelle. Earlier he had managed to acquire the small house in Bordentown, where as soon as the progress of the war gave him any leisure he went to work on a project for an iron bridge supported by an arch of girders arranged on the principle of the spiderweb.

He had hoped that the Pennsylvania legislature or Robert Morris and his associates would try out this plan for a single span across the Schuylkill. When they proved unwilling to take a chance on so novel an experiment he decided to take his model to Paris to get its principles endorsed by the highest authority in engineering matters, the French Academy of Sciences. Such an endorsement might convince the doubting Pennsylvanians. He would visit the old people in England on the way back.

It was hardly as a refugee that he sailed from New York on the French packet for Havre. He had money in his pocket. He was buoyed up by expectations of the fortune his bridge would bring him. He was received in France as a man who had already made his mark in the world, as a Master of Arts of the University of Pennsylvania, a member of the American Philosophical Society and a friend of the great Dr. Franklin. Jefferson and Lafayette between them smoothed every path for him in Paris. The reformers around Lafayette's dinner table greeted him as an authority on the art of statebuilding.

Though he did not speak a word of French his dealings with the Parisian enthusiasts confirmed him in the notions he had expressed in his reply to the Abbé Reynal's illdigested writings on America a few years before: "Perhaps no two events ever united so intimately

and forcibly to combat and expel prejudice as the Revolution of
America and the alliance with France . . . We see with other eyes;
we hear with other ears; and think with other thoughts than those we
formally used. We can look back on our own prejudices as if they
had been the prejudices of other people."

He found the same ferment working in France which had driven
him to his own private revolt against the limitations of the life of a
poor tradesman in England. The American revolution had sparked
the revolution of the world.

He was still Quaker enough to feel testimony imperative when the
spirit moved. Doing good was still more important to him than making
a fortune out of his invention. From the conversation of the men he
was introduced to in Paris he became convinced that peace was the
immediate cause. The revolution of the world must develop in an era
of peace. Right away Paine bought paper and sharpened his quill pens.

The French engineers, perhaps urged on by Lafayette's persuasive
powers, were prompt in examining the plans for his bridge. The day
after their Academy handed him a satisfactory endorsement of the
principles on which it was to be constructed, Paine set out for London. In his pocket he carried a statement of the peaceful intentions of
the French foreign office which he was to hand to Edmund Burke.

The first thing he did when he arrived in London was to hurry his
article to the printers. The next was to climb into the coach for Thetford. His father the old Quaker corsetmaker was dead. His mother
was in good health but living in desperate poverty. While he corrected the proofs on his plea to the British government to preserve the
peace of Europe, he spent some time with her that fall in the moldy
little Lincolnshire river town where he had spent the first miserable
seventeen years of his life.

2. ". . . the head which worked such mickle woe to courts and kings"

The five years after Paine's return to England were his years
of greatest glory. In his early fifties he was at the full flush of his
powers. A notable Yorkshire ironworks was building a large scale
model of his bridge. He was wined and dined by the whole circle of
radical literary people who had been the intimates of the bookseller
Johnson's table. When he tired of his somewhat too public life at The
White Bear on Piccadilly, he made his home at the house of his admiring and affectionate old crony, Rickman, now a bookseller in London, who had named his eldest son after him.

The author of *Common Sense* was a nine days' wonder among the noble Whigs of the Rockingham contingent. Edmund Burke invited him to spend a week at the Gregories. He was entertained at the nearby seat of the Duke of Portland who after Rockingham's death inherited the leadership of his branch of the Whigs. Lord Fitzwilliam, the Marquis of Rockingham's nephew, interested himself in the progress of the iron bridge. The restless Earl of Shelburne, who had been the chief architect of the American peace, now retired among his great gardens at Bowood as Marquis of Lansdowne, sounded Paine out on his lordship's favorite project of bringing the United States back into the British fold again. He had friendly talks with Charles James Fox, the statesman about town who had elevated parliamentary opposition to a par with horseracing and the prize ring and betting at Brooks' as a fashionable sport among the highliving beaux of the Prince of Wales' set. He was received as an equal by Franklin's friends of the Royal Society, Sir Joseph Banks the geographer, and Unitarian dissenters like Priestley the great chemist, and the favorite whig preacher and economist Dr. Price.

Royall Tyler, the humorous Vermonter who was one of the first American dramatists, in London in the course of his grand tour, was taken to see Paine as he was taken to Vauxhall and Westminster Abbey and the Tower of London. His report was not without malice: "He was dressed in a snuffcolored coat, olive velvet vest, drab breeches, coarse hose. His shoebuckles of the size of a half dollar. A bobtailed wig covered that head which worked such mickle woe to courts and kings . . . It is probable that this was the same identical wig in the shadow of whose curls he wrote *Common Sense,* in America years before. He was a spare man, rather under size, subject to the extreme of low, and highly exhilerating spirits; often sat reserved in company; seldom mingled in the common chitchat. But when a man of sense and elocution was present, and the company numerous, he delighted in advancing the most unaccountable, and often the most whimsical paradoxes."

3.   *George in a Straight Waistcoat*

The English had their own plans for electoral reform. With the failure of his American policy and the collapse of Lord North's government the third George lost most of the patronage by which, painstakingly plying the arts of corruption, he had managed to muster a majority of King's Friends at every division of the House of Commons. "Every man has his price" and "I will have no innovations in my time" had been the two tenets on which George based his politics. In spite of him there had appeared the dreadful innovation of the transatlantic republic; wherever he looked new innovations threatened.

Pitt had begun his administration with a plan for parliamentary reform in his pocket. That had been shelved, to the King's great relief, but in spite of the corruptions of Parliament, Pitt was reorganizing the antiquated fiscal structure bit by bit as he carried on the daily business of government. He sought and received the backing of the moneymen. Like Hamilton in America, he was the darling of the exchanges. In the fall of 1788 Pitt's government had been presented with an acute constitutional problem. The King went off his head.

Whether it was the frustrations of the American war or the humiliations of his brother monarch Louis was undergoing at Versailles or the dreadful prospect of innovations in England; or, as some of his loving subjects claimed, the effect of sitting too long in wet stockings after a four-hour walk in the country when he already had a rash on his legs, George began to behave so strangely that he had to be respectfully restrained.

The courtiers remembered that during the summer at Windsor his speech had seemed even more rapid and incoherent than usual. He made advances to one of the ladies in waiting in a manner quite shocking in a man of his impeccable morals. His notes to Pitt, usually so neat and precise, straggled wildly over the paper. He complained of feeling weak and stiff. He broke out in hives. He had welts all over his body. He did not lose his spirit. "You suppose me ill beyond recovery," he stammered to Lord Thurlow, "but whatever you or Mr. Pitt may think or feel, I that am born a gentleman shall never lay my head on my last pillow in peace so long as I remember my American colonies."

His speech and his eating became faster and faster. He beat an attendant with his fists. At last it was all that four pages could do to hold him down. His physicians ordered him into a straight waistcoat. Even they began to admit in their communiqués that His Majesty was seriously unwell. One of them gave the show away by suddenly selling a large block of securities. This produced such a serious break in the stock markets that poor George, pale and shaking, had to be produced at a royal levee.

The courtiers found him somewhat emaciated, but still the same popeyed "Farmer George" who had won his subjects' affection by his frugal life and his painstaking devotion to his duty as he saw it through many a disastrous year. When his wits returned as mysteriously as they had left him he found himself more popular than ever. The thought that their good King had lost his mind only endeared him to the English more.

4. Burke's Reflections

England was still primarily an agricultural country. In spite of the growth of the industrial towns which attracted the disfranchised poor as fast as the enclosures and the destruction of small holdings drove them off the land, the bulk of the population still depended on farming and grazing for a living under the rule of the gentlemen who sat in the assizes and the parsons who represented God and the King in the pulpit. When King George declared, "I will have no innovations in my time," yeomen and gentry of every hamlet and cathedral town in England breathed a profound amen.

It was in Scotland, where people took their learning seriously, and in Ireland, where daily oppressions made innovation an obvious necessity, and among the middleclass nonconformists of the cities that people read and debated and that thought stirred. There revolutionary ideas took hold.

Now Tom Paine, the Thetford staymaker, found himself for a short time the spokesman of the radical nonconformists who were elbowing their way to equality with the gentry. Their zeal for reform had led them to take up the cause of the American colonists, and now that that battle was won they were pressing forward to demand regular parliaments elected by some sort of truly representative system.

Already during the American war Dr. Price, the favorite economist of the Whigs and, as a Unitarian, the favorite divine of the party of the buff and blue, was writing of the colonists: "They have fought with success for themselves and the world; and in the midst of invasion and carnage, have established forms of government favorable in the highest degree to the rights of mankind"; and glorifying the American achievement as "a revolution by which Britons themselves will be the greatest gainers."

The news of the storming of the Bastille was received with cheers by this whole segment of the British reading public. Fox cried out in Parliament: "How much the greatest event it is that ever happened in history, how much the best!"

Dr. Price made the great event the text of a sermon "On the Love of Our Country" which he preached on the fourth of November at the meetinghouse in old Jewry before the members of the Revolution

Society. This society was a highly respectable group, of which Pitt's brotherinlaw, the inventive and mechanicalminded Earl Stanhope, was chairman. These gentlemen made a habit of celebrating the day of the "Glorious Revolution," from which they dated their constitutional principles by listening to a sermon on some patriotic topic, and then adjourning convivially to the London Tavern where for 7/6 they were served a good dinner and as much sherry and punch and port as they could drink.

"I have lived to see thirty millions of people indignant and resolute," they heard in the peroration of Dr. Price's sermon on this fourth of November, "spurning at slavery and demanding liberty with an irresistible voice, their king led in triumph and an arbitrary monarch surrendering himself to his subjects. And now methinks I see the ardor for liberty catching and spreading, a general amendment beginning in human affairs; the dominion of kings changed for the dominion of laws, and the dominion of priests giving way to the dominion of reason and conscience." This was revolution as Jefferson saw it.

Edmund Burke, ever since he had attained fame by his eloquence on behalf of the colonists in the early days of the American war, had been the mouthpiece of the whig conscience in Parliament. He had risen as high as a man of his origins could. The malicious Wilkes used to say it always made him think of whiskey and potatoes to hear Burke speak. It was only Burke's brogue and his poverty and the fact that he was a mere attorney's son from Dublin that kept him from the great offices in the cabinet. Now when the printed version of Dr. Price's sermon came under his eyes, instead of reading it with edification, Burke read it with abhorrence.

The English constitution had done well by Edmund Burke. Edmund Burke responded by a passionate affection for every mossgrown inconsistency in that massive and paradoxical edifice. His interest in reform was the interest of a man who reforms in order to conserve.

To Tom Paine in his youth, as to a whole generation of young radicals, Burke was the great parliamentary idol, the symbol of how far a man of moderate fortune could rise by his own efforts. Already when Paine, fresh from America, visited him in fashionable Buckinghamshire, Paine had been disappointed at the tone of his conversation. As the years went on they had some correspondence about the French Revolution. Abolishing the aristocracy was the point Burke stuck at. "Do you really imagine, Mr. Paine," Burke answered categorically to some suggestion of Paine's that a similar revolution might do old England good, "that the constitution of this kingdom requires such innovations, or could exist with them, or that any reflecting man could seriously engage in them? You are aware that all my life I have opposed such schemes of reform, because I know them not to be Reform."

In the sober preaching of the elderly Dr. Price, Burke suddenly saw the rash idealists of the National Assembly on the march to attack British institutions. He felt himself hurt to the quick by the sufferings of the rich and wellborn displaced and destroyed by the great upheaval. All his deepest convictions and sensibilities, his hopes for his own advancement, his touching determination to make a career for his son among the great men of England, his love of dignity and order combined to make his *Reflections on the Revolution in France* a most eloquent plea.

Even in his greatest days in Parliament he had trouble in getting his fellow members to hear him through. In the *Reflections* he molded a prose style that gave the effect of oratory without the tedium of it. Although written in the form of a letter to a French friend it was an oration set to paper. His readers could imagine the gestures of the man himself. They could hear the modulations of his voice: "I do not like to see anything destroyed; any void produced in society; any ruin on the face of the land."

A national constitution he saw as the slow accretion of the social habits of centuries, laid down layer after layer like a coral reef. He pleaded for gradual reform instead of destruction: "Rage and phrensy will pull down more in half an hour than prudence deliberation and foresight can build up in a hundred years . . . The true lawgiver ought to have a heart full of sensibility. He ought to love and respect his kind, and to fear himself. His movements . . . ought to be deliberate. Political arrangement, as it is a work for social ends, is to be wrought by social means. There mind must conspire with mind. Time is required to produce that union of minds which alone can produce all the good we aim at."

Even before he got hold of the text Paine, who had been hearing echoes of the fulminations of the great orator in the Commons, had been planning a reply. As soon as he laid eyes on the work he saw that Burke had laid himself open to charges of special pleading, of distortion of the facts, and of outrageous appeal to the prejudices and the insular selfsatisfaction of ruling circles in England. "No innovations in my time."

Paine could not wait to demolish Burke's arguments. He wrote the first part of *The Rights of Man* at top speed in a rural inn in Islington. He held up Burke's thunderous periods to the light of the cool disenchanted reasoning of the ordinary townsman sitting in the coffeehouse over the gazettes. He pointed out that the incidental cruelties of the Paris mob, which Burke made so much of, and which he disliked as much as Burke did, had been taught them by their despotic government. Burke's sympathy went out only to the suffering aristocrats. He forgot what the people had suffered before. "He is not affected by the reality of distress but by the shadowy resemblance of it striking his imagination; pities the plumage, but forgets the dying bird."

5. The Appeal from the New to the Old Whigs

Both Paine's and Burke's books were enormously read. King George, who was a great bibliophile though hardly a reader, kept a number of elegantly bound copies of the *Reflections* on hand to distribute to worthy persons. Translated into French, the work became the bible of émigré opposition to the French Revolution. Reading it was said to have strengthened Marie Antoinette's resolution to resist.

The Revolution Society and the Society for Constitutional Information and the democratic societies that were springing up in imitation of the Jacobin clubs of France distributed *The Rights of Man* over all England. While the gentry were reading Burke in the manor house parlors, the mechanics and artisans were reading Paine in their thatched cottages. At first the literate opinion of England was overwhelmingly on Paine's side of the argument. *The Rights of Man* was one of no less than thirtyeight answers to Burke.

The French Revolution and its consequences were Burke's obsession from now on. He devoted an immense amount of time and money to caring for French refugees. His political realignment was dramatized by a grand scene in the Commons between Burke and his old disciple Fox which immediately became the talk of the kingdom.

Burke, with another of his great orations swelling within him, had been looking for an opportunity to explain and justify his reactionary attitude which many old supporters were decrying as a reversal of his whole life's course. Pitt, who wanted no rash debates to interfere at that time with his administration's cold neutrality towards events in Europe, tried to stave him off, and was abetted by Fox, from the opposition benches. At last, during the debate on the Quebec Act, which was to apportion representation in the new Canadian parliament between the French and Englishspeaking populations, Burke managed to get the floor. Though there was little connection between revolutionary France and Catholic Quebec, Burke managed to launch himself into a tirade on events in France.

It had become a habit to walk out on Burke. Fox was following some of his supporters out into the lobby when he suddenly thought

better of it and came back, biting into an orange, in time to hear
Burke's hoarse peroration: he would quit his best friends and join his
most avowed enemies to oppose the least influence of such a spirit in
England. With his last words he would gasp out, "Fly from the French
constitution."

Fox leaned across the aisle to his old friend and whispered, "But
there is no loss of friendship."

Burke faced Fox coldly and said, "There is."

The scene between Fox and Burke was reenacted in every walk of
life in England. The French Revolution divided old associates, broke
up families, even invaded the peaceful courtyards of Oxford and
Cambridge.

When Paine came back with a fresh spate of arguments against
Burke in the second part of *The Rights of Man*, the book was distributed by the corresponding societies from Land's End to John o'
Groats. This time he dedicated his work to Lafayette, then at the
height of his prestige as the Washington of France. The common
people of England were beginning to look to Tom Paine as their
leader. The corresponding societies became daily bolder in their agitation for a parliament which would represent the nation instead of
twelve thousand electors.

The Americans had amended their government through a constitutional convention. American securities were quoted high on the
exchanges. To the discontented in England as well as in France the
word convention took on a musical sound. Along with agitation for a
convention in England went talk of manhood suffrage, lowered taxes,
of putting an end to pressgangs and primping; if Parliament would
not reform itself the people would have to reform Parliament.

6.   "... a litter of revolutions."

The speeches of liberalminded members of the Royal Society
hailing the new dispensation in France aroused in Pitt neither enthusiasm nor alarm. The first part of *The Rights of Man* was printed uniform
with Burke's *Reflections* and sold for three shillings. It was only when
the corresponding societies began distributing Paine's works by the
thousands in cheap editions that any plowman could afford that Pitt
found himself agreeing with Burke that the proper answer to such
arguments was a criminal prosecution.

First he hired a government clerk named Chalmers to write a book
refuting Paine's doctrines. Chalmers brought out a scandalmongering

biography. Defamation of their hero only stimulated the corresponding societies to greater efforts. Repression became the policy of Pitt's
administration. Parliament, with Burke and his supporters voting with
Pitt's Tories, approved a royal proclamation against "wicked and seditious writings, printed, published, and industriously dispersed." Even
before the proclamation, on the plea that Paine himself could not be
found, a summons was served on Paine's publisher, Jordan.

As it turned out, events in France were to play into the hands
of Pitt's administration and to justify to all except the most convinced
republicans Burke's wild denunciations. The constitution which Lafayette had charged with such great hopes was no sooner sworn to at the
Festival of the Federations than the Assembly started picking it to
pieces again. Everybody had a notion of how to improve it. Lafayette
stood almost alone in its defense. "I am still tossed about in the ocean
of factions and commotions of every kind," he complained to Washington. "For it is my fate to be on each side and with equal animosity
attacked both by the Aristocratic, Slavish" — here he meant the West
India colonials who opposed the emancipation of their slaves — "Parliamentary, Clerical, in a word by all enemies to my free and levelling
doctrine, and on the other side by the orleanoise, factious, AntiRoyal,
licentious and pillaging parties of every kind, so that my personal
escape from amidst so many hostile bands is rather dubious."

Mirabeau's death left him again the most popular man in France.
When Louis bolted from the Tuileries disguised as a footman and fled
north to join the emigration it was Lafayette who ordered his recapture. The King was found eating his usual copious dinner at Varennes.
When the royal family were brought back to the Tuileries, Lafayette
could think of nothing but his precious constitution. He was hurt that
the King did not take kindly to his advice. Gouverneur had lost
patience with him entirely. "Unfortunately," he reported to Washington, "both for himself and his country he has not the talents which
this situation requires."

A year after the royal family's shamefaced return to their imprisonment, Gouverneur was dining with Short and a group of Americans at
the legation on the Fourth of July. The guest of honor as usual was
Lafayette. Paine was among them, come over from London to write an
article for a republican newspaper which he and Condorcet had
founded.

Paine had already burned his bridges behind him. His advice to the
French was to treat the King's attempt to escape as an abdication. You
will be better off without him: set up a republic. The Paris streets were
placarded with his manifesto. He had been threatened with arrest by

the monarchists in the Assembly. Gouverneur by this time loathed Paine. "Payne is here," he noted in his diary, "inflated to the eyes and big with a litter of revolutions."

7. *Liberty Stifled in Blood*

Gouverneur has convinced himself by this time that the revolution has gone too far already. Any further agitation he considers criminal. "This unhappy country," he writes Washington, "bewildered in the Pursuit of metaphysical Whimsies, presents to our Moral View a Mighty Ruin . . . The Sovereign, humbled to the Level of a Beggar's Pity, without Resources, without Authority, without a Friend. The Assembly at once a Master and a Slave, new in Power, wild in Theory, raw in Practice. It engrosses all Functions tho incapable of exercising any, and has taken from this fierce ferocious People every Restraint of Religion and of Respect . . . Such a State of Things cannot last."

Able operators have discovered that immense things can be accomplished by skillful use of the armed mob. One bloody explosion follows another. In the abandoned convents and in the gardens of the Palais Royale orators call for blood in the name of Condorcet's trinity of liberty, equality, and reason. Treasons and aristocratic plots become the morning fare of the newspapers. To be a revolutionary means to demand the death of traitors. The great phrases from the Declaration of Rights hover like birds of prey over the Paris streets.

Lafayette had set himself desperately to stem the torrent. He had spent all the money he could raise from his estates to bolster his political party. He had threatened and complained, sought military appointments and resigned them. He even had retired for a while to his château in Auvergne, but the attraction of the whirlpool of Paris was too great. Always he saw himself like Washington as the patriot general of a citizen army.

When the Declaration of Pillnitz, in August 1791, had seemed to threaten an émigré invasion backed by the despots of Germany, the Assembly appointed Lafayette to command one of the northern armies. He threw himself in his carriage and drove off at top speed to Metz. "I will send you an exact return of my Army when it is finally arranged," he wrote Washington, "for I always consider myself, my dear General, as one of your lieutenants on a detached command."

Lafayette's army is fated never to be "finally arranged" because its commander cannot keep his mind on his soldiering. He keeps flying back to Paris to defend his reputation.

The Constituent Assembly gives place to the Legislative Assembly. The seating of the new deputies in their redecorated hall becomes suddenly significant. On the right are Lafayette's constitutionalists, on the left the new shrill voices that hail from the Gironde, from the Jacobins, from the Cordeliers, from the municipality of Paris. The madmen crowd into the extreme top benches of the left; they are already known as the Mountain.

The map of France is reorganized again. The decimal system is established. Monopolies are abolished. The farmers-general are herded into jail. Old abuses and old vested interests are legislated away, but the strife and hatred between factions makes orderly government impossible. Ambitions flare on every street corner. Ministry follows ministry. The armies of the coalition of kings are advancing. Fear of retribution by the triumphant reaction fills the streets of Paris with madness. Behind every shuttered window men see an avenging aristocrat.

The Assembly where Lafayette's constitutional party still has a thin majority is helpless before the ambitions of men who have learned the dangerous science of evoking the mob. Only war to the death can save the nation. In April of 1792 the Assembly declares war on Austria. In June the mob, goaded by news of defeats of the national armies, attacks the Tuileries. The Bourbon princes have instigated the coalition. The royal family is a nest of traitors.

The Bourbon does not lack courage. Louis calmly walks out on a balcony wearing a liberty cap on his head and carrying a glass of wine in his hand, and stands looking stolidly down on the waving pikes and the red caps. His fumbling quiet demeanor quells the insurrection.

"The Constitution," Gouverneur Morris, who has just got news of his appointment as American minister to France, notes in his diary, "has this Day I think given its last groan."

The moment Lafayette hears the news of this fresh uprising, forgetting his military command he sets off posthaste for Paris. He is forever flinging himself into his traveling carriage. When he arrives at the town house of de la Rochefoucauld, his old friend is astonished at his state of frenzy. Lafayette appears at the bar of the Assembly and by a passionate speech staves off a vote of censure. He tries to call out the National Guard to support the constitution, to protect the person of the King and the liberty of the citizens. The time has come for the Washington of France to show himself on his white horse. The National Guard is to gather on the Champs Elysées and to discipline the Parisians. Only a hundred men show up. While the Assembly is pronouncing the nation in danger, Lafayette is already in his carriage again driving off to rejoin his army. His supporters are still strong enough in the Assembly to reject a motion for his impeachment.

By August 10, 1792, the extremists will be ready for their coup d'état. The mob will storm the Tuileries again. The King will tell his Swiss guards not to fire. The Swiss will be massacred almost to a man.

In a safe in the royal study documents will be found to incriminate half the moderates in France, among them letters of Lafayette, who has been trying to arrange a fresh flight of the King, this time to Compiègne.

The hour of the republic has come. The deposed King is confined in the Temple. Commissioners to the armies announce the new regime that will complete the revolution. Lafayette claps three of them into jail and musters his troops on the famous plain of Sedan. When he adjures his soldiers to defend the King and the constitution murmurings and mutterings are the only reply. On a sudden impulse he throws up his career as the Washington of France and rides off into the gathering dusk.

About twenty of his staff officers follow him. "Je me suis abandonne à mon sort," he writes. The little troupe rides vaguely northward in search of neutral soil. There is no more neutral soil in Europe. Near a Belgian village they stumble on an Austrian detachment. When the officer in charge arrests him, Lafayette haughtily announces that since he has resigned from the French service he is an American citizen. He demands to be taken to the American legation at the Hague. Instead he is hustled off to a dungeon in Magdeburg. First the Austrians, then the Prussians keep him imprisoned. Through the years at Olmütz through prison walls he is to hear muffled echoes of the tragedy of liberalism in France: the massacre of his friends in the Paris prisons in September; the Convention; the trial of the King; the timely invention of the guillotine by a humanitarian Paris physician whose aim was to abolish inhuman punishments; the carnival of blood presided over by Robespierre, that meticulous provincial notary who is such a fanatic for the rights of man that he can find no man good enough to enjoy them. "In a word," as Lafayette writes in a letter smuggled out of his dungeon, "natural liberty, civil liberty, religious liberty, political liberty stifled in blood."

8. *Paine the Outlaw*

Mobs rose in England too, but they started from the other side of the street. Already in Birmingham the loyal English had celebrated the Bastille's second anniversary by rioting for two days. They burned dissenting churches. They harried members of the brilliant group of scientists and philosophers congregated about Boulton and Watt's ironworks where the first steam engines were being built. On the rumor that Joseph Priestley was going to attend a dinner of the Constitutional Society a drunken crowd rushed his house, wrecked his laboratory, destroyed his papers and his library, and burned the place to the ground. Priestly himself barely escaped with his life. The annual dinner of the Revolution Society could find no tavern to accommodate it. On Guy Fawkes Day the crowds at the street corners now burn Tom Paine in effigy instead of the Pope.

Paine's friends, more afraid of the mobs than of the Attorney General, kept urging him to leave the country. William Blake, the poet of the inner illumination, reported to be the only man in London who carried his enthusiasm for the French Revolution to the point of wearing a red liberty cap around the streets, came to Paine at Rickman's one night and warned him, in a voice as full of prophecy as one of his own apocalyptic drawings, to flee at once.

A few days later Paine is able to depart for France without laying himself open, at least so he thinks, to the taunt of running away from his trial. A certain Citizen Audibert has crossed the Channel to announce to him that the Pas-de-Calais have elected him its representative in the National Convention now convening with the purpose of establishing a last and perfect constitution to take the place of the discredited one Lafayette wrecked his career trying to defend. The customs officers rummage in Paine's papers until they find a personal letter from George Washington which so awes them that they let the embattled staymaker depart in peace.

His packet has hardly cleared the harbor jetties when a rider comes galloping into Dover with a warrant for his arrest.

In Paris, Paine, working through an interpreter because he still knows no French, devotes himself to the heady business of dictating the clauses of a perfect constitution. If he had not felt he had a higher duty to perform in France he would have stayed in England, not to "defend himself but to defend his principles," he writes the Attorney General from Paris. "The duty I am now engaged in is of too much importance to permit me to trouble myself about your prosecution."

He asks him as one man to another whether the prosecution is intended against a Thomas Paine or against "the right of the people of England to investigate systems and principles of government." He calls "the government of England . . . the greatest perfection of fraud and corruption that ever took place since governments began . . . Is it possible that you or I can believe," he adds recklessly, "or that reason can make any other man believe, that the capacity of such a man

as Mr. Guelf, or any of his profligate sons, is necessary to the government of a nation?" He ends with a threat: "I know also that I speak
what other people are beginning to think."

All the Attorney General has to do to ruin the great liberal lawyer
Thomas Erskine's carefully calculated defense of the right of free
speech is to read Paine's letter to the jury. They bring in an immediate
verdict of guilty. When the Prince of Wales hears himself described
as Mr. Guelf's profligate son he so far fails to see the humor of the
situation as to discharge Erskine as his household lawyer.

The news of Paine's condemnation in absentia to outlawry in England will appear in the official Paris gazette the same day in which he
stands up in the Convention, after Louis Capet's conviction for treason, to beg that howling assembly to stop and think, to reconsider the
sentence of death. It is the most courageous act of his life. He is
described as standing modestly in the tribune, a sharpfaced man with
handsome dark eyes in a suit of quakerish snuffcolor, wearing his
same old bobtailed wig, while another deputy translates his plea for
mercy in a trembling voice.

Marat answers with a shout that the great Paine is being mistrans-
lated. As a Quaker his opinion is worthless. The Mountain roars. Even
so the motion to confirm the vote to execute Louis Capet is carried
by only a single voice. From that moment Paine's life is in very great
danger. Ten months later he himself will be immured in the Luxembourg to await execution.

Meanwhile in England the news of the guillotining of Louis XVI will
be hardly printed in the gazettes before they will be announcing the Convention's declaration of war. All the force of outraged patriotism will
rise up against any sympathizer with regicide France, and particularly
against democratic societies which corrupt the lower orders. Loyalist
societies will take their place. They will make it their business to circulate simple versions of Burke's arguments. Hannah More's pamphlets will be distributed by the tens of thousands. Patriotic and
charitable ladies will egg on the revivalist ministers to encourage the
workingman to substitute for the hope of a reformed social order in
this world the hope of salvation in the world to come.

The promotors of the Edinburgh convention will be prosecuted as
traitors. Habeas corpus will be suspended. Parliament will pass laws
against unlicensed assemblies. In London a dozen members of the
Corresponding Society will be arrested for high treason and sent to the
Tower. Far from being discouraged by his difficulties with Paine's
case, Thomas Erskine will successfully defend them in one of the great
state trials in English history.

Others will not be so lucky. In Scotland the courts will deal out savage sentences to radicals. A group of men whose only crime is advocating parliamentary reform will be sent to Australia on a convict ship. A Baptist minister will be fined two hundred pounds and sent to jail for two years for complaining of oppressive taxation in a sermon. In Edinburgh a young man named Muir will be sentenced to fourteen years transportation to Botany Bay for recommending *The Rights of Man* to his barber. Pitt is to take no further chances with freedom of thought for the lower orders.

XI   The Spirit of Party and Faction

1.   *The United States Bank*

Jefferson had barely managed to spend a month with his family at Monticello during the summer of 1790. He had hardly time to talk things over with his overseers, or to ride the circuit of his farms, or to make a few projects for rebuilding the hilltop house which, after all he had seen in Europe, now smacked too much of the literal style of the Palladian textbooks to please him, or to renew old intimacies with his neighbors in Albemarle, or to settle back into the warm affections of family life. Martha was already big with her first child.

Before the four weeks were out Jefferson had to be driving over to Orange County to pick up Madison for the trip to Philadelphia. The two men had found so much to talk about on the way down that they had decided to return to the seat of government in the same style. They stopped off at Mount Vernon.

Washington had been beguiling his own scanty leisure by filling the mails with explicit instructions to Tobias Lear as to the furnishing and arrangement of one of Robert Morris's two big downtown houses that had been rented for his use in Philadelphia. He had improved his health by the early morning canters he so loved. He had taken the time to ride from corner to corner of the ten miles square that included what *The Times and Potowmack Packet* of Georgetown was already referring to as "the Grand Columbian Federal City."

Most of the talk between Washington and Madison and Jefferson over the dinner table at Mount Vernon must have been about the federal city: how could they make the project an accomplished fact before some realignment in Congress should repeal the settlement act?

The first thing needed was buildings. Jefferson and Madison had concluded that if the states of Maryland and Virginia could each be induced to appropriate funds to build ten good private dwelling houses every year, the capital's location on the Potomac would be assured. All three men were united on the urgency of the work. Washington was planning to put up some houses himself. It was a topic on which the President and his Secretary of State agreed perfectly.

Years before, Washington had written Jefferson telling him how it pleased him that Jefferson, who could expect no personal advantage from the Potomac and Ohio Canal, was backing the project, in which, he admitted, he himself had a financial as well as a public interest. Now Jefferson's and Madison's enthusiasm for the location on the Potomac was whetted by the hope that moving the capital west would get Congress out of reach of the businessmen and speculators with whose lobbies they had had bitter experience in New York.

At the seat of government both Virginians went to board with Mrs. House until they could find themselves more permanent quarters. Soon they were joined there by their mutual friend Monroe, appointed by the Virginia Assembly to the Senate to take the place of William Grayson, who had been one of the victims of the influenza in New York during the past spring.

James Monroe was now thirtytwo. Although Monroe and Madison had differed about the Constitution, he and Jefferson were of one mind on the question of setting up new states in the West. Through his uncle Joseph Jones' interest in the old Ohio Company, Monroe had been brought up with his imagination full of the Western Waters. He had ably assisted Jefferson in securing the adoption of the first ordinance for the government of the Northwest.

After Jefferson sailed for France, Monroe had ridden out to the new settlements to see for himself. While he sat in the Continental Congress he made two extensive and strenuous trips through the western country. Passing through New York on one of these trips, he met a girl of some wealth in the circle of the Stirlings and of Lady Kitty Duer, who, in spite of her tender years, was already very much the great lady. Elizabeth Kortright was the daughter of a flourishing New York merchant. When Monroe rather stiffly proposed to her, to the surprise of their acquaintances she accepted him. When he took his bride to Virginia it was to open a law office and take up his residence in his uncle's house in Fredericksburg. As soon as he was able, he bought them a home of their own in Charlottesville, and a tract of land near Carter's Mountain where he could eventually build a country house near his friend Jefferson.

Monroe had been particularly outspoken against Jay's submission to Spain's shutting off the free navigation of the Mississippi. The fact

that he had run against Madison for the House in the elections for the
First Congress hardly interfered with their friendship. It was as a
westernfacing man more or less of Patrick Henry's anti-Federalist
stripe that, in spite of the opposition of another young lawyer from
the northeastern part of the state, the enthusiastic continentalist John
Marshall, he had been chosen for the Senate. He arrived in Philadelphia fresh from the vigorous protest of the Virginia legislators against
funding and assumption.

Monroe was a staunch, somewhat slow witted man, one of those men
whose character and intelligence develop gradually. In the Senate he
would prove a loyal confederate to Madison and Jefferson. His suspicion of everything Hamilton stood for, so obviously typical of the
attitude of the plain people in the South and West, went far towards
toughening their opposition to the plans of the Treasury. With Monroe on their side, they felt they had the people on their side. In spite
of his wife's social relations with the hightoned families of New York,
the young lawyer from the Northern Neck had the feelings of the
farmers and settlers and the western pioneers in his blood. He was a
man furthermore to whom personal loyalties were highly important.
His politics were sometimes blundering, but they were all of one piece.
Jefferson, who had great affection for him, wrote of him years later
as "a man whose soul might be turned wrong side outwards without
discovering a blemish to the world."

On December 13 Hamilton asked the House of Representatives,
sitting in the brick building the Pennsylvanians had built for the use
of Congress next to their own State House, for an increased excise on
spirits. The same day he followed it up with a proposal for a national
bank modeled on the Bank of England. Immediately the rift among
the administration supporters, which had appeared on the question
of assumption, began to assume the proportions of a real cleavage
between parties.

Madison, basing his argument on his clear recollection of the debates of the Constitutional Convention, insisted that, desirable as
private or state banks were, the delegates had explicitly refused to
give the general government the right to incorporate such an institution. His arguments were eagerly seconded by a newly elected congressman from Virginia, William Branch Giles, a twentyeight year old
Petersburg lawyer who had been a classmate of John Beckley's and
of Jefferson's devoted friend Short at William and Mary, and had
studied law under George Wythe and grown up a passionate addict
of Thomas Jefferson and everything he stood for. Jackson of Georgia
pointed out that this particular plan for a bank "was calculated to

benefit . . . the mercantile interest only; the farmers, the yeomanry will derive no advantage from it."

Fisher Ames as a representative of the merchants and moneyed men of Massachusetts defended the bank bill on the ground of implied powers. He was joined by most of the members from the northern and middle states. Giles, listening to the debate with the fresh ear of a newcomer, deplored "a radical difference of opinion between gentlemen from the Eastern and Southern states" and expressed the fear "that the operation of that cause alone might cast ominous conjecture on the promised success of this much valued Government." The bill passed early in February by a vote of 39 to 20.

Madison now found himself the leader of the opposition in the house, but in so far as Madison was concerned it was still very fervently the President's loyal opposition.

Washington, as he always did when he had a tough nut to crack, asked for written opinions from his cabinet. The Virginians, Jefferson and Randolph, prepared careful statements advising him not to sign the bank bill. In substance they repeated what Madison had been saying on the floor of the House. Incorporation did not come within the delegated powers. As Jefferson put it: "To take a single step beyond the boundaries thus especially drawn around the powers of Congress, is to take possession of a boundless field of power, no longer susceptible of any definition."

Hamilton, with his boyish ingenuousness of manner, took advantage of his "commander and favorite aide" relationship with Washington to induce the President to let him take Jefferson's and Randolph's opinions home to study. In one of his whirlwind compositions, cleverly evading the question of what class of people would profit most from the type of bank he advocated, he wrote his famous opinion that became the political gospel of the American centralism to which John Marshall so ably played St. Paul in later years. Hamilton answered his colleagues' arguments point by point. "Every power vested in a government is by nature *sovereign* and includes by the *force* of the *term,* all the means requisite and fairly applicable to the attainment of the ends of such power."

Washington was a practical man. He had no head for abstract theories of government. Hamilton convinced him that a national bank was a practical necessity. He signed the bill.

When Fisher Ames mailed a copy of Hamilton's report to a friend he included a note of explanation that told another side of the story: "The late surprising rise in public stocks is supposed to be owing in part to this report, because it affords an opportunity to subscribe three fourth paper and one fourth silver into the bank stock."

William Maclay, the senator from Pennsylvania who represented the settlers and farmers of the western hills, had been particularly upset over the passage of the excise act increasing the tax on home-distilled whiskey. He made the entry in his diary: "Congress may go home. Mr. Hamilton is all-powerful and fails in nothing he attempts."

"If there is treason in the wish I retract it; but would to God this same General Washington were in heaven," he had written a few days before. "We would not then have him brought forward as the constant cover to every unconstitutional and irrepublican act."

2. Freedom's Guardian

The First Congress adjourned sine die on March 3, 1791. Men viewed its achievements in the light of their hopes and fears and of their diverse desires as to the shape of the nation they were building, but on the whole both the Treasury party and the still disorganized opposition had some reason for satisfaction. The central government worked. The national credit had been established. Due to Washington's respect for the law as he saw it and to his spirit of accommodation the machinery of the administration had been set smoothly in motion. Every one of the thirteen original states had ratified the Constitution, and the admission of two new states, Vermont and Kentucky, was already assured. The farmers were prosperous. The merchants were making money. The towns were booming.

Washington always preferred to see things with his own eyes rather than to rely on "information." As soon as he could shake himself loose from the levees and the protocol and the confining paperwork of his office he set out for a tour of the states to the southward from which most of the "animadversions" had come about the monarchical trend of the administration. His fellow citizens would see for themselves that he was still the same old General Washington of wartime. He took only one secretary along but he could not help traveling with a certain pomp.

Even though Mrs. Washington stayed in Philadelphia he rode in his fine new creamcolored carriage just imported from England. "My equipage and attendance," he noted in his diary, "consisted of a Charriot and four horses drove in hand — a light baggage Waggon and two horses — four saddle horses besides a led one for myself — and five — to wit; — my Valet de Chambre, two footmen, Coachmen and postillion."

He followed Madison's and Jefferson's route across Chesapeake Bay, but without their luck with the weather. After a stormy crossing his boat went aground in the mouth of the Severn, "the night being immensely dark with heavy and variable squalls of wind, constant lightning and tremendous thunder," there was no way of getting her afloat till daybreak. The President lay all night "in my Great Coat and Boots, in a birth not long enough for me by a head and much cramped." The governor of Maryland made it up to him next morning by greeting him with fifteen guns when he landed and the citizens of Annapolis set him up to a public dinner at the same tavern where young Tom Shippen had so enjoyed the turtle.

After a night at Bladensburg (he must have laughed over the story of Mrs. Adams' privy) he reached Georgetown in time for dinner. There he delivered to Congressman Carroll and to his close friend Dr. Stuart and to Judge Thomas Johnson of Maryland their appointments as the commissioners for the federal district. Riding in a drizzly mist about the site of the new city to cast his professional eye over the staubs and stakes of the survey, he managed to talk the local landholders who had lots to sell into working together, instead of blocking progress by trying to cut each others' throats: "Arguments were used to show the danger which might result from delay and the good effects that might proceed from a Union."

He spent a week visiting his plantations at Mount Vernon and then set out for the Carolinas. Crossing the Colchester ferry, he had a mishap that nearly cost him his fine new English carriage. One of the lead horses slipped overboard in the middle of Occaquan Creek and dragged the other three after him, so that only with great difficulty horses, harness and carriage were saved. The President drove south through Fredericksburg, so full of memories of his childhood and his crochety old mother, to Richmond where he was delighted as Jefferson had been with the progress of the James River canal. Jefferson's old friend Carrington, who was now federal marshal and who had been traveling all over the state as Hamilton's representative in charge of collecting the excise, assured the President that the people of Virginia were "favorable towards the Central Government" and only needed "to have matters explained to them in order to obtain their full assent to the Measures adopted by it."

He found the flour mills on Appomattox Creek at Petersburg flourishing though the main business of the town still was the export of tobacco. Wheat was beginning to compete with the Indian weed as Virginia's main cash crop. Between Petersburg and the first North Carolina settlements the road was a cloud of dust before a rain and a bed of mud afterwards: "but few good Houses with small appearances of wealth."

In New Bern, which had been a more modest Williamsburg in

colonial days, the lodgings were "exceeding good" and the President attended a dancing assembly in the evening, which was graced by "abt. 70 ladies." The road south to Wilmington led "through the most barren country I ever beheld." There were no inns so he had to accept the hospitality of private houses.

After entering South Carolina his horses pulled the chariot "with ease and celerity" for sixteen miles along a hardpacked ocean beach. In Georgetown he was acclaimed by "about 50 ladies who had assembled at a tea party on the occasion."

A twelveoared barge rowed by twelve ship captains carried him across the Cooper River to Charleston amid a welcoming flotilla of small boats. Bands played and guns roared out salutes. When the President had installed himself in the fine house on Church Street which had been swept and garnished for his use — at about the same charge as he would have paid at an inn, he was careful to note — he was called on, in a flock, "by a great number of the most respectable ladies of Charleston — the first honor of the kind I had ever experienced, and it was flattering as it was singular."

On this whole trip he was much impressed by the numbers — often with his penchant for exact figures, he noted the count of heads in his diary — and the well-dressed and "respectable" appearance of the ladies who turned out to do him honor. The adulation of the lovely ladies touched him more than the salvos of musketry or the parading militia or the endless reduplication of welcoming addresses hailing him as "Our Beloved Chief," "Freedom's Guardian," "Mankind's Best Friend" and the like.

He pushed south along the coast as far as Savannah, which was about as far south as a carriage could go, and then turned inland up the Georgia side of the Savannah River to Augusta. He was particularly anxious to find out how the people of Georgia, where the legislature had been parceling out Indian lands, took his insistence that all dealings with the Indians should be through the general government. It was in the hope of putting a quietus on the operations of the frontier speculators that he had signed his treaty with the Creeks. He visited South Carolina's new inland capital at Columbia, which he found "laid out on a large scale," but mostly still "an uncleared wood," and drove by long difficult stages, where his horses suffered for lack of water, up into the piedmont region of North Carolina and so home to Virginia through the old unhappy battlegrounds past Guilford Court House.

The President noted that everywhere he went the people appeared "happy, contented and satisfied with the government under which they were placed — Where the case was otherwise, it was not difficult to trace the cause to some demagogue or speculating character."

Washington rested up a couple of weeks at Mount Vernon before starting back to Philadelphia. In Georgetown on the way he superintended the signing of the deeds for the land needed for Washington City by the adjoining landowners, explained to them L'Enfant's plat with its radiating avenues, and rode out to make his final choice of a location for the capitol on Jenkins Hill. He celebrated Independence Day in York, Pennsylvania, and from there drove briskly over a good road to Philadelphia.

In a fit of sanguine spirits unusual to him he took up his presidential duties again. "The Country appears in a very improving State," he wrote David Humphreys, who had been despatched with his and Jefferson's common blessing on a secret mission to Europe to sound out the Spanish court on the question of the Mississippi, "and Industry and Frugality are becoming much more fasionable than they have hitherto been there. Tranquility reigns . . . and with it that Disposition towards the General Government which is likely to preserve it. They begin to feel the good effects of equal Laws and equal Protection. The Farmer finds a ready Market for his produce and the Merchant calculates with more certainty on his Payments."

In his last circular letter to the states as commander in chief of the Continental Army, Washington had spoken of the citizens of America "as sole Lords and Proprietors of a vast Tract of Continent comprehending all the various soils and climates of the World, and abounding in all the necessaries and conveniences of Life."

Before his election he had made a last rugged trip on horseback to the Ohio. As President and with added gusto he had pushed his official journeys first northward and now southward. As a farmer he loved to ride through croplands, good or bad, studying them with a professional eye. As a merchant of wilderness real estate, he loved appraising the possibilities of new country for settlement and development. As President of the United States his progresses had a deeper meaning. In that last circular he had spoken of the Americans as "Actors in a most conspicuous Theatre; which seems particularly designated by Providence for the display of human greatness and Felicity," with "a fairer possibility for political Happiness, than any other Nation has ever been favored with." When he took his oath as commander in chief he had given his life to a nation that had not yet come into being. Through the hammering griefs and frustrations of the war years amor patriae had become his religion. There was no more intense delight for him than to discover that the projected nation had come to be. Now in his progresses through the country he was managing to impart to the people who turned out to greet him that feeling of triumphant patriotism.

"We were educated in royalism," Jefferson had written Madison from Paris in a letter discussing the prospects for free institutions; "the rising race are all republicans," he had added. Until that new generation should establish new habits of thought it was the tall figure of Washington riding into town on his white stallion that filled the gap left in men's imaginations by the elimination of King George. Instead of the King's birthday it was Washington's birthday they celebrated now. Instead of "Gentlemen the King" it was "General Washington" they toasted at their banquets. Speedily the figure grew in American imagination until the myth eclipsed the man.

3. *Political Heresies*

While the President was seeing the southern states with his own eyes, Jefferson and Madison were off on a junket of their own to the northward, riding in Jefferson's phaeton, each with a single servant to attend to the horses. They met in New York. Madison arrived there first. It was rumored that the little bachelor was paying his addresses to an intellectual widow of that city named Mrs. Colden. Among conversations with anti-Federalist republican friends at Mrs. Elsworth's boardinghouse it is highly likely the two men talked over the prospects for the coming presidential election with New York's new senator, a successful lawyer a couple of years younger than Hamilton even, whose name was Aaron Burr.

A New Jersey man, Aaron Burr was a grandson of one president of the college at Princeton and the son of another. His mother was the daughter of the intense New England divine, Jonathan Edwards. Burr graduated at Princeton some years before the Revolutionary War with a reputation for restless inquisitiveness of mind that verged on impertinence. He was on Arnold's staff in the illfated Quebec expedition and made himself such a name for courage and energy that Washington took him into his own military family with the rank of major. His irreverence and lack of decorum offended the general, who liked a certain deference in his young men, and as early as the Battle of Long Island, Burr was serving under Rufus Putnam.

Burr from his youth was a disenchanted man. He was never one of Washington's admirers. He was among the discontented spirits at Valley Forge. The close of the war found him studying law under William Paterson, soon so ably to represent New Jersey at the Philadelphia convention. He married the widow of a British colonel who had been the gay beloved hostess for young officers at her Hermitage at Paramus in the Jerseys during the Hudson River campaigns. In

THE SPIRIT OF PARTY AND FACTION

spite of being ten years her junior he astounded his friends, whom he had taught to think of him as a headlong rake, by being devotedly true to her as long as she lived. When she died he transferred that complete devotion to their one small daughter Theodosia. He opened a law office in New York City and became the friendly rival of Hamilton at the bar.

When Hamilton moved to Philadelphia with the general government, Burr managed to supplant him as Manhattan's chief political organizer. He exercised a fascination over less audacious men second only to Hamilton's.

Burr was another short dapper man, very much of Hamilton's height and build except that he was dark where Hamilton was fair. Like Hamilton, he was a very bantam cock to strut about the hens. Few women, or few juries when he argued a case, could resist his saturnine charm. People remarked on the extraordinarily piercing glance of his black eyes.

Martling's Long Room was the social center of the Society of Tammany, which, though eternally convivial, was taking on a political cast. When Burr's young supporters presided over the sessions there they aped his confident offhand manner and his bold freethinking talk. Though they rarely saw him in person, through his political henchmen he became the hero of the tradesmen and apprentices and the mechanics' organizations Hamilton had marshaled in support of the Constitution.

The graver heads among his associates were already dismayed by his unblushing lack of scruple. A man without hypocrisy, perhaps; but those who resisted his fascination worried. He frightened them. They found a streak in him of pure theological evil which his grandfather Jonathan Edwards had so eloquently portrayed.

George Clinton had appointed Aaron Burr attorney general of New York. By making himself useful in a legal way as a link between the governor and the Livingston connection in an unwholesome deal in state lands, Burr managed to get himself chosen senator in place of Hamilton's devoted fatherinlaw Philip Schuyler, whose influence in the affairs of the state waned from then on.

The New York politicians felt that Burr was a man with a future. His position was that of a moderate Federalist. They were looking forward to a contest for the vice presidency in 1792. New York was already a pivotal state. There as elsewhere all factions agreed that George Washington must serve again, but the diverse opponents of the hightoned centralizing tendency had one thing in common; they wanted to put out John Adams. For Vice President, Burr was their man.

Philip Schuyler's defeat was a serious setback for Hamilton. Jefferson and Madison had hardly started on their sightseeing and botanizing excursion when Hamilton's adherents were reading political implications into it. "There was every appearance of a passionate courtship," Hamilton's old Albany friend Robert Troup warned him from New York in mid-June, "between the Chancellor" — Robert R. Livingston — "Burr, Jefferson and Madison, when the latter two were in town." Troup was in a position to know, because as a very young man he had been Burr's most intimate friend. "They had better be quiet," he added ominously, "for if they succeed they will tumble the fabric of government in ruins to the ground."

Jefferson was all his life somewhat surreptitious about politics. He liked to think of himself as the disinterested natural philosopher aloof from personalities and from the illtempered wrangling and abuse of the debates between parties. He agreed with Washington that the sort of factional strife that had made the local politics of Pennsylvania a nightmare during the war years should be eliminated from the general government. At the same time he had passionate convictions and personal feelings he could not keep to himself. They fired other men to action on a far from philosophic plane.

Now he was telling everyone that what he wanted was to get away from national affairs, to enjoy the summer weather and the pleasures of adventuring along unknown roads among trees and plants and animals new to him. He trusted to the fresh air to rid him of another migraine headache.

In Philadelphia he had been made chairman of a committee of the American Philosophical Society to study the Hessian fly that ravaged the wheat which had become the American farmer's most successful cash crop. The letters he wrote on the trip dealt almost entirely with his researches into the habits of the pestiferous fly and with the loveliness of the northern mountains.

Late in May Jefferson and Madison embarked the phaeton and their horses on board one of the broadbottomed Dutchtype fore and aft rigged vessels that plied the Hudson River and proceeded by water through the magnificent mountain gap under Storm King to Poughkeepsie. From there they drove up by Albany, where Hamilton's supporters claimed they had a sinister political conference with Governor Clinton, to Lake George.

Jefferson wrote his daughters on sheets of birchbark. "Lake George is, without comparison, the most beautiful piece of water I ever saw," he wrote Martha, "finely interspersed with islands, it's water limpid as crystal, and the mountainsides covered with rich groves of thuya,

silver fir, white pine, aspen and paper birch down to the water-edge
. . . an abundance of speckled trout, salmon trout, bass and other fish
have added to our amusements the sport of taking them."

They pushed up into Lake Champlain against a head wind and a
high sea. At the house where they lodged opposite Crown Point they
were delighted with the abundance of squirrels.

They drove across the Green Mountains to Bennington. Madison
was an enthusiastic botanist; the two friends admired the north woods
trees; the paper birch, an aspen with a velvet leaf, a wild gooseberry,
a shrubby willow new to them. They argued about the botanical name
of a rosypink fragrant azalea.

In Bennington, nestled in its hills, they were regaled with information about parties and policies in Canada. Jefferson reported to
Washington that in spite of the statesmanlike management of the
formidable Lord Dorchester the dominion was dividing into French-
Canadian and Anglo-Canadian factions. In the same letter he complained of the encroachment of a British ship enforcing the customs
into American waters on Lake Champlain. He was silent about the
political opinions of the Vermonters. Jefferson was keeping to himself
what he learned of the political sympathies of this new state of self-
willed mountaineers. He filled his letters with something he enjoyed
much more: an account of their maple sugar industry.

The Vermont law against Sunday travel held them an extra day in
Bennington. From there they followed the Connecticut River Valley
almost to the sea and then cut over to Guilford where they ferried
across the Sound. They drove back down the whole length of Long
Island. Jefferson bought up the entire stock of sugar maples at a nurs-
ery they visited on the way to send home for planting on his Monticello hilltop.

Back in Philadelphia, very much refreshed, he wrote Martha that
his health had been perfect throughout the trip. He remarked that he
felt the heat more in the North than he did in the South. In spite of
the sultry weather the pleasure of the jaunt had freed him from the
headache that had tortured him through the entire winter, which he
attributed to the drudgery of the State Department.

While Jefferson drove back to his paperwork in Philadelphia, Madison stayed on in New York. He was joined there by John Beckley,
who was on his way to Massachusetts and New Hampshire to sound
out public sentiment. The country was dividing into political parties
like the parties in England. Madison was already being written of in
the newspapers friendly to his views as the American Charles James
Fox. Hamilton was the American Pitt. The clerk of the House of Rep-

resentatives was not wasting his time on the Hessian fly or on the
study of sugarbushes. He was a man whose entire life was devoted
to politics.

Because his horse was off his feed from so much traveling; or because the heat had brought on a return of the "bilious dispositions"
that worried his friends; or on account of Aaron Burr's amusing conversation; or perhaps because of the charms of the widow Colden,
Madison let Beckley ride off alone on his listening trip into New
England. Not even his old college friend, the debonair Henry Lee of
light horse fame, could tempt him out of New York. He was getting
to enjoy politicking as much as John Beckley. He was much less dismayed than Jefferson by the factional cleavage in the President's
court.

"Mr. Adams seems to be getting faster and faster into difficulties,"
he wrote Jefferson maliciously. "His attack on Paine, which I have
not seen, will draw the public attention to his principles, more than
anything he has published." He was referring to a series of letters
signed "Publicola" which had started to appear in *The Columbian
Centinal* of Boston while the two of them were still happily catching
trout and shooting squirrels in the north woods.

With the appearance of these Publicola letters the war of words
that had already been raging in England for a year over the principles
and practices of the French Revolution broke out on American soil.

Earlier that spring Beckley, who had correspondents among the
reforming English Whigs, received a copy of the first part of Paine's
Rights of Man and passed it on to Madison, who in turn gave it to
Jefferson to read. Jefferson read, approved and, with Beckley jogging
his memory because the printer was impatient to get the pamphlet set
up, sent it to press with a covering letter in which he said:

> I am extremely pleased to find it will be reprinted here,
> and that something is at length to be publickly said against
> the political heresies which have sprung up among us.
>
> I have no doubt our citizens will rally a second time round
> the standard of Common Sense.

The printer placed Jefferson's words on the flyleaf. *The Rights of
Man* was immediately as widely read in America as in England. Jefferson's endorsement was so often quoted that Jefferson began to fear
that his old friend John Adams would be offended. The word "heresies" could apply only to his *Discourses on Davila* which had run all
winter in *The Gazette of the United States*. Before starting on his
jaunt with Madison, Jefferson had written Washington, who had himself a friendly feeling for Tom Paine, in explanation of this seeming
breach in the solidarity of the administration: ". . . I am afraid the

indiscretion of a printer has committed me with my friend John Adams, for whom, as one of the most honest & disinterested men alive, I have cordial esteem, increased by long concurrence of opinion in the days of his republicanism; and even since his apostasy to hereditary monarchy & nobility, though we differ, we differ as friends should do . . . I tell the writer freely that he is a heretic, but certainly I never meant to step into a public newspaper with that in my mouth."

4. The Appeal to the Reading Public

The Hamilton faction in Philadelphia immediately raised a hue and cry against Jefferson. Major Beckwith, with whom Hamilton was on confidential terms, suggested that the endorsement by a member of Washington's administration of Paine, whom Pitt was treating as a dangerous subversive, would give offense at Westminster.

Now it was Jefferson's turn to be offended. Publicola not only gave Paine a thorough dressing down but he dusted Jefferson's jacket for endorsing him. Jefferson, like every other newspaper reader, had jumped to the conclusion that Publicola was the Vice President. It was Beckley who brought the news back to Madison from Boston that the articles were actually the work of John Adams' precocious and scholarly son, John Quincy.

Madison pointed out sarcastically when he wrote Jefferson that they were too concisely written to be by John Adams himself. The articles restated in more compact form John Adams' strictures on the danger of placing all the powers of government in the hands of a single body like the French Assembly. They advocated his theory of a balance of powers, and summarized effectively the heart of Burke's position, which was that the unwritten British constitution, as the accretion of the habits and customs of centuries, was superior to any newfangled written constitutions whatsoever. In the latter part of the series, young Adams beat a retreat. Defending himself against a flock of letters to the editor from Brutuses, Agricolas, and Republicans, he hastily explained that his criticisms were not intended to apply to the American written Constitution, which he loved and revered, but merely to that of the French.

For six months Madison had been conniving to set up an opposition newspaper in Philadelphia. Hamilton had already captured Fenno's *Gazette of the United States* which had followed the seat of government when it moved from New York. John Fenno was an obsequious fellow who had conducted a writing school in Boston; his ambition,

which George Washington highly approved, was to publish an imitation of the court journals of Europe, to print news of government appointments and proclamations, and discreetly to retail the debates in
the House of Representatives. Any more critical discussion of government affairs Washington was wont to describe as "scurrility and
nonsensical declamation." He had no more use for journalists than he
had for clergymen.

Hamilton from the beginning subsidized Fenno by giving him the
Treasury announcements (which amounted to an income of some two
thousand dollars a year) and occasionally by lending him money out
of his own pocket. Fenno was delighted to print anything the generous
Secretary of the Treasury suggested. Hamilton from his early youth
had understood the importance of the press. With Jay's and Madison's
help he had carried on the successful newspaper campaign for the
Constitution. Now it was obvious to Madison and to his eager partisans like Beckley that if the opposition were to make any headway
against the Treasury interest they must have a paper of their own.

They had trouble convincing Jefferson of the need to take action.
Jefferson, while theoretically he understood the importance of newspapers as organs of republican government, still retained an odd
oldfashioned diffidence about using them. There lingered in his mind
the country gentleman's prejudice; there was something undignified
about publication.

He apologized for his *Notes on Virginia*. Whenever in his public
career he found it necessary to leak some document to a gazette it
was with a disclaimer. All explanations notwithstanding, under the
impulse of Hamilton's report on the bank, he was induced to write
Madison's friend Freneau in New York offering him the job of trans-
lator for the State Department at the salary of $250 a year. The un-
stated condition was that he would edit a paper in Philadelphia.

Philip Freneau, the son of a devout family of New Jersey Huguenots, was a friend of Madison from their salad days at Princeton. As
undergraduates he and Madison and Hugh Brackenridge were tremendous patriots together in the American Whig Society. They ex-
coriated the Tories in doggerel diatribes in the style of Churchill and
of Hudibras. Young Freneau started to write a picaresque novel with
Brackenridge. Madison turned from satiric verse to statebuilding and
Brackenridge took up the law out among the raw hills of fast growing
Pittsburgh but Freneau had stuck to his doggerel.

He was an adventurous fellow. First as a seaman and then as a
skipper of his own small coastwise ships he earned a precarious living
at sea during the period of the war. His spare time he devoted to

writing patriotic verses for the newspapers. Captured on a merchant-man by the British, he nearly died aboard one of the prison ships in New York Harbor and wrote a lively poem about his experiences. His rousing verses were reprinted in the Revolutionary press and heart-ened the patriots in the days when many men despaired of the "glorious Cause." He had recently married and was now trying to make a living writing for Child's *Daily Advertiser* in New York.

Madison and Jefferson found the crusty sailor sitting across the table from them one day when they dined at Mrs. Elsworth's board-inghouse while they were getting ready for their trip into the north woods. Madison was fond of Freneau. He knew him to be a man of talent. He wanted to help him; he felt that with his flair for invective he was just the man to edit a political newspaper. Freneau, it turned out, was no man to jump at a proffer of help even from an old friend. He refused to commit himself. His wife was in a family way and he did not want to move before the baby was born.

It was months before Madison could induce him to accept the State Department post which Jefferson held open for him. At last in the fall of 1791 he consented to move to Philadelphia and to edit a paper from the printshop of Child's Philadelphia partner Swaine.

Hamilton was not slow in pointing out that Child and Swaine were playing both sides of the street. Their New York publication was Federalist and their Philadelphia publication Republican. No matter who owned the press Freneau insisted on his independence. He was a passionate republican of the school of 1776. He was far too touchy to take any man's orders. Both Madison and Brackenridge contributed. It was a revival of the old patriot triumvirate of collegiate days. Though Freneau's editorials and verses appeared under pseudonyms, as editor he scorned any pretense of anonymity; he printed his name square on the masthead of *The National Gazette*.

In the early issues there appeared little that could be construed as criticism of the Secretary of the Treasury. There was criticism of the excise on spirits and of funding and assumption. "A Farmer" deplored the fact that the "accumulation of that power which is conferred by wealth in the hands of a few is the perpetual source of oppression and neglect to the rest of mankind." "Brutus" found that the funding system exalted the moneyman and victimized "the industrious me-chanic, the laborious farmer, and generally the poor and middling class." "Sidney" pointed out somewhat forcefully that the Secretary of the Treasury's methods of securing support for his measures bore too close a resemblance to the bribery and corruption which were the daily practice of British prime ministers. In May the poet echoed the popular cry in his own brand of doggerel:

> Public debts are public curses
> In soldiers hands there nothing worse is!
> In speculators' hands increasing
> Public debt's a public blessing.

In the interest of fair play, he continued during most of his first winter to devote many columns to printing Alexander Hamilton's entire Report on Manufactures.

5. *The Report on Manufactures*

This third and most elaborate of Hamilton's reports was presented to Congress on December 5, 1791. The Report of Manufactures was the result of an immense amount of work by the Secretary and by his assistant Tench Coxe. The idea had been in the air for some years. Tench Coxe had anticipated much of its reasoning in newspaper articles and in speeches before a Pennsylvania society for the encouragement of new industries. Just as the funding and assumption bills were a revival of measures Robert and Gouverneur Morris had failed to get through the old Congress when they were running the Finance Office, it was the census of American industries they had undertaken which Hamilton now completed. For months he had been writing Treasury agents up and down the Atlantic seaboard asking for details of manufacturing establishments actually in operation. Some of the manufacturers were chary of their answers because they were afraid the Secretary would use his information as a basis for new taxes.

Among the answers was a letter from Moses Brown of Rhode Island, who had succeeded in accomplishing something that Tench Coxe and his Philadelphia friends had been trying to do for years. He had laid his hands on a model of Arkwright's continual process mechanical loom. "Late in the fall," he wrote, "I recd. a Letter from a young man then lately Arrived in New York from Arkwright's works in England."

The young man, by name Samuel Slater, had managed, in spite of acts of Parliament forbidding under heavy penalties the export of plans for mechanical improvements or the emigration of mechanics, to smuggle himself aboard a ship bound for New York. Slater had no need to conceal any drawings. He carried the entire plan of Arkwright's new loom in his head. The State of Massachusetts had been experimenting unsuccessfully with a model based on a hearsay description. Here was a man who was not only an inspired mechanic but who had worked with Arkwright himself. Brown invited him to

Providence and before long the two of them were duplicating Arkwright's machinery in a Pawtucket mill which proved to be the foundation of a great textile industry.

The Foreign Office was already alerted. Sir John Temple, the popular British consul in New York, who may not have been as deaf as he pretended to be, was writing to Whitehall about the improvements in American handicrafts. He spoke of the excellence of the cabinetwork, the "perfectly tolerable" cheese, the carriages, the saddlery and men's and women's shoes being turned out "as good as any in England."

As soon as George Hammond, His Majesty's new minister to the United States, an able Yorkshireman of Pitt's own generation, had settled himself at the republican court in Philadelphia he reported to Lord Grenville with dismay that complete models of Arkwright's looms were "in possession of the American government."

Hamilton's report furnished a vivid picture of the industries of the young republic.

Iron ore was being worked with pick and shovel. Even before the war the colonies had outrun the mother country in production of pig iron. Now the Treasury agents reported an increase in the manufacture of sheet iron and nails and farmers' tools and castiron pots and hollow wares.

There were the beginnings of a steel industry. The Germans on the Rappahannock and the Pennsylvania gunsmiths had produced accurate rifles during the Revolution.

A few foundries for copper and brass had sprung up. Brick kilns were plentiful. They made lead bullets in Richmond, Virginia.

The shipbuilders of New England were second to none. There were cabinetmakers in Philadelphia hardly inferior to those of Europe. Glassblowers were flourishing. The cult of homemade textiles during the war years had fostered the weaving of worsteds and cotton and linen fabrics. The seaport towns were producing sailcloth and shipbuilders' supplies and rope and cable in abundance. There were tanners and harnessmakers' shops to compete with British leather goods. Paper was being made. Books were being printed. Lampblack and painters' colors and starch and sugar and hairpowder and gunpowder were available of home manufacture, and of course whisky and rum. Some of these industries were merely in embryo, but they were ready to grow up and flourish under the government's fostering care.

Many members of Congress shared the Secretary of the Treasury's enthusiasm for improving American manufactures, but their ardor cooled when he listed his panaceas for encouraging them. Not even the Federalists were ready yet to go along with a protective tariff, direct bounties to new enterprises, cash premiums for valuable inventions, the exemption of raw materials from the impost, all measures which Hamilton argued could properly be set in motion under the general welfare clause in the Constitution. The Secretary's industry and his prose style were much admired, but the report was laid on the table. Hamilton was having hard sledding that winter.

With characteristic energy, he had not waited for Congress to take action on his plan for manufactures. As a private citizen he had already plunged into an enterprise which he hoped would be the model for future industries. The Society for Establishing Useful Manufactures — S.U.M. it was known for short — was encorporated by the New Jersey legislature a month before Hamilton presented his report to Congress. Tench Coxe published an advance glimpse of the project in *The American Museum* and sent his detailed prospectus to the Secretary of State with the suggestion that something of the sort might fit in with Jefferson's and Washington's plans for the federal city. Hamilton, Coxe explained, was working out the financing of the New Jersey enterprise.

Though the original project may well have been Coxe's the push and enthusiasm to put it across came from Hamilton. He had little hope that Congress would be farseeing enough to take action on his report right away. He intended to proceed as he had with the bank. All his arguments about the need for national banks had fallen on deaf ears until the Bank of North America had proved itself a going concern. Businessmen had made money on it. Now they could not set up banks fast enough. He hoped it would be the same with S.U.M.

In the end Hamilton's enterprise which started out with such fair prospects ran on the rocks because the "art magick" of high finance had turned the heads of his financial associates. Hamilton had no access to speculative funds. His good friend William Duer naturally took the lead in raising the money. Hamilton himself scrupulously refrained from investments that might be affected by his public acts as Secretary of the Treasury; he had no scruples at all about using his public powers to help political supporters. Since Duer had resigned from the Treasury, Hamilton had proved his regard for him by getting him the contracts to supply the small federal army being raised to defend the settlements west of the Ohio against the Indians. To the chagrin of Henry Knox, Hamilton used his influence with Washington to transfer procurement, that great source of political patronage, away from the War Department.

6. *Misadventures of a Favorite Minister*

For Hamilton the Treasury meant the Administration. While

he was building his career in Philadelphia, young William Pitt, at Westminster, with whom he had so much in common, was taking advantage of the reaction against French ideas to mold the Prime Minister's office into an organ of the greatest personal power any British statesman had enjoyed in a century. As Hamilton saw it the secretaries of War and State should be subordinate officers as they were in England. How far he had succeeded could be judged by the budgets for the three departments: in the budget presented to Congress in January 1791 about $57,000 was allotted to the Treasury, $6500 to the War Department and a mere $6200 to Jefferson's Department of State.

Even before Jefferson joined the administration, Hamilton was conducting the informal negotiations over the frontier posts through Beckwith with Lord Dorchester in Quebec. As soon as George Hammond set up a legation in Philadelphia as King George's formal representative, he managed to establish himself on a confidential footing with Hamilton. The Secretary of the Treasury now went so far as to give him to understand that Jefferson's note protesting against the way the Navigation Acts were being enforced against American shipping "did not contain a faithful exposition of the sentiments of this government." Hammond was hurrying Hamilton's indiscretions to the Foreign Office in a series of private reports.

The administration had weathered Arthur St. Clair's disgraceful defeat the past autumn by the Indians in the Northwest Territory without too many "animadversions." The story was going around that when Captain Ebenezer Denny, who had been St. Clair's aide, came riding worn and miserable into Philadelphia with the bad news, the President blew up in one of his famous fits of temper, shouting, "I told him to guard against surprise." Still all that Denny noted in the diary he was still keeping up in which he had described ten years before that "most delightful music" at Yorktown, was how kindly he was treated by the President and by General Knox when during a family breakfast at the President's table he described the sudden yells of the Indians in the edges of the clearing about the camp; and the murderous accuracy of their fire; and their capture of the artillery; and the ruts in the roads of the army's retreat covered with flintlocks and cartridge boxes and discarded regimentals; and the wounded left to their fate; and how it was only because the redskins gave up the pursuit to loot the camp that even a shattered remnant was saved. So great was the country's reverence for Washington that not even the extreme anti-Federalists raised any public outcry against him or against his favorite minister.

Hamilton was still invincible in the legislative branch. In spite of the increased representation in the Second Congress the unwritten entente between the northern merchants and the slaveholders of the deep South which had appeared in the latter days of the Constitutional Convention still persisted. Hamilton had a bare majority in the Senate but he was sure of a subservient majority in the House. He had the support of the whole mercantile and financial interest. He knew exactly how far he could depend on Washington's confidence in him. He had managed so far to parry every political blow.

Hamilton made his way not only by his abilities, but by his personal charm. He was accustomed to being indulged in his little peccadilloes. His weakness was the overconfidence of the selfmade man. A case of odd recklessness in his private life came to light which had unfortunate consequences for the future.

By a hardly credible series of imprudences he managed, during the hot summer of 1791, to fall into the clutches of a group of blackmailers. He told the story himself in an odd and revealing pamphlet he printed a few years later after the dingy little tale had been aired by the opposition party in the press.

A young woman named Maria Reynolds, who must have possessed certain charms, came to call on the Secretary of the Treasury one day at his modest country house out near Robert Morris's grand villa on the Schuylkill. Showing every evidence of great perturbation of mind, she sobbed out her story. She was the daughter of a Mr. Lewis of New York, and the sister — there was no effort to explain the discrepancy of names — of a Mr. G. Livingston, presumably one of the mighty Livingstons of that state. Her husband had treated her cruelly and had left her for another woman, and she was destitute and was taking the liberty of applying to Hamilton's humanity for assistance so that she could return home to her family and friends.

Hamilton prided himself on being a gay dog with the ladies. In this case his humanity may have been especially kindled by a glint in the young woman's eye. As he had no money on him at the time he asked for her address. "In the evening I put a bank bill in my pocket and went to the house. I enquired for Mrs. Reynolds and was shown up the stairs, at the head of which she met me and conducted me into a bedroom. I took the bill out of my pocket and gave it to her. Some conversation ensued, from which it was quickly apparent that other than pecuniary consolation would be acceptible . . . After this I had frequent meetings with her, most of them at my own house; Mrs. Hamilton with her children being absent on a visit to her father." Hamilton was hooked.

Gradually Mrs. Reynolds let it be known that Mr. Reynolds, instead of having made off into the blue, was right there in Philadelphia and that he had been speculating in the funds and that he had information about the conduct of certain people in the office of the Treasury which might be useful to the Secretary.

Hamilton sent for Reynolds, who turned out a voluble fellow. At this point Hamilton did not doubt that he was actually her husband. This Reynolds unfolded a tale to the effect that Duer, while the Treasury was still in New York, had let him have a list of names of war veterans of the Virginia Line who had claims for back pay. He used the list, presumably, to buy up their paper cheap. "As Mr. Duer had resigned his office some time before," wrote Hamilton, betraying a strange lightmindedness about the public trust, "this discovery, if it had been true, was not very important — yet," he added in a Casanova mood, "It was the interest of my passions to appear to set value upon it, and to continue the expectation of friendship and good offices."

Reynolds seems to have claimed at that time to be a Virginian. He discreetly took a trip south, which left Hamilton the field so far as the lady was concerned. When he came back he importuned Hamilton for a job in the Treasury. Hamilton refused. He had heard no good of Reynolds in the meanwhile, and he seems to have already been trying to disentangle himself from the lady.

All winter she wrote him desperate letters. One of them fell under the eye of the unsuspecting husband. Reynolds wrote Hamilton in high dudgeon: "She was a woman. I should as soon sespect an angiel from heven. and one where all my happiness was depending. and I would Sacrefice almost my life to make her Happy. but now I am determined to have satisfaction. it shant be only one family that's miserable."

Reynolds was threatening to bring the story to Mrs. Hamilton's ears. It was not his doting Betsey whom Hamilton was worried about; she was used to his infidelities; it was the President. None of Washington's associates could face the prospect of one of his outbursts of Olympian rage without flinching.

Hamilton charmed everybody. In the correspondence he later published traces appeared of a certain dim congeniality between him and Reynolds. They had several more interviews. It is possible that some evening after drinking a little more wine than usual at dinner Hamilton boasted to him, as Reynolds afterwards claimed, that he could tell him how to make a fortune in the funds. He would do "something clever for him," he promised.

Reynolds came up with a proposal of his own, "give me the Sum of thousand dollars and I will leve the town and take my daughter with me" — this was the first mention of a child — "and go where my Friend

shant here from me and leve her to Yourself to do for her as you
thing proper." His agitation or else the rum toddy he had drunk kept
getting the better of his spelling. The thousand dollars was paid in
two installments and Reynolds, draping the mantle of a man of honor
about him, scrupulously wrote out his receipts.

Reynolds did not leave town. Quite the contrary, he reconciled himself to the situation too rapidly for Hamilton's comfort. "I have not the
Least Objections to your Calling," he wrote in January of 1792, "as a
friend to Boath of us. and must rely intirely in your and her honnor . . .
and I rely on your befriending me if there should anything Offer that
would be to my advantage."

All through that spring, in the turmoil and excitement of public
business Hamilton's life was haunted by that drab figure. Reynolds
with his winy talk of his fortune in the making kept appearing at his
elbow as a grimy caricature of the great speculators and capitalists
Hamilton was trying to interest in S.U.M. With Duer's help Hamilton
was managing to attract much of the wealth of New York and New
Jersey to the enterprise. Stately Elias Boudinot and astute Governor
Paterson became directors; three of the Livingstons were interested;
and the furtrader Alexander Macomb who owned the fine mansion
where the President had lived in Manhattan; and William Constable,
Duer's associate in many a farflung enterprise. Plans were laid for the
subscription of stock. The State of New Jersey authorized a lottery
to raise funds.

The production of textiles would be the first objective. A tract of
land was contracted for at the falls of the Passaic. L'Enfant, who was
already running afoul of the Potomac landowners by the highhanded
way he laid out the streets and avenues of Washington City, and who
kept promising to the President's commissioners sketches for the public buildings of the national capital which never materialized, added
to his other duties the planning of a great industrial city to be named
Paterson after the governor. The project was grandiose enough to
appeal to him. Mechanicalminded gentlemen were sent off to scour
Europe for further improvements in textile machinery. Hamilton wrote
the prospectus. Everything went swimmingly until, before the members of Congress could get their teeth into Hamilton's report, S.U.M.
came near swamping in the sudden cataract of the panic of 1792.

The moneymen were so full of enthusiasm for Hamilton's measures
that every fresh report he presented to Congress brought a rise in
the securities on the stock markets. Duer, like Robert Morris, had for
years been dazzled by a dream of the vast wealth that would fall into
the hands of the man who should corner the markets in American
government paper. During the winter prices were bouyant. Hamilton

used government funds to support the speculative market. It looked as if values would go on rising forever. In the early spring of 1792 Duer and Alexander Macomb came to an agreement to buy six percents in New York. Duer threw every cent he could lay his hands on into the speculation, including ten thousand dollars of the funds of S.U.M. he had to his account as treasurer. He even sold Lord Stirling's estate, Lady Kitty's old home.

The corner kept eluding him. More cash was needed every day. Macomb endorsed his notes for incredible amounts. Duer borrowed from every Tom, Dick and Harry at high rates of interest. So great was his reputation for successful finance that merchants, storekeepers, draymen, oystermen, market women, widows and orphans crowded into the office of his borrowing agent to lend him money. The vestries of churches offered him their funds. He was said to be investing thirty million dollars.

Meanwhile another group of speculators, mostly identified with the Livingston interest, were betting on a fall in prices. Every time prices started to slip a little they sold. Before long the slide became catastrophic.

Hamilton had already written Duer warning him that embarrassing rumors were going around about his activities: "I know you too well to suppose you capable of such views as were implied in these innuendoes, or to harbor the most distant thought that you would wander from the path either of public good or private integrity." Early in March Duer was forced to wander so far from the path of private integrity as to stop payment, on various pretexts, on some of his notes. Hamilton did what he could to keep prices up, but particularly as the trustees of the sinking fund, of whom Jefferson as Secretary of State was one, were dragging their feet, he found the funds he had at his disposal insufficient to keep the market from crashing.

At the same time precise young Oliver Wolcott of Connecticut, who had recently been appointed comptroller at Hamilton's insistence instead of Tench Coxe whom Jefferson wanted for the job, discovered in going over the books of the retired Assistant Secretary that Duer had neglected to account for nearly $250,000 in public funds which had been placed to his credit. He insisted that Duer must make good, and fast.

This time there was nothing Hamilton could do for his friend. March 14 he wrote him . . . "It was too late to have any influence upon the event you were apprehensive of, Mr. Wolcott's instructions having gone off yesterday" — to the United States district attorney to take Duer into court if he did not pay up immediately. Hamilton added he hoped the district attorney would use discretion and avoid

any "pernicious éclat." He gave Duer a piece of his mind: "Act with
fortitude and honor . . . Do not plunge deeper . . . Take all the care
you can in the first place of the institutions of public utility" — meaning S.U.M. — "and in the next of all fair creditors . . . I have experienced all the bitterness of soul on your account a warm attachment
can inspire. I will not pain you now with any wise remarks, though if
you recover from the present stroke I shall take great liberties with
you. Assure yourself in good and bad fortune, of my sincere friendship and affection."

More frantic letters passed between them. It was too late to save
Duer from ruin or to recover what he owed the United States. March
23 Duer allowed himself to be arrested and placed in the debtors'
prison while a mob of creditors filled the common outside and howled
for his blood. His friends agreed that jail was the safest place for him.
A few days later Macomb failed too and joined his associate. Walter
Livingston, who had been a member of the Treasury Board under the
old Congress, soon followed them into custody. The New York debtors' prison was packed to the very bars.

While Hamilton was on tenterhooks over the financial panic, dashing off desperate letters to his agents in New York and receiving in
return Duer's even more desperate pleas for help, he was conning, as
a sort of doleful counterpoint to the misfortunes of the rich and wellborn, the illspelled notes from Maria Reynolds and the shabby gentleman who claimed to be her spouse.

On March 24, while Hamilton was waiting with desperate im-
patience for news from Duer, before the post from New York had
time to bring an account of his arrest, he found himself reading a note
from Reynolds that struck a disquietingly intimate tone: "what would
you do in such a Case. Would you have acted as I have done. I have
consented to things which I thought I never could have done. but I
have dun it to make life tolerable . . . I find that when ever you have
been with her. She is cheerful and kind. but when you have not in
some time she is quite the Reverse."

A few days later Hamilton was reading tearstained words from
Maria: "Let me once more se you and unbosom myself to you perhaps
I shall be happier after It I have mutch to tell which I dare not write
And which you ought to know oh my dear Sir give me your advice
for once In an Affair on wich depends my Existence Itself."

The thousand dollars were either spent or lost in speculation because a few days later Reynolds was asking for a "lone of about thirty
Dollars." He had evidently already had sixty because, clinging to some
pathetic shred of selfrespect, he enclosed a receipt for Ninety. Next
he was asking for fortyfive; then for thirty; then for three hundred,

which he explained he needed to buy stock in the Lancaster turnpike — he had a chance to make five hundred dollars in a week — then fifty dollars more because he did not want to sell his turnpike stock at a loss; and so it went. The ragtag and bobtail of the speculative fever.

This was the sort of madness Jefferson had foreseen and dreaded as the result of Hamilton's policies. "The failure of Duer, in New York," he wrote his soninlaw, "soon brought on others, & these still more, like ninepins knocking one another down, till at that place the bankruptcy is become general, every man concerned in paper being broke . . . it is computed there is a dead loss in New York of about 5 millions of dollars, which is reckoned the value of all the buildings of the city; so that if the whole town had been burnt to the ground it would have been just the measure of the present calamity . . . in the mean time building & other improvements are suspended. workmen turned adrift. country produce not to be sold at any price . . . notwithstanding the magnitude of this calamity, every newspaper almost is silent on it, Freneau's excepted, in which you will see it mentioned." To Jefferson and his friends this seemed the moment to make a great effort to rid the government of the influence of the moneymen.

7. The Treasury Interest

Hamilton turned with unusual savagery on his political opponents. Under the stress of the financial troubles of that spring and of his private worries he wrote in May a long and revealing letter to Jefferson's old friend Carrington who had become, as an employee of the Treasury, one of Hamilton's political lieutenants in Virginia.

"Mr. Madison," Hamilton wrote, "cooperating with Mr Jefferson, is at the head of a faction decidedly hostile to me and my administration; and activated by views in my opinion, subversive of the principles of good government."

Madison's defection still smarted. He could not get used to the idea that the studious little man with whom he had cooperated so happily in defense of the Constitution would not remain on his side on every public question. He laid Madison's change of heart to Jefferson's evil communications. Jefferson had opposed the bank "in a style and manner which I felt as partaking of asperity and ill humor towards me." Madison and Jefferson had inspired newspaper writers to "represent funded debt in a most odious light as a Pandora's box . . ." "In Almost all questions great and small Mr Jefferson and Mr Madison have been found among those who are disposed to narrow the federal authority." They were trying to represent him to the public as a monarchist. They were doing their best to bring about his resignation.

Though he was not then seeking any elective office he ended his letter with a statement of first principles intended for circulation in Virginia as his personal platform during the coming election: "I am affectionately attached to the republican theory. I desire above all things to see the equality of political rights, exclusive of all hereditary distinctions, firmly established by a practical demonstration of its being consistent with the happiness of society . . . I have strong hopes of the success of that theory; but in candor I am far from being without doubts. I consider its success yet a problem."

He violently rejected Jefferson's accusation that he was trying to establish an Englishstyle government. He accused Jefferson and Madison of a "womanish attachment to France and a womanish resentment against Great Britain."

He laid it all to Jefferson's envy of the power of the Treasury. The Secretary of State had come into the government "with the expectation of a greater share in the direction of our councils than he actually enjoyed . . . He aims at the presidential chair." He was a dangerous demagogue.

"If I were proposed to promote monarchy and overthrow state governments," he added significantly, "I would mount the hobby horse of popularity; I would cry out 'usurpation', 'danger to liberty', etc. etc.; I would endeavor to prostrate the national government and then 'ride the whirlwind and direct the storm'. There are men acting with Jefferson and Madison who have this in view I verily believe. I could lay my finger on some of them."

It is likely that he already had Senator Burr of New York in mind. Burr was taking part in the partisan maneuvers, of which Jefferson expressed firm disapproval, by which the election of Hamilton's candidate John Jay over Clinton as governor of New York was set aside by the Clinton machine. "That Madison does not mean it I verily believe; and rather believe the same of Jefferson, but I read him on the whole thus: a man of profound ambition and violent passions."

Hamilton was carrying the war into the enemy country. His Treasury agents furnished him with the framework of a nationwide political machine. In looking about for political support in Virginia he had lit upon a lanky sardonic young lawyer who came from one of those backhill counties that Jefferson most relied on for support. John Marshall of Fauquier had made a name for himself as an extreme Federalist in the Richmond convention that ratified the Constitution.

Though he was not a reading man and lacked formal schooling he was already a leader of the Richmond bar. In June Jefferson wrote Madison, who had gone home to Montpellier when the houses adjourned, that Hamilton was backing John Marshall for Congress, and suggested a way of heading him off: "I am told that Marshall has half a mind to come. hence I conclude that Hamilton has plied him well with flattery & solicitation, and I think nothing better could be done than to make him a judge."

Not content with merely lining up a political party behind the Treasury, Hamilton threw himself with all the frenetic energy at his command into the war of words. He had convinced himself that the forces behind *The National Gazette* were aiming not only to drive him from office but "to prostrate the national government." He was determined to attack.

8. ". . . Internal Dissension . . ."

That summer of 1792 he had the seat of government to himself. The President was at Mount Vernon. The members of Congress had gone home. A few days after Jefferson left for his vacation at Monticello with his grandchildren and his daughters, Hamilton fired his first big gun. Writing in Fenno's *Gazette of the United States* under the signature "T.L.," he asked whether Philip Freneau was being paid a salary by the Department of State for his translations or whether it was "to vilify those to whom the voice of the people has committed the administration. In common life," he added, "it is thought ungrateful for a man to bite the hand that puts bread into his mouth; but if the man is hired to do it, the case is altered."

Hamilton was gunning for bigger game than the thinskinned poet. Writing as "An American," he came out with the charge that Freneau was merely "the faithful and devoted servant of the head of a party" and that this head of a party was Thomas Jefferson, who had opposed the national government and its Constitution from the beginning.

Freneau prided himself on his independence. He denied that his paper had published a line from Jefferson's pen. He appeared before the Mayor of Philadelphia and swore out an affidavit to the effect that Jefferson had nothing to do with the negotiations for establishing *The National Gazette*.

"An American" intimated that he was a liar. "Facts speak louder than words under certain circumstances louder than oaths." "Catullus" jumped into the fray with a rank distortion of Jefferson's attitude

towards government finance and particularly foreign loans, claiming
that the Virginian had been all along for welching on the government's obligations.

An "Aristides," thought by some to have been Edmund Randolph,
answered "Catullus" with a carefully reasoned defense of Jefferson.
According to "Aristides," in office or out the Secretary of State had
every right to express his opinion of a financial system of which he
disapproved.

Hamilton took the form of a slapstick sort of lout he labeled
"Scrouge" to abuse "Aristides" and repeated the charges he'd made as
"An American" and as "Catullus" that "Mr. J—— was the promoter
of national disunion, national insignificance, public disorder and discredit." If Jefferson did not like the way the administration was being
run he was perfectly free to resign.

The row in the Philadelphia press was echoed all over the country.
Local papers eagerly reprinted the contending articles as fast as they
were brought in by the postriders or by chance travelers or by the
slow stages.

Washington tried at first to ignore the conflict. It was the sort of
factional strife he most hated and feared. Now in retirement in Mount
Vernon for the summer, he found his peace interrupted by its echoes.
Already both Jefferson and Hamilton had stated their position on the
financial system for him in writing. Jefferson added to his statement
that while he felt it absolutely necessary for Washington to serve
another term he felt it would be much better if he himself resigned
at the end of the year. "Multitudes can fill the office in which you
have been pleased to place me, I therefore have no motive to consult
but my own inclination, which is bent irresistibly on the tranquil enjoyment of my family, my farm and my books. I should repose among
them, it is true, in far greater security, if I knew that you remained
at the watch."

Washington had not yet quite made up his mind to serve again,
but as long as he was in office he was determined that the members
of his cabinet should work in harmony. He wrote both men begging
them to be charitable of each other's opinions. He pointed out the
precarious state in which St. Clair's defeat had left the western frontier. "How unfortunate and how much it is to be regretted," he wrote
Jefferson, "that whilst we are encompassed on all sides by avowed
Enemies and insidious Friends internal Dissension should be gnawing
at our Vitals."

The President could not understand why the members of his cabinet
could not argue out their differences in private like gentlemen. He
pleaded with Jefferson: "My earnest Wish, my fondest Hope, there-

fore is, that instead of wounding Suspicious and irritable Charges, there may be liberal allowances, mutual forbearances and temporizing yieldings on all sides." To Hamilton he used almost the same words: "My earnest wish," he insisted, "is that Balsam may be poured into all the Wounds that have been given."

At the same time the President felt that criticism of any part of his administration was criticism of himself. He had approved Hamilton's measures; they were his measures now: "If the Government and the Officers of it are to be the constant theme of newspaper Abuse," he angrily wrote Edmund Randolph, "and this too without condescending to investigate the motives or the facts, it will be impossible, I conceive, for any Man living to manage the Helm."

Both Hamilton and Jefferson gave him answers which increased his misgivings about the wisdom of his serving another term. Each man considered himself the injured party. Jefferson reiterated his intention of resigning, but promised that while he remained in office he would do nothing to stir up further strife in the public press. He would wait until he had retired from office: "I reserve to myself then the right of appealing to my country, subscribing my name to whatever I write, & using with freedom & truth the facts & names necessary to place the cause in it's just form before that tribunal."

It was in the course of that correspondence that Jefferson first spoke of the Republican party. For some time Hamilton's supporters had been describing themselves as Federalists. In spite of everything that Washington could do the spirit of party and faction was splitting his administration under his feet.

9. "A Vindication of Mr. Jefferson"

When the time came to go back to Philadelphia for the fall term, Jefferson made a point of stopping off at Mount Vernon for a personal talk with the President. "Had a full free & confidential conversation with the President," he wrote Madison. "He declares himself quite undecided about retiring, desirous to do so, yet not decided if strong motives against it exist."

Jefferson had made another visit the day before that had moved him deeply. On the way to Mount Vernon, he told Madison, "I called at Gunstonhall, the proprietor just recovering from a dreadful attack of the cholic. he was perfectly communicative . . ." George Mason's mind had been roaming back over the days of the Constitutional Convention. He was trying to fix in his memory the point where the plan for a new system of government had departed from the decentralized yeoman's republic he and Jefferson in their hearts both desired. Mason told him that it was in the last days of the convention that the coalition between the three New England States and the slaveowning delegates changed the whole plan. Up to then he could have conscientiously put his name to it. From then on the Hamiltonian trend was inevitable. "He said he considered Hamilton as having done us more injury than Great Britain and all her fleets and armies."

The old man went on to expatiate on what his plan for funding would have been "but I could not in discretion," Jefferson explained, "let him talk as much as he was disposed." George Mason had been disappointed in his deepest aspirations. He was brokenhearted over the failure of the general government to put a stop to slavery. He felt that the cause of civil liberty had suffered a check. He was one of the men Jefferson most revered in the world. A few days after Jefferson left him George Mason was dead.

It is hardly likely that Jefferson said much at Mount Vernon about his visit to Gunston Hall. Washington and Mason had not spoken for months. That Washington himself was not entirely aloof from "the spirit of party and faction" is evidenced by his referring to George Mason scornfully in one of his letters when he listed "my neighbor and quondam friend Colo. M" as one of the irreconcilable enemies of his administration.

Now Jefferson and Washington went rather fruitlessly over the same ground they had covered in their letters. In his notes Jefferson quoted Washington as declaring that he did not believe there were ten men in the United States who wanted to turn the government into a monarchy. Jefferson explained that he thought Hamilton was using the Treasury's power to corrupt the legislature "to make an English constitution of it . . . The President" — in a phrase very typical of his cast of mind — "observed that experience was the only criterion of right which he knew . . . He had seen our affairs desperate and our credit lost." Hamilton had restored it "to the highest pitch . . . I told him all that was ever necessary to establish our credit, was an efficient government and an honest one . . . He finished by another exhortation to me not to decide too positively on retirement, and here we were called to breakfast."

After Jefferson had caught up enough with the routine business he found on his desk in Philadelphia to get a chance to look over the newspapers that had collected in his absence, he found that his friends Madison and Monroe were at work defending him from Hamilton's attacks. Using quotations from his letters to both men about the Constitution written while he was minister in Paris, in the first of a series of articles entitled "A Vindication of Mr. Jefferson" Madison had taken the argument back into the realm of cool and thoughtful discussion. Monroe was more aggressive. In the following piece he demanded that the author of "these most illiberal and contemptible efforts to injure the character of a respectable citizen" come out from behind the mask of his pseudonyms. "It is to be wished this writer," he wrote in the last of the series, "would exhibit himself to the public view, that we might behold in him a living monument of that immaculate purity, to which he pretends, and which ought to distinguish so bold and arrogant a censor of others."

This was a telling blow. Only a few days before the last article was published in *The American Daily Advertiser,* Monroe was present at an interview which presented Hamilton in a sorry light. Reynolds had landed in jail and Reynolds was threatening to talk.

10. "... *that immaculate purity to which he pretends* ..."

All through the summer Hamilton, as fast as Reynolds drank it up or speculated it away, had been paying him hushmoney, demanded on various pretexts. Once it had been two hundred dollars to fix up a house (on which Hamilton had already paid the rent) so that Mr. and Mrs. Reynolds could support themselves by taking in boarders.

Reynolds and a certain Jacob Clingman had been putting their heads together as to how they could use Reynolds' list of government creditors "to improve their setivation." They tried to collect the sums in the name of two of the men on the list through forged affidavits, but so clumsily that the watchful comptroller, Oliver Wolcott, who could not have known that he was uncovering a hornets' nest for the man he most admired in the administration, had the pair of them arrested for subornation of perjury. In jail they raised an uproar. Reynolds claimed he had it in his power "to hang the Secretary of the Treasury."

Clingman, it turned out, was a clerk in the office of the first Speaker of the House, Frederick Augustus Muhlenberg, of that brilliant Pennsylvania German family of Muhlenbergs who, among other achievements, brought the Lutheran Church to America. Muhlenberg induced Clingman to confess his crime and to return the certificates he had collected. Then, taking with him his friend Senator Burr of New York, Muhlenberg went to call on Hamilton to see if there was not some way he could get his erring clerk let off. At that moment they had no suspicion of how deeply Hamilton was involved.

Hamilton told them to apply to Oliver Wolcott, who had framed the charges. Wolcott said he would let the men off if they would tell him how they got the list. Clingman talked. The culprit was not Duer. Clingman accused a clerk named Fraunces, who was promptly fired. Clingman was released, but Reynolds, still in jail, tried to talk himself out of his fix by hinting that he had grave revelations about the Secretary of the Treasury's private speculations.

This news was a harvest for Hamilton's foes. If the Republicans could implicate Hamilton they could force him out of office. John Beckley had been bringing Jefferson so much gossip about defalcations at the Treasury that Jefferson had become a little shy of his tales. He noted in the *Anas* that what Beckley heard with his own ears he trusted, but not what he brought him secondhand. December 17 Jefferson made an extremely cautious entry about the Reynolds' story in his notes.

Three days before, Monroe and Representative Venable of Virginia, who had been told that a Virginian was in trouble, went to see Reynolds in jail. They found him full of mystery but could get nothing out of him they felt they could rely on. They did discover that he was not a Virginian at all but a New Yorker. His story that day was that he was being kept in jail through the machinations of someone high up in the Treasury whom he refused to name.

Wolcott by that time had heard enough to realize that he had better let Reynolds go. Besides, there was no way of prosecuting him without prosecuting Clingman.

As soon as Monroe heard Reynolds was turned loose, he hurried around to Reynolds' house, taking Muhlenberg with him, to try to get to the bottom of the story. Reynolds was not to be found. They did find the lovely Mrs. Reynolds, who indulged them with nods and shrugs and hints about how Mr. Hamilton had been exerting pressure to get her husband to leave town. She brought another name into the case.

She declared that Mr. Wadsworth had "been active in her behalf." Jeremiah Wadsworth, the wealthy senator from Connecticut, had the reputation of being somewhat of a lecher. Like Hamilton, he was a family man, but like Hamilton he was far from secretive about his frequent strayings from the path of virtue. Maybe he was poaching on Hamilton's preserve. Mrs. Reynolds hastily explained that she had appealed to him because Reynolds' father had been a commissary under him in the late war.

The same day Clingman, at Muhlenberg's insistence, made a sworn statement of his version of the facts. Monroe, Muhlenberg and Venable went solemnly to call on Hamilton with the statement in their hands. Dryly they asked for an explanation. The interview had been prearranged and Hamilton had asked Wolcott to be present.

Hamilton was embarrassed, but he did not lose his selfpossession. He read Mr. and Mrs. Reynolds' letters aloud. It was obvious they were both of them congenital liars. He smiled his boyish smile. He made a clean breast of his folly and pointed out that if he had planned to speculate in the public funds he would not have used a creature like Reynolds as an intermediary. They had seen Mrs. Reynolds. Hamilton admitted his weakness for the ladies. What could men of the world do but declare themselves satisfied?

11. "... the torment of hatred & aversion ..."

"The ensuing year will be the longest of my life and the last of such hateful labors," Jefferson wrote his daughter Martha in the spring of 1792 as soon as he made his decision to resign as Secretary of State when the first four-year presidential term was up. "The next we'll sow our cabbages together," he added, remembering the pleasant French expression. Now back in harness in Philadelphia in the fall he was already counting the days and hours which still lay between him and his resignation.

He was fortynine. He had spent the last twenty years almost entirely in the public service. There was a great deal he wanted to do on his own account while he still had time.

Architecture was as much his passion as statebuilding. This was the period of his most inventive architectural thinking. He wanted to try out a whole new set of ideas based on his study of the temple at Nîmes and of the disreputable Landgrave of Salm-Kribourg's beautiful little domed hôtel on the left bank of the Seine. He wanted to rebuild Monticello in a fresher lighter style. He was helping Madison revamp his father's mansion at Montpellier. He was engaged in a plan for the hall of Congress in the federal city, which, trying as usual to keep himself behind the scenes, he submitted anonymously to the judges in the contest under the initials A Z.

The remodeling of Monticello would cost a great deal of money. He had to have some time at home to see what he could do to put his rundown estates in order. Living in Philadelphia cost him far more than his salary.

He was no more a city man than Washington was. At the seat of government his only real pleasures were the meetings of the American Philosophical Society and the business, which he superintended personally to the last detail, of issuing patents for new inventions. The rest of his official work was drudgery.

He could not get over being hurt by the personal antagonisms that went along with political strife. Already that spring he had been writing Martha that the "heats and tumults" of conflicting parties had become a torment to him. Now in the fall of the year, after the bitterness of the newspaper war with Hamilton and the tender summer interlude with his family at Monticello, he found life in Philadelphia hardly supportable.

Even his vacation had been laced with anxiety. His baby granddaughter Anne had been ill, "at death's door," he wrote. Martha's confinements were a special source of worry to him because of her mother's illnesses at those times. It was the aftermath of childbearing that had carried her off in the prime of her life and left him eternally bereaved. Martha had relieved his anxiety by presenting him with a fine new grandson and he had left the family brood in the best of health.

He was comforted on that score, but as soon as he settled back to his confining paperwork in his office in the narrow little house on High Street he found himself once more struggling among the hatreds and tensions of the political conflict he so hated. The division between parties had passed the bounds of reasonable argument.

Jefferson described his feelings in a letter to Hamilton's sisterinlaw. Angelica Church was the most gifted of the Schuyler girls. Some thought her one of the loveliest women of her time. She was a painter of talent. Jefferson had known her during the period when he was the favored gallant of pretty, flighty Maria Cosway during those sentimental Parisian days of gay excursions, strolls in formal gardens, heartfluttering suppers, raptures in art galleries, when Jefferson for a few months had enjoyed to the full the pays du tendre of the old regime. Answering a letter of Angelica Church's, he told her what he knew of the fate of various acquaintances belonging to their lively circle of Parisian friends who were now fallen on evil days through the revolution. He too, he implied, was suffering from the bitterness of political struggles.

"Party animosities here have raised a wall of seper'n" — separation; the letter is full of oddly telescoped words, as if written in a great hurry or under the stress of feeling — "between those who differ in political sentim'ts." He wrote next: "the oldest friends will cross the street to avoid meeting each other," and crossed it out as if he felt it too strong an expression. "They must love misery indeed who would rather at the sight of an honest man feel the torment of hatred & aversion than the benign spasms of benevolence and esteem," he wrote instead.

He was probably thinking of the old banker Willing's daughter, lively Mrs. Bingham, for whom abroad he had indulged in one of his half fatherly, half flirtatious friendships and who now ruled Philadelphia society from the pomp and splendor of her banker husband's magnificent mansion. It was painful to him to be denied the society of spirited and fashionable women.

As if to assure Angelica that his political differences with Hamilton had made no difference in his feeling for her, he ended the letter: "Accept assurances of the unalterable attachment of your sincere & affect. friend and servant."

Jefferson loathed controversy, yet when ever he opened a newspaper he found himself carried away by "heats and tumults" which as a philosopher he felt he should be aloof enough to ignore. Personal gibes that invaded the sacredness of his country gentleman's privacy rankled particularly. As the contest between them sharpened Jefferson and Hamilton were thrown into an odd intimacy of dislike, tinged by the respect each one of them felt for the other's abilities.

They saw each other almost every day. They could not help being interested in each other's conversation. The federal office holders scattered about the fringes of Philadelphia were no more numerous than a weekend crowd in a large country house. It was almost a family group. The members of the cabinet were constantly thrown together. When they met at the dinner table or at cabinet meetings Hamilton was smoothly polite. His manner was always disarming. Even his enemies he could not help charming with his boyish smile.

It was different with Hamilton's supporters. They made no effort to hide their animosity. The moneymen were in the saddle; they wanted no back talk from spokesmen for the lower orders. The only Philadelphians who invited the Secretary of State to their table were of the limited circle of the Philosophical Society: the Rittenhouses or the Logans, or broadminded William Thomson, the retired secretary of the old Congress who was filling his leisure by translating the Greek text of the Bible into English. Jefferson's congenial friend, the whimsical composer Francis Hopkinson, was dead. He had the friendship of dogmatic Dr. Rush and of idealistic Dr. Hutchinson, but most of the adherents of the rich and wellborn would cross the street rather than wish him good day.

Jefferson was a moderate drinker and cared nothing for the cardplaying and late hours of the fashionable set, but like every other man of brains of his age, much of the pleasure and relaxation of his life came from good talk over a bottle of wine after dinner. It was painful to him to be cut off from the ordinary genialities of social intercourse.

He had a scholar's capacity for burying himself in his work. Now at the end of every avenue of accomplishment in his department he found the busy figure of Hamilton crossing his path. No matter what the topic was he needed to bring up with the President, Hamilton had brought it up first. Organizing the postriders to speed communications was the sort of thing Jefferson enjoyed; Hamilton insisted that the Post Office belonged to the Treasury.

In the course of his tedious negotiations with the British minister about His Majesty's government's procrastination in giving up the forts on the northwest frontier the Secretary of State kept coming on frustrating traces of Hamilton's interference. Though he did not know to what extent Hamilton had undercut him in his negotiations with George Hammond, he could not help suspecting that Hammond had other sources of communication with the administration than through the Department of State.

Jefferson's bargaining position with the British had been weakened by St. Clair's defeat as it was. Hammond was an able opponent and behind Hammond was the masterly strategy of Lord Dorchester in Quebec, who was trying to salvage an empire for Great Britain in North America by setting up the region between the lakes and the Mississippi River as an independent Indian reservation under British control. The fur trade was the stakes.

Jefferson was trying to counter the predominance of British power by increasing American commerce with France. When the French dethroned their King and proclaimed a republic, war between France and England became highly likely. The United States had a good deal to gain from such a war. The problem was how to protect the neutrality of American shipping.

To Jefferson's mind Hamilton's policy of seeking an agreement with Great Britain at almost any cost was throwing away the whole advantage of the French connection. He hoped to use such a war to rescue the carrying trade of the Atlantic ports from the oppressions of the Navigation Acts. That would be wiping out the last vestiges of colonial subjection. He wanted American merchants to be free to sell to both sides. Neutral bottoms make neutral goods was his motto.

12. *Jefferson's Longest Year*

1793 opened auspiciously for the Republicans. Governor Clinton, with the help of Burr's New York City machine, had made a showing against John Adams for the vice presidency. The congressional elections of the autumn before had on the whole been encouraging and so had the state elections in Pennsylvania and Massachusetts. Jefferson's partisans in Philadelphia, Madison, Monroe, Giles, Beckley

THE SPIRIT OF PARTY AND FACTION

and their friends, remembering Hamilton's discomfiture in the Reynolds business and the popular outcry against Duer, made plans to pry Hamilton out of the Treasury during the new year.

No one knew whether the President had heard the gossip about Hamilton's entanglement with the Reynolds family but it seemed to Jefferson that the French victory of Valmy, where Dumouriez's and Kellermann's well placed artillery checked the Duke of Brunswick's coalition army, made an impression on Washington's military imagination. After a talk with the President on December 27 during which they agreed on the terms they should work for in a new treaty with France, Jefferson noted: "I was very much pleased with the tone of these observations. it was the very doctrine which had been my polar star, and I did not need the successes of the republican arms in France, lately announced to us, to bring me to these sentiments."

The President was a practical man and a military man; the success of the republican army meant more to him than all Hamilton's and Jefferson's theoretical disputations.

In France republicanism was carrying all before it. The King was deposed. A National Convention had taken the place of the Legislative Assembly. A vigorous central government seemed to be in order. Early in January, Jefferson wrote in highly optimistic mood to his soninlaw: "Our news from France continues to be good & promises a continuance. the event of the revolution there is little doubted of even by its enemies, the sensations it has produced here, and the indications of them in the public papers, have shown that the form our own government was to take depended much more on the events in France than anybody before imagined. the tide which, after our former relaxed government, took a violent course towards the opposite extreme and seemed ready to hang everything round with the tassles and baubles of monarchy, is now getting back as we hope to a just mean, a government of laws addressed to the reason of the people, and not to their weaknesses."

Jefferson had every reason to hope that the moneymen were losing their influence in the government. Washington's secretary, Tobias Lear, who combined Republican principles with complete loyalty to the President, was friendly with the Republican leaders. He gave them to understand that the President was becoming somewhat disenchanted with Hamilton's and Adams' notions. He went out of his way several times that winter to reassure Jefferson as to the President's politics.

Late in February John Adams' soninlaw, William Stephens Smith, arrived in Philadelphia fresh from cordial conversations with the chief men of the Convention. He had been at work on a private deal to sell arms to the French. In Paris he had seen a great deal of his old friend

Miranda. Miranda had managed to get himself a command in the revolutionary army under the triumphant Dumouriez and was enthralling the salons of the ruling Girondins with plans for carrying the Revolution of the World to his homeland. Colonel Smith was a sanguine fellow. He brought glowing tales of the plans the new French Minister for Foreign Affairs, Lebrun, was forming to throw the French West Indies open to American trade, to accept payment of the American debt in provisions, and to send a fleet of fortynine ships of the line to liberate South America from the Spanish yoke. Miranda was to be in command; he planned a landing on the Mexican coast. Lebrun had told Smith he would have no objection if the Americans took over the two Floridas. He wanted the sister republics to join hands in bringing freedom to the New World.

This would mean the opening of South American ports to American shipping; the thought of the glory to be won and the money to be made had dazzled Smith ever since his first intimacy with Miranda ten years before. Now he reported to Washington that the new French regime, in order to cement their fraternal ties with the United States, was sending one of the most brilliant young men in their diplomatic service to Philadelphia with full powers "to give us all the priviledges we can desire in their countries." Meanwhile the foreign minister Lebrun had entrusted him with a letter to George Washington, announcing that Colonel Smith would unfold to him these plans "worthy of his great mind."

Smith further reported that the French ministers had shut their doors to Gouverneur Morris. As a private citizen Smith had refused to be the bearer of a letter asking for the sharpspoken tall boy's recall, but he explained to Jefferson that Gouverneur was far too open in his association with monarchists and constitutionalists and other proscribed elements in Paris to be of any further use as American envoy.

Gouverneur was always getting into trouble from the freedom of his epithets. At his own table and in front of a mixed company of guests and servants, he was reported to have denounced the Convention's ministers as a set of damned rascals. He had handled funds for the royal family. He had helped proscribed aristocrats to escape across the frontiers.

Smith had much the same story to report of William Short, Jefferson's favorite disciple in the diplomatic corps whom Jefferson, when he failed to induce Washington to appoint him to Paris, had switched to the Netherlands to make way for Morris. Short's crime, in the eyes of the Parisian revolutionaries, was that he had cried out with horror at the indiscriminate September massacre of suspects and hostages in the Paris prisons which had prepared the way for the elections to the Convention. The ministers through their secret agents were undoubt-

edly aware of the fact that Short was the lover of de la Rochefoucauld's young widow and had been deeply shocked by the murder of
the liberal duke, and that he lived in daily fear for his Rosalie's life
and for the lives of the poor survivors at la Roche Guyon. Like
Gouverneur, he showed too much courage in helping his friends to be
acceptable to the rancorous Convention.

Washington liked Colonel Smith. In the slippery paths of civilian
politics it was a relief to talk to one of his old aides; he had confidence in the young men who had served him well in the war. He
was so much impressed by the news he brought, coming on top of
the news of Valmy, followed by an Austrian defeat at Jemappes and
Dumouriez's conquest of Belgium, that he immediately took up with
Jefferson the matter of reshuffling their European envoys. He suggested that if Jefferson did not care to remain as Secretary of State
he might like to go to Paris in place of Gouverneur Morris. It would
be a chance, Washington slyly intimated, for him to see at first hand
the revolution he so admired.

To Jefferson this proposition seemed a scheme of Hamilton's to
remove him from the political stage at home; he replied that, as the
French were sending a new envoy with full powers to negotiate a
treaty, he felt he could make himself more useful in Philadelphia. He
suggested that Gouverneur Morris should be accredited to the Court
of St. James, where his opinions would be congenial, and that Thomas
Pinckney, who charmed everyone with his agreeable manners, should
be sent to Paris.

Jefferson had made up his mind to stay on in the administration
for a few more months. He wrote Martha, "Under an agitation of
mind which I scarcely ever experienced before," that he would have
to postpone coming home. At the same time he proved he was in
earnest about resigning by giving up his town house and renting a
cottage out on the Schuylkill for the summer. His furniture was already
on its way to Virginia.

His friends had been working on him not to let Hamilton push him
out of office. He was investing more hopes than he liked to admit in
the effect of a series of resolutions he helped draw up, which young
Giles was introducing in the House, calling for a detailed explanation
by Hamilton of his use of the public funds. Jefferson relied on their
passage to restore the administration to what he described as "a just
mean."

Events in France, he wrote his soninlaw, were having a paramount
influence on political opinions in America. He insisted on viewing the
September massacres which had so horrified Short as a last spasm
before the installation, with the election of a convention which would

furnish France with a permanent constitution, of a selfgoverning republic. He wrote Short scolding that unhappy young man for letting
his personal feelings stand in the way of his duty.

"Many guilty persons fell without the forms of trial," he admitted,
"and with them some innocent. these I deplore as much as anybody,
& shall deplore some of them to the day of my death. but I deplore
them as I should have done had they fallen in battle. it was necessary
to use the arm of the people, a machine not quite so blind as balls
and bombs but blind to a certain degree. a few of their cordial friends
met at their hands the fate of enemies . . . the liberty of the whole
earth was depending on the issue of the contest and was ever such a
prize won with so little innocent blood? my own affections have been
deeply wounded by some of the martyrs to this cause, but rather than
it should have failed, I would have seen half the earth desolated. were
there but an Adam & an Eve left in every country, & left free, it would
be better than as it now is. I have expressed to you my sentiments
because they are really those of 99 in a hundred of our citizens. the
universal feasts and rejoicing which have been lately been had on
account of the successes of the French showed the genuine effusions
of their hearts."

News from Europe was always scarce during the winter months.
With the coming of spring, dispatches and gazettes poured in from
England and France heavy with portentous events. Louis XVI had
been tried and executed. The guillotine ruled Paris. The Convention
had declared war on England. France was in arms against all the
courts of Europe.

Little by little the "99 in a hundred of our citizens" which Jefferson
had claimed as sympathizers in the worldwide republican cause began to show signs of misgivings. Only extreme Republicans like Freneau were willing to be called Jacobins. Up and down the coast the
Republican enthusiasts set up political discussion societies modeled on
what they had heard of the Jacobins and Cordeliers of Paris.

The Federalists, on the other hand, felt at once that the cause of
England and of the old regime was the cause of civilization. They
read Burke. Burke's *Reflections* were in every drawing room. Pitt's
anti-Jacobin propaganda roused them to extremes of righteous indignation. They began to tax the Republicans at home with the crimes of
the French. In Philadelphia, Hamilton was holding his own. "If all the
people in America were now assembled to call on me to say whether
I am a friend of the French revolution, I would declare that I have
it in abhorrence," he told Edmund Randolph. With every dispatch
from France more Americans came to agree with him.

Two days before the second inauguration of George Washington and John Adams, the most important of Giles' resolutions failed to pass the House.

"He & one or two others were sanguine enough to believe that the palpableness of these resol'ns rendered it impossible the house could reject them" — Jefferson betrayed his disappointment by the bitterness of his comment in his private notes — "those who knew the composition of the house 1. of bank directors 2. holders of bank stock 3. stockjobbers 4. blind devotees, 5. ignorant persons who did not comprehend them 6. lazy & goodhumored persons . . . the persons who knew these characters foresaw . . . that they would be rejected by a majority of 2. to 1. but they thought that even this rejection would do good, by shewing the public the desperate & abandoned dispositions with which their affairs were intrusted."

He next included in the *Anas* a list, which Beckley made up for him, of the members of the two houses whose fortunes depended on government paper and who were therefore tied by every bond of self-interest to Hamilton's measures. He listed as "papermen" nineteen representatives and seven senators.

Washington went to Mount Vernon as soon as Congress adjourned after inauguration. When the news of the war between France and England reached him there he hurried back to Philadelphia and called a meeting of the cabinet to decide whether the United States should follow England's lead in refusing to recognize the French Republic. In spite of Hamilton's objections the advice of the cabinet was that the treaty made with the Bourbon government should be considered still binding, and that the new envoy should be received when he arrived as the representative of the people of France. A proclamation of neutrality should be issued.

"I fear that a fair neutrality," wrote Jefferson, who had reconciled himself with Washington's opinion, "will prove a disagreeable pill to our friends, tho' necessary to keep out of the calamities of war."

That summer's conflict between Jefferson and Hamilton in the administration was over what constituted a fair neutrality.

Edmond Charles Genêt, the Convention's envoy, sailing in convoy with some British prizes captured at sea, arrived in Charleston in the spring on the French frigate *Embuscade*. He brought with him a gust of the ardor and rhetoric of the early days of the Convention. He was a somewhat lightheaded young man who had been a youthful prodigy in the foreign office at Versailles. He had been brought up backstairs at the court. His father translated dispatches for Vergennes. His sisters were ladies in waiting to Marie Antoinette. He was a natural linguist. He made a name for himself by his translations from the Swedish at the age of fourteen. He claimed to have been the one who announced to old Vergennes the news of Cornwallis's surrender. He was a typical careerist of the enlightenment. He showed a suitable interest in steam engines and agriculture and botany. He exchanged letters on philosophical subjects with de la Rochefoucauld and Condorcet. He had started early on a diplomatic career and had endeared himself to the then dominant Girondin party, which, since the collapse of Lafayette's constitutionalists, had attracted the enthusiasts for moderate American methods among the French revolutionaries, by being declared persona non grata as chargé d'affaires in St. Petersburg by Catherine of Russia. Although his sisters were among the most courageously loyal of Marie Antoinette's attendants, he managed to convince the politicians round Madame Roland's drawing room that he was completely devoted to the republican cause.

He could speak with authority of the sentiments of the Girondin leadership because he was privy to one of their most secret plans: the royal family — the famille Capet, as good republicans were careful to call them — were to be sentenced to exile instead of to death and Genêt was to take them aboard his frigate already waiting at Rochefort and to set them up as plain citizens in America. This was the plan that Tom Paine had got himself locked up in the Luxembourg for promoting.

The Mountain and the Commune of Paris ruled otherwise. Louis Capet's head had already rolled in the sand when Genêt arrived in America exuding from every pore the philosophical enthusiasms of the salons of the Gironde and the martial ardors of the "Marseillaise." In order to make sure that the powers that were should forget his courtly past he had to be a little extra loud in his republicanism.

He was met with an outburst of the old fire out of the early days. Even in Federalist Charleston he was welcomed with banquets and cheering, public receptions and bandmusic and liberty caps. Democratic societies toasted him wherever he went. "I live here in the midst of perpetual fêtes," he delightedly wrote back to Lebrun.

Genêt brought along a satchel full of letters of marque. Privateering had traditionally been considered a profitable enterprise by American sailors. Long before the Revolution they had developed great skill in evading the British cruisers that enforced the Navigation Acts. It was risky business but the stakes were high. Even an ordinary seaman's share in the sale of one rich prize would set him up as a substantial citizen. If the shipowners were mostly pro-British, the skippers and crews were overwhelmingly republican. Genêt was immediately surrounded by young hotheads eager to fit out the *Embuscade's* prizes as privateeers and to take their chance at outsailing the British frigates and neutrality be damned.

It was not only at sea that Genêt embarked on grandiose adventures. He was not waiting for Miranda's expedition to revolutionize the continent. The Canadians must immediately revolt from Great Britain and Louisiana from Spain. He wrote to the French settlers in Illinois. He was in correspondence with George Rogers Clark in Kentucky. Through him he would finance a Revolutionary and Independent Legion of the Mississippi which would carry the liberty cap down the river to New Orleans. As he made his way northward from Charleston, jouncing slowly over the dusty ruts of the wandering roads, he was met with "cries of joy, addresses of congratulation, writings aflame with patriotism."

In every town and hamlet "the true democrats feel that their fate is intimately linked with ours," he wrote home, "that their evident interest is to unite with us to beat down the monster of despotism that has sworn their undoing as well as ours." Genêt was a shrewd young man in some ways, but revolutionary verbiage had gone to his head.

There was no question about the popular enthusiasm. "The war between France & England," Jefferson wrote Monroe from Philadelphia "seems to be producing an effect not contemplated. all the old spirit of 1776 is rekindling. the newspapers from Boston to Charleston prove this; & even the Monocrat papers are obliged to publish the most furious philippics against England."

The new energy with which the French Republic was waging war at sea had been brought home to the seat of government. "A French frigate took a British prize off the capes of Delaware the other day & sent her up here," Jefferson told Monroe. "Upon her coming into sight thousands and thousands of the *yeomanry* of the city crowded & covered the wharves. never before was such a crowd seen here and when the British colors were seen reversed & the French flying above they burst into peals of exultation." He was afraid this enthusiasm might go too far. "I wish," he added, "we may be able to repress the spirit of the people within the limits of a fair neutrality."

Genêt made it his business to do just the opposite. Although he greeted the administration on his arrival in Philadelphia with a grand declaration of the affection the Convention bore towards the United States, and produced a letter telling George Washington "he was the only person on earth who can love us sincerely & merit to be so loved," not many weeks went by before Genêt was on the outs not only with Washington but with Jefferson too.

Jefferson was cold, Genet complained to Lebrun. Washington was a "Fayettiste." It was from Washington that Lafayette had acquired his constitutionalist obsessions. While the ci-devant marquis was planning to make Louis Capet constitutional monarch of France, Washington had been planning to crown himself constitutional monarch of America. That was why good republicans were greeted with disgust in Philadelphia while liberticide nobles and constitutionalists received every help. "My position you can see is difficult but my courage is not affrighted."

The news arrived of Dumouriez's defection to the coalition of kings. In Santo Domingo the slaves had risen against the whites. The Mountain was denouncing the Gironde. French ships were heading into every American port to take refuge from anarchy and war in the West Indies. Each ship brought a story that conflicted with the rest. A hundred and one sail of them had entered Chesapeake Bay. The Revolution of the World was progressing far from smoothly. Genêt drowned his misgivings in a flood of oratory.

By the end of June Jefferson was writing Monroe: "I do not augur well of the mode of conduct of the new French minister; I fear he will enlarge the circle of those disaffected with his country. I am doing everything in my power to moderate the impetuosity of his movements."

Nothing could moderate the impetuosity of Genet's movements. He felt he was riding a tidal wave. Acting with sublime disregard of public sentiment, before another month was out he had managed to insult the President by threatening to appeal to the people against the rulings of his administration on the status of British ships captured by the French in American waters, and had embroiled himself with Jefferson and with the Pennsylvania authorities over the arming of the British prize the *Little Sarah,* which he was equipping as a privateer to be called *Le Petit Démocrate.*

His every word, and he hardly ever stopped talking, put fresh ammunition into the hands of the Hamilton faction. The only thing that preserved any balance at all was that the officers of His Majesty's navy were as highhanded as the French. The belligerent powers were both treating the United States as if their national sovereignty did not exist.

It was a hot summer. Dissension in the press echoed dissension in the cabinet. The almost daily cabinet meetings rasped on the nerves of the five men who had to make the decisions. Particularly they rasped on the President's.

"The President is not well," Jefferson wrote Madison in June. "Little lingering fevers have been hanging about him for a week or ten days, and have affected his looks most remarkably. he is also extremely affected by the attacks made & kept up on him in the public papers. I think he feels these things more than any person I ever met with."

Jefferson was convinced that the Hamiltonians were inspiring some of the more violent attacks on the President in the Republican press in order to drive him into the ranks of their party. Beckley had brought him the story that one particularly virulent piece attacking Washington was the work of an Irishman who was a clerk for Oliver Wolcott in the comptroller's office. The state of factions had reached a point where a man could believe anything of an opponent.

At a cabinet meeting on August 22 Jefferson and Hamilton argued at length about what Hamilton considered the dangers of the democratic societies. Hamilton claimed that Genêt was trying to use them to overthrow the government. Hamilton wanted to suppress them as Pitt was suppressing them in England. Jefferson dryly pointed out that repression would only inflame public feeling.

They all agreed that it was necessary to ask for Genêt's recall. Jefferson wanted to do it privately and civilly. Dissension with France would be "liberty warring against itself." Hamilton wanted the protest to take the form of a public statement.

The President agreed with Hamilton. Furthermore he said that Robert Morris, whose opinion as a successful businessman he valued so much, had counseled at dinner the other day an appeal to the people and had assured him that he would support it and that his business connections up and down the coast would support it. "This shows," noted Jefferson suspiciously, "that the President has not confidence enough in the virtue & good sense of mankind to confide in a government bottomed on them and thinks other props necessary."

At this point Knox, to Jefferson's great annoyance, showed the President a cartoon which depicted him and James Wilson, now leader of the Pennsylvania conservatives, on their way to the guillotine. "The President was much inflamed," wrote Jefferson, "got into one of those passions when he cannot command himself, ran on much on the personal abuse which had been bestowed on him, defied any man on earth to produce one single act of his since he had been in the govt which was not done on the purest motives, that he had never repented but once the having slipped the moment of resigning his office, & that was every moment since, that *by god* he had rather be in his grave than in his present situation. that he would rather be on his farm than to be made *emperor of the world* and yet that they were charging him with wanting to be a king. that that *rascal Freneau* sent him 3 of his papers every day, as if he thought he would become the distributor of his papers, that he could see in this nothing but an impudent design to insult him. he ended in this high tone. there was a

pause . . . some difficulty in resuming our question . . . he desired we
would meet at my office the next day to consider that should be done
with the vessels armed in our ports by Mr. Genet & their prizes."

A few days later the President called on Jefferson at his little rented
house under the trees by the Schuylkill where he was enjoying freedom from the hated city. It was a delightful spot. "I never before
knew the full value of trees," he had written Martha. "my house is
entirely embosommed in high planetrees, with good grass below: and
under them I breakfast, dine, write, read and receive my company."

As they chatted in their old friendly fashion under the trees, the
President begged Jefferson again to put off his resignation. The President cried out that as for himself there was nothing he would like
better than to resign. Resignation was in the air. Even Hamilton was
planning to resign. "He expressed great apprehensions at the fermenta-
tions which seemed to be working in the mind of the public," wrote
Jefferson; the President was worried about the makeup of the new
Congress; "if I would only stay to the end of it it would relieve him
considerably."

Jefferson had written Madison two months before that his own
determination to retire from public life was unshakable. "The motion
of my blood no longer keeps time with the tumult of the world."
Madison had been urging him to stay on. "Never let there be more
between you and me on this subject," Jefferson curtly ended his letter.

This time Jefferson convinced the President that he meant what he
said. Their conference ended with a discussion of whom to appoint
in his place.

It was not only the behavior of Genêt and the writings of Pitt's
propagandists and ever fresh tales of tumult and bloodshed in France
that had set Americans against the French revolutionists. In the South
slaveholders were profoundly disturbed by the tales told by the refugees who kept arriving from the French West Indies. What had been
a brisk contest between royalist and republican factions among the
whites in Santo Domingo was interrupted by an insurrection of the
slaves. The Negroes were taking seriously all this talk about the rights
of man. The only way they saw to attain their freedom was to massacre the slaveholders as the mobs in Paris were massacring the old
aristocracy. They killed every white man, every white woman and
every white child who did not manage to escape by sea. The lovely
creole city of Cap François was gutted and burned. The only Frenchmen left alive were a few groups holding on in fortresses along the
coast. Along with the insurrection yellow fever raged. Shiploads of
ruined planters were joining the shiploads of titled émigrés from
France that arrived in every port.

Early in summer the governor of South Carolina had become so alarmed by what he heard of an unusually virulent epidemic of yellow fever in the islands that he forbade entry to ships from the West India ports. The question came up in the cabinet as to whether such an act was not an infringement of federal prerogative. The unanimous opinion was that even if it were it was too slight to take notice of. "Therefore let it lie," noted Jefferson.

It was not long before they were taking notice at cabinet meetings of a plague that no quarantine could forbid entry to: yellow fever broke out in Philadelphia. Along with the contagion of the terror of a slave uprising the French refugees brought with them, there came a contagion carried by a wan little lowflying mosquito that nobody at that time imagined carried death in its feeble sting. "A malignant fever," Jefferson wrote Madison, who was happily home at Montpellier, "has been generated in the filth of Water Street."

Devoted Dr. Rush attributed it to some damaged coffee which had putrefied on one of the wharves — "about 70. people died of it two days ago & as many more were ill of it," Jefferson continued. "It comes on with a pain in the head, sick stomach, then a little chill, black vomiting and stools, and death from the 2nd to the 8th day. everybody who can is flying from the city and the panic of the country people is likely to add famine to the disease. tho' becoming less mortal, it is still spreading and the heat of the weather is very unpropitious. I have withdrawn my daughter" — that was Maria, Polly he usually called her, the younger and prettier one who looked like her mother; she was living with him while she attended a Philadelphia school — "from the city but am obliged to go there every day myself."

A few days before Dr. Rush, who continued night and day, with total disregard of his own safety, trudging from afflicted household to afflicted household, dosing the victims with calomel and jalap, had written his wife, whom he had urged to stay out near Princeton with the children, "I enjoy good health and uncommon tranquility of mind. While I depend upon divine protection and feel that at present I live, move and have my being in God alone, I do not neglect to use every precaution that experience has discovered to prevent my taking the infection. I even strive to subdue my sympathy for my patients; otherwise I should sink under the accumulated loads of misery I am obliged to contemplate. You can recollect how much the loss of a single patient once in a month used to affect me. Judge then how I must feel in hearing every morning of the death of three or four."

The war of words in the press, the dissensions in the cabinet were stilled by the silence of the pestilence. Only the Negroes were untouched. Every white man who could fled the city.

"The President goes off the day after tomorrow as he had always intended," Jefferson wrote Madison at the end of the first week of September, making sure that no one could take him to mean that George Washington had been scared out of the city by a few cases of yellow fever. "Knox then takes flight," he added sarcastically. Plump Henry Knox had been too much involved with the moneymen to please him. What he wrote of Hamilton reflected the bitterness of his state of mind: "Hamilton is ill of the fever, as it is said. he had two physicians out at his house the night before last."

One of them was the Ned Stevens who had been Hamilton's great chum when he kept store on St. Croix, the boy to whom he had boyishly written, "Ned my ambition is prevalent." Stevens had come to America with him and had taken up medicine instead of statebuilding. After his recovery Hamilton made a great deal of the success of Dr. Stevens' treatment, which consisted of quinine and cold baths, and published a pamphlet on it.

"His family think him in danger & he puts himself so by his excessive alarm," Jefferson continued spitefully. "He had been miserable several days before from a firm conviction he would catch it. a man as timid as he is on the water" — Jefferson was referring to some incident on the schooner the time three years before when Washington, hoping he could teach them to work together in friendly fashion as he felt his cabinet members should, took the pair of them out deep sea fishing off Sandy Hook — "as timid on horseback, as timid in sickness would be a phaenomenon if his courage of which he has the reputation on military occasions were genuine."

Jefferson disposed of Hamilton's yellow fever in a final sentence: "his friends who have not seen him suspect it is only an autumnal fever he has."

The yellow fever was real enough in most cases. The French consul was dead. Except for Dr. Rush who was convinced his life was being saved by direct divine interposition, the city's doctors were dead or in flight. Few dared visit the sick. Bodies were left to rot in the streets. At night a few faithful colored men went around with carts to carry the dead off for burial. Dr. Rush hurried from shuttered house to shuttered house with his jalap and calomel. People chewed garlic, built bonfires in the street, shot off guns to dispel the infection. Dr. Rush's patients kept on dying but he still was confident of his remedy. The fever spread till somewhere between four and five thousand people had been carried off.

A cemetery quiet pervaded the city. Nothing stirring at the French legation. Genêt had rushed off to New York to quell a mutiny in another fleet of French ships that had fled Santo Domingo.

"I would really go away," Jefferson wrote Madison, "because I think there is a rational danger, but that I had before announced that I should not go before the beginning of October, & I do not like to exhibit the appearance of panic. besides I think there might serious ills proceed from there not being a single member of the administration in place. poor Hutcheson dined with me on Friday was sennight, was taken that night on his return home and died day before yesterday. it is difficult to say whether the republican interest has suffered more by his death than by Genêt's extravagance."

Dr. Hutchinson, professer of chemistry at the University of Pennsylvania medical school where he was one of the pillars of the anti-Federal party in Pennsylvania politics, was a rival of Dr. Rush's. He had refused to take Dr. Rush's prescription of jalap and calomel. "This evening Dr. Hutchinson breathed his last," Rush wrote his wife. "It is remarkable that he denied the existence of a contagious fever in our city for above a week after it appeared among us, and even treated the report of it with contempt and ridicule. The reason, I fear, was the first account of it came *from me.*" Dr. Rush was telling everyone that poor Dr. Hutchinson had contracted the disease on account of the full meal he unwisely ate sitting with Mr. Jefferson out in the open air under the trees on the banks of the Schuylkill.

It was not until the end of October that frost brought the disease to an end. Dr. Rush was amazed to find himself still living. "Sometimes seated in your easy chair by the fire," he wrote his wife, "I lose myself looking back upon the ocean I have passed, and now and then find myself surprized by a tear in reflecting upon the friends I have lost."

Jefferson left for Monticello in mid September. "Having found on my going to town, the day you left it," he wrote Washington, "that I had but one clerk left, and that business could not be carried on, I determined to set out for Virginia as soon as I could clear my letter files. I have now got through it so as to leave not a single letter unanswered."

Sitting in his phaeton besides his little Polly, whose charming ways reminded him of her mother, while his fine horses carried them briskly over the graveled road through the lovely farming country towards Wilmington, like Dr. Rush he must have lost himself looking back upon the bitter ocean of conflict and fear he had just passed.

13. "... & so it ended"

Jefferson had about a month in Albemarle to rest before, leav-

ing Polly with the Randolphs, he had to be on his way back to the
seat of government for the final windup of his business as Secretary
of State. It was not for long. Instead of taking his own carriage he
traveled on the stages.

He found Congress convening in cramped quarters in Germantown.
Nobody dared to go into Philadelphia. The neat Pennsylvania Dutch
village was so crowded he had to sleep on a cot in the corner of a
public room at a tavern. There Jefferson put the finishing touches on
a report on the foreign trade of American shipping, which he hoped
would prove the basis of a policy of fair neutrality between France
and England. At cabinet meetings Hamilton continued to check his
every move.

Genêt was still the obsession. It was not understood yet in America
that since the arrest of the Girondin leaders poor Genêt was no longer
a problem to anybody. While Genêt thundered and roared his friends
in Paris were following Louis Capet and his sisters' dear queen to the
guillotine. The Girondins were executed two days before Jefferson
reached Germantown.

While Jefferson and Hamilton chivvied each other over whether
they should dismiss Genêt or wait for his recall, the order was on its
way. The order minced no words. In the name of the Committee of
Public Safety of the Republic One and Indivisible it was signed:
Barrère, Hérault, Robespierre, Billaud-Varennes, Collot d'Herbois, St.
Just, names that were soon to be read with a chill of horror the world
over. The September massacres, instead of being the end as Jefferson
thought, had been the beginning. Terror ruled the Convention.

Although the hard pressed American officials meeting in Germantown were far from knowing the whole story the news from France
filled the word republic with nightmare for them.

In the arguments in cabinet meetings the President inclined more
and more to Hamilton's opinion. Jefferson and Randolph were in the
minority. "Questions & answers were put & returned in a quicker
altercation than I ever before saw the Presdnt use . . . Hamilton . . .
spoke much of the dignity of the nation . . . touched on the Pr's personal feelings," Jefferson noted.

He was helpless. He had no more place in Washington's administration. "The Presidt. lamented there was not unanimity among us; that
as it was we left him exactly where we found him & so it ended."

January 1, 1794, Jefferson's resignation became effective. He packed
his papers and went home. "I am going to Virginia," he wrote Angelica
Church in high spirits. "I am then to be liberated from the hated
occupations of politics, and to remain in the bosom of my family, my
farm and my books. I have my house to build, my fields to farm, and

to watch for the happiness of those who labor for mine." Once again he was convinced, as he had been convinced twelve years before when he retired from the governorship of Virginia, that his political career was over.

XII   Hamilton's Heyday

1. *Mr. Madison's Resolutions*

On January 5, 1794, Alexander Hamilton, settling back into the cordial winter round of his Philadelphia friendships as the government departments straggled back into town after the fear of the yellow fever subsided, had the satisfaction of learning that his great opponent had boarded the southbound stage. That left only Edmund Randolph, who took Jefferson's place as Secretary of State, to represent the Virginia Republicans in Washington's administration.

In spite of Randolph's ability as a constitutional lawyer his efforts to assume the posture of a man superior to party considerations was costing him the esteem of Federalists and Republicans alike. "He is the poorest cameleon I ever saw," Jefferson confided to Madison in a moment of irritation, "having no color of his own and reflecting that nearest him." When Washington, during their last long confidential conversation under the plane trees by the Schuylkill on the subject of Jefferson's successor, asked Jefferson what the general opinion was of Randolph, Jefferson had evaded the question. "I knew," he noted in his *Anas*, "that the embarrassments in his private affairs had obliged him to use expedients which had injured him with the merchants and shopkeepers, and affected his character for independence."

Randolph and his wife, who was one of that Nicholas family which was so closely entwined with Jefferson's career, had fallen heir to several plantations, but they were always in money trouble. Not even the very considerable fees Randolph collected as the most esteemed lawyer in Virginia kept him out of debt.

Randolph himself was painfully aware that his financial difficulties combined with his hairsplitting legal mind and his somewhat too finicky conscience to make his friends feel he was politically unreliable. "I know it," he wrote Washington in some agony of mind, "— that my opinions, not containing any systematic adherence to party, but arising solely from my views of right, fall sometimes on the one side and sometimes on the other." His connections "by friendship, by marriage, by country, and by similitude of opinions, where republicanism and good order meet, with the leaders of the southern politicks," might give birth to suspicion among the Federalists that he was trying to influence the President against them. "I see among them men whom I respect, and who, if their duplicity be not extreme, respect me. I see others who respect no man but in proportion to his subserviency to their wishes."

He hastened to explain: "I have no reason to suspect Col. Hamilton of any unkind disposition towards me . . . Even to your confidential ear I have never disclosed an idea concerning him which he might not hear . . ." He begged the President not to take amiss the fact that he occasionally disagreed even with him: "Your character is an object of real affection to me; there is no judgment, no disinterestedness, no prudence in which I ever had equal confidence . . . No danger can attend us so long as the persuasion continues, that you are not, and cannot become, the head of a party. The people venerate you because they are convinced that you choose to repose yourself on them . . . the inference which I submit to your candor is, that the measures adopted by you should be tried solely by your own and unbiassed mind."

It turned out that these apprehensions which the new Secretary of State was so guardedly trying to disclose to his chief were only too well founded. He was in the camp of the enemy. He lacked the political acumen to understand how hazardous his position was. Hamilton's supporters were letting their partisan feelings blind them to every other consideration. George Washington at sixtytwo was aging fast. Whenever Randolph had convinced him of one thing, Hamilton was always ready to talk him around the other way again.

As Jefferson put it years later when he was getting his manuscript notes of the period into shape for the binder: "From the moment of my retiring from the administration the federalists got unchecked hold of Genl. Washington." Jefferson laid it to the early senility Washington had so often complained of as being characteristic of his family: "his memory was already sensibly impaired by age, the firm tone of his mind for which he had been remarkable, was beginning to relax, it's energy was abated; a listlessness of labor, a desire for tranquility had crept on him, and a willingness to let others act and think for him."

Acting and thinking for the President became second nature to

Hamilton. Outside of Randolph the cabinet was willing putty in his hands. Henry Knox, though a devoted servant of his old commander in chief, was so involved in high living and in land speculation that he was letting the diligent Secretary of the Treasury take over more and more his functions in the War Department. The new Attorney General, William Bradford, had been a close friend of Madison's in college but he had married into the Boudinot connection and had made his career as a lawyer in the highflying financial circles of Philadelphia which the aged Willing and his aggressive soninlaw William Bingham presided over. In the subordinate officers Hamilton had fanatical supporters such as sedulous Oliver Wolcott as comptroller and gaunt selfrighteous Pickering as Postmaster General.

About the only friend of Jefferson's left at the seat of government was Tench Coxe as Commissioner of Revenue. Coxe had no access to Washington, and Randolph could be readily bypassed. It was Hamilton who acted and thought for the administration.

Hamilton had already decided that he must retire from office himself as soon as he could. He was no more solvent than Randolph was. His salary did not support his family. He was in the embarrassing position of having to accept help from his fatherinlaw. He was continually borrowing small sums of money from his friends. Though Hamilton enjoyed an argument much more than Jefferson did, even that tireless debater was weary of the private bickering and the name-calling in the public press. He dreamed of a trip to England to visit his affectionate relations John and Angelica Church, whose extensive money affairs in America he had in charge. After that he wanted to go back to the practice of the law.

Before he could resign Hamilton felt he had to dispose of two powerful reminders of Jefferson's influence in Congress. The first was the movement led by noisy young Giles to demand a fresh investigation of Hamilton's stewardship as Secretary of the Treasury. The other was a set of resolutions which Madison introduced in the House to implement the report "on the priviledges and restrictions on the commerce of the United States in foreign countries" which Jefferson had presented before retiring from office.

Though Hamilton, like Jefferson, and like Pitt himself for that matter, believed theoretically in Adam Smith's principles of free trade, he felt, as Pitt did, that the present instance, when France and Britain were at war, was no time to apply them. The merchants on both ends of the Atlantic trade tended to agree with him. The war added to their risks, but it enormously multiplied their prospects of gain. They did not care to risk their present profits in behalf of an abstract theory no matter what rosy future it held out. More than three quarters of the business of the American seaport towns was with England.

To Hamilton, Jefferson's foreign policy, based on his insistence that the ocean was the common property of all nations and that neutral bottoms should make neutral goods in wartime, seemed impractical as long as the United States had no navy to enforce it. Hamilton's fiscal system was based on the impost on imports. Anything that threatened Anglo-American trade threatened the national credit. He considered the measures Jefferson was advocating — meeting high duties with high duties, discrimination with discrimination — as merely a pretext for siding with revolutionary France against conservative England.

Hamilton knew that Jefferson had held back this report, which he had been working on off and on with occasional assistance from Madison and Coxe ever since he took office in New York, until the moment he thought it would do the Federalists the most harm. Now Madison with his dry logic and cool marshaling of uncontrovertible facts was advocating a policy of tit for tat.

Hamilton saw in Madison's resolutions a challenge to his entire system. Hitherto the Republican opposition had appealed mostly to the southern planters who felt they were being charged unjust interest on their longstanding debts to British merchants, to the small farmers who hated taxes and hard money, and to the settlers on the Western Waters who felt that the administration was neglecting their interests for those of the seaboard, but here was a move to undercut Hamilton in New England, which was the Federalist citadel.

Pitt's total blockade of France was beginning to hurt the American shipowners. Two hundred American ships had been taken into port by British cruisers in the West Indies under the Order in Council of November 6, 1793, that made foodstuffs contraband. The majority of them were treated as prizes, their crews imprisoned on feverridden hulks, their skippers despitefully treated by the goldbraided officers of His Majesty's navy. Every New England seaport abounded with friends and relatives of American seamen impressed aboard British warships where the cat o' nine tails ruled. To add to the indignant uproar among seafarers and shipowners came the news that Portugal, well known to be a British pawn, had signed a treaty with the Bey of Algiers which amounted to an encouragement to the Barbary pirates to pursue neutral ships out into the Atlantic.

Madison's even sarcastic voice defending his resolutions in the House gave the Federalists cold chills. They had to avoid a vote on Jefferson's report. Hamilton's ardent supporter Fisher Ames immediately asked for a week's postponement of the debate in order to give his party time to improvise a strategy.

Fisher Ames was the ablest representative of the young generation in New England in full reaction against the dogmas and enthusiasms of 1776. Democracy was their bugbear. They felt themselves well-born, they intended to be rich. The Great Britain they looked to as a model was not the old rural England of the whig oligarchy but the new Britain of aggressive merchants and sailors where Pitt was assiduously welding the wealth of the City with old landowning interest into a renovated ruling class. These young men felt that they were part of that class.

As mob rule and massacre overwhelmed the moderates in France, they felt that Burke's most hysterical fears had been justified. Their interests as bankers and insurance men and merchants were inextricably intertwined with those of the great mercantile firms of the City of London. They were willing to suffer almost any loss and indignity for the feeling of security this solidarity with the powerful rulers of England afforded them.

Hamilton felt all this strongly. The problems Pitt was facing to save his England for the rich and wellborn were the same that he was facing in America. He could see clearly that the United States must have peace. The country had no navy and what little army there was had suffered two disgraceful defeats at the hands of the Indians across the Ohio.

He took advantage of the postponement of the debate in the House to throw himself into the writing of a persuasive lawyer's brief that countered such of Madison's arguments as could be countered and evaded the rest. Since he could not deliver it himself he found a faithful Federalist, William Smith of South Carolina, to deliver it for him on the floor of the House.

More had to be done. The indignation against the British Orders in Council was too great to be ignored. Hamilton placed himself at the head of the movement for putting the country into a state of defense. Federalists and Republicans alike voted for a bill to fortify the seaports from the Penobscot to Savannah, Georgia. Work was resumed on the construction of the six frigates projected years ago while Robert Morris was Agent of Marine.

The islands of the Caribbean which produced nothing but sugar, in spite of the Navigation Acts and a halfhearted effort to supply them from Nova Scotia, still depended on United States shipping for their daily needs. It was hoped the West India planters would bring pressure on the Admiralty to use tact in enforcing the blockade. A month's embargo on sailings from American ports was voted and proclaimed by the President. Bills were introduced into Congress to raise an army of fifteen thousand men.

It was clear to Hamilton that war with England would play into the hands of the Francophile Republicans. Some immediate agreement with Westminster on navigation and commerce was necessary if the Federalists were to preserve their gains at home.

There was never a doubt in Hamilton's mind that saving his party meant saving his country.

2. Mr. Jay's Weak Side

In spite of Hamilton's confidential relationship with the British minister George Hammond, who had formed new ties with Federalist circles by marrying the daughter of a Philadelphia merchant, he made no progress even after the departure of the marplot Jefferson towards prying loose from the Crown the frontier posts that furnished the Indians a base for their warfare against the western settlers, or in reducing the oppression of the Navigation Acts. Quite the contrary, disturbing rumors were coming in of an inflammatory speech Lord Dorchester had made to the Indians which gave them to understand that a fresh war was imminent between Great Britain and the United States and that King George not only had no intention of giving up the posts but that he would help the Indians regain their lost hunting grounds. An envoy extraordinary must immediately be sent to England.

Hamilton himself was the first candidate of the Federalists. Robert Morris, in whom Washington still had great faith as a practical man, in spite of his notorious financial difficulties and the ridicule he had exposed himself to by the ostentation of the marble palace L'Enfant was building for him in downtown Philadelphia, was induced to talk the project up with the President. Hamilton, although he dearly craved a trip to England and a sight of his charming sisterinlaw Angelica, refrained from pushing his own candidacy. He and Robert Morris between them politely squelched Washington's suggestion that either John Adams or Thomas Jefferson should be chosen. At last, talking the matter over with his closest political associate Rufus King, now senator from New York, and with Oliver Ellsworth of Connecticut and the two Massachusetts senators, Caleb Strong and George Cabot, he lit upon John Jay as the most reliable man for the mission. Washington, who was at his wit's end, yielded reluctantly. Though he himself had great respect for the Westchester Aristides he knew how unpopular he was in the South and West.

John Jay was Chief Justice, and as the Supreme Court rode circuit in those days, he had just arrived in Philadelphia for the spring term. Everybody admitted that he was a man of flawless private and public morals, with a cool devotion to impartial justice as he saw it, but he

was hated by the Westerners on account of his disregard of their interests in the negotiations with Spain years before. Recently he had
earned the sympathy even of some Republicans because of the crass
manipulations by which Clinton and Burr had managed to cheat him
out of the governorship of New York.

Hamilton and his four senators trooped around to see Chief Justice
Jay at Mrs. Gibbon's boardinghouse on Spruce Street and managed to
convince him that he was the indispensable man for the mission. It
was agreed that Jay need not resign as Chief Justice. He agreed to
risk the ocean crossing, to separate himself from his adored wife, and
to postpone his ambition to be elected governor of New York in spite
of the Clinton machine.

By mid April his appointment was hurried through the Senate
against the opposition of Burr and Monroe. The United States already
had a minister in England, the popular Thomas Pinckney of the great
South Carolina family of Pinckneys. What could Jay do that Pinckney
could not? The Federalists answered that a special mission was essential. There was no time to be lost. As early as May 12, with a long
letter of instructions from Hamilton in his dispatch case to which he
paid great attention and another from the Secretary of State to which
he paid no attention at all, John Jay sailed for England on the ship
Ohio out of New York.

In Philadelphia the ungrateful task was left to Randolph of explaining to Joseph Fauchet, who had arrived to supplant Genêt as a representative of the incorruptible Robespierre, why the Americans were
failing to carry out the provisions of their treaty with France. Although
it was daily becoming more apparent that in the cabinet he was the
fifth wheel of the coach, Randolph was trying as usual to satisfy both
parties. The result was that he disgusted Fauchet and drifted into a
public scolding match with Hammond. Randolph's position was further weakened by the fact that, while the Secretary of State and His
Majesty's minister were berating each other in the newspapers, Hammond and Hamilton were carrying on a series of cozy and confidential
chats over their wine at the British legation.

The two men seem to have been genuinely congenial. One of Hamilton's greatest charms was his defenseless candor. Hammond was able
to take advantage of this friendship and perhaps of the West Indian's
innate respect for His Majesty's service, to extract from him a number
of highly indiscreet statements which Hammond promptly retailed in
his dispatches to Lord Grenville.

William Wyndham, Baron Grenville, a close friend of Pitt's,
was one of the ablest men ever to enter the Foreign Office at
Whitehall. He shared Pitt's disenchanted preoccupation with the

weaknesses of men. Between them they had the best intelligence service in Europe. By the time John Jay landed, seasick and shaken after a rough spring crossing, at Falmouth in the west of England and posted up to London, showing his son Peter Augustus, whom he brought along as his personal secretary, the splendors of Bath and the castles and cathedrals on the way, Lord Grenville knew a great deal more about the intentions and opinions of the leadership of Washington's administration than Jay did; and almost as much about John Jay.

Long before the American envoy wrote his lordship politely to announce his arrival at the Bath Hotel where he was met with a warm and generous greeting by Thomas Pinckney, Grenville knew that the all powerful Hamilton had no interest in the doctrine of the freedom of the seas which Jefferson, as minister to France and as Secretary of State, had worked so hard to establish as part of the law of nations. He knew that Hamilton was willing to acquiesce in the Admiralty's famous Rule of 1756 on the seizure of belligerent goods on neutral ships which Jefferson and Randolph had spent so much time and so much ink to prove inadmissible. He also knew that Hamilton would not budge on the surrender of the string of forts from Niagara to Detroit which had been conceded to the Americans by the treaty of peace, and that he intended to hold out for trade with the West Indies in American bottoms.

England needed the Atlantic trade as much as the Americans did. England needed America's benevolent neutrality in the war with France. Grenville was prepared to make concessions.

Grenville had been carefully posted on the American envoy's private character. "He argues closely but is longwinded and selfopinionated," wrote one of his lordship's correspondents. "He can bear any opposition providing regard is paid to his ability . . . Every man has a weak and assailable quarter but Mr. Jay's weak side is Mr. Jay."

Grenville spared no effort to assure Mr. Jay a cordial and flattering reception. The Jays, father and son, found themselves dining in circles to which no American envoy had yet been admitted. All classes treated them with sedulous hospitality. Lord Grenville entertained them in state at his own table. Nobody could be more affable than the Lord Chancellor. When John Jay was introduced at a royal levee, King George, who had been forewarned, scolded a little at Jay's having been doubtful as to the sort of reception he would get. Then he beamed on him and asked in a cascade of royal verbiage whether any doubts still remained in his mind as to the success of his mission, what? what?

Grenville knew his own bargaining position was weak. When he and Pitt put their heads together over rivers of port in endless late meetings at Downing Street, since neither of them had any capacity

for selfdelusion, they could find little to please them about the course
of the war.

His Majesty's navy had done well. The French West India islands
were caving in one by one. A few days before Jay landed in Falmouth,
morose and elderly Admiral Howe (Black Dick his crews lovingly
called him) had given a French fleet, which was trying to convoy a
group of provision ships from the Chesapeake into Brest, a thorough
trouncing in the Channel.

On land it was another story. Marching to the roar of the "Marseillaise" and lashed forward by the hoarse oratory of republican
heroism and the frantic butcheries of the Terror, the French republicans crushed the royalist rising in Brittany, retook Toulon in the
south, and drove the coalition armies back across the Rhine in the
north. In the Low Countries they captured Charleroi and, with Belgium in their hands, were threatening the Channel ports.

At home on the green isle of Britain money was short. The country
was sullen under the regime of pressgangs and high taxes. The lower
orders were not taking the repression of the democratic societies and
the suspension of habeas corpus in the proper patriotic spirit.

A blockade of France was Pitt's last expedient.

The greatest danger to the success of the blockade to Grenville's
mind was a revival of the League of Armed Neutrality by the Baltic
powers. Ever since he had heard of the explosions of popular indignation the ship seizures had caused in every American seaport, one
of his chief preoccupations had been to keep the Americans from
joining with Sweden and Denmark in agreement on a common policy,
which would stem logically from Jefferson's and Randolph's conduct
of foreign affairs, to protect the freedom of the seas.

Though Jay neglected Randolph's instructions to start exploratory
conversations with the Scandinavians, he did allow himself to be seen
in friendly conversation with the Swedish ambassador. At Whitehall
Lord Grenville was accessible and congenial. During the preliminary
talks Jay found his lordship full of the spirit of accommodation. Jay
was a suspicious man. He knew he was in the hands of sharpers. He
was determined to play his cards carefully. "As yet I do not regret
any step that I have taken," he wrote Hamilton. "I wish I may be able
to say the same thing at the conclusion." He did not know, as he
cautiously canvassed the points at issue between the two countries,
that it was his friend Hamilton who had unwittingly placed a trump
in his opponent's hand.

His lordship's mind was set at rest on armed neutrality by a dispatch
from Hammond that reached him in mid September. Hamilton, wrote
the exultant envoy, had assured him "that it was the settled policy of
this government, in every contingency, even in that of an open contest

with Great Britain, to avoid entangling itself with European connections." From that moment Grenville, who had been all affable eagerness to meet the Americans halfway, became a little hard to see. He made no further concessions. He knew now that he could dictate his own terms. Jay struggled on against increasing difficulties. In the end the treaty he signed was so little to his liking that the best thing he could say of it in his guarded letter to Randolph which accompanied the text was, "My opinion of the treaty is apparent from my having signed it. I have no reason to believe or conjecture that one more favorable to us is attainable."

3. *The Whiskey Boys*

Once John Jay was hustled aboard ship for England, Hamilton had to exert himself to get the reins of government into his hands again. The administration's hold on Congress had been weakened by the resentment aroused against England among Federalists and Republicans alike. Now the Secretary of the Treasury could damp down the hotheads with the argument that since negotiations with Pitt's government were under way nothing should be done to disturb them.

Before Congress adjourned in early June of 1794 Hamilton's supporters managed to abort two retaliatory measures against the British. Each had aroused the absent Jefferson's enthusiasm. One of Jefferson's eternal preoccupations was how to develop some action other than war to meet foreign aggression. He had seen a beginning of such a method in the pending nonintercourse bill and in Washington's proclamation of an embargo on shipping. "I love peace," he wrote hopefully to Tench Coxe from Monticello. "I am anxious that we should give the world still another useful lesson by showing them other modes of punishing injuries than by war, which is just as much of a punishment to the punisher as to the sufferer."

After a two months' trial the embargo was allowed to lapse. The nonintercourse bill failed only by John Adams' casting vote against it. The whole Hamiltonian system had been in jeopardy. In the Senate the Federalists, to be sure, managed to show their vigor and cohesion by denying a seat to a clever young Swiss named Albert Gallatin who was the senator elect from western Pennsylvania. The pretext was that although he had admittedly resided for thirteen years in the United States he had not been a citizen for the nine years required by the Constitution.

The Federalists split hairs against Gallatin primarily because he was a Republican; but he was a Republican who spoke with a French accent and a westernminded man into the bargain. For some years now he had represented the settlers on the Western Waters in the Pennsylvania Assembly. He had made himself particularly obnoxious to Hamilton by being one of the most articulate leaders of the opposition to his excise on spirits.

Albert Gallatin had landed in Boston at the age of nineteen, towards the end of the Revolutionary War, with the usual pocketful of letters from Benjamin Franklin and to Robert Morris. He came of one of the great families of that thoughtful Geneva aristocracy that had made their tiny republic the resort for aspiring innovators in literature and philosophy. His grandparents had been close friends of Voltaire's and as a child he ran in and out of the aged philosopher's salons at Ferney. Left an orphan at nine, he graduated from the Geneva Academy the first in his class in mathematics and in science. His family wanted him to accept a commission in the Hessian army. He hated war; and since he could expect only a tiny inheritance and wanted at all costs to avoid the career of the poor relation under the thumb of the conseil de famille, he ran away, in the company of a likeminded friend, to America. Rousseau had a hand in his decision; all his life Gallatin had an ethnologist's interest in the savages of the forest.

Unlike most of the lettered European immigrants, he developed a real taste for frontier life. He spent two winters in a coastal settlement near Machias down in Maine. There he saw some militia service against the British. His trading venture failed down east, and he took up the life of a roving immigrant, picking up a living as best he could. He taught French at Harvard College. The country was full of French refugees; when everything else failed he served as interpreter. Wherever he went he made friends. In Philadelphia he ate in the same boardinghouse at Pelatiah Webster.

He got along famously with the Virginians. In Richmond he married the daughter of a family that kept a French pension for exiles. There Patrick Henry, whose whole life was now wrapped up in western lands, took a fancy to him and sent him off across the mountains to the Ohio country with letters to the frontier surveyors in his saddlebags.

He was keeping store at George's Creek across the Pennsylvania line when he met George Washington slogging through the glades and the gulches to look over his landholdings the summer after he had resigned his command. It was said that the general offered to make the sharp young Swiss his land agent, but Gallatin stuck to his store and to his private speculations.

He managed by the careful use of small sums of money picked up in trading to get title to some rich bottomlands on the Monongahela. When a couple of his countrymen came to America to join in his venture they named their settlement New Geneva. On the bluffs above he started building himself a home which he called Friendship Hill. In a district where there were not too many men who could read and write, he found himself called upon to take down the minutes at every political meeting.

When he first appeared in the United States Senate at the age of thirtythree he still spoke with an accent. He had already accumulated legislative experience in the Pennsylvania Assembly where he did the detail paperwork on committee after committee, drafting bills and writing reports. He worked there for universal manhood suffrage and for improved public schools and for the extension of highways. He was the author of a resolution calling for an end to Negro slavery.

He made himself outstandingly disagreeable to the Treasury by acting as clerk to a meeting at Pittsburgh that advocated resistance against Hamilton's tax collectors. The whole western country was up in arms against the excise on spirits. In the course of these resolutions Gallatin explained the reason for their opposition. The farmers across the Alleghenies were in a predicament. Since the Mississippi was closed to them they had no way of getting their abundant crops of barley and rye and wheat and corn to market. Grain was too bulky to transport profitably by muletrain across the mountains. They had no money to pay the excise tax with even if they wanted to. Cash was unobtainable in the country. Whiskey was the medium of exchange. "We are therefore distillers through necessity, not choice; that we may comprehend the greatest value in the smallest size and weight."

Even before he met Jefferson he had Jefferson's fellow feeling for the farming community. He loved the backcountry people. Raised in the spartan school of Calvinist Geneva, he was shocked by the pomp and ostentation of the parvenu rich of Philadelphia. He wrote proudly back to Switzerland from Friendship Hill: "From the suburbs of Philadelphia to the banks of the Ohio I do not know a single family that has any extensive influence. An equal distribution of property has rendered every individual independent, and there is amongst us true and real equality. In a word," he confessed, "as I am lazy, I like a country where living is cheap; and as I am poor, I like country where no person is very rich."

It was not only his public career that brought Gallatin into conflict with Hamilton. Gallatin's second marriage was to a daughter of that Commodore Nicholson who had been a crony of Tom Paine's. The house on William Street in New York to which that doughty old sea dog had retired as the highest ranking officer of the discarded Continental Navy was a center for the friends of Jefferson and Burr. There was every reason for Hamilton to feel that with the factions so evenly balanced in the Senate, it would be a danger to his party to allow the

young Swiss to take his seat. The vote to unseat him was too close for
Hamilton's comfort, at that.

With Congress adjourned and Jay on the high seas bound for
England and Gallatin sent back to the Monongahela, Hamilton was
able to turn his attention to giving Gallatin's constituents a much
needed lesson.

For years the Secretary of the Treasury had felt that the general
government should establish its authority by a show of force. The men
of the western counties must be forced to pay the excise. There followed a tussle in Washington's cabinet like one of the old tussles with
Jefferson. Edmund Randolph argued for moderate measures. Hamilton, who had already virtually taken over Knox's functions as Secretary
of War, wanted to raise an army. The small regular army under
General Wayne was already busy with the expedition which was soon
to retrieve the ground St. Clair had lost against the Indians across
the Ohio.

Washington let himself be persuaded by Randolph to seek a compromise. He had already addressed proclamations to the disorderly
frontiersmen. Now he would send three commissioners to demand that
the western counties submit to the excise law. If that failed he would
call out the militia. "We are going the old way 'Slow'," Washington
wrote Jefferson in a letter dealing with the subject of green manures,
a topic dear to the hearts of both men and into which politics did not
enter. "I hope events will justify me in adding 'and sure.'"

The whiskey boys, as they had come to be known, of Fayette and
Washington counties in western Pennsylvania were giving Hamilton
some justification for his show of force. Congress before adjourning
had yielded to one of their chief demands, which was that infractors
of the excise laws should be tried in their home counties instead of
in Federal Court in Philadelphia. In spite of that, mobs and armed
posses rose up in fury against the United States marshal and his
agents when they tried to serve writs against distillers for nonpay-
ment of taxes. Led by a scatterbrained young man named David
Bradford whom Gallatin described as "a tenth rate lawyer and an
empty drum" and by a half imaginary backwoodsman who set up
liberty poles and signed misspelled posters calling for resistance under
the name of "Tom the Tinker," the whiskey boys ran riot. They intim-
idated lawabiding citizens who were offering their submission to
Washington's commissioners. They tarred and feathered officers of
the law.

The uproar reached its height when they laid siege to the house of
General Neville, the inspector of revenue. The house was defended

by a small detail of regulars from the old fort at Pittsburgh. A whiskey boy was killed. There were several wounded on both sides. The whiskey boys set fire to Neville's house and barns, and the soldiers, to keep from being burned alive, had to march out under a flag of truce while the inspector of revenue and his friends barely escaped with their lives out of the back of the house into the hills.

When news of this outrage reached Philadelphia the President gave Hamilton his head and instructed the governors of Pennsylvania, New Jersey and Virginia to call out their militia to the number of fifteen thousand men. When Jefferson heard of it at Monticello, not being able to imagine that such a force could be needed to intimidate a few distillers, he wrote optimistically that he hoped the President was using the whiskey boys as a pretext to have a force ready on the Ohio to back up Wayne's expedition and perhaps to take Detroit from the British.

Hamilton had been preparing the public mind for punitive measures by a series of articles in the newspapers signed "Tully": the functioning of a republican government depended on acceptance of majority rule. The people's representatives had passed an excise law. Four counties, representing one sixtieth part of the nation, were defying the collective will of the nation as a whole. With his lawyer's skill, in his final article he managed to confound the fomenters of the insurrection in "a dark conspiracy" with opponents of the Treasury's financial measures and of his policy of conciliating the British Crown.

4. A Daring and Factious Spirit

It was not too hard to convince the President that the outrages of the whisky boys were the logical outcome of the agitation of the democratic societies. Ever since the row with Genêt he had held them in detestation. He spoke of them wrathfully as "selfcreated bodies, forming themselves into permanent Censors under the shade of Night in a conclave, resolving that acts of Congress, which have already undergone the most deliberate and solemn discussion by Representatives of the people . . . are unconstitutional . . . or . . . pregnant with mischief." He denounced them in every letter to his militia generals. When he issued a final proclamation against the western rebels he called on all good men to abandon them. "And I do moreover exhort all Individuals, Officers and Bodies of men to contemplate with Abhorrence the Measures leading to these Crimes . . . to check . . . . the efforts of misguided or designing Men to substitute their Misrepresentation in the place of Truth and their Discontents in the place of Stable Government."

The President's dander was up. In crushing the insurrection he saw an opportunity to subdue the "daring and factious spirit" the democratic societies represented. Otherwise "we may bid adieu to all government in this country except Mob and Club Govt. from whence nothing but Anarchy and Confusion can ensue." As an old soldier he could not help longing a little for the jingle of harness and the snap of presented arms, and perhaps even for a sniff of gunpowder. He decided to ride out himself to take charge of the marshaling of the expeditionary force.

Eager as a schoolboy, Hamilton begged to go along. Knox had somewhat unexplainedly taken the month off to attend to his wife's landholdings in Maine. The business of the Treasury could be delegated to the capable hands of Hamilton's assistant, Oliver Wolcott. Hamilton explained that it was his duty as acting Secretary of War to take the field. "In a government like ours it cannot but have a good effect for the person who is understood to be the adviser or proposer of a measure, which involves danger to his fellow-citizens, to partake in that danger."

Calling out the militia was a popular move. Even the administration's opponents felt it was the first step towards putting the country on a war footing in case of hostilities with the British. Governor Richard Howell of New Jersey, a lawyer of some musical talent, who had been one of Washington's secret agents during the war, marched his men across the fat Pennsylvania farmlands to the tune of a song he composed for the occasion: "Dash to the Mountains, Jersey Blue."

Restless Henry Lee, the Light Horse Harry who had so brilliantly commanded the cavalry at Paulus Hook and Eutaw Springs, was already drilling the Virginia levies as that commonwealth's governor. Only Governor Mifflin of Pennsylvania, who had never been an admirer of George Washington anyway, exhibited qualms as he marshaled his troops: he did not relish the idea of pumping lead into his constituents. Washington had his best horses led out of his stable, dusted off his buff and blue uniform and the threecornered hat with the black cockade and rode out to review the expedition, exhibiting once more, in his saddle with the leopardskin housings, the magnificent seat and erect posture that were the admiration of the age.

In Carlisle the President had to quiet the ardor of the militia officers. Lashed up by Hamilton's campaign in the press and by the rumormongers who were busily linking the whiskey boys, according to the politics of their hearers, either with the insidious British or the rascally Jacobins, they were pounding on the inn tables and shouting that by God they would hang the traitors without trial. Patiently Washington went about explaining that the purpose of the expedition was to apprehend the guilty so that they might be tried fairly and squarely by the civil courts.

He had to take measures too to restrain the rank and file who were showing their enthusiasm for law and order by burning the farmers' rail fences and plundering the countryside. "In some places," he wrote Hamilton, who was hurriedly cleaning up his paperwork in the Treasury and the War Department in order to join in the outing, "I am told, they did not leave a plate, a spoon, a glass or a knife."

Washington's perplexities were much relieved by the good news from Anthony Wayne that reached him on the road. That able fire eater succeeded in drilling the disorganized troops he took over from St. Clair into an aggressive fighting force. He taught them the lessons of forest warfare so successfully that they gave a large band of Indians, stiffened by some white agents of the Montreal fur dealers, such a trouncing at Fallen Timbers that they lost stomach for the war. He burned their villages and their crops and chased the remnant back under the guns of the British fort on the Miami River. After an exchange of military billingsgate with the British commander he marched his men, with many an Indian scalp hidden in their haversacks, back to base in good order.

After riding as far west as Fort Cumberland to visit his own Virginia troops, Washington, leaving Henry Lee in military command of the expedition, with Alexander Hamilton really in charge as a combination of presidential deputy and Secretary of the Treasury and acting Secretary of War, started back in his coach to Philadelphia in order to reach the seat of government in time for the assembling of Congress. As he drove in the rain through the roads rutted and mired by the army wagons he reflected bitterly on the wickedness of the "selfcreated" democratic societies that had caused all this trouble.

"Against the malignancy of the discontented the turbulent and the vicious," the President wrote John Jay from his mansion in Philadelphia while he was waiting impatiently for Congress to assemble a quorum, "no abilities; no exertions; nor the most unshaken integrity are any safeguard."

Referring to a possible war with England if Jay's mission should fail, he assured him that "measures, as far as depends on the Executive preparatory for the worst, while it hopes for the best, will be pursued." He expressed the fear that the western insurrection would be taken in England "as an evidence of what has been predicted, that we are unable to govern ourselves." Then he returned to the obsession

which filled his letters during that summer and fall against the democratic societies. "That they have been the fomenters of the Western
disturbances admits of no doubt in anyone who will examine their
conduct," he wrote, rather reflecting Hamilton's arguments than any
facts that had been brought to light, "but fortunately they have pre-
cipitated a crisis for which they were not prepared; and thereby have
unfolded views which will I trust effectuate their annihilation."

He went on with enthusiasm to describe "The Spirit which blazed
out on this occasion!" He had seen "instances of General Officers
going at the head of a single Troop . . . of field Officers when they
came to the places of rendezvous and found no command for them in
that grade, turning into the ranks and proceeding as private Soldiers,
under their own Captains, and of numbers, possessing the first fortunes in the Country, standing in the ranks as private men and marching day by day with their knapsacks and haversacks on their backs,
sleeping on the straw with a single blanket in a Soldiers tent, during
the frosty nights we have had . . . These things have terrified the
Insurgents . . . Their language is much changed indeed but their principles want Correction." He had no more doubts that the people of
the United States were ready to defend their Constitution and the
financial system which had established its credit in the world.

Meanwhile Hamilton and Henry Lee were riding in the rain at the
head of their troops through the slippery mountain trails and the
muddy glades down into the deep valley where the raw shacks of
Pittsburgh clustered round the old earthworks of Fort Pitt at the junction of the Allegheny and Monongahela rivers. Though they were
irritated by occasional tales of liberty poles being set up at the crossings of trails, not an insurgent showed his head. Rumors, but rumors
only, came to them of armed men led by that mysterious Tom the
Tinker massing beyond the rivers. There was no resistance along the
road.

Their strategy was to move fast and to seize the ringleaders in their
beds before they could carry out their "dark conspiracy." From his
camp at Roshaven, Hamilton wrote Washington that an attempt would
be made to round up the traitors in one night's raid. "All possible
means are using to obtain evidence and accomplices will be turned
against the others . . . This step is directed by that principle of law
that every man may of right apprehend a traitor."

Catch the big fish and let the little minnows go, Hamilton and Lee
had been telling their staff officers. In Fayette County the big fish was
Albert Gallatin, but he had already ruined Hamilton's plans by taking
the lead, at great personal risk, in the campaign for submission to the
federal officers. In the Pittsburgh region the big fish was H. H. Brack-

enridge, whom Hamilton described to Washington as "the worst of all scoundrels."

This was the same Brackenridge who had joined with Madison and Freneau in the infamous publications of *The National Gazette* that had caused such heartburnings in the Treasury. Gallatin would probably slip from his clutches, but if Hamilton could pin the insurrection on Brackenridge it would be capturing Tom the Tinker himself.

5. *A Character Fit for an Example*

Hugh Brackenridge was a Scot from Campbeltown on the west coast. Brought to Newcastle as a child, he worked his way up from poverty, teaching school, tutoring, clerking in law offices in various Pennsylvania towns. At Princeton where he was the literary mentor of young Madison's poetical coterie in which so many literary patriots had first sharpened their quills, he tutored Henry Lee.

He was a chaplain in the Continental Army and since he moved out to the western country had made a name for himself as a lawyer and as a novelist. The third volume of his *Modern Chivalry,* much esteemed in those days, which he had printed in Pittsburgh, was the first work of literature published west of the Alleghenies.

Besides being an enthusiastic Republican, Brackenridge was a whimsical character whose elvish remarks made him enemies. Among his most virulent illwishers was a brother lawyer named Woods whom he was opposing in that fall's congressional election and General Neville, the inspector of revenue, who had escaped from his burning house to run for his life across the mountains.

Neville and his numerous family connections held patents to most of the best land in the region: the greater part of Brackenridge's practice was defending squatters' and settlers' rights against the demands of speculators. As Neville and his friends rode back across the mountains with Hamilton and Lee they were loudly discussing their plans to get even for the losses and humiliations they had suffered.

They filled Hamilton's ears with denunciations of that worst of all scoundrels. Brackenridge was the principal catch that Hamilton was thinking of when he wrote again to the President from his camp opposite Pittsburgh, "Tomorrow the measures for apprehending persons and seizing stills will be carried into effect."

Brackenridge himself, in his *Incidents of the Insurrection in the Western Parts of Pennsylvania,* described his arrest and inquisition: "The right wing of the army had now crossed the mountain, and were in the western country. It was like the approach of a tempest to me. I could hear the thunder at a distance; every day new accounts of butchery denounced against me, without judge or jury. I began to hear General Neville raise his voice: 'the damndest rascal that there ever was on God Almighty's earth.'"

It had been discovered that Brackenridge, who like Gallatin in the adjoining county had been riding around securing signatures to the articles of submission, had been so busy getting other men to sign before midnight of the final day set in the President's proclamation that he had forgotten to sign himself. Here was a character fit for an example. "In the examination of all the witnesses the burden of the song was, 'What do you know of Brackenridge?' I knew well that secretary Hamilton would have a predisposition against me. He would rather find the opposition to the law to have originated in the plan of some leading individuals, than with the mass of the people: for the excise law being the result of the funding system, of which the secretary was an advocate, it would save the pride of judgment, to have it thought opposed by the seditious arts of one, or a few, rather than by the feeling of common sense of many. I reflected also, that the secretary would have observed in my letter to Tench Coxe . . . that I was not a friend to the funding system itself."

Brackenridge was arrested in the course of the raid on the night of November 13, long remembered in the western country as a night of terror, and interned in his own house in Pittsburgh.

The next day Henry Lee took over Brackenridge's house for his headquarters. Brackenridge fidgeted around in the back room listening through the wall to the cheerful chatter of the officers' mess as they ate his food and drank his drink. In all his distress of mind he could not help playing a kind of prank: ". . . I had just before this time, got a large cocked hat, and buff under dress with a coat of military blue; and now and then occasionally shewed myself in the street, imitating, as well as I could, the grave deportment, and stately gait of a general officer. A variety of detachments of horses had come to town, and I found it was a matter of curiosity, to see the leader of the insurgents. I would sometimes hear it said, when not supposed to hear it, 'He has the appearance of a military man.'"

Meanwhile Hamilton rode into Pittsburgh to set up his inquisition. The schoolboy dream of conquest was fading fast. This tiny log town, hemmed in by the hills and by the old earthworks of the fort, where the coalsmoke hung low over the loghouses; the deeprutted mud of the streets full of dogs, drays, oxcarts, rooting hogs, dirtyfaced children running underfoot; this was nothing like the panoply and show of the old days at Yorktown, and Cornwallis so elegantly dressed, and his fine officers so straight and stern. From all over the country poor devils dragged out of their beds were being driven in through the rain and the mud at the breasts of the soldiers' horses. The settlement was small, the houses were small; everybody was on top of everybody. These were not an Alexander's conquests.

Brackenridge was taken before the Secretary for questioning: "I was received by Hamilton with that countenance, which a man will have when he sees a person, with regard to whom his humanity and his sense of justice struggles; — he would have him saved, but is afraid he must be hanged . . . He began by asking me some general questions, with regard to any system or plan, within my knowledge, of overthrowing the government. I had known of nothing of the kind . . ."

After a number of questions about the Jacobin revolution, which Hamilton had convinced himself and the President was being planned by the democratic societies in the western country, for which Brackenridge found no answer because no such conspiracy existed, Hamilton asked him to tell what he did know. As Brackenridge talked the Secretary covered a long sheet of paper with his rapid small handwriting.

"I gave him the outlines of the narrative . . . until I came to the particular, where after the burning of Neville's house, I represented the people called on Bradford" — Bradford, the "empty drum" who had played soldier riding at the head of the mob in a militia uniform, had already escaped downriver in a flatboat headed for Louisiana — "and Marshall to come forward, and support what was done, under the pain of being treated as Neville himself had been. At this the secretary laid down his pen and addressed himself to me;

" 'Mr. Brackenridge,' said he, 'I observe one leading trait in your account, a disposition to excuse the principal actors; and before we go further, I must be candid and inform you of the delicate situation in which you stand; *you are not within the amnesty; you have not signed upon the day.*' "

Brackenridge answered that he knew that all too well, but that he was telling the truth and that there was nothing else to tell. In the middle of his narrative Hamilton was called away to dinner. Brackenridge went back home, "but declined dining with General Lee that day, though pressed by several messages. I could not bear to show myself in that company, in the doubtful predicament in which I stood."

Meanwhile there was a conversation at Hamilton's lodgings that Brackenridge only learned about later: "A treasonable letter of mine addressed to a certain Bradford had fallen into the hands of my adversaries. It was dark and mysterious, and respected certain papers, a duplicate of which I wished him to send me, having mislaid the first copy; that these were so essential, I could not go on with the business without them. This letter was now brought forward.

" 'What do you make of that?' said secretary Hamilton to James Ross, who was present: 'you have averred as your opinion, that Brackenridge has had no correspondence with Bradford; look at that, is it not the handwriting of Brackenridge?'

" 'It is the handwriting,' said James Ross, pausing for some time; 'and there is only this small matter observable in the case, that it is addressed to William Bradford, attorney general of the United States, and not to David Bradford.'

"When a blast, transverse, takes a shallop on the river, and throws her on her beam ends, with all her sails set: or when a scud of wind takes the standing corn of the farmer, and on the field bows the stalks to the earth, so languished my brother of the bar." — Woods, his opponent in the election — "The old general" — Neville — "stood motionless and speechless, and to this hour had been standing, had not secretary Hamilton broken the silence;

" 'Gentlemen,' said he, 'you are too fast; this will not do.' "

Brackenridge, who was a nervous man, had been bolting a little food and pacing up and down the back room of his house. "At three o'clock I returned to my examination; Mr. Hamilton entering the room where I had been waiting for him, appeared to have been reflecting, and said:

" 'Mr. Brackenridge, your conduct has been horribly misrepresented.' "

Hamilton questioned him about the townmeeting at Pittsburgh when the inhabitants of the town, led by Brackenridge, marched out to join the whiskey boys — an assemblage of trappers, Indian fighters, settlers and lumbermen all wild as hares and five thousand strong — who swarmed on the level land across the river where Washington as a young man had seen Braddock's redcoats meet their great defeat. "I stated it as moved by me" — in townmeeting, Brackenridge explained — "that we should march out and affect to join the people at Braddock's fields." The whiskey boys were threatening to take the town by storm if they didn't. "I saw the secretary pause at this and sink into deep reflection. It staggered him."

Brackenridge had convinced his neighbors that they had better put up a pretense at least of offering their help, before the whiskey boys started helping themselves. The townspeople set them up to refreshments. "I thought it better," Brackenridge explained, "to be employed extinguishing the fire of their thirst, than of my house . . . 'Was it any more,' said I, 'than what Richard the second did when a mob of 100,000 men assembled on Blackheath? the young prince addressed them, put himself at their head, and said, What do you want, gentlemen? I will lead you on!'

"My narrative now continued. After some time the secretary observed:

"'My breast begins to ach, we shall stop tonight; we will resume it tomorrow morning at 9 o'clock.'

"I withdrew but was struck by his last expression. I was at a loss to know whether his breast ached for my sake, or from his writing . . . Waiting on the secretary at 9 o'clock, my examination recommenced. In the course of the narrative, his countenance began to brighten and having finished the history there was an end.

"'Mr. Brackenridge,' said he, 'in the course of yesterday I had uneasy feelings, I was concerned for you as a man of talents; my impressions were unfavorable; you may have observed it. I now think it my duty to inform you, that not a single one remains. Had we listened to some people, I do not know what we might have done. There is a side to your account; your conduct has been horribly misrepresented.'"

Hamilton was letting off his chief "character fit for an example." Even in the heat of partisan conflict he was personally incapable of framing an innocent man. The show of force had failed.

Volunteers were signed up for a corps which was to stand guard over the western counties all winter. They were paid in good United States currency. Since like good soldiers they spent most of their pay on whiskey they thus furnished the distillers with cash to pay their taxes. The suppression of the insurrection solved the currency problem for the Pittsburgh region.

Hamilton had quelled the whiskey boys, but there was little satisfaction to be gained from his victory. In the election which had been quietly going on through all the turmoil of marching men the hated Gallatin was elected to the House of Representatives.

Since the big fish had either fled or proved their innocence there was nothing to it but to indict a few of the minnows. The light horse troop made up of young men of the wealthy families of Philadelphia demanded the honor of guarding the captives back to the seat of government. The general opinion was that their attempt at a Roman triumph was a sorry business. James Carnahan, later president of the college at Princeton, sourly described the triumphal entry of the gentlemen's corps into Canonsburg:

"The contrast between the Philadelphia horsemen and the prisoners was the most striking that can be imagined. The Philadelphians were some of the most wealthy and respectable men of that city. Their uniform was blue, of the finest broadcloth. Their horses were large and beautiful, all of a bay color, so nearly alike that it seemed that every two of them would make a good span of coach horses. Their trappings were superb. Their bridles, stirrups, and martingales glittered with silver. Their swords, which were drawn, and held elevated in the right hand, gleamed in the rays of the setting sun. The prisoners were also mounted on horses of all shapes, sizes and colors; some large, some small, some with long tails, some short, some fat, some lean, some every color and form that can be named. Some had saddles, some blankets, some bridles, some halters, some with stirrups, some with none. The riders were also various and grotesque in their appearance. Some were old, some young, some hale, respectable looking men; others were pale, meagre, and shabbily dressed. Some had great coats, — others had blankets on their shoulders. The countenance of some was downcast, melancholy, dejected; that of others, stern, indignant, manifesting that they thought themselves undeserving such treatment. The Philadelphia horsemen rode in front and then two prisoners, then two horsemen and two prisoners . . . throughout a line extending perhaps half a mile. When they rode into Philadelphia the prisoners had papers lettered with the word Insurgent pinned on their hats."

When they were brought to trial the evidence against them impressed the courts as little as it had the public. Most of them were dismissed as soon as their cases came up. Two men only were convicted of treason and sentenced to death. The President pardoned them and published a general amnesty. The Republican press led by Bache's *Aurora* roasted Hamilton for his military exploits.

In spite of the publication, even before Hamilton's expedition, of a series of resolutions by the chief democratic societies condemning the western insurrection, the President remained convinced that they were at the bottom of it. Jefferson from the first had seen Hamilton's hand in the President's denunciations of them. "It is wonderful indeed," he wrote Madison from Monticello, "that the President should have permitted himself to be the organ of such an attack on the freedom of discussion." He saw Hamilton's repressive measures as part of a general attack on the liberties of the Englishspeaking peoples. "The servile copyist of Mr Pitt thought he too must have his alarms," he wrote Monroe, "his insurrections and plots against the Constitution. hence the incredible fact that the freedom of association of conversation & of the press, should in the 5th year of our government, have been attacked under the form of a denunciation of the democratic societies, a measure which even England, as boldly as she is advancing to the establishment of an absolute monarchy, has not yet been bold enough to attempt . . . & all this under the sanction of a name that has done too much good not to be sufficient to cover harm also."

Hamilton took high ground. "It is long since I have learned to hold popular opinion of no value," he wrote the President from Pittsburgh. "I hope to derive from the esteem of the discerning, and an internal consciousness of zealous endeavors for the public good, the reward of those endeavors."

Back in Philadelphia, he found himself suddenly sick to death of the whole business. He had accomplished what he had set out to do. He had answered triumphantly every question the congressional investigating committees had raised on his conduct of affairs. He had established the credit of the United States and fostered a group of moneyed men to form the nation's ruling class. He had established the authority of the general government by a show of force. He had defeated Jefferson's and Madison's foreign policy, wrenched the country away from its alliance with revolutionary France and thrown it into the orbit of conservative England. He had kept the peace; Jay's negotiations with Lord Grenville were far enough along so that he knew that war had been averted. Outside of the "esteem of the discerning" the only thanks he got was to be held up to ridicule in the public press. He wrote out his resignation as Secretary of the Treasury to take effect the last day of January of the coming year.

"Don't let Mr. Church be alarmed at my retreat," he explained to his devoted sisterinlaw Angelica in London. "All is well with the public. Our insurrection is most happily terminated. Government has gained by it reputation and strength, and our finances are in a most flourishing condition. Having contributed to place those of the Nation on a good footing, I go to take a little care of my own."

6. *The Dark Conspiracy*

Hamilton retired from office at the height of his reputation. His policies had on the whole been successful. His skill and probity had been vindicated before Congress. In the law offices and the countinghouses and among the Cincinnati he had devoted adherents. "The more you probe, examine and investigate Hamilton's conduct," a supporter wrote him, "rely upon it, the greater he will appear."

He was immediately busy with his own affairs. It was time he paid more attention to his family. His wife, whom he tenderly loved in spite of his philanderings, had suffered a miscarriage and was still gravely ill. He felt that worry about his safety when he was riding against the whiskey boys might have brought it on. His eldest son Philip, now thirteen and a likely lad, needed his company. There were four more children to care for. Before he settled down to the law in New York City where the business was, he moved his whole family up

over the snowy roads to the Schuylers' great brick mansion in Albany.
In every crisis it was a pleasure to settle back for a while into the
family nest. Whatever he and his doting Elizabeth planned old General Schuyler was sure to be ready with sympathetic support and
assistance.

McHenry, Hamilton's friend since they were aides under Washington together, wrote lyrically from Baltimore to welcome him back to
private life. He compared his own carefree life with Hamilton's: "I
have built houses. I have cultivated fields. I have planned gardens. I
have planted trees. I have written little essays. I have made poetry
once a year to please my wife, at times got children and at all times
thought myself happy. Why cannot you do the same, for if a man is
only to acquire fame or distinction by continual privations and abuse
I would incline to prefer a life of privacy and little pleasures." Mc-
Henry looked at politics from the vantage of the profits of the general
store he had inherited from his father and brother. He dealt in marine
supplies. His fortunes had thriven with the Baltimore boom.

Hamilton was primarily an advocate. As a lawyer he was unbeat-
able. He immediately found his docket crowded with cases. In financial
organization he was felt to have the golden touch. Every group of
speculators in the coffeehouses scheming how to get quickly rich by
ventures in western lands or in flour for Europe or in government
securities wanted his advice. He took particular interest in the new
and growing field of insurance. A great deal of his time was taken up
by complicated transactions carried on for John Barker Church, whose
financial interests on both sides of the Atlantic were becoming formidable. Though he was involved in enormous transactions for others
it never occurred to him to get rich himself. In spite of his fame his
fees remained, as they had always been, scrupulously moderate. Going
over his financial situation after his retirement from the Treasury, he
found himself considerably in debt.

When he was faced with the possibility of a duel during the summer of 1795 he wrote Robert Troup asking him to act as his executor
in case of his death. About all he had to list in the way of assets was
the hope that his practice would bring in enough to pay his debts.
His liabilities were not those of a rich man. He owed Church five
thousand pounds, he had a $500 note at the bank, he owed a Phila-
dephia winemerchant a small balance on his bill. He was worried
about Robert Morris's slowness in repaying some large sums of
Church's money he had loaned him at interest, for which he felt himself responsible. He listed some retaining fees from clients for whom
he had as yet performed no services which he felt should be refunded
in case of his death. Perhaps Church, who could afford it, could be

prevailed on to pay off his debts. Especially he would like to feel that some way would be found to keep up the remittances to his father, who was still living the life of a ruined bankrupt in the islands and whom he had never been able to induce to come to America. Meanwhile his law practice brought him in enough to support his family in comfort in the modest house he rented on Pine Street in New York.

In spite of his preoccupation with the law, which he really enjoyed, he followed from day to day, with all the anxiety of a hen separated from her chicks, the actions of the men he trusted to continue his policies in Philadelphia.

When he heard that his plan for taking up the unsubscribed debt had failed to pass the House, he wrote Rufus King in despair: "To see the character of the government so sported with — exposed to so indelible a blot, puts my heart to the torture. Am I then, more of an American than those who drew their first breath of life on American ground? Or what is it that thus torments me, at a circumstance so calmly viewed by almost everybody else? Am I a fool, a romantic Quixote, or is there some constitutional defect in the American mind?"

Hamilton's supporters in the administration were abject in their devotion. They consulted him on every move they made. Oliver Wolcott as Secretary of the Treasury prided himself on conducting every detail of the government's business as Hamilton would have done it. Timothy Pickering, the cadaverous New Englander with such a mob of children to support who had been promoted from being Washington's quartermaster to Postmaster General and who now, since Knox's resignation, was Secretary of War, though an opinionated man, set in his own ways as only a New Englander could be, deferred humbly to Hamilton. The President himself asked Hamilton's opinion on every public question.

Meanwhile Rufus King in the Senate and Fisher Ames in the House saw to it that the Federalists were apprised almost daily of their great mentor's views. From his law office in New York Hamilton had as much influence in the administration as when he sat slaving to all hours over the paperwork at the Treasury in Philadelphia.

7. The Treaty of Amity and Commerce

It was not long before Hamilton was faced with a new dilemma to "put his heart to the torture." Although several drafts of Jay's treaty were sent off from England as soon as they were signed, no copy reached Philadelphia until March 7, 1795. In spite of Howe's victory the French fleet was all over the Atlantic that winter. The draft Grenville sent to Hammond on the British packet had to be dropped overboard to escape capture. The Virginia sea captain to whom Jay entrusted his copy managed to hide the bundle when his ship was searched for contraband by a French privateer. He brought it safe into the Delaware and hurried with it to Edmund Randolph.

When Randolph and Washington glanced over the treaty its terms gave them goose flesh. What a source of "animadversions." Their first thought was that no inkling of its contents should leak out until it should be presented to the Senate when Congress assembled in June. Washington locked the text in his desk and clamped his jaw tight in one of his impenetrable silences.

As soon as Randolph heard that John Jay, who had remained in London all winter nursing his rheumatism and hoping for news of ratification before he sailed for home, was due to arrive in New York, he wrote him in great perturbation of mind a list of questions. Randolph was taking it for granted that the administration was bound to ratify; but how, he asked, were they going to explain to the American public why Jay had allowed the British a whole year in which to turn over the posts, why there was nothing said about the impressment of American seamen or the restitution of captured American property. What about the West India trade?

The President and his Secretary of State agreed to leave these problems up to the Senate. Meanwhile they shared their uneasy secret.

The treaty could not be kept in the President's desk forever. The moment the text was read aloud, although the senators were sworn to secrecy, the humiliating terms began to leak out. Since Hammond had not yet received his copy Hamilton's friend Rufus King seems to have felt that there was no harm in furnishing him with an abstract. Hammond found the terms delightful. At the same time Oliver Wolcott, who had inherited Hamilton's intimate relationship with the British legation, began confiding in Hammond what difficulties the administration faced in securing the treaty's ratification.

Rumors of the terms imposed on Jay, which amounted to an abrogation of the old treaty with France and the return of the Americans to a colonial status on the high seas, threw the French legation into a fever.

Fauchet was packing up to go home. He had been the creature of Robespierre's Committee of Public Safety. Once Tallien and his friends in the Convention, in a last desperate move to save their own heads, managed to cut off Robespierre's and to give the panicstricken representatives of the sovereign people of France a chance to reassert their authority by suppressing the Jacobins and hurrying the rest of the terrorists to their own guillotine, his recall was inevitable. A certain Pierre Adet was arriving to replace him.

The reshuffle of diplomatic posts was general. The summer before, Washington, still trying to keep the peace with the Virginia Republicans, had reluctantly recalled Gouverneur Morris, whose letters he enjoyed, and sent Jefferson's friend Monroe to Paris in his stead. Monroe, whom Fauchet praised as a sincere patriot and republican in high revolutionary style in his dispatches, after an enthusiastic initial reception was spending his days at the French capital trying to get Tom Paine out of jail and parrying embarrassing questions about the negotiation with England, on which neither the administration in Philadelphia nor John Jay saw fit to enlighten him.

Thomas Pinckney, although he freely admitted that Jay's appointment over his head had put his nose out of joint, had stood manfully by to give Jay what help he could. Now he was consoled by being sent on a special mission to Madrid to take over negotiations there from young Short. Jefferson's hardworking and capable protégé had followed the wanderings of the Spanish court for many weary months trying to keep open the question of the navigation of the Mississippi. To soothe the hurt feelings of John Adams, who felt he was too little consulted during the negotiation with England, John Quincy Adams was sent to take over Short's post in the Netherlands. The only diplomat to lose out in this game of musical chairs was Short, who found himself with no post and no salary. He showed his public spirit by consenting to remain in Spain at his own expense while he instructed Pinckney in the infinite complications of a government presided over by the libidinous María Luisa and her handsome young guardsman, Godoy.

At the same time Lord Grenville, anxious to accommodate Jay in all matters he felt unimportant, consented to recall George Hammond from Philadelphia. Jay had explained to him that Hammond had made himself unpopular with a large segment of American opinion by the vigor of his expressions in his public argument with Edmund Randolph.

One of the first acts of Pierre Adet on arriving in Philadelphia, to show how much more successfully he could intervene in American politics than his predecessor, was to get hold of an abstract of Jay's treaty, purchased from a senator, so he claimed to his government, and to see that it was made public in Bache's *Aurora*. As soon as the Senate voted for ratification, Washington made a virtue of necessity by authorizing Randolph to publish the treaty himself. The same day he found the complete text in a copy of the *Aurora* that came to him fresh from the press.

Stevens Thomson Mason, appointed from Virginia to the Senate seat left vacant by Monroe when he accepted the mission to France, let it be known that he was no longer bound to secrecy and took the text to Bache himself. This young man was the son of George Mason's brilliant and indolent brother Thomson; he had been brought up in his uncle's libertarian school; the keystone of George Mason's carefully reasoned objections to the Constitution was his objection to what he considered a dangerous new concept by which the arrangements set forth in a treaty with a foreign power should become the law of the land.

To the average citizen it was obvious that the Jay treaty meant submission to the very Navigation Acts which had been one of the causes of the Revolution. It was an admission that the independence the colonies had won was only a partial independence after all. Not only the partisan Republicans were furious; the outcry was universal.

Bache filled his saddlebags with printed sheets of the treaty and rode up through New England, distributing it from town to town. Every newspaper copied it. Indignant citizens declaimed against the treaty in public meetings from Maine to Georgia. Mobs paraded. Attacks were made on British warships in port to free impressed seamen. Straw men were dragged through the streets and labeled "John Jay" and burned.

It was up to Hamilton to make the best of a bad bargain. Immediately, with his wonderful lawyer's facility, he began to sketch out a brief to fit the needs of his clients. His articles signed "Camillus" in the *New York Argus* furnished his supporters with a set of plausible arguments to stand up to their opponents.

Jefferson was appalled by the effectiveness of Hamilton's plea. "Hamilton is really a Colossus to the Anti-Republican party. without numbers he is a host within himself," he wrote Madison, begging him to pick up his quill and to "give a fundamental answer." He saw immediately that Hamilton would use the constitutional rule that treaties were the paramount law of the land for his own political purposes at home. He could not help admiring the man's audacity. "A bolder party stroke was never struck."

8. *"... a Colossus to the Anti-Republican party"*

Casting Jay's treaty in a favorable light taxed even Hamilton's dialectical skill. The task was made increasingly difficult by the news published in every gazette that the British had rammed home their determination to go on treating the United States as merely a dissident part of their empire, by publishing a fresh order to their cruisers to seize neutral ships carrying foodstuffs to the enemy. Raising wheat for wartime European markets was the basis of the American farmers' prosperity. Flour mills were flourishing. The carrying trade in food products to the belligerent powers was immensely profitable. Even Hamilton could not help exclaiming that this new order was "atrocious." He suggested that a special agent be appointed to see if he could not induce Lord Grenville to get it rescinded.

Washington was driving back and forth between Philadelphia and Mount Vernon in an agony of indecision. Now that the Senate had voted and gone home ratification depended on him. On him the onus would fall.

Randolph gave it as his opinion that the President should not put his name to the treaty until he received some reassurance about the seizures of provision ships. Randolph's notions had very little weight with the President any more. He was listening to Hamilton, or to Hamilton's opinions brought him indirectly by Pickering and Wolcott. In July Washington wrote his Secretary of State from Mount Vernon that he still had the same opinion of the treaty as when he had first read it: "namely not favorable to it, but that it is better to ratify in the manner the Senate have advised (and with the reservation now mentioned)" — the Senate had refused to ratify clause 12 which limited to seventy tons American ships in the West India trade — "than to suffer things to remain as they are, unsettled."

The frenzy of opposition hardened the Federalist demand for ratification into an obsession. To Hamilton's friends it seemed that only Jay's treaty stood between them and bloody revolution. Washington himself was by this time as firmly convinced as Hamilton pretended to be that opposition to any act of his administration was opposition to law and order itself. Hamilton had so dinned it into his head that there existed a "dark conspiracy" of designing men working through the democratic societies to overthrow the general government which Washington was devoting the ebbing strength of his last years to setting up, that he could only see in these farflung protests the working of some Jacobin plot against everything he held most dear.

Whenever his mail caught up with his comings and goings over the dusty roads during that broiling summer, it was full of addresses: the selectmen of Boston reported the vote of a townmeeting against ratification; protests came from a meeting in Richmond presided over by George Wythe, the first legal light of the Commonwealth; brash young Giles' constituents in Petersburg sent in an address couched in terms the President considered too indecent to deserve a reply. Reports of indignant meetings arrived from Philadelphia and New York — this one drafted by John Adams' soninlaw, the President's old aide William Stephens Smith — they came in from Charleston and Wilmington and Trenton and Portsmouth, New Hampshire; from the citizens of Lexington, Kentucky; from meetings in Bordentown and Crosswicks and Black Horse and Reckless Town, New Jersey.

All these protests seemed to Washington to smack dangerously of seditious criticism of his administration, in fact of criticism of the President himself. He was stung by them. "The cry against the treaty is like that against a mad dog," he wrote disgustedly, "everyone, in a manner, seems engaged in running it down."

He answered such addressed as were couched in terms his dignity could brook, warning his correspondents in identical terms against "sudden impressions" which "when erroneous will yeild to candid reflection" and explaining that his system for "securing the happiness of my fellow citizens" was "to overlook all personal local and partial considerations; to contemplate the United States as one great whole." The gist of it was that the public had no right to meddle while the father of his country was making up his mind.

By the end of July the President, in spite of his letter to Randolph, had not yet put his name to Jay's treaty. Randolph was so sure the treaty was dead that he wrote Monroe that the text would be returned to London for negotiation and that would be the end of it. Randolph had fatally underestimated the men he was dealing with.

9. Wolcott's Fortunate Discovery

Early in August Washington, who still lingered at Mount Vernon, received a letter from Timothy Pickering: "On the subject of the treaty I confess that I feel extreme solicitude; and for a *special reason* which can be communicated to you only in person. I entreat therefore that you will return with all convenient speed to the seat of government. In the meantime, for the reason referred to, I pray you to decide on no important political measure, in whatever form it may be presented to you."

One of the byproducts of the puritan education of the New Englanders was a knack for putting their opponents in the wrong. They felt that it was Edmund Randolph's legalistic hairsplitting that was holding up the President's signature. Now they had a document in their hands that would take care of Mr. Randolph. Carefully they were preparing a trap for the Secretary of State. They even gave themselves the satisfaction of seeing to it that he should help dig his own grave. "Mr. Wolcott and I (Mr. Bradford concurring)," Pickering's letter to Washington read, "waited on Mr. Randolph, and urged his writing to request your return. He wrote in our presence" — sure enough, the unsuspecting Randolph's letter reached Mount Vernon in the same pouch — "but we concluded a letter from one of us also expedient. With the utmost sincerity I subscribe myself," concluded Pickering, who was trying without giving anything away to let the President have an inkling of the deep importance of the occasion, "yours and my country's friend." He added mysteriously: "This letter is for your eye alone."

The Federalist leaders were in a state of nerves. On this same July 28 that Pickering wrote Washington, Wolcott wrote Hamilton begging him to come to Philadelphia for the next session of the Supreme Court. His influence was needed. Randolph kept talking the President around.

Hamilton himself was violently agitated. He and his friends had been driven off the street by a protesting crowd in New York. He was hit in the face with a stone when he attempted to address a massmeeting at the City Hall. The same day that Wolcott wrote him, he was dashing off a hurried note to Wolcott asking him please to see to it that the federal troops which were in New York should be ordered to stay in the city a few days more. "Our Jacobins meditate serious mischief to certain individuals."

Hamilton was in fear of his life. At the same mass meeting where he and his friends were howled down by the crowd, he allowed himself to be drawn into an altercation with Gallatin's fatherinlaw, roughspoken old Commodore Nicholson. The old sea dog had been loudly asserting that Hamilton was stacking away large sums in the English funds and that he could prove it. Seconds were sent off with the customary demands for explanations. It was only by the quick action of George Clinton's young nephew DeWitt that an accommodation was patched up. It was with this duel hanging over his head that Hamilton had written his friend Troup on the shabby state of his finances and had begged him to become his executor in case of his death.

Wolcott was as nervous as Hamilton. He could only see the President's delay in ratifying the treaty as part of the "dark conspiracy." Randolph was being unconscionably slow about drafting the memorial on the subjects at issue which was to accompany the ratified treaty when that document was presented to Hammond. Randolph was the obstacle.

Hammond was impatient. He was packing up to go home. He would have to sail any day now. His obsequious American friends wanted him to have the pleasure of taking the signed treaty to Lord Grenville in person. "I cannot but suspect *foul play* in persons not generally suspected," Wolcott wrote Hamilton. The delay was part of a Franco-

phile plot. "Everything is conducted in a mysterious and strange manner by a certain character here," he added ominously.

Hammond kept complaining of the delay. He invited Wolcott to a
family dinner at the British legation and in this cozy atmosphere expressed his disappointment at having to leave without the ratified
treaty. "But what must the British government think of the United
States," Wolcott repeated Hammond's complaint to Hamilton, "when
they find the treaty clogged with one condition by the Senate, with
another by the President; no answer given in precise form after forty
days: no minister in that country to take up negotiations proposed by
ourselves; the country rising into a flame; their minister's house insulted by a mob; — their flag dragged through the streets, as in
Charleston before the doors of the Consul."

Hammond was not quite as uneasy as he made out. Grenville's intelligence service had come to his rescue. About the same time as he
received his orders to return home, sweetened by congratulations on
the success of his mission, Hammond received from his lordship copies
of several of the highly colored dispatches which the French minister
Fauchet had been sending home to his government during the past
winter. These were found in a mail pouch thrown overboard too late
when the crew of His Majesty's Ship *Cerberus* overhauled and captured a French corvette just as she was about to slip into a Breton
port. Grenville had only to give them a glance to discover that they
contained matter which might be highly useful to Hammond. They
were hurried off to him by the first packet.

After the company rose from the table at Hammond's family dinner
the British minister beckoned the Secretary of the Treasury into a
private room and showed him a few words about Mr. Randolph in a
communication of Fauchet's marked No. 10. He did more. He furnished him with a certified copy. "I hardly dare *write* and hardly dare
think of what I *know* and *believe* respecting a certain character whose
situation gives him a decided influence," Wolcott wrote Hamilton
all agog.

As soon as Wolcott could excuse himself from the obliging Britisher's hospitality he hurried off to Pickering's house with what he later
called his "fortunate discovery." Pickering, who knew little more
French than Wolcott did, went eagerly to work to make his own translation with a dictionary. Fauchet was giving his government an account, which though obviously inaccurate in details did not seem too
farfetched to be believable, of the struggle for the advantage of the
President's prestige between what he called the aristocratic and the
republican parties in the United States.

Fauchet tried to give the impression of knowing more than he really did. He told how Mr. Randolph had come to him with "précieuses confessions" to the effect that George Washington was really a republican and a Francophile at heart. Hamilton's military party was using the western insurrection with the intention of ruining the President's popularity and making him their tool in the introduction of "le pouvoir absolu."

Since Fauchet was writing with the hope that his report would come under the eyes of the terrible Robespierre he dressed his tale up in the terms of revolutionary oratory. He made Randolph appear as the head of a party which, through the governor and the secretary of state of Pennsylvania, controlled the local democratic society, which in turn controlled the democratic societies all over the nation. Randolph's faction, according to Fauchet, was still balancing between the French party and the English. Two or three days after the President's proclamation to the insurgents, he said Randolph came to him "avec an air fort empressé" and made him "the overtures described in his report no. 6."

The implication which Wolcott and Pickering jumped at with enthusiasm was that Randolph asked for French money to be used to keep the democratic societies on the Francophile side. With his audience in mind, Fauchet wound up in the style of the Committee of Public Safety's denunciation of Danton, "So with some thousands of dollars the Republic would have decided for peace or for civil war! Thus the consciences of the pretended patriots of America have already their price!"

The impression intended seemed to be that if his government would only furnish Fauchet with more funds he would be able to influence the course of events in America and to restrain "the already visible trend towards aristocracy."

The combination of "democratic societies" with Edmund Randolph's name in what could be presented as an effort to shake down the French minister for a subsidy for the Republican cause filled Wolcott and Pickering with holy enthusiasm. They knew Washington's phobias. They were convinced they had in their hands the means to ensure the President's signature to the treaty. They took their documents to the Attorney General. Bradford fell in with their plan to confound Randolph with Fauchet's dispatch. "I shall take immediate measures with two of my colleagues who are *firm* and *honest* men," Wolcott wrote Hamilton. "We will if possible, to use a French phrase, *save our country.*"

Meanwhile the President was postponing a raft of private business at Mount Vernon in connection with his farm and his landholdings and the progress of Washington City. He set off in a hurry for Philadelphia. As soon as he arrived he sent for Pickering, who years later wrote a gleeful account of the scene that followed:

"I hastened to the President's house, where I found him at the table; and Randolph — cheerful and apparently in good spirits — also at the table. Very soon, after taking a glass of wine, the President rose, giving me a wink. I rose and followed him into another room. 'What,' (said he,) 'is the cause of your writing me such a letter?' 'That man,' said I, in the other room (pointing towards that in which we had left Randolph) 'is a traitor'. I then in two or three minutes gave the President an intimation of what Fauchet, in his intercepted letter, said of Randolph."

As Wolcott and Pickering had expected, the linking of the words "democratic societies" with Randolph's name threw the President into a passion of blind rage. He had known his Secretary of State since Randolph was a boy. Randolph had faithfully performed all manner of personal legal services for him and had been from the beginning the member of his administration most assiduous in carrying out the President's wishes. In spite of all that, he concluded immediately that Randolph was as Pickering had said, a traitor.

" 'Let us return to the other room' said the President" — so Pickering remembered the scene — " 'to prevent any suspicion of our withdrawing.' "

The President had immediately made up his mind to follow Hamilton's advice. Hamilton would talk the people around. "From New York," Washington wrote just before he left home, "there now is, and I am told there will further be, a Countercurrent." He had suspected all along that Randolph's arguments sprang from a secret sympathy with the bloody revolutionaries of France. "I told Mr. Randolph I thought the postponement of ratification was a ruinous step." Now everything was clear. Randolph had been bribed. In a cold fury Washington decided that before he sprang the trap on Randolph, in order to avoid "animadversions," he must get the Secretary of State's signature on the treaty.

At the cabinet meeting next day, after the usual heated argument, in which Randolph asked for delay and in which Pickering described the opposition to the treaty as a nefarious conspiracy, to Randolph's complete astonishment, the President suddenly ended the discussion by getting to his feet. "I will ratify the treaty," he said. With his jaw set he walked out of the room.

During the week that followed the President saw Randolph every day, hanging over him while he slaved over the wording of the conciliatory memorial, so different from the protest he had planned, to be presented to the British minister along with the ratified treaty. Washington invited him to dinner and even made an informal call on him when he sat at home with his wife and children. Not a word passed his lips on the subject of the Fauchet letters. He insisted that Randolph deliver the documents to Hammond in person. "When he delivered it to me," Hammond wrote home to Lord Grenville, "Mr. Randolph did not attempt to conceal his chagrin upon the occasion, but voluntarily confessed his opinion had been overruled in the cabinet."

In the account of the affair which Randolph published in vindication of his own honesty, along with full quotations from Fauchet's dispatches, Randolph described how he fell into the pit Wolcott and Pickering had so carefully prepared.

"On Wednesday the 19th of August 1795 I was going to the President's as usual at 9 o'clock in the morning; when his steward . . . informed me that the President had desired me to postpone my visit, until half after ten . . . Accordingly I turned to the office, and at the appointed hour called on the President . . . Upon being informed that Mr. Wolcott and Colonel Pickering had been there for some time I went upstairs . . . When I entered the President's room he with great formality rose from his chair; and Mssrs. Wolcott and Pickering were also marked in their efforts to a like formality . . . He put his hand in his pocket, and, pulling out a large letter, said something of this nature: 'Mr. Randolph here is a letter which I desire you to read, and make such explanations as you choose . . .' "

". . . The President desired us to watch Randolph's countenance while he perused it," Pickering recalled years later. "The President fixed his eye upon him; and I never before saw it look so animated . . .

"He silently perused it with composure till he arrived at the passage which refers to his 'precious confessions' when his embarrassment was manifest"; so Wolcott remembered the scene. "When the perusal was completed he said with a smile I though forced: 'Yes sir, I will explain what I know . . .' "

". . . On reading the letter I perceived," Randolph continued, "that two of the most material papers, which were called dispatches no 3 and no 6 were not with it . . . being thus suddenly and without any previous instruction, called before a *council* which was minutely prepared at every point . . . I could only rely on two principles, which were established in my mind; the first was that, according to my sincere belief, I never made an improper communication to Mr. Fauchet; the second was that no money was ever received by me from him . . . The President desired Mssrs. Wolcott and Pickering to put questions to me."

Randolph, who had grown up thinking of Washington, one of his uncle Peyton's best friends, as almost another uncle, was bitterly wounded; "this was a style of proceeding to which I would not have submitted."

He could not imagine why the President had not asked him for an explanation in private: "While I was appealing to the President's memory for communications which I had made to him on this subject; and after he had said with some warmth that he should not conceal anything . . . he was called out to receive from Mr. Willing the copy of an address which was to be presented to him next day by the merchants." This was one of the addresses in favor of the treaty, which Hamilton and his friends were drumming up in all the seaport towns, from friendly bankers, merchants, and chambers of commerce, to counteract the public meetings. "Upon his return the President desired me to step into another room while he should converse with Mssrs. Wolcott and Pickering upon what I had said. I retired and upon revolving the subject I came to this conclusion, that if the President had not been worked on to prejudge the case, he would not have acted in a manner so precipitate in itself, and so injurious and humiliating to me . . . After an absence of three quarters of an hour I returned into the President's room; when he told me that as I wished to put my remarks on paper, he desired I would . . . I answered as soon as possible. But I declared to him at the same instant that I would not continue in office one second after such treatment."

Randolph stalked off, locked up his office and sent the keys to the President, and wrote out his letter of resignation. Already he was meditating his *Vindication*. He had to have copies of those dispatches No. 3 and No. 6 which Fauchet had mentioned in his No. 10. Fauchet had turned over the French legation to Pierre Adet and gone on board a French frigate to run the British blockade.

At five the next morning Randolph was at the French legation. Would Mr. Adet furnish him with copies of the dispatches? Adet could not make the dispatches available but he did furnish him with the information that Fauchet's ship the *Medusa* had been chased back into Newport by a British cruiser. Randolph went posting off to Newport.

When he reached that island seaport ten days later he found the *Medusa* bottled up in the harbor by His Majesty's Ship *Africa* which was cruising in the channel between the islands off Newport Light. He found Mr. Fauchet at the French consul's house. In a stormy scene he implored him to explain what he had meant in dispatch No. 10. Mr. Fauchet suggested disarmingly that as he spoke only French and as Mr. Randolph, who was proud of his French, spoke to him in mixed French and English, perhaps there had been times when they had not understood each other too well. He protested "that on his part he had never suspected the most distant corruption." He would write the whole affair down in a procès verbale.

Next morning when Randolph called before breakfast at the consulate a servant brought him word that Mr. Fauchet was still writing; would Mr. Randolph come back at noon? During the forenoon Randolph noticed that the *Medusa* was hoisting her sails. He hurried back to the consul's. Fauchet had gone, bag, baggage, papers and all. Taking advantage of a rising gale which had driven the Britisher to take refuge in Narragansett Bay, the captain of the *Medusa* had cut his cables and was beating out of the harbor. Randolph hired a swift pilotboat to chase after her with a desperate note begging the Frenchman to make good his word. The pilotboat came back reporting that the *Medusa* had shown a clean pair of heels and vanished into the fog.

While Randolph in black despair was calling Fauchet every kind of a scoundrel another pilotboat slid with wet sails out of the fog into the wharf. Aboard was a Captain Caleb Gardner who had taken out the *Medusa* as pilot. He brought Randolph a letter. Fauchet had sent the promised documents in his diplomatic pouch to the legation in Philadelphia. Mr. Adet had charge of them.

Randolph went posting back to Philadelphia. There Adet very graciously turned over to him Fauchet's packet. Fauchet's explanations were confusing but they were explicit in affirming that no money had changed hands. This could be proved by examining his account at the New York bank. He explained the talk of money as being a reference to the difficulties of certain flour merchants under contract to the French who needed an advance to withstand the financial pressure of certain British agents. Randolph hurried to the printer's with the whole illorganized mess of dispatches, with his correspondence with the President and his secretaries, along with a letter complaining of the President's incomprehensible failure of friendship towards him. All that he could be blamed for was an occasional indiscretion, exaggerated by the difficulties of translation and by Fauchet's confusion of mind. Men read his *Vindication* and found Randolph innocent or guilty strictly in accordance with their political convictions.

"His greatest enemies will not easily persuade themselves that he was under a corrupt influence of France," Madison declared, "and his best friend," he added tartly, "can't save him from the self-condemnation of his political career as explained by himself." Jefferson agreed: "his narrative is so straight & plain," he wrote Giles from Monticello, "that even those who did not know him will acquit him in the charge of bribery; those who knew him had done it from the first. Tho' he mistakes his own political character in the aggregate he gives it to you in detail. He supposes himself a man of no party . . . the fact is that he has generally given his principles to one party and his practice to the other; the oyster to one, the shell to the other. Unfortunately the shell was generally the lot of his friends the French and republicans & the oyster of their antagonists."

Hamilton wrote Wolcott with frank satisfaction from New York: "As to Randolph I shall be surprised at nothing; but if the facts come out, his personal influence is at all events damned." He wrote the President soothingly about Randolph's pamphlet: "I consider it as amounting to a *confession of guilt* . . . His attempts against you are viewed, by all whom I have seen, as base. They will certainly fail of their aim and will do good, rather than harm, to the public cause and to yourself." He advised Washington to take no public notice of Randolph's attacks. Washington was so hot under the collar Hamilton feared some indiscretion.

A land agent of Washington's years later told Hamilton's son John Church of arriving at the President's house for breakfast the morning after the great man had read Randolph's *Vindication*: "Mrs. Washington was sitting in the parlor completely awestricken and in the corner Nelly Custis her niece, cowering like a partridge. Mr. Murray" — William Vans Murray, McHenry's great friend, a convinced Federalist from the Eastern Shore of Maryland — "came in and addressing himself to the President, asked him if he had seen Mr. Randolph's book?" Murray was a brave man. "Washington replied in a voice swelling with indignation, 'Yes Sir I have read every line, every letter of it, and a damneder scoundrel God never permitted to disgrace humanity.'"

Hamilton had not stooped to the dirty work himself, but it had been well done.

Amid the crowds of noble exiles from France Hamilton felt free to entertain at his table now that he was a private citizen was a certain ci-devant bishop who, being very anxious to keep his subtle head on his slight shoulders, had found it expedient to travel in America until the Parisians should get over their fad for the guillotine. Talleyrand was taken with immense admiration for Hamilton. With a professional eye he watched the little New Yorker's manipulation of the general government. Later he was to rank Hamilton with Pitt and Napoleon as the great men of the age. The greatest praise Talleyrand knew for Hamilton was "Il a deviné l'Europe." Their admiration was mutual. Hamilton was quoted as calling Talleyrand "the greatest of modern statesmen because he had so well known both to suffer wrong to be done and to do it."

Hamilton had carried everything before him. Jay's treaty was ratified. Washington was a prisoner of the Federalists. The United States was their oyster. Through his puppets at the seat of government Hamilton had the President, the cabinet and the Senate in his hands. Only the House of Representatives held out. Now he had to carry the House.

Jefferson was writing his friends describing the Hamilton treaty as "a treaty of alliance between England & the Anglomen of this country against the legislature & people of the United States." Jefferson's ardent supporter John Beckley, who from the vantage point of clerk of the House of Representatives was becoming the chief political manager for the Republican Party, wrote dejectedly to DeWitt Clinton in New York: "Is it not a painful reflection, my friend, that the machinations and intrigue of a British faction in our Country should place our good old President in the distressing situation of singly opposing himself to the almost unanimous voice of his fellow Citizens, and of endangering the peace, happiness and Union of America, as well as destroying his own tranquility, peace of mind, good name and fame?"

10. "... the Aera of strange vicissitudes"

On Sunday afternoon early in May 1796 George Washington sat at his desk in Philadelphia writing confidentially in his bold round even hand to Alexander Hamilton in New York. Hamilton had forwarded him a letter from Gouverneur Morris in Europe. The tall boy was still one of the President's most trusted informants on European affairs. Now Gouverneur reported that the newest of new French governments, improvised out of the wornout remnants of the Convention the summer before, had become so firmly established, through the skillful way a young Corsican officer had used his artillery to drive the Paris mob off the streets, that its executive Directory was planning to dispatch a fleet to the Delaware to demand in peremptory terms an explanation of Jay's treaty.

"You will in effect be called on to take Part decidedly with France," Gouverneur wrote. "Mr. Munroe will no Doubt endeavor to convince the Rulers of that Country that such Conduct will force us into the War against them, but it is far from impossible that the usual Violence of their Councils will prevail."

Monroe, the last of Jefferson's friends to hold an office of importance under Washington's administration, had been placed in a hopelessly false position in France by Pickering's delay in informing him of the terms of Jay's treaty. His career in Paris had begun auspiciously. Received in a full session of the Convention not long after Robespierre and his Committee of Public Safety perished under the guillotine, he poured forth an oration about the rapproachement between the two sister republics in the fervid periods fashionable at the time. Merlin de Douai, the constitutional lawyer who was then president of that assembly, was so moved that he smacked him on both cheeks in what was described "as a simple and touching republican embrace." This scene caused heartburnings at Whitehall which were immediately transmitted to Hamilton's friends in Philadelphia. Messrs. Wolcott and Pickering lost no time in pointing out to the President that such conduct was highly reprehensible in an American envoy.

Monroe meanwhile had made some progress towards inducing the French to restore the privileges for American shipping called for by the original treaty of 1778, but he was daily badgered by his friends in the Directory's foreign office for information as to the terms of the new agreement with the British. When Jay did vouchsafe him this information it was by sending the painter John Trumbull, who was secretary of his mission, over to Paris to tell Monroe about the treaty orally and in confidence. Monroe refused to listen: if he were not free to pass it on to the French the information would be of no use to him. The State Department claimed that Monroe was refusing to present the administration's side of the story. The Directory, puffed up with the glory of Bonaparte's victories, was threatening to treat the United States as an ally of England.

Pickering, who had a secret service of his own, now filled the President's ears with the contents of a private letter he managed to intercept from Monroe to Jefferson's quaker friend George Logan. Monroe's letter emphasized the stability of the new French government and the need, through John Beckley's kind offices and through Bache's newspaper, to get correct information as to the course of events in France to the American people, who were being deceived by the lying reports in the British gazettes.

To Washington in his present state of mind corresponding with Bache was corresponding with the devil. Immediately he decided that Monroe must be recalled and wrote Hamilton to ask whom he suggested for a successor.

This threat of trouble with France was particularly irksome to the President as a possible obstacle to the retirement he had decided on at the end of his second term — "One would think," he wrote Hamilton of the French, "that even Folly and Madness on their parts would hardly go to such lengths, without supposing a stimulus of a more serious nature than the Town meetings and the partial resolutions which appeared in the course of last Summer and Autumn on ours."

Messrs. Wolcott and Pickering were hinting that Monroe was putting the French up to their intransigent attitude. Hamilton added his fuel to the President's suspicions by forwarding to Wolcott a rumor of financial wrongdoing by Monroe in connection with Treasury funds placed for transmission to Holland in the hands of the consul Fulwar Skipwith, another Virginian belonging to a family which had close relations with Jefferson. There had been a mysterious robbery of some silver ingots from the consulate.

Washington had already noted with distaste what he described as the imperious tone of Monroe's communications. Monroe, helplessly fretting in Paris while he nursed Tom Paine, whom he had finally managed to extricate almost at the point of death from prison fever from his cell in the Luxembourg, had every reason to feel aggrieved. When the French Minister for Foreign Affairs did learn the terms of Jay's treaty he read them in a London newspaper. To the French that treaty meant only one thing; the Americans were cooperating with the British to starve them into submission.

Washington meanwhile was puzzling over how best to replace Monroe by someone whose ideas were more congenial to the administration. He was through with Republicans; he was remembering Randolph; he had once trusted a man named Benedict Arnold. "Yet as it seems to be the Aera of strange vicissitudes, and unaccountable transactions," he told Hamilton, "attended with a sort of irresistible fatality in many of them, I shall not be surprised at any event that may happen."

As he sat writing in Robert Morris's fine square mansion on Market Street there were reasons why he could "ruminate over the information received," in spite of the "Folly and Madness" of the French and the wickedness of the Republicans, with a certain equanimity.

11. *Thomas Pinckney's Treaty*

A number of happy events had occurred to justify his policies. Only five days before, the House of Representatives, after three months of skillful and stormy opposition, with Madison and Giles and Gallatin in the forefront of the debate, had passed the appropriations bills needed to set in motion Jay's treaty. Just as Bonaparte had cleared the streets of Paris by a few well timed discharges of grapeshot, the President had confounded the parliamentary rebels against his treaty by his cool refusal, on the constitutional grounds which Hamilton suggested to him, to let them see his private papers dealing with the negotiation.

The Federalists in Congress secured their victory by threatening to hold up ratification of two other treaties which the President had placed before the Senate. These treaties were popular in exactly the quarters where Jay's treaty was most unpopular. They were Wayne's agreement with the Indians and Thomas Pinckney's treaty with Spain.

The agreeable South Carolinian had arrived in Spain just at the moment when María Luisa's favorite, the husky young guardsman Godoy, had convinced the giddy Queen and the cuckold King and all the scatterbrained court which Goya was painting for all the world to see, that the Spaniards ought to wriggle out of their alliance with Pitt's anti-Jacobin coalition and to join forces with France. Godoy was worried about the British reaction to what they would consider his treachery, and was looking for some arrangement in America which would secure the borders of Spain's enormous colonies there. At last he was willing to talk about the navigation of the Mississippi.

Thomas Pinckney found that the ground had been well prepared for him by unhappy young Short. He took advantage of this first favorable turn of affairs. He handled the negotiation so well, calling for his passports in the best diplomatic style at just the right moment, that he got the Spaniards not only to agee to opening the Mississippi to American trade, and to a boundary for West Florida south of the rich Yazoo River delta which was the center of such frenzied land speculation in Georgia, but to grant the Americans a free port and depot in New Orleans for three years. When the South Carolinian sailed for home there was no doubt in anybody's mind that he was in line for the presidency.

The advantages of Pinckney's treaty, coming on top of Anthony Wayne's success at Fallen Timbers, which forced the Indians to give up virtually the whole territory that was soon to be the state of Ohio, more than counterbalanced, in the minds of all westernminded men, the disadvantages of Jay's.

Even Jay's treaty produced a few concessions. While the Admiralty remained overbearing towards American shipping, the Foreign Office under the subtle Grenville was sufficiently impressed by Wayne's successes and swayed by Jay's arguments to try to sweeten the bitter pill. Not only George Hammond, but Lord Dorchester was recalled. Dorchester's recall from Quebec signified the abandonment of that great empire builder's policy of trying to hem the United States in by creating an Indian dependency in the Northwest. The British were furthermore preparing to fulfill their part of the agreement by evacuating their forts from Niagara to Detroit.

On this same Sunday afternoon that he wrote Hamilton, Washington penned another note which must have given him great pleasure. It was to Hamilton's bosom friend, and his own intimate from the days of his military family, the easygoing Baltimorean McHenry, who had been made Secretary of War when Pickering was moved into the State Department to displace the disgraced Randolph. "Let the march of the troops wch. are to take possession of the Posts be facilitated as much as possible."

Unless the mad Frenchmen pushed their dissatisfaction with Jay's treaty to the point of war, Washington felt he had at last accumulated sufficient credits on the balance sheet of his administration to retire with honor to Mount Vernon. "If the people of this country have not abundant cause to rejoice at the happiness they enjoy," he wrote Gouverneur, "I know of no country that has. We have settled all our disputes and are at peace with all Nations. We supply their wants with our superfluities and are well paid for doing so. The earth generally for years past has yeilded its fruits bountifully. No City, Town, Village, or even farm but what exhibits evidences of increasing wealth and prosperity." Then he remembered the articles in Bache's *Aurora*. "Yet by second sight; extraordinary foresight or some other sight" — he was always a little facetious when he wrote the tall boy — "evils afar are discovered." He was sick and tired of the criticism and abuse of those mistaken people who would not admit that the father of his country knew best.

He unburdened himself to John Jay: "I am *Sure* the Mass of Citizens in these United States *mean well.* and I firmly believe they will always act well . . . but in some parts of the Union . . . great Pains are taken to inculcate a Belief that their Rights are assailed, and their Liberties endangered . . . To this source all our Discontents may be traced and from it our Embarrassments proceed . . . Indeed the trouble and Perplexities which they occasion," he wrote bitterly, "added to the Weight of Years which have passed over me have worn away my Mind more than my Body; and renders Ease and Retirement indispensably necessary to both during the short time I have to stay here." He added that nothing short of events which might render a retreat dishonorable would prevent the public announcement of his decision to retire.

With this declaration off his chest he was able to turn with a freer mind to writing his overseer at Mount Vernon about the things he really enjoyed; he was worried about his chicory, he regretted that the peas had not been sown in February as they should, he hoped the recent rains would bring up the clover, he wanted to know how much cash his fishery had brought in, and the exact date when his two coach mares "went to Jack." He wanted more mules for his farm work.

12. *Thoughts and Reflections in the Form of an Address*

Once the question of Jay's treaty was settled the administration measures moved smoothly through the Fourth Congress. Even before the two houses adjourned Washington began to work on the announcement of his retirement he was planning to publish in the newspapers. He had previously asked Hamilton to help him, as he had on so many state papers, on this final and definitive formulation of his policies. Both men agreed that this statement must crown the glory of the administration.

"As it is important that a thing of this kind should be done at great care and, much at leisure, touched and retouched," Hamilton wrote from New York, "I submit a wish that as soon as you have given it the *body* you mean it to have, it may be sent to me." Washington hoped particularly to appeal to the good sense of the yeomanry. "My wish is," he wrote when he answered Hamilton a few days later, "that the whole may appear in a plain Stile; and be handed to the Public in an honest; unaffected; simple Garb."

In his first draft Washington included a long quotation from the original farewell, which Madison had written out for him in 1792 when he planned to retire at the end of his first term. "I am attached to the Quotation," he explained to Hamilton, "as it is not only a Fact that such an Address was written, and on the point of being published, but known also to one or two of those Characters" — he meant Jefferson and Madison — "who are now strongest and foremost in the Opposition to the Government and consequently to the person Administering it contrary to their views . . . Having struck out the reference to a particular Character" — meaning Madison — ". . . I have less (if any) objection to expunging those Words which are contained within Parenthesis's."

The first parenthesis he referred to contained the statement couched in Madison's terms, that one of the reasons for his retirement was "that an early example of rotation in an office of so high and delicate a nature, may equally accord with the republican spirit of our constitution, and the ideas of liberty and safety entertained by the people."

Right after Congress adjourned in early June Hamilton tore himself away from his law business long enough to spend a few days in Philadelphia. As he worked over the wording of the address he tried loyally to make Washington's sentiments his own. In the final draft the word republican occurred only once, where the President spoke — and with some justification, since Bonaparte's armies were already rampaging through Europe — of republican liberty as being particularly — more than the "monarchical liberty" that the British enjoyed, the reader was led to infer — vulnerable to subversion through overgrown military establishments.

The word republican had taken on a partisan connotation to Washington's ears as it had to Hamilton's. Under Hamilton's influence many an early predilection and many an early friendship had gone by the board. The President had let himself be convinced, with real grief, because he had always had confidence in the bookish little man from Montpellier, that Madison was deeply compromised in the conspiracy of the democratic societies.

The cast of Jefferson's mind had never been too congenial to Washington's, though there had been moments when their collaboration was warmed by real cordiality. He had not forgiven Jefferson for backing "that rascal Freneau." Now rumors of fresh critical remarks from Monticello kept coming to his ears. Henry Lee, who hated Jefferson, reported that Jefferson was accusing the President of partiality to England. "There could not have been a trace of doubt on his mind of Predeliction of mine towards G. Britain or her Politics," Washington wrote back angrily, "unless (which I do not believe) he has set me down as one of the most deceitful and uncandid Men living: because, not only in private Conversation between ourselves on this Subject, but in my Meetings with the confidential Servants of the Public, he has heard me often, when occasions presented themselves, express very different Sentiments with an Energy that could not be mistaken by *anyone* present."

First it had been Freneau and now it was Bache. The tall young Philadelphian was taking advantage of a certain eminence he enjoyed as Benjamin Franklin's grandson to publish not only virulent attacks but downright lies and slanders in his *Aurora*. Bache's publication which had raised the latest storm among the Federalists was that of one of the President's confidential sets of questions to the members of his cabinet, at the time of the arrival of Genêt, on what sort of balance should be kept between what Washington was fond of referring to as the Scylla of France and the Charybdis of England. "Are the United States obliged to Consider Treaties binding" — referring to the Franco-American treaty of 1778 — "(as applying to the present situation of the parties)?" Since only four men, Hamilton and Knox, Jefferson and Randolph, had ever seen the paper, Washington was blaming the leak on Randolph, whom he had come to despise and to detest.

Jefferson hastened to write from Monticello to assure Washington that he himself was not the guilty party and to deplore that the gossip of a malicious person, referring of course to Lee, "dirtily employed in sifting the conversations of my table" had represented him to Washington "as still engaged in the bustle of politics, & in turbulence & intrigue against the government." He made his usual pious disclaimer of any connection with the press, but maintained: "I have never conceived that having been in public life requires me to belie my sentiments, or ever to conceal them."

"As you have mentioned the Subject yourself," Washington answered illhumoredly from Mount Vernon, "it would not be frank, candid or friendly to conceal, that your Conduct has been represented as derogatory from that Opinion *I* had conceived you entertained of me." What most rankled was Jefferson's accusation, which Lee had reported, that Washington was "a person under dangerous influence," and that dangerous influence was Hamilton. He maintained that he had as often ruled against Hamilton as for him. "The first wish of my Heart was, if parties did exist to reconcile them . . . I had no Conception," he went on bitterly, "that parties would or even could go to the Length I have been witness to . . . that every act of my Administration would be tortured, and the grossest and most insidious mis-representations of them be made (by giving one side only of a Subject, and that too in such exaggerated and indecent Terms as could scarcely by applied to a Nero; a notorious Defaulter; or even to a common Pickpocket)."

In the last pages of his letter Jefferson had tried to bring the President back to the old friendly ground, as one farmer to another: "I put away this disgusting dish of old fragments," he wrote, "& talk to you of my peas & clover." Washington now put himself out, a little stiffly perhaps, to reply in kind.

There was nothing he loved better than green manures. He told of getting a ton of clover to the acre, discussed the various varieties of peas Jefferson had mentioned and wished him good luck in his experiments with a movable threshing machine "for nothing is more wanting and to be wished for on our Farms." Jefferson had concluded with "very affectionate compliments to Mrs. Washington." The President replied that "Mrs. Washington begs you to accept her best wishes." And so their correspondence ended.

In spite of Albany peas and chicory and threshing machines and the great interest in the wellbeing of the federal city they had in common there was no more friendship between them.

As Jefferson had suspected for some months the Federalist administration meant no good to his friend Monroe. Washington was looking about for a successor. Ever since Edmund Randolph's mysterious misadventure Washington had been finding it difficult to induce men of prominence to accept offices in his government. The President offered Monroe's post to John Marshall, who was one of the new generation of Virginians in whom he found a certain likemindedness that attracted him, but Marshall shrewdly refused. The President talked over with Hamilton the possibility of sending McHenry or of getting Thomas Pinckney to stay overseas a few more years. McHenry was reluctant, and neither Washington nor Hamilton, while they loved him as a friend, had much respect for his abilities; and Thomas Pinckney was already bound homeward to reap his laurels. At length Hamilton suggested Thomas's brother, another South Carolina grandee, General Charles Cotesworth Pinckney.

As soon as the welcome news of General Pinckney's acceptance reached Mount Vernon Washington arranged to meet him and his lady in Philadelphia to prepare with him personally those explanations of Jay's treaty which Pickering was insisting that Monroe had willfully refused to offer to the French. Washington set out immediately for the seat of government, although the roads were seas of mud from unusually heavy midsummer rains.

He would lose no time in breaking the last link between his critics in America and the triumphant republicans of France. When he wrote Monroe from Philadelphia complaining that one of his private letters to Gouverneur Morris, meant for his friend's eyes alone and possibly for the eyes of Lord Grenville, had fallen into the hands of the French Directory, he said not a word about his fellow Virginian's recall. He was treating him as he had treated Randolph. He had decided that General Pinckney should hand him his recall in person.

A few days before leaving Mont Vernon he received a complete rough draft of the address from Hamilton. "I have endeavored to make it as perfect as my time and engagements would permit," Hamilton wrote with understandable pride in the accompanying letter. "It has been my object to render this act importantly and lastingly useful, and . . . to embrace such reflections and sentiments as will wear well . . . How far I have succeeded you will judge." Washington read it with approval. This was what he wanted to say. "I have given the paper herewith enclosed several serious and attentive readings," he said when he shipped it back to New York from Philadelphia for a final polishing, "and prefer it greatly to the other drafts . . . more dignified on the whole; and with less egotism."

He could hardly wait to get his farewell to the press. He was on tenterhooks for fear something should come up to delay his retirement from public life. Ten days later he wrote Hamilton that, as his steward was on his way to New York on other business, if Hamilton could quickly finish his final revision the steward would bring it back with him to Philadelphia when he came. Since he had had intimations that the Republicans were prying into his letters he was not willing to trust to the mails this document in which he took such pride.

As soon as he had this final draft in his hands he turned it over to Messrs Wolcott and Pickering for their inspection and to Charles Lee, his old Alexandria associate who was now Attorney General. The moment they had approved it, he sent out his favorite secretary

Tobias Lear, now back in his service after a trip to Europe on business on his own, to fetch David Claypoole, the printer and editor of *The Daily American Advertiser.*

When Claypoole arrived at the President's house, he was ushered into the drawing room. There he found Washington sitting alone. The President received him kindly, offered him a seat beside him and began to talk. For some time, he said, he had contemplated retiring from public life; he had some thoughts and reflections in the form of an address which he wished to appear in Claypoole's paper. Claypoole burst into protestations of delight and started to thank him profusely for showing him this mark of confidence in the way he conducted his paper. The President merely nodded at this, and asked him abruptly how soon he could print his address. The following Monday, Claypoole replied. Very good, he should have a corrected draft the next morning.

When the bewildered editor had departed, walking on air at the thought of the honor the President was bestowing on his newspaper, and possibly at the thought of the sales he could look forward to for this issue, Washington settled down to a final loving revision of the much amended composition:

"Friends and Fellow Citizens: The period for a new election of a Citizen, to Administer the Executive government of the United States, not being far distant, and the time actually arrived, when your thoughts must be employed in designating the person, who is to be cloathed with that important trust, it seems to me proper . . . that I should now apprise you of the decision I have formed, to decline being considered . . ." He explained that though he felt no diminution of zeal for the future interest of his fellow citizens, he now was convinced that public affairs wore such a favorable aspect that he had a right to consult his own needs and inclinations. "While choice and prudence invite me to quit the political scene patriotism does not forbid it."

He thanked the American people for their unfailing support "amidst appearances sometimes dubious, vicissitudes of fortune often discouraging, in situations in which not infrequently want of Success has countenanced the spirit of criticism." He offered his fervent hope that "the happiness of the people of these States, under the auspices of liberty, may be made complete, by so careful a preservation and so prudent a use of this blessing as will acquire them the glory of recommending it to the applause, the affection, and adoption of every nation which is yet a stranger to it."

He added a few "disinterested warnings of a parting friend: . . . the Unity of Government is now dear to you . . . it is of infinite moment that you should properly estimate the immense value of your national

Union . . . indignantly frowning upon the first dawning of every attempt to alienate any portion of our Country from the rest . . . Is there a doubt, whether a common government can embrace so large a sphere? Let experience solve it."

He warned against parties, particularly against parties based on "*Geographical* discriminations." He declared that "the very idea of the power and the right of the People to establish Government presupposes the duty . . . of every individual to obey the established Government . . .

". . . It is important, likewise, that the habits of thinking in a free Country should inspire caution in those entrusted with its administration, to confine themselves within their respective Constitutional spheres . . . A just estimate of that love of power, and proneness to abuse it, which predominates in the human heart is sufficient to satisfy us of the truth of this position.

". . . Religion and morality are indispensible supports . . . Let it simply be asked where is the security for property, for reputation, for life, if the sense of religious obligation *desert* the oaths, which are the instruments of investigation in Courts of Justice?

". . . Promote then as an object of primary importance, Institutions for the general diffusion of knowledge. In proportion as the structure of government gives force to public opinion, it is essential that public opinion should be enlightened.

". . . Cherish public credit.

". . . Observe good faith and justice towds. all Nations . . . against the insidious wiles of foreign influence (I conjure you to believe me fellow citizens) the jealousy of a free people ought to be *constantly* awake . . . there can be no greater error than to expect or calculate upon real favors from nation to nation." As regards the war in Europe neutrality had been his plan ever since his proclamation of April 22, 1793: "A predominant motive has been to endeavor to gain time to our country to settle and mature its yet recent institutions . . .

". . . Though in reviewing the incidents of my Administration, I am unconscious of intentional error, I am nevertheless too sensible of my defects not to think it probable I may have committed many errors. Whatever they may be I fervently beseach the Almighty to avert or mitigate the evils to which they may tend. I shall also carry with me the hope that my Country will never cease to view them with indulgence; and that, after forty five years of my life dedicated to its service, with an upright zeal, the faults of incompetent abilities will be consigned to oblivion, as myself must soon be to the Mansions of rest."

Bright and early Friday morning Lear appeared at Claypoole's printshop with the completed text. "After the proof sheet had been carefully compared with the copy and corrected by myself," wrote

Claypoole, telling later of the greatest moment of his life as a newspaper editor, "I carried two different Revises, to be examined by the President; who made but few alterations from the original except in punctuation, in which he was very minute."

When Claypoole brought the original back to the President's house after the type was set up he told the President how loath he was to part with it, "upon which in the most obliging maner, he handed it back to me, saying that if I wished for it I might keep it."

The copy in Washington's letterbook was taken from Claypoole's printed version. On the margin the President in his large round hand noted these instructions to his clerk: "Let it have a blank page before and after it, so as to stand distinct. Let it be written in a letter larger and fuller than the common recording hand."

The Farewell Address, as it came to be called, was reprinted in every newspaper in the country from Portsmouth to Savannah, from Boston to Pittsburgh. As soon as Washington had consigned these final "counsels of an old and affectionate friend" to the public prints, he set off to Mount Vernon to fetch Mrs. Washington and her grandchildren for their last official winter in Philadelphia.

XIII The Federalists on the Car of State

1. *The Bustle of Politics*

Ever since Jefferson reached his hilltop home at Monticello in time for the slow delicious coming of spring in 1794, he had been vowing and protesting to his friends that nothing in the world would induce him ever again to accept public office. As he rode over his steep farms, enjoying the sweet air of his heights and the smell of budding woods and plowed lands, noting in his little book the dates of the early bluebirds, of the blackbirds' first swirling in the sky, of the blooming of his almond trees, he was determined to go on as long as he lived "like an antediluvian patriarch among my children and grandchildren and tilling my soil."

His private affairs were crying for attention. His farms had run down during his ten years' absence. Like Washington, he was full of enthusiasm for the new farming methods foreshadowed by the experiments of the English agriculturists. He was planting red clover to bring fertility back to his exhausted hillsides. He could never get anything done right except when he was there on the spot. Improving the land by plowing under green manures was a long term business that would need his supervision for a number of years.

His children and grandchildren needed him. Thomas Mann Randolph, his soninnlaw whom he loved as a son, was turning out, like so many of the Randolphs, a hypochondriacal character, full of dark moods and strange pains interspersed with moments of considerable intellectual energy. Martha needed her father's help in raising her growing family. Polly was reaching marriageable age. His nephews, Dabney Carr's boys, had grown up to a wild and flighty manhood. They needed his restraining hand.

Outside of educating the young people and managing his plantation he had enough projects for work to keep a dozen men busy. He had come home from abroad with his head full of new architectural ideas. At heart he was as much an architect as he was a statesman. He wanted to rebuild the Monticello house according to a new design, lighter and more compact than the old. He was planning country houses for his friends in which he could develop in modern style Palladio's theory of the ferme ornée. He was engaged in completing those calculations for the most efficient shape for the moldboard of a plow which had first occurred to him when he saw the clumsy instruments the peasants were tilling the land with on a drive back from the Rhineland across northern France during the first year of the French Revolution. As a sequel to his work with Pendleton and Wythe during the early days of independence he was planning the codification and editing of the complete laws of the State of Virginia.

Then there were his studies of the weather, his Indian vocabularies, his experiments in methods of calculating the height of the surrounding mountains, his collecting of the fossil bones of prehistoric animals. He thought of himself as a philosopher; philosophy meant the study of all the aspects of nature and man.

All these plans called for funds. Even the most successful Virginia planters were perennially short of cash. Jefferson was uncomfortably in debt. As a way of getting some immediate profit out of his slaves he was starting a small shop for making nails. "I now employ a dozen little boys from 10. to 16. years of age, overlooking all the details of their business myself & drawing from it a profit on which I can get along till I can put my farms into a course of yeilding profit," he wrote a French refugee who had asked his advice about how to make a living in America. "There is no such thing in this country as what would be called wealth in Europe," he explained, "the richest are but little at ease, and obliged to pay rigorous attention to their affairs to keep them together." In spite of his nailery Jefferson found himself so little at ease that before a year was out he was having to give a second mortgage on his slaves to a Dutch firm of bankers to raise two thousand dollars.

All the while his friends were quietly taking it for granted that he would be available for the presidency when Washington retired. In spite of Jefferson's disclaimers of any interest or knowledge of politics, Madison was keeping him regularly informed of the progress of the political organization he was spreading, with the help of the indefatigable John Beckley, through the middle Atlantic states.

In an effort to head off his own candidacy Jefferson tried to turn the tables on his little friend from Montpellier. Since he had married his lovely Quaker widow, the warm and managing Dolley Todd, Madison was a much less diffident character than in the old days when Jefferson and all his friends had worried so over his confirmed bachelorhood. Madison was the leader of his party in the House of Representatives. His marriage had given him new social poise. It was Madison who should be the Republican candidate.

"There is not another person in the U.S.," Jefferson wrote him, "who being placed at the helm of affairs, my mind would be so completely at rest for the fortune of our political bark . . . My retirement from office," he went on to insist, "had been meant from all office high or low, without exception . . . the little spice of ambition I had in my younger days has long since evaporated, and I set still less store by a posthumous than a present name."

As Jefferson followed the agitation against Jay's treaty in the letters of his friends and in the newspapers and pamphlets they kept him well supplied with his resolution to abstain from politics weakened. Though he still insisted on his abhorrence of the prospect of seeing "the scenes of 93. revived as to myself, & to descend daily into the arena like a gladiator, to suffer martyrdom in every conflict," he began tacitly to admit that if he were elected President he would have to serve. The question was still so much touch and go that as late as the end of September of the campaign year, Madison was writing Monroe, "I have not seen Jefferson and have thought it best to present him no opportunity of protesting to his friends against being embarked in the contest."

While the Federalists pictured him as deep in political machinations Jefferson was chiefly preoccupied with rebuilding Monticello. He had started to tear down the central part of the house. In spite of the ruinous state the mansion was left in he did not discourage political visits. Though he hoped to avoid playing a part himself he was never loath to urge on others to the fray. His visitors found him busy with the dust and confusion of masonry and bricklaying. "Do not let this discourage you from calling on us," he wrote Giles." . . . We shall have the eye of a brick-kiln to poke you into, or an Octagon to air you in."

Beside Giles, room was somehow found to put up Talleyrand's friend Volney, who was making a grand tour of the American backwoods. Volney was the fashionable French philosophe. His elegiac *Ruines, ou méditations sur les révolutions des empires* was one of the key literary productions of the period.

Les Ruines, published in 1791, had stirred the deep enthusiasm of such diverse characters as Jefferson and Joel Barlow and Napoleon Bonaparte, and as a product of French revolutionary rhetoric had aroused the sacred ire of the followers of Edmund Burke. The "atheist Volney's" visit to Jefferson stirred the bile of the Federalist editors, and when they learned that Aaron Burr had also been entertained at Monticello that summer they gave tongue indeed: the leading Republicans of America were meeting with agents of France in Albermarle: a Jacobin plot was hatching to seize the government and murder honest men in their beds.

During wheat harvest another Frenchman came to admire the view of the mountains and valleys from Jefferson's terrace. The surviving Duke de la Rochefoucauld-Liancourt, like every other literate exile, was noting down his adventures in the American wilderness for publication. He described Jefferson's system of rotation of crops, his threshing machine, his mechanical drill for planting seed: "I found him in the midst of the harvest, from which the scorching heat of the sun does not prevent his attendance. His negroes are nourished, clothed, and treated as well as white servants could be. As he cannot expect any assistance from the two small neighboring towns, every article is made on his farm; his negroes are cabinet makers, carpenters, masons, bricklayers, smiths, etc. The children he employs in a nail factory, which yeilds already a considerable profit. The young and old negresses spin for the clothing of the rest." — The slaves did their own weaving too and operated a gristmill in the swift Rivanna at the foot of the hill. — "He animates them by rewards and distinctions; in fine his superior mind directs the management of his domestic concerns with the same abilities, activity, and regularity which he evinced in the conduct of public affairs."

Though it is hardly likely that he brought the subject up with his foreign visitors Jefferson's mind was far more occupied with political topics than he liked to admit. There was one foreigner he did unburden himself to. It was a long time since he had written his old friend, the bustling and often pestiferous Mazzei. Perhaps distance lent enchantment to the voluble Tuscan. Jefferson had an account to render of various financial and legal chores he had performed for him. In the course of a long friendly letter he included a frank discussion of his hopes and fears for the coming campaign: "In place of that noble love of republican government which carried us triumphantly thro' the war, an Anglican monarchical & aristocratical party has sprung up, whose avowed object is to draw over us the substance as they have already done the forms, of the British government. the main body of our citizens, however, remain true to republican principles; the whole landed interest is republican, and so is a great mass of talents. against us are the Executive, the Judiciary . . . all the officers of the government, all who want to be officers, all timid men who prefer the calm of despotism to the boisterous sea of liberty, British merchants & Americans trading on British capitals, speculators & holders in the banks & public funds . . . it would give you a fever were I to name to you the apostates who have gone over to these heresies, men who were Samsons in the field & Solomons in the council, but who have had their heads shorn by the harlot England. in short, we are likely to preserve the liberty we have obtained only by unremitting labors & perils. but we shall preserve them; and our mass of weight & wealth on the good side is so great, as to leave no danger that force will ever be attempted against us. we have only to awake and snap the Lilliputian cords with which they have been entangling us during the first sleep which succeeded our labors."

It was the passage of Jay's treaty and the failure of the Republican majority in the House to block its implementation that convinced Jefferson that he might have to sacrifice his inclinations to help snap those Lilliputian cords. "It has been to them a dear bought victory," he wrote Monroe in France. "it has given the most radical shock to their party which it has ever received . . . they see that nothing will support them but the Colossus of the President's merits with the people, and the moment he retires, that his successor, if a Monocrat, will be overborne by the republican sense of his Constituents, if a republican he will of course give fair play to that sense and lead things into a channel of harmony between the governors & governed." He saw a chance, in the turn of phrase he loved, to put the vessel back on the republican tack.

The Republicans, though they had been beaten in Congress on foreign policy, were far from being the disorganized opposition that had suffered humiliating defeats in the grim year of '93 that Jefferson remembered with so much pain. They dominated the South and West in spite of the powerful South Carolina Federalists. The East would fall to John Adams. That left Pennsylvania and New York as the area where the greatest effort must be made.

Though the appointment of presidential electors was still in most cases in the hands of the legislatures, in these two states the popular vote, restricted to be sure by property qualifications, already counted. Aaron Burr through his own peculiar charm had fascinated as many diverse elements in New York as Hamilton had. If Hamilton held the countinghouses and their dependents enthralled, Burr through his influence in the Tammany Society swayed the artisans and mechanics and the wild Irish pouring off ships at the Battery with hatred of England as the first law of their lives. To them he could add the erratic but vastly powerful Livingston connection and George Clinton's upstate contingents now reinforced by the emergence of the old governor's personable and liberalminded nephew DeWitt. Burr was using Hamilton's own methods to turn the tables on him.

In Pennsylvania as the summer wore on John Beckley was at work distributing handbills and copies of Madison's pamphlets, and urging his friends to set to work with their families to write out lists of the Republican electors so that the voters could make no mistake at the polls. Printed ballots were not allowed by the Pennsylvania election law; each voter had to write out the names of the fifteen presidential electors on his ballot. Beckley in Pennsylvania, like Hamilton and Burr in New York, was conducting a methodical campaign at the district level.

"In a few days a select republican friend from the City will call on you with a parcel of tickets to be distributed in your county," Beckley wrote a supporter in Carlisle. " . . . He is one of two republican friends, who have undertaken to ride through all the middle & lower counties on this business, and bring with them 6 or 8 thousand tickets to be distributed in your County." By mid October he could report to Madison that "30,000 tickets are gone thro' the State, by Express, into every county." Beckley and his associates circulated so much Republican literature and wrote out their tickets so industriously that Jefferson won fourteen out of the fifteen electoral votes in the state. "Let us cultivate Pennsylvania," Jefferson was to write Madison a little later, "& we need not fear the universe."

Meanwhile Hamilton was sparing no horses. "There is no inferior degree of sagacity in the combinations of this extraordinary man"— Beckley had described his methods to Madison, when he first matched his talents as party manager against Hamilton's in the campaign for the vice presidency four years before — "with a comprehensive eye, a subtle and contriving mind and a soul devoted to its object, all his measures are promptly and aptly designed, and like the links of a chain, dependent on each other, acquire additional strength by their union and concert."

This time Hamilton's plan was a little too subtle to be effective. And his opponents had schooled themselves in his political methods.

Hamilton had set his heart on heading off John Adams although he knew that the majority of Federalists, particularly in New England, were taking it for granted that the Quincy lawyer was next in line for the presidency. He had tried hard, working through John Marshall and Carrington in Virginia, to induce Patrick Henry to run. Hamilton wanted a man he could dominate as he had dominated Washington during the old general's last years in office. John Adams was far too erratic and independent to suit his purpose.

Presidential elections were still conducted on the clumsy system by which top man in the vote in the electoral college got the presidency and second man the vice presidency. Hamilton's plan, suggested to his supporters by various roundabout means, was to get so many votes for Thomas Pinckney as Vice President that he would be elected President. It failed completely. Pinckney's treaty had made him a popular figure but he did not have the appeal of stalwarts of 1776 like Jefferson and Adams.

The canvass dragged on for weeks. Communications were slow; it was early November before the news straggled into Monticello that Jefferson was very probably elected Vice President. The vote was said to stand seventyone for Adams, sixtyeight for Jefferson, fiftynine for Thomas Pinckney and thirty for Aaron Burr.

Immediately Jefferson started explaining to his friends that he was delighted with the result. "I know the difficulty of obtaining belief to one's declarations of a disinclination to honors," he wrote Madison, insisting again that he had not wanted to be President; "pride does not enter into the business; for I think with the Romans that the general of today should be a soldier tomorrow if necessary. I can particularly have no feelings which would revolt at a secondary position to mr. Adams. I am his junior in life, was his junior in Congress, his junior in the diplomatic line, his junior lately in the civil government."

Always sanguine, he was wondering if he could not do something with Adams. He was genuinely fond of the man. He respected his learning. Their minds were congenial. There was a certain type of discussion of the philosophy of statebuilding he could engage in with no one else. "If mr. Adams can be induced," he told Madison, "to relinquish his bias to an English constitution, it is to be considered whether it would not be to the public good to come to a good understanding with him as to his future elections. he is perhaps the only sure barrier against Hamilton's getting in."

At the same time John Adams was sagely intimating to his friends that he thought he could wean Thomas Jefferson away from the Jacobins: "I hope we can keep him steady," he wrote.

A truce had been patched up between Quincy and Monticello since their row about the *Rights of Man*. The winter before, Adams had sent Jefferson a book by a Swiss writer on government. In a cordial letter of thanks Jefferson picked up their old discussion on how to curb the abuses of power. He had doubts about the efficacy of a plural executive which the French were trying out. He thought the American system of a single executive better.

He was searching for a common ground with his old friend as he wrote. Maybe the patriotism which was the deepest emotion of their lives could be the bond between them. He let his high hopes for American institutions run wild: "Never was a finer canvass presented to work on than our countrymen, all of them engaged in agriculture or the pursuits of honest industry, independent in their circumstances . . . this I hope will be an age of experiments in government . . . if ever the morals of a people could be made the basis of their own government, that is our case."

He pressed the argument against the Federalists as far as he dared: "& who could propose to govern such a people by the corruption of a legislature, before he could have one night of quiet sleep must convince himself that the human soul as well as body is mortal."

He knew that Adams shared his suspicions of the moneymen: "I am sure from the honesty of your heart, you join me in a detestation of the corruptions of the English government, & that no man on earth is more incapable than yourself of seeing that copied among us, willingly." He admitted ingenuously: "I have been among those who have feared a design to introduce it here, & it has been a strong reason with me for wishing there was an ocean of fire between that island and us."

Adams answered in the old highflying style, but in friendly fashion. "Reasoning has been all lost" — he was still in a pet against the French —"Passion, Prejudice, Interest, Necessity has governed and will govern; and a Century must roll away before any stable and quiet System will be established. An Amelioration of human Affairs I hope and believe will be the Result but you and I must look down from the Battlements of Heaven if we are ever to have the Pleasure of seeing it."

Now that he and Adams had been elected to the two highest offices in the land Jefferson sat down to write his old friend a letter of congratulation. If he and Adams could keep that lofty attitude of being above the pulling and hauling of party politics they might work together to defeat Hamilton's schemes.

"The public & the papers have been much occupied lately in placing us in a point of opposition to each other," he wrote in his clear rapid script. "I trust with confidence that less of it has been felt by ourselves personally." He laid on a little of the flattery he knew his old friend loved: "I knew it impossible you should lose a vote north of the Delaware, and even if that of Pennsylvania should be against you in the mass yet that you would get enough South of that to place your succession out of danger."

He knew John Adams' vanity and Abigail's fierce partisanship for her husband and her brood. He tried to direct against Hamilton any hurt feelings the couple might harbor on account of Adams' bare majority. He referred to Hamilton's scheme to elect Pinckney as "a trick worthy the subtlety of your arch-friend of New York who has been able to make of your real friends tools to defeat their and your just wishes."

It was a hard letter to write. He was sweating over it. "My inclinations place me out of his reach" — Hamilton's — he continued, "I leave to others the sublime delights of riding in the storm better pleased with sound sleep and a warm birth below. no one of them will congratulate you with purer disinterestedness than myself . . . I have no ambition to govern men."

He added that he hoped that Adams would be able to avoid the war with France that seemed so threatening. "If you are the glory will be all your own; and that your administration may be filled with glory . . . is the sincere wish of one who, tho' in the course of our own voyage through life, various little incidents have happened or been contrived to separate us, retains still for you the solid esteem of the moments when we were working for our independence."

Jefferson was not completely satisfied with his letter. It was a laborious piece of work. He felt some doubt as to how it would be received. Instead of sending the letter direct to Adams he sent it to Madison for advice. Madison advised him to hold it back until they saw how the land lay.

Jefferson had convinced himself he did not want to be President. When he answered a letter from Dr. Rush notifying him of his election as president of the American Philosophical Society in place of Rittenhouse who was dead, he cheerfully described his *"escape"* from the presidency, "an office where it would be impossible to satisfy either friends or foes . . . a more tranquil & unoffending one could not have been found for me," than the vicepresidency, he added; "it will give me philosophical evenings in winter & rural days in summer."

He spoke of his election to the leadership of the Philosophical Society as "the most flattering event of my life." He was bringing with him for the inspection of the society "some bones of the lion kind, but of most exaggerated size. I have been disappointed in getting a femur as yet, but shall bring on the bones I have, if I can, for the Society."

Jefferson was already planning to take as much pomp as he could out of the business of being Vice President. He wrote his soninlaw he was planning to ride the public stages on his trip north. "I mean to get into Philadelphia under shadow of the stage and unperceived to avoid any formal reception (which was practiced on a former occasion). I do not let it be known that I go in the stage, and have announced a later arrival than I mean actually to effect."

The Randolph family had been driven out of Monticello by

Jefferson's building operations. Half the house was uninhabitable. No one could take a step without falling over stacks of bricks. Leaving everything higgledy piggledy on his hilltop, the Vice President elect set out towards the end of February for Philadelphia. He had been tactfully suggesting to friendly members of Congress that it would be a good idea to notify him of his election through the mail instead of going to the trouble and expense of sending a formal committee.

Jefferson drove his own horses as far as Georgetown. From Georgetown he traveled by stage to Baltimore, then by vessel across Chesapeake Bay from North Point to Rock Hall on the Eastern Shore and then by stage again to Philadelphia.

He had long ago discovered that traveling by stage for all its discomfort had advantages. "I prefer that conveyance to travelling with my own horses," he wrote Volney, "because it gives me what I have long been without, an opportunity of plunging into the mixed characters of my country, the most useful school we can enter into, and one which nothing else will supply the want of. I once intimately knew all the specimens of characters which compose the aggregate mass of my fellow citizens" — he was thinking of his lawyer days when he rode circuit through Virginia — "but age office and literature have too long insulated me from them." Enormous changes were taking place in the makeup of the population; new immigrants, French refugees were everywhere: half the younger people he met were on the move westward: everybody was speculating in land. "I find that either their features or my optics have considerably changed in twenty years," he confided to Volney.

The narrow margin by which John Adams won the presidency — actually if certain irregularities had been ironed out, it was only by one electoral vote — filled the Federalists with anguish. "I groan, my dear sir, at the disgraceful course of our affairs," Hamilton wrote Oliver Wolcott. "I pity all those who are officially in the vortex." Wolcott's father, old Governor Wolcott of Connecticut, had been writing the Secretary of the Treasury that he would consider Jefferson's election to the presidency a sufficient reason for dissolving the Union.

Pickering's long face under its lank black hair crowned by his narrow bald head must have looked unusually cadaverous when he sat in his office writing Jefferson that his certification of election was being forwarded through the kind offices of young Mr. Bloodworth, the son of a senator from North Carolina.

Whether it was distaste for the news he was carrying or the inclemency of the weather, young Mr. Bloodworth had barely reached Wilmington when he took sick. He wrote back to the Secretary of State a few days later that he had fallen into such a fever there, accompanied by delirium, that he had quite forgotten the purpose of his mission. Even so Jefferson did not manage to go jouncing unobserved into Philadelphia, with his bag of fossil bones under his seat on the hard planks of the stage. At the Artillery Park, as he drove in, he was greeted by a discharge of sixteen rounds from two twelve pounders and by a banner inscribed with the words, "Jefferson the friend of the People."

He put up with James Madison and his charming Dolley and immediately went to call on the President elect, whom he found, since Abigail had remained in Quincy to nurse John Adams' aged mother, in bachelor quarters at Francis's Hotel. The next morning John Adams returned his call and they had a long cordial conversation shut up in Jefferson's room at the Madisons' which Jefferson recorded in his *Anas*.

The subject was the crisis in relations with France. Before coming to see Jefferson, Adams had been visited by Fisher Ames, who was retiring from Congress to nurse his health. Fisher Ames, who had been discussing the matter with Hamilton, had strenuously urged the new President to appoint Madison and George Cabot of Massachusetts to form a commission with Charles Cotesworth Pinckney to negotiate with the French Directory. General Pinckney had already been left five months cooling his heels in Paris without being received.

Though a bigoted Anglophile, Fisher Ames like Hamilton felt that hostilities with France, at a moment when the country was completely unprepared, must be avoided at all cost. Now Adams, who was equally determined to avoid a war, was consulting Jefferson.

The Directory had taken the abrupt recall of Monroe, whom they had felt was trying to play fair with them, as virtually an act of war. They were likely to take the election of a Federalist president as representing the triumph in the United States of the party which was willing to submit to any national indignity for the furtherance of Pitt's savage blockade. The interruption of grain imports from America was pinching the French with famine and bringing about riots and insurrections against the government of the republic.

Ames argued that it was as essential now to send "a commission extraordinary" to France with full powers to accommodate all differences as it had been to send Jay to England two years before. Adams' first thought had been to appoint Jefferson, but now he agreed with Jefferson that it would be improper for the Vice President to leave the country. Would Jefferson try to induce Madison to accept the appointment?

Remembering Monroe's fate at the hands of a Federalist administration, and knowing that Adams had asked the members of Washington's cabinet to remain on, Jefferson was cool to the proposition. He said he would at least see what Madison had to say.

2. *"the sublimest scene . . ."*

Inauguration Day was a Saturday. The Senate assembled at ten o'clock with General Washington and Thomas Jefferson in attendance. To Senator Bingham, the banker, fell the honor, which it is hardly likely that he enjoyed, as the Binghams had been leaders in the movement to freeze Jefferson out of Philadelphia high society, of administering the oath to the Vice President.

After swearing in the new senators the body was called to order to hear a short speech by Jefferson, in which he pointed out in his low indistinct voice that he would consider it his business to draft a set of parliamentary rules for the Senate's proceedings and to apply them with inflexible impartiality, "regarding neither persons, their views, nor principles, and seeing only the abstract proposition subject to my decision."

The new Vice President then led the senators into the hall of the House of Representatives. As soon as the doors were thrown open the crowd poured in. When the erect figure of General Washington was seen moving across the floor the chandeliers shook and tinkled with applause, and again, when rotund little John Adams, dressed in his best, and wearing one of those large halfmoonshaped black hats that were coming into style, marched up the aisle followed by Messrs. Wolcott and Pickering and McHenry and by lawyer Lee.

John Adams' inaugural address disappointed the Federalists without pleasing many of the Republicans. He declared he had never had an idea of promoting any alteration in the Constitution which the people themselves, in the course of their experience, should not feel to be necessary and expedient. He was for peace and for a rigid neutrality between the warring nations. He spread a little healing balm towards the French: his seven years' residence off and on in their country had left him with a feeling of "personal esteem" for the French nation.

John Adams himself was not too sanguine about the effectiveness of his speech, though he did report a favorable comment from the Republican side. "A solemn scene it was indeed," he wrote his Abigail next morning, "and it was made more affecting to me by the presence of the General whose Countenance was as serene and unclouded as the Day . . . Methought I heard him say 'Ay! I am fairly out and you are fairly in! . . . See which of us will be happiest' . . . In the Chamber of the House of Representatives was a Multitude as great as the Space could contain, and I believe scarsely a dry Eye but Washington's. The Sight of the Sun setting half orbed, and another rising, though less splendid, was a novelty. Chief Justice Ellsworth administered the Oath and with great Energy. Judges Cushing, Wilson and Iredell were present. Many Ladies. I had not slept well the Night before and did not sleep well the Night after. I was unwell and did not know whether I should get through or not. I did, however. How the Business was received I know not, only I have been told that Mason, the Treaty Publisher" — George Mason's nephew, the enthusiastically Republican Stevens Thomson Mason — "said we should lose nothing by the Change, for he had never heard such a Speech in public in his Life."

He could not help strutting for Abigail a little. His sun was risen. He had managed to play his part in the drama. "All agree that, taken altogether, it was the sublimest scene ever exhibited in America."

President Adams took his seat but as soon as the polite clapping subsided he rose, bowed and marched solemnly out of the hall. With his usual modest politeness Jefferson motioned to Washington to precede him, but Washington insisted on following Jefferson down the aisle to the wide central doors. The crowd shouted and cheered.

As in Washington's previous farewells uncontrollable weeping seized many of those present. John Adams felt that these tears had been exaggerated in the newspapers. He wrote Abigail a couple of days later: "It is the general Report that there was more Weeping than there has ever been at the Representation of the Tragedy. But whether it was Grief or Joy, whether from the Loss of their beloved President, or from the Accessibility of an unbeloved one . . . *I know not;* one thing I know, I am a Being of too much Sensibility to act any Part well in such an Exhibition."

The Fourth Congress had adjourned without day. Monday morning John Adams held his first cabinet meeting. The first subject under discussion was the mission to France. Messrs. Wolcott and Pickering were skeptical of the usefulness of any fresh mission.

Oliver Wolcott had screwed himself up to the point of standing up against Hamilton, who wrote him daily and insistent letters from New York calling for the nomination of the sort of embassy which Fisher Ames had recommended. Hamilton's argument was that it would be good politics to send along a prominent Republican; it would soothe the hurt feelings of the French; if the mission failed the Republicans would share in the discredit.

When Adams insisted on the need for a commission extraordinary and began to speak "of the fine talents and amiable qualities and manners of Mr. Madison," Pickering began to glower. The smooth Wolcott asked coolly whether it had been determined to send Madison. Adams hesitated; no, it deserved consideration. Wolcott suggested that such an appointment would raise a storm among Federalists in

Congress and out of doors and through the states. Were they forever going to be overawed by party passions? Adams asked with spirit. "Mr. President, we are willing to resign," was Wolcott's rejoinder.

John Adams looked about him. "We," Wolcott had said. There was no question that he spoke for the four of them. The four principal cabinet officers had been so well drilled by Hamilton to act in concert that they continued to do it even when they were going against his wishes. Though he had his tantrums Adams was a much milder man than he pretended to be. He had none of Washington's administrative skill and training. He had none of the general's divine obstinacy. Nor his judgment of men. He was appalled at the prospect of going out to find himself a new cabinet at this juncture with the country on the brink of war. He dropped the subject. John Adams was in the hands of Messrs. Wolcott and Pickering from that moment on.

Adams and Jefferson both dined with General Washington the same afternoon. They walked home together down Market Street after dinner. When Jefferson began to explain why Madison could not accept an appointment to France, Adams cut him short. "He immediately said that, on consultation some objections to that nomination had been raised," Jefferson noted in his *Anas*, "and was going on with excuses which evidently embarrassed him, when we came to Fifth Street where our road separated, and we took leave; and he never after said one word to me on the subject, or ever consulted me as to any measures of the government."

Their road separated and they took leave. Jefferson immediately made up his mind that as Vice President his only duties should be to preside over the Senate. Madison was right. There was no way he could collaborate in his old friend's administration.

3.   *". . . some bones of the lion kind"*

He stayed on for another week in Philadelphia to preside at a meeting of the American Philosophical Society. While he waited he bought clover seed for Monticello, arranged a power of attorney so that John Barnes, his tobacco agent, could collect his salary from the Treasury when it came due, and promptly borrowed a hundred and fifty dollars from him on account. Five thousand dollars a year was no great sum, but to Jefferson it meant that he had at least one source of income not already garnisheed for the service of debts.

He went shopping. He roamed about the streets of Philadelphia. He made purchases for Monticello, he bought an instrument case for his soninlaw and a fleecy waistcoat and a cloth coat and a pair of

boots for himself. He went around to Bache's printshop and took out
a year's subscription for the *Aurora* to be sent to another young family connection: John Randolph. The day of the meeting he paid twentyfive cents to see an elephant and then, with his paper on the
megalonix in his pocket, full of pleasant anticipation, walked around
to the assembly rooms of the society.

He had many warm friends there. There was aged Charles Thomson who had been the secretary of the old Congress and Dr. Rush,
and Dr. Logan the Quaker and Tench Coxe and Dr. Thornton the
architect of the Capitol building in Washington City, and Beckley
and Tom Shippen and that young Swiss from western Pennsylvania
whose speeches on finance Jefferson had so admired in the House,
Albert Gallatin. He was looking forward to meeting the famous Priestley who had taken refuge in America from the English mob and from
Pitt's persecution of republican ideas. Jefferson revered Priestley as a
great experimental chemist and for his liberal politics but at the same
time he deplored his polemical theology.

Priestley, as dogmatic in theology as he was pragmatic in science,
had recently been belaboring Jefferson's friend Volney's philosophy in
the public prints. In the French traveler's cult of reason and progress
Priestley detected a brimstone stench of atheism. When Jefferson was
introduced to him, he found him delightful. Priestley recommended a
new type of specially accurate thermometer for the weather observations at Monticello.

Jefferson produced his fossil bones and read his paper describing
the clawed quadruped found in a limestone cave in the Blue Ridge,
which he called the megalonyx. He added some stories picked up
from the Indians about gigantic creatures of the lion kind prowling
round their campfires along the Cheat River, and read an extract from
an article in a British scientific journal about the remains of another
extinct monster hailing from the River Plate which was thought to
be a gigantic sloth.

He always enjoyed collecting proofs of the size of American animals:
each one was another refutation of Buffon's ridiculous theory, which
offended Jefferson's most profound and naïve patriotic feelings, that
animals and men were smaller, feebler and less fertile in America
than in Europe. He listened to another paper based on Indian legends,
this time about a huge hairless bear that had preyed on the redskins,
and to a disquisition on the varying behavior of air currents over land
and over water. Discussion followed on into the midafternoon. The
members of the society were good trenchermen; the proceedings ended
with a dinner copiously irrigated with toasts in claret and madeira.

A couple of days later, having paid seventyfive cents to see some
elks that morning, taking leave of the Madisons, who as Madison had

refused to run for the next Congress were packing up for the journey back to Montpellier, Jefferson boarded the Baltimore stage.

He reached home in time to find asparagus thrusting up in his garden and spinach on his table. The peaches and cherries were in bloom. The prospect of being on salary for four years encouraged him to start negotiations with his Dutch bankers for another two thousand dollar loan which he sorely needed to finish rebuilding his house.

4. *Embarked in the Contest*

Back at Monticello, Jefferson had hardly nursed himself through a bout of rheumatism and begun to enjoy "the soft genial temperature of the season just above the want of fire," and "the reanimation of birds, flowers, the fields forests and gardens" he wrote Volney about, when he received a call back to Philadelphia.

The Directory had expelled General Pinckney from France and were piling decree on decree abrogating the clauses favorable to American shipping in the treaty of 1778. Henceforth French cruisers would treat American merchant ships exactly as the Americans allowed themselves to be treated by the British. In practice they were treating them a great deal worse. The British at least paid for contraband flour when they confiscated it. With the news of the latest decree came news of seizures in the West Indies, drumhead prize courts, and the imprisonment and abuse of American seamen. To put the country in a state of defense against these outrages, President Adams was calling the Fifth Congress into special session.

Aching and feverish after a grueling ride on the stage, Jefferson arrived at Francis's Hotel in time to call the new Senate to order on May 15 of 1797. He found the Federalists in control of the Senate and strong enough in the House to reelect Jonathan Dayton as Speaker. Dayton was a New Jersey lawyer, a close friend of Burr's and a Federalist in politics. This time Priestley, who had almost been chosen the last time his name was put up, got only twelve votes for chaplain. John Beckley, whose meticulous attention to duty had endeared him even to congressmen who disagreed with his politics, lost by one vote the clerkship which he had held ever since the inauguration of the new government.

The French spoliations were proving a godsend to the Federalists. Dominant in all three branches, and taking their cue from Pitt's proscription of the radicals in England, they were in the mood to treat any criticism of their conduct of the government as treason against the United States.

Jefferson heard John Adams spur them on with a warlike address to the two houses in which he denounced the terms of the French Directory's leavetaking with Monroe as an effort to drive a wedge between the American people and their government. Adams asked for laws to stop the equipping in American ports of the very French cruisers and privateers that were raiding American shipping. He asked Congress to put the army and the navy on a war footing. His high tone swept all waverers into the administration camp. The hotter heads among the Federalists were looking forward to a war with France as sure ruin for the Republican opposition.

Jefferson saw them take over with a heavy heart. "For when General Washington was withdrawn," he wrote years later in his preface to his notes for the period, "these *energumeni* of royalism" — by royalism he meant, as always, the English system of rule by a hierarchy of men of property and birth — "kept in check hitherto by the dread of his honesty, his firmness, his patriotism and the authority of his name, now mounted on the car of State and, free from control, like Phaeton on that of the sun, drove headlong and wild."

Jefferson made up his mind that, as opposition Vice President, he should take no part in the political fray. He would devote himself to the technical aspects of his job. He made no further effort to come to an understanding with John Adams. Instead he amused himself, while the war measures moved steadily through the Senate, in putting together his manual of parliamentary procedure which was to become the basis of the rules of debate for successive congresses.

His efforts to remain above the battle were to prove unavailing. Although in the Senate sessions he managed to maintain an attitude of impartiality, his name had already descended "like a gladiator," as he put it, into the arena of the public prints.

The day before Adams' inauguration, vindictive young Bache, as a sendoff for General Washington whose majestic reputation he considered the mainstay of Federalist wrongdoing, published a long diatribe by Tom Paine against the retiring President. Paine had come out of the Luxembourg prison convinced that Gouverneur Morris directly and George Washington indirectly had intrigued to place his neck under the guillotine. Though Washington had always tried to help him in times past he saw Washington's failure to protest his imprisonment as a case of personal ingratitude to a man whose writings had done so much to assure victory to the revolutionary cause.

Paine's pen had lost none of its fire. His letter was scorching: too much so to be of any help to the Republicans. The old general was held in such veneration by Americans of all classes and opinions that any personal attack was sure to lose more sympathy than it attracted. Monroe had done his best to head Paine off. It was in Monroe's house

in Paris that the old exciseman had brewed the bitter dish. After
Monroe dug Paine out of jail, there was nothing he could do but take
him home and nurse him back to health. The man was sick and penniless and in a desperate state of nerves. Monroe admired his talent and
sympathized with the ardor of his republicanism. He could not put
Tom Paine out on the street.

When Paine began his fulminations against Washington and Morris, Monroe tried to explain to him how awkward it would be for the
American minister if a guest at the legation published an attack on
the President. Far too selfrighteous to see the point, for all Monroe
could do, Paine managed to send the letter off to America.

The moment his "Letter to George Washington" appeared in the
Aurora it furnished the Federalist press with ammunition against
Monroe himself and against Jefferson and the whole Republican cause.
Now Pickering could shake his lank locks and exult with smooth Wol-
cott over the eternal rightness of their judgment in recalling this
patron of the venomous Paine.

Soon after Jefferson reached Philadelphia the Federalist editors
were able to hold up to public scorn another evidence of the depravity
of the opposition. Mazzei had no sooner received Jefferson's letter of
the preceding summer than, all in a dither to prove how deeply he was
in the great man's confidence, he hurried to the nearest newspaper
with it. French journalists picked it up from the Italian press and an
English gazette retranslated it back into its original tongue. Now it
was reprinted in America garbled and with comments. Where Jefferson wrote that the Federalists had introduced the *forms* of British
government, meaning presidential birthdays, levees, processions to the
opening of Congress and the like, the text was construed to read *form*,
which implied that, as the Federalists had been claiming, he opposed
the Constitution itself. The reference to "Samsons in the field and
Solomons in the council," in which he had referred to the Cincinnati
in general, was interpreted as a direct impeachment of Washington's
integrity.

Jefferson, who suffered whenever he saw his name in print, experienced great agony by the publication of Mazzei's letter. What
should he do to mend matters? At length he came to the conclusion
that it would be best neither to avow nor disavow. It would be impossible for him to explain his disapproval of the celebration on February 22, he pointed out when he wrote for Madison's advice on the
subject, "without bringing about a personal difference between Genl
Washington & myself, which nothing before the publication of this
letter has ever done. it would embroil me with all those with whom
his character is still popular, that is to say, nine tenths of the people
of the U S; and what good would be obtained by my avowing the

letter with the necessary explanations? very little indeed in my opinion, to counterbalance a good deal of harm. from my silence in this instance it can never be inferred that I am afraid to own the general sentiments of the letter."

Meanwhile, he told Madison, he had explained exactly what he meant to tell Mazzei to "several friends at Philadelphia." It is highly likely that John Beckley, who was the sort of man Jefferson told things to when he wanted them to get around, was one. John Beckley at that moment was having his own difficulties with the Federalist press.

Still smarting from his disappointment at not being reelected to the office about which his whole life had revolved for the past eight years, he was so stung by an article accusing him of miscounting the votes in the House of Representatives that he went in a rage to the editor of *Porcupine's Gazette* and threatened to horsewhip him.

This editor, William Cobbett, who, writing under the name of Peter Porcupine, gleefully abused the Republicans wherever they showed their heads, was a far more dangerous opponent than the sanctimonious Fenno.

He was a big towheaded man with small gray eyes set close in his head, the son of an impoverished yeoman of Surrey who, an extreme Whig in his day, had filled his boy's head with admiration for George Washington. As a lad, furthermore, young Cobbett had worked as a gardener in the royal gardens at Kew where he had been impressed by the rustic virtues of England's own George, the voluble squire of Windsor.

To see the world young Cobbett took the King's shilling and, being a man of energy and brains, soon found himself sergeant major in an infantry regiment stationed in New Brunswick. There he was much thrown with New England loyalists from whom he heard sad tales of revolutionary ferocity.

Forced out of the army, where a man of his lowly birth had no chance of preferment, for taking up the grievances of the rank and file, much as Tom Paine a generation before had been forced out of the excise service, he took part in publishing a pamphlet which described the sufferings of the private soldier and even had the effrontery to try to get some officers courtmartialed for stealing the men's rations.

Pitt's agents were harrying radical agitators. Cobbett fled with his family to France. He was soon disgusted by the bloody unreasonableness of the French. The United States was the haven of the world's discontented. As soon as he could scrape up the passage money he took ship for the Delaware and landed in Wilmington.

He had learned some French; he made his living during his first years in America teaching English to the French political refugees who abounded in Wilmington and Philadelphia. For that purpose he published an English grammar for Frenchmen. One publication led to another.

When Priestley took refuge in Pennsylvania from the mobs and the vindictive law courts of England, Cobbett was so riled by the welcome the democratic societies gave the unitarian chemist that he took the hide off him in a scurrilous pamphlet as "the firebrand philosopher."

Cobbett claimed to have learned to write by reading and rereading Swift's *Tale of a Tub*. His abuse was couched in plain vigorous English that stood out amid the provincial circumlocutions of Claypoole and Fenno. The Federalists delighted in his cheerful cudgeling of their opponents.

The subtle Talleyrand and Robert Liston, the British minister who had replaced Hammond, both seem to have hinted to him that they could use the services of Peter Porcupine. The story Cobbett told was that he informed the ci-devant bishop that he was "no trout to be caught by tickling" and sent him limping off with a flea in his ear. Though the Republicans claimed that he was in Liston's pay, they were unable to prove it. Possibly he threw himself into polemics for the sheer pleasure of satisfying the prejudices of a trueborn Englishman.

When he opened a bookstore in Philadelphia for the sale of anti-Jacobin literature such as Burke's complete works and *The Bloody Buoy Thrown out as a Warning to the Political Pilots of All Nations* and *The Cannibal's Progress* and his own *History of Jacobinism* and the *Anti-Jacobin Review* which Pitt subsidized, and other highly spiced accounts of republican atrocities, he adorned its windows with an enormous portrait of King George, a garishly painted battlepiece of Lord Howe's defeat of the French fleet and with prints and woodcuts of the crowned heads of Europe. He imported the works of Hannah Moore. He made his shop the depot for all the products of the anti-republican presses Pitt and Dundas were fostering in Great Britain. Cobbett was the first really literate exemplar of the obstinate rural Toryism to which Pitt's administration trusted to pull the tight little island through the disasters and despairs of the wars with the French.

Beckley's fracas with Cobbett in his shop ended without any broken heads. Though Cobbett claimed never to retract a word, he consented to print Beckley's explanation of the single incident of a mistaken count immediately corrected which Peter Porcupine had made much of. Beckley called him a damned scoundrel and walked out of the shop.

The Republican party manager in Pennsylvania had seen for some time the need for Republican batteries more capable of replying to Cobbett's great guns than shrill young Bache. Ben Bache was so pro-

French that he laid himself open to the reproach of being a French-man by education if not by birth. Beckley had been working with another journalist refugee from Pitt's persecution of the press who was to prove a damned scoundrel indeed. This was a Scottish printer named Callender.

Callender had published a little chronicle, half statistics half scan-dal, called *The Political Progress of Britain*, about the time of the arrest of the leaders of the Edinburgh Convention and had escaped out of Britain with the catchpoles at his heels. Landing in Philadelphia, he was taken up by the Republicans as one of Liberty's martyrs. They found him a job reporting congressional debates for *The Philadelphia Gazette*.

When his book was reprinted it interested Madison and Jefferson as an exposure of the failure of Pitt's fiscal system, which they claimed had been Hamilton's model. This encouraged Callender to describe the American scene. He brought out a rambling gossipy chronicle which he called *The History of the United States for 1796*. Amid a number of odds and ends, such as complaints of the discomfort of the stages and of the overcrowding of American cities, and an abusive anonymous letter to John Beckley which for no particular reason he attributed to Oliver Wolcott, he printed a few of the actual letters that had passed between Hamilton and Muhlenberg, Venable and Monroe at the time of their investigation of Reynolds' accusations of financial malfeasance when Hamilton was in the Treasury. They were so arranged as to leave grave doubts as to Hamilton's honesty in the readers' mind. This was a shot below the waterline for the Federalists.

Jefferson evidently felt that the *History* was an effective piece of campaign material. On June 19 he noted in his account book that he had bought copies to the value of $15.14. The public airing of Hamil-ton's four year old scandal so stirred the dregs of that controversy in the town that Andrew G. Fraunces, the man who had lost his job as a clerk in the Treasury as a result of Reynolds' forgeries, improved the shining hour by touching Jefferson for four dollars. He must have been an insistent beggar because Jefferson took the trouble of writing him that he was out of cash and leaving town. He probably felt some sympathy for him as a victim of Hamilton's and Wolcott's reprisals.

5. *A View of the Executive*

The day following Jefferson's interview with Fraunces, Monroe and his wife and daughter arrived in Philadelphia from France. Mon-roe was coming home in a boiling temper. He was a man slow to

anger. He had excellent personal relations with many of the leading
Federalists, especially in New York where he was linked to them
through Mrs. Monroe's family connections. Rufus King and his wife
had visited the Monroes in Paris and, having agreed to hang their
political differences on a peg, the two men became warm friends.
Now Monroe felt that Messrs. Wolcott and Pickering had intentionally,
out of partisan spite, ruined his chances of reaching a sensible agreement with the French and of coming home with a difficult mission
successfully accomplished. They had impugned his honesty and had
embarrassed and humiliated him. "I think I can ride any storm if I
get safe to port upon the sea upon which I am now embarked. Surely
no man was ever in the hands of such a corps as I am at present," he
wrote Jefferson from Paris. He bitterly resented Washington's having
allowed a fellow Virginian to be so grossly mistreated, but he considered Hamilton's machinations as the fountainhead of his difficulties.

Randolph's *Vindication* had not done Randolph much good but it
had done the administration harm with fairminded men. Monroe was
determined to publish his own story of his mission to France. Already
he was collecting corroborative testimonials. First he wanted to force
Pickering to state the reasons for his abrupt recall. Pickering refused
to state his reasons.

Giles of Virginia had been trying to pin down the vague charges
aired in the House by dandified young Harper of South Carolina who,
though elected as a Republican, became a redhot Federalist under the
influence of the Philadelphia high society that revolved around the
rich and lovely Mrs. Bingham. Cobbett was helping Harper write his
speeches. After a bitter debate and acid correspondence all Giles
could report were rumors and innuendoes about Monroe's failure to
explain Jay's treaty to the French, his patronage of Paine, and the
theft of a silver ingot from the consulate in Paris, a loss which Fulwar
Skipwith made good out of his own pocket; Oliver Wolcott was refusing to honor his claim for repayment by the government. These
were all charges too vague to be answered. Monroe decided to publish the record of his mission entire.

From the moment he arrived in Philadelphia he was besieged by
Republicans eager for a firsthand account of his adventures in France.
With Jefferson he spent two hours talking to Burr, who though no
longer in the Senate had a way of happening to be in Philadelphia
when news of importance was stirring, and to Representative Gallatin.
Gallatin wrote his wife: "from my conversation with Monroe, from
his manner and everything about him (things which are more easily
felt than expressed) I have the strongest impression upon my mind
that he is possessed of integrity superior to all the attacks of malign-
ity . . . I am also pretty well convinced that the American Administra-

tion have acted with a degree of meanness only exceeded by their
folly . . ." "We give tomorrow a splendid dinner to Monroe at Oeller's
hotel," he added in his next letter, "in order to testify our approbation
of his conduct and our opinion of his integrity. Jefferson, Judge Mc
Kean the governor and about fifty members of Congress will be there;
for which I expect the Administration, Porcupine & Co., will soundly
abuse us."

6. The Events of Europe

Jefferson and Monroe had to have a thorough private talk before they parted. They had a feeling of being spied on at the hotel.
Partisan emotions were in such an exacerbated state that it was not
possible for two Republicans to be seen together without the Federalist press raising a hue and cry about a Jacobin conspiracy.

"The passions are too high at present to be cooled in our time,"
Jefferson was writing despairingly to General Pinckney's brotherinlaw,
his old Charleston friend from Continental Congress days, Edward
Rutledge; "men who have been intimate all their lives cross the streets
to avoid meeting, & turn their heads the other way lest they should
be obliged to touch their hats." The ill feeling was worse than in the
rancorous summer of '93. Jefferson felt too old for this endless strife,
he was telling Rutledge: "this may do for young men with whom
passion is enjoyment. but it is afflicting to peaceable minds. tranquility is the old man's milk."

To find the peace and tranquillity they needed for a thorough discussion of the political scene Jefferson drove Monroe out to their
Quaker friend Dr. Logan's farm out on the Germantown road. Under
the huge trees and the famous hemlocks that were thought to have
been planted by William Penn, on the green lawns that bordered the
slow meanderings of Wingohocking Creek, they spent the day together at Stenton in conversation with the tolerant Quaker. The present was dark but they could see glimmerings of light ahead. The
more sanguine Republicans were already congratulating each other
on the possibility of a revolution in England which might bring about
a lasting peace between the three great republics of Great Britain,
France and America.

Jefferson had outlined for his friend Rutledge the "events of Europe
coming to us in astonishing & rapid succession" on which he founded
his hopes of a speedy victory for the republican cause. Pitt's government was bankrupt. The suspension of specie payments by the Bank
of England on the last day of the preceding February was spreading

financial panic among the British merchants trading in America and the American merchants trading on British capital who Jefferson felt were the backbone of Federalist power. The British fleet was in a state of mutiny. The mutineers on the warships off Spithead had only been brought back to their duty by the exhortations of their beloved Black Dick, the aged Admiral Howe, and by lavish promises of better treatment from the Admiralty. The United Irishmen were in arms and a French landing to liberate the insurrectory isle was expected any day. Bonaparte had beaten the Austrians in the campaign of the quadrilateral in northern Italy and forced them to an armistice. He was assembling shipping on the Channel coast for an invasion of England itself. These events had visibly shaken the Federalists; "and above all," Jefferson wrote Rutledge, "the warning voice of Mr King, to abandon all thought of connection with Great Britain, that she is going down irrevocably & will sink us also if we do not clear ourselves . . . brought over several to the pacific party."

To all this Monroe could add the rumor that Pitt's agents were suing for peace. George Hammond was said to have joined Lord Malmesbury at Lille in a fresh attempt to negotiate with the Directory. At home Pitt's repressive measures against the Jacobins had been only partly successful. His prosecution of the leaders of the democratic societies had failed in the courts. In spite of sedition laws an English mob had stoned the royal coach proceeding in solemn procession to the opening of Parliament. King George himself had been shot at with intent to kill from a mysterious weapon some thought to be a blowgun.

Pitt's England was the mainstay of Federalist hopes. Even the Federalists admitted that England was in peril of revolution within and from invasion from without. John Barker Church and his charming Angelica, who was one of Jefferson's favorite ladies and for whom Hamilton was supposed to entertain warmer feelings than a brother-inlaw should, had recently arrived in New York. The Churches made no bones of the fact that they were taking refuge in America because they thought England's end was near. It was they who had brought Hamilton the warning letter from Rufus King.

Excluded as they were from the national councils, the Republicans were aware that Hamilton was doing everything he could to hold tight rein on his highflying supporters. In letter after letter to McHenry and to Messrs. Pickering and Wolcott he was urging that a commission must be sent to patch up a peace with France. This was not the time for the United States to plunge into war. Some weeks before he had been scolding Oliver Wolcott over the militant tone of the House's reply to John Adams' inaugural address: "*Hard words* are very rarely useful in public proceedings," he wrote. "*Real firmness* is good for everything. *Strut* is good for nothing."

The day after their excursion to Stenton, Jefferson and Monroe parted with the promise of meeting again at Monticello during the summer. Jefferson's companion on the southbound stage was Monroe's uncle and erstwhile guardian, Joseph Jones, bound for his Fredericksburg home. Jefferson was turning over the conduct of the Senate to a president pro tem while the Federalist majority went to work to expel William Blount who represented — along with old William Cocke the pioneer of the Holston River settlement, and a Jeffersonian — the new State of Tennessee. Jefferson saw in these proceedings merely a partisan move to eliminate one more Republican from Congress. He refused to sanction them by his presence.

A week after leaving Philadelphia he was driving into Montpellier to bring Madison up to date on the latest complications of congressional news. Next day he was back at Monticello setting his bricklayers and carpenters to work on the house again. The time had come to take off the roof.

7. The Navigation of the Mississippi

In the halls of Congress the Federalist phalanx was on the move against Senator Blount. William Blount was one of the most popular men in the Mississippi Valley. He had represented North Carolina in the old Congress and in the Constitutional Convention. Moving west with a great body of his constituents, he became a leader of the settlers in the Southwest Territories and presided over the convention that wrote a constitution for the State of Tennessee. Like most of the men he represented he was in a fever to take in fresh lands to the westward. Finding little encouragement for these enthusiasms among the Federalists, he let his disgust with the rule of the New Englanders in Philadelphia drive him to the point of entering into a correspondence with the British which, if not treasonable, was certainly indiscreet.

Jefferson got an inkling of an enterprise being brewed against the Spaniards some months before when he dined with Blount in the company of Jefferson's fellow member of the American Philosophical Society, the artful General Wilkinson of Kentucky. At that point Blount and Wilkinson might well have been mulling over some scheme for settlement on the lands the Spaniards had not yet evacuated along the Mississippi. The Pinckney treaty had granted the Americans the right of navigation and a free port in New Orleans, but the Spanish officials in the river ports had developed a certain capacity for obstruction. The boundary commission was working slowly. Every man who tried to move goods downriver, by raft or flatboat or bateau, found himself entangled in a web of intrigue, conniving and corruption for which, as it later became clear, the Spaniards were not solely responsible. Wilkinson, with his gift for getting on the right side of a great many different kinds of men, had known how to disarm Jefferson with accounts of Indian customs and burial mounds and of the traces of a vanished civilization. When the table was cleared after dinner at Senator Blount's a "hardy brawny weatherbeaten man" appeared who was introduced as Captain Chisholm. With the first glass of wine he began to boast that he had such influence at the campfires of the Creeks and the Cherokees that he could turn them against the Spaniards and take over West Florida with their help. Jefferson made it immediately clear that much as he wanted to see New Orleans in American hands his interest in the Creeks and the Cherokees at this point was purely scientific.

Not being able to entangle any member of the administration in his scheme, Blount steered Chisholm towards Robert Liston, the British minister. Liston, who knew that ever since the days when John Jay inserted a secret clause in the first treaty of peace there had been a body of American opinion which preferred to see the Floridas and New Orleans in British hands than under the Spaniards or the French, listened to Chisholm's drunken harangue with interest. He was so much interested that he used some of his secret service funds to pay Chisholm's passage to England, where a certain Dr. Romayne, a New Yorker, was already in touch with the ministry in behalf of Blount and the restless settlers of the Western Waters. "A man of consequence has gone to England about the business," Blount wrote one of his confidants, an Indian agent at Tellico Blockhouse, named Carey, "and if he makes the arrangements he expects, I shall myself have a hand in the business, and probably shall be at the head of the business on the part of the British."

Chisholm held forth about his plans in a Philadelphia tavern the night before he sailed and when he arrived in London created such a scandal that Lord Grenville, like Jefferson, refused to listen to him and demanded that he be shipped back to America forthwith. Blount's letters meanwhile had been intercepted by agents of Pickering's and placed on the President's desk. John Adams read them with one of his bursts of indignation and forwarded them to Congress for action.

Blount's attitude on being confronted with his "conspiracy" was that he would intrigue with the devil himself to get the Mississippi territory away from the Spaniards. His letters, he wrote home ruefully, "make a damnable fuss here. I hope however the people of the Western Waters will see nothing but good in it, for so I intended it, especially for Tennessee."

The Federalists in Congress, led by Robert Goodloe Harper and James Asheton Bayard of Delaware, made a great show of righteous indignation and proceeded to expell Blount from the Senate and to prepare impeachment proceedings against him in the House "for high crimes and misdemeanors." Liston publicly disavowed any connection with the business; privately he wrote Lord Grenville that bringing the matter to light was another example of Pickering's lack of tact.

8. *The Reynolds Papers*

Monroe meanwhile had set off for New York. He wanted to have further consultations with the resourceful Burr as to how he could best defend himself against the attacks of Messrs. Wolcott and Pickering. There was the business of his accounts to take up with the administration. There was property of his wife's to attend to. There was the question of the coming elections.

The night before Monroe left Philadelphia he was handed a puzzling and threatening missive from Alexander Hamilton. Hamilton was in a state over *The History of the United States for 1796*. Ignoring the fact that it was fairly obvious that, since he had refused to be bound by any promise of secrecy, John Beckley must be the man who had furnished Callender with the Reynolds correspondence, Hamilton seemed to be trying to hold Monroe responsible for a breach of confidence.

As soon as he read Hamilton's letter Monroe tried to find Venable and Muhlenberg, who had been the other two members of the informal congressional committee that had taken the matter up with Hamilton in the first place. As they were not at their quarters he could get no light from them. All he knew was that Hamilton had published an angry statement in Fenno's paper attributing Callender's disclosures to a Republican plot to tarnish his good name.

Monroe had hardly settled in his lodgings in New York when he received a visit from Hamilton in person. With him came his brotherinlaw, John Barker Church. Burr's friend, David Gelston, whose sons Monroe had looked out for when they went through Paris on the grand tour, was present at their interview and took down minutes of what was said.

"Col. H. appeared very much agitated upon his entrance into the room." He came in proclaiming that he presumed Monroe knew why he had come. He began a recital at great length of what had taken place at their last meeting with Muhlenberg and Venable four years before. "Colo M. asked what all that meant and said *if you wish me to tell you anything in relation to the business all this history is unnecessary* . . . some warmth appeared in both gentlemen."

Monroe insisted that his knowing anything about the business was purely accidental in the first place. He had heard that a Virginian named Reynolds was in trouble and at the jail had discovered that the man was not a constituent of his, but a New Yorker. After the interviews with Hamilton which had developed from Reynolds' pretended revelations he had sealed up the papers Hamilton furnished and sent them "to his friend in Virginia" — most likely his uncle, Joseph Jones —and had known nothing about their publication until he arrived home from Europe a few days before. He was sorry they had been published. There was nothing more to be said.

Hamilton demanded to know why Monroe had not answered his letter. Church, who was there to act as a second in case of need, now fished two of Callender's pamphlets out of his pocket and showed Monroe the statements he and Venable and Muhlenberg had signed. Monroe said that he had wanted to refresh his memory by consulting these gentlemen before answering. Hamilton burst out that his letters to Venable and Muhlenberg had been answered. He had expected an immediate answer from Monroe "to so important a subject in which his character, the peace and reputation of his family were so deeply interested. Colo. M. replied that if he Colo. H. would be temperate or quiet for a moment or some such word he would answer him candidly."

Monroe tried to explain that he had received Hamilton's letter at ten o'clock at night and had not been able to get hold of the other two before boarding the New York stage first thing next morning. He felt they should make a joint answer to Hamilton's inquiry.

Hamilton cried out: "This as your representation is totally false (as nearly as I recollect the expression)," noted Gelston, who was smudging the paper in his hurry to scratch down everything exactly as it was said, "upon which both gentlemen instantly rose. Colo. Monroe rising first and saying do you say I represent falsely, you are a scoundrel. Colo. H. said I will meet you like a gentleman. Colo. M. said I am ready get your pistols."

At that point Gelston and Church stepped between them. "Gentlemen, gentlemen, be moderate," Church was pleading. Gelston suggested that they let the matter rest until Monroe had time to talk with Venable and Muhlenberg. Hamilton consented. They both agreed to treat any intemperate expressions as if they had never been said. Hamilton allowed himself to be led away. "The interview continued about an hour or a little over. Myself being present through the whole," noted Gelston and carefully dated his notes and signed them.

A few days later Hamilton received a letter from Philadelphia signed jointly by Muhlenberg and Monroe, repeating their four year old statement that nothing had come up in their inquiry to justify the suspicion that Hamilton had been using Treasury funds for personal speculation. However they pointed out that they had been somewhat surprised by Hamilton's treating the affair as a party maneuver in his letter to *The Gazette of the United States.* At the time he had thanked them for their understanding attitude.

Hamilton wrote back peevishly demanding an explanation from Monroe of another letter written as far back as January 1793 which had referred to Clingman's offer to turn state's evidence. Hamilton wanted Monroe to make a formal statement that all the charges against him were false. Monroe answered that this was a matter upon which he had formed no opinion. Hamilton immediately wrote back asking whether Monroe considered him guilty of having fabricated the Reynolds scandal to cover up something worse. He demanded an answer; yes or no. Monroe stood his ground. He had not accused Hamilton of anything.

Hamilton answered angrily that he considered Monroe's having had any communication with Clingman in regard to his affairs was "indelicate and improper."

Monroe answered that he considered Hamilton's last letter "indelicate and improper." He had not accused Hamilton of anything. Since he understood that Hamilton was publishing his account of the transaction he reserved to himself the liberty of forming an opinion after reading Hamilton's defense.

In a state of furious excitement Hamilton made a trip to Philadelphia to procure the affidavit of a lodginghouse keeper to the effect that Mrs. Reynolds really existed and that the letters attributed to her were in her handwriting. At the same time he somehow got hold of two notes which Jefferson had just written Fraunces, the discharged clerk, in which he gently resisted his demands for assistance. Hamilton insisted on dragging Jefferson's name into the affair.

He added to the lot an affidavit by that doughty schoolmaster Noah Webster to the effect that no threat of scandalous disclosures had ever scared him off suggesting Hamilton's name for the presidency in his newspaper. Webster's *Minerva* had become, with good reason, because Webster did not stoop to personal abuse, the most respected Federalist journal in New York. A suggestion of Webster's would have carried weight among the moderates of the party. The implication was that if Hamilton had ever entertained any hope of the presidency that hope was now dashed to the ground.

While attending to the publication of his pamphlet in Philadelphia Hamilton hurried off to Monroe the sort of letter which would ordinarily have led to a duel, accusing him of motives "malignant and dishonorable, nor can I doubt that that will be the universal opinion, when the publication of the whole affair which I am about to make shall be seen." This letter was handed to Monroe at his inn by Hamilton's old associate on Washington's staff, the Major Jackson who had been secretary of the Constitutional Convention, now surveyor of customs at Philadelphia and married to one of the wealthy Willing girls. Hamilton had chosen him as his second. Before the major had a chance to deliver it, Hamilton unaccountably hurried off to New York again.

Monroe answered soberly that he was sorry he could not satisfy Hamilton's demands but that he was only interested in the truth. He had not made up his mind as to what the truth was. He regretted that Hamilton had placed the matter on a basis of personal honor.

Hamilton was in a fury. He could not let well enough alone. He kept writing Monroe fresh notes in terms that placed the controversy on very personal grounds. The last thing Monroe wanted was a duel with Hamilton. His whole soul was set on collecting the necessary materials to publish a defense of his behavior as American envoy in Paris which would preserve his reputation from the slanders of Messrs. Wolcott and Pickering. He felt that these men were egging Hamilton on against him. "I am satisfied," he wrote Aaron Burr, whom he had asked to be his second in case he were forced into a duel, "he is pushed on by his party friends here who to get rid of me wod. be very willing to hazard him."

To finish the business once and for all he sent a note to Burr in New York to deliver to Hamilton in person. In this he declared formally that he had no intention of challenging Hamilton to fight but that if Hamilton intended to challenge him let him say so to Colonel Burr, who was authorized to make any arrangements that might be necessary.

After talking with Burr, who was a gentleman very much at home with delicate points of honor, Hamilton wrote disarmingly that it had been his impression all along that Monroe was challenging him, but that since he was not, there was nothing more to be said.

Hamilton bundled up all the letters he could lay his hands on that had any connection with the business, prefaced them by a hasty diatribe against the spirit of Jacobinism which endeavored to accomplish its purpose by calumny, and sent them to John Fenno for publication. He added, in an odd footnote which gave the whole affair a surprising twist, that two of the still unpublished letters of Mrs. Reynolds were signed "Maria Clingman." The implication was that she had been Clingman's wife instead of Reynolds' all the time.

As in the case of Randolph's pamphlet and of Monroe's some

months later, men approved or disapproved the publication in accord with their partisan passions. Hamilton's revelations in the Reynolds pamphlet cleared him from the charge of speculating in government funds, which not even his enemies believed, but they made it impossible for him to be seriously considered ever again for an elective office.

So secure was Hamilton in the affections of his family that to her dying day his wife Elizabeth blamed the whole scandal on Monroe.

9. "... dissensions and discords"

Hamilton's publication of the Reynolds letters was a fillip to the Republicans. The strangely lightminded tone of his confession and his gullibility throughout the proceedings eliminated any prospect of his nomination for the presidency. New England would never vote for a confessed adulterer.

"I have not yet seen Hamilton's pamphlet," Jefferson wrote John Taylor in high spirits in the fall of 1797, "but I understand that, finding the strait between Scylla and Charybdis too narrow for his steerage he has preferred running plump into one of them." Jefferson never believed that Hamilton was financially dishonest, but he pointed out to Taylor that the retired Secretary of the Treasury had certainly laid himself open to suspicions: "his willingness to plead guilty as to the adultery seems rather to have strengthened than weakened the suspicion that he was in truth guilty of the speculation."

This John Taylor of Caroline County was already an intellectual leader among Virginia Republicans. Brought up in the law by his cousin, Edmund Pendleton, Jefferson's friend and admired opponent in many an argument over the principles of English law and American government in the early days of independence, Taylor was a man of highly original cast of mind. Jefferson loved and respected Edmund Pendleton. Now he was finding in his protégé, whose wits had been sharpened by the old lawyer's rigorous training, a worthy contestant on constitutional problems. Taylor and Jefferson had another enthusiasm in common; they were both experimenting with the new agriculture. Even more than Jefferson, Taylor considered himself as a planter first and foremost. In his copious correspondence with all the leading Republicans Taylor's analytic intelligence was developing, couched in sarcastic and incisive phrases, the principles of what was to become the agrarian creed.

Jefferson believed that all the evils of government could be mitigated. Taylor never forgot the deep conflict of interest between the governors and the governed: "No one can be so weak to believe," he wrote to tease Monroe about his predicament with the Federalist administration, "that your letter to Logan" — the letter to Dr. George Logan which Pickering had intercepted — "or your purpose to amuse yourself scribbling about the affairs of France, were either of them offensive to the government; nor is it conceivable that they thought your successor could serve his country better with the French than you could. Your attempts to do this were your great error. You had not discovered a distinction between the government and the nation, which it is expected every executive man should clearly discern, and you had unluckily looked into your instructions for the true intent and meaning of your mission. An example therefore became necessary in order to teach diplomatic men the distinction betwen the public good and the will of the Government, and to inform them which they should cling to. You was therefore sacrificed."

While Jefferson, in the midst of his preoccupation with the details of farming and architecture that gave him so much pleasure, turned his experiences at the seat of government over in his mind, his correspondence with John Taylor became the repository of his frankest convictions. The theoretical framework of the practical Republican party, which was to give reality to at least some of the aspirations of 1776, was being put together in a fourway correspondence between Jefferson and Taylor and Madison and Monroe.

Jefferson was busy that summer. Besides superintending his farms and his nailery he was getting ready to build a domed roof over the Monticello house. In spite of his construction work he kept enough rooms in condition to receive Madison and Monroe and their families.

Monroe came, bringing along his mass of records and diplomatic correspondence, seeking the peace of the Albemarle countryside and planning to settle permanently in the cottage Jefferson had designed for him at Ash Lawn within sight of Monticello. Monroe was burning with a sense of outrage; he could hardly wait to turn the tables on his tormentors. He was at work on his *View of the Executive.*

A procession of political visitors climbed Jefferson's steep road. On court days in August Charlottesville filled up with Republican leaders. Jefferson had given up trying to evade his responsibilities as leader of the Republican party. He had entered into a contest in which defeat was unthinkable.

His political discussions did not keep him away from his drafting board. He was advising the Madisons on the proportions of the classical portico they were adding to Montpellier. He was at work on plans for a house for the Randolphs at Edgehill. He even had a scheme to rebuild his father's old house at Shadwell which burned when he was a very young man. At the same time he was remodeling Pantops, his plantation across the valley from Monticello, for his daughter Polly.

Maria, as he called her since she had grown to young womanhood, was engaged to marry a son of the Eppes family of Eppington to which Jefferson and the wife he had never ceased mourning were linked by lifelong affection. Jack Eppes was a cousin on her mother's side. He was one of the many young men whose education Jefferson had supervised. This marriage filled Jefferson with delight. Like Martha's, it would link the family closer and add a son to the "antediluvian patriarch's" huge household.

After the bride and groom and the wedding guests had departed, the need to drive through the reroofing of the house before winter set in kept Jefferson so long at Monticello that it was December 4 and Congress had been several weeks in session before he took the road for Philadelphia. He found very little to please him at the seat of government.

John Adams had agreed with Hamilton on the need for a new mission to France. While they waited for news from the two men he had sent overseas to join in General Pinckney's interrupted negotiation with the Directory the two houses of Congress were marking time.

Adams had picked Elbridge Gerry, the Marblehead fish merchant, a fussy dapper little man for whom Jefferson felt more affection than respect, to represent the Republican interest on his commission extraordinary. To represent Virginia he had lit on John Marshall, who was George Washington's favorite among the rising Federalists of his home state. Jefferson rated Marshall a man of ability but he distrusted his ambition and disliked the authoritarian bent of his mind. To Jefferson it looked as if the purpose of the mission were rather to make war than to make peace.

Communication with Europe was always faulty in winter. As ship after ship entered the Delaware without news from the negotiators, but with ever fresh accounts of the spoliation of American commerce by the French in the West Indies and of captures of American ships, the Federalists in the House amused themselves with preparations to impeach William Blount for treason.

They were itching for a show of force. They were getting ready to treat the Republicans in America as Pitt was treating them in England. Already a federal judge had stirred up a grand jury to bring an indictment for criminal libel against one of the Cabells, who was representing Jefferson's own district in the House of Representatives, for calumnies "against the happy government of the United States" in a letter to his constituents.

As he watched the Federalists hardening their hearts against the constitutional guarantees in the Bill of Rights, Jefferson sat bored and discouraged in the chair of the Senate. "We are lounging our time away,'" he wrote his daughter Martha, "doing nothing and having nothing to do. it gives me great regret to be passing my time so uselessly when it could have been so importantly employed at home . . . Nor are we relieved by the pleasures of society here. for partly from bankruptcies, partly from party dissentions, society is torn up by the roots."

Although the moneymen were triumphant pclitically, the speculators among them were in the grip of a financial panic. Bonaparte's successes, shipping losses due to Pitt's blockade of France and the Directory's counterblockade on the high seas, combined with the failure of the Bank of England, had brought dire consequences to the Federalist magnates in America. Money was tight. Western lands were not selling. Bankruptcies were increasing. Associate Justice James Wilson of the Supreme Court, whose level head and constitutional learning had been the mainstay of popular sovereignty in the 1787 convention, had let his mania for speculating in land wreck his career. Having fled from his creditors in Philadelphia, he was dying penniless at Justice Iredell's house in North Carolina crying out in his delirium that he was being hunted like a beast.

Washington's lifelong friend Robert Morris, who as Financier was the most powerful man in America and reputed the richest, was forced to sell the unfinished marble hulk of the palace L'Enfant was building him at such enormous cost on Chestnut Street and to retire to his famous country place across the Schuylkill where he was besieged by bailiffs out to arrest him for debts mounting into the millions. His partners in a grandiose scheme to corner the lots in the federal city had either fled the country or landed in jail. In New York and Philadelphia the debtors' prisons were again filling up with ruined men.

The business depression made partisan differences bitterer than ever. According to their politics men blamed their troubles on the bludgeoning British or on the murderous French. Each side claimed its political opponents were in the pay of the enemy. The imminent breakup of the Union was already the subject of private conversation. Hamilton in New York and Jefferson in Philadelphia were having to exert all their influence over their respective followers to keep them from calling publicly for secession.

Uriah Tracy, the senator from Connecticut who had been assigned the job of answering Monroe's attack on Federalist foreign policy, spoke for many of the leaders of the commercial oligarchy in New England when he wrote excitedly to Hamilton: "The southern part of

the union is increasing by frequent importation of foreign scoundrels"
— he meant the Irish who were fleeing their embattled isle in greater
numbers than ever before — "as well as by those of home manufacture . . . in both Houses of Congress the Northern States will soon be
swallowed up & the name & real character of an American soon be
known only as a thing of tradition." He considered "a separation" —
from the slaveholding South — "absolutely necessary to preserve our
independence, in a part, which could not be done united. We are
really so different in manners & in opinion and in activity & *exertion.*"
As he put it, "the northern states were carrying the southern on their
backs." Hamilton's cure for these admitted ills, so he told his corre-
spendents, was a stronger central government.

At the same time Jefferson was arguing with his supporters to the
southward. John Taylor was broaching plans for the establishment of
a separate southern confederacy. "It is true that we are completely under the saddle of Massachusetts and Connecticut and that they ride
us very hard, cruelly insulting our feelings as well as exhausting our
strength and substance," Jefferson wrote him from Philadelphia; "the
body of our countrymen," he insisted, "is substantially republican
through every part of the Union. it was the irresistable influence and
popularity of General Washington, played off by the cunning of Hamilton, which turned the government over to anti-republican hands . . .
he delivered it over to his successor in this state, and very untoward
events, since improved with great artifice, have produced on the public mind the events which we see; but still, I repeat it, this is not the
natural state."

Jefferson had come to agree with Madison that party dissensions,
instead of being an unmitigated disaster, as he would have thought
them a few years back, were a vital part of the machinery of selfgovernment. "In every free and deliberating society there must, from
the nature of man, be opposite parties and violent dissentions and
discords," he explained to Taylor. "but, if, on a temporary superiority
of the one party, the other is to resort to a scission of the Union, no
federal government can ever exist. if to rid ourselves of the present
rule of Massachusetts and Connecticut we break the Union, will the
evil stop there? suppose the New England States alone cut off, will
our natures be changed? . . . immediately we shall see a Pennsylvania
and a Virginia party arise in the residuary confederacy, and the public
mind will be distracted with the same party spirit . . . seeing therefore
that an association of men that will not quarrel with one another is a
thing which never yet existed, from the greatest confederacy of nations to a town meeting or a vestry, seeing that we must have somebody to quarrel with, I had rather keep our New England associates
for that purpose than to see our bickerings transferred to others.

"They are marked like the Jews," he added in a jocular tone, "with such a peculiarity of character as to constitute from that circumstance the natural division of our parties. a little patience and we shall see the reign of the witches pass over, their spells dissolve, and the people, recovering their true sight, restore the government to its true principles. it is true that in the meantime we are suffering deeply in spirit . . . but who can say what would be the evils of a scission and when and where they would end. better keep together as we are, haul off from Europe as soon as we can, and from all attachments to any portions of it. and if we feel their power just sufficiently to hoop us together, it will be the happiest situation in which we can exist. if the game runs sometimes against us at home we must have patience till the luck turns, and then we shall have the opportunity of winning back the *principles* we have lost, for this is a game where principles are the stake."

While Jefferson sat presiding over the Senate, cut off from immediate political activity by the impotence of his office, he pondered the behavior of the politicians about him. What he saw and heard jarred indeed on the ideal of government by passionless men oblivious of anything but the public good which had fired him in the ardent early days of the Continental Congress. He knew already he could never urge them on all the way to his great goals. His youth was far behind him. The question for a man of his age was how much could he accomplish that was worth while with the refractory materials that came to his hand.

He was fiftyfour, a longlimbed loosejointed man in what was considered late middle age. People claimed that he was a careless dresser. He usually wore a plain dark longtailed coat and buff breeches. Powder was going out among the Republicans. His sandy hair was combed loosely back and tied in a cue behind his head. Political opponents claimed he never looked straight at them when he addressed them. In the Senate he spoke without gestures and made his rulings in a low, barely audible voice.

He still could not abide criticism. He had never got used to the personal spite he saw in the faces of those who disagreed with him. It still pained him that notwithstanding his patiently contrived attitude of political neutrality he could not utter a sentence without its being torn to pieces in the press. Critics swarmed about him like hornets.

Luther Martin, whom Jefferson referred to humorously among his friends as the Federalist bulldog, led the pack. That most intemperate of debaters was filling the Maryland newspapers with columns of abuse on account of a few words Jefferson had published years before in his *Notes on Virginia*. In denying Buffon's claims as to the incapacity and degeneracy of the American Indians, he had cited as a proof of their oratorical gifts a speech a Mingo chief named Logan made to Lord Dunmore which was much quoted in the gazettes during the last years of colonial rule. Logan had been the white man's friend until a group of whites murdered his family in an unprovoked attack.

In cadences which the schoolmasters compared to Cicero and Demosthenes at their best, Logan told why he had waged bloody war against them. ". . . I had even thought to have lived with you but for the injuries of one man. Col. Cresap, the last spring, in cold blood, and unprovoked, murdered all the relations of Logan, not sparing even my women and children. There runs not a drop of my blood in the veins of any living creature. This called on me for revenge; I have sought it: I have killed many: . . . who is there to mourn for Logan? — Not one."

This Michael Cresap had become a man of power and prominence in western Maryland and along the Ohio and Luther Martin had married his daughter. Violently selfrighteous, and with a muleskinner's gift for abusive language, Martin set out to take Logan's charges against his fatherinlaw out of Jefferson's hide.

His articles were reprinted. Others joined in the hue and cry. *Notes on Virginia* became a sourcebook for Federalist vilification. The *Notes* betrayed the rational outlook of an experimental scientist. On that account Jefferson was denounced as an atheist in half the pulpits in the land. "O! that mine enemy would write a book! has been a well known prayer against an enemy," he wrote a friend in the West in almost comic dismay. "I had written a book, and it has furnished matter of abuse for want of something better."

Jefferson was refusing to let himself be lured into a public discussion, but at the same time he was privately collecting the mass of evidence proving the truth of Logan's charge which he added as an appendix to a later edition of *Notes on Virginia*. He was waiting with invincible optimism for the tide to change. The time to refute his tormentors had not yet come. Meanwhile he was using exaggerated precautions to keep his name out of the newspapers. "It is hardly necessary to caution you," he added in a P.S. to John Taylor, "to let nothing of mine get before the public. a single sentence got hold of by the Porcupines will suffice to abuse and persecute me in the newspapers for months."

Just at the moment when it seemed that the Republicans' luck might be turning, when it seemed that the chilly reception of the taxes on land and houses and slaves and of a tax on transactions similar to the famous stamp tax that had brought revolutionary ardor to a boil thirty

years before might cause Congress to pause and consider, there occurred some events which Jefferson referred to as very untoward, to
throw all the power of popular indignation behind the Federalist
policies.

10. The Commission Extraordinary

        In mid-February of 1798 Jefferson dined with John Adams.
The President from the head of the table had been deploring high
rentals and the exorbitant wages that were being paid for labor; they
had managed to agree in blaming the high cost of living on the inflation of paper money that resulted from the Hamiltonian policies Wolcott was pursuing in the Treasury; the President went off into one of
his favorite tirades about the need for a permanent Senate. It is possible that Jefferson put up an argument on that point, tactfully to be
sure, because he knew how easy it was to send his old friend off into a
pet; he reported in his notes that Adams closed the conversation by
declaring in his oracular way that anarchy did more mischief in one
night than tyranny in an age. The President was overwrought. Jefferson could see he had something on his mind.

Four days later President Adams delivered a bitter message to
Congress reporting an affront to his envoys in France. Messrs. Wolcott
and Pickering had received the first dispatches from John Marshall
in Paris and had passed them on to the President with unfeigned satisfaction. Here were "untoward events" which would brand republicanism with infamy. Adams' whole stubby rotund frame swelled with
indignation.

John Marshall, whose personal popularity had acquired him the
title of General in the Virginia militia, had joined General Pinckney
in Amsterdam. There they received encouraging news. Talleyrand,
who had been on such good terms with Hamilton and Rufus King in
New York, and Henry Knox's partner in land speculations in the forests of Maine, was foreign minister to the Directory. The September
coup d'état by which Bonaparte's friends had seized supreme power
in France, through the simple expedient of arresting all the members
of the legislature who voted against them, had changed the personnel
of the Paris ministries. Through the machinations of Madame de
Staël's salon, Talleyrand had established a foothold in the government.
Even though it was the peace faction in the Directory that had been
defeated it was hoped that the ci-devant bishop would listen to reason.
Driving down through Belgium and northern France, Generals Mar-

shall and Pinckney marveled at the high state of cultivation of the countryside since the peasants had taken advantage of the political confusion to make themselves the owners of the fields they worked. Their first impression of Paris was of hands held out for the pourboire. They settled themselves in their lodgings and waited for an invitation to call at the foreign office. Meanwhile they were besieged by the skippers of American ships interned by the French.

A few days later Eldridge Gerry appeared in Paris from Rotterdam. He was full of his adventures on the journey. He had sprained his ankle going aboard ship and had suffered from an infected finger by pricking it with the pin of his stock. The crossing was stormy. They rigged ropes in his cabin so that he could limp about. He just missed capture by a French privateer supposed to be cruising for the American envoys in order to carry them off to the West Indies. In the Channel his vessel was threatened by a British patrolboat. He was astounded at the density of the European population; jingling in his post chaise through the Low Countries and into France, he passed through twenty cities and an untold number of villages.

Although Gerry did not think much of the lodgings his fellow envoys had picked he was enjoying the adventure. "The Ministers of the U.S. are under one roof, have separate tables, families and carriages and live sociably," he wrote Mrs. Gerry. General Pinckney, who had his daughter with him, had appropriated to himself the grands appartements aux premier. Gerry and Marshall had to be content with a bedroom and parlor each, barely furnished and without carpets. The chimneys smoked, "& to complete my happiness there was a stable underground." In the night Gerry was startled by loud noises that sounded like someone trying to break through the wall. He slept with a pair of pistols under his pillow.

His first morning in Paris the envoys extraordinary and plenipotentiary were serenaded. "The morning after my arrival I was waited on by the musicians of the supreme executive and the succeeding morning by a deputation of *Poissardes* or fishwomen for presents." They demanded fifteen or twenty guineas from each of the ministers. With the help of Major Rutledge the secretary," so Gerry wrote Mrs. Gerry, "I avoided the kind caresses of these ladies and an interview with the gentlemen"; but the fishwomen smothered his colleagues with "their delicate kisses."

A few days later the envoys dressed in their best; Elbridge Gerry and General Pinckney adjusted their wigs; John Marshall combed out his untidy dark hair; and they drove out in state to call on the Minister for Foreign Affairs, whose offices, they discovered, were in the state apartments of his home. They found the Portuguese ambassador waiting in Talleyrand's lobby. When the Citizen Minister came out to see them he appeared strangely preoccupied. He was preparing a report on American affairs. Everything was very difficult. President Adams had said things in a speech; the Citizen Directors were angry. When the Americans spoke of presenting their credentials in form Talleyrand stalled them off. He would see that they were furnished with guest cards. They could remain in Paris as guests. He would advise them on what steps to take. They returned crestfallen to their lodgings. Days passed.

While the three envoys waited they entertained themselves with the sights of the autumnal city, the picture galleries and the opera and the parks and public walks filled with incroyables and merveilleuses in astonishing garb modeled on the antique as seen through the canvases of the painter David. John Marshall took a certain partisan satisfaction in noting in his letters to Washington that in this great center of the hopes of the world's republicans there was neither liberty of the press nor of assembly nor liberty of any kind. The envoys were beginning to suffer from that unhappy sensation of being cut off from the life about them so common to foreigners among the Parisians, when they were called upon at their hotel in rapid succession by a number of gentlemen and by at least one lady. Their visitors gave every evidence of sympathizing with their plight.

First it was a Swiss gentleman, a banker by the name of Hottinger. He explained with gesticulation of upspread palms that the personal feelings of the Citizen Directors had been hurt by the tone of President Adams' addresses to Congress. He intimated slyly that since the news of the defeat of their allies, the Dutch, in the North Sea there might be ways of inducing the Directors to moderate their indignation. The loss of the Dutch fleet was a setback for the French. After dinner, with shrugs and nods he let fall a remark about "something for the pocket." He rubbed his thumb and forefinger together significantly. He mentioned the sum of 1,200,000 livres, a mere £50,000 sterling, he pointed out. It had been the custom of ambassadors to make presents to the kings of France: diplomatic usage. The Directors in their antique togas were investing the victorious republic with all the attributes of royal sovereignty. The Portuguese ambassador had seen it to his advantage to offer a large sum. The Americans pretended not to understand.

Next day Citizen Hottinger turned up early in John Marshall's parlor in the company of a Citizen Bellamy, whom he introduced as a Genoese. They had with them a copy of John Adams' speech. They rolled their eyes and tapped on the paper with their forefingers and shook their heads lugubriously. Breakfasting together in private in Gerry's quarters, the three puzzled Americans talked the situation over. They were dumbfounded. Marshall and Pinckney insisted that they should not negotiate with anybody until they had been accredited in due form. Gerry urged no precipitation.

The day the signing of Bonaparte's peace with the Austrian Emperor was announced, while the distant boom of cannon fired in celebration still resounded through the city, Citizen Bellamy seized the moment when Pinckney and Gerry were at the opera to call on John Marshall, who may have appeared to him to be the most rustic and gullible of the envoys. Bellamy took a threatening attitude. He read Marshall the clauses of the treaty imperial Austria had submitted to. He told of Bonaparte's preparations to invade England. The Directory was intensifying the blockade by ordering the capture of every neutral vessel with English goods aboard. Marshall put him off by saying he would consult his colleagues. Next day Hottinger found the three envoys together. John Marshall began to talk of the wrongs suffered by American shipping. Hottinger was pained; how could the Americans be so thickheaded? "Gentlemen," he pleaded, "you do not speak to the point; it is money; it is expected that you will offer money."

General Pinckney's face was red to the jowls. "No, not a sixpence," he roared.

Hottinger shook his head. He was patient. He was dealing with forward children. He introduced the gentle word "douceur." He became confidential. Merlin de Douai, he whispered, wanted no part of the money; the French privateersmen had him in their pay. But the other Directors and their dear friend Talleyrand, who had so many intimates in America and was only too anxious to be of service . . . The free city of Hamburg had paid handsomely for terms. The Americans paid subsidies to the Algerines and even to the wild redskins, did they not? "Nothing," he announced firmly as he took up his hat to leave, "can be obtained here without money."

The day following a Citizen Hauteval most considerately took Gerry for a private call on Talleyrand. After cooling their heels for an hour they found the Minister for Foreign Affairs in a testy mood. The Directors were furious. They would require a disavowal by President Adams of the wounding remarks he had made in his speech. A substantial loan, said Talleyrand, might repair the insult to the French Republic. Gerry tried to make him laugh by suggesting that a million livres was a rather high price to pay for seeing the plays and operas of Paris, but if that were paid, he went on to ask, would that mean that the captured vessels would be released? Talleyrand shook his head. Gerry left him with the remark that though they would certainly have to consult their home government perhaps the Americans would not mind spending a little money if it would result in a really friendly spirit in France.

At Gerry's breakfast table Bellamy and Hottinger brought the matter up again. This time they took high ground. Bellamy threatened the United States with the fate of Venice. Bonaparte had sent the Venetian senate packing earlier in the year and taken over the republic. England was ruined, Bellamy said. Bonaparte had an expedition of a hundred and fifty thousand men ready to overturn the British throne. The French party in America would rise at a word. The American envoys had better come to terms while they could. Otherwise, he hinted, things might turn out unpleasantly for the envoys themselves. Hottinger was more conciliating: if they paid the douceur of £50,000 the foreign minister might arrange for one of them to remain in Paris while the other two sailed to American to consult their government about the loan. Bellamy came out with an ultimatum: The Americans had eight days to make up their minds. The Directors were preparing an arrêté on American affairs that would not be to their taste. It could still be avoided, but once an arrêté was signed, it would be unchangeable.

After a few days' consideration John Marshall and General Pinckney announced that they would have no further conversations with anyone until they were officially accredited as ministers of the free and independent republic of the United States. John Marshall, who was gradually taking the lead, retired to his parlor to prepare a formal letter to Talleyrand outlining the American case.

Late in November Marshall and Gerry moved from their uncomfortable quarters to the elegant hôtel of Madame de la Villette on the left bank of the Seine. There Gerry for twelve French guineas a month installed himself in the suite the British ambassador had occpied. John Marshall, Gerry wrote Mrs. Gerry with some satisfaction, had only three rooms on the ground floor. Marshall wrote home that his quarters were delightful and that he was enjoying the conversation of his charming landlady. This Madame de la Villette had been brought up in Voltaire's château at Ferney on the Lake of Geneva. Voltaire spoke of her as "la belle et la bonne" and considered her his adopted daughter. Her house had been his home in Paris during his last years. Although she was a lady of the purest morals and très religieuse she was said to burn a grain of incense before the dead philosopher's bust in her boudoir every day.

Late in December, after further refusals by Marshall and Pinckney to carry on any negotiations until their credentials were received, and a flat refusal by Gerry, when he was cornered by Hottinger and Bellamy in Talleyrand's own dining room, to hand over any douceur, a new figure appeared on the scene.

Caron de Beaumarchais, the first advocate of the American cause in the early days of the sixteenth Louis' reign; the gay intriguer who had used the mask of Roderique Hortalez et Cie. to ship the Americans their first munitions and had made himself a fortune in the process; the impudent dramatist who had lampooned the old regime with his *Figaro* and whose own life had been as full of rascally plots and counterplots as his plays, was the epitome of everything most pro American in the old regime. He had escaped with his life by a hair's breadth in the September massacres, he had slipped out from under a denunciation by Robespierre, he had wormed his way out of King's Bench prison and from the dungeons of the German despots. Now he was back in Paris, trying to get his proscription as an émigré erased from the rolls, trying to get his fine house and gardens at the entrance to the faubourg Saint Antoine restored to him and to rebuild his publishing house at Kehl on the Rhine from which had emanated the first great collected editions of Voltaire and Rousseau. He was an old man. His claim for compensation for his losses mounted into the millions. One of these millions he claimed was still owed him by the American states. Talleyrand, who during his own exile had played the whole gamut of claims and speculations in America, cannot have been ignorant of the fact that the lawyer who was pressing Beaumarchais' claim for a million livres tournois against the Virginia Commonwealth in Richmond was none other than the lanky and rustic appearing John Marshall.

Beaumarchais, in his sixtyseventh year still the wittiest, the most delightful of men, dined with the Americans. After dinner Bellamy appeared and whispered in their ears that from his love of America and his ardent desire for peace the generous Beaumarchais was willing to forget his grievances against the United States. If £50,000 were turned over to Talleyrand he would abate his claim by that amount. Marshall and Pinckney answered shrewdly that if the decrees against American shipping were withdrawn they would see what they could do. Beaumarchais explained sadly that payment must come from the Americans first. "France," he explained, "considers herself sufficiently powerful to give the law to the world, and exacted from all around her . . . money . . . to finish the war against England." Talleyrand called for some proof of friendship; he declared himself hurt that Marshall and Pinckney would not call on him as private individuals. Gerry called continually but rarely had found him in.

The Americans had been in Paris for months. Their tempers were wearing thin. Marshall and Pinckney had a number of altercations with Gerry, who claimed that Marshall particularly was too suspicious. Gerry claimed they should hold out the possibility of a loan. "I told him," Marshall declared in his journal, "that my judgement was not

more perfectly convinced that the floor was wood, or that I stood on
my feet and not on my head, than that our instructions would not
permit us to make the loan."

The Directors had already lost patience. Marshall and Pinckney
were handed their passports. Marshall was subjected to the special
humiliation of being forced to apply through his consul for his safe
conduct as a private citizen. Talleyrand sent word privately that
Gerry, who seemed a good republican, might be able to accomplish
something by staying. "We shall both be happy if by remaining without us Mr. G. can negotiate a treaty which shall preserve the peace
without sacrificing the independence of our country," was Marshall's
entry in his journal. When he got home he told a different story. Pinckney was allowed to take his daughter to the South of France for her
health before leaving the country, but Marshall had to clear out on
twentyfour hours' notice, without being given time to lay in a stock
of wine as he had intended or to get his foul linen washed.

Gerry did not leave till early August, 1798, after John Adams had dis-
patched the brig *Phoebe* with orders to bring him home. The day he
went on board he received a copy, from the hands of Talleyrand, of a
fresh arrêté of the Directors, which somewhat mitigated the harsh
measures against American shipping. He reached home convinced that
war with the United States was the last thing the French wanted.

The dispatches of the three envoys, mostly from John Marshall's
persuasive pen, arrived in Philadelphia before them. They furnished
Messrs. Wolcott and Pickering with the pretext for an explosion of
righteous indignation. Between them they dressed up the story into
an international mystery by designating the agents of corruption as
W X Y and Z.

John Marshall was no scholar in international law but he was a
debater of unparalleled skill who never missed an opportunity to put
his opponent in the wrong. He presented the Federalist case in clear
and compelling language. His eloquence carried the President off his
feet. Here was justification for all the doubts John Adams had been so
abused for expressing as to the efficacy of popular rule. Here was an
instance of highhanded corruption which would damn democracy
forever. He transmitted the X Y Z dispatches to Congress with a
hightoned message calling for all defensive measures short of war.
John Marshall's arguments were reprinted in every newspaper in the
country.

In reply to the addresses from indignant patriots that every postrider brought into Philadelphia the Republicans could only mumble
that there must be some mistake; the commissioners had been taken
in by swindlers. Even good Republicans were forgetting to dwell on

their wrongs at England's hands in the face of this insult from the French.

Atrocity stories abounded. A Baltimore skipper had been taken on board a French cruiser and tortured with thumbscrews to make him admit his cargo was owned in England and therefore contraband. Francis Hopkinson's son wrote patriotic words to "The President's March." In every tavern they were singing "Hail, Columbia." In Philadelphia young men stuck Washington's black cockade in their hats and scoured the streets for Jacobins. The Republicans retorted by flaunting the tricolor. Rival gangs fought in the alleys. For a whole day peaceable men did not dare venture out of doors.

Congress immediately passed an act permitting merchant ships to arm for their own defense. The old treaties with France were abrogated and the exequaturs of the French consuls revoked. To take some of the load off McHenry's shoulders a navy department was established to speed the completion of the six frigates that had been authorized years before. A marine corps was established. An act was passed authorizing the President to raise a provisional army of ten thousand men and to appoint a lieutenant general and three major generals to officer it.

John Adams appointed Benjamin Stoddert, an industrious and farsighted Maryland shipowner who had built up a large import and export business at Georgetown in the federal district, as Secretary of the Navy. Stoddert went immediately to work to improvise a fleet.

Two frigates, the *United States* in Philadelphia and the *Constitution* in Boston, had already left the ways. Their hulls had been designed by a Philadelphia shipbuilder named Joshua Humphreys at the time of the threatened war with the Algerine pirates. Humphreys was determined, since he felt the Americans would never be rich enough to compete in number of ships with the navies of Europe, to build menofwar that could outshoot and outsail anything afloat. His frigates were longer and broader and lay lower in the water than any ships sailed by the British or the French. They were of unusually sturdy construction. Their timbers were liveoak and red cedar. Humphreys poured the experience and skill of a hundred years of American shipbuilding into the new frigates to make them the fastest and most maneuverable ships on the sea. So seriously did they take their work that his carpenters almost killed Ben Bache, the editor of the Francophile *Aurora*, when he went on board the *United States* to take a look.

Every shipyard on the coast resounded with the hammer and the adze. Seasoned skippers like John Barry who had made his fame on the *Alliance* during the Revolutionary War, and the old Commodore Nicholson's younger brother, and Thomas Truxtun the privateersman, and the elder Decatur were speeding construction with an

impatient eye, spoiling to take their ships into battle. American seamen had been raised as privateers and blockade runners. They re-
joiced at the chance of turning the tables on their tormentors. As soon
as the necessary authorization went through Congress the *Ganges*, a
converted East Indiaman of 24 guns, slipped out between the capes
of the Delaware to patrol the coast. In every port merchantmen were
mounting cannon. As fast as they were gunned and manned the
frigates left port to scour the Caribbean sea lanes.

When Truxton early in the following winter overhauled the crack
French frigate *Insurgente* off Nevis and to the dismay of her captain,
who had orders to avoid combat with the Americans, forced him to
fight, he shot her rigging full of holes and captured her after an hour
and a quarter's engagement. The French suffered heavy losses, but
the Americans had only one man killed, a waverer whom the lieutenant had to run through with his sword when he left his station on
deck. From then on the *Insurgente* sailed the Atlantic under the Stars
and Stripes. The flag with the sixteen stars began to be treated with
respect by the seafarers of the world. Not only at home but abroad,
Humphreys' low long frigates proved a turning point in naval architecture. The thrifty shipowners of New England were remarking that
the drop in insurance rates alone had more than made up for the ten
millions the taxpayers had to spend on their fleet.

11. *Silence and Patience*

While the Federalists were securing popular support for their
foreign policy by the energy and efficiency with which they went to work
to fit out a fleet, they prepared to move against their enemies at home.
They rushed a bill through Congress tightening the requirements for
naturalization. They launched another giving the President the power
to deport aliens at his discretion. More violent measures were to come.

"They have brought into the lower house a sedition bill," Jefferson
wrote Madison early in June of 1798, "which among other enormities,
undertakes to make printing certain matters criminal, tho' one of the
amendments to the Constitution has so expressly taken religion, printing presses &c out of their coertion. Indeed this bill & the alien bill
both are so palpably in the teeth of the Constitution as to shew they
mean to pay no respect to it."

Republican members of Congress were leaving for home in despair
of bucking the fury of the Federalist majority. Some like William
Branch Giles resigned their seats and stood for election in the state
legislatures. The state legislatures were to be the last bulkhead against

the high Federalist tide. It was a tactic in which Madison and Burr had led the way. Burr was already busy in the lower house in New York. It would not be long before Madison would be forced to give up those delights of private life all the politicians of the time made so much of to lead the Republican element in the Virginia Assembly.

Jefferson was not too happy about this strategy at first. He complained to Madison that, had it not been for the absence of so much of the leadership, a Republican move to adjourn Congress before any more harm was done would have succeeded. He now felt so hopelessly in the minority, he told Madison, that he had ordered his horses to wait for him at Fredericksburg and would be arriving at Montpellier before the end of the month. No more than during the expulsion of Blount of Tennessee did he intend to give his sanction to highhanded proceedings in the Senate by presiding over them: "For the present . . . nothing can be done," he explained. "Silence and patience are necessary for a while; and I must pray you, as to what I now write, to take care it does not get out of your own hand, nor a breath of it in a newspaper."

Meanwhile Jefferson's Quaker friend and fellow member of the Philosophical Society, George Logan, had come after much earnest mediation to the decision that he must act on his convictions. As a member of Quaker meeting he abhorred war. The inner voice was telling him that it was his personal and private duty to go to France himself to try to restore peace. He sold a farm to raise money for the journey. Quite aware of the risk he was taking, he made over his property to his wife, just in case Congress should see fit to attaint him in his absence, and quietly slipped out of the Delaware on a ship bound for Hamburg.

As credentials he carried a certificate of American nationality signed by Jefferson as Vice President and another from Thomas McKean, the Republican Chief Justice of Pennsylvania. When the news of his departure leaked out the Federalist press set up a clamor. "Can any sensible man hesitate to suspect," wrote Brown's *Pennsylvania Gazette*, "that his infernal design can be anything less than the introduction of a French Army, *to teach us the genuine value of true and essential liberty* by reorganizing our government, through the brutal operation of the bayonet and guillotine. Let ever American now gird on his sword."

Dr. Logan conducted his selfappointed mission with the wisdom of the dove. His choice of the free city of Hamburg as a base of operations showed an understanding of the state of affairs in Europe. All through the French Revolution the old Hanseatic port was a neutral clearinghouse for diplomatic intrigue.

As soon as he arrived there he discovered that Lafayette, finally released at Bonaparte's insistence by the Austrian emperor from his long captivity, was nursing his sick wife at a country villa a few miles out of town. The faithful Adrienne had been allowed to join her husband in his dungeon at Olmütz. Prison had ruined her health. While the romantic nobleman looked amazedly about him at this undreamed scene of a continent dominated by the revolutionary France that had come into being during the years when he had been cut off from the light of day, he wrote George Washington in the old affectionate enthusiastic style. It never occurred to Lafayette that Washington would have come to dread his arrival in American more than the plague, and that the man he most revered in the world was writing Lafayette's own dear friend Hamilton for advice as to how to stave it off.

Dr. Logan lost no time in posting out to Lafayette's villa. The ci-devant marquis greeted the Quaker with all his old fervor for things American. With what nobler gesture could Lafayette reappear on the world stage than as peacemaker between his native land and the land of his adoption?

Lafayette was already in friendly communication with the authorities in Paris. He arranged for Dr. Logan's safe conduct and gave him a letter to Merlin de Douai, whom Lafayette had known as an expert on French feudal law in the days when the National Assembly was writing the first constitution, and who now had reached the pinnacle of power as one of the toga clad Directors. Thus armed, Dr. Logan drove to Paris. Though Joel Barlow and Fulwar Skipwith and other resident Americans gave him little encouragement, he managed skillfully to bypass Talleyrand and to get his letter directly into Merlin's hands. The august Director invited him to dinner and listened to what he had to say. The Quaker's arguments were so effective that he was able to take home with him the assurance that France did not want war with the United States and that a new mission would be received with honor.

The fact that Britain's one eyed and one armed Horatio Nelson was cruising the Mediterranean and threatening to cut off communication with Bonaparte's Army of Egypt may well have made the Directory think twice about raising themselves up a new enemy on the high seas. To prove their sincerity they lifted their embargo on a number of American ships in Atlantic ports and let a hundred American seamen out of jail. Meanwhile Cobbett in Philadelphia was calling for the pillory for Dr. Logan if he dared show his face again at the seat of government.

Before boarding the stages for Fredericksburg Jefferson drove out to Stenton to reassure Mrs. Logan. When he arrived there he told her that his movements were continually dogged by Federalist spies.

He had come by the most roundabout road he could find to throw his shadowers off the trail. Years later so good a Republican as Dr. Rush admitted shamefacedly that he had been carried away by the war spirit to the point of letting himself be talked into joining a secret committee set up to spy on the Logans.

Mrs. Logan had the Quaker firmness too. She was able to tell Jefferson that the grand old conservative John Dickinson, whose great wealth and standing in both Delaware and Pennsylvania made him proof against Federalist attacks, had sent word that he was watching over her. Levelheaded men of both parties were becoming aroused by the highhanded doings in Philadelphia.

The seat of government was in an uproar. The mail of prominent Republicans was intercepted. Republican congressmen were booed and insulted at the theater. Gangfighting between the black cockades and the red white and blue continued in the streets. In the House, Robert Goodloe Harper, the wildest of the warhawks, as Jefferson was calling them, was on his feet daily echoing the wildest declamations of Cobbett and the Federalist press. He was linking Dr. Logan's journey with Bache's publication in the *Aurora* of a conciliatory letter from Talleyrand as part of a Republican plot to introduce a French army into the country and to overturn the government. Treating as treasonable any correspondence with France, he kept hinting of more serious revelations to come.

At the height of the outcry against Dr. Logan's conspiracy news reached Philadelphia that John Marshall had disembarked in New York from the good ship *Alexander Hamilton*.

"I had supposed to have set out on the 20th," Jefferson wrote Madison, "but on the morning of the 19th we heard of the arrival of Marshall at New York and I concluded to stay & see if that circumstance produced any new projects. no doubt he there received more than hints from Hamilton as to the tone required to be assumed. yet I apprehend he is not hot enough for his friends. Livingston" — Edward Livingston, the Republican congressman from New York — "came with him. M told him they had no idea in France of a war with us."

Jefferson went on to describe John Marshall's reception as a conquering hero: "M was received here with the utmost éclat. the Secretary of State" — longfaced baldheaded Timothy Pickering — "& many carriages with all the city cavalry, went to Frankfort to meet him, and on his arrival here in the evening the bells rung till late in the night, & immense crowds were collected to see & make part of the shew, which was circuitously paraded through the streets before he was set down at the city tavern."

Jefferson called on Marshall next morning. Marshall was out. Jefferson left a note which afforded Marshall some amusement. He used to tell his friends that the wording read: "Thomas Jefferson presents his compliments to General Marshall. He had the honor calling at his lodgings twice this morning, but was so *lucky* as to find him out." Marshall made great sport of the fact that Jefferson had had to caret in a little *un* above the line to make the word *lucky* read *unlucky*.

Jefferson was explaining that "a pre-engagement would prevent him the satisfaction" of attending the public dinner which was being offered in General Marshall's honor that day but that he would very much like to talk to him privately. It was amid the cheers and shouts of that dinner that Marshall's name became linked with a toast offered on the occasion: "Millions for defense but not one cent for tribute." He was far too shrewd a man to let Jefferson get a word with him.

Although Jefferson and Marshall were cousins there were a dozen reasons why they could never agree. Their mothers were both of the Randolph blood, but Jefferson was born rich while Marshall was born poor. Jefferson cultivated a scholar's aloofness from the crowd while Marshall's great stock in trade as a lawyer and as a politician was the gladhanding philistinism of the man of the people. Though Jefferson believed in popular rule and Marshall did not, Marshall, like that other great trial lawyer old Patrick Henry, was adept at working on the prejudices of illeducated men. He played cards, he drank whiskey, he poked fun at booklearning and philosophy. When he ran for Congress from the Richmond district he was seen dancing with his supporters round a bonfire where they were burning the opposition tickets in front of the polling table.

Marshall's perennial disesteem of Jefferson had another source. His wife was Mary Ambler, the daughter of the Becky Burwell whom Jefferson had courted and had some falling out with during his student days at Williamsburg. Becky Burwell had married on the rebound into the Ambler family. The Amblers were of the group of tidewater magnates who never forgave Jefferson for his part in the repeal of the laws of entail and for his critical attitude towards slavery. Hatred of Jefferson was becoming a tradition in Tidewater. The Ambler girls almost split their sides over the story of Jefferson's running out of Monticello with Tarleton's troopers at his heels during his last days as governor of Virginia.

Marshall was one of a large family of brothers and sisters. Most of them made good marriages and achieved positions of wealth and power. His brother Thomas married Robert Morris's daughter Hester. As a lawyer John Marshall represented the Morris interests in Virginia. It was through Robert Morris's good offices that he and his brother, in somewhat occasional association with land crazy Henry

Lee, another enemy of Jefferson's, managed to purchase the Fairfax claim to a hundred and sixty thousand acres of valuable land in the Northern Neck. The Republicans in the legislature were the great stumbling block to the establishment of their claim. When Robert Morris went bankrupt, the Marshall brothers had to find money to meet scheduled payments or else lose their whole stake. John Marshall made no bones of the fact that it was this need for cash that induced him to accept the mission to France. Messrs. Wolcott and Pickering, while they were niggardly with Republicans, were openhanded with Federalists. Marshall came home from his excursion abroad some nineteen thousand dollars the richer.

The thought of any man's profiting by the public service offended Jefferson's fastidious sense of noblesse oblige. His influence furthermore had always been thrown behind the small landowners and sometimes even behind the squatters on unoccupied lands. They were the raw material for the ideal republic of his dreams. This was the yeomanry the Marshall brothers would have to dispossess if they succeeded in making good the Fairfax claim. The efficacy of that claim depended upon the carrying out by the courts of the terms of the Jay treaty which Jefferson had been so abused for denouncing in his letter to Mazzei. There was every reason why the two Virginians should be incompatible.

When Jefferson found there was no way of getting a private talk with John Marshall, in whose practical good sense he had confidence in spite of their political and temperamental differences, he turned over the chair of the Senate to a president pro tem and set off for home. He would spend the summer concocting with Madison and Monroe and Wilson Cary Nicholas and his other Virginia friends a set of measures aimed to counteract the dreadful results of what he called "the delusion of the people."

The strength of the Republicans was in the state legislatures. To defend the principles of selfgovernment he had to define the relationship between the states and the general government in the terms of his theory of statebuilding.

Before Jefferson left Philadelphia, Congress had passed a law barring American ships from the ports of France or of the French colonies in the West Indies. News of the passage of the Alien Act and the Sedition Act came posting after him. A whole set of new taxes was being levied. With George Washington's appointment to lead the provisional army the Federalists had managed, in spite of these unpalatable measures, once more to cloak themselves in the old general's mighty fame.

12. *"This damned army . . ."*

Though Washington was the figurehead Hamilton was the animating force behind the new army. Writing tirelessly to McHenry and Wolcott and Pickering from New York, he outlined every phase of its organization. This was how he came into collision with John Adams.

John Adams, a New Englander brought up at Braintree in the smell of the salt breezes, was all for a navy, but he felt much as Jefferson did about the danger of a standing army. Congress had authorized him to appoint a lieutenant general and three major generals to muster a provisional force. He intended it to remain provisional.

When Adams discussed nominations with Messrs. Wolcott and Pickering they all agreed that George Washington should have the top rank. In fact they were in such a hurry to appoint him commander in chief that they caused heartburnings at Mount Vernon by sending him his commission before asking him if he would accept it. The old general complained that his dignity had been slighted and the agreeable McHenry had to be sent off posthaste to the banks of the Potomac to explain.

Washington laid down as a condition of his acceptance that he should be allowed to choose his subordinates. Ever since the "warhawks" had started their turmoil in the halls of Congress he had been in constant communication with Hamilton. He and his old aide had agreed that the executive command should be in Hamilton's hands as inspector general and that Generals Knox and Charles Cotesworth Pinckney should rank immediately under him. Washington felt that Hamilton was the only man left from his old staff competent for the job.

Messrs. Wolcott and Pickering emphatically agreed. They felt that their associate McHenry, for all his engaging manners and literary tastes, lacked organizing drive. Hamilton, in spite of his affection for the discursive Baltimorean, was itching to take over his office. Even in peacetime the heads of departments Adams had inherited from Washington's cabinet were continually writing Hamilton for advice. Neither Wolcott nor Pickering had too much confidence in their own abilities. Without the prop of Hamilton's administrative skill and his ability to marshal men they dreaded the responsibility of waging war. "I wish you were in a situation not only 'to see all the cards' but to play them," Pickering wrote him, "with all my soul I would give you my hand."

President Adams already considered Hamilton, as he wrote of him later, "the most restless, impatient, artful, indefatigable and unprincipled intriguer in the United States if not in the world." John Adams' mind was at home in broad general ideas; in some ways he was a shrewd observer of men; but he had none of Washington's or Jefferson's aptitude for detail. He didn't like what his Secretaries were doing but he had not one idea in the world as to how to make a change. He disliked Wolcott's fiscal program because it was a continuation of Hamilton's but he had no alternative to offer in its place. He did almost come to a breaking point with Wolcott over the interest rate on the war loan. Wolcott was blandly insisting that nothing less than eight percent would attract the investments of the financial community. Adams held out as long as he could for six. When he finally gave in it was with a peevish explosion of temper. "All right," he cried, "I cannot help it. Issue your proposals as you please . . . This damned army will be the ruin of the country."

Adams yielded on the war loan but he refused to appoint Hamilton as a major general to outrank Pinckney and Knox. Knox, Pinckney, Hamilton; in that order they had ranked in the Continental Army. In that order he intended to write their commissions. When Messrs. Wolcott and Pickering tried to insist he ordered his carriage in a huff and went trundling off to Braintree with the commissions in his pocket.

Meanwhile Jefferson, back home in the Virginia foothills, had been consulting with Madison about how to go about instigating some statement which would shake people out of the delusions of what he was beginning to call "the year of X.Y.Z." Monroe was finding country life dull after the excitement of Parisian politics; he was itching to get back into the fray. John Taylor was still talking about secession. Wilson Cary Nicholas was often in the neighborhood and whenever he could find safe conveyance was in communication with his fat brother George, who was now a member of the Kentucky legislature. His friend James Breckinridge was its intellectual leader. Out of the unannounced meetings and messages exchanged with great privacy, because the Republican leaders were being very careful not to expose themselves to a trial for sedition at the hands of the catchpoles of the administration, grew the Kentucky Resolutions and the resolutions Madison drafted for the Virginia Assembly.

While Jefferson slaved over the wording of the resolutions Breckinridge was to introduce in Kentucky, he saw to the laying of the new floors in his house and superintended the installation of mantles and moldings in his drawing room and hall modeled in the delicate low relief the Adam brothers had made fashionable in England. The press of politics had forced him to postpone the complete reorganization of crop rotation he intended for his farm. He did take the time to refresh his spirits by copying out for an English etymologist the notes he made when he was a law student of a new and original scheme for the study of the Anglo-Saxon language.

The Sedition Law was proving highly effective in curbing the Republican press, but Jefferson was trusting to the reaction against it that was sure to come. Callender, whose publications had given a mortal wound to Hamilton's political aspirations, had taken refuge from the repressions of the Federalists in Richmond, where at least the courts were still willing to grant writs of habeas corpus, and wrote Jefferson begging for financial help. In a letter asking Stevens Thomson Mason to arrange the details of a handout of fifty dollars for Callender at Jefferson's expense, Jefferson described the political scene: "The X Y Z fever has considerably abated . . . and the alien & sedition laws are working hard. I fancy that some of the State legislatures will take strong ground on this occasion . . . I consider those laws as merely an experiment on the American mind, to see how far it will bear an avowed violation of the constitution. if this goes down we shall immediately see attempted another act of Congress declaring that the President shall continue in office during life, reserving to another occasion the transfer of the succession to his heirs, and the establishment of the Senate for life . . . that these things are in contemplation I have no doubt; nor shall I be confident of their failure, after the dupery of which our countrymen have shewn themselves susceptible."

The legislatures were the last line of defense for the principle of selfgovernment by the people. It was Jefferson's business to find arguments to bolster the states at this juncture. In the Kentucky Resolutions, which he hoped would eventually be introduced in a majority of the legislatures of the sixteen states Jefferson, in somewhat more drastic terms than Madison was to use in Virginia, laid down the proposition that there had never been any constitutional intent to unite the states on any principle of unlimited submission: "When the general government assumes undelegated powers its acts are unauthoritative and of no force." Therefore, he argued, acts of Congress which conflicted with constitutional provisions such as those forbidding arrest without due process of law or interference with the freedom of the press were automatically null and void. It should be the business of the state legislatures to declare them so. The electorate could take care of the abuse of delegated powers by the officers they elected to the general government, but in the case of the assumption of undelegated powers the proper recourse was nullification by the states.

Jefferson sent his resolutions off to Breckinridge with every precaution of secrecy. "The infidelities of the post office and the circumstances of the times are against my writing fully & freely," he wrote John Taylor, "while my own dispositions are as much against mysteries, innuendos & half-confidences. I know not which mortifies me most, that I should fear to write what I think, or my country bear such a state of things. yet Lyons' judges" — turbulent Matthew Lyon, the Vermont Irishman who represented his state in the House, had just been sent to prison for statements disrespectful to the President — "are objects of rational fear." These were dark days for Republicans.

Hamilton, meanwhile, was riding high in New York. He was General Hamilton now. His childhood ambition for military glory was being realized. He had virtually given up his law practice. On a citizen's committee with Aaron Burr he was at work on the fortification of the Narrows and Sandy Hook. He was telling McHenry it would be a good idea for McHenry to call him and Henry Knox immediately to Philadelphia to help reorganize the War Department. In that case, Hamilton suggested tactfully, he would have to start collecting his salary; he had a wife and six children and his law practice was shelved. (The President's delay in signing the commissions had held up the salaries of the general officers.) At the same time Hamilton was urging Messrs. Wolcott and Pickering, who were in full charge while Adams sulked at Braintree, to avoid a full scale war with France. He was for meeting force with force but he was opposed to reprisals.

Particularly he was urging moderation in the enactment of repressive legislation; "let us not be cruel or violent," he wrote Pickering. He felt that some of the provisions of the Sedition Law were "highly exceptionable." He feared they might lead to civil war. "Let us not establish a tyranny," he wrote Wolcott. "Energy is a very different thing from violence."

His Majesty's navy was giving the Federalists no help. Encouraged by Nelson's successes, British cruisers were harrying neutral shipping. The more condemnations the more prize money. "How vexatious," Hamilton wrote Rufus King in London, "that at such a juncture there should be officers of Great Britain who, actuated by a spirit of plunder, are doing the most violent things calculated . . . to furnish weapons to the enemies of government . . . The British cabinet must at this time desire to conciliate this country. It is to be hoped they will not want vigor to do it with effect."

While he kept insisting in his letters to Philadelphia that he must be second in command under Washington, and advising McHenry how to soothe Knox's hurt feelings, and writing daily letters to the old general outlining the immediate steps to be taken to comb the Cincinnati for good officers, he was carrying on a correspondence with Rufus King about a projected use of the provisional army far different from the defense against a French invasion which Congress had intended. Bonaparte's incredible victories had stirred up all the old boyhood dreams of military glory. King's letters were full of it too; even sensible Rufus King had fallen under the lyrical spell of Francisco Miranda's rhetoric.

That perennial liberator of the Spanish colonies was in communication with Pitt again. The ruin of Spanish sea power off Cape St. Vincent had laid open to British initiative a far more profitable enemy than the stubborn French. Godoy's infatuated policy of a French alliance, of which the first fruits for the United States had been the opening of the Mississippi, had exposed Spain's huge possessions, sprawling from the Mississippi to Cape Horn, to British raids. Miranda, irrepressible as ever, whose efforts to get French help for his revolutionary plans for Venezuela had almost cost him his head, turned to England again as soon as England's mastery of the seas became assured. He had had a sympathetic hearing and considerable hard cash from Pitt in times past.

Before Monroe's recall from Paris Monroe had suspected that something was brewing in that quarter and had sent his secretary, Burr's young stepson Prevost, to sound out the grandiloquent liberator on his plans. Miranda was suspicious; he had had his fill of republicanism. He was claiming that Monroe had become "a regular Marat." After refusing to talk to Prevost he wrote Hamilton telling him how he had evaded a Jacobin trap.

He managed to get himself expelled from France soon after and had made his way to England. There he was finding Pitt again willing to listen to his plans. Nelson's great victory over the French in the battle of the Nile had made Britain supreme on the seven seas. The opening of South American and Mexican ports to British ships would double Great Britain's foreign trade. It would be a source of specie for the Bank of England; it would pay the whole cost of the war with France. Pitt was definitely interested.

Anxious to engage his American friends in this dazzling enterprise, Miranda presented to Rufus King a scheme by which the Americans and British should outfit a joint expedition. The British would furnish the naval force and the Americans their new army under General Alexander Hamilton. At the sight of the great Miranda the Spanish colonists would rise as one man to throw off the hated yoke. While he organized the government — a "moderate" government, Hamilton advised — the British and Americans would share the commerce that had hitherto been a Spanish monopoly.

The project filled Hamilton's head with giddy dreams. ". . . I wish it much to be undertaken," he wrote King, "but I should be glad that the principal agency be in the United States — they to furnish the whole of the land force if necessary. The command in this case would very naturally fall upon me, and I hope I shall disappoint no favorable

anticipations . . . Are we yet ready for this undertaking? Not quite,"
he admitted; "but we ripen fast," he added hopefully.

The provisional army was not ripening as fast as George Washington would have liked. Procrastination at the seat of government was
allowing the spirit and enthusiasm of his officers to evaporate. He was
finding it impractical to try to raise an army while his headquarters
were in Virginia and his second in command was in New York. He
got little assistance from the administration. Messrs. Wolcott and
Pickering were not men of enough stature to transcend the routine of
their departments. McHenry was no organizer. The commander in
chief could not plan his chain of command until the question of precedence was solved among his major generals. Knox was refusing to
be outranked by Hamilton. Pinckney, who was bringing his ailing
daughter home from France by slow stages, had not yet arrived. From
President Adams at Braintree there came no news at all. Mrs. Adams
was ill.

To make matters worse, yellow fever broke out in Philadelphia.
The epidemic was even more severe than that of 1793. Thousands
died. The seat of government was abandoned to the Negroes and the
rats. The indomitable Dr. Rush, who by this time had become an
authority on the subject, moved patiently among the stricken and bled
them and dosed them with mercury and jalap. Very few survived.
Among the dead were John Fenno, who had aspired to a life of calm
respectability as the President's court printer, and young Ben Bache
of the reckless pen.

Messrs. Wolcott and Pickering moved their departments to Trenton.
When the cool October days came John Adams joined them there. He
explained the fact that he had made himself inaccessible for three
months by saying: "My dear Mrs. Adams has been at death's door."

It was at Trenton that Dr. Logan, after a prosperous return voyage
from the shores of France, found the President when he sought him
out to report his conversation with Merlin de Douai. He assured John
Adams, as had Elbridge Gerry, that the French government did not
want war with the United States. John Adams listened to him politely.
He seemed in a very good humor. When Dr. Logan suggested he send
a fresh mission he answered with a quizzical smile, "I suppose if I
were to send Mr. Madison or Mr. Giles or Dr. Logan they would
receive either of them. But I'll do no such thing. I'll send whom I
please."

"And whoever you do send will be received," Logan told him.

The earnest Quaker met with quite a different reception from the
Secretary of State. Peace with France was the last thing the high
Federalists wanted at that moment. Logan told his wife afterwards

that Pickering, who had lashed himself into believing that there was something treasonable about any communication with the French, had been extremely agitated, though not personally abusive, throughout their interview. "Sir it is my duty to inform you that the government does not thank you for what you have done," were his last words when he showed him the door.

The Federalist press raved against Logan. The polemical writers fastened on the fact that he had sailed with a passport from Jefferson. They went so far as to circulate a spurious memorial to the French government supposed to be Logan's work which Robert Goodloe Harper read out in the House. Immediately the Federalists introduced a bill making it a felony for any private citizen to take it upon himself to conduct negotiations with a foreign government. Their orators claimed that Jefferson was at the bottom of the business.

Jefferson, in the other hand, in a letter to the venerable Edmund Pendleton, who had come out with a manifesto against the unconstitutional Federalist measures, and whom he was trying to induce to write a pamphlet for general circulation giving a reasonable and understandable account of the XYZ business, disclaimed any part in Logan's mission: "From long acquaintance he knew my wishes for peace and my political sentiments generally, but he received no particular declaration of them nor one word of authority to speak in my name . . . it was an enterprise founded in the enthusiasm of his own character. he went on his own ground & made his own way. his object was virtuous, and the effect meritorious."

When Dr. Logan asked a clergyman who was a mutual friend to introduce him to Washington the old general treated him with all the studied rudeness of which he was capable. Washington wrote afterwards with some glee that he had affected not to know who the Quaker was, had neglected to offer him a chair and when he insisted on telling his story had not listened to a word of it. He was getting a little deaf anyway, and ever since they had pestered him with petitions on the abolition of slavery while he was President he had little use for the Quakers.

General Washington, tired of fretting and fuming at Mount Vernon, had traveled to Philadelphia to meet Hamilton as soon as the danger of the yellow fever abated. He took lodgings with a Mrs. White on Eighth Street and immediately plunged with all his old energy into setting the tangled command situation to rights.

His military family was around him again. The voluble accurate efficient Hamilton was at his elbow again to anticipate his every suggestion. The inspector general had come to the seat of government prepared to relieve his old commander in chief of all the tiresome paperwork, and of the important decisions too, if he would let him. Grizzled officers out of the Continental Army crowded in to salute their general with moist eyes.

Handsome General Pinckney had at last arrived from France and as usual did the handsome thing. He declared that he would serve in any capacity in which he could be useful and order of rank be damned. Henry Knox could hardly refuse to serve now, though he was so distracted with money troubles brought on by his land speculations that his work devolved on Hamilton; until after a couple of months' tenure he resigned his commission, a bankrupt in the hands of the bailiffs, and left Hamilton to cope with the artillery along with the other problems of the provisional army.

In picking their officers Washington and Hamilton had one criterion; none need apply "who are known enemies to their own gov't." To Washington that meant any critic of the Federalist administration. They turned down Aaron Burr, whose appointment would have conciliated many moderates in the middle states, as brigadier general — an intriguer, Washington called him — but gave a commission to that prince of intriguers James Wilkinson, whom even the easygoing McHenry could not stomach. Their refusal of a commission to one of the erudite Muhlenberg brothers who dominated the Lutheran Church resulted in the alienation of the whole Pennsylvania German vote from the Federalists. While they cultivated Charles Cotesworth Pinckney they neglected his cousin, the other Charles, in South Carolina. As Jefferson put it, the old general had lost the sound judgment that had characterized him all his life through. Hamilton, without the little Corsican's shrewd ruthlessness, was trying to emulate Bonaparte's career.

Washington spent his mornings conferring with Hamilton and Pinckney; afternoons he dined with old friends. Often in his comings and goings he was attended by groups of the Philadelphia light horse in their handsome blue uniforms. The ostentatious Binghams and old Jacob Read of South Carolina spread their tables for him and his old aides Major Jackson and McHenry, and the Oliver Wolcotts who were always so deferential, and Robert Liston the canny British minister who had been an agreeable visitor at Mount Vernon, and Robert Morris's brotherinlaw the bishop.

When he dined with Robert Morris himself, instead of at The Hills where the asparagus and strawberries were always so fine in the spring and the apricots and plums in summer and the pears and hothouse grapes in the fall, and where the claret and madeira and the roast meats were of the rarest, he dined with his old friend in a dim ill-smelling room with barred windows at the Prune Street jail.

For the fifteen years since his resignation as Financier, the man whose financial judgment and whose taste in worldly things Washington had always deferred to had managed somehow to keep in the air, by endless juggling of paper and kiting of promissory notes, an unbelievable structure of interlocking partnerships, land options, loans, mortgages, speculations in everything from ships' timbers to snuffbottles. With the tightening of credit that followed the failure of the Bank of England the whole thing crashed; ingenious men figured that Morris and John Nicholson, his latest partner in dishonor, were in default, when the bailiffs at last seized hold of them, of something like thirtyfour millions of dollars.

When George Washington, erect and stately in his buff and blue uniform with the shining epaulettes, strode with a jingle of spurs into the prison room which Mrs. Morris had worked hard to make a little homelike with a few faint evidences of former grandeur, he found them both pale and shrunken after their ordeal of that summer. As soon as he had heard of the yellow fever Washington, who knew they were in financial difficulties but did not realize to what extent, had written to his old friends to come at once to stay with him at Mount Vernon. When Washington's letter reached Robert Morris the doors were already locked on him.

His wife, who had taken what Abigail Adams, who called on her there when she returned to Philadelphia after her illness, described as a small neat room nearby, refused to leave him. Together they braved the yellow fever. The streets around were filled with dead. Imprisoned debtors died in the adjoining rooms. They had been spared. They were grateful to God. Even in this last extremity Morris could not keep his sanguine spirits down. He was already revolving vast new schemes by which he could take advantage of some sudden rise in values to pay off his creditors and spend himself into wealth once more.

13. *"the event of events . . ."*

From his house a little out of town John Adams watched the doings of the military with a bilious eye. The triumvirate, he scornfully called Washington, Hamilton and Pinckney. They had left him the fifth wheel of the coach. He was planning to put a spoke in theirs for a change. He was planning to make peace with the French.

Adams had been in constant communication with William Vans Murray, McHenry's bosom friend, whom Adams had appointed minister to the Netherlands when he planned to move his son young John

Quincy to balmier climes in Lisbon. Murray was a man he trusted. In long chatty letters Murray reported that he had received assurances that Talleyrand would respectfully receive a new envoy. Dr. Logan and Elbridge Gerry had been right. Marshall and Pinckney had been wrong. Without a word to his Secretary of State, John Adams sent Murray's name to the Senate for minister to France.

"But the event of events was announced to the Senate yesterday," Jefferson wrote Madison in high spirits on February 19, 1799. "Soon after Gerry's departure overtures must have been made by Pichon" — Monsieur Pichon, now chargé d'affaires at the Hague, had been favorably known and liked by all factions during the years when he was secretary to the French legation in Philadelphia — "they were so soon matured, that on the 27th of Sept, 98, Talleyrand writes . . . approving . . . of his having assured Murray that whatever Plenepotentiary the govent of the U S should send to France would . . . be received with the respect due to the *representative of a free, independent & powerful nation* . . . Yesterday the P nominated to the Senate W V Murray Mr. Pl to the French republic." He added gleefully: "this had evidently been kept secret from the Feds of both house, as appeared by their dismay." There were some satisfactions in presiding over the Senate.

With his friends at least Jefferson had given up any pretense of not being the active leader of his party.

As he sat lounging on one hip with his legs sprawled out in front of him in the chair on the little platform from which he presided over the Senate, he could see the rift widening between John Adams and the Hamiltonian Federalists. Here was an opportunity for a fresh appeal to the intelligence of reasonable and thoughtful men.

In every letter he urged his friends to devote their time to writing and their money to the printing and distribution of newspapers and pamphlets. "They say . . . from all quarters," he wrote Madison, "that they wish to hear *reason* instead of disgusting blackguardism. the public sentiment now being on the creen, and many heavy circumstances being about to fall into the republican scale, we are sensible that this summer is the season for systematic energies & sacrifices. the engine is the press. every man must lay his purse & his pen under contribution."

At the same time his curious private inhibition in regard to the press kept him from entering the lists himself. Bitter experience had taught him that anything he wrote would be misinterpreted. He knew he could never curb his own penchant for incisive and radical phrases. He had long ago discovered that, in order to be effective as a politician, he would have to keep the philosophic and theoretical part of his mind separate from the part of his mind that was engaged in the practical business of statebuilding. He had learned that men could be influenced only just so far even in their own interest. As he saw it the coming campaign had the limited objective of getting the helm of administration away from the authoritarian Federalists and putting the vessel back "on the republican tack."

He made no secret of his principles; he felt they were the principles of the majority of his fellow citizens. He believed these principles contained the original essence of the enthusiasms of 1776. His first duty was to steer his party to victory, but from a distance.

For the public his policy was silence. He would busy himself with his architecture and his farming and remain shrouded in the rural solitude of Monticello until a decision was reached. That fall during the hottest of the campaign he wrote John Taylor: "I cease from this time during the ensuing twelvemonth to write political letters, knowing that a campaign of slander is now open to me, and believing that the postmasters will lend their inquisitorial aid to fish out any new matter of slander they can to gratify the powers that be. I hope my friends will understand and approve the motives of my silence."

14. Miranda's Scheme

Hamilton with very different feelings was watching the growth of a hostile spirit towards the general government. He had so long been teaching his followers that any opposition to the measures of the Federalist administration meant opposition to the Union itself that, like many another good lawyer, he had begun to be taken in by his own special pleading. As he fretted over each new hitch in the smooth development of his schemes he began to be more and more incensed at John Adams. Without Adams' misunderstanding of military matters and his mulish obstinacy, the public mind would even now be ripening towards the great undertakings Hamilton had in mind. In spite of old Adams he had to move fast; while the war spirit was still in the flood. The Kentucky Resolutions, behind which he saw Jefferson's devious hand, appeared to him a forewarning of a revolt that must be nipped in the bud. He must exert the whole power of the federal government to curb the Republicans before they had time to frustrate his plans.

Hamilton was throwing all his enthusiasm into the organization of his army. Since Washington had gone home to Mount Vernon the whole weight of the work rested on his shoulders. His mind teemed with projects.

He already had in hand an operation which would try out on a small scale Miranda's scheme for a joint Anglo-American expedition to the southward. British naval officers were encouraging a Negro chief named Toussaint L'Ouverture, who since the flight of the French from their end of the sugar rich island of Santo Domingo and the discomfiture of the Spaniards at the other end, had set up a government there. Hamilton managed to get the law enforcing nonintercourse with the French colonies repealed as regards that island and to arrange the appointment of his own boyhood friend and personal physician Dr. Stevens as consul general. The British were falling in with his plan to recognize the independence of the revolting Negroes. Hamilton even took the time to draw up a scheme of military government which he felt would suit their situation. American merchant ships were flocking to their ports.

At the same time Hamilton was trying to counteract Jefferson's influence in Kentucky through a correspondence of his own. His correspondent was the major general in command of the old federal force along the Mississippi, the same James Wilkinson who was so assiduously helpful to Jefferson in his researches in the languages, the customs and the archaeology of the Indian tribes.

James Wilkinson was a Marylander originally, born and raised on Hunting Creek off the Patuxent River. The Revolutionary War interrupted his study of medicine at the College of Philadelphia. In the Continental Army as a convivial confiding young officer he developed an extraordinary gift for finding himself in the company of important commanders in moments of stress. He was with Charles Lee when that dogloving Britisher was so ignominiously captured. He ingratiated himself with Horatio Gates and became the confidant of his vainglorious dreams of supplanting Washington after Saratoga. It was young Colonel Wilkinson whom Gates picked to carry the news of Burgoyne's surrender to Congress. Though he was still only twenty, in spite of some grumbling over the unconscionable time he had taken to arrive, he was made a brigadier general for his pains. As a result of certain indiscretions through which some disrespectful remarks exchanged by Gates and his friend Conway about the commander in chief's abilities came to Washington's ears, the young general and his patron, the middleaged Gates, were soon at loggerheads. They fought a duel in which the powder mysteriously flashed in the pans of their pistols so that no one was hurt. Wilkinson's second in this affair was General Philip Schuyler's new soninlaw, a young Englishman named John Barker Church, who under an assumed name was laying the foundation of a great fortune by procuring supplies for the Continental troops.

Finding himself unpopular both with Gates' friends and Washington's as a result of these misunderstandings, young Wilkinson, who had managed to get himself appointed secretary of the Board of War, resigned his commission and with it the prospect of spending a miserable winter at Valley Forge and settled in Philadelphia. There he married the daughter of a respectable Quaker innkeeper named Biddle. He managed to convey such damaging insinuations to Joseph Reed, who presided over the Executive Council, that he got Benedict Arnold discharged from his post of clothier general and though still only twentytwo obtained the appointment for himself. As clothier general in the year of Yorktown he was better known as leader of the Philadelphia cotillion than for the efficiency of his services. The peace found him the owner of a sequestered tory estate, an assemblyman for Bucks County and adjutant general in the Pennsylvania militia.

Finding the going hard in Pennsylvania in the depressed years after the peace, he moved his family to Lexington, Kentucky. There he ran a general store. He practiced a little medicine occasionally; so some claimed, even playing the part of man midwife. He appeared in the law courts and dazzled the frontiersmen by letting himself be frequently seen in the uniform of a major general in the Continental line. His free spending and lavish entertaining made him popular wherever he went. When Jay's understanding with the Spaniards cut off the Mississippi traffic to the settlers Wilkinson managed by methods as mysterious as they were successful to open it up again. Two trips to conciliate the Spanish authorities in New Orleans resulted in his becoming marvelously good friends with the generous Dons; so much so that any Kentuckian who wanted to ship produce downriver found he could do so by making arrangements, for a price, through General Wilkinson. He served in Kentucky's various constitutional conventions and by the time Kentucky was admitted to the Union under the general government had made himself such a reputation as a fighter and fixer of Indians and as an entrepreneur in the river traffic that President Washington, forgetting Wilkinson's bad odor among the military during the war, sent him a commission to command a regiment in the newly organized army of the United States. Evil tongues told scandalous stories, but nobody could prove that Wilkinson had obtained his monopoly of the Mississippi trade by swearing allegiance to the Spanish Crown and was even then receiving a sizable pension from His Catholic Majesty. Wilkinson busied himself undermining Anthony Wayne's reputation along the Western Waters and, when that great soldier conveniently died soon after taking over Detroit from the redcoats, stepped into his shoes as ranking officer of the federal army.

With Washington in retirement at Mount Vernon, General Hamilton was the great man in the general government. Hamilton and Wilkinson corresponded eagerly on all the Mississippi topics. Wilkinson started sending boxes of pecans and West Florida oranges to the wife of his old friend Church, Hamilton's adorable Angelica. Hamilton was showing a feverish interest in all Wilkinson had to tell him. Since John Adams was blocking his hopes of service against the French, Miranda's scheme was becoming the basis of Hamilton's grand strategy. If Godoy and his helpless Bourbon court let Louisiana slip back into the hands of France, Hamilton had to be in a position to forestall an invasion of the Mississippi Valley by Bonaparte's bloody battalions, with their bayonets and their guillotine and their Marseilleise. The liberation of Mexico and the lands to the south through an alliance with His Majesty's navy was his answer to that threat.

The vistas opening into the future through the collapse of French and Spanish power in the Americas were too brilliant to let the scruples of a few blockheads stand in the way. If the people of the United States would not come along willingly on the majestic path Hamilton was indicating for them they must be driven. An army along the Mississippi could be used to chasten the Kentuckians.

15. ". . . a very pernicious tendency . . ."

In a long letter to Burr's friend Jonathan Dayton, Speaker of the House and a brigadier general in the new army, Hamilton outlined his plan to establish federal authority. The state of the popular mind, which aroused such hopes in Jefferson, to him meant disaster. "Notwithstanding the unexampled success of our popular measures at home and abroad," he wrote Dayton — "notwithstanding the instructive comments afforded by the disastrous and disgusting scenes of the French Revolution — public opinion has not been ameliorated . . . among the most numerous class of citizens errors of a very pernicious tendency have not only preserved but have extended their empire . . . opposition to the government has acquired more system than formerly . . . The opposition party in Virginia . . . have followed up the hostile declarations which are to be found in the resolutions of their General Assembly by an actual preparation of the means of supporting them by force . . . they have taken measures to put their militia on a more efficient footing . . . and, (which is unequivocal proof of how much they are in earnest) have gone so far as to lay new taxes on their citizens."

The remedy he advised was "vigorous measures of counter-action." He would like to see each of the large states subdivided into small states and these cut up into districts, each presided over by a federal court appointed by the President to enforce the federal laws at the

county level, like the British assizes. He wanted a federal system of
turnpikes and canals to open up communications; and particularly he
called for "arrangements for confirming and enlarging the powers of
the federal government." A step in this direction would be the introduction of the English common law concepts of libel and sedition into
the federal courts "to preserve confidence in the officers of the general
government, by preserving their reputations from malicious and unfounded slander."

He told Dayton that the government should "act upon the hypothesis that opposers of the government are resolved . . . to make its
existence a question of force." He had already led an army to put
down opposition to his excise in western Pennsylvania. Now he would
lead his army into Virginia and Kentucky to put down their much
more dangerous opposition to the Alien and Sedition Laws. "Possessing as they do now all the constitutional powers" — he was speaking
of Adams' administration — "it will be an unpardonable mistake if
they do not exert them to surround the Constitution with more ram-
parts and to disconcert the schemes of its enemies." Hamilton wanted
someone better qualified than himself to emphasize these matters for
John Adams' private ear.

16.   ". . . an Aegis very essential to me"

Hamilton's commander in chief meanwhile was spending his
days at Mount Vernon in an afterglow of the glories of the Continental
Army. Washington wrote letters, he signed dispatches. He was in daily
confidential communication with his inspector general at the seat of
government. After he had finished his dispatches he rode over his
fields and saw to his mill and superintended his real estate transactions
and his land sales. He was building some houses in the federal city.
At dinner after he got back from his daily ride he entertained a continual stream of visitors. They were all Federalists or foreigners;
hardly a Republican, except his faithful secretary Tobias Lear whose
aberrations he indulged, dared darken the doors of Mount Vernon.

The old robust health that had stood him in good stead through so
many campaigns had failed him. He was weary of making decisions.
He was only too glad to let Hamilton carry the load. At the beginning
of September of 1799 he suffered a severe return of the chills and
fevers. After a few days in bed and liberal doses of "bark" he was able
to take up his daily rides again.

The winter came on early. The night of December 11 the old general observed a large circle round the moon. Next day while he was

riding the usual circuit of his plantations it began to snow. As he rode the snow turned into hail and then into a settled cold rain. "He did not return home till past three," Lear noted in his diary. "I observed to him that I was afraid he had got wet, he said no his great Coat had kept him dry, but his neck appeared to be wet and the snow was hanging upon his hair. He came to dinner (which had been waiting for him) without changing his dress."

The next day it snowed heavily. Washington complained of a sore throat but seemed cheerful and went out to mark some trees between the house and the river he wanted cut down to improve his view. In spite of his hoarseness, when they came back in the house he read Lear entertaining snatches from the newspapers that came in the morning mail. He asked Lear to read aloud the debates from the Virginia Assembly. "On hearing Mr. Madison's observations respecting Mr. Monroe" — complimentary, no doubt — "he spoke with some asperity on the subject."

Lear suggested he take something for his cold.

"No you know I never take anything for a cold. Let it go as it came."

The general went to bed early.

Between two and three in the morning he woke Mrs. Washington. He was in great discomfort; he was shaking with ague and could hardly breathe. They sent a horseman off for Dr. Craik. During the forenoon, before the doctor came, the general insisted on being bled. One of the foremen knew how to do it. The general's throat was so sore he could not speak. As soon as Dr. Craik had taken a look at his old friend he asked Lear to send at once for Dr. Brown from Port Tobacco. Meanwhile he tried to get the general to gargle and bled him some more. When Dr. Brown arrived he brought with him a Dr. Dick. The three physicians consulted solemnly together and bled the general again.

At this point Washington roused himself and asked Mrs. Washington to go to his desk and fetch him two wills she would find there. He directed her to burn one.

When she had moved to the other end of the room he whispered to Lear, "I find I am going. My breath cannot last long. I believed from the first this disorder would prove fatal."

He asked Lear to arrange his military papers in order and to balance up his account books for him.

He suffered greatly during the afternoon. He kept changing his position in bed. "Doctor I die hard," he whispered to Dr. Craik, "but I am not afraid to go."

The doctor pressed his hand but could not say a word. He walked over to the fire and sat there absorbed in grief. Martha Washington had for a long time been sitting motionless at the foot of the bed, Lear near its head. From time to time the house servants came trembling to the door of the white bedroom with its spindly mahogany furniture. At the end of the afternoon the doctors, after another consultation, tried to prop the general up with pillows. "I feel myself going, I thank you for your attentions but I pray you take no more trouble about me." His voice was barely audible. "Let me go off quietly. I cannot last long."

During the evening he kept asking Lear what time it was.

Around ten o'clock he made several efforts to speak. "I am just going," he whispered to Lear. "Have me decently buried and do not let my body be put into the vault less than three days after I am dead." Lear wrote in his diary that he could only nod his head in assent, he could not speak. The general managed to make himself heard. "Do you understand me? 'Tis well," he said.

"About ten minutes before he expired (which was between ten & eleven o'clock) his breathing became easier, he lay quietly. He withdrew his hand from mine and felt his own pulse . . . The General's hand fell from his wrist. I took it in mine and put it in my bosom. Dr. Craik put his hands over his eyes and he expired without a struggle or sigh."

The news of Washington's death sped along the muddy Virginia lanes. Bells tolled in Dumfries, in Alexandria, in Georgetown across the Potomac. Men's voices failed when they told each other the news.

The political leaders whose minds were set on the partisan battle to the exclusion of every other thought appraised his death as to whether it would hurt or help their cause. To the Virginia Republicans it came as a blessing; no longer could the Federalists wrap themselves in the old general's cloak.

Hamilton, when he heard the news, was busy hurrying back and forth between his law office in New York and his military duties in Philadelphia. Answering Lear's note telling him of the general's death, he wrote that the event "filled my heart with bitterness. Perhaps no man in this community has equal cause with myself to deplore his loss." He added in a flash of selfrevelation "I have been much indebted to the kindness of the General and he was an *Aegis very essential to me*." He underlined the words.

XIV The Republican Tack

1. *The Scourge of Aristocracy*

As Hamilton in New York and Messrs. Wolcott and Pickering in Philadelphia felt the tide of public opinion rising against them they turned to the courts for protection against the sort of criticism which might result in a loss of votes in the coming elections. The federal judges were not waiting for the fresh legislation Hamilton was calling for to enforce the Sedition Act. Urged on by Pickering's circulars to the federal district attorneys to silence the Republican press, they were reviving the English common law principle that any utterances which tended to bring the officers of government into disrepute were in themselves seditious.

The campaign was carefully planned by Pickering in the State Department. John Adams, all for upholding the "splendour and majesty" of his office, went along for a while. The first indictment secured was against Matthew Lyon, who represented the unruly Vermonters, a man of great force and energy whose activities both in Congress and out of doors were considered dangerous to the federal cause.

Matthew Lyon was an Irishman. The story went that he had learned the printer's trade as a boy at the press that published *The Freeman's Journal* in Dublin. His father was executed by the British. Arriving friendless and penniless in Boston on a stinking immigrant ship, he was put on the auction block for his passage money and indentured to a Connecticut man who worked him in Ethan Allen's foundry. When he scraped up enough money to buy his liberty he married the daughter of one of Ethan Allen's brothers and moved up with the family into Vermont.

There at Fair Haven on Lake Champlain he inaugurated a sheaf of enterprises based on the abundant water power the place afforded. He set up a sawmill, a nailery and a gristmill and exploited a nearby vein of iron ore for a foundry. During the Revolution he was out with the Green Mountain Boys. Like most of the Vermonters, he had almost as many runins with the officers of the Continental line as he did with the British. After the peace the state Assembly authorized him to run a lottery for six hundred bushels of wheat to raise the capital—in wheat, which was the currency of the time—to set up a furnace to make "flatirons, spiders, bakepans and dishkettles." He cast his own type and on paper made from the bark of the basswood tree by a process of his own invention published a newspaper which he titled *The Scourge of Aristocracy.*

When he arrived to take his seat in Congress he was greeted by Cobbett in *Porcupine's Gazette* with a characteristic broadside:

"*The Lyon of Vermont*—Tomorrow morning at eleven o'clock will be exposed to view the Lyon of Vermont. This singular animal is said to have been caught in the bog of Hibernia, and when a whelp, transported to America; curiosity induced a New Yorker to buy him, and moving into the country afterwards exchanged him for a yoke of young bulls with a Vermontese. He was petted in the neighborhood of Governor Chittenden, and soon became so domesticated that a daughter of his excellency would stroke and play with him as a monkey." After his first wife died Lyon married a daughter of Vermont's often reelected governor. "He differs considerably from the African lion, is more clamorous and less magnanimous. His pelt resembles more the wolf or the tiger, and his gestures bear a remarkable affinity to the bear; this however may be ascribed to his having been in the habit of associating with that species of wild beast on the mountains: he is carnivorous but not very ferocious—has never been detected in having attacked a man, but report says he will beat women."

The townbred Federalists in Congress echoed Cobbett's taunts at Lyon's lowly birth and lack of formal education and jibed at him with a tale that fertile slanderer had dredged up of cowardice in wartime until the frontiersman was goaded into spitting in the face of Representative Griswold of Connecticut. Griswold retorted by attacking Lyon from behind with a hickory cudgel as he sat quietly at his desk next morning waiting for the House to be called to order. Lyon snatched the tongs out of the fireplace and there followed an affray which gave great delight to the cartoonists.

His indictment was on the pretext of a letter to *The Vermont Journal* at Windsor in which he spoke of "the continual grasp for power . . . an unbounded thirst for ridiculous pomp, foolish adulation,

and selfish avarice" on the part of the Executive; and for having read
at a public meeting a letter of Joel Barlow's from Paris disapproving
of Monroe's recall and criticizing the administration's conduct of
relations with the French.

Justice Paterson of the Supreme Court, Hamilton's associate in
S.U.M. and the constitutional arbiter of the State of New Jersey, sitting
at Rutland on circuit, overruled Lyon's plea that the Sedition Law
was unconstitutional, sentenced him to four months imprisonment and,
blandly expressing regret that the defendant's financial affairs were
said to be in such bad order that he feared he would have a hard
time raising the money, to a thousand dollar fine. During his absence
in Congress Lyon's mills and foundries were indeed at sixes and
sevens; like so many others, he was making great personal sacrifices
to serve the public.

The United States marshal turned out to be a personal enemy of
Lyon's and hurried him to jail at Vergennes, forty snowy miles from his
home. Until his friends made a noise he was denied the use of writing
materials.

As soon as paper, ink and quills were furnished he wrote Stevens
Thomson Mason, the senator from Virginia, describing his situation:
"On Wednesday evening last I was locked up in this room, where I
now am; it is about sixteen feet long by twelve wide, with a necessary
in one corner which affords a stench about equal to the Philadelphia
docks in the month of August. This cell is the common receptacle for
horse-thieves, money-makers, runaway-negroes or any kind of felons.
There is a half-moon hole through the door sufficient to receive a
plate through, and for my friends to look through and speak to me.
There is a window place on the opposite side, about twenty inches by
sixteen, crossed by nine square iron bars: all the light I have is through
this aperture; no fireplace in the cell, nor is there anything but the
iron bars to keep the cold out" — this in midwinter in Vermont —
"consequently I have to walk smartly with my greatcoat on, to keep
comfortably warm some mornings . . . The Marshal paid me a visit on
Thursday evening, he examined the cell, looked on my little table to
see what was there; but he found nothing but Volney's Ruins, the
late laws, some of the President's messages, and a list of the petit
jury." Lyon apologized to Mason for "this long prolix account of the
fruits of this *beloved* sedition bill. You may remember that I told you,
when it was passing, that it was doubtless intended for the members
of Congress, and very likely would be brought to bear on me the very
first; so it has happened, and perhaps I, who have been a football for
dame fortune all my life, am best able to bear it."

In spite of the lynching spirit against Republicans fomented by the
publication of the XYZ dispatches, public feeling rose so high when

stories of Matthew Lyon's treatment by his jailers spread through the
Green Mountains that a crowd surrounded the jail threatening to
tear the building apart to get him out. It was only Lyon's voice through
the bars refusing to leave that dispersed them. He had no intention of
giving the Federalists an excuse for further repressions. His wife was
a woman of equal spirit; when his friends another time suggested a
jailbreak while she and her sisters were visiting him, "That he shall
not do," she cried out, "if I stand sentinel myself."

While he was still serving his term Lyon was reelected to the House
of Representatives by a very large majority. The United States
district attorney riposted by bringing charges against another Republican, Anthony Harwell, the publisher of *The Vermont Gazette* in
Bennington, for the wording of an advertisement published in his
paper announcing a subscription to pay Representative Lyon's fine.
Harwell was a much respected editor and a close friend of Chittenden
and of the Allen brothers. He was duly tried under Judge Paterson at
the next term of the circuit court, convicted and sentenced to two
months in jail and a $200 fine: the result was greatly to increase the
Republican vote in the State of Vermont.

2.   *". . . vigorous measures of counter-action"*

With Matthew Lyon behind the bars as an example to the
minority in Congress, the administration proceeded to move against
the opposition press in general. The five most important Republican
newspapers were Abijah Adams' *Independent Chronicle* in Boston,
Greenleaf's *Argus* in New York, *The Aurora* in Philadelphia, *The
Examiner* in Richmond, and *The American* in Baltimore. The *Boston
Chronicle* had already been crippled by a prosecution in the state courts
for the crime of approving the Virginia and Kentucky resolutions.

In New York Hamilton himself moved against the *Argus*. A story
had been going the rounds of the Republican press that annoyed him
exceedingly: it was that Hamilton had joined with Robert Liston in an
effort to buy the Philadelphia *Aurora* by the use of British secret
service funds. The *Argus* was owned by the widow of the same Greenleaf who had been the original publisher of the *Federalist Papers*.
Always gallant, General Hamilton, explaining that he wanted to avoid
prosecuting a lady, brought charges against a journeyman printer in
her employ named Frothingham. Since Hamilton as inspector general
of the army was a public official the district attorney charged the
printer with seditious libel for setting up the *Aurora* story in type.
From the bench one of the judges on the Mayor's Court made the

point that although the federal Sedition Law allowed evidence of the truth of a libel to be admitted in defense, this case was being tried under the old common law principle. The question for the jury to decide was: did this writing expose General Hamilton to hatred, contempt and ridicule? Frothingham admitted on the witness stand that he did not believe the story to be true but claimed that as an employee he had no control over what was printed in the newspaper. In spite of an able speech in his defense by Brockholst Livingston, a son of witty old Governor William Livingston of New Jersey, the jury found him guilty but with a recommendation for clemency.

Frothingham threw himself on the mercy of the court, claiming that the *Argus* had only reprinted a story published in Newark by *The Centinel of Freedom* and by *The Epitome of the Times* in Norfolk, Virginia: he had a wife and six small children, the eldest twelve, and only made eight dollars a week. "If the defendent was poor, he should have thought of that before he committed his offence," the judge remarked from the bench as he sentenced him to four months in the Bridewell and a hundred dollar fine, and further to find sureties for good behavior to the amount of two thousand dollars.

The efforts of the Federalists in Philadelphia to suppress *The Aurora* itself were meeting resistance. William Duane, the new editor, was an able man, somewhat more circumspect in his polemics than Ben Bache, who had been brought up in his grandfather's lighthearted school of tongue-in-cheek journalism.

Although Duane was raised in Ireland he was able to defeat efforts to deport him under the Alien Act by proving that he was born in upper New York State. He came, so it was said, of a family of some wealth. After his father's death his mother had carried the boy back to Ireland with her. When she disowned young Duane for marrying a Protestant he took up the trade of printer. Emigrating to India, he amassed a small fortune there and started a newspaper in Calcutta. His taking up the grievances of the troops in their employ got him on the bad books of the East India Company. His capital and even his library and personal effects were confiscated and he was shipped back to England as poor as the day he arrived. In England he served as parliamentary reporter for *The General Advertiser*, which was soon to be transformed into *The Times* of London. He became a friend of Horne Tooke and of the radicals of the democratic societies and sailed for America in time to avoid going with them to the Tower as traitors. His first wife had meanwhile died. In Philadelphia he published a history of the French Revolution and became Ben Bache's assistant. A month after the death of Franklin's grandson in the yellow fever of 1798 Duane married Mrs. Bache and inherited the newspaper, and with it the detestation in which Bache was held by the Federalists. Under his management it became the leading opposition journal.

No one quite understood why Duane's early indictment in the Federal Court was not pushed with more energy. Possibly, since the ill success of the trial of the whiskey boys, the Attorney General was loath to risk a Philadelphia jury. In October 1798 an additional prosecution was instituted in the city court against Duane and several others for riot and assault in connection with an altercation which occurred when a placard was posted outside the Catholic Church one Sunday which called on the congregation to sign a memorial to Congress for repeal of the Alien Act. In the same indictment a true bill was found against an Irish physician for pointing a pistol at a man.

The prosecutor for the Commonwealth was a son of Jefferson's friend Hopkinson, the composer. Joseph Hopkinson was highly esteemed among the party of the rich and wellborn as a Federalist lawyer and as the author of "Hail Columbia." Alexander Dallas and John Beckley appeared as counsel for Duane. The doctor managed to prove that he had only brandished the pistol in selfdefense after he had been knocked down and repeatedly kicked by a young man with a club. Duane and his friends were acquitted on all counts.

The Federalists had little more success with Duane when they cited him to appear at the bar of the Senate. His crime was the publication of the action of the Federalist caucus in favor of a bill introduced by Senator Ross of Pennsylvania to establish a congressional commission to superintend the coming presidential election. Duane pointed out that such a commission could steal the election for the Federalists no matter how the popular vote came out, and was duly summoned for contempt of the Senate. On advice of the leading Republican lawyers he answered coolly that he would refuse to appear unless assisted by proper counsel, and managed to stave off the proceedings from week to week until Congress adjourned, leaving the summons still pending.

In their campaign to stamp out opposition the Federalists found in one of Washington's appointees to the Supreme Court an energumen of great legal learning and extraordinary violence of character. Samuel Chase was in his late fifties, a six foot Marylander with a broad red face—a bacon-face, his enemies called it—and a beetling brow under a thatch of white hair. Although his father was a Baltimore clergyman Chase was brought up on the Eastern Shore. He started public life during the Stamp Act agitation as a Son of Liberty so violent that he was denounced by the mayor of the city as "a foulmouthed and inflaming son of discord." He rose through the Maryland Assembly to the Continental Congress, signed the Declaration of Independence and continued through thick and thin a vehement defender of General Washington. He did business in commodities. In Philadelphia his speculations at the time of Robert Morris's attempted corner of flour became so notorious that the Maryland legislature passed a special bill forbidding their delegates to Congress to engage in commerce. One of the first of the efforts to impeach him that checkered his career failed in the Assembly. When the general government was formed Chase, then a noisy anti-Federalist, was holding in his grasping hands in spite of popular outcry the positions of Chief Justice of the General Court of the State of Maryland and of the Criminal Court. He was described as moving perpetually "with a mob at his heels."

McHenry suggested him to George Washington for the national Supreme Court and the President, remembering perhaps Chase's sturdy advocacy of Washington's measures during difficult moments under the old Congress, appointed him in the face of grumbling from the New Englanders, who feared his anti-federalism. After Washington's retirement Chase transferred his allegiance to John Adams and stumped for him vigorously off the bench and on. The Republican papers described with glee the scene one Sunday morning when enormous Samuel Chase was seen holding what was then a novelty, an umbrella, over stubby little John Adams' head as he escorted him to church down the sunny Baltimore street. Outside of George Washington and John Adams, Judge Chase was said to respect no man or woman either. Mrs. Bingham, the banker's wife, was the most courted hostess in Philadelphia and inordinately proud of her French chef; dining one day at the Binghams', the justice threw up his hands at the sight of a procession of ragouts and fricassees and called for a beefsteak. "There madam, I have made a sensible dinner," he exclaimed when he had finished, "but no thanks to your French cook."

While the Federalists in Congress were harassing Duane without managing to interrupt the circulation of his newspaper, Judge Chase during the spring term of 1800 defended the authority of government by a number of mighty blows from the bench. His first victim was the learned Thomas Cooper, Priestley's bosom friend and housemate at Northumberland.

Thomas Cooper, a younger man than Priestley, was an associate of long standing of the Unitarian chemist's. He came of a family of dissenters. He was kept from a degree at Oxford by his scruples against signing the Thirty Nine Articles. He studied law and medicine and chemistry and was the partner in charge of the dyeworks in a concern that printed calicos in the Midlands. Ardent for parliamentary reform, he became the leading spirit of the Manchester Constitutional Society. He was a man of immense learning and immense industry but such an enthusiastic exponent of American republicanism that Priestley could not get him admitted to the Royal Society.

When Cooper was sent to France in 1792 along with James Watt Jr., the son of the inventor and builder of steam engines in Birmingham, to carry fraternal greetings from the English democratic societies to the Jacobin club of Paris he was greeted by Robespierre, not yet a member of the Committee of Public Safety, with an apostrophe to "the English flag united and entwined with the threecolored flag of France and the thirteen stripes of the brave Americans." As a result he was picked out for special attention by Edmund Burke in his thunderings against revolution in the Commons. Burke described the Manchester delegates as "locked in the fraternizing embrace. They received the fraternizing kiss . . . and kissed the bloody cheek of Marat." In spite of the fact that the two Englishmen soon fell out with the Jacobins and were pursued back to England by Robespierre's denunciations as agents of Pitt, Cooper found the English Tories calling for his blood. He emigrated to Pennsylvania along with Priestley and Priestley's sons. Cooper, a man whose every passing notion found its way into print, was a voluminous writer. He immediately produced a tract on emigration in which he gave first circulation to the phrase "a government of the people and for the people."

The two philosophers had hardly settled to their writing and teaching and to their chemical experiments in the rural quiet of Northumberland when Cobbett began to bombard them with insults. In fact it was on Priestley that Cobbett cut his teeth as a professional slanderer. He denounced them as renegade Englishmen. He made fun of their erudition. Priestley he called "the malignant old Tartuffe of Northumberland."

Priestley was all his life an extremely naïve man in his personal relations. In England during the days of John Adams' mission to the Court of St. James he had known Adams well and had come to consider him as a warm personal friend. Adams as Vice President attended every one of Priestley's Philadelphia lectures with seeming approval. Consequently when Adams became President, Priestley did not feel it presumptuous to recommend his friend Cooper to him as a possible appointee as one of the American representatives on the mixed commissions to settle claims set up under Jay's treaty. Since Cooper had added a mass of information on international trade to his general encyclopedic knowledge he was so much the obvious man for the position that Robert Liston was suggesting that, in spite of his politics, he might get him appointed to represent the Crown. Cooper already considered himself an American citizen. He let it be known that he would prefer to represent his adopted country. The

Northumberland philosophers were appalled to find that their somewhat diffident suggestions to the President were being published and
held up to ridicule in the Federalist press.

Thomas Cooper was a very small completely humorless man with a
very large head. Somebody said he looked like an egg balanced on top
of a wedge. The publication of his letter to Adams outraged him to
the very core. Although he already edited his own newspaper in
Northumberland he published a dignified remonstrance in *The Reading Weekly Advertizer*: "Nor do I see any impropriety in making this
request of Mr. Adams." He could not help taking a dig with his quill:
"At that time he had just entered into office; he was hardly in the
infancy of political mistake; even those who doubted his capacity
thought well of his intentions." He continued with a few more specific
criticisms of the President's policies, accused him of setting up a
standing army, of saddling the country with a navy, and of paying
exorbitant interest on the public debt.

Cooper had already made himself obnoxious to Messrs. Wolcott
and Pickering by his opposition to the Alien and Sedition Acts, which
he described as the very governmental tyranny he had left Pitt's
England to escape. He was known to have offered Duane his legal
assistance in Duane's difficulties with the Senate. Adams was the
touchiest of men. To Pickering it seemed an excellent opportunity to
put one more Republican behind the bars. In the April session of the
United States Circuit Court Cooper found himself in the prisoner's
dock with Judge Chase glaring down at him from the bench.

Cooper insisted on conducting his own defense. He began by asking
for subpoenas for the President and for a long list of members of
Congress. Chase refused to subpoena the President, but the attendance
of a number of congressmen was arranged. In fact men from both
parties crowded eagerly into the courtroom to see the show. "Have we
advanced so far on the road to depotism in this republican country,"
Cooper asked the jury, "that we dare not say our President may be
mistaken?"

Judge Chase with Judge Peters beside him on the bench conducted
the trial with a show of moderation; at the same time he made no
effort to conceal from the jury or the spectators his reliance on the old
courtroom adage: the man who is his own lawyer has a fool for a
client. His attitude on the bench was one of illrestrained mirth. In
his charge to the jury he developed the Federalist theory of malicious
libel much more effectively than the prosecuting attorney did. He
spoke of Cooper's letter as "the boldest attempt I have ever known to
poison the mind of the people." He made a telling point against
Cooper by challenging his criticism of Adams for encouraging a
standing army as a falsehood because enlistments in General Wilkin-

son's western army were for five years only, and in Hamilton's provisional army were to terminate with the end of hostilities with the French.

"This publication is evidently intended to mislead the ignorant, and inflame their minds against the President, and influence their votes on the next election," Judge Chase proclaimed in ringing tones. "You will please to notice, gentlemen," he continued, giving his own interpretations to the clause in the Sedition Act the Federalists had claimed would protect the rights of free speech, "that the traverser in his defense must prove every charge he has made to be true; he must prove it to the marrow. If he asserts three things and proves but one, he fails."

The jury returned a verdict of guilty. Judge Chase sentenced Cooper to six months in jail, to pay a four hundred dollar fine and to find surety for good behavior.

With the learned Dr. Cooper packed off to the jail across the Common, where he went to work to write up his record of the trial in a pamphlet which immediately became, along with Erskine on libels, a classic in the literature of the oppressive use of laws against seditious writings, Judge Chase proceeded to a case which dealt with deeds instead of words. A certain John Fries of Bucks County, Pennsylvania, an auctioneer, was charged with treason as the leader of an insurrection against the house tax. Although ably defended by Alexander Dallas and William Lewis, outstanding Republican lawyers, he had been found guilty at the previous term of court; but at the last moment Judge Iredell and Judge Peters had let him slip through their fingers and granted him a new trial. This time it was up to Judge Chase to maintain the majesty of the law.

The direct tax on lands, slaves and houses which Hamilton's friends had put through Congress, as one of the fiscal measures needed to meet the expense of the provisional army and of the fine new frigates and of the eight percent interest Oliver Wolcott was paying to the financiers for the money he borrowed for the Treasury, was met with grumbling and protest everywhere, but only in some eastern counties of Pennsylvania did popular indignation reach the point of armed resistance. There it was more the manner of assessment than the tax itself that provoked people.

Assessors demanded entrance into dwelling houses and assessed their value by measuring the size of the windows. This invasion of privacy rankled particularly with the withdrawn and secluded farmers of German peasant origin who grew such fine crops in Bucks and Northampton and Montgomery counties. Men took to throwing the assessors bodily out of their houses. One woman poured hot water on an assessor's head.

The United States marshal was called. He swore in deputies and went around arresting people who had resisted the tax assessors. He herded his prisoners into the Sun Tavern in the Moravian mission town of Bethlehem, with the intention of marching them into Philadelphia for trial.

An angry crowd collected round the tavern, demanding that the prisoners be tried in their home counties. Treasury agents were chivvied and hustled. The turmoil was compounded by the fact that many of the farmers were illiterate and that very few of them knew English. A good deal of liquor went around. Some of the people were announcing that they were for Jefferson and against federal taxes. Others claimed that they were for John Adams but that no such law as a window tax had been passed by Congress. Others spread the news that someone had received a letter from George Washington in support of their protest. For adherents of the federal officers they revived the old epithet "stampfers" that had been used against the Tories in the Stamp Act agitation. In the end John Fries, a popular auctioneer who had seen service as an officer in the Revolutionary War, found himself leading an armed band to quell the excitement and demand the release of the prisoners. Fries was well known throughout the Pennsylvania Dutch country by his little black dog named Whiskey that was forever at his heels. He had helped write a petition of remonstrance a few days before. He conducted a formal parley with the United States marshal, who by this time had retreated with his deputies to the upper floor of the inn. There was shouting and abuse but nobody was hurt. The United States marshal yielded to superior force; the prisoners were released and everybody went home to his farm.

At the seat of government Messrs. Wolcott and Pickering painted these disturbances in the blackest light and induced John Adams to call for the state militia. William MacPherson, who led an intensely Federalist corps of young men much admired for their fine blue uniforms and their close order drill on parade, was made a brigadier general in the United States Army and told to quell the insurrection. Robert Goodloe Harper went along as adjutant. MacPherson's Blues had already played a large part in the "cockade riots" against the Jacobins. Before leaving town a group of them visited Duane's bookstore and printing shop and would have beaten the Republican editor to death if his friends had not appeared in force to save him. When they reached Reading they dragged a man named Schneider who edited the chief German language newspaper of the region, *Der*

Readinger Adler, out of his office into the middle of the market square. There they tore off his clothes and had begun to flog him on the bare back when a less frantic detachment of militia came along and took their prisoner away from them.

When the Blues reached the region round Bethlehem they found the country quiet, the houses shuttered and the farmers working in the fields. They rode through the country looking for ringleaders. John Fries they found plying his trade at the sale of a farmhouse, standing on a barrelhead with his bell in his hand, about to auction off a fire shovel. They proceeded to treat the crowd at the auction as a seditious gathering and charged them with bare sabers. People ran in all directions; the least fleet of foot were arrested. John Fries hid in a thicket in a marsh, but his hiding place was given away by the sight of his inseparable little dog Whiskey. Fifteen prisoners were dragged off to the Philadelphia jail charged with treason and twenty or thirty charged with lesser crimes and misdemeanors. In the end only three men were tried, though the bulk of them were kept in jail for a year. When the yellow fever broke out in the late summer the warden had the humanity to march his prisoners out to Norristown and to allow them to work for the neighboring farmers if they would promise to be back in custody every night. At that a number of them died of prison fever.

When John Fries came up for trial a second time Judge Chase determined to shorten the proceedings by publishing, before counsel for the defense had a chance to argue their theory of the case, his opinion that Fries was being tried for treason and no lesser crime and by ruling out any argument as to the propriety of the wording of the indictment. Dallas and Lewis refused to defend their client on those terms. "Then by the blessing of God," Judge Chase told the trembling Fries, "the court will be your counsel and will do you as much justice as those that were your counsel."

The testimony from the first trial was all recited again. Nobody denied that the marshal had been forced by threats to let his prisoners go. In his charge to the jury Judge Chase reiterated his theory that any resistance to the officers of the United States was levying war against the United States and therefore treason. The jury found Fries guilty for a second time. Judge Chase in a moving address pointed out the particular heinousness of the crime of treason under a freely elected republican government and called on Fries to repent of his sins: "I suppose you are a Christian . . . Your day of life is almost spent; and the night of death fast approaches . . . the judgement of the law is and this court doth award that you be hanged by the neck until dead and I pray God Almighty to be merciful to your soul."

John Adams had been watching with misgivings the progress of the trials of the Northampton insurgents. He had been on the outs with his cabinet ever since he had forced approval of his new mission to France through Congress against the disguised opposition of Messrs. Wolcott and Pickering. The long struggle over the order of precedence of the major generals had left rancor behind. The President was becoming aware that General Hamilton, through his puppets in the cabinet, had been making a fool of him for years; and was now planning to harness the provisional army and the entire federal government if he could manage it to the vague grand expedition he was planning with Miranda in London against the Spanish dominions to the south and west.

Messrs. Wolcott and Pickering were demanding that the execution of Fries be allowed to proceed. The agreeable McHenry, who was the most obvious mouthpiece in the cabinet of his bosom friend Hamilton, backed them up. Though his worst enemy could not accuse him of courting popularity it had occurred to Adams that allowing Fries to be executed would ruin him with the common run of American yeomanry forever; perhaps that was what Hamilton wanted. To cap these musings came news from New York of a victory for what was becoming known as the Democratic-Republican party in the state elections. Hamilton could not even carry his own state; now was the time to rid the administration of his influence. McHenry was the man closest to Hamilton. May 5, 1800, the President wrote a short note to his Secretary of War: "The P. requests Mr. McH's company for one minute."

The minute was a long one. John Adams had lashed himself into a tantrum. He accused the astonished Secretary of War of personal infidelities and breaches of confidence. McHenry could find no words to reply. The President couched his accusations in the most wounding and abusive language. McHenry immediately wrote out his resignation.

A few days later the President struck out again. He wrote Timothy Pickering a short note demanding his resignation. Pickering had thwarted him in a number of ways. Adams had only recently discovered that it was Pickering's personal lobbying that had made the course of a commission as brigadier general for his soninlaw William Stephens Smith so difficult in the Senate. Then too Pickering had been making Elbridge Gerry's life almost as miserable as he had made James Monroe's by haggling over his accounts with the State Department of expenditures during his mission to France. Though Gerry was a Republican he was a personal friend and supporter of John Adams. Adams was coming to consider Pickering's insulting treatment of Gerry as a personal affront. The fact that Pickering refused to resign with the impudent plea that he needed the job to support his family did nothing to sweeten John Adams' temper. He promptly dismissed him.

Next he called a meeting of his rump cabinet and put to Wolcott and Stoddert and Charles Lee a series of questions as to the advisability of hanging John Fries. He had been gathering information privately on the trials. Devoted as Adams was to "the splendour and majesty" of his office, he was even more devoted to his own private notion of justice. He had sent his son Thomas to the defense lawyers to ask them to send him their briefs. Wolcott replied that all three ring-leaders should be executed. Stoddert and Lee were willing to settle for one, with pardon for the rest.

John Adams listened in silence to their arguments and then went home and wrote out a proclamation granting amnesty to all the prisoners held in jail pending trial. The Federalist press let out a roar. Hamilton raged from New York. Already, since George Washington's death, his provisional army in which the inspector general had placed his hopes of military glory, had been crumbling away before his eyes. Congress had cut off further enlistments. And now Adams was not only making peace with the French but he was courting popularity and an accord with the Jeffersonians at home. The President's reply was to grant an unconditional pardon to John Fries and the two other convicted ringleaders. The Federalist party was split in two.

3. *These Young Gentlemen of the Virginia Bar*

Judge Chase meanwhile continued on his circuit to the south-ward, breathing fire and brimstone against seditious writings. There was a case waiting for him in the circuit court at Richmond, Virginia, that would give him an opportunity to confound the Republicans on their home grounds. When he arrived in Richmond in June he was announcing to everyone who would listen that he was going to take these Virginia lawyers over his knee and give them a good spanking.

The prisoner at the bar was James Thomson Callender, Hamilton's gadfly, whom Jefferson had encouraged to take asylum from prosecution in Virginia. His newest crime was the publication of some abuse of John Adams in a campaign pamphlet called *The Prospect Before Us*. "The reign of Mr. Adams has been one continual tempest of malignant passions," he began. Though the immediate target was Callender it was well understood that the whole Republican press was on trial. As counsel Callender had two close friends of Jefferson's, one of the

Nicholas brothers and Patrick Henry's biographer William Wirt. George Hay, the attorney general of the Commonwealth who had recently married Governor Monroe's daughter, also appeared for Callender. Their defense was the truth of the statements alleged to be libelous.

The defense first moved for a postponement until a list of eminent witnesses, among them Timothy Pickering, Tenche Coxe and Stevens Thomson Mason, could be collected to testify. Motion denied. After a good deal of argument and a disquisition from the bench on the law of libels according to Coke's *Littleton*, John Taylor of Caroline was sworn as the first witness for the defense. Judge Chase asked what the witness intended to prove. John Taylor was prepared to swear that President Adams had made statements approving of aristocracy and monarchy. Was he ready to testify that the whole statement charged in the indictment was true? Nicholas explained that the defense intended to prove the truth of some statements by one witness, some by another.

This was a new doctrine, inculcated in Virginia, roared Judge Chase. In tones that set the spectators to tittering he kept referring to the learned counsel, who were well along in middle years, as "these young gentlemen." Nicholas sat down. William Wirt rose with the argument that, since the common law had been adopted by the Commonwealth of Virginia, the jury, according to common law practice, had the right to judge on the law as well as on the facts. He began to develop at some length the theory that as the Constitution was the supreme law of the land the jurors would violate their oaths if they found a traverser guilty under a law which was an infraction of the Constitution.

"Take your seat sir if you please," roared Judge Chase.

Chase then proceeded to read a long opinion which he had prepared ahead: it was no business of the jury's whether a law was constitutional or not. "The jury have a right to consider the law and since the constitution is law," Wirt insisted, "the conclusion is certainly syllogistic that the jury have a right to consider the constitution."

"A non sequitur Sir!" roared Judge Chase.

Mr. Wirt sat down a second time.

George Hay took up the argument but was so browbeaten that he folded up his papers and refused to proceed. Judge Chase concluded with an overwhelming harangue to the effect that the constitutionality of laws was for the courts and not for the juries to decide. The case went to the jury without witnesses being heard for the defense. The jury was out two hours and returned a verdict of guilty. Judge Chase sentenced Callender to nine months in jail and to pay a two hundred dollar fine.

When Judge Chase clambered heavily back in his coach to be driven north he had made an enemy of every lawyer in Virginia. Even John Marshall was reported by his friends to have been shaken by Chase's conduct of Callender's trial.

4. The Rush-Light

While the repressive measures of the Federalists were multiplying the number of Republican voters throughout the country, in Philadelphia the opinionated Dr. Rush was turning the tables on their ablest mouthpiece in the press. During the terror and agony of the yellow fever epidemic in 1793 Rush convinced himself that such of his patients as had survived the disease were cured by his copious bleedings and his purgings with mercury and jalap. He set himself up as an authority on the yellow fever and engaged in a polemic on the origin of the disease with the members of the College of Physicians: they claimed it was an infection imported from the West Indies and demanded quarantine against it; he claimed it arose from the putrefying filth of the waterfront and demanded sanitation. Rush was so confident that he had the temerity to announce in the newspapers that there was no more danger to be apprehended from the yellow fever than from the measles or influenza. He ran advertisements boasting that he could cure the disease with ten grains of calomel, fifteen of jalap and phlebotomy. The pharmacies eagerly advertised Dr. Rush's specific.

Cobbett, whether he was in Liston's employ or not, was making it his business as a trueborn Englishman to make sport of everything that savored of republicanism in America. It was enough for him that Rush had favored Jefferson in the election of 1796. In a series of satires that even the doctor's friends couldn't help laughing at he lampooned poor Rush as the Dr. Sangrado of Philadelphia. Dr. Sangrado, the comic quack in Le Sage's Gil Blas, was as much one of the literary characters of the age as Uncle Toby or Corporal Trim. He was the phlebotomist incarnate. He was made to claim in the novel that it was "a gross error to suppose that blood is necessary to the conservation of life."

Cobbett was implacable. "Purge and bleed! Purge and bleed resounded through the halfdeserted city, while the responsive howling of the dogs gave dreadful note of preparation," he wrote. He ran a want ad: "Wanted, by a physician, an entire new set of patients, his old ones having given him the slip; also a slower method of dispatching them than that of phlebotomy, the celerity of which does not give time *for making out the bill.*"

Peter Porcupine never let up on Rush's description, in one of his pamphlets, of his assistants during the epidemic: "A Popish Priest, a German Apothecary, and Auctioneer and a brace of negro parsons . . . 'They spent all the intervals in which they were not burying the dead' "—here he was quoting Rush himself—" 'in visiting the poor who were sick and in bleeding and purging them agreeably to directions.' " This to Rush, who had risked his own life unstintingly, whose sister had died trying to help him, who had lost three esteemed apprentices, whose battle against the yellow fever had been a forlorn hope carried on with the extremest dedication: it was more than the dogmatic doctor could bear.

To make matters worse, when summer after summer the epidemics emptied the city of inhabitants Dr. Rush's patients kept justifying Cobbett's strictures by dying on his hands. *Porcupine's Gazette* vied with the death cart in making mock of his methods. Fenno's old paper joined in the hue and cry. The good doctor's practice, from being the largest in the city, dropped off to a point where he began to wonder how he could go on supporting his family. In despair he brought suit against Cobbett for libel.

Cobbett was already in trouble with the Pennsylvania courts. The Spanish ambassador, the dandified Marquis de Casa Yrujo, had appealed years before to the general government for protection against Cobbett's spitefully personal tirades which had followed Godoy's abandonment of the British alliance. Unable to get any satisfaction from Pickering's Department of State, Yrujo brought suit in the Pennsylvania court. Cobbett, with the help of his Federalist lawyer friends, managed a series of postponements.

The Spanish ambassador's standing with the Republican leadership in Pennsylvania meanwhile was improved by his marriage to a daughter of Chief Justice McKean. When in the fall of 1799 Judge McKean was elected governor of the state, Cobbett began to fear he would no longer be able to stave off a judgment. Even the high Federalists were tiring of Peter Porcupine. In pressing his suit Rush was able to call in the help of the ablest lawyers in Philadelphia. The ardent Federalist Joseph Hopkinson took up his case. This was the last straw. Cobbett had gone to such lengths that all Cobbett's lawyers could do was play for time. When in the fall of 1799 Robert Goodloe Harper found he could no longer keep the case from trial, Cobbett packed up his family and left for New York.

He published a last editorial in a farewell number of *Porcupine's Gazette*: "I began my editorial career with the Presidency of Mr.

Adams; and my principle object was to render his administration all the assistance in my power. I looked upon him as a stately wellarmed vessel sailing on an expedition to combat and destroy the fatal influence of French principles; and I flattered myself with the hope of accompanying him through the voyage, and of partaking in a trifling degree, of the glory of the enterprise; but he suddenly tacked about and I could follow him no longer. For a firstrater like Mr. Adams to beat up suddenly in the very teeth of former maxims, professions and declarations, might, for aught I know, be not only safe and prudent, but magnanimous also in the highest degree; but for a poor little cockleboat like me, rigged only for a right-foreward course, to attempt to imitate the adventurous manoeuvre would have been the very extreme of vanity and presumption."

The jury awarded Rush five thousand dollars damages. Cobbett abandoned the stock in his bookstore and some printing presses to the judgment of the court. Meanwhile he delivered himself of some of the most amusing publications of his career in a series printed in New York which he entitled *The Rush-Light*. These lampoons so infuriated the Rush family that the doctor's younger son John hurried off to New York to call Cobbett out to fight. Cobbett, who had never made any pretense to gentility, laughed in his face. Young Rush was driven to publishing diatribes in the press, where he was no match for his father's defamer.

Cobbett was no fool, he understood that even with the Federalists he had worn out his welcome. With the split in their ranks Porcupine's market was gone. Even before Cobbett ran out of Philadelphia subscriptions had begun to drop off. Hamilton was defending him with a rear guard action in the New York courts. What with the yellow fever and universal suffrage, there was no living in America for an honest man, he announced. In June 1800 he sailed for the old country.

He stopped in Halifax on the way and was greeted as a great man by the loyalist Nova Scotians. "When I was last in Halifax," he wrote proudly back to Edward Thornton, the Secretary of the British legation in Philadelphia, "I helped as a soldier on fatigue to drag the baggage from the wharf to the Barracks; and when my wife was here last, she was employed in assisting her poor mother to wash soldiers' shirts." His services to the anti-Jacobin cause had made him a career.

In England his reputation was enormous. He was sought out wherever he went. George Hammond greeted him enthusiastically. When he reached London from Portsmouth in August he was able to write back to Thornton describing a dinner with a group of Hammond's eminent associates in the anti-Jacobin campaign. Not only were cabinet ministers delighted to dine with the erstwhile sergeant major but Mr. Raike, the governor of the Bank of England, came to offer him funds for a newspaper. The Prime Minister himself, the unapproachable Pitt, sat at the table with him.

In Philadelphia Benjamin Rush had difficulty collecting his five thousand dollars. Although he had won his libel suit his selfconfidence was more shaken than he dared admit. He would have fretted himself to death if his family and friends had not rallied to him loyally. Cobbett had ruined his medical reputation. John Adams, who admired Rush's devotion to humanitarian causes more than he deplored his politics, had already consoled his hurt pride and assured him a small income by appointing him Treasurer of the Mint.

5. *The Crucial Seventh Ward*

From the moment John Adams presented William Vans Murray's name to the Senate in order to reopen negotiations with the French, Hamilton's carefully woven plans and prospects for empire building to the southward began to unravel. When after Washington's death President Adams showed no sign of treating his inspector general as commander in chief, Hamilton took to spending less of his time at the seat of government and more in his law office in New York.

A large part of Hamilton's business was connected with his brotherinlaw's investments. Like everyone else in the financial community, Church had claims against Robert Morris. In pressing some of these Hamilton came into conflict with Gouverneur Morris, who, having left fragments of his capacious heart in the laps of all the noble émigrée ladies of the old regime scattered among the German courts, had come back to Morrisania still unmarried and was setting to work to salvage what he could for Mrs. Robert Morris out of the ruins of her husband's speculations. Then Church was involved in the complicated deals of a group of Dutch investors in western lands operating in New York under the name of the Holland Land Company. He held title to tens of thousands of acres upstate in his own right. He had a large business in marine insurance and underwriting. Under Hamilton's sponsorship he had become a director of the Bank of New York.

John Barker Church's pretension to leadership among the moneymen who crowded the coffeehouses on Hanover Square was matched by the vivacious Mrs. Church's brilliance as a hostess. Her manners caused dismay among Hamilton's conservative supporters. Harrison Gray Otis, the Massachusetts Federalist, claimed that although she pretended to be "extremely affable and free from ceremony" she was actually "the mirror of affectation."

Her balls were the most magnificent yet seen in New York. Their tone marked a subtle change that had come over the world of fashion. In spite of Edmund Burke's sonorous preachings against everything French, the manners and costumes that the incroyables and the merveilleuses of Paris had copied off the canvases of David were invading the London West End. Angelica Church had brought them with her from England. The young people who besieged her drawing rooms were garbed in the latest Grecian modes.

In the chitchat of these affairs Bonaparte's victories had taken the place of the cruelties of the Jacobins and the sufferings of the powdered heads of the old regime. Marie Antoinette was forgotten. As the ladies wriggled into the highwaisted robes of the new style, wondering just how much of their bosoms they dared expose, it was the legend of a certain Josephine de Beauharnais and of the classical beauties of the salons of victorious Paris that was teasing them on; as the young men tightened their stocks and slipped into sleek swallowtail coats over tight white kneebreeches their beau ideal was Bonaparte, the man of decision, the saturnine young officer of artillery who with a few short scornful orders quelled the mob or destroyed the armies of the archdukes. His likeness—the pale face, the haunted eyes, the raven lock over the forehead—was appearing in the print shops. Busts of Bonaparte were already in demand.

The gallant who escorted the delightful Angelica while she queened it, under the flicker of the chandeliers, over this somewhat disapproving New York society was not her garrulous ungainly husband; it was General Alexander Hamilton in his uniform with the gold eagle of the Cincinnati gleaming at his breast.

Hamilton had been told so often that no woman could resist him that he had come to believe it. Angelica had never made any effort to conceal her passionate devotion to her brotherinlaw. Their lightheaded disregard of the proprieties set envious tongues to work. "Though not yet in the field of Mars," Hamilton's old crony Troup wrote Rufus King in London, "he maintains an unequalled reputation for gallantry —such at least is the opinion entertained of him by the ladies."

In that backbiting provincial society the Churches were already losing the social glamor they had brought with them from London. A few weeks later Troup wrote King again, still shaking his head over their doings: "Poor Church is fast declining in respectability. He talks too much—is too fond of premiums—and too unwilling to pay losses." Troup feared that the whole Schuyler clan, of which Hamilton was the chief luminary, was already deeply compromised. He had even begun to doubt Church's financial powers. "Church is said to be much pushed for money—and indeed family affairs are in a train which in my opinion will by & by cause an explosion which will spread general ruin around it—I mean the ruin of almost the whole connexion. I consider it unfortunate that he ever removed with his family to this country."

This last letter of Troup's was written on the very day that John Barker Church met Aaron Burr on the dueling field at Hoboken.

Under the influence of Hamilton's growing bitterness against his chief rival at the bar and at the polls and in the boudoirs of the lovely ladies, Church was overheard indiscreetly repeating some disparaging remark about Burr's transactions with the Holland Land Company. The inference was that Burr had been bribed to use his influence in the state Assembly to repeal a law that discriminated against foreign landowners. Burr, who was smarting from having lost twenty thousand dollars he did not have through his failure to complete the payments within the specified period on a tract of land he had been trying to buy through that very company, resented Church's statements and called him out to fight.

A Republican journalist named Matthew Davis wrote an account of the duel. Davis was a devoted follower of Burr's and one of his chief henchmen in New York City politics. He was taking over *The Time-Piece* from Philip Freneau. That restless versifier, wearying of his endless doggerel lambastings of the bulldog Cobbett, was again giving up journalism for the sea. Davis was turning the journal into an organ of Burr's own private brand of republicanism. Bonapartism his enemies called it. According to Davis, Burr, who hardly let a day go by without practicing with his pistols, had been explaining to his second on the way across to the Jersey shore a special system he had for loading them.

Burr's second in this duel was Aedanus Burke, the original enemy of aristocracy and of the Cincinnati, who was now a South Carolina judge. Burr's pistols shot a particularly small ball which needed to be greased and wrapped in chamois skin before being pressed home against the charge with a ramrod. Judge Burke could hardly have been listening very carefully because, when Burr handed him his pistol case after they landed from the boat, it was noticed that he was having trouble loading. After the preliminary civilities and the pacing off of the distance, Burr turned to him for his pistol. The judge was not ready. Burr, with his usual expression of quiet disdain, stood watching the judge struggling to force the bullet home by pounding on the ramrod with a stone. "I forgot to grease the leather," the judge stammered, "but you see he's ready. Don't keep him waiting. Just take a crack at him as it is. I'll grease the next one."

Burr bowed and shot the pistol as it was. A coat was creased. Church apologized for his remark. Burr announced himself satisfied and the parties allowed themselves to be rowed back across the Hudson.

Wherever Hamilton moved he found himself in competition with Aaron Burr. They had long been rivals in the law courts. Now Burr was managing to build up a financial interest to rival Hamilton's. The Federalists, since the foundation under Hamilton's auspices of the New York branch of the Bank of the United States, so completely dominated banking in the city that they were able to put pressure on their opponents by cutting off their credit. After leaving the United States Senate to get himself elected to the Assembly, Burr managed to use his influence at Albany and his careful manipulation of the rancors and prejudices of the Livingston and Clinton interests in the Council of Revision to secure a charter for a concern he named the Manhattan Company.

This company was allowed to engage in business without too much opposition because the ostensible purpose was to furnish pure water to the city householders. The lack of decent drinking water had long been a trial to New Yorkers. They had to buy their water at a high price from carts that brought it from what was known as the teawater pump uptown. Burr's company went to work immediately to establish a reservoir. An engineer named Nicholas Roosevelt was hired to furnish a steam pump from which the water would flow through wooden conduits to the houses. The water system was such a success that Church, whose money knew no politics, was glad to serve on the board of directors. When it turned out that the charter of the Manhattan Company was written in such terms as to allow the establishment of a bank and of a trading concern as well as a water system the whole Hamiltonian interest raised the cry of chicanery and deception against Burr. An independent bank was a threat to their monopoly of the money market.

Hamilton's exasperation over the Manhattan Company's banking business was increased by the inroads he found Burr to be making in the ward politics of the city where in the days of the great procession in celebration of the Constitution Hamilton had reigned supreme.

Long since, Burr's eager young disciples like Davis and the Swartwouts and the Van Ness brothers had made themselves preeminent in the Tammany Society. They contributed mightily to swell the vote for Jefferson in the presidential election of 1796 and helped defeat Hamilton's scheme to elect Thomas Pinckney instead of John Adams President.

The election of the spring of 1799, held in the height of the fluster over the XYZ dispatches, had gone well for Hamilton's friends. Burr himself lost his seat in the Assembly. Now in the spring of 1800 it was on everybody's lips that this year's New York election was as much of nationwide concern as the election that Hamilton had so brilliantly carried during the struggle for the ratification of the Constitution. In New York the presidential electors were chosen by the Assembly. Upstate the vote furnished by the Clinton and Livingston connections on the Republican side would be about matched by the vote controlled by the Schuyler connection and by the admirers of John Jay, who was still governor, on the other. The election in the city and county of New York would determine the electoral vote of the state.

Hamilton and Burr exerted themselves to the uttermost. In past elections Hamilton's friends among bankers and moneylenders had found it useful to bring pressure to bear on the merchants so that they would see to it that their employees voted the right way. "We have at last prevailed upon the merchants to exert themselves," Troup wrote Rufus King. "In the last election they were essentially useful. They told the cartmen that such of them as supported the democratic ticket would be dismissed from their employ. The consequence was we had strong support from the cartmen . . . Mr. John Murray – the president of the Chamber of Commerce–spent one whole day at the poll of the Sev'th Ward sometimes called the cartmen's ward or the Livingston stronghold–and his presence operated like a charm."

Burr thought of a countermeasure. He sent his young men out to encourage poor Republicans, recent Irish immigrants most of them, to establish themselves as voters by clubbing together to buy fortyshilling freeholds in common. As each tenant in common had a legal right to the whole parcel he could register as a voter at least for the assemblymen and for the representative in Congress. To vote for a state senator a man had to show that he was worth £120, a sum out of the reach of most of the laborers and tradesmen and mechanics who made up the Republican vote in the city wards. In specially deserving cases money was furnished out of the very considerable campaign fund which Burr was raising, by assessing his friends and supporters according to their ability to pay, to help set up these tenancies in common.

Hamilton had lost his early flair for popular politics. He was bent on repeating the machiavellian tactics which had come so near losing his party the presidential election of 1796. The Federalists were agreed that their candidates for the fall of 1800 would be John Adams and Charles Cotesworth Pinckney. John Adams would bring in the solid New England vote and General Pinckney the southern slaveholding conservatives. With McKean's election in Pennsylvania there was a good chance that that state with its large electoral vote would go

Republican. Although his more independent friends pointed out to him that personal feelings should be sacrificed to keep New York State Federalist, all Hamilton could think of was how to defeat John Adams, who had thwarted his great plans. In picking the slate of candidates for the state Assembly and the House of Representatives in the city election he thought more of their pliability to his orders than of their appeal to the voters.

John Adams, after his retirement to Quincy, described the situation in a retrospective letter: "Hamilton made a Journey to Boston, to Providence & c, to persuade the People and their Legislatures but without Success, to throw away some of their Votes, that Adams might not have the unanimous Vote of New England consequently that Pinckney might be brought in as President and Adams as Vice President. Washington was dead and the Cincinnati were assembled at New York to chose Hamilton for their new President. Whether he publicly opened his Project to the whole Assembly of the Cincinnati or not, I will not say; but of this I have such proof that I cannot doubt, namely that he broached it privately to such Members as he could trust; for the learned and pious Doctors Dwight and Babcock, who having been chaplains in the Army, were then attending as two reverend Knights of the Order, with their blue Ribbons and bright Eagles at their sable Buttonholes, were heard to say repeatedly in the Room where the Society met 'we must sacrifice Adams', 'we must sacrifice Adams' . . . Hamilton soon after called another more secret Caucus to prepare a list of Representatives for the City of New York . . . He fixed upon a List of his own Friends, People of little Weight or Consideration in the City or the Country. Burr, who had Friends in all Circles, had a copy of this List brought to him immediately. He read it over, with great gravity folded it up, put it in his Pocket and without uttering another Word said Now I have him all hollow."

Burr started collecting the most prominent and independent candidates possible for his ticket. So that he could devote all his time to the campaign in the city the Republican caucus decided to run Burr himself for the Assembly in Orange County where he would be virtually unopposed. He put all his persuasive powers to work to induce George Clinton, the perennial governor of the state who had been defeated by John Jay; and Robert Morris's inveterate enemy in the old Congress, the retired Postmaster General, Samuel Osgood; and old General Gates who had moved to New York from Berkeley Springs, to join Brockholst Livingston in heading the ticket. He was ably seconded by Albert Gallatin's fatherinlaw Commodore Nicholson. Clinton and Osgood and Gates had announced repeatedly that they would not allow their names to be used. After agonizing discussions Burr talked them around. These names had far more than local appeal.

The rest were men who had strong support in the various city wards.

The polls were open for the last two days of April and closed at sunset on May 1. During the three days nobody slept or ate. Hamilton rode from polling place to polling place on a white horse. Burr, who outside the law courts was chary of public appearances, made repeated speeches to the voters assembled round the whiskey barrels. When the two men met they exchanged the most courtly civilities.

At midnight on May 1 Matthew Davis scratched off a hurried note to Albert Gallatin in Philadelphia. Gallatin as leader of the Republican minority in the House was in the position of national manager for the Democratic-Republicans. Through his close ties with the Nicholsons he was in daily touch with the New York election. Like a good journalist, Davis began his letter with a headline: "Republicanism Triumphant . . . Dear Sir, it affords me the highest gratification to assure you of the complete success of the Republican Assembly ticket in this city." Dr. Mitchill, their candidate for the House, was elected by a hundred votes and the whole ticket would show a probable majority of three hundred and fifty. "To colonel Burr we are indebted for everything. This day has he remained at the poll of the Seventh Ward ten hours without intermission." This year there was to be no intimidating of the cartmen. "Pardon this hasty scrawl; I have not ate for fifteen hours."

A few days later, after Davis had caught up on his sleep a little, he wrote Gallatin more at length:

"Dear Sir;—I have already informed you of the complete triumph which we have obtained in this city . . . The approaching election for President and Vice President will decide in some measure on our future destiny. The result will clearly evince whether a republican form of government is worth contending for . . . The management and industry of Colonel Burr has effected all that the friends of civil liberty could possibly desire . . . I believe it is pretty generally understood that Mr. Jefferson is contemplated for President. But who is to fill the Vice President's chair?" Obviously, Davis explained, the candidate must be from New York. Davis disposed of Clinton as too old and of Chancellor Robert R. Livingston too vaccilating. "Colonel Burr is therefore the most eligible character . . . If he is elected to the office of V. P. it would waken so much of the zeal and pride of our friends in this State as to secure us a Republican governor at the next election (April, 1801). If he is not nominated, many of us will experience much chagrin and disappointment . . . Please inform me by post . . . I feel very anxious."

Next day Gallatin wrote his wife, who was staying with her father in New York, that he had to make a decision within a few days between

Clinton and Burr and wanted "correct information of the wishes of the New York Republicans."

Immediately the commodore wrote back that the election "has been conducted and brought to an issue in so miraculous a manner that I cannot account for it but from the intervention of a Supreme Power and our friend Burr the agent . . . His generalship, perseverance, industry and execution exceeds all description, so that I think I can say he deserves anything and everything of his country; but he has done it at the risk of his life," he added mysteriously. He would explain when they next met. "I am informed he is coming on to you. Perhaps he will be the bearer of this. I shall conclude by recommending him as a general far superior to your Hambletons"—the old commodore didn't have enough use for the inspector general to try to spell his name right—"as much so as a man is to a boy; and I have but little doubt that this state, through his means and planning, will be as Republican in the appointment of electors as the state of Virginia."

Mrs. Gallatin wrote her husband by the same post: "Burr says he has no confidence in the Virginians; they once deceived him, and they are not to be trusted." Burr was holding out for assurances that the Virginians would really vote for him and not cast their second ballot for General Pinckney, as they had for Thomas Pinckney in the last election. "His name must not be played the fool with," insisted the commodore.

May 12, the same day that John Adams wrote Pickering to demand his resignation, Gallatin wrote his wife from Philadelphia: "We had last night a very large meeting of Republicans, in which it was unanimously agreed to support Burr for Vice President."

Meanwhile Hamilton was counseling desperate measures. While he wrote his friends urging them to see that General Pinckney got a majority in the electoral college, he wrote Governor Jay suggesting that measures should be taken to circumvent the New York vote: "The moral certainty therefore is, that there will be an anti-federal majority in the ensuing Legislature; and the very high probability is that this will bring *Jefferson* into the chief magistracy unless it be prevented by a measure which I shall now submit to your consideration, namely the immediate calling together of the existing Legislature."

Hamilton was suggesting that the old legislature which the Federalists controlled should be called into special session to change the system of choosing presidential electors. If the vote were by districts, as it was in Massachusetts, they might hope for a Federalist majority.

"It will not do to be overscrupulous," Hamilton wrote, fully conscious of his friend's somewhat exaggerated rectitude. *"It is easy to sacrifice the substantial interests of society by a strict adherence to ordinary rules . . .* They ought not to stop the taking of a legal and constitutional step to prevent an atheist in religion and a fanatic in politics, from getting possession of the helm of state."

Hamilton paused for breath and began a new paragraph: "You sir, know in a great degree the anti-federal party; but I fear you do not know them as well as I do. It is a composition indeed of very incongruous materials, but all tending to mischief—some of them to the Overthrow of the Government, by stripping it of its due energies; others of them, to a Revolution after the manner of Bonaparte."

Burr had mysterious ways of learning of the plans of opponents. When Hamilton wrote John Jay, he was repeating his advice to the Federalist caucus held immediately after the counting of the votes. An anonymous correspondent the very next day wrote a letter to Philadelphia describing the scheme. Duane featured it in his *Aurora*. The Federalists immediately denounced this story as a Jacobin calumny. "Where is the American who will not detest the author of this infamous Lie," wrote one New York editor in high dudgeon. Governor Jay never answered Hamilton's letter. It was found among his papers with a note in Jay's neat meticulous handwriting across the back: "Proposing a measure for party purposes which I think it would not become me to adopt."

6. Gabriel's Conspiracy

Jefferson left Monticello on November 24, 1800, to preside over the second session of the Sixth Congress, the first to be held in the long projected capital city at the head of navigation of the Potomac. Winter was settling in early. The roads were already deeply rutted. He had three ferries to cross. He drove slowly. He was timing his journey so as to be sure not to be in the presiding officer's chair when John Adams made his opening address. "I shall set out for Washington so as to arrive there as soon as I suppose the answer to the speech is delivered," he wrote Monroe, who was governor in Richmond. "It is possible some silly things will be put into the latter on the hypothesis of it's being valedictory, & that these may be zealously answered by the federal majority in our house. they shall deliver it themselves therefore."

He added he was sorry he had missed Monroe's last trip to Albemarle by having gone to his plantation in Bedford County. Poplar Forest was becoming his island of refuge when he felt he had to escape the continual tramping of visitors, political, social and philosophical, through Monticello. And now in view of the probability that he would be the next President the parade of officeseekers was beginning.

The reason he so wanted to talk to Monroe was a grim one. Gabriel's conspiracy had been discovered among the Negroes around Richmond. "I wished to learn something of the excitements, the expectations & extent of this negro conspiracy, not being satisfied with the popular reports," he wrote.

This conspiracy, supposed to have been fomented by mulatto revolutionists arriving in Norfolk full of French ideas of liberty and equality on ships that traded with Santo Domingo, had caused sardonic amusements among the New England Federalists. They took no pains to conceal their satisfaction at seeing the Virginia Jacobins hoist by their own petard. The slaves were taking these ideas of liberty and equality in dead earnest. They would emulate their brothers in Santo Domingo. The first step would be to massacre their white masters. The leader, "General" Gabriel, was a great Bible reader. He announced that he was appointed of God, like Samson, to set his people free. His plans were discovered when two Henrico County Negroes warned their master that his life was in danger.

The news of it filled Jefferson, who saw no immediate way of inducing his fellow citizens to rid his country of the curse of slavery, with bitter meditations. The conspiracy had been quelled with the usual severity. Fortyone Negroes had been hanged in Richmond. "Where to stay the hand of the executioner is an important question," Jefferson wrote Monroe from Monticello on the first news of it; "those who have escaped from the immediate danger, must have feelings which would dispose them to extend the executions. even here, where everything has been perfectly tranquil, but where a familiarity with slavery, and a possibility of danger from that quarter prepare the general mind for some severities, there is a strong sentiment that there has been hanging enough. The other states & the world at large will forever condemn us if we indulge a principle of revenge, or go one step beyond the absolute necessity."

Jefferson never forgot the cruel paradox on which the southern Republicans were impaled. They were for liberty for everyone except the slaves. He could see how the brutal reprisals which were part of the very structure of the slave system would appear in the eyes of people who made freedom their creed. "They cannot lose sight of the rights of the two parties & the object of the unsuccessful one," he wrote as tactfully as he could to Monroe.

7.   *"The greatest service which can be rendered . . ."*

The summer and fall that had just gone by had been for

Jefferson a period of deep searching and selfappraisal. As it became more and more probable that he would succeed John Adams as President he began to turn over in his mind ways and means of accomplishing some of the things he wanted to accomplish.

His publication that spring of a new and revised edition of his *Notes on Virginia* had two aims. The most immediate was to put an end to the bickering and backbiting of the Cresap connection by printing the true facts, which he had gone to great trouble to discover, on which the Indian Logan's charges against Michael Cresap were based. The other was to express clearly his underlying philosophy of government, his fears and forebodings on the subject of slavery, his aspirations for his country. To make his position even clearer he printed in additional appendices his latest draft of a constitution for . the State of Virginia and his act for establishing religious freedom. He felt these two writings expressed as clearly as anything he had ever written his matured philosophy of government.

He was immensely sensitive to criticism. He never pretended not to be pained by the virulence of the attacks on him by the New England divines. Taking their cue from the English parsons who had long been cribbing their sermons out of Burke's denunciations of French atheism, libertinism and bloodshed, the clergy of New England, since the political campaign began, had, almost to a man, been lashing up their parishioners to exert themselves in the Federalist cause by holding up to common obloquy as atheistic Jacobins Robespierre, Tom Paine and Jefferson.

Jefferson had been pondering a project of trying to set the record straight by publishing some formulations of his own religious creed based on his careful and continuous reading of the New Testament. "I have a view of the subject," he wrote Dr. Rush, whom he knew to be a man of profound and somewhat dogmatic religious convictions, "which ought to displease neither the rational Christian nor Deists, and would reconcile many to a character"—he meant Jesus—"they have too hastily rejected. I do not know that it would reconcile the *genus irritabile vatum* who are up in arms against me," he added wryly. He explained that he felt a good deal of their spleen came from their belief that he was opposed to any religion established as a ward of the state. "And they believe rightly for I have sworn on the altar of god eternal hostility against every form of tyranny over the mind of man."

Jefferson, sitting pondering and worrying at his desk some time during this period, jotted down a page of notes:

"I have sometimes asked myself whether my country is the better for my having lived at all? I do not know that it is. I have been the instrument of doing the following things. but they would have been done by others; some of them, perhaps, a little better."

It was second nature to him to make lists. He listed first the work
he did the year he came of age to get the red Rivanna that flowed
past the foot of his hill between Charlottesville and Monticello cleared
of obstructions and opened to navigation by flatboat and canoe; then
the Declaration of Independence; the Virginia law for religious freedom; the law putting an end to entails which he believed would,
through the division of property among numerous heirs, hinder the
growth of landowning aristocracy; the act prohibiting further importation of slaves; his naturalization act which established "the natural
right of man to expatriate himself at will," and his act establishing
labor in solitary confinement as a penal measure.

On a level with these achievements he noted his importation of
olive plants and upland rice into Georgia and South Carolina. "The
greatest service which can be rendered any country is, to add an
useful plant to its culture; especially a bread grain; next in value to
bread is oil."

At the end of the page he listed one of his failures: "Whether the
act for the more general diffusion of knowledge will ever be carried
into complete effect I know not," he wrote wistfully, and noted that
even the small part of his project that had passed the Virginia
legislature, the section which set up free grammar schools, had been
rendered ineffectual by making the schools optional with the counties.
Now the prospect of being in a position to put the prestige of the
presidency behind it had encouraged him to revive another part of
his great project.

Among his political friends in Virginia he had been talking up the
part of his plan that dealt with higher education. He wanted a great
Virginia university "on a plan so broad & liberal & modern . . . to
be a temptation to the youth of other states to come and drink the
cup of knowledge and fraternize with us," he explained when he
wrote to Priestley for advice about a curriculum.

Their plans for a national university as part of their great scheme
for a national capital had been one of the last of the common projects
in which his mind had met on friendly ground with Washington's
before the rancors and misunderstandings of political partisanship
divided them forever. Now Jefferson was full of hope that once republicanism should triumph over the nation he could push his scheme
for free public education so long held in abeyance. When he wrote
for Priestley's advice he did not fail to apologize for the persecutions
he and his friend Cooper had suffered at the hands of the Federalists,
"but their glass is nearly run out and the day I believe is approaching
when we shall be as free to pursue what is true wisdom as the effects
of their follies will permit."

8. The Grand Columbian Federal City

Jefferson was not a man to remain long discouraged. As he ferried his carriage across the smooth Potomac to the clustered houses of Georgetown under their great trees he could hardly have avoided a feeling of elation. After so many years' delay, the transfer of the capital away from the influence of the moneymen of Philadelphia and New York had actually been accomplished. Every sign of new building he saw filled him with sanguine hopes for the future.

He drove through the gullied streets of Georgetown, crossed the new stone bridge that spanned Rock Creek and then plunged into a mile and a half of well drained level land grown up in bushes, interspersed with clearings where fifty or more brick houses stood, some singly, but most of them in attached rows like London houses, before reaching the fine new structure of white Aquia sandstone that Hoban had modeled on the Duke of Leinster's mansion in Dublin.

Jefferson, who had approved the plans, studied the work with a professional eye. The President's house was far from finished. Hogan was shorthanded; he was running advertisements in the newspapers offering as high as two dollars a day for qualified carpenters and joiners. Still the President and Mrs. Adams, even though the fireplace smoked and collecting enough wood to heat its vast apartments was a daily miracle, were managing to live in some state in one corner of it. The great reception hall had recently been plastered; Mrs. Adams used it for her laundress to dry the washing in. The grounds were still a tangle of brush fenced in by a few rough palings. Across the road were some more brick houses and a scattering of log shacks where the workmen lived.

Flanking the handsome edifice on one side was the scorched hulk of the three story building which had accommodated the War Department that had burned a few days before. On the other was the small brick house of the Treasury, from which careful Oliver Wolcott, scenting the change in the political winds, had announced his resignation for the end of the year.

Possibly resisting an impulse to call on his old friend, Jefferson drove on from the President's house across a broad uneven causeway, full of ruts and potholes, which was already known as Pennsylvania Avenue. This causeway ran straight across the tidal marshlands drained by a small stream which Jefferson had encouraged the early promoters to call the Tiber instead of Goose Creek. Where the banks of the little river rose above high tide level they were shaded by groves of enormous tulip poplars. The flats were full of snipe that offered excellent shooting. The soggy quality of the land, often flooded

on high tides, and the dread of fevers in the "sickly season" had kept
any houses from being built until the high ground was reached on
which the enormous edifice of the Capitol was under construction.

The work on Thornton's project had lagged. Congress made niggardly appropriations. There had been disputes among the architects
as to the feasibility of the arches. Thornton's designs, like L'Enfant's,
had the epic sweep, but found it hard to cope with simple practical
details such as the headroom on the stairways or the lighting of the
lobbies. Although most of the foundation was laid, only part of the
north wing was in a state to be occupied. Visitors wrote home about
the excellent quail hunting in the weeds and long grass on the hillside
under its high walls pieced with pedimented windows in the style of
Michelangelo. The scaffoldings and piles of brick and stone round the
Capitol were the center of another little village where most of the
members of Congress lived.

Gallatin, the Republican leader in the House, on whom Jefferson
depended for his keen head for figures, wrote his wife: "Our local
situation is far from being pleasant or even convenient. Around the
Capitol are seven or eight boarding houses, one tailor, one shoemaker,
one printer, a washing-woman, a grocery shop, a pamphlet and sta-
tionery shop, a small drygoods shop and an oyster house."

From Capitol Hill you could see the rest of the unfinished city. "At
a distance of three fourths of a mile, on or near the Eastern branch" —
which Jefferson insisted on calling by its Indian name of Anacostia —
"lie scattered . . . half a dozen houses, a very large but perfectly empty
warehouse, and a wharf graced by not a single vessel. And this makes
the whole intended commercial part of the city, unless we include in
it what we call the Twenty Buildings, being so many unfinished houses
commenced by Morris and Nicholson" — the bankruptcy of these
worthies had interrupted work on their development — "and perhaps
as many undertaken by Greenleaf, both of which groups lie, at a
distance of a half a mile from each other, near the mouth of the Eastern
Branch and the Potowmack, and are divided by a large swamp from
the Capitol Hill and the little village connected with it."

Jefferson, like Gallatin, put up at Conrad and McMunn's boardinghouse a couple of hundred paces from the Capitol. These enterprising
Caledonians had prepared for the arrival of Congress by erecting
stables and carriage houses and a building to accommodate transients
on the south flank of the hill. In addition, for the housing of residents
of distinction they leased a spacious brick house from Thomas Law, an
eccentric Englishman who had married one of Martha Washington's
Custis granddaughters.

Margaret Bayard Smith, the wife of the editor of *The National*

Intelligencer whom Jefferson had induced to come on from Philadelphia, where he had served as secretary of the American Philosophical Society, to set up a Republican print shop, wrote her friends enthusiastically of the location of the Law house and of the romantic views from its southern and western windows. "It was on top of the hill," she noted in her journal, "the precipitous sides of which were covered with grass, shrubs and trees in their wild uncultivated state. Between the foot of the hill and the broad Potomac extended a wide plain, through which the Tiber wound its way . . . the whole plain was diversified with groves and clumps of forest which gave it the appearance of a fine park . . ." She noted how unhappy the felling of these magnificent trees for firewood made Mr. Jefferson. "It was partly from this love of nature, that he selected Conrad's boarding house . . . Here he had a separate drawingroom for the reception of his visitors; in all other respects he lived on a perfect equality with his fellow boarders, and eat at a common table. Even here, so far from taking precedence of the other members of Congress, he always placed himself at the lowest end of the table. Mrs. Brown the wife of the senator from Kentucky, suggested that a seat should be offered him near the fire, if not on account of his rank as vice-President, at least as the oldest man in company. But the idea was rejected by his democratic friends and he occupied during the whole winter the lowest and coldest seat at a long table at which a company of more than thirty sat down."

Gallatin had a less high opinion of the little village on Capitol Hill than Mrs. Smith. Writing his wife, he described somewhat enviously the superior advantages of the northwesterly settlement grouped round the President's house which he figured might well in the course of a few years become as flourishing as Lancaster, newly chosen as capital of Pennsylvania, or even as Annapolis. "But *we* are not there; the distance is too great for convenience from thence to the Capitol; six or seven of the members have taken lodgings at Georgetown, three near the President's house, and all the others are crowded in the eight boardinghouses near the Capitol. I am at Conrad & McMunn's, where I share the room of Mr. Varnum," — senator from Massachusetts — "and pay at the rate, I think including attendance, wood, candles and liquors, of 15 dollars per week. At table, I believe, we are from twenty-four to thirty, and, was it not for the presence of Mrs. Bailey and Mrs. Brown, would look like a refectory of monks. The two Nicholas, Mr. Langdon, Mr. Jefferson, General Smith. Mr. Baldwin & & make part of our mess."

The Washington lodging houses were filling up strictly according to party lines. Mrs. Bailey was the wife of a Republican representative from New York. Wilson Cary Nicholas, senator from Virginia, and

John his brother, the representative, were both old supporters of
Jefferson's. John Langdon was a moderate, but his appointment as
senator from New Hampshire was a symptom of the growing Republican groundswell in New England. General Smith was a wealthy
Baltimore shipping man who inclined to the Jeffersonian side. Abraham
Baldwin, a Yale man who had set up a law practice in Georgia and
whose sister Ruth was Joel Barlow's wife, was a pioneer in public
education and one of the ablest Republicans in the Senate.

"The company is good enough but it is always the same," complained
Gallatin to his wife, "and, unless in my own family, I had rather now
and then see some other persons. Our not being able to have a room
each is a greater inconvenience. As to our fare, we have hardly any
vegetables, the people being obliged to resort to Alexandria for
supplies; our beef is not very good; mutton and poultry good; the
price of provisions and wood about the same as in Philadelphia."

Peglegged Gouverneur Morris, appointed to fill an uncompleted
term as senator from New York, had arrived in the new capital
a few days before Jefferson. He came full of memories of his ten
years in Europe, full of scorn for his fellow man and full of that
appetite for adventure that never left him. He found two inches of
snow on the ground and enjoyed the fine frosty air. He described to
his female correspondents overseas the beauty of the landscape, the
piles of brick and stone, the sites for magnificent dwellings; it was the
city in the world where you best could live in the future.

"All we lack is houses, winecellars, kitchens, educated men, amiable
women and other little bagatelles of that nature," he wrote in his
florid French to the Comtesse de Tour et Taxis. Whenever he closed
his door his room filled with smoke from a faulty chimney. One afternoon when he drove out to dinner a couple of miles from his lodging
a thaw came on. His coach sank so deep in the mud the horses would
not pull it and he had to spend the night. "Here I follow the trade
of Senator and I find a nonchalant amusement in watching the little
intrigues, the mad Hopes and the vain Projects of that proud and
feeble Animal which is Man."

He found his Federalist friends grumbling desperately over the
discomforts of the place. Brought up in their tight little seaboard cities
which still looked to London as the metropolis of thought and fancy,
they could not reconcile themselves to this new raw western world
where everything was in the future. They felt doom ringing in their
ears. Their nerves were jangled by the overcrowding of the rattletrap
boardinghouses they had to live in. They were huddling together for
a last stand again the changes the very success of their revolution had
brought about. Their minds were pitched to the politics of despair.

9. "As to politics ... "

"As to politics," wrote Gallatin, "you may suppose that being all thrown together in a few boardinghouses, without hardly any other society than ourselves, we are not likely to be either very moderate politicians or to think of anything but politics. A few indeed drink and some gamble, but the majority drink naught but politics, and by not mixing with men of different or more moderate sentiments they inflame one another."

Through a cold December, Congress was marking time over the new treaty with France which Governor Davie had brought home. The intransigence of the British members of the mixed claims commission set up under the Jay treaty, combined with the continued impressment of American seamen on the high seas, had convinced the wing of the Federalist party which revered John Adams that the President should be supported in his efforts to seek an accommodation with the French. Even Hamilton was urging his friends to make the best of a bad business. All the extreme Anglomen could do was obstruct the progress of ratification.

Just in case they had to concede Jefferson's election to the presidency the Federalists in both houses were pushing through a bill very much extending the federal judiciary. They were going part way to meet Hamilton's specifications in his letter to Jonathan Dayton for a series of courts which would enforce every fiat of the general government.

Meanwhile they hoped against hope. With New York lost they looked to South Carolina to bring in Federalist electors. In South Carolina even the powerful Pinckneys were divided. General Pinckney's cousin Charles, who had played so large a part in the constitutional convention, came out vigorously for Jefferson and Burr. Though in the election for the Seventh Congress South Carolina voted Republican, it would still be the Federalist legislature that appointed the electors. Furthermore they hung their hopes on an odd stalemate in the Pennsylvania legislature. The state had gone overwhelmingly Republican when McKean was elected governor. Now the holdover Senate was balking at passing any electoral law at all. That would mean that Pennsylvania would lose its vote in the presidential election. When news came of a compromise by which the Republicans would be allowed a bare majority of the state's electoral vote even John Adams had to admit that the election would go to Jefferson and Burr.

A few Federalist newspapers were still claiming a victory for Adams and Pinckney. Harrison Smith's *National Intelligencer* was claiming 84 votes for Jefferson. By the middle of December it was generally admitted that the vote in the electoral college would be Jefferson 73; Burr 73; Adams 65; Pinckney 64 and John Jay 1. That meant that

according to the confused wording of the Constitution, which pre-
scribed no way of keeping the votes for President and Vice President
separate, the House of Representatives of the Sixth Congress, where
there was still a Federalist majority, would have to choose between
Jefferson and Burr. The Republican Seventh Congress could not meet
until after March 4.

Hamilton sat at his desk at 26 Broadway writing and writing. The
complete victory of the coalition between the Burr, Clinton and Livingston factions had eliminated him for the time being from New
York politics. Now he was trying to reassume his dominance of the
national scene which he had lost when he lost his aegis, George
Washington.

To further his scheme of contriving more votes for General Pinckney
than for John Adams in the electoral college he wrote a long denunciation of *The Public Conduct and Character of John Adams Esq., President of the United States.* Most of the damaging detail came from
notes furnished him by Messrs. Wolcott and Pickering, who at Hamilton's request had been beguiling their spare time during their term
in office by collecting a dossier against their chief. Hamilton intended
this diatribe for the private consumption of the party leaders but to
save time in copying he rashly ordered copies of it printed. Some
journeyman or printer's devil, possibly wanting to get back at hightoned General Hamilton for Frothingham's imprisonment, saw to it
that a copy found its way to Aaron Burr at Richmond Hill.

Burr immediately distributed Hamilton's denunciation of Adams far
and wide. *The Aurora* gleefully published an abstract. Every casual
reader of the gazettes could appreciate the extent of the split in the
Federalist party. "Alexander Hamilton and the New York Feds have
split upon the Adamantine rock," exulted Duane; "he says that John
Adams must not be President, they say that John Adams must — so
says the proverb where thieves fall out honest men must come into
their own."

When Hamilton discovered that Adams and Pinckney were both
irrevocably lost and that the choice was to be between Jefferson and
Burr his feelings underwent a complete transformation. His Federalist
friends were beginning to work for the election of Burr by the House
of Representatives as the lesser of two evils. His brotherinlaw Church
was already jokingly referring to Burr as "our Chief Consul." This
must not be. Hamilton threw all the energy of his flowing pen into
begging his friends to defeat Burr.

"Jefferson is to be preferred," he wrote Oliver Wolcott. "He is by
far not so dangerous a man; and he has pretensions to character. As to

Burr, there is nothing in his favor. His private character is not defended by his most partial friends. He is bankrupt beyond redemption except by the plunder of his country."

At about the same time Hamilton's friend Troup was writing Rufus King that if Burr became Vice President his salary would not even pay the interest on his debts.

"His public principles," ranted Hamilton, "have no other spring or aim than his own aggrandizement, *per fas et nefas*. If he can he will certainly disturb our institutions, to secure himself permanent power and with it wealth. He is truly the Cataline of America."

The prospect of Burr's election robbed him of his sleep. "Let it not be imagined," he wrote Wolcott again next day, "that Mr. Burr can be won to the federal views. It is a vain hope . . . To accomplish his ends he must lean on unprincipled men, and will continue to adhere to the myrmidons who have hitherto seconded him . . . He is too cold-blooded and too determined a conspirator ever to change his plan." Burr made it a point, wrote Hamilton in scandalized vein, to toast Bonaparte at his dinner parties. "Adieu to the Federal Troy if they once introduce this Grecian horse into their citadel.

"Trust me my dear friend, you cannot render a greater service to your country than to resist this project." It would be far better to obtain assurances from Jefferson on four chief points: 1. preservation of the fiscal system, 2. neutrality in the war between England and France, 3. preservation of the navy, 4. continuance of Federalists in office, "except in the great departments, in which he ought to be left free," added Hamilton, who, for all his partisan fury, understood the exigencies of administration.

The fear that his friends might elect Aaron Burr to the presidency became an obsession. He could not enjoy his family or his delightful plans for the country house he was building or Angelica Church's gay parties. The day after Christmas he wrote Gouverneur Morris, who as usual was wavering and getting a perverse pleasure out of his own indecision, that Burr's elevation could only "promote the purposes of the desperate and profligate . . . If there be a man in the world I ought to hate," he added, "it is Jefferson. With Burr I have always been personally well. But the public good must be paramount to every private consideration."

As it became certain with the approach of the New Year that the election would go into the House of Representatives, Hamilton threw all his powers of persuasion into a letter to James Bayard, who as sole representative from Delaware would play a pivotal role in the coming contest. "As a politician," he wrote of Burr, "his whole spring of action is an inordinate ambition . . . without probity . . . a voluptuary by system — with habits of expense that can be satisfied by no fair expedi-

ents. As to his talents, great management and cunning . . . daring and
energy . . . to a man of this description, possessing the requisite talents,
the acquisition of permanent power is not a chimera . . . I am sure
there are no means too atrocious to be employed by him."

As the fatal February 11 set for the scrutiny of the electoral vote
by the two houses of Congress drew near he wrote Bayard again. He
deplored the news that kept coming to him that the Federalists were
planning to support Burr. He repeated that he, Hamilton, was the last
man in the world to become an apologist for Jefferson: "I admit that
his politics are tinctured with fanaticism; that he is too much in earnest
in his democracy; that he has been a mischievous enemy to the
principle measures of our past administration; that he is crafty and
persevering in his objects; that he is not scrupulous about the means
of success, and that he is a contemptible hypocrite." He went on to
analyze very acutely Jefferson's political character. "While we were
in the administration together, he was generally for a large construction
of the executive authority and not backward to act on it in cases
which coincided with his views . . . To my mind a true estimate of
Mr. Jefferson's character warrants the expectation of a temporizing
rather than a violent system . . . Add to this that there is no fair
reason to suppose him capable of being corrupted."

He went back to gnawing on the old bone of Burr's tactics again.
He would use the Federalists for his own purposes if they went along
with him. "Ambition without principle was never long under the
guidance of good sense . . . the force of Mr. Burr's understanding is
much overrated. He is far more cunning than wise, far more dextrous
than able." Then in a passage marked *Very very confidential* Hamilton
related an anecdote: "He has blamed me for not having improved the
situation I was once in to change the government. That when answered
that this could not have been done without guilt, he replied" — in the
words of their mutual friend Talleyrand — " 'les grandes ames se souci-
ent peu des petits moraux'; that when told that the thing was never
practicable from the genius and situation of the country, he answered,
'That depends on the estimates we form of the human passions and
our means of influencing them.' Does this prove that Mr. Burr would
consider a scheme of usurpation as visionary?"

Ever since the New York victory Burr and Jefferson had been
exchanging careful communications. Jefferson wrote Burr to congratulate him on his certain election to the vice presidency. Burr rejoined
that it had never occurred to him that the people in voting had any
other intention than to choose Jefferson for the chief post and himself
for the second. Jefferson expressed regret that Mr. Burr's being Vice
President would make it impossible to consider him for "one of the

great offices." Burr hastily wrote back that he would hold himself at Jefferson's disposal to fill whatever post he was offered. He would be just as glad to resign as Vice President if he could head a department. Jefferson said no more about the "great offices."

Burr smothered his disappointment. He went about his business, a small sallow darkeyed man driving about in an enormous coach. When he arrived at some house he had a habit of walking in with his chin sunk on his breast, without looking to the right or the left. He responded to questions with scornful and ambiguous monosyllables. A man of many mysteries. That winter, on top of his duties as assemblyman at Albany, he was busy with his daughter's wedding. His adored Theodosia was marrying a rich young man named Alston from South Carolina.

The name of Burr was in every man's mouth. The New England parsons, having convinced themselves that Thomas Jefferson was the fiend incarnate, began to noise it abroad that Burr had good blood in him. Though they admitted his reputation for profligacy and Jacobinism, he was the son and grandson of two great divines. The old stock would prevail in the end. When the time came he would have sown these wild oats and would stand out as a godly man and a true Federalist.

John Adams wrote in astonishment of Burr's sudden rise to fame. "Mr. B's good Fortune surpasses all ordinary Rules," he exploded to Elbridge Gerry, "and exceeds that of Bonaparte. All the old Patriots, all the splendid Talents, the long Experience, both of Federalists and antifederalists must be subjected to the Humiliation of seeing this dextrous Gentleman rise, like a Baloon, filled with inflammable Air, over their Heads."

10. *The Setting Sun*

The last year of John Adams' administration had been full of a sort of splendor of conflict that he rather enjoyed. He had asserted himself at last. He was making peace with the French; his young navy was displaying the excellence of American seamanship. Even as the negotiations went on, the ports were filling up with captured French privateers and letters of marque. Since he had torn himself loose from the web of Hamilton's intrigue in which he saw Pickering and McHenry as the chief manipulators he had found a fresh rapport with his fellow citizens. He was personally beloved by the seamen and merchants and small businessmen of the seaport towns. At dinners tendered to him on his stately progresses to and from his seashore home to the seat of government he allowed himself more and more to fall into the old oratory of 1776. He found himself denouncing the Anglomen of Hamilton's faction with all the old fervor. Wherever he went he was applauded.

He viewed his political failure as a martyrdom for honest principles. He even managed to take a magnanimous attitude towards Hamilton's denunciations. "It will do him more Harm than me," he wrote. "He has Talents, if he would correct himself which might be useful," he added condescendingly. "There is more Burnish, however, on the Outside than sterling Silver in the Substance." He and Abigail would miss the salary but they were resigned to retirement from public life. He would lay down the reins with relief but he was determined to assert himself up to the last moment. "After the 3rd of March I shall be a private Citizen and your brother Farmer," he wrote a supporter. "I shall leave the State with all its coffers full and the fair Prospect of a Peace, with all the World smiling in its Face, its Commerce flourishing, its Navy glorious, its Agriculture uncommonly productive and lucrative."

John Adams' complacency in the face of the ruin of his party disgusted the more farseeing Federalists. "I keep clear of Mr. Adams," Gouverneur wrote his old associate Robert Morris, who was eagerly awaiting the passage of a bankruptcy law to free him from jail, "because I find that in his Eagerness to provide for Relations, Flatterers and Favorites he does everything in his Power to render the Government contemptible."

Indeed John Adams was showing every day his lack of administrative powers. In Stoddert he had a public spirited Secretary of the Navy. Since Wolcott had left the sinking ship the War and Treasury departments were drifting along under the management of an undistinguished Massachusetts lawyer named Dexter. What little coherence the administration retained was due to the very peculiar qualities of John Marshall, whom Adams had appointed Secretary of State.

After his first political success in stirring up the XYZ frenzy John Marshall had proved a disappointment to the extreme Federalists. Except for his extraordinary argumentative powers, which had at one point won from even Gallatin the admission that he was unanswerable, he gave the impression of drifting with the tide. The lanky Virginian had played a waiting game. Sedgwick, the Speaker of the House, complained that his affectionate indolent nature would keep him from making his mark in the world. His habits were too convivial. As Secretary of State he was everybody's friend. "He is disposed on all popular subjects to feel the public pulse and hence results indecision and an expression of doubt. Doubts suggested by him create in more feeble minds those which are irremovable," Sedgwick wrote Rufus King.

The Republicans underestimated John Marshall as much as the Federalists did. Jefferson wrote his cousin off as a mere timeserver. The only man at that early day who seemed to have any conception of the force of Marshall's character was his brother lawyer William Wirt who described him inside and out in his *Letters of a British Spy.* He sketched his appearance: "Tall, meagre, emaciated; his muscles relaxed . . . head and face small in proportion to his height; his complexion swarthy; the muscles of his face being relaxed give him the appearance of a man of fifty years of age . . . while his black eyes possess an irradiating spirit which proclaims the imperial powers of the mind that sits enthroned within. This extraordinary man, without the aid of fancy, without the advantages of person, voice, attitude, gesture, or any of the ornaments of an orator, deserves to be considered as one of the most eloquent men in the world; if eloquence may be said to consist in the power of seizing the attention with irresistible force, and never permitting it to elude the grasp, until the hearer has received the conviction the speaker intends."

Washington had appreciated Marshall's qualities. Patrick Henry, turning out, with all the desperate conservatism of old age in the last sickly year of his life, to defeat the Jeffersonians in Virginia, wrote in a letter widely circulated during Marshall's campaign for his seat in Congress, "Tell Marshall I love him" — referring to Marshall's part in the XYZ business — "because he felt and acted as a republican, as an American."

For some time now John Adams' regime had lacked a Chief Justice. Ellsworth had resigned. John Jay had refused. The President was at his wit's end to find reputable men for his heads of departments. Particularly since the burning of the Treasury building gave the Republican gossipmongers the opportunity to proclaim jeeringly that the Federalists were covering their tracks, no man who valued his reputation wanted to be connected with John Adams' crumbling administration. Gallatin wrote his wife that he did not believe the fires were set, but that they did give rise to suspicions. One conflagration of government documents might be laughed off, but two . . .

On the spur of the moment John Adams appointed his accommodating Secretary of State Chief Justice of the United States. John Marshall was just the man he needed to help him staff the new courts established under the Judiciary Act as a last Federalist bulwark against Jacobinism. Not even John Adams could have suspected what an authoritarian rock he was setting up in the general government, a rock against which the spring tides of democracy would beat in vain.

Adams, like Washington, felt that in Marshall he had a man he could trust to keep clear of libertarian notions. Marshall was ready to meet objections with a hearty laugh while he relieved the President of the troublesome detail of thinking up suitable nominations. With his usual good nature he consented to administer both offices during the final month of the retiring President's term.

11. *The Seven Days' Suspense*

On February 11, a Wednesday, the Senate and House meet in joint session for the scrutiny of the ballots of the electoral college in the handsome new Senate chamber with its tall columns with giltedged capitals. The ample gallery is crowded with ladies and gentlemen in their best clothes. A heavy snowstorm rages outside. For days Washington and Georgetown have been filling up with citizens come from far and near to follow the results of the election. Every bed is filled to bursting. Men are sleeping in their greatcoats on the floor of the common rooms of the inns.

Thomas Jefferson as Vice President breaks the seals on the certificates from the sixteen states and hands them to the tellers. The count turns out as expected: Jefferson 73, Burr 73, Adams 65, Pinckney 64, Jay 1.

Immediately the representatives return to their cramped uncomfortable quarters on the other side of the north wing, where water drips from leaks in the shingled roof, to choose a President. The doors are closed. A motion is passed not to adjourn or to take up further business until an election is completed. The newspapers liken them to cardinals shut up in the Consistory to choose a Pope.

It is already known, from the news that has seeped out from the caucuses of the two parties, that the first result will be a tie. Among the Federalists the New Englanders take the lead. Theodore Sedgwick of Massachusetts, at first inclined to agree with Hamilton, has been talked around. The Federalists vote must be solid for Burr.

Among the Republicans coolheaded Gallatin, with his long sharp nose and his meticulous speech, is in command. His first success is in detaching one vote from the South Carolina delegation. The Marylanders prove to be evenly divided. Joseph Nicholson of Chestertown, a nephew of the old commodore and of the Captain Nicholson who commands one of the new frigates, is sick in bed with a high fever. With his wife and his physician in attendance he has himself dragged on a cot through the driving snow to the capitol. He stays through every ballot.

The vote is by states. On the first ballot the result is eight states for Jefferson, six for Burr, two divided. No majority. The New Englanders are solid for Burr, except for Vermont, which is divided; Matthew Lyon for Jefferson, Lewis Morris, Gouverneur's nephew whom some claimed to be completely under his uncle's thumb, for Burr. The middle states, except for Delaware, show majorities for Jefferson: Bayard, in spite of Hamilton's pleading, votes for Burr. Maryland is divided 4 to 4. Nicholson's presence prevents a Federalist majority. Virginia, North Carolina, Georgia, Kentucky and Tennessee are for Jefferson; South Carolina, except for the one member who breaks party lines, go for Burr.

As the balloting continues both parties hold firm. At three o'clock in the morning of the twelfth one of the Virginia Tazewells writes Monroe, who is on tenterhooks in Richmond: "We have been up all night and have balloted twentytwo times, the result the same as the first . . . Fatigue has born down most of my friends but those who still bear up remain firm . . . we never more adjourn but to proclaim Jefferson the President."

By eight o'clock the same morning they have balloted twentyseven times. The balloting is suspended for four hours to let the members get some sleep. The snowstorm continues outside. Through Friday and Saturday the balloting goes on without change. At last the exhausted members decide to take the Lord's Day off. The next ballot is set for Monday at noon.

Gouverneur listens with pleasure to "an excellent sermon" by Bishop Claggett at the interdenominational church services held in the House chamber. Meanwhile expresses ply back and forth riding hard through the snow and the slush and the mud between Washington and Albany where Burr continues to attend the New York legislature. The mails bring conflicting reports. Some say that Burr is giving the Federalists assurances that he will respect Hamilton's four points. Some say he refuses to commit himself.

John Armstrong, the same Armstrong who as a hasty youth penned the Newburgh addresses, comes to call on Jefferson in his parlor at Conrad and McMunn's. General Gates' old aide has married a Livingston and moved to New York. As a result he finds himself Gouverneur Morris's colleague in the Senate. He brings Jefferson the tale that Gouverneur has been heard expressing surprise that Jefferson is inactive while Burr's agents are hard at work in the lobbies to get him the presidency. Matthew Lyon reports that he has been offered anything he wants, money or office, to change his vote. Edward Livingston arrives breathless with the story that Samuel Smith has been approached with an offer of the Secretaryship of the

Navy in Burr's cabinet. Jefferson is already considering Smith for the same post in his. Gallatin has hopes of inducing the man who represents the district around Washington City to change his vote. Both sides are working hard on the Marylanders.

Bayard of Delaware meanwhile, through this same Samuel Smith, is trying to get an assurance from Jefferson that he will conform, if elected, to Hamilton's four points: respect of the fiscal system; retention of the navy; neutrality in the European war; no wholesale purge of Federalist officeholders. When Jefferson meets Gouverneur Morris pegging down the steps of the Capitol one day, the New Yorker takes him aside and tells him, in his blunt way, that all Jefferson needs to secure his immediate election is to make these assurances.

Out of doors conjecture is busy. A theory has been launched that since it is impossible to break the tie Congress will have to appoint a President. The congenial gentleman who holds the two highest offices is rumored to be of this opinion.

John Marshall has found himself a newspaper. Ever since John Adams' prostration by the news of the death of his son Charles in New York in the past November removed him from direct contact with day to day politics, Marshall has been interesting himself in the administration organ, *The Washington Federalist*. In its columns a certain Horatius has been arguing that in default of an election Congress would be justified in appointing an officer to act as President. It is the general opinion that John Marshall is Horatius.

Between the Republican candidates the Chief Justice refuses to take sides. On being questioned he is noncommittal about Burr, but he does make the statement that he considers Jefferson unfit: "The morals of the writer of the letter to Mazzei could not be pure."

The tale goes around that Marshall himself was to be the officer named by the Senate.

Marshall is attacked for this project in *The Richmond Examiner*. The Virginia Republicans are loud in denouncing him. Governor Monroe lets it be known that at the first word of an attempt at usurpation he will assemble a special session of the legislature to call out the Virginia militia. Governor McKean of Pennsylvania writes from Lancaster that the Pennsylvania militia is ready to march. Armed bands are rumored to be already assembling in the snowy outskirts of Washington ready to plunge their daggers into the heart of any President chosen by unconstitutional means.

Jefferson's soninlaw Thomas Mann Randolph writes Monroe from Albemarle that he has visited the federal arsenal at New London on the James, where many of the British arms captured at Yorktown are still stored. The guard is negligible. It will take a hundred wagons to haul the stores away.

Monroe's mail is full of offers to volunteer. A veteran of the Revolutionary War asks to be allowed "to fight the infernals . . . I wish for an opportunity of sacrificing the Devils and sending them to Moloch their King."

This prospect of civil war sends Jefferson riding over to the President's house to call on his old friend John Adams. He implores him to veto any act that may be passed authorizing an unconstitutional election. There is no arguing with John Adams. "You can have no idea of the meanness, indecency, almost insanity of his conduct, especially of late," the tolerant Gallatin is writing confidently to his wife. At the same time Stevens Thomson Mason describes Adams to Monroe as "a soured mulish and disappointed executive." Adams turns on Jefferson like an old bull at bay. The appointment of a President would be quite justifiable, he tells him. The stalemate is Jefferson's fault; all he needs to do to secure the election is to make the declaration the Federalists demand.

On Sunday, February 15, while the Representatives are catching what sleep they can in their crowded boardinghouses, Jefferson writes Monroe: "If they could have been permitted to pass a law for putting the government into the hands of an officer, they would certainly have prevented an election. but we thought it best to declare openly and firmly, one & all, that the day such an act passed the middle states would arm & that no such usurpation, even for a single day, would be submitted to. this first shook them; and they were completely alarmed at the recourse for which we declared, to wit, a convention to reorganize the Govt & amend it. the very word convention gives them the horrors, as in the present democratical spirit of America, they fear they would lose some favorite morsals of the Constitution. many attempts," he adds, "have been made to obtain terms and promises from me. I have declared to them unequivocally that I would not receive the government on capitulation, that I would not go into it with my hands tied."

That same Sunday Jefferson betrays some of the feelings he is concealing from his associates in a hasty note to his dear little Maria, who is down at Bermuda Hundred on the James with her husband. She has been in bad health since her child's birth; she has her mother's build; how can he help remembering her mother's constant illnesses? He is trying to get Maria up into the healthier climate of Albemarle; whichever way the matter was decided, he tells her, he expects to leave Washington by the middle of March. "I hope I shall find you at Monticello. the scene passing here makes me pant to be away from it;

to fly from the circle of cabal, intrigue and hatred to one where all is love and peace."

In the Republican caucus Gallatin remains cool and firm. They will go on voting for Jefferson until March 4 if need be. They will acquiesce in a fair election of Burr, but they will oppose usurpation with their lives. All they need is to hold their ground, he tells his supporters.

Jefferson himself is surprising friends and foes alike by the lack of agitation with which he goes about his daily routine and the unhurried courtesy of his manner. Perhaps he takes some of the political emissaries who besiege his door to visit a trained pig on show in another part of Conrad and McMunn's versatile establishment. The Learned Pig is advertised in the newspapers as being able to read writing and printing, to tell time off a watch, to give dates, to distinguish colors and to add, multiply or divide. Admission is fifty cents. There is no report of the pig's having been asked to prophesy the result of the election.

Monday, February 16, Gallatin informs Commodore Nicholson in New York: "I am sorry I cannot yet relieve you from the present general anxiety. We have balloted for the 34th time this morning and the result is still the same. Mr. Bayard had positively declared on Saturday to some of his own party that he would this day put an end to the business by voting for Mr. Jefferson. He acted otherwise."

Next day, Tuesday, February 17, Gallatin is able to write with enormous relief to his wife: "We have this day after 36 ballots chosen Mr. Jefferson President. Morris of Vermont withdrew." That leaves the whole vote of Vermont to be cast by Matthew Lyon, an act which possibly makes up for some of his sufferings in his wintry prison at Vincennes. The rest of New England votes for Burr till the end. Bayard votes blank. The four Maryland Federalists put in blank ballots. So does South Carolina. "Thus ended the most wicked and absurd attempt ever tried by the Federalists," is Gallatin's summing up.

As the expresses carry the news east and south and west through the country the people receive it with a wave of rejoicings unequaled since the celebrations that followed the ratification of the Constitution. "The assembled crowds," writes Mrs. Smith in her journal, "without the Capitol rent the air with their acclamations and gratulations, and the Conspirators as they were called, hurried to their lodgings under strong apprehensions of suffering from the just indignation of their fellow citizens." "The people got so clamorous," one Republican writes exultingly to Monroe, "that some members expected to be shorter by the head." Jefferson's parlor is crowded with a motley throng of well wishers.

That night the residents of New Jersey Avenue put candles in the windows of their houses. Mr. William C. C. Claiborne of Virginia and Kentucky, who has been fishing for appointment as governor of the Mississippi Territory, illuminates his house with his own hand and sets up his neighbors to a public supper at which Thomas Jefferson is toasted with sixteen cheers and John Adams with four. The revelers stand with bowed heads in a moment of silence in memory of George Washington. Gallatin is toasted. "Matthew Lyon and the Liberty of the Press" is greeted with sixteen cheers and so is the name of the generous gentleman who is furnishing the entertainment. The final toast before the company disperses across the rutted tracks through the snowy wastes to their lodgings is: "To the American Fair; may they instruct their offspring to remember the 17th day of February, 1801."

At the President's house meanwhile John Adams in conspiratorial mood, with the help of his obliging Chief Justice and Secretary of State, is writing out commissions for the appointment of federal judges and court officers under the new Judiciary Act. They choose the hardest shelled Federalists they can think of. This is their answer to the Republican election. They are still busy at this congenial work as late as nine o'clock in the evening on March 3. In the Republican press these commissions are lampooned as "the midnight appointments."

Without saying goodbye to anybody, leaving Abigail to follow with the carriages and the servants and the baggage, John Adams rises before dawn on March 4 to catch the northbound stage. As a fellow passenger on the hard board seat he finds Speaker Sedgwick. Neither of them will grace Thomas Jefferson's inauguration with his presence. John Adams arrives home at Quincy on March 18 to find a northeaster blowing and what he estimates to a friend as a hundred loads of seaweed, an excellent fertilizer for his farmlands, washed up into his front yard.

To Benjamin Stoddert he pens his own political requiescat: "No Party that ever existed knew itself so little, or so vainly overrated its Influence and Popularity as ours. None understood so ill the Causes of its own Power or so wantonly destroyed them. If we had been blessed with Common Sense we should not have been overthrown by Philip Freneau, Duane, Callender, Cooper and Lyon; or their great Patron and Protector."

XV A Philosopher in the President's House

1. " . . . the world's best hope . . . "

March 4 was ushered in by a discharge of artillery. Riflemen of the local militia paraded with fife and drum in front of Thomas Jefferson's boardinghouse. The scattered clearings and building lots of the city presented, according to *The National Intelligencer,* "a scene of uncommon animation." Such a concourse of people as had never been seen crowded up Jenkins' Hill.

At noon the President elect walked over from Conrad and McMunn's to the Capitol. "His dress as usual that of a plain citizen without any badge of office." As he entered the building the artillerymen started shooting off their blank charges again. Jefferson was met at the entrance of the Senate chamber by the dapper figure of Aaron Burr with his brooding dark eyes and his sharply chiseled profile. Burr had just been sworn in as Vice President. Burr directed him to the presiding officer's chair under the crimson damask canopy. Jefferson sat quiet awhile to let the largest audience that had ever been crowded into the Senate chamber and visitors' gallery settle into what space they could find. The assemblage was estimated at a thousand. The senators gallantly gave up half their seats to the ladies. When the rustling and coughing subsided Jefferson read his inaugural address.

The National Intelligencer found Jefferson's delivery "plain, dignified and unostentatious," his style "chaste appropriate and eloquent," his principles "pure, explicit and comprehensive." Gouverneur Morris, on the other hand, noted in his diary that the speech was too long by half, "and so he will find it himself before he is three years older." Federalists and Republicans agreed that they had trouble hearing what the new President was saying. Jefferson's voice was weak as ever and the acoustics in the handsome new Senate chamber were wretched. Jefferson took the oath from John Marshall. The Sixth Congress adjourned without delay. The members hurried through the mud over to Samuel Harrison Smith's printshop, where they stood waiting in line while the slow handpresses turned out copies of the inaugural address.

When they read the wet smudged print of the address the Federalists breathed a sigh of relief and the extreme Republicans felt their high hopes dampened. Jefferson was putting into words his theory of politics. He intended to pursue, as President as he had throughout his political career, moderate and roundabout methods to set the course of the general government in the direction of the principles of 1776. His first effort was towards conciliation.

"During the contest of opinion through which we have passed the animation of discussions and exertions, has sometimes worn an aspect which might impose on strangers unused to think freely & to speak & to write what they think.

"But this being now decided by the voice of the nation, enounced according to the rules of the constitution, all will of course arrange themselves under the will of the law, & unite in common efforts for the common good. all too will bear in mind this sacred principle, that tho the will of the Majority is in all cases to prevail, that will, to be rightful, must be reasonable; that the Minority possess their equal rights, which equal laws must protect & to violate would be oppression . . . let us restore to social intercourse that harmony and affection, without which liberty, & even life itself are but dreary things . . . every difference of opinion is not a difference of principle . . . we are all republicans; we are all federalists.

"If there be any amongst us who wish to dissolve this union, or to change its republican form, let them stand undisturbed, as monuments of the safety with which error of opinion may be tolerated where reason is left free to combat it.

"I know indeed that some honest men have feared that a republican government cannot be strong; that this government is not strong enough. but would the honest patriot, in the full tide of successful experiment, abandon a government which has so far kept us free & firm, on the theoretic & visionary fear that this government, the world's best hope, may be possibility want energy to preserve itself?

"I trust not. I believe this, on the contrary, to be the strongest government on earth."

"This day a new era commences: the era of principle," wrote Samuel Harrison Smith in the lead editorial in his *Intelligencer*. Mrs. Smith wrote her sister that evening: "There has been a constant succession

of persons coming for the papers. I have been interrupted several
times in this letter by the gentlemen of Congress, who have been to
bid their adieus; since three o'clock there has been a constant succession . . . You will smile when I tell you that Gouverneur Morris, Mr.
Dayton" — Burr's intimate and Hamilton's correspondent, the New
Jersey Federalist — "and Bayard drank tea here; they have just gone
after sitting near two hours." James A. Bayard had a few days before
refused a last minute nomination by Adams as minister to France. It
was not too unnatural that he should drink tea with Mrs. Smith; he
was her cousin and foster brother; but to a certain extent it was a
sign of the lion lying down with the lamb.

Jefferson went about his reorganization of the government in a
leisurely way. Since the members of Congress were all hurrying home
after the inauguration, he slipped away to Monticello for a month.
There he could be tolerably free from importunate officeseekers.
There he could talk the new administration over in quiet with his
Secretary of State. James Madison had been detained at Montpellier
by one of the sickly fits he was subject to and by his beloved old
father's final illness. Jefferson had been assuring him that a change
of air to the Territory of Columbia would do him good. There had
been no doubt in either man's mind that if Jefferson were elected
President his closest friend should become his first assistant. As
Jefferson planned the executive, the Secretary of State, in charge of
foreign affairs, should be the chief officer under the President.

The Treasury must go to Gallatin, whose levelheaded management
of the opposition in Congress ever since Madison's retirement from
the House had met its final proof in his quietly successful leadership
of the Jefferson faction to victory in the presidential election. Jefferson,
who lacked confidence in his own competence in fiscal matters, had
been entranced by the clarity of Gallatin's speeches and writings on
public finance. He shared Gallatin's skepticism of Pitt's and Hamilton's
sinking funds and perpetual debentures. He agreed with Gallatin that
the government must use any balance of income after expenditure to
pay off debts. He trusted to Gallatin, as he had written Madison ten
years before, to reduce what he considered Hamilton's elaborately
contrived "chaos" to order, and to "present us with a clear view of
our finances, and put them into a form as simple as they will admit
. . . the accounts of the United States ought to be as simple as those
of a common farmer, and capable of being understood by common
farmers."

Jefferson and Madison had been mulling over the makeup of a
cabinet ever since a Republican victory had become a near certainty
round the first of the year. Apart from the two chief offices they
planned their appointments to conciliate New England and the com-

mercial interest. The Secretary of War was a Lieutenant Dearborn, a New Hampshire man who after distinguished services in the Continental Army had moved to a farm on the Kennebec in the District of Maine. Levi Lincoln, a Massachusetts lawyer whose articles signed "A Worcester Farmer" had done much to undermine the Federalists on their home ground, was Attorney General.

The two Virginians had trouble finding a suitable Republican to take over the Navy Department. The shipping men were all highflying Federalists. Jefferson played for a while with the notion of casting aside party considerations and offering the post to Robert Morris, but no one could think of any way of getting the fallen financier out of the Prune Street jail. His next choice was Robert R. Livingston, the New York State chancellor, with whom he had been having an absorbing correspondence on the possibilities of applying steam engines to the navigation of ships. Livingston, deaf, opinionated, keenminded and eccentric, had made up his mind that if he could not be Secretary of State he would like to go to Paris as minister plenipotentiary. Jefferson, who considered him a very able man, made the appointment with pleasure. Meanwhile he asked Rufus King to stay on in London. Since the chancellor had to have time to get his private affairs in order before sailing, Monroe's scapegrace halfbrother Representative Dawson of Virginia was sent off to France with the Senate's ratification of the new treaty. With him he carried a letter to Tom Paine which, when it was published, was to cause great outcry in the Federalist press. Jefferson invited the old staymaker back to the country he had served so well and offered him passage on an American frigate.

General Samuel Smith, the Baltimore shipowner, who had been the gobetween in the efforts of the Federalists to force commitments on Jefferson before they would consent to his election, had, since Stoddert's resignation, taken temporary charge of the Navy Department. The work there was urgent because Jefferson was planning to send three frigates and an armored sloop immediately to the Mediterranean to cut down, by a show of force, the outrageous pretensions of the Barbary pirates. When Samuel Smith's wife, who was a social leader in Baltimore, declared she would rather die than spend her life among the weedgrown building lots of Washington City, the post of Secretary was foisted off on the general's younger brother Robert.

It was on the Fourth of July that the inhabitants of Washington and Georgetown had their first official view of their new President. Jefferson aimed to substitute the nation's birthday for George Washington's as a national holiday. For six weeks now Jefferson had been settling his small household into Hoban's still unfinished building and was already planning flanking colonnades and improvements in the classical revival

style. Accustomed as he was to the continual construction work at
Monticello, the smell of fresh masonry and new plaster had no terrors
for him. Mrs. Samuel Harrison Smith, who had been filling her letters
to Philadelphia with accounts of the new gaiety that had come over
the city with the new administration, was among those who paid their
respects at the President's house. "We found about 20 persons present
in a room," she wrote her sister, "where sat Mr J surrounded by five
Cherokee chiefs. After a conversation of a few minutes, he invited
his company into the usual dining room, whose four large sideboards
were covered with refreshments, such as cakes of various kinds, wine,
punch & c. Every citizen was invited to partake . . . The company soon
increased to near a hundred, including all the public officers and
strangers of distinction. Martial music soon announced the approach
of the marine corps of Capt. Burroughs, who in due military form
saluted the President, accompanied by the President's march played
by an excellent band attached to the corps . . . All appeared to be
cheerful, all happy. Mr Jefferson mingled promiscously with the
citizens, and far from designating any particular friends for consultation, conversed for a short time with everyone that came his way."

Mrs. Smith was referring to Jefferson's rule of pêle mêle, by which,
to the derision of the Federalist press and to the especial distress of
Mr. Anthony Merry, King George's minister, Jefferson threw into
discord all the protocol modeled on that of the Court of St. James
which had been carefully elaborated at the levees of George Washington and John Adams. He remembered with pleasure the informal
manners of the French liberal noblesse of the old regime when they
had received him in their own gardens and salons. He was determined
to receive visitors distinguished and undistinguished in the President's
house exactly as he received them at Monticello.

Mrs. Smith and her husband, who was the chief administration
editor, often dined with Jefferson. "He had company every day," she
wrote, "but his table is seldom laid for more than twelve. This prevents
all form and makes the conversation general and unreserved. I happened to sit next to Mr. Jefferson and was confirmed in my prepos-
sessions in his favor by his easy, candid and gentle manners . . ."
This time charming Mrs. Madison presided at the tea urn. "About
six o'clock the gentlemen joined us, but Mr. Jefferson's and Mr.
Madison's manners were so easy and familiar that they produced no
restraint. Never was a plainer set of men."

Along with the plainness of the manners at the President's house
went a change in dress and behavior that affected all ranks of society.
Powdered heads were becoming an exception. Men's clothes, influenced
by the plainness of Bonaparte's dress, were becoming simpler every
day. Long hair was disappearing. When timeserving General Wilkinson

who appeared in Washington to ingratiate himself with the President
upon his inauguration — he ingratiated himself with Gouverneur
Morris too, by arranging for him to receive an occasional pound of
fresh butter from the farm of a friend in Frederick — went home to
his troops in their frontier posts along the Mississippi, in his first
general order he told them to cut off their queues. The Federalists
claimed that Jefferson received visits in his dressing gown and in down
at the heel slippers. "At Headquarters," Gouverneur Morris wrote
Hamilton in a captious mood, "there is such an Abandonment of
Manners and such a Pruriency of Conversation as would reduce even
Greatness to the Level of Mediocrity."

When the Seventh Congress assembled in the fall, Jefferson had the
pleasure of seeing his old campaign manager, the assiduous John
Beckley, elected to his old post of clerk of the House. Jefferson, who
was interesting himself in forming a library for the education of the
legislators, soon after appointed him the first librarian of Congress.

Ohio, the seventeenth state, was represented in that session for the
first time. Among the representatives of the still Federalist settlements
which had been settled from New England was the Reverend Manasseh
Cutler, that busy land salesman and divine who kept such a complete
record of his travels. Like most westernminded men accustomed to
the rawness of the new settlements, Cutler found Washington City
delightful. He wrote home describing the beauty of the Potomac
scenery, the magnificence of the Great Falls, the impressiveness of
the view from Jenkins' Hill. He described with relish the meals he
ate at the President's house when, in due rotation, his turn came to
be one of a dozen congressmen invited to dine at the President's oval
table. He wrote with enthusiasm of the rice soup, the round of beef,
the turkey, mutton, and ham, the loin of veal, the cutlets of mutton
or veal, the fried eggs, and fried beef with which the table was piled.
The cookery had a European flavor. He regarded with some suspicion
a newfangled "pie called macaroni, which appeared to be a rich crust
formed with the strilions of onions . . . very strong and not agreeable,"
he added. He found the ice cream marvelous: "crust wholly dried,
crumbled into thin flakes." Then there was "a dish like a pudding,
inside white as milk or curd, very porous and light, covered with
cream sauce," which he found very fine.

After dinner Mr. Jefferson took his company into what he called
"the mammoth room" to see the five hundred pound cheese the Republican citizens of Cheshire, Massachusetts, had sent the President
with the advice that not a crumb of Federalist curd had gone into
the making of it. Those who were interested were allowed to examine
odds and ends of bones of an actual mammoth and the Indian sculp-

tures and paintings which were already beginning to accumulate there.

The Reverend Cutler, perhaps mollified by the excellence of the desserts, was surprised to find the President's conversation less licentious than he had expected and his dress "quite decent." He was astonished too, so he wrote his family, to see him at the church services held in the new temporary House of Representatives which had been erected during the preceding summer in the foundations of the south wing of the Capitol.

These services, conducted each Sunday by a preacher of a different denomination — once a woman officiated in the pulpit — became as much as the horseraces and the picnics at the Great Falls one of the diversions of the new capital. They were the main gathering place of Georgetown and Washington society. Everyone came dressed in his best. The services were enlivened by the brassy strains of Captain Burrough's marine band. Mr. Jefferson, who arrived with his loose-limbed mountaineer walk, tall and erect in his buffcolored clothes and woolly waistcoat, with his rusty graying hair still caught in a queue behind his long head, was usually accompanied by his secretary, slight darkhaired Captain Meriwether Lewis. Two seats towards the front were invariably reserved for them.

2. The Western Waters

Jefferson had chosen as his secretary an army officer of twenty-eight whose life was linked with his in many various ways. Meriwether Lewis came of that great family of Lewises that was scattered through the valley and piedmont sections of Virginia. One great uncle had married Washington's sister. Another was the diarist of the pioneering survey of the confines of the Fairfax grant carried on by Jefferson's father Peter and Joshua Fry in 1746. Through his mother he was descended from the Quaker Meriwethers, who were the first settlers in Albemarle County. When Meriwether's father died his mother married one of the Franks family Jefferson was allied with by his sister's marriage. He went to school in Albemarle with Matthew Maury, who was continuing his father James Maury's school where Jefferson got most of his education. This James Maury, a Huguenot pedagogue of original and inquisitive cast of mind, was the chief propounder of Peter Jefferson's and Thomas Walker's scheme for an exploration of the great rivers up into the western mountains and through to the western ocean. These plans were thwarted by the French and Indian War and the subsequent restriction of colonization to the westward while Jefferson was still a boy.

Jefferson had first become interested in Meriwether when as a youngster in Albemarle, besides being a famous coon and possum hunter, he showed more than a mere woodsman's interest in the birds and beasts and insects and the vegetation of the forests. A captain at eighteen, he was detached for recruiting service at Charlottesville. Immediately he started pestering Jefferson to let him go along on the French naturalist Michaud's botanizing and exploring expedition into the Western Waters. The dream of his life was to explore the headwaters of the Missouri. As soon as Jefferson was elected President he had Meriwether Lewis detached from Wilkinson's command on the Mississippi for service in Washington. Immediately the two of them started plotting a reconnaissance of the continent. Singular John Ledyard, whom Jefferson had encouraged while still minister to France to try to explore the northwest coast starting from a Siberian port, had failed due to the obstructions the Russians threw in his way and later died, a frustrated explorer, in Cairo. Now as President, Jefferson was at last in a position to turn all these long dreamed of plans and projects into reality. In Captain Lewis he found a deputy whose life was what his life might have been if he had been a man of action instead of a man of letters.

The planning of the expedition to explore the westernmost of the Western Waters went along with the conduct of a strange game of hazard with the unpredictable Bonaparte. In this game Livingston and Talleyrand in Paris and Madison and the French minister Pichon in Washington all played their parts; the grand strategy was Jefferson's.

Ever since Talleyrand had spied out the land during his exile among the Americans, the ci-devant bishop had nourished an ambition to restore to France preponderance in America. For that purpose he egged Bonaparte on to force the Bourbon court of Spain to restore to him, by a secret treaty signed at San Ildefonso, the great Louisiana tract west of the Mississippi which included New Orleans on the eastern bank and which France had transferred to Spain in the weak-kneed days of the dying liberal monarchy. There had been many rumors as the intrigue proceeded, but the people of Ohio and Kentucky and Tennessee got their first concrete intimation of the new status of Louisiana when the Spanish Intendant suddenly suspended the right of deposit at New Orleans. As soon as Jefferson heard the news he knew he had to move fast if he was to "give the world still another useful lesson," as he had written Tenche Coxe years before, "by showing them other modes of punishing injuries than by war, which is as much a punishment to the punisher as to the sufferer."

For once the interests of the Mississippi and Ohio settlers coincided with those of the eastern shipowners, whose vessels were rotting in port since the British and French had patched up a peace. From both ends of the country could be heard the shrill screeching of the war-hawks.

Livingston was in Paris to negotiate the points still at issue between France and the United States. He had already been instructed to try to trade American claims for the spoliation of their commerce against the French for New Orleans or at least for a port in West Florida. Now Jefferson sent off Monroe, whose term had expired as governor of Virginia, as minister extraordinary to both France and Spain with instructions to offer anything within reason, to whichever government he should discover to have the territory near the mouth of the Missis-sippi in its control, for its cession to the United States. His bargaining point was the threat of an alliance with England in the new war which already loomed large on the horizon. Jefferson admired Livingston's keenness and wit; but in Monroe he had absolute confidence; besides it gave him pleasure to right the wrong done his fellow Virginian under the administration of Messrs. Wolcott and Pickering.

Bonaparte meanwhile, having dropped his dreams of eastern empire into the trashbasket, had begun to interest himself in Talleyrand's plans for expansion to the west. First the revolting Negroes of Santo Domingo must be crushed, slavery restored there, and that island fitted out as a base for a landing in Louisiana. Bonaparte sent off one of his best generals, the Leclerc who had married his handsome sister Pauline. With him went a brilliantly equipped expedition. Leclerc drove the Negro bands into the hills; by cajolery he won over Toussaint L'Ouverture's lieutenants, Dessalines and Christophe; through their treachery he managed to lay hands on Toussaint himself and to ship him off to France. Bonaparte promptly sent him off to die of pneumonia in a stone cell in the high Jura mountains. Faced with the restoration of slavery, the Haitian Negroes were resolved to fight until they died. With the removal of Toussaint, who had been encouraged by the British and by Hamilton's emissary Dr. Stevens to try to set up a civilized regime, all moderation ceased. It became a war of massacre and countermassacre. The Negroes vanished into the hills.

An enemy had early appeared that Leclerc could not drive off into the hills. Bonaparte's brotherinlaw saw three fourths of his army die before the yellow fever took him. Reinforcements under the son of old Rochambeau of Yorktown fame died as fast as they landed from the ships. As Bonaparte, lolling in the tubful of warm water clouded with eau de cologne in which he did his private thinking at St. Cloud, scrutinized the butcher's bill of his Louisiana venture he decided suddenly that to fight the Haitian Negroes, the yellow fever, and the British fleet was too great odds. To keep Louisiana out of the hands of England he would cede it to the United States. He needed cash money quickly to meet the expenses of the coming war; he must drive a hard bargain. Since he could not trust Talleyrand to destroy the imperial web he had been so long weaving he placed the negotiation in the experienced hands of François de Barbé-Marbois, who had been attached to the French legation in Philadelphia during the Revolutionary War. It was Marbois' questionnaire which had elicited from Jefferson the first draft of his *Notes on Virginia*.

Livingston proved a good horsetrader. Though in his first surprise he fumbled a little and tried to insist that New Orleans and West Florida were all he was authorized to buy, by the time Monroe arrived in Paris the two parties had virtually agreed on the cession of Louisiana in return for a sum which, including the damages for spoliation which the United States agreed to pay to its own citizens, amounted to approximately twenty million dollars. Monroe's arrival with full powers clinched the deal.

When Jefferson and Lewis first planned the expedition to the sources of the Missouri it had been thought necessary to procure passports from the French minister. Now the whole journey could be made on American territory, unless they should stumble into the region the sea otters came from, in the mistily imagined sounds north of the Columbia River, which still formed a dim no man's land where British and Spanish and American and even Russian claims conflicted. Lewis had induced one of the redheaded Clarks of Virginia and Kentucky whom Jefferson had known all his life, George Rogers' younger brother William, to go along as joint leader, and was already recruiting his explorers out of the western settlements. Jefferson took such pleasure in writing their instructions that they scanned like poetry:

> The object of your mission is to explore the Missouri River & such principle stream of it, as, by it's course & communication with the waters of the Pacific Ocean, may afford the most direct & practicable water communication across this continent, for the purposes of commerce . . .
> Your observations are to be taken with great pains & accuracy, to be entered distinctly, & intelligently for others as well as yourself, to comprehend all the elements necessary, with the aid of the usual tables, to fix the latitude and longitude of the places at which they were taken.

Jefferson himself had experience as a surveyor as a young man.

> Several copies of these, as well as your other notes, should be made at leisure times and put into the care of the most trustworthy of

your attendants, to guard by multiplying them, against the accidental losses to which they will be exposed. a further guard would
be that one of these copies be written on the paper of the birch,
less liable to injury by damp than common paper.

Jefferson had written his daughters on birchbark from Lake George.
One of his hobbies was finding uses for the natural products of the
American forest.

"You will therefore endeavor to make yourself acquainted," he
went on,

With the names of the nations and their numbers;
  the extent & limits of their possessions;
  their relations with other tribes or nations;
  their language, traditions, monuments;
  their ordinary occupations in agriculture, fishing, hunting, war,
    arts, & the implements for these;
  their food, clothing, & domestic accommodations;
  the diseases prevalent among them, & the remedies they use;
  moral & physical circumstances which distinguish them from the
    tribes we know;
  peculiarities in their laws, customs & dispositions;
  and articles of commerce they may need or furnish & to what
    extent.
And considering the interest which every nation has in extending
& strengthening the authority of reason & justice among the people
around them, it will be useful to acquire what knolege you can of the
state of morality, religion & information among them, as it may better
enable those who endeavor to civilize & instruct them, to adapt their
measures to the existing notions & practises of those on whom they
are to operate.
Other object worthy of notice will be
  the soil & face of the country, it's growth & vegetable productions;
    especially those not of the U.S.
  the animals of the country generally, & especially those not known
    in the U. S.
  the remains and accounts of any which may deemed rare or
    extinct;
  the mineral productions of every kind; but more particularly
    metals, limestone, pit coal & salpetre; salines & mineral waters,
    noting the temperature of the last, & such circumstances as
    may indicate their character.
Volcanic appearances.
climate as characterized by the thermometer, by the proportion
  of rainy, cloudy & clear days, by lightning, hail, snow, ice, by
  the access & recess of frost, by the winds prevailing at different
  seasons, the dates at which particular plants put forth or lose

their flowers, or leaf, times of appearance of particular birds, reptiles or insects.

Jefferson further instructed Lewis to treat the Indians he would come into contact with "in the most friendly and conciliatory manner which their own conduct will admit . . . if a superior force . . . should be arrayed against your further passage, & inflexibly determined to arrest it, you must decline it's further pursuit, and return. in the loss of yourselves, we should lose also the information you will have acquired. by returning safely with that, you may enable us to renew the essay with better calculated means . . . we wish you to err on the side of your safety, & bring back your party safe, even if it be with less information."

Lewis and Clark carried out Jefferson's instructions to the letter. When they returned to St. Lewis two years later with only the loss of a single man they had laid open a path of empire to American settlement.

General Wilkinson, always on hand for a historic event, and Governor Claiborne of Mississippi have the pleasure of standing side by side on December 20, 1803, to see the tricolor hauled down from the flagstaff in front of the Cabildo in New Orleans and the striped flag with the seventeen stars hauled up. General Wilkinson takes advantage of the goodfellowship of the ensuing festivities to shake down the captain general of Cuba for several thousand dollars to write him a report on how the Spaniards could best defend their frontiers west of the Mississippi from American encroachment. Always a thrifty fellow, he sends a slightly amended copy of the same report to Secretary Dearborn and President Jefferson as proof of his continued diligence in the service of the United States.

3. The Tragedy of the Romantics

The Louisiana Purchase and the public enthusiasm it aroused threw consternation into the hearts of the extreme Federalists. They saw a horde of new states rising up to the westward to rob them of their preponderance forever. Their remedy was secession. Already in January 1804 Timothy Pickering, now senator from Massachusetts, was exhorting George Cabot, his fellow member of a small group of New Englanders to which their critics gave the name of the Essex Junto, "And shall we sit still, until this system shall universally triumph? The principles of our Revolution point to the remedy — a separation . . . I do not believe in the practicability of a long-continued union. A northern confederacy would unite congenial characters . . . But New York must be associated; and how is her concurrence to be obtained? She must be made the center of the confederacy."

As the presidential election of 1804 approached, New York again became the political pivot. The prospects were that everywhere else the Democratic-Republicans would sweep the country for the re-election of Jefferson. In New England the gentlemen of the Essex Junto wrote each other panicky letters describing the rise of the democratic tide into their own sacred precincts. Only in New York did they see a flicker of hope. There Burr was running for governor in the spring election against Morgan Lewis, the Chief Justice of the state, who was supported by the Clinton and Livingston factions, with the approval of the Jeffersonians to the north and to the south. Burr, with the support of his enthusiastic adherents in Martling's Long Room, seemed to have the New York wards in the palm of his hand. Once more the balance of power was thought to lie in the New York City vote. The extreme New England Federalists who had tried to elect Burr President of the whole Union now saw in him the possible popular leader of a northern confederacy.

"I have engaged to call on the Vice President as I pass through New York," Matthew Lyon's old enemy, Roger Griswold of Connecticut, wrote Oliver Wolcott from Washington. "The manner in which he gave me the invitation appeared to indicate a wish to enter upon some explanation. He said he wished very much to see me, and to converse, but his situation in this place did not admit of it; and he begged me to call on him at New York. This took place yesterday in the library. Indeed I do not see how he can avoid a full explanation with Federal men. His prospects must depend on the union of the Federalists with his friends; and it is certain that his views extend much beyond the office of Governor of New York. He has the spirit of ambition and revenge to gratify, and can do but little with his 'little band' alone."

Burr and his "little band" had reason to be disgruntled. Though Jefferson treated his Vice President with cordial politeness he remained deaf to any hints about the "great offices." As the two men got to know each other better they became even less congenial than they had been while they were seeking each other's collaboration in the building of the Republican Party. In private Burr cursed the ingratitude of the Virginians. The only one of his supporters whose dreams of office were satisfied was John Swartwout, who was made United States marshal in New York. For all Gallatin, who was in touch with the Burrites through his wife's family, could do to stop him, Burr's devoted Matthew Davis followed Jefferson clear to Monticello in pursuit of his claims to an appointment. Jefferson never let him open his mouth on the subject. "It is not to be doubted," Gallatin wrote regretfully to Jefferson, "that this refusal will by Burr be considered as a declaration of war."

And so it was. As early as August 1802 Wilson Cary Nicholas was regretting in a letter to DeWitt Clinton the loss of Burr to the Republican cause. "Our situation was like that of a man who submits to the loss of a limb to save his life."

Burr remained as closemouthed as ever. His casting votes on two ties in the Senate on the repeal of John Adams' Judiciary Act left both parties confused. He added to the mystery of his proceedings by appearing at a strictly Federalist dinner on Washington's birthday and giving the enigmatic toast "To the Union of All Honest Men."

As the spring election for governor drew near a personal bitterness such as had never been seen before pervaded the political contest in New York. Each of the three factions in the city had a newspaper. Washington Irving's elder brother Peter edited the *Chronicle and Express* in favor of Burr. Hamilton and Troup were subsidizing a young man named Coleman on *The Evening Post*. An Englishman named Cheetham, who had been a hatter in the Midlands, filled his columns with scurrilous attacks on anyone who opposed the Clinton faction. The courts were full of suits and countersuits for libel and slander.

With the help of several of the Livingstons, DeWitt Clinton, recently appointed United States senator, now the acknowledged leader of his uncle's faction in politics and in business, took advantage of Burr's desperate financial condition to put him and his friend Swartwout off the board of directors of Burr's own Manhattan Company. In the resulting row Swartwout accused Clinton of trying to destroy Aaron Burr to further his own ambition. Clinton lost his temper and called him a liar.

As a result the United States senator and the United States marshal had themselves rowed in two fouroared barges one morning over to the Jersey shore. Since the New York authorities were enforcing the state law against dueling, such affairs of honor took place on the rocky ledges below the Palisades. Clinton and Swartwout exchanged a number of pistol shots, punctuated by the usual suggestions from their seconds that their honor had perhaps already been satisfied, but without result. Then Clinton, who was a first rate shot, hit Swartwout in the leg and sent word by his second to ask him if he were satisfied. Swartwout swore he would only be satisfied by a written apology and the duel went on. Clinton hit him in the leg again. By that time the United States marshal was so weak from loss of blood that the surgeon insisted the duel go no further. Clinton walked over to Swartwout

where he lay faint and bleeding on a rock and apologized for having
hurt him so badly. "I don't want to hurt him," he said to the seconds
as he walked back to his barge, "but I wish I had the principal here.
I'll meet him when he pleases."

One duel led to another. John Swartwout's brother Robert and
DeWitt Clinton's second used each other for targets without too much
damage. Hamilton's protégé Coleman shot a Republican named
Thompson. The first duel of the series had already caused the death
of Hamilton's adored firstborn son Philip.

The fall after Jefferson's inauguration eighteen year old Philip, in
whom Hamilton believed he had a son whose career would surpass
his own but whom the family friend Robert Troup considered "a sad
rake," got into an argument with a group of Republicans. He used
fighting words to a lawyer named Eaker, who mortally wounded him
over in Weehawken a few mornings later. "Never did I see a man
so completely overwhelmed with grief as Mr. H. has been," Troup
wrote Rufus King. "The scene I was present when Mrs H. came to
see her son on his deathbed (he died about a mile out of the city) and
when she met her husband and son in one room beggars description."

In New York State at that time, so one observer put it, outside of
the city wards which Burr controlled, the Livingstons had numbers,
the Clintons had power, and the Schuyler connection, representing
the waning Federalists, had Hamilton.

From the time of Philip's death there had been an inner emptiness
in Hamilton's life. He had his devoted family and the pleasures of
gardening at The Grange. His law practice just about kept up with his
debts. He was president of the Cincinnati and had many devoted
friends; they listened to what he had to say with interest, but his
influence among the Federalists had frittered away. Ever since the
fatal attack on John Adams his friends were telling each other that
Hamilton lacked discretion.

His mind turned more and more to religion. He pondered a new
grand scheme to form a Christian Constitutional Society which would
link hightoned religion with hightoned politics to sweep the atheistic
Republicans out of office. Always a kindhearted man, now friends like
Chancellor Kent noticed a new tenderness in his manner. He tried to
lead the Christian life. He took to reading the Episcopal service to
his assembled family Sunday mornings at The Grange.

Jefferson's successful and peaceful purchase of Louisiana at the
very time Hamilton was vociferously demanding, through the columns
he dictated to Coleman for *The Evening Post*, the mustering of a new
army and all his favorite war measures, placed him in a quandary. In

the old days of his feverish correspondence with Miranda, the cession of Louisiana and the two Floridas had been part of the price tentatively agreed upon by Pitt and the revolutionary junta in return for Hamilton's leadership of an American army in support of the liberating expedition to South America. Now, while he could not agree with his Federalist friends in condemning the purchase, he at least could give himself the satisfaction of belittling Jefferson's part in it.

He had to admit the purchase "would give éclat to his administration. Every man, however, possessed of the least candour or reflection," he announced in a lead article he dictated to Coleman late one night in his office, "will readily acknowledge that the acquisition has been solely owing to a fortuitous concurrence of unforeseen and unexpected circumstances, and not to any wise or vigorous measures on the part of the American government."

Much as he wanted to belittle Jefferson's statesmanship he could not go along with his old supporters Messrs. Pickering and Wolcott in their use of the Louisiana Purchase as a pretext for breaking up the very federal union which he had devoted so much of his life to attaining. "Dismemberment of our empire will be a clear sacrifice of great positive advantages, without any counterbalancing good; administering no relief to our real disease which is Democracy," he told Theodore Sedgwick in one of the last letters he ever wrote.

Their plan to rely on Aaron Burr to lead a new confederacy distressed Hamilton immeasurably. Although his *Evening Post* had defended Burr against the scurrilous attacks of DeWitt Clinton's press, he had been doing everything in his power to prevent Burr's election. At a dinner party in Albany, encouraged by the emphatic agreement of his friend Chancellor Kent, he discoursed to a tableful of politicians on his favorite theme of Burr as the Catiline or Bonaparte of America. A certain Dr. Cooper—not Priestley's learned friend—wrote a letter describing his outburst. It seems to have been Hamilton's devoted fatherinlaw, old General Schuyler, who saw to it that the letter should appear in the columns of *The Albany Register*. Though he carried New York City, where the toast at Martling's was "Aaron's rod shall blossom in New York," Burr was defeated by Judge Lewis's sweeping majority upstate.

Once more Burr's great unrevealed plans are frustrated. Jefferson has checked him in Washington, now Hamilton checkmates him in New York. A couple of weeks after the results of the election are known Burr writes Hamilton a letter which he hands to one of the Van Ness brothers to deliver in person. He demands that Hamilton retract his and Chancellor Kent's statement quoted by Dr. Cooper, that Burr is a "dangerous man who ought not to be trusted with the reins of government"; he further demands that he explain and retract the implications of some remark on "still more despicable" traits of Burr's, over which Dr. Cooper has drawn a veil. Hamilton answers with a quibbling lawyer's letter. Burr refuses to be satisfied. The correspondence passes into the hands of their seconds, Van Ness for Burr and a Judge Pendleton for Hamilton. As letter follows letter each man writes himself into a position from which, according to the code of the hour, there is no retreat but an interview at Weehawken. They agree to put off their encounter until the end of the term of the circuit court before which Hamilton has cases to argue.

On Independence Day the two men sit side by side at a holiday banquet, Hamilton at the head of the table and Vice President Aaron Burr on his right as the most distinguished guest. The painter John Trumbull sees them there and makes an entry in his diary: "The 4th of July I dined with the Society of the Cincinnati, my old military comrades, and there met, among others Gen. Hamilton and Col. Burr. The singularity of their manner was observed by all but few had any suspicions of the cause. Burr contrary to his wont was silent, gloomy, sour, while Hamilton entered with glee into all the gaety of a convivial party, and even sang an old military song."

The circuit court adjourns on July 10. Both men spend the rest of the day writing. Burr writes his daughter telling her how to handle his debts if he should suffer some mischance, and what to do with bundles of letters from his lady friends tied with various colored ribbon which he enumerates with lingering care. "I am indebted to you my dearest Theodosia for a very great portion of the happiness which I have enjoyed in life. You have completely satisfied all that my heart and affections hoped or even wished." He begs her to keep up her classical studies. "Let your son have occasion to be proud he had a mother. Adieu. Adieu."

Among a mass of notes explaining to his friends in hairsplitting detail why, although opposed to dueling from religious conviction, he cannot avoid meeting this particular challenge, Hamilton leaves two letters to his browneyed Elizabeth:

"If it had been possible for me to have avoided the interview, my love for you and my precious children would have been alone a decisive motive," he writes in the first one. "It is not possible, without sacrifices which would have rendered me unworthy of your esteem ... Fly to the bosom of your God, and be comforted. With my last idea I shall cherish a sweet hope of meeting you in a better world."

The scruples of a Christian (he writes in his second letter), have determined me to expose my own life to any extent, rather than to subject myself to the guilt of taking the life of another. This much increases my hazards, and redoubles my pangs for you. But you had rather I should die innocent than live guilty . . . Once more,

Adieu my darling, darling wife.

The morning of July 11 Burr and Van Ness are first on the ground. They take off their coats and spend the time waiting for Hamilton's boat to arrive clearing a space among the weeds with their canes. When Hamilton's party disembarks the seconds mark out ten paces. After the formalities are concluded Hamilton asks for a pause to put on his glasses. He has trouble seeing in the early light. This time Burr's pistol is properly loaded. At the command "One, two, three . . . Fire," he neatly puts a bullet through Hamilton's waistcoat.

As Hamilton falls his pistol goes off into the air. A few leaves flutter down as his ball nicks the branches above Burr's head. Burr's ball has passed through the liver and lodged in the spine. "This is a mortal wound, Doctor," Hamilton says as his surgeon kneels beside him.

Burr's second, Van Ness, opens an umbrella over Burr's head so that Matthew Davis and others of his friends who are hiding in the bushes can testify, if they should be called into court, that they have not recognized Hamilton's opponent, and hurries him to his boat. When he reaches the New York shore he drives off posthaste to Richmond Hill. From there he flits in the ensuing days to another country place farther up the Hudson.

Hamilton has fainted. He revives a little on the boat. When he is carried up from the landing to a friend's house on Jane Street it is obvious that he is in horrible pain. When the doctors undress him and lay him on a bed they try to quiet his pain without much avail with massive doses of laudanum.

By nine o'clock the news is all through the city. A notice is posted in the Tontine Coffee House that Colonel Burr has mortally wounded General Hamilton in a duel. Hamilton's every fault is forgotten; Burr from that moment becomes the enemy of mankind. Friends flock to the house on Jane Street. Oliver Wolcott, who happens to be in the city, hurries there.

"I have just returned from Mr. Bayard's—where Hamilton is," he writes his wife. "I did not see him—he suffers great pain—which he endures like a Hero — Mrs Hamilton is with him, but she is ignorant of the cause of his Illness, which she supposes to be Spasms—no one dares tell her the truth—it is feared she would become frantic . . . Gen'l Hamilton has of late years expressed his conviction of the truths of the Christian Religion, and has desired to receive the Sacrament—

but no one of the Clergy who have yet been consulted will administer it . . . Thus has perished one of the greatest men of this or any age."

Before Hamilton died the next day his friend Bishop Moore of Trinity Church allowed himself to be convinced that Hamilton was not morally a duelist. He had sacrificed his life with no intention of harming his opponent. The bishop administered Communion, "as a sign" Hamilton weakly whispered.

All classes joined in mourning Alexander Hamilton. The merchants of the city, the Common Council, the gentlemen of the Bar, the students of Columbia College, the militia companies, Tammany Hall, the Mechanics and Tradesmen, the St. Andrew's Society, the Cincinnati all passed resolutions of mourning. Indictments for murder were introduced against Aaron Burr in New York and New Jersey. No more talk among the Federalists of making Burr their standard bearer. The men who had been agitating for a convention to discuss the secession of the northern states behaved as if they had never heard of the scheme.

Gouverneur Morris pronounced the funeral oration from the portico of Trinity Church. In his diary he disclosed the preplexities he suffered writing it. He had hurried in from Morrisania to the house on Jane Street. He found Hamilton unconscious. "The Scene is too powerful for me," he wrote . . . "I am obliged to walk in the Garden to take Breath. After having composed myself I return and sit by his Side until he expires." Gouverneur promised to deliver the valedictory "if I can possibly command myself. I am wholly unmanned by this day's Spectacle."

When Gouverneur started composing his speech, the old perverse spirit returned: "The first Point of his Biography is that he was a Stranger of illegitimate Birth; some Mode must be contrived to pass over this handsomely. He was indiscreet, vain and opinionated; these Things must be told . . . in such a Manner as not to destroy the Interest. He was in Principle opposed to republican and attached to monarchical Government . . . His Share in forming our Constitution must be mentioned, and his unfavorable Opinion of it cannot therefore be concealed . . . He was in Principle opposed to duelling, yet he has fallen in a Duel. I cannot thoroughly excuse him without criminating Colonel Burr, which would be wrong . . . I can find no way to get over the Difficulty which would attend the Details of his Death . . . I must not either dwell on his domestic Life; he has long since foolishly published the Avowal of conjugal Infidelity. Something, however must be said to elicit public Pity for his Family, which he has left in indigent Circumstances."

"Fellow citizens," Gouverneur declaimed in his fine voice broken with emotion to the crowd that filled the yard in front of the Trinity Church and the Broad Way beyond. "You know how well he performed the Duties of a Citizen. You know that he never courted your Favor by Adulation, or the Sacrifice of his own Judgement. You have seen him contending against you, and saving your dearest Interests as it were in spite of yourselves. And now you feel the Benefits resulting from the firm Energy of his Conduct. Bear this Testimony to the Memory of my departed Friend. I charge you to protect his Fame."

Though there was many a sob in the crowd Gouverneur felt afterwards his great oration was a failure. Perhaps he leaned too far back to avoid stirring up a lynching spirit against Burr. "How easy it would have been," he noted in retrospect, "to make them for a Moment absolutely mad."

In spite of his high office Burr's life became that of a fugitive from justice. Someone who hated him left a scrawled note written in some country house on the North River. It was after Hamilton's death. "That little devil is coming." Burr arrived in an enormous carriage drawn by six horses, a short ugly man who cursed continuously. When he walked into the house with bowed head and rapid gait, they could hear the funeral guns booming in New York. All night they heard Burr's steps as he walked back and forth in the upper passage of the house. A servant was with him. In the morning he practiced with his pistol on the riverbank. He shot twelve balls into a white birch tree.

At Monticello Thomas Jefferson set up Alexander Hamilton's bust in his domed entrance hall among his collection of great men.

Spence's Point
June 23, 1956

Acknowledgments

Most of the letters and journals quoted are to be found among the
Jefferson, Washington, Monroe, Marshall, Madison and Gouverneur
Morris papers in the Library of Congress manuscript room, where the
distracted researcher continues to meet with unfailing helpfulness and
hospitality. The extracts from Elbridge Gerry's letters to his wife and
some of the Jefferson materials are by courtesy of the Massachusetts
Historical Society. A couple of quotations from letters of John Beckley
in the De Witt Clinton Papers are by permission of the Columbia
University Libraries. Gelston's eyewitness account of the big scene
between Hamilton and Monroe is to be found in the archives of the
Pennsylvania Historical Society.

Among published collections, the Princeton Edition of Jefferson's
papers now takes its place beside Fitzpatrick's writings and diaries of
George Washington as basic for the study of the period. This work is
enormously indebted to it. I have quoted fairly extensively from the
correspondence of Benjamin Rush made available in Lyman Butter-
field's *Letters of Dr. Rush*. For most of the quotations from Gouverneur
Morris's letters and diaries and for a letter of William Short I relied on
Beatrix Cary Davenport's *A Diary of the French Revolution: 1789-1793*,
published by Houghton Mifflin in 1939. Part of a memorial of Tom
Paine's is from the *Complete Writings*, edited by Philip Foner in 1945.
A couple of Lafayette's letters are from Gottschalk's *Letters of Lafayette
to Washington*. I drew heavily on Max Farrand's *The Framing of the
Constitution* for the debates and for the letters of members of the Philadelphia Convention of 1787. The quotations from St. George Tucker
are from Mary Haldane Coleman's *Citizen of No Mean City*. The ex-
cerpts from McHenry's and Murray's chatty epistles are from Steiner's
Life and Correspondence of James McHenry. The paragraph from
Gouverneur Morris's father's will I found in *The Livingstons of Livingston Manor*, by Edwin B. Livingston. Some of the quotations from
Genêt's letters are lifted out of Meade Minnigerode's *Jefferson, Friend
of France* and *Life and Times: Four Informal Biographies*. Jefferson's
note to Marshall I found in Beveridge's *Life of John Marshall*, which
in spite of its Federalist bias remains an extremely useful book. The
quotations in the last chapter from Mrs. Samuel Harrison Smith's
journals and letters are from *The First Forty Years of Washington
Society*, published by Scribners in 1906.

INDEX

THE MAINSTREAM OF AMERICA SERIES

THE aim of this new approach to history is to tell the story of America in narrative form. The *Series*, when complete, will cover the entire sweep of our nation's history from the earliest days of exploration to the recent days of turmoil and achievement . . . and this history will be told in the terms of the *people* who made it.

THE MAINSTREAM OF AMERICA SERIES is edited by Mr. Lewis Gannett, distinguished critic of the New York *Herald Tribune*.

Books published thus far in THE MAINSTREAM OF AMERICA SERIES are:

> *The Age of Fighting Sail,* by C. S. Forester
> *The Age of the Moguls,* by Stewart H. Holbrook
> *From Lexington to Liberty,* by Bruce Lancaster
> *Glory, God and Gold,* by Paul I. Wellman
> *The Land They Fought For,* by Clifford Dowdey
> *New Found World,* by Harold Lamb
> *Men to Match My Mountains,* by Irving Stone
> *This Hallowed Ground,* by Bruce Catton
> *The Men Who Made the Nation,* by John Dos Passos

Under contract to write future volumes are: Hodding Carter, Stewart H. Holbrook, Saunders Redding, David Lavender, Henry Steele Commager, and George Willison.

The 1956 Carey-Thomas Award — "for the best example of creative publishing" — was given to Doubleday & Company, Inc. for the publication of THE MAINSTREAM OF AMERICA SERIES.